LAW OF EDUCATION

SECOND EDITION

LAW OF EDUCATION

SECOND EDITION

Oliver Hyams

Barrister , Devereux Chambers

JORDANS

2004

Published by
Jordan Publishing Limited
21 St Thomas Street
Bristol BS1 6JS

British Library Cataloguing-in-Publication Data

A catalogue record for this book is available from the British Library.

ISBN 0 85308 803 9

Typeset by Jordan Publishing Limited
Printed by The Cromwell Press Limited, Trowbridge, Wiltshire

PREFACE

In a knowledge-based economy, education may be seen as a key commodity. However, some highly successful entrepreneurs and business managers have achieved their success without the foundation of an intensive education. Such an education is therefore not a prerequisite of economic success. Yet the ability to read and write effectively could sensibly be said to be essential in the modern world. In any event, it is of immense value to the individual. As Lord Scott put it in *Adams v Bracknell Forest Borough Council*:[1]

> 'Subject to the Limitation Act point I would be in no doubt but that if the [claimant] can establish that in failing to teach him to read the schools were in breach of the duty they owed him he would be entitled at least to general damages. The ability to read is a benefit that nobody who is able to read would dream of undervaluing. It is not simply a benefit of economic value leading to enhanced employment prospects, although it certainly is that. It is a benefit that transforms the whole quality of life of the person who acquires it.'

In any event, in order to be able to practise professionally in many areas, certain educational qualifications are a prerequisite.

It is for these reasons that mention is first made here of the developments in the law of negligence concerning the provision of education which have occurred since December 1998, when the first edition of this book was published. At that time, the extent of the liability in negligence of an education provider for failures in relation to the provision of education to an individual was unclear (although that lack of clarity developed too late to be reflected in the text of that edition). The House of Lords had, in *X v Bedfordshire County Council*,[2] ruled that such liability may arise in at least some circumstances, but the manner in which that ruling had been applied in several subsequent cases, most notably by the Court of Appeal in *Phelps v Hillingdon London Borough Council*,[3] had put the effect of *X v Bedfordshire County Council* in doubt. The House of Lords has subsequently, on appeal in *Phelps*,[4] affirmed its ruling in *X v Bedfordshire County Council* and in some respects removed the limits which it had placed in that case on the liability of an education provider.[5] Nevertheless, as Lord Hoffmann stated in *Adams v Bracknell Forest Borough Council*,[6] the damages which are likely to be awarded for negligence in relation to the provision of education are 'likely to be modest'. This, however, must be seen as the result of the difficulty of proving that the educational failures led to the claimed loss, with the result that there is no universally applicable rule that the damages will be modest. In any event, educational negligence claims are here to stay.

---

[1] [2004] UKHL 29, [2004] 3 WLR 89, para 67.
[2] [1995] 2 AC 633.
[3] [1999] 1 WLR 500.
[4] [2001] 2 AC 619.
[5] See para **14.56**.
[6] Ibid, para 55.

A number of other cases of interest and significance have been reported since the first edition of this book was published, but they are not all mentioned here if only because this preface would have become unduly lengthy if they had been. One only is mentioned, and that is the case of *A v Head Teacher and Governors of the Lord Grey School*.[1] It is mentioned because it is one of the few cases in which the Human Rights Act 1998 has been of significant value to the claimant and because the fact that there have been so few cases in which that Act has assisted a claimant in a case concerning education may be surprising.

At the time of the publication of the first edition, given the enactment in 1998 of the School Standards and Framework Act 1998 and the Teaching and Higher Education Act 1998, it might reasonably have been thought that at least the statutes relating to school education and higher education were unlikely to be the subject of substantial change as long as the then majority party in Parliament remained in power. However, despite the return to power of that party in 2001, substantial changes have been enacted to both areas since 1998. The Education Act 2002 made substantial changes in particular to the law relating to school education, and the Higher Education Act 2004 will, when it is in force, effect considerable change to the law relating to the provision of higher education. There are in addition two other primary enactments which have affected the provision of education significantly since 1998. One is the Learning and Skills Act 2000, concerning principally the provision of further education and related matters, and the other is the Special Educational Needs and Disability Act 2001, which, in addition to making some changes to the law relating to special education, applied (with modifications) the principles of the Disability Discrimination Act 1995 to the education sector.

The number of statutory instruments affecting the provision of education has, as ever, been great. Indeed, the text of this book will be slightly out of date as soon as it is published. Developments up to the beginning of August 2004 have, as far as possible, been taken into account by final proof changes made at that time.

Textual matters

An apology is in order about the use of the words 'he', 'him' and 'his' instead of 'he or she', 'him or her', and 'his or hers' respectively. This usage has been adopted for the sake of simplicity. In mitigation it is pleaded that the same usage is adopted in modern statutory provisions. In contrast, however, in most (but not all) current statutory provisions, a local authority is referred to as 'they', but in this book a local authority is referred to as 'it' (although the members of such an authority are of course referred to here in the plural as 'they'). The same is true of a local education authority and the governing body of a school. In mitigation in this respect, it is pleaded that the usage adopted in this book is grammatically correct. Less grammatically correct, but preferable on the basis that the written text flows rather better when read, is the use of the abbreviation 'LEA' as a word in itself. Thus it is referred to as 'an LEA'.

---

[1]   [2004] EWCA Civ 382; [2004] 2 WLR 1442. See para **18.124** for the relevant ruling.

Grateful acknowledgements

Various parts of the text of this book have been the subject of helpful comments and suggestions by a number of lawyers whose expertise concerns, or includes, the law of education, and I am very grateful indeed to them for taking the time to read through and comment on drafts of parts of the text. They are Paul Bogle, Beth Coxon, Malcolm Gilbert, John Hall, Jo Honigmann, Sian Jones-Davies, Gaynor Lloyd, Mark Radford, Nick Saunders, and Andrew Warnock. I am grateful also to several other lawyers who have read through parts of the text and whose positive comments on that text have in themselves been helpful. They include Deborah Alexander, Tracey Eldridge-Hinmers, and Tom Lewis-Brooke. The responsibility for any errors in, or omissions from, the text is, naturally, mine alone.

Indeed, as far as omissions are concerned, although it has been my aim to state the law of education as comprehensively as possible, the text is not fully comprehensive. A book of this sort is necessarily only something of a signpost, but in some areas more than in others the indications are relatively brief. A salient example is the law relating to the National Curriculum, the number of statutory instruments concerning which is such that in a number of respects reference is made only to the primary statutory provision concerning the matter. In mitigation I plead that the relevant secondary legislation is now available over the Internet (on the HMSO website) at no cost to the user other than the cost of access to the Internet itself.

My thanks are due to the staff at Jordans for their unfailing kindness and consideration since the time when the typescript of this book was first due and to Gary Hill, who edited the book on behalf of Jordans, for his flexibility, courtesy, and general efficiency after the typescript was finally delivered.

Last, but by no means least, thanks are due to my wife, Gill, and daughters Sarah and Katy, for their forbearance and patience while the text of this book was in preparation.

Oliver Hyams

Devereux Chambers
London

August 2004

CONTENTS

TABLE OF CASES

TABLE OF STATUTES

TABLE OF STATUTORY INSTRUMENTS

TABLE OF EUROPEAN MATERIALS

References are to paragraph numbers

TABLE OF OTHER MATERIALS

TABLE OF ABBREVIATIONS

ALI	Adult Learning Inspectorate
CA 1989	Children Act 1989
CA 1993	Charities Act 1993
CETW	National Council for Education and Training for Wales
CJCSA 2000	Criminal Justice and Court Services Act 2000
CRE	Commission for Racial Equality
DDA 1995	Disability Discrimination Act 1995
DFE	Department for Education
DfEE	Department for Education and Employment
DfES	Department for Education and Skills
EA 1921	Education Act 1921
EA 1944	Education Act 1944
EA 1981	Education Act 1981
EA 1986	Education Act 1986
EA 1993	Education Act 1993
EA 1994	Education Act 1994
EA 1996	Education Act 1996
EA 1997	Education Act 1997
EA 2002	Education Act 2002
EAF	Education Action Forum
EAT	Employment Appeal Tribunal
EAZ	education action zone
ECHR	European Court of Human Rights
ECJ	European Court of Justice
ERA 1988	Education Reform Act 1988
ESA 1992	Education (Schools) Act 1992
DRC	Disability Rights Commission
FEC	further education corporation
FHEA 1992	Further and Higher Education Act 1992
GTC	General Training Council for England
HASAWA 1974	Health and Safety at Work etc Act 1974
HEC	higher education corporation
HEFC	Higher Education Funding Council
HEFCW	Higher Education Funding Council for Wales
HRA 1998	Human Rights Act 1998
LEA	local education authority
LSA 2000	Learning and Skills Act 2000
LSC	Learning and Skills Council for England
POCA 1999	Protection of Children Act 1999
RRA 1976	Race Relations Act 1976
RSA 1987	Reverter of Sites Act 1987
SDA 1975	Sex Discrimination Act 1975
SEN	special educational needs

SENDA 2001   Special Educational Needs and Disability Act 2001
SIA 1996   School Inspections Act 1996
SOC   school organisation committee
SSA 1841   School Sites Act 1841
SSFA 1998   School Standards and Framework Act 1998
THEA 1998   Teaching and Higher Education Act 1998
TTA   Teacher Training Agency
TUPE   Transfer of Undertakings (Protection of Employment)
                Regulations 1981
Welsh GTC   General Training Council for Wales

GLOSSARY OF TERMS AND PHRASES

Academy	See para **3.68**
Care Standards Tribunal	the tribunal established under s 9 of the Protection of Children Act 1999
compulsory school age	See paras **2.40–2.41**
delegated budget	see para **7.140**
higher education	see para **17.7**
institution within the further education sector	see para **16.2**
institution within the higher education sector	see para **17.14**
maintained school	see para **7.7**
a member of the Inspectorate	see para **12.13**
National Assembly	National Assembly for Wales
parent	see paras **5.3** et seq
primary education	see para **7.3**
registered pupil	see para **5.8**
religious character within the meaning of section 69(3) of the SSFA 1998	see para **7.26**
school	see paras **7.2** et seq
school session	see para **7.157**
secondary education	see para **7.4**
Secretary of State	this term should be read as applying also to the National Assembly unless specifically stated otherwise; this will be the result either of the transfer of the Secretary of State's functions to the National Assembly by SI 199/672, or of the provisions in the legislation conferring the function if it was enacted after SI 1999/672 came into force
walking distance	see para **5.39**

Chapter 1

INTRODUCTION AND HISTORY OF THE LAW OF EDUCATION

INTRODUCTION

1.1   Today, the law of education is mainly statutory. Before Parliament became involved in its formulation,[1] the law of education, such as it was, consisted of a branch of the law of charities, if only because private education (as opposed to that funded directly by public authorities) was often provided by charitable schools and universities. However, although the relatively recent introduction by the Education Reform Act 1988 (ERA 1988) of statutory education corporations[2] has brought back to the fore the question of the impact of charity law on the provision of education, modern education law is concerned primarily with statutory provisions. This is not to say, of course, that the role of charity law ever lost its place in the law of education, since charity law has always been highly relevant in the university and independent school sectors, and continues to be so.

1.2   The statutory provisions which apply in the field of education today, among other things, effect a channelling of resources from central government to public bodies which are amenable to judicial review. As a result, the principles of public law are often prominent in the context of education, and it is necessary always to keep them in mind when considering practical problems in the context of the public provision of education.

1.3   An understanding of the history of the law of education is probably essential for an understanding of the network of legal provisions which apply today. Although the history of aspects of the law of education is referred to below where necessary to either clarify or set aspects of the present law in context, an overview is in addition helpful. The rest of this chapter accordingly consists of a brief history of the law of education.

---

[1]   This book describes the law of education only in England and Wales.

[2]   In the form of the governing bodies of grant-maintained schools (which have now been abolished; they are in any event not to be confused with schools which were called 'direct grant' schools) and higher education corporations. The other main kind of education corporation resulting from the current legislative regime is the further education corporation. The incorporation of maintained school governing bodies resulted in a different kind of corporation from that referred to here: see further paras **7.205–7.208**.

HISTORY OF THE LAW OF EDUCATION

Schools

1.4   The change from the position in which the common law and equity were the predominant sources of education law, came in the nineteenth century. Although the history of the period before then has been told many times before,[1] a brief overview will nevertheless be given here.

1.5   The system of support for education in the form of government funding in this country began in 1833, when Parliament first voted that a sum of money (not exceeding £20,000) be made available:

> 'to be issued in aid of private subscriptions for the erection of school houses for the education of the poorer classes in Great Britain.'[2]

However, no specific administrative machinery was set up to carry out the distribution of this sum, and the Treasury was left to do the job. Without such machinery, the Treasury, in order to determine whether applications for grants were meritorious, relied on reports from the two main societies which promoted charitable schools, the National Society (which advanced the interests of the Church of England with regard to what was then called elementary education) and the British and Foreign Schools Society (which represented the interests of the Nonconformists in the same sphere).[3]

1.6   This led to the establishment of the Committee of the Privy Council on Education, on 10 April 1839, to have responsibility for the administration of the grants which had by now become annual. (The establishment of the Committee did not require legislation, since it required only an Order in Council. The setting up of the administrative arrangements in this way therefore minimised the possibility of disagreement between the rival religious parties. It was in fact the then accepted method of catering for new executive functions.) The Committee's decisions were published in the form of minutes of the Committee of Council on Education, and those minutes contained among other things the conditions on which grants would be made to the promoters of schools.

1.7   Initially, grants had been made only towards the cost of school buildings and not towards the running of schools, and one of the acts of the new Committee was to make available in exceptional circumstances grants to help meet the current expenses of schools as well as the cost of constructing and maintaining their buildings.[4] It should be noted, however, that the only schools to which grants were made were what

---

[1]   See, for example, SJ Curtis, *History of Education in Great Britain* (University Tutorial Press, 7th edn, 1967) and PHJH Gosden, *The Development of Educational Administration in England and Wales* (Basil Blackwell, 1966). It is also told in a succinct and informative way in the judgment of the Court of Appeal in *Fraser v Canterbury Diocesan Board of Finance* [2001] Ch 669, at paras 3–11 and (more fully) at paras 3–31 of the judgment of Lewison J in *Fraser v Canterbury Diocesan Board of Finance (No 2)* [2003] EWHC 1075 (Ch), [2003] NPC 62.

[2]   Gosden, op cit, p 1.

[3]   Gosden, op cit, pp 1–2.

[4]   Gosden, op cit, p 3.

would now be called voluntary schools. What would now be called community schools first appeared only after 1870, when the Elementary Education Act 1870 was enacted. In 1856, a new Education Department was set up, as a formal administrative vehicle to deal with the work of the Committee of Council.[1]

1.8   The Committee of Council developed its administration for the inspection of schools which were in receipt of a grant from the Committee over the next few years (and indeed the Committee survived until 1899, when the Board of Education Act 1899 created the Board of Education). Curiously, the Committee of Council was unaffected by the enactment of the Elementary Education Act 1870, which first introduced a statutory system for the provision of education, and which was the first major piece of legislation affecting the provision of education in England and Wales. Equally curiously, in addition, the minutes of the Committee were given the force of law by ss 3, 7 and 97 of the 1870 Act. Section 7 provided that public elementary schools among other things:

'shall be conducted in accordance with the conditions required to be fulfilled by an elementary school in order to obtain an annual parliamentary grant.'

Section 97 provided, among other things, that:

'The conditions required to be fulfilled by an elementary school in order to obtain an annual parliamentary grant shall be those contained in the minutes of the Education Department in force for the time being.'

Section 3 provided that:

'The term "Education Department" means "the Lords of the Committee of the Privy Council on Education".'

1.9   The Education Department published an annual Code for its inspectors, in which the standards of elementary schools, the subjects which might be taught and curricular matters generally, were set out.[2] Since the code was published in the minutes of the Committee, the code can be seen as a predecessor of the National Curriculum.[3] This effect of s 7 may well have been unintentional.[4]

1.10   The 1870 Act introduced school boards. These were *not* school governing bodies, but rather, in effect, what would now be called local education authorities (LEAs). The school boards had a discretion with regard to the establishment of a separate tier of management for individual elementary schools. Where such a separate tier was set up, the persons who were responsible for the running of the school were

---

[1]   Gosden, op cit, p 8; this was done under the Education Department Act 1856.
[2]   Gosden, op cit, p 18.
[3]   There was much opposition from the teaching profession to the introduction of the National Curriculum under the ERA 1988, since at that time, the curriculum in schools had been unregulated for many decades: see NS Harris *Law and Education: Regulation, Consumerism and the Education System* (Sweet & Maxwell, 1993), pp 27 and 198–199.
[4]   See, for the proposition that giving the Code the force of law was unintentional, Gosden, op cit, p 17.

referred to as 'managers'.[1] The school boards obtained their finance from the rates and were empowered, where they considered it necessary, to establish and maintain schools for the provision of elementary education.

1.11   There are now, broadly, five kinds of state school: community schools, voluntary schools, foundation schools, Academies (and city technology colleges and city colleges for the technology of the arts) and pupil referral units.[2] Only community and voluntary schools have any obvious predecessors in the kinds of school which were funded by the school boards from 1870 onwards until their abolition by the Education Act 1902. The predecessors of community schools were called 'provided' schools, and were so called because they were provided by the school boards. The predecessors of voluntary schools were the schools which had previously been receiving grants from Parliament via the Education Department. These came to be known as 'non-provided' schools. Such schools were not expressly catered for in the provisions of the 1870 Act regarding school boards, and it was intended that such schools would continue to receive funding as before, in the form of annual grants from the Treasury administered by the Education Department. Indeed, it was probably intended that non-provided schools should not be supported from the rates. However, s 25 of the 1870 Act did allow the school boards to pay the whole or part of the fees of children who could not otherwise afford them, with the result that a number of school boards channelled rate money to the non-provided schools in their areas.

1.12   The need for a new central authority with responsibility for the administration of education became more and more apparent during the 1890s, but the Board of Education[3] only began to function as such an authority after the enactment of the Education Act 1902. That Act was the second pivotal step in legislative terms in the context of education. It effected a fundamental change to the administration of education, since it abolished school boards and gave all local functions with regard to education to LEAs (albeit that they were in a rather different form from those of today, since there were different types of LEA, and more overall than today). The 1902 Act also brought the non-provided schools into the state system, in that although the managers of such schools were to continue to be responsible for the provision, and the majority of the repair of the school buildings, the day-to-day running costs of the schools were now to be met from the rates.[4]

1.13   Although there were important measures after the 1902 Act, and that Act and related provisions were consolidated in the Education Act 1921, the third pivotal change in legislative terms in the context of education was brought about by the Education Act 1944 (EA 1944). Under that Act the Board of Education was replaced by a Minister of Education. In addition, the Act made many major changes in regard to the provision of schools by LEAs.

---

[1]   See s 15 of the Elementary Education Act 1870.
[2]   See further, Chapter 7 regarding such schools.
[3]   Established, as noted above, under the Board of Education Act of 1899.
[4]   See s 7 of the Education Act 1902.

1.14   From 1944 until 1980, there was relatively little legislative activity in the field of education. Changes were certainly made, but they were minor compared with those made from 1980 onwards. The first changes after 1979 came in the Education Act 1980, which introduced the principle of parental choice in respect of state schools. Then came the Education Act 1981 (EA 1981), which was designed to revolutionise the provision of special education. This was followed by the Education (No 2) Act 1986 (EA 1986), which, among other things, effected many changes in regard to the governance and management of schools. Then came the Teachers' Pay and Conditions Act 1987, which removed from the employers of teachers in state schools the power to determine many of the terms of employment of teachers in such schools. The ERA 1988 introduced among other things the National Curriculum, grant-maintained schools, city technology colleges and higher education corporations. The latter were established to be responsible for the running of polytechnics and colleges of higher education which were, at the time of the passing of that Act, maintained by LEAs. The next piece of primary legislation was the Further and Higher Education Act 1992 (FHEA 1992), under which further education colleges and sixth-form colleges were also separated from LEAs, and were also (in the main) to be run by new statutory corporations, with funding provided by the further education funding councils (one for England, one for Wales). The Education (Schools) Act 1992 was enacted in the same year. In the following year, the Education Act 1993 (EA 1993) was enacted, one result of which was that two Funding Agencies for Schools were to be established to acquire some of the functions of an LEA where the number of grant-maintained schools in the authority's area was above a certain threshold. The EA 1993 also introduced education associations. In 1996, Parliament helpfully consolidated much (but not all) of the then existing legislation relating to education in the Education Act 1996 (EA 1996) and the School Inspections Act 1996 (SIA 1996). The Education Act 1997 made a number of miscellaneous changes to the law concerning education provided to persons of school age. However, there was then a general election, a new government was formed, and the School Standards and Framework Act 1998 (SSFA 1998) was enacted. It abolished grant-maintained schools and education associations, enacted a new set of provisions concerning the maintenance of state schools, and introduced a range of new bodies, such as school organisation committees and adjudicators. In addition, the Teaching and Higher Education Act 1998 (THEA 1998) was enacted. That is a shorter enactment than the SSFA 1998, but its practical effect was also considerable: it introduced a new regime for the provision of financial support to students in further or higher education, and provided for the establishment of two new General Teaching Councils: one for England and one for Wales.

1.15   In 1999, there was a major change in relation to responsibility for the provision of education in Wales. That change occurred as a result of the transfer of almost all of the Secretary of State's functions in relation to education, to the National Assembly for Wales.[1]

1.16   In 2000, the Learning and Skills Act 2000 (LSA 2000) was enacted. One of its major effects was the abolition of the further education funding councils and the introduction of new bodies by which public money was to be channelled to the

---

[1]   See the National Assembly for Wales (Transfer of Functions) Order 1999, SI 1999/672, Art 2, Sch 1.

providers of further education. These are local learning and skills councils, the Learning and Skills Council for England (LSC), and the National Council for Education and Training for Wales (CETW).

1.17   The year 2001 brought the Special Educational Needs and Disability Act 2001 (SENDA 2001). In addition to amending the provisions in the Education Act 1996 regarding children with special educational needs (SEN), it provided for the application, with modifications, of the Disability Discrimination Act 1995 (DDA 1995) to the education sector (the DDA 1995 having originally applied in only a limited way to that sector).

1.18   The most recent primary enactment directly concerning the provision of education other than higher education is the Education Act 2002 (EA 2002). It made a number of significant changes to the legislation governing the manner in which education is provided in schools, including independent schools. One major aim of the Act was to liberate successful schools from the legislative regime governing the provision of education, introducing 'a lighter touch schools framework, with more devolution and more decision-making at school level'.[1] This was effected in part by ss 1–10 of the Act. Another (related) aim was to 'move significant detailed prescription out of primary legislation', in the place of which the intention was to 'make regulations that will be less detailed and less prescriptive [in order to] reduce burdens on schools'.[2] The areas of the law which were affected by this move included the law relating to admissions to and exclusions from maintained schools.[3] Also affected were the detailed primary statutory provisions concerning the governance of such schools.[4] This was only 4 years after the enactment of the SSFA 1998 containing the most recent set of such provisions.[5] One of the difficulties caused from the point of view of an exposition of the law by the EA 2002 is its enactment of a number of provisions which relate to England only.[6]

Universities

1.19   The ancient universities also became subject to some statutory regulation in the nineteenth century, when the Oxford University Act 1854 and the Cambridge University Act 1856 were passed. These Acts were designed to modernise the governance of those universities; for example, discussions in Council could now take place in English instead of Latin. However, the 'old' university sector was left relatively untouched by statutory intervention until the FHEA 1992, and even under that Act the intervention took the form in the main of the alteration of the funding mechanism for universities. The Higher Education Act 2004 (HEA 2004), enacted shortly before this book was published, will effect more substantive change to the law of higher education than has occurred as a result of previous legislation. Among other things, it will abolish the jurisdiction of the visitor to higher education institutions for

---

[1]   Per Mr David Miliband, the Minister for School Standards, on 15 July 2002: *Hansard*, HC vol 389, col 73.
[2]   Ibid.
[3]   See Chapter 3 of Part 3 of the EA 2002.
[4]   See Chapter 1 of Part 3 of the EA 2002.
[5]   Sections 36 and 37 of, and Schs 9–11 to, the SSFA 1998.
[6]   See, for example, ss 70–73.

almost all practical purposes, and it will require such institutions to make and comply with plans for 'fair access' to the instuitutions if they wish to charge fees above a certain level.[1]

Generally

1.20 Curiously, in several respects, the law of education appears to have turned full circle. For example, as indicated above,[2] the National Curriculum had a predecessor in the Codes contained in the minutes of the Committee of Council on Education, the influence of which was progressively diminished until, for a period of almost half a century (from 1944, when the EA 1944 repealed the original legislation, until 1988, when the ERA 1988 was enacted), there was no national regulation of the curriculum.[3] Yet, even before 1944, the control which was exercised had diminished over time.[4] Although control over the secular curriculum was mostly placed in the hands of LEAs under s 23 of the EA 1944, in practice it was left to the teaching profession to determine that curriculum.[5] Therefore, the provisions concerning the National Curriculum in the ERA 1988 involved a complete reversal of both policy and practice. In addition, the fact that the new statutory corporations are in most cases exempt charities has brought back to the fore the question of the impact of charity law.

1.21 The introduction of the new statutory corporations had an additional, perhaps unforeseen, result: it helped to bring back to life the law of corporations per se – a subject which had by and large fallen into desuetude except as a branch of the law of companies and of the law of local government.

1.22 On a more practical level, many of the changes introduced since 1979 appear to have been made with a view to promoting the policies of freedom of choice and of giving power to the consumer. However, in at least one respect those policies have not been entirely successful. This is because the freedom of parents to choose the school at which their children are educated, the intended result of the Education Act 1980, seems at the present time at least in some cases to be largely illusory. This is because a popular school cannot expand indefinitely, with the result that there will always be disappointed parents.

---

[1] See further, paras **17.126** et seq.

[2] See para **1.9**.

[3] The main original provision, s 7 of the 1870 Act, was contained in the consolidating Education Act 1921, as s 27. Section 97 (which referred to 'the minutes of the Education Department') was, however, replaced by s 120 of and the Sixth Schedule to the Education Act 1921, but the effect of the latter provisions was so far as relevant the same as that of s 97 of the 1870 Act. The Sixth Schedule in fact referred to 'the education code' rather than to 'the minutes of the Education Department'.

[4] NS Harris, *Law and Education: Regulation, Consumerism and the Education System* (Sweet & Maxwell, 1993), p 199, quotes from JP White *Towards a Compulsory Curriculum* (1973), where it was said that before 1926 'there was a fairly strict centralized surveillance of the content of elementary education', but from 1926, when a new elementary code was issued by the Education Department, 'individualism ... was given free rein'.

[5] See Harris, op cit, p 27.

PURPOSE OF THIS BOOK

1.23   This book is primarily intended to be of use to all those who practise in the field of education. Accordingly, in what follows, an attempt is made to draw out the practical effects rather than the theoretical underpinning of the law of education today, although on occasion in order to understand the practical effects, it is necessary to refer to that theoretical underpinning.

Chapter 2

THE STATUTORY FRAMEWORK AND GENERAL PRINCIPLES

2.1   An overview is given in this chapter of the statutory framework governing the provision of education in England and Wales, and the general statutory and common law principles applicable to such framework and provision (excluding the law of negligence, an outline of which is set out in Chapter 14). Chapters 3 and 5 are concerned with a number of specific powers of (1) the Secretary of State and the National Assembly for Wales, and (2) LEAs. Certain functions of the Secretary of State and the National Assembly are nevertheless referred to here on the basis that they are so central to the statutory framework that they fit more naturally in this chapter. The same is true of a number of LEAs' functions.

THE SECRETARY OF STATE AND THE NATIONAL ASSEMBLY FOR WALES

Introduction

2.2   The foundation of the public education system of England and Wales is to be found in ss 10 and 11 of the EA 1996. The terms of s 10 are as follows.

'The Secretary of State[1] shall promote the education of the people of England and Wales.'

2.3   Section 11 fleshes out this duty, although it confers no extra power. Section 11 provides that the Secretary of State:

'shall exercise his powers in respect of those bodies in receipt of public funds which –

    (a)   carry responsibility for securing that the required provision for primary, secondary or further education is made –
        (i)   in schools, or
        (ii)   in institutions within the further education sector, in or in any area of England or Wales; or
    (b)   conduct schools or institutions within the further education sector in England and Wales,

for the purpose of promoting primary, secondary and further education in England and Wales.

(2) The Secretary of State shall, in the case of his powers to regulate the provision made in schools and institutions within the further education sector in England and Wales,

---

[1]   'Secretary of State' here means 'one of Her Majesty's Principal Secretaries of State': Interpretation Act 1978, s 5 and Sch 1.

exercise his powers with a view to (among other things) improving standards, encouraging diversity and increasing opportunities for choice.'

2.4   The omission of a reference in ss 10 and 11 of the EA 1996 to higher education and higher education institutions was deliberate, with the result that s 11 has no impact on universities.[1] The omission of a reference to LEAs was also deliberate.[2] Thus LEAs are now merely one of a number of bodies which are in receipt of public funds for distribution onwards to education institutions. The bodies other than LEAs are further referred to below where relevant. The main ones are mentioned here merely for the purpose of giving an overview. They are the Learning and Skills Council for England,[3] the National Council for Education and Training in Wales,[4] the Higher Education Funding Councils for England and Wales[5] (which are responsible for distributing funds for higher education[6]) and the Secretary of State himself, as a provider of funds to city technology colleges, city colleges for the technology of the arts, and Academies.[7]

2.5   However, in Wales, most of the Secretary of State's powers are exercised by the National Assembly for Wales. In relation to enactments before 1998, this is a result of the National Assembly for Wales (Transfer of Functions) Order 1999,[8] made under the Government of Wales Act 1998. Since the establishment of the National Assembly for Wales, specific provision has been made in most (but not all) relevant primary legislation for the National Assembly for Wales to exercise functions in Wales which in England are to be exercised by the Secretary of State. References below to the Secretary of State should accordingly, unless there is a contrary indication, be read in relation to Wales as references to the National Assembly for Wales.

The National Curriculum and related matters

2.6   The Secretary of State has considerable powers in relation to the National Curriculum and public examinations. These are considered in depth in Chapter 11.

---

[1]   *Hansard*, HL vol 546, cols 1083 and 1098, per Baroness Blatch, Minister of State. But note s 11A of the Education Act 1994, which requires the Secretary of State when exercising his functions under ss 10 and 11 of the EA 1996 to make 'such arrangements as he considers expedient for securing that sufficient facilities are available for the training of teachers to serve in [state schools and further education institutions]'.

[2]   This was indicated by the then Secretary of State, John Patten: *Hansard*, HC vol 220, cols 158–162.

[3]   See s 1 of the LSA 2000.

[4]   See s 30 of the LSA 2000.

[5]   See s 62 of the FHEA 1992.

[6]   It has to be said that slightly less control can be exercised by the Secretary of State with regard to the distribution of funds to higher education institutions than in relation to the funding of schools and further education.

[7]   See EA 1996, ss 482 and 483, and paras **3.68** et seq.

[8]   SI 1999/672, Art 2, Sch 1. The only exceptions are EA 1996, ss 333(5) and (6), 334(2), 335 and 336 (which relate to the Special Educational Needs Tribunal); the regulation-making functions under ss 492–494 (which concern recoupment); ss 492(5), 494(4) and 495 so far as they relate to a dispute to which only one party is in Wales; and Sch 34, para 5 (the power to pay members of an Independent Schools Tribunal remuneration and allowances), in relation to Wales. The enactment of s 195 of the EA 2002 (providing for the Special Educational Needs Tribunal for Wales) has reduced the impact even of these limited exceptions.

Funding powers

2.7   Perhaps the most important function which the Secretary of State has in regard to the provision of education is his power to provide funding for it. Many of his funding powers were conveniently re-enacted in Part 2 of the EA 2002, s 18 of which repealed a number of powers in various enactments. Under s 14(1), the Secretary of State may give, or make arrangements for giving,[1] financial assistance to any person for or in connection with the purposes set out in s 14(2). These purposes include the provision, or proposed provision, in the United Kingdom or elsewhere, of (a) education or educational services, and (b) 'childcare' or 'services related to childcare'.[2]

2.8   With one exception, assistance may be given under s 14 'in any form',[3] including by way of grants, loans, guarantees, or by the incurring of expenditure for the benefit of the person assisted.[4] The exception is that financial assistance may not be given by the Secretary of State under s 14 to an LEA by way of a loan or guarantee.[5] The terms on which assistance may be given under s 14 are set out in s 16, and include that the recipient may be required to pass funding on to another person.[6] Section 16(3) states that the person receiving assistance under s 14 must comply with the terms on which it is given, and that 'compliance may be enforced by the Secretary of State'. Since there is no method stated for such enforcement in the section (or elsewhere in the EA 2002), this provision presumably has the effect that if money is given and it is used otherwise than in accordance with the conditions subject to which it was given, then it will be repayable as a statutory debt.

2.9   As a result of s 27 of the LSA 2000, the Secretary of State may make grants to the LSC, subject to conditions.[7] However, these conditions 'may not ... relate to the Council's securing of the provision of financial resources to a particular person or persons'.[8]

School teachers' pay and conditions

2.10   The Secretary of State has under Part 8 of the EA 2002 the power to determine the pay and conditions of service of teachers in maintained schools in both England and Wales.[9] That power first appeared in the Teachers' Pay and Conditions Act 1987. The full effect of that Act and its ramifications are considered in Chapter 15

---

[1]   Including by way of delegation under s 17: see s 17(1).

[2]   EA 2002, s 14(2)(a) and (b). It is of note that there is no definition in the EA 2002 or elsewhere in the Education Acts of the word 'childcare'. Presumably, it is self-explanatory. See further, para **2.94** regarding s 14.

[3]   EA 2002, s 15(1).

[4]   Ibid, s 15(2).

[5]   Ibid, s 15(3).

[6]   Ibid, s 16(2)(b).

[7]   LSA 2000, s 49 contains equivalent provision concerning the National Assembly for Wales, in relation to the CETW.

[8]   Ibid, s 27(5) and, in relation to Wales, s 49(5).

[9]   See EA 2002, s 122(3), which for this purpose has to be read in conjunction with ss 35 and 36 of that Act.

(which concerns the training, qualification and principles relating to the remuneration of teachers).

Power to compel a rationalisation of places in maintained schools

2.11   Under Sch 7 to the SSFA 1998, the Secretary of State may direct what is called (only) in the title to that Schedule the 'rationalisation of school places'. This is a power by order to direct an LEA to make proposals under ss 28–31 of the SSFA 1998 and/or the governing body of a foundation, voluntary, or foundation special school to exercise their powers to make proposals for the alteration of their school under s 28(2)(b) or s 31(2)(a). This power is considered in more detail in paras **7.48** et seq.

Limits on infant class sizes

2.12   Section 1(1) of the SSFA 1998 requires the Secretary of State by regulations to 'impose a limit on class sizes for infant classes at maintained schools' and to specify the school years in relation to which such limit is to have effect. The limit imposed by s 1 must 'specify the maximum number of pupils that a class to which the limit applies may contain while an ordinary teaching session is conducted by a single school teacher'.[1] The regulations may impose different limits, and fix different dates, according to the age groups into which the pupils in infant classes fall, and may provide for circumstances in which any limit is either not to apply, or is to apply in a manner specified in the regulations.[2]

2.13   The obligation to comply with the limits set out in regulations made under s 1 of the SSFA 1998 is not absolute: rather, the LEA and the governing body of a school to which a limit applies under the regulations 'shall exercise their functions with a view to securing that that limit is complied with in relation to that class'.[3]

2.14   The Secretary of State is empowered by the Education (Infant Class Sizes) (Grant) Regulations 1999[4] to pay grants to LEAs 'in respect of expenditure incurred or to be incurred by them for the purpose of securing that the limit imposed by Regulations made under s 1 of the SSFA 1998 is complied with in relation to infant classes at [schools maintained by them]'.[5]

Education action zones

2.15   Section 10(1) of the SSFA 1998 enables the Secretary of State, if he 'considers that it is expedient to do so with a view to improving standards in the provision of

---

[1]   SSFA 1998, s 1(2) as amended by EA 2002, Sch 21, para 87. 'School teacher' means a person who is a school teacher for the purposes of s 122 of the EA 2002. See paras **15.61** et seq regarding s 122.

[2]   SSFA 1998, s 1(4). Regulations made under s 1 include SIs 1998/1943, 1998/1947, 1998/1968 and 1998/1973.

[3]   Ibid, s 1(6). Section 2 of the SSFA 1998 required statements to be made by LEAs setting out the arrangements which they proposed to make for the purpose of securing that the class size limits in s 1 were complied with, but since the date by which that had to be done (16 October 1998 in England and 27 November 1998 in Wales: see SI 1998/1971 and SI 1998/1942 respectively) is now long passed, no further mention of s 2 is made here.

[4]   SI 1999/13, made under s 3 of the SSFA 1998.

[5]   Regulation 3.

education at any particular eligible schools', by order[1] to provide for those schools to constitute collectively an 'education action zone' (EAZ) for the purposes of ss 10–12 of the SSFA 1998.[2] An 'eligible school' is either a maintained school, a nursery school, a pupil referral unit, or an independent school.[3] The EAZ must in the first instance exist for 3 years, but the Secretary of State may by an order made before the end of that period extend its life for a further 2 years.[4] Furthermore, the Secretary of State may create or extend the duration of an EAZ only with the consent of the governing body of every school which it is proposed should be a member of the EAZ (referred to as a 'participating school').[5] Unless the Secretary of State by order otherwise provides, no EAZ may be created in Wales.[6] An EAZ may be expanded by an Education Action Forum.[7]

Education Action Forums

2.16   Where an order is made under s 10(1) of the SSFA 1998 establishing an EAZ, the order must 'provide for the establishment of an Education Action Forum for the zone'.[8] The Education Action Forum (EAF) is a body corporate.[9] The constitution of the EAF must comply with s 11A of the SSFA 1998. An EAF may not borrow money.[10] An EAF must be dissolved by an order made by the Secretary of State with effect from the time when the EAZ to which it relates ceases to exist.[11]

2.17   The main object of an EAF is 'the improvement of standards in the provision of education at each of the participating schools'.[12] With the consent of the Secretary of State, an EAF may also 'carry on any other activities which it considers will promote the provision of, or access to, education whether in a participating school or otherwise'.[13] The EAF may discharge any 'prescribed function of [the governing body of a participating school] relating to the conduct of the school' under arrangements made by the governing body.[14] The EAF may either '(a) discharge that function on behalf of the governing body until such time as they may specify in a request to the Forum to cease discharging the function on their behalf; or (b) assume full responsibility for the discharge of that function during the whole of the period for which the Forum remains in existence'.[15] Regulations making provision in relation to (a) the circumstances in which such arrangements may be made, (b) the procedure to

---

[1]   The order must be made by statutory instrument: see SSFA 1998, s 138. The same is true of any other order relating to an education action zone, except one made under s 11(5) of the SSFA 1998: s 138(2).

[2]   SSFA 1998, ss 10–12 were amended considerably by EA 2002, Sch 15.

[3]   SSFA 1998, s 10(1A).

[4]   Ibid, s 10(2).

[5]   Ibid, s 10(4). For the definition of 'governing body', see s 10(6)(a) as substituted by EA 2002, Sch 15, para 2(3)(a).

[6]   Ibid, s 10(8).

[7]   Ibid, s 11B. See the following paragraph regarding such a forum.

[8]   Ibid, s 11(1).

[9]   Ibid, s 11(2). See SSFA 1998, Sch 1, and the Education Action Forum (Proceedings) Regulations, SI 1998/1964, in relation to the proceedings of the EAF.

[10]   SSFA 1998, Sch 1, para 1(2).

[11]   Ibid, s 11(5). The order need not be made by statutory instrument: SSFA 1998, s 138(2)(a).

[12]   Ibid, s 12(1).

[13]   Ibid, s 12(1A).

[14]   Ibid, s 12(2).

[15]   Ibid.

be followed by the governing body of a participating school in connection with the making of such arrangements, and (c) the procedure to be followed by the EAF when discharging any function in accordance with such arrangements, may be made under s 12(3) of the SSFA 1998.[1] Regulations may also apply, with prescribed modifications, statutory provisions concerning governing bodies of maintained schools to an EAF when discharging any function under s 12(2)(b).[2] The Secretary of State may, by a direction, provide for a scheme of financial delegation (that is, local management) to be modified where an EAF is discharging any function by virtue of s 12(2)(b).[3] Such an EAF may therefore be made responsible in place of the governing body of a participating school for certain employment law functions.[4]

Appointment of adjudicators for the purposes of the School Standards and Framework Act 1998

2.18   A further function of the Secretary of State is the duty to appoint adjudicators for England for the purposes of the SSFA 1998.[5] The tenure of office, remuneration, staff, accommodation, procedure, and other relevant matters relating to such an adjudicator, are provided for in Sch 5 to the SSFA 1998 and regulations made under para 5 of that Schedule.[6] An adjudicator is entitled to an indemnity from the Secretary of State 'against any reasonable legal costs and expenses reasonably incurred by him in connection with any decision or action taken by him in good faith in pursuance of his functions as an adjudicator'.[7] The adjudicator is subject to the supervision of the Council on Tribunals.[8] The functions of adjudicators are (1) those under s 26 of the SSFA 1998 concerning school organisation plans,[9] (2) those arising under Sch 6 to the SSFA 1998 concerning the approval in certain circumstances of proposals in relation to the establishment, alteration or discontinuance of maintained schools,[10] (3) those arising under Sch 7 to the SSFA 1998 relating to the rationalisation of school places[11] and (4) matters relating to admissions to maintained schools.[12]

2.19   Section 27 of the SSFA 1998 empowers the making of regulations under which the Secretary of State may appoint adjudicators, or panels of adjudicators, for Wales.[13]

---

[1]   No such regulations have been made.

[2]   SSFA 1998, s 12(3)(d). No such regulations have been made.

[3]   Ibid, s 12(5). See paras **7.132** et seq regarding financial delegation. The Secretary of State must consult the LEA before giving a direction under s 12(5): s 12(6).

[4]   This is a product of s 12(5). See further, para **15.75** as to the employment law functions in question.

[5]   See SSFA 1998, s 25.

[6]   See the Education (References to Adjudicator) Regulations 1999, SI 1999/702, and the Education (Adjudicators Inquiry Procedure etc) Regulations 1999, SI 1999/1286, as amended by SI 2001/1339.

[7]   SSFA 1998, Sch 5, para 7.

[8]   Ibid, Sch 5, para 10.

[9]   See paras **2.54–2.56** regarding school organisation plans.

[10] See, for example, para **7.37**.

[11] See paras **7.48** et seq.

[12] See paras **9.9**, **9.11** and **9.12** et seq.

[13] No such regulations have been made.

Powers in s 2 of the Education Act 2002[1]

2.20   The Secretary of State has power under s 2(1) of the EA 2002 (a) to confer exemption or relaxation from any requirement imposed by education legislation[2] on any 'qualifying body',[3] (b) to enable such a body to 'exercise any function conferred on any other qualifying body (either concurrently with or in place of that other body)', and (c) to make consequential modifications of any provision of education legislation. The purpose of this power is to 'facilitate the implementation by qualifying bodies of innovative projects that may ... in the opinion of the Secretary of State, contribute to the raising of the educational standards achieved by children in England'.[4] In forming such an opinion, the Secretary of State must have regard to the need for the curriculum 'for any school affected by the project to be a balanced and broadly based curriculum which promotes the spiritual, moral, cultural, mental and physical development of children and society', and must 'consider the likely effect of the project on all the children who may be affected by it'.[5]

2.21   An order under s 2 of the EA 2002 may not have effect for longer than 3 years initially,[6] but it may be extended (no more than once) for up to 3 years.[7] However, no order under s 2 may be made after 4 years after the commencement date of s 2.[8] Thus no order made under s 2 may be in force after 10 years after the commencement date of the section.

2.22   The power in s 2 is exercisable only on the application of a qualifying body. Such an application must be refused if it appears to the Secretary of State that the proposed order would be likely to have a detrimental effect on the education of children with SEN.[9] The Secretary of State may give guidance as to the matters which he will take into account in deciding whether to grant an application for an order under s 2.[10] No order under s 2 which relates to ss 119–129 of the EA 2002 may be made by the National Assembly for Wales without the consent of the Secretary of State.[11]

2.23   The power in s 2 includes a power to amend a previous order made under the section so as to extend the requirements or functions to which the order applies or

---

[1]   Currently, ss 2–5 are in force only in relation to England.

[2]   That is (1) any of the Education Acts as referred to in s 578 of the EA 1996, (2) the LSA 2000, and (3) any subordinate legislation made under those enactments: EA 2002, s 1(3).

[3]   This means: (1) an LEA, (2) an EAF, (3) the governing body of (a) a community, foundation or voluntary school or a community or foundation special school, (b) a maintained nursery school, (c) a city technology college, a city college for the technology of the arts, or an Academy, and (4) the proprietor of a special school which is not maintained by an LEA but is for the time being approved by the Secretary of State under s 342 of the EA 1996: see EA 2002, s 1(3).

[4]   EA 2002, s 1(1)(a). See s 1(1)(b) in relation to Wales.

[5]   Ibid, s 1(2). A child for this purpose is a person under the age of 19: s 1(3).

[6]   Ibid, s 2(2).

[7]   Ibid, s 3(2).

[8]   Ibid, s 2(7) and (8).

[9]   Ibid, s 2(5).

[10]   Ibid, s 2(6).

[11]   Ibid, s 2(4). This is consistent with the fact that the power in s 122 is exercisable only by the Secretary of State (and not the National Assembly for Wales).

the qualifying bodies to which it applies,[1] and a power (exercisable without the application of a qualifying body to which the order applies) to revoke such a previous order.[2]

2.24   An application made under s 2 must comply with any requirements as to its form and the information supplied with it imposed by the Secretary of State under s 4(1), and before making such an application, the qualifying body making it must consult as required by s 4(2). The Secretary of State may, but only with the consent of the applicant qualifying body, include in an order under s 2 provisions which are different from those requested in the application.[3] If the power in s 2 is exercised in any academic year, then the Secretary of State must prepare a report on all the orders made by him in that year and lay it before each House of Parliament.[4]

Power in ss 6–10 of the EA 2002 to disapply curriculum and/or pay and conditions provisions[5]

2.25   Under ss 6–10 of the EA 2002, a 'qualifying school'[6] may be granted exemption from the requirements of (1) a 'curriculum provision' (that is, a provision of the National Curriculum[7]), and/or (2) a 'pay and conditions provision' (that is, a provision in an order made under s 122 of the EA 2002, which concerns the pay and conditions of teachers[8]). Such requirements must be designated for the purpose under regulations made under s 7(1). Such regulations may designate a curriculum provision or a pay and conditions provision which attracts exemption as of right, or a modification of such a provision which is available as of right.[9] They may also designate such a provision which attracts discretionary exemption, or a modification of such a provision which is available on a discretionary basis.[10]

2.26   The Secretary of State may, on the application of the governing body of a qualifying school, by order[11] provide that any pay and conditions provision designated under s 7(1)(a) or (b) is not to apply in relation to school teachers employed at the school, or is so to apply with modifications.[12] Similarly, the Secretary of State may, on

---

[1]   EA 2002, s 3(1)(a).

[2]   Ibid, s 3(1)(b).

[3]   Ibid, s 4(3).

[4]   Ibid, s 5(1). The National Assembly for Wales must, where it has made any order under s 2 in any academic year, prepare and publish a report on all such orders made by the Assembly during that academic year: s 5(2). An academic year for this purpose is the period 1 August to 31 July: s 5(3).

[5]   Sections 6–10 of the EA 2002 are not yet in force.

[6]   This means a community, foundation or voluntary school, or a community or foundation special school, of a prescribed description which satisfies prescribed criteria relating to one or more of: '(a) the performance of the school, (b) the quality of the leadership in the school, and (c) the quality of the management of the school': s 6(1).

[7]   See s 6(4), which must be read for the purpose with ss 87(1) and 108(1) of the EA 2002.

[8]   See s 6(4).

[9]   EA 2002, s 7(1)(a) and (c). Such regulations may be made by the National Assembly for Wales only with the consent of the Secretary of State: s 7(5).

[10]   Ibid, s 7(1)(b) and (d).

[11]   Made by statutory instrument, which is subject to neither the negative nor the positive resolution procedure: see EA 2002, s 210.

[12]   EA 2002, s 7(2)(a) and (b).

the application of a qualifying school, by order[1] provide that any curriculum provision designated under s 7(1)(b) is not to apply in relation to the school, or is so to apply with modifications specified in the order.[2] Either such order may be revoked or varied on the application of the governing body of the school to which the order relates.[3] Such an order may also be revoked, or its effect may be restricted, by the Secretary of State without any application by the governing body where the school ceases to be a qualifying school.[4] The Secretary of State may give guidance as to the matters which he will take into account in determining whether to grant applications for discretionary orders under s 7(2).[5] An order under s 7(2) may with the consent of the applicant include provisions different from those requested in the application.[6]

2.27 An application under s 7(2) must be in such form and contain such information as is required by the Secretary of State.[7] Before making the application, the governing body must consult the LEA, the parents of registered pupils at the school where the application concerns a curriculum provision, the school teachers employed at the school where the order relates to a pay and conditions provision, and 'such other persons as appear to them to be appropriate, having regard to any guidance given from time to time by the Secretary of State'.[8]

2.28 Where an order is made under s 7(2) in relation to a pay and conditions provision, the governing body of the school to which the order relates must determine the remuneration and other conditions of employment of each school teacher employed at the school to the extent that the pay and conditions provision does not apply to him as a result of the order, but pending such determination his pay and conditions remain unchanged.[9] The Secretary of State may by regulations provide for the application of s 122(2) of the EA 2002 where an order made under s 7(2) is revoked or subsequently restricted by a further order.[10]

Power to form, participate in forming, or invest in companies

2.29 Under s 13 of the EA 2002, the Secretary of State may, if he considers it expedient to do so for purposes connected with any function of his relating to education,[11] form or participate in forming, any company[12] to carry on any activities

---

[1]   Which is also made by statutory instrument subject to neither the negative nor the positive resolution procedure: see EA 2002, s 210.
[2]   EA 2002, s 7(2)(c) and (d).
[3]   Ibid, s 7(2(e).
[4]   Ibid, s 9(1).
[5]   Ibid, s 7(4).
[6]   Ibid, s 8(3).
[7]   Ibid, s 8(1).
[8]   Ibid, s 8(2).
[9]   Ibid, s 10(1).
[10]   Ibid, s 10(2).
[11]   This includes vocational training and social and physical training, but it does not include higher education: s 13(2).
[12]   This means a company within the meaning of the Companies Act 1985: EA 2002, s 13(3).

which he considers likely to secure or facilitate the achievement of those purposes.[1]
He may also invest in any such company in the same circumstances.[2]

Regulatory powers regarding the provision of education in state schools

2.30   The Secretary of State's powers in relation to the making of regulations concerning the conduct of maintained schools, special schools and independent schools are mentioned here for the sake of completeness.[3] The brevity of the mention is no way related to the extent or importance of this power (the results of whose exercise are referred to where relevant below).

Duty to issue and revise code of practice under s 127 of the School Standards and Framework Act 1998

2.31   The Secretary of State is under a duty as a result of s 127 of the SSFA 1998 to issue, and has a power under that section from time to time to revise, a code of practice containing:

> 'such practical guidance as he thinks appropriate with a view to securing effective relationships between local education authorities and the schools maintained by them –
>
> (a)   in relation to promoting high standards of education in such schools; and
> (b)   in relation to the discharge of relevant functions of such authorities in relation to such schools.'[4]

2.32   The 'relevant functions of such authorities in relation to such schools' include those referred to in s 127(6) of the SSFA 1998. They are all functions under the SSFA 1998, namely under ss 6 and 7 (regarding education development plans[5]), s 15(2) (regarding the giving of warnings to schools the standards of performance of whose pupils are in the view of the authority 'unacceptably low'[6]), s 16(1) (concerning the appointment of additional governors to such schools and to those with serious weaknesses or subject to special measures[7]), s 17(1) (regarding the LEA's power to suspend the right of such schools to a delegated budget[8]), s 62(1) (re-enacting the LEA's reserve power to prevent a breakdown of discipline[9]), paras 1 and 2 of Sch 15 (concerning the suspension of delegation for mismanagement[10]), and s 25 of the

---

[1]   EA 2002, s 13(1)(a).

[2]   Ibid, s 13(1)(b).

[3]   See, for example, EA 2002, ss 19 and 21, read with s 212(1) of that Act, which provides that in that Act ' "regulations" means regulations made under this Act by the Secretary of State (in relation to England) or by the National Assembly for Wales (in relation to Wales)'.

[4]   The current code in England came into force on 1 April 1999: see Art 9 of the School Standards and Framework Act 1998 (Commencement No 6 and Saving and Transitional Provisions) Order 1999, SI 1999/1016; that for Wales came into force on 30 June 1999: see the Education (Code of Practice on LEA-School Relations) (Appointed Day) (Wales) Order 1999, SI 1999/2022.

[5]   See paras **2.64–2.66**.

[6]   See para **12.33**.

[7]   See para **12.36**.

[8]   See para **12.37**.

[9]   See para **10.26**.

[10]   See para **7.144**.

School Inspections Act 1996 (SIA 1996) (which confers on an LEA the power to cause an LEA officer to inspect a school maintained by it[1]). The Secretary of State may add further functions to the discharge of which the code of practice made by him under s 127 of the SSFA 1998 will apply.[2]

2.33   The LEA, the governing body, and the head teacher of every maintained school are under a duty to 'have regard' to 'any relevant provisions of the code'. The crucial question in regard to the code is, therefore, the effect of the duty on these bodies to 'have regard' to its provisions. This is a question which arises in relation to a number of aspects of the legislation governing the provision of education.

Impact of a duty placed on a public body to 'have regard' to something

2.34   As a matter of principle, it seems clear that the only result of a duty to have regard to the provisions of a document such as the code of practice made under s 127 of the SSFA 1998 should be that the provisions of the code will be factors which the relevant bodies will have to take into account, and that they will accordingly be factors in the light of which (but not only in the light of which) the decisions of such bodies should be judged when determining whether or not their determinations were *Wednesbury* unreasonable[3] or otherwise unlawful. However, in several cases, statutory guidance has been regarded by the courts as requiring more. For example, in *R v Islington London Borough Council, ex parte Rixon*,[4] Sedley J said in relation to the duty of a local authority under s 7 of the Local Authority Social Services Act 1970, which requires local authorities when exercising social services functions to act 'under the general guidance of the Secretary of State', that:

> 'Parliament in enacting s 7(1) did not intend local authorities to whom ministerial guidance was given to be free, having considered it, to take it or leave it. ... [I]n my view, Parliament by s 7(1) has required local authorities to follow the path charted by the Secretary of State's guidance, with liberty to deviate from it where the local authority judges on admissible grounds that there is good reason to do so, but without freedom to take a substantially different course.'[5]

The comment of Sedley J in the same case that 'a failure to comply with the statutory policy guidance is unlawful and can be corrected by means of judicial review'[6] must be read in the light of the statement set out immediately above. If not, then it is suggested here that comment on any view goes too far. In regard to a set of guidelines relating to the matter issued by the Department of Health, but not under a specific statutory provision, Sedley J also said that:

---

[1]   See para **12.49**.

[2]   See SSFA 1998, s 127(6), which requires no particular method for the addition by the Secretary of State of functions for this purpose: all that is required is a determination by the Secretary of State.

[3]   That is, unreasonable in the narrow sense referred to by Lord Greene MR in *Associated Provincial Picture Houses Limited v Wednesbury Corporation* [1948] 1 KB 223, or simply irrational (to use the term used by Lord Diplock in *Council of Civil Service Unions v Minister for the Civil Service* [1985] AC 374).

[4]   [1997] ELR 66.

[5]   Ibid, at 71B–C.

[6]   Ibid, at 73D–E.

'While such guidance lacks the status accorded by section 7 of the 1970 Act, it is ... something to which regard must be had in carrying out the statutory functions.'[1]

2.35   *R v Police Complaints Board, ex parte Madden*[2] could probably be distinguished in this context, but nevertheless provides some further guidance. There, a slavish following of guidance issued by the Secretary of State to which the Complaints Board was obliged by statute to 'have regard', was quashed. This was on the basis that the Board had acted unlawfully and in any event had fettered its discretion, by allowing itself to be bound by the approach of the Director of Public Prosecutions in relation to disciplinary charges (to which the guidance referred). The case of *De Falco v Crawley Borough Council*[3] is perhaps more relevant. There, the Court of Appeal ruled that guidance to which the respondent local authority was under a duty to 'have regard' was of no direct statutory force or effect, and that the authority was not bound to follow it in any particular case.[4] This suggests that Sedley J went too far in *ex parte Rixon* in relation to the duty to have regard to statutory policy guidance, such as is contained in the provisions of the code of practice required by s 127 of the SSFA 1998. The judgment of Dyson J in *C v Special Educational Needs Tribunal*,[5] so far as it concerned the application of the code of practice regarding the education of children with SEN made under s 313 of the EA 1996, is consistent with the ruling in *De Falco*,[6] and is therefore contrary to that of Sedley J in *ex parte Rixon*. It is of note that Dyson J's approach towards non-statutory guidance is also contrary to that of Sedley J in *ex parte Rixon*. *C v Special Educational Needs Tribunal* concerned (among other things) the degree of precision required in setting out the SEN in a statement of SEN, and Dyson J commented that although the then relevant DES circular, 22/89, impliedly required the statement to specify the provision in detail, the circular had no statutory force, and it was a matter for the LEA to decide 'with what degree of precision it wished to specify the special educational provision'.[7]

2.36   It therefore seems clear that the proposition set out at the beginning of para **2.34** is capable of being sustained by reference to the relevant case-law, *ex parte Rixon* notwithstanding. Indeed, in *S v Brent London Borough Council*,[8] the court (which included Sedley LJ) said in relation to the code of practice issued under s 68 of the SSFA 1998 concerning exclusions from maintained schools (to which governing bodies, LEAs and appeal panels established under para 2 of Sch 18 to that Act were obliged to 'have regard') that:

'Appeal Panels, and schools too, must keep in mind that guidance is no more than that: it is not direction, and certainly not rules. Any Appeal Panel which, albeit on legal advice,

---

[1]   [1997] ELR 66, at 79G. The reference at that point in the ELR report is to s 7 of the 1990 Act, but the report in *The Times* of 17 April 1996 (as well as the context) makes it clear that the reference was to the 1970 Act. The approach of Sedley J is to be contrasted with that of Dyson J in *C v Special Educational Needs Tribunal* [1997] ELR 390, as to which see para **2.35**.

[2]   [1983] 2 All ER 353.

[3]   [1980] QB 460.

[4]   See ibid, at 482D–E and 478A.

[5]   [1997] ELR 390.

[6]   See ibid, at 398E–F.

[7]   Ibid, at 398H. See now paras **6.69–6.71** regarding the degree of specificity required in a statement of SEN.

[8]   [2002] ELR 556, para 15.

treats the Secretary of State's Guidance as something to be strictly adhered to or simply follows it because it is there will be breaking its statutory remit in at least three ways: it will be failing to exercise its own independent judgment; it will be treating guidance as if it were rules; and it will, in lawyers' terms, be fettering its own discretion. Equally, however, it will be breaking its remit if it neglects the guidance. The task is not an easy one.'

2.37 In any event, the provisions of the code are likely to be at the very least influential in relation to determinations of the local government ombudsman.[1]

Powers of the National Assembly for Wales in relation to the making of regional provision for special educational needs

2.38 Sections 191–194 of the EA 2002 empower the National Assembly to direct two or more LEAs in Wales to make regional provision for children with SEN. Section 191(1) empowers the National Assembly to direct all or some LEAs in Wales to 'consider whether they (or any of them) would be able to carry out their special educational functions, in respect of children with the special educational needs specified in the direction, more efficiently or effectively if regional provision were made'. If the National Assembly is of the view that two or more LEAs in Wales would be able to carry out their special educational functions in respect of a particular class of children more effectively or efficiently if regional provision were made, then the Assembly may, under s 192, by order (which does not need to be made by statutory instrument[2]) direct two or more such LEAs and/or the governing body of a foundation, voluntary or foundation special school, to take certain kinds of action in order to secure that such regional provision is made, including the publication of proposals for the establishment, alteration or discontinuance of schools. Under s 193, the National Assembly may itself make proposals of the sort which have, or might have, been made under the direction. Section 194 makes consequential amendments to ss 14 and 318 of the EA 1996, which, of course, apply only in relation to Wales.

LOCAL EDUCATION AUTHORITIES

The duty in s 14(1) of the Education Act 1996 and related functions

2.39 An LEA is under a duty as a result of s 14(1) of the EA 1996 to 'secure that sufficient schools for providing (a) primary education and (b) education that is secondary education by virtue of section 2(2)(a), are available for their area'.[3] This duty does not extend to children under compulsory school age.[4]

2.40 'Compulsory school age' is now defined by s 8 of the EA 1996 as amended by s 52(1)–(3) of the EA 1997. A person begins to be of compulsory school age when he

---

[1]   Under the provisions of Part III of the Local Government Act 1974.
[2]   See EA 2002, s 210(1) and (2).
[3]   The duty is therefore not to provide schools, but rather, merely to secure that they are available. For the definition of primary and secondary education, see s 2 of the EA 1996, as to material parts of which, see paras **7.2–7.5**.
[4]   EA 1996, s 14(4), as amended by EA 1997, Sch 7, para 12.

attains the age of five 'if he attains that age on a prescribed day, and ... otherwise at the beginning of the prescribed day next following his attaining that age'.[1] A person ceases to be of compulsory school age:

'at the end of the day which is the school leaving date for any calendar year –

(a) if he attains the age of 16 after that day but before the beginning of the school year[2] next following,
(b) if he attains that age on that day, or
(c) (unless paragraph (a) applies) if that day is the school leaving date next following his attaining that age.'

2.41   The Secretary of State may by order (which must be made by statutory instrument[3]) specify the prescribed days in each year for the purpose of determining under s 8(2) when children begin to be of compulsory school age, and the day which is to be the school leaving date for that year.[4]

2.42   The schools available for an area:

'shall not be regarded as sufficient for the purposes of [s 14(1)] unless they are sufficient in number, character and equipment to provide for all pupils the opportunity of appropriate education.'[5]

2.43   'Appropriate education' for this purpose means:

'education which offers such variety of instruction and training as may be desirable in view of –

(a) the pupils' different ages, abilities and aptitudes, and
(b) the different periods for which they may be expected to remain at school,

including practical instruction and training appropriate to their different needs.'[6]

2.44   Section 14(6) of the EA 1996 requires an LEA to have regard to the 'need for securing that primary and secondary education are provided in separate schools', to the need for securing that special educational provision is made for pupils who have SEN, and to the:

'expediency of securing the provision of boarding accommodation (in boarding schools or otherwise) for pupils for whom education as boarders is considered by their parents and the authority to be desirable.'

---

[1]   EA 1996, s 8(2)
[2]   'School year' is now defined by EA 1996, s 579(1) as amended by EA 1997, Sch 7, para 43.
[3]   EA 1996, s 568.
[4]   Ibid, 8(4), as substituted by s 52(3) of EA 1997. The school leaving date has been set for 1998 and successive years as the last Friday in June, by the Education (School Leaving Date) Order 1997, SI 1997/1970. The Education (Start of Compulsory School Age) Order 1998, SI 1998/1607 prescribes 31 August, 31 December and 31 March as the relevant dates for determining when a child begins to be of compulsory school age.
[5]   EA 1996, s 14(2).
[6]   Ibid, s 14(3).

2.45   Section 16(1) and (2) of the EA 1996 empower an LEA to establish, maintain and assist primary and secondary schools, both within and outside their area.[1] However, this power does not extend to establishing a school to provide part-time education suitable to the requirements of persons of any age over compulsory school age, or to provide full-time education suitable to the requirements of persons who have attained the age of 19.[2]

2.46   An LEA is both entitled and required to take into account the provision made in all schools in its area in order to determine what numbers and sorts of schools must be provided in order to secure that there are sufficient schools of the sort required by s 14.[3] If, however, it is a condition of entry that a fee be paid, then the school cannot be taken into account in the determination.[4] However, under s 18 of the EA 1996, an LEA may make arrangements for the provision of primary and secondary education for pupils at schools which are maintained neither by them nor by another LEA. When they do so, they must comply with the provisions of s 517 of the EA 1996 regarding the payment of fees.[5] Presumably, when they pay the relevant fees, they may take into account the accommodation which is as a result available.

2.47   Section 18 of the EA 1996 will be repealed and replaced by a new s 18, to be inserted by s 128 of the SSFA 1998 when the latter is brought into force. Under s 18 of the EA 1996 as substituted by s 128 of the SSFA 1998:

'(1)   Subject to subsection (2), a local education authority may –

(a)   assist any primary or secondary non-maintained school[6] (whether inside or outside their area);

(b)   make arrangements for pupils to be provided with primary or secondary education at such schools.'

2.48   Section 18(2) and (3) as substituted will permit LEAs to make grants or other payments in respect of fees or expenses for pupils at non-maintained schools only in circumstances specified or determined in accordance with regulations, and require them to make such grants or other payments in other circumstances so specified or determined.

---

[1]   SSFA 1998, ss 20(4) and 22 make it clear that the LEA is under a duty to maintain schools of the type referred to in the latter section.

[2]   EA 1996, s 16(3). See, however, paras **2.81–2.83** concerning an LEA's functions in relation to further education.

[3]   *R v Secretary of State for Education and Science, ex parte Avon County Council (No 2)* (1990) *The Times*, June 15; (1990) 88 LGR 737n. Although there is no reference in either of these reports to the principle stated in the text to this note, the summary of the case in PM Liell, JE Coleman and D Wolfe, *The Law of Education* (Butterworths, London, looseleaf) at para F[99] indicates that that is what the Court of Appeal said. In any event, the principle is a sound one, albeit that it must be read against the background of the existence then of grant-maintained schools.

[4]   'The accommodation in the school cannot be said to have been made "available" for children if they are refused admission unless and until their parents comply with some request to pay money which the statutes do not confer upon the local education authority any right to demand': *Gateshead Union v Durham County Council* [1918] 1 Ch 146, 160 per Swinfen Eady LJ.

[5]   See paras **4.49** et seq.

[6]   Meaning a school which is not maintained by any LEA: s 18(4).

2.49   The duty of an LEA under s 8 of the Education Act 1944 (which was the predecessor to s 14 of the EA 1996) was described by Woolf LJ in *R v Inner London Education Authority, ex parte Ali*[1] as only a 'target' rather than an 'absolute' duty. In that case, the LEA had insufficient teachers to staff its schools with the result that approximately 300 pupils were deprived of a primary school place. However, because the LEA was doing all that it reasonably could to rectify the situation, it was not in breach of s 8.

2.50   Although an LEA is obliged by s 14(1) of the EA 1996 to provide staff,[2] as a result of *Meade v Haringey London Borough Council*[3] it is clear that there can be circumstances where an LEA can close schools without being in breach of the duty in s 14(1). Those circumstances are likely to be ones of emergency,[4] but the LEA must be acting legitimately in furtherance of the duty placed upon it by s 14(1) and not in total disregard of its responsibilities as an LEA.[5]

2.51   The duty in s 14(1) of the EA 1996 is to be enforced (at least primarily) by means of a complaint to the Secretary of State under s 497 of that Act.[6] The duty in s 14(1) must be read as subject to the duties placed on LEAs not to discriminate against pupils on the ground of their race, sex, disability or other status within the meaning of Art 14 of the European Convention on Human Rights. Those duties are considered in Chapter 18.

School organisation committees

2.52   Section 24(1) of the SSFA 1998 requires every LEA in England to establish a 'school organisation committee for their area'. The committee must be constituted in accordance with regulations made by the Secretary of State,[7] and must have among its members at least one member of the LEA, at least one person nominated by the Diocesan Board of Education for any diocese of the Church of England any part of which is comprised in the LEA's area, and at least one person nominated by the bishop of any Roman Catholic Church diocese any part of which is situated in the LEA's area.[8] The functions of the school organisation committee are to consider the

---

[1]   [1990] 2 Admin LR 822, 828B; (1990) *The Times*, February 21; [1990] COD 317; and see the note of NS Harris in (1990) 2 *Education and the Law* 174. There is also an extensive analysis of the case in P Meredith, *Government, Schools and the Law* (Routledge, London, 1992), pp 106–111, during the course of which relevant extracts from the LEXIS transcript of the case are set out.

[2]   *R v Liverpool City Council, ex parte Ferguson* (1985) *The Times*, November 20.

[3]   [1979] 1 WLR 637.

[4]   *Meade*, ibid, at p 650b–c, per Eveleigh LJ.

[5]   *Ex parte Ferguson*, per Watkins LJ.

[6]   *Watt v Kesteven County Council* [1955] 1 QB 408, CA; but note *R v Inner London Education Authority, ex parte Ali* (see footnote 1 above), where Woolf LJ said that he 'would not accept that the language of the default powers contained in s 68 and s 99 of the [1944] Act indicate that Parliament intended the jurisdiction of the courts to be ousted from considering the issues which can be considered by the Secretary of State under those sections' ([1990] Admin LR 822, 831B; see also at 836C). See further, paras **3.30** et seq regarding s 497 of the EA 1996.

[7]   SSFA 1998, s 24(2); see the Education (School Organisation Committees) (England) Regulations 1999, SI 1999/700.

[8]   SSFA 1998, s 24(3). See SSFA 1998, Sch 4, and the Education (School Organisation Committees) (England) Regulations 1999, SI 1999/700; the Education (School Organisation Plans) (England) Regulations 1999, SI 1999/701 (amended by SIs 2001/783 and 2003/1201); the Education (Maintained

LEA's school organisation plan (as to which, see paras **2.54** et seq) and to consider proposals relating to the establishment, alteration or discontinuance of maintained schools, under Sch 6 to the SSFA 1998.[1]

2.53 Section 27 of the SSFA 1998 empowers the making of regulations providing for the establishment by LEAs in Wales of school organisation committees. No such regulations have been made.

Duty to prepare school organisation plan under s 26 of the School Standards and Framework Act 1998

2.54 Section 26 of the SSFA 1998 requires every LEA to prepare a school organisation plan for their area, and new ones at prescribed intervals. A school organisation plan is a statement which sets out:

'(a) how the authority propose to exercise their functions during the prescribed period with a view to securing the provision of primary and secondary education that will meet the needs of the population of their area during that period; and

(b) any facilities which the authority expect to be available outside their area for providing such education.'[2]

2.55 A school organisation plan prepared by an LEA in England must be approved by the school organisation committee for the LEA's area[3] or the adjudicator.[4] The preparation and approval of school organisation plans are subject to the Education (School Organisation Plans) (England) Regulations 1999[5] and the Education (School Organisation Plans) (Wales) Regulations 2003.[6] In preparing a school organisation plan, the LEA must have regard to the plans of any relevant local learning and skills council ('local LSC') published under s 22 of the LSA 2000.[7] A local LSC is relevant if

---

Special Schools) (England) Regulations 1999, SI 1999/2212, the Education (School Organisation Proposals) (England) Regulations 1999, SI 1999/2213 (amended by SIs 2000/2198, 2001/1405 and 2003/1229); the Education (Change of Category of Maintained Schools) (England) Regulations 2000, SI 2000/2195 (and see the Education (Foundation Body) (England) Regulations 2000, SI 2000/2872); the School Organisation Proposals by the Learning and Skills Council for England Regulations 2003, SI 2003/507; and the Education (Additional Secondary School Proposals) Regulations 2002, SI 2003/1200 regarding the proceedings and expenses of a school organisation committee. The members of the committee are entitled to allowances payable under s 173(4) of the Local Government Act 1972 (SSFA 1998, Sch 4, para 3), and are entitled to an indemnity from the relevant LEA 'against any reasonable legal costs and expenses reasonably incurred by those members in connection with any decision or action taken by them in good faith in pursuance of their functions as members of the committee': Sch 4, para 8.

[1] Those functions are considered in Chapter 7.

[2] SSFA 1998, s 26(2). A school organisation plan must also 'deal with such matters, and take such form, as may be prescribed': s 26(3); see the Education (School Organisation Plans) (Wales) Regulations 1999, SI 1999/499, as amended by SI 2001/3710, and the Education (School Organisation Plans) (England) Regulations 1999, SI 1999/701 (as amended by SIs 2001/783 and 2003/1201), regarding some such matters.

[3] As to which, see para **2.52**.

[4] SSFA 1998, s 26(5). See para **2.18** regarding the adjudicator.

[5] SI 1999/701, made under s 24(5) and (6). See footnote 3 above regarding the amendments to those regulations.

[6] SI 2003/1732.

[7] SSFA 1998, s 26A(1), as inserted by the LSA 2000. See para **16.31** concerning local LSCs.

its area falls within the area of the LEA.[1] When considering a school organisation plan, a school organisation committee and the adjudicator also must 'have regard to the plans of any relevant' local LSC.[2]

2.56   While there is no school organisation committee in existence in Wales and no adjudicator, a school organisation plan in Wales must be adopted, in accordance with a procedure set out in regulations for the preparation and adoption of such plans, by the LEA (rather than approved by a school organisation committee for the authority's area).[3] In preparing such a plan, an LEA in Wales must have regard to the plans of the CETW published under s 43 of the LSA 2000.[4] If, however, school organisation committees are established and adjudicators are appointed in Wales under regulations made under s 27(1) of the SSFA 1998, then the school organisation plan for an LEA's area will have to be approved in accordance with the regulations, which may apply (among other things) any provision of s 26 of the SSFA 1998.[5] The school organisation committee or the adjudicator must then have regard to the plans of the CETW published under s 43 of the LSA 2000.[6]

Duty to contribute to the development of the community

2.57   Section 13(1) of the EA 1996 (as amended by the LSA 2000) is in the following terms:

> 'A local education authority shall (so far as their powers enable them to do so) contribute towards the spiritual, moral, mental, and physical development of the community by securing that efficient primary education and secondary education are available to meet the needs of the population of their area.'

2.58   However, this duty does not extend to matters in respect of which any duty is imposed on (1) the LSC or the CETW, or (2) the higher education funding councils established under s 62 of the FHEA 1992.[7]

2.59   It has been held that an LEA does not have power under what is now s 13(1) of the EA 1996 to institute legal proceedings for the interpretation of a will purporting to create a charitable trust: *Re Belling, London Borough of Enfield v Public*

---

[1]   SSFA 1998, s 26A(4).

[2]   Ibid, s 26A(2) and (3).

[3]   Ibid, s 26(7). See further, s 26(8) regarding the content of the regulations to be made under s 26(7). For the current regs, see footnote 6 at para **2.55**.

[4]   Ibid, s 26B(1), inserted by the LSA 2000.

[5]   See ibid, s 27(2).

[6]   Ibid, s 26B(2) and (3).

[7]   EA 1996, s 13(2). See paras **16.9** et seq for the relevant functions of the LSC and the CETW and **17.8** et seq regarding relevant functions of the higher education funding councils.

Trustee.[1] It is of interest that although it has been thought that s 13 is declaratory only,[2] in R *(Rhodes) v Kingston upon Hull City Council,*[3] Goldring J said:

'How could a reasonable or rational Secretary of State not intervene [under s 496 or s 497 of the EA 1996] when a local education authority is in breach of its statutory duty under s 13(1)?'

Duty of an LEA under s 13A of the Education Act 1996 to promote high standards of education

2.60   Section 13A(1) of the EA 1996 requires every LEA to:

'ensure that their functions relating to the provision of education to which this section applies are (so far as they are capable of being so exercised) exercised by the authority with a view to promoting high standards.'

2.61   The section applies to education for persons of compulsory school age (whether at school or otherwise), and education for persons of any age above or below that age who are registered as pupils at schools maintained by the authority.[4]

Duties of an LEA under ss 175 and 176 of the Education Act 2002

2.62   Mention needs to be made here of the duty of an LEA under s 175(1) of the EA 2002 to:

'make arrangements for ensuring that the functions conferred on them in their capacity as a local education authority are exercised with a view to safeguarding and promoting the welfare of children.'

However, Parliament did not intend this duty to give rise to any right to damages in the event of its breach.[5] It should be noted that s 175(4) provides:

'An authority or body mentioned in any of subsections (1) to (3) shall, in considering what arrangements are required to be made by them under that subsection, have regard to any guidance given from time to time (in relation to England) by the Secretary of State or (in relation to Wales) by the National Assembly for Wales.'

---

[1]   [1967] Ch 425. Section 222 of the Local Government Act 1972 allows a local authority to bring proceedings in the interests of the inhabitants of their area. It has therefore probably reversed the effect of *Re Belling,* because it would probably allow an LEA to make an application similar to that made in *Re Belling.*

[2]   As noted by KP Poole, in *Education Law* (Sweet & Maxwell, 1988), at paras 1.67–1.68, although it was questioned in the House of Commons whether s 7 of the EA 1944, the predecessor to s 13 of the EA 1996, was indeed declaratory (397 HC Deb 95, 15 February 1944), in both Houses, Government spokesmen described it as such.

[3]   [2001] ELR 230, at para 49.

[4]   EA 1996, s 13A(2).

[5]   Baroness Ashton of Upholland, the Parliamentary Under-Secretary of State, Department for Education and Skills, speaking on Report in the House of Lords on 26 June 2002, said that 'the clause does not intend to give rise to private law actions by individuals against an education authority, school or FE institution for breaches of the statutory duties it contains' (*Hansard,* HL vol 636, col 1458). Section 175 is currently in force in England only: see SI 2004/1318.

2.63   A duty of equally wide scope, but which is even weaker, is that which is imposed by s 176(1) of the EA 2002. That provides that an LEA must, in the exercise of any of its functions relating to maintained schools, pupil referral units, or the provision of education for children of compulsory school age otherwise than at school, 'have regard to any guidance given from time to time by the Secretary of State (in relation to England) or the National Assembly for Wales (in relation to Wales) about consultation with pupils in connection with the taking of decisions affecting them'. Such guidance must, as a result of s 176(2), 'provide for a pupil's views to be considered in the light of his age and understanding'.

Duty to prepare education development plans under s 6 of the School Standards and Framework Act 1998[1]

2.64   Section 6(1) of the SSFA 1998 requires every LEA to 'prepare an education development plan for their area, and [to] prepare further such plans at such intervals as may be determined by or in accordance with regulations'.[2] Such a plan must set out proposals by the LEA 'for developing their provision of education for children[3] in their area, whether by – (i) raising the standards of education provided for such children (whether at schools maintained by the authority or otherwise than at school), or (ii) improving the performance of such schools, or otherwise'.[4] It must also have annexes, which must contain 'such material as may be prescribed'[5] and may contain such other information as the authority considers relevant to the proposals set out in the statement.[6]

2.65   The statement of proposals must 'deal with such matters, and relate to such period, as may be determined by or in accordance with regulations'.[7] In the course of preparing an education development plan, the LEA must consult (a) the governing body and head teacher of every school maintained by the authority, (b) the appropriate diocesan authority for any foundation or voluntary school in the LEA's area which is a Church of England, Church in Wales or Roman Catholic Church school, and (c) 'such other persons as they consider appropriate'.[8] The LEA must

---

[1]   The exercise of functions under ss 6 and 7 of the SSFA 1998 may be affected by (and is currently mentioned in) the code of practice empowered by s 127 of the SSFA 1998, as to which see paras **2.31**– **2.33**. The duty in s 6 may be contracted out by an LEA, except that the LEA may not authorise another person to approve the plan for the purpose of its submission to the Secretary of State for approval or to adopt it: Contracting Out (Local Education Authority Functions) (England) Order 2002, SI 2002/928, Sch 2.

[2]   The current regulations are the Education Development Plans (England) Regulations 2001, SI 2001/3815 (as amended by SI 2002/423) and the Education Development Plans (Wales) Regulations 2002, SI 2002/1187.

[3]   'Children' means 'persons of compulsory school age (whether at school or otherwise), or ... persons of any age above or below that age who are registered as pupils at schools maintained by the authority': s 6(3).

[4]   SSFA 1998, s 6(2)(a).

[5]   Regarding which, see now the Education Development Plans (England) Regulations 2001, SI 2001/3815 and the Education Development Plans (Wales) Regulations 2002, SI 2002/1187.

[6]   Ibid, s 6(2)(b) and (5).

[7]   Ibid, s 6(4)(a). See SI 2001/3815 (as amended by SI 2002/423) and SI 2002/1187.

[8]   Ibid, s 6(7). For what is a maintained school, see SSFA 1998, ss 142(1) and 20(7).

also, when performing its functions under s 6, 'have regard to any guidance given from time to time by the Secretary of State'.[1]

2.66 The statement of proposals made in the education development plan must be approved by the Secretary of State under s 7 of the SSFA 1998,[2] which contains detailed procedural provisions. Once the statement of proposals in the plan has been approved by the Secretary of State under s 7 and he has notified the LEA of that approval, the LEA must implement the proposals set out in the statement, so far as approved by the Secretary of State, as from such date as he may determine.[3] The LEA must also publish the plan 'in such manner and by such date as may be prescribed, and ... provide such persons as may be prescribed with copies of that plan or of a summary version of that plan'.[4]

Nursery education and childcare

Introduction

2.67 As a result of s 118(1) of the SSFA 1998, an LEA must 'secure that the provision (whether or not by them) of nursery education for children who – (a) have not attained compulsory school age, but (b) have attained such age as may be prescribed, is sufficient for their area'.[5] In determining whether the provision of such education is sufficient for their area, the LEA may have regard to any facilities which they expect to be available outside their area for providing such education, and must have regard to any guidance given from time to time by the Secretary of State.[6]

2.68 As a result of s 118A(1) of the SSFA 1998,[7] an LEA must 'review annually the sufficiency of childcare provision for their area'. In doing so, it may have regard to any facilities which it expects to be available outside its area for providing childcare, and must have regard to any guidance given by the Secretary of State.[8] An LEA must also establish and maintain 'a service providing information to the public relating to the provision of childcare and related services to their area',[9] and in relation to the 'function, form and content' of such service, must have regard to any guidance given by the Secretary of State.[10]

2.69 'Nursery education' is defined by s 117 of the SSFA 1998 to mean 'full-time or part-time education suitable for children who have not attained compulsory school

---

[1]   SSFA 1998, s 6(9). For the impact on a public body of a duty to 'have regard' to something, see paras **2.34–2.36**.

[2]   See ibid, ss 6(4)(b) and 7(1).

[3]   Ibid, s 7(3).

[4]   Ibid, s 7(9); see reg 6 of SI 2001/3815 and reg 6 (in different terms) of SI 2002/1185 regarding publication and the provision of copies.

[5]   Regarding the prescribed age, see (for England) SI 1999/1329 as amended by SI 2002/2466 and (for Wales) SI 2003/893.

[6]   SSFA 1998, s 118(2). See paras **2.34–2.36** concerning the impact of the requirement to 'have regard' to something.

[7]   Section 118A was inserted by s 149 of the EA 2002.

[8]   SSFA 1998, s 118A(2).

[9]   Ibid, s 118A(3).

[10] Ibid, s 118A(4).

age (whether provided at schools or elsewhere)'.[1] In contrast, the word 'childcare' is not defined in any Education Act.[2] Parliament presumably thought it to be self-explanatory.

Early years development and childcare partnerships

2.70   Every LEA must 'establish for their area a body to be known as an early years development and childcare partnership'.[3] The LEA must 'have regard'[4] to any guidance given from time to time by the Secretary of State when 'establishing the partnership and determining its constitution'.[5] The LEA may establish a sub-committee of the partnership for any part of its area.[6] The LEA must 'make arrangements (a) for the meetings and proceedings of the partnership and any such sub-committee, and (b) for the partnership (and any such sub-committee) to be provided with accommodation and with such services as the authority consider appropriate'.[7]

2.71   The functions of the partnership are to work with the LEA (1) in reviewing (a) the sufficiency of the provision of nursery education for the LEA's area for the purposes of s 118 and (b) the sufficiency of childcare provision for the LEA's area for the purposes of s 118A, and (2) in preparing early years development and childcare plans under s 120 of the SSFA 1998.[8] The Secretary of State may by order (made by statutory instrument) confer additional functions on early years development and childcare partnerships.[9]

Early years development and childcare plans

2.72   Every LEA must prepare, in conjunction with the early years development and childcare partnership for its area, 'an early years development and childcare plan for their area'.[10] They must prepare new such plans at intervals determined by or in accordance with regulations.[11] Such a plan consists of (a) a statement setting out the LEA's proposals for complying with its duty under s 118, (b) a statement setting out the LEA's proposals for providing or promoting the provision of childcare for its area, and (c) background and supporting statements.[12] The statement setting out the LEA's proposals for complying with its duty under s 118 must 'deal with such matters, and relate to such period, as may be determined by or in accordance with

---

[1]   For 'compulsory school age', see paras **2.40** and **2.41**.
[2]   The word first appeared in the LSA 2000.
[3]   SSFA 1998, s 119(1) as amended by s 150(5) of the EA 2002, which amended the term 'early years development partnership' wherever it appears in Part 5 of the SSFA 1998 so that those words are now to be read as meaning 'early years development and childcare partnership'.
[4]   See paras **2.34–2.36** for the impact of a duty to 'have regard' to something.
[5]   SSFA 1998, s 119(2).
[6]   Ibid, s 119(3).
[7]   Ibid, s 119(4).
[8]   Ibid, s 119(5) as amended by s 150 of the EA 2002. See para **2.72** regarding early years and childcare development plans.
[9]   Ibid, ss 119(6) and 138. No such order has been made.
[10]   Ibid, s 120(1)(a) as amended by s 150(5) of the EA 2002.
[11]   SSFA 1998, s 120(1)(b). For the intervals, see in relation to England, SI 1999/1329 as amended by SI 2002/2466 and, in relation to Wales, SI 2003/893.
[12]   Ibid, s 120(2) as amended by s 150(2) of the EA 2002.

regulations',[1] and in relation to the form and content of the statements regarding childcare and the background and supporting statements, the LEA must have regard to guidance given by the Secretary of State.[2] The Secretary of State must approve the early years development and childcare plan under s 121 of the SSFA 1998,[3] which contains a detailed régime for (1) the obtaining of such approval, (2) the obtaining of the Secretary of State's approval for any modifications to the plan, and (3) for the publication of the plan. Once the plan (or modification of it) is approved, the LEA must implement the plan as from a date determined by the Secretary of State.[4]

Nursery education for children with special educational needs

2.73   An LEA which provides nursery education, and any other person who is in receipt of financial assistance given by an LEA and whose nursery provision is taken into account by the authority in formulating proposals for the purposes of s 120(2)(a) of the SSFA 1998, must (unless already required to do so by s 313(2) of the EA 1996) 'have regard to the provisions of the code of practice issued under' s 313 of the EA 1996.[5] So must any person employed by such an authority or other person, or who is 'otherwise engaged to provide his services, in the provision of such education'.[6]

2.74   If that code of practice does not include 'practical guidance in respect of the provision of relevant nursery education for children with special educational needs in circumstances where functions under Part IV of the Education Act 1996 do not fall to be discharged', the Secretary of State 'shall publish a document explaining how the practical guidance contained in that code applies in circumstances where functions under Part IV of the Education Act 1996 do not fall to be discharged', and the duty imposed by s 123(1) of the SSFA 1998 'includes a duty to have regard to the provisions of that document'.[7]

2.75   Where: (1) an LEA or other person providing relevant nursery education[8] for a child makes special educational provision for the child because it is considered that he has SEN; (2) no statement of such needs is maintained under s 324 of the EA 1996 for the child; and (3) the parent has not previously been informed of the special educational provision being made for him, the LEA or such other person must inform the child's parent that such provision is being made for the child because it is considered that he has such needs.[9]

---

[1]   SSFA 1998, s 120(3) as amended by EA 2002, s 150(3). See SI 1999/1329 as amended by SI 2002/2466 and SI 2003/893 regarding the prescribed matters and periods.
[2]   SSFA 1998, s 120(4) as inserted by EA 2002, s 150(3).
[3]   As amended by EA 2002, s 150(4).
[4]   SSFA 1998, s 121(3)(b) as amended.
[5]   Ibid, s 123(1) and (4). See paras 6–19 regarding that code of practice. See paras **2.34–2.36** concerning the impact on a public body of a duty to have regard to something.
[6]   Ibid.
[7]   Ibid, s 123(3).
[8]   That is, of the sort referred to in the first sentence of para **2.73**.
[9]   SSFA 1998, s 123(3A) and (3B), inserted by SENDA 2001, s 7(2).

Power to make teachers available for day nurseries

2.76 An LEA has power under s 515(1) of the EA 1996 to make available to a day nursery[1] the services of a teacher employed by the LEA in a nursery school or in a primary school having one or more nursery classes. Where, however, the teacher is employed in a foundation or voluntary school, the governing body of the school must consent to the arrangement.[2] In addition, the teacher must agree to provide his services for the purposes of the arrangements.[3]

Power to direct admissions to schools

2.77 Under s 96 of the SSFA 1998, an LEA may direct a maintained school[4] to admit a child in the LEA's area where the child has either been refused admission to, or has been permanently excluded from, each school which is a reasonable distance from his or her home and which provides 'suitable education'.[5] However, the power to direct the admission of a child only applies in respect of a school which is a reasonable distance from the child's home and from which the child has not been permanently excluded.[6] Accordingly, by implication, if a pupil has been permanently excluded from each school which is a reasonable distance from his or her home and which provides suitable education, then no direction may be made under s 96. Further, a direction under s 96 may 'not specify a school if his admission would result in prejudice of the kind referred to in section 86(3)(a) by reason of measures required to be taken as mentioned in subsection (4) of that section'.[7]

2.78 There is no right of appeal under s 94 of the SSFA 1998[8] against a refusal of admission to a school as a result of a decision to direct the admission of a child to another school under s 96.[9] Section 97(1) of the SSFA 1998 requires the LEA before deciding to give a direction under s 96 to consult the parent of the child concerned and the governing body of the school which the LEA propose to specify in the direction. An LEA which has decided to give a direction under s 96 must serve notice of that fact on the governing body and the head teacher of the school.[10] The governing body may, within the period of 15 days beginning with the day on which

---

[1] By 'day nursery' is meant a nursery provided as part of the day care provided by a local authority under s 18 of the Children Act 1989 (CA 1989): s 515(4) of the EA 1996. It should be noted that under s 29 (as amended) of the CA 1989, a local authority may charge a parent for the provision of day care under s 18, although no charge may be levied where the parent is in receipt of income support under Part VII of the Social Security Contributions and Benefits Act 1992, of any element of child tax credit other than the family element, of working tax credit, or of an income-based jobseeker's allowance: s 29(3).

[2] EA 1996, s 515(2). It is odd that this provision was extended by SSFA 1998, Sch 30, paras 57 and 136 to apply to a foundation school, since the governing body of the school is the employer of its staff: see para **7.9**. Thus the extension appears to have been mistaken. Section 515(2) appears to have application only in relation to a voluntary controlled school, the contractual employer of whose staff is the LEA: see now EA 2002, s 35(1) and (2).

[3] EA 1996, s 515(1)(b).

[4] That is, a community, foundation or voluntary school: SSFA 1998, s 84(6).

[5] 'Suitable education' means 'efficient full-time education suitable to his age, ability and aptitude and to any special educational needs he may have': SSFA 1998, s 96(7).

[6] SSFA 1998, s 96(2).

[7] Ibid, s 96(4). See para **9.6** regarding s 86(4).

[8] As to which, see paras **9.59** et seq.

[9] SSFA 1998, s 94(1)(a).

[10] Ibid, s 97(2).

the notice was served, 'refer the matter to the Secretary of State', and if they do so then they must inform the LEA accordingly.[1] The Secretary of State has a power, but is not under a duty, to determine which school is to be required to admit the child.[2]

Securing attendance at school

2.79 The power in s 96 of the SSFA 1998 was conferred in part to support the duty of an LEA contained (now) in Chapter II of Part VI of the EA 1996 to take various steps to secure the attendance at school of pupils of compulsory school age. That duty is considered in detail in Chapter 5.

Special education

2.80 The law relating to the provision of special education is considered in detail in Chapter 6, and reference is accordingly made here only to the fact that one of the major roles which LEAs currently have is that in relation to special education. Section 321 of the EA 1996 has the effect that the primary responsibility in relation to children with SEN is held by LEAs. They do not necessarily have to provide the education required by those children with such needs, but they do have to both identify[3] and assess[4] certain children in their area who have SEN. If it is necessary to determine the special educational provision to be made for a child, then the LEA comes under a duty to make and maintain a statement of SEN for that child.[5] The LEA then in practice (at least usually) comes under a duty to fund the special educational provision specified in that statement.[6]

Further education

2.81 An LEA may 'secure the provision for their area of full-time or part-time education suitable to the requirements of persons over compulsory school age who have not attained the age of 19, including provision for persons from other areas'.[7] This power includes power to secure the provision of (a) training, including vocational, social, physical and recreational training, and (b) organised leisure time occupation which is provided in connection with the provision of education or such training.[8] In exercising these functions, an LEA must in particular have regard to the

---

1 SSFA 1998, s 97(3).
2 EA 1996, s 97(4).
3 Ibid, s 321(1).
4 Ibid, s 323.
5 Ibid, s 324(1).
6 See further, paras **6.87** et seq.
7 EA 1996, s 15A (which was inserted into the EA 1996 by the SSFA 1998 and then amended by the LSA 2000), which replaced s 15 of that Act as originally enacted. Section 15 imposed a duty regarding the provision of further education and a power which was in similar terms to that in s 15A. In *R v Further Education Funding Council, ex parte Parkinson* [1997] ELR 204 it was held that the power to provide further education in s 15 was only a 'target' power. See further, paras **16.52** et seq concerning the functions of an LEA with regard to further education. The term 'other areas' seems clearly to mean the areas of other LEAs, and not areas outside the UK.
8 EA 1996, s 15A(1A); 'organised leisure time occupation' means (see EA 1996 ss 15A(1A)(b) and 2(6)) 'leisure-time occupation in such organised cultural training and recreative activities as are suited to their requirements, for any persons over compulsory school age who are able and willing to profit by facilities provided for that purpose'.

needs of persons with learning difficulties within the meaning of s 13(5) and (6) of the LSA 2000.[1] An LEA may do 'anything which appears to them to be necessary or expedient for the purposes of or in connection with the exercise of their functions under [s 15A]'.[2]

2.82   An LEA may also 'secure the provision for their area of full-time or part-time education suitable to the requirements of persons over compulsory school age who have attained the age of 19, including provision for persons from other areas'.[3] This power does not apply to higher education.[4] As with s 15A, this power includes power to secure the provision of (a) training, including vocational, social, physical and recreational training, and (b) organised leisure time occupation which is provided in connection with the provision of education or such training.[5] Also, as with s 15A (1) in exercising these functions, an LEA must in particular have regard to the needs of persons with learning difficulties within the meaning of s 13(5) and (6) of the LSA 2000,[6] and (2) an LEA may do 'anything which appears to them to be necessary or expedient for the purposes of or in connection with the exercise of their functions under [s 15B]'.[7]

2.83   An LEA in England must 'secure the provision of education and training (and connected leisure-time occupation) in accordance with any provisions included in a plan under' s 22(3) of the LSA 2000.[8] If it does not do so, then the Secretary of State may direct it to do so.[9] However, the LEA will be obliged to comply with the direction only if the LSC provides it with 'any financial resources which the authority reasonably requires to enable it to do so'.[10]

Higher education

2.84   LEAs may (1) secure the provision of such facilities for higher education as appear to them to be appropriate for meeting the needs of the population of their area, and (2) secure the provision of higher education for persons from other areas.[11] In exercising this power, the LEA must have regard to any facilities for higher education provided by institutions within the higher and further education sectors and other bodies which are provided for, or available for use by people living in, its area.[12]

---

[1]   EA 1996, s 15A(3).
[2]   Ibid, s 15A(4).
[3]   Ibid, s 15B, which was inserted by the LSA 2000.
[4]   Ibid, s 15B(5).
[5]   Ibid, s 15B(2); 'organised leisure time occupation' means (see EA 1996 ss 15B(2)(b) and s 2(6)) 'leisure-time occupation, in such organised cultural training and recreative activities as are suited to their requirements, for any persons over compulsory school age who are able and willing to profit by facilities provided for that purpose'.
[6]   Ibid, s 15B(3).
[7]   Ibid, s 15B(4).
[8]   LSA 2000, s 23(1).
[9]   Ibid.
[10]   Ibis, s 23(2).
[11]   ERA 1988, s 120(3). See footnote 5 at p 33 regarding the meaning of the term 'other areas'.
[12]   Ibid, s 120(4). See further, paras **16.52** et seq concerning LEAs' functions in relation to higher education.

The organisation of a local education authority in relation to its education functions

2.85 The organisation of a local authority in general is outside the scope of this book. Accordingly, only the particular statutory provisions relating to LEAs are considered here. In addition, only the main relevant issues which are likely to arise in practice for an LEA are discussed below. The current situation in which those education functions which are given to local authorities are held by only one authority (such as the county council where there are still two tiers of authorities) as the LEA and are not divided between two or more different kinds of local authority, is, however, noted. Although relatively recent partial reorganisation of local authorities has in some cases altered the body responsible as the LEA for an area, that has not altered this fundamental principle.[1]

Education committee

2.86 Section 6(2) of, and Part II of the First Schedule to, the EA 1944 imposed on an LEA a duty to establish an education committee. Those provisions were repealed by s 296 of the EA 1993. This does not, of course, affect the power[2] of an LEA to exercise its functions by delegating them to a committee, or of a local authority's executive to act in relation to certain of those functions.[3] Indeed, the combined effect of s 296 of the EA 1993 and the simultaneous repeal of s 101(9)(a) of the Local Government Act 1972[4] has liberated LEAs from the need to carry out acts of delegation themselves, rather than via their education committees.[5]

2.87 The Secretary of State has power (under s 499 of the EA 1996) to direct the appointment of persons who appoint foundation governors[6] for voluntary schools in the area of a local authority to committees and sub-committees of the LEA. A direction has been given, and it is contained in the Annex to DfEE Circular 19/99. The direction applies to 'any committee appointed by a local authority in accordance with section 102 of the Local Government Act 1972 wholly or partly for the purpose

---

[1]   Such reorganisation occurred as a result of the Local Government Act 1992. There is in KP Poole, *Education Law* (Sweet & Maxwell, 1988), at paras 1.14–1.25 and 1.28–1.35 a history of the situation up to 1988. The events preceding and the process involved in the abolition of the Inner London Education Authority are described in Professor NS Harris' *Law and Education: Regulation, Consumerism and the Education System* (Sweet & Maxwell, 1993), at pp 39–42.

[2]   Conferred by ss 101 and 102 of the Local Government Act 1972 (as amended).

[3]   See the Local Government Act 2000, s 13 and SIs 2000/2853 and 2001/2291.

[4]   By para 49 of Sch 19 to the EA 1993.

[5]   Section 101(2) authorises subdelegation by a committee or a sub-committee to an officer (unless, in either case, the local authority otherwise provides). However, s 101(9)(a) provided that Part II of the First Schedule to the 1944 Act (which required an LEA to have an education committee) was unaffected by s 101, with the result that in *R v Birmingham City Council, ex parte National Union of Public Employees* (1984) *The Times*, April 24, it was held to be unlawful for the education committee of an LEA to delegate its powers to a chief officer and that the delegation had to be carried out instead by the full council. This may continue to be relevant for some purposes. It is noted that the power contained in s 101 to delegate functions to an officer appears to have been overlooked by Lord Donaldson MR in *Devon County Council v George* [1989] AC 573, at 586E.

[6]   The definition of 'foundation governors' in relation to Wales is currently contained in SSFA 1998, Sch 9, para 2 (the SSFA 1998 falling to be read as one with the EA 1996: see SSFA 1998, s 142(8)). In relation to England, the definition is provided for in regulations made under EA 2002, s 19(2)(e) (which is currently in force only in relation to England); see para **7.64** for the current regulations.

of discharging any of the authority's functions with respect to education which are conferred on the authority in its capacity as a local education authority' as well as to any such committee which is appointed by two or more LEAs for the joint discharge of their education functions.[1] The representative of a diocesan body which appoints foundation governors of a voluntary school in the area of an LEA must be appointed to such a committee,[2] unless there is more than one such body, in which case the LEA can appoint one person as the representative of both or (as the case may be) all such bodies.[3] Such a representative may vote on any matter which relates to schools maintained by the LEA or to pupils who are educated in schools maintained by the LEA or who are educated by the LEA otherwise than at school, except the determination of the LEA's total revenue expenditure on education or the determination of its capital expenditure on education.[4]

2.88　Section 499(6) of the EA 1996 (as amended) enables regulations to require any education committee or sub-committee, or joint education committee or sub-committee, 'to include one or more persons elected, in accordance with the regulations, as representatives of parent governors at maintained schools in relation to which the committee or sub-committee acts'.[5] In R *(Transport and General Workers Union) v Walsall Metropolitan Borough Council*,[6] Harrison J held that an LEA's decision to exclude such elected representatives of parent governors from its Education and Community Services Committee when it was deciding which caterers were to be awarded a contract mainly for the provision of school meals on the basis that this was not 'a matter which relate[s] to schools ... or pupils who are educated in schools maintained by the local education authority' within the meaning of the then current regulations,[7] was unlawful.

Acting through agents

2.89　The power of a local authority to act via agents should also be noted. That there is such a power was clarified by the House of Lords in *Provident Mutual Life Assurance Association v Derby City Council*.[8] It was held in that case that an officer in the department of the officer to whom a function had been formally delegated under s 101[9] could validly exercise that function. In passing it is noted that if it were otherwise then there would be a major difference between the situation concerning civil servants under the principle in *Carltona Ltd v Commissioner of Works*[10] and that concerning local authorities. It seems that the thinking behind the statement in *Carltona* that: 'it cannot

---

1　See para (3) of the Annex to the Circular.
2　Ibid, paras (4) and (8), subject to para (7).
3　Ibid, para (6).
4　Ibid, para (5).
5　Section 499(7)–(9) empowers the making by regulations of related provision. The current regulations are the Education (Parent Governor Representatives) (England) Regulations 2001, SI 2001/478 and the Education (Parent Governor Representatives) (Wales) Regulations 2001, 2001/3711.
6　[2002] ELR 329.
7　SI 1999/1949.
8　[1981] 1 WLR 173.
9　Although Lord Bridge, who dissented, was the only judge to refer specifically to s 101, it seems clear from the only other reasoned speech, that of Lord Roskill (with whom the other three law lords agreed), at 181B–C, that the delegation was carried out under s 101.
10　[1943] 2 All ER 560.

be supposed that ... in each case, the minister in person should direct his mind to the matter'[1] must apply just as much to the operations of a modern local authority as to the operations of the civil service. However, a rather more restrictive view has tended to be taken in regard to local authorities, perhaps because of the existence of the specific powers of delegation and subdelegation contained in ss 101 and 102 of the 1972 Act.[2] In contrast, though, and somewhat surprisingly, Neill LJ in *Credit Suisse v Allerdale Borough Council*[3] did not rule out the possibility that a local authority could lawfully use a wholly owned subsidiary under its direct control as a means of carrying out certain of its functions. According to Neill LJ, the company 'might then be the agent of the council'.[4] However, Neill LJ specifically declined to rule on the question.[5] Further, what he said in this regard was quite clearly obiter. Accordingly, it should be treated with caution.

Contracting out

2.90   Since that case was decided, some subordinate legislation has considerably altered the position regarding the use of agents. Under the Contracting Out (Local Education Authority Functions) (England) Order 2002,[6] which was made under the Deregulation and Contracting Out Act 1994, many functions of an LEA may 'be exercised by, or by employees of, such person as may be authorised in that behalf by the local education authority whose function it is'. The list is long, and the brevity of the mention made here of the Order and its potential effect is unrelated to the potential importance of the Order.

Chief education officer

2.91   Although an LEA is no longer obliged to appoint an education committee, it is still obliged to appoint 'a fit person to be the chief education officer of the authority'.[7]

Local management of schools

2.92   The situation of what is known as the local management of maintained schools under a scheme of delegation made under Chapter IV of Part II of the SSFA 1998, needs to be considered here as well as below in Chapter 7. Under ss 45, 49 and 50 of the SSFA 1998, it is the duty of an LEA to delegate to the governing body of a school which is maintained by the LEA[8] a 'budget share'[9] for a financial year, where such delegation is required or permitted by or under a scheme of delegation made under s 48 of that Act. As a result, it is clear that the governing body is given delegated power of a special (if not unique) sort, to spend the school's budget share.

---

[1]   [1943] 2 All ER 560, at 563, per Lord Greene, MR.
[2]   See, generally, paras **2.209** et seq of the *Encyclopedia of Local Government Law* (Sweet & Maxwell).
[3]   [1997] QB 306.
[4]   Ibid, at 912F.
[5]   Ibid.
[6]   SI 2002/928.
[7]   EA 1996, s 532.
[8]   For the meaning of which, see SSFA 1998, s 45(3).
[9]   By which is meant 'such amount as the local education authority may determine, in accordance with regulations, to allocate to the school out of the authority's individual schools budget for that year': SSFA 1998, s 47(1). See SSFA 1998 s 45A, as inserted by s 41 of the EA 2002, regarding the determination of the LEA's 'individual schools budget'.

2.93   It is noted that this means that the governing body will not enter into contracts entered into by it when spending the school's budget share on its own behalf. Rather, it will do so on behalf of the LEA. It is irrelevant that the governing body of a maintained school is a corporate body [1] and that such a body has power to enter into contracts on its own behalf.[2] Section 49(5) of the SSFA 1998 confirms this.

Funding

2.94   The funding of a local authority in general terms is not considered in detail in this book. However, mention needs to be made here of the funding powers in Part 2 of the EA 2002. These powers are conferred on the Secretary of State.[3] They are powers to give, or make arrangements for the giving of, financial assistance for the purposes set out in s 14 of the EA 2002. Those purposes include the provision, or proposed provision, whether in the United Kingdom or elsewhere, of education or educational services. They also include the provision, or proposed provision, whether in the United Kingdom or elsewhere, of childcare or services related to childcare. Section 14 also confers powers to provide financial assistance to enable any person to undertake any course of education,[4] or higher education provided by an institution within the further education sector, including by providing for his maintenance while he undertakes the course. Power is also conferred by s 14 to fund the training of teachers (other than higher education teachers) and non-teaching staff, the promotion of the recruitment and retention of such teachers and non-teaching staff, and the remuneration or provision of other benefits to such teachers and non-teaching staff. Funding may in addition be provided under the section for the promotion of learning and research and for the promotion of the use of educational buildings or facilities for purposes other than those of education. Sections 15–18 of the EA 2002 make consequential provision. Section 18 repealed a number of regulatory funding powers which were to be found in various places in the Education Acts, and the enactment of Part 2 of the EA 2002 accordingly resulted in a welcome simplification of the situation. However, s 18 did not replace all of the statutory funding provisions relating to education, and the salient remaining ones are referred to below. Section 15 specifies the manner in which financial assistance may be given under s 14 (and it is of note that it may not be given to an LEA by way of loan or guarantee). Section 16 is of particular importance, because it has conferred on the Secretary of State power to provide for the repayment of any financial assistance given under s 14 which is not used in accordance with any of the conditions under which it has been so given. Section 16(3) also provides for the enforcement by the Secretary of State of compliance with any such conditions. The manner of enforcement is not specified, but it is presumably by means of an application to the Administrative Court for a mandatory order.

---

[1]   See SSFA 1998, s 36(1) and EA 2002, s 19(1).

[2]   See ibid, Sch 10, para 3(2)(c) and EA 2002, Sch 1, para 3(3)(c).

[3]   For the avoidance of doubt, references to the Secretary of State here are to be read as including references to the National Assembly.

[4]   'Education' is defined by s 14(3) among other things not to include higher education. 'Higher education' means (see EA 2002, s 212(3) and (4) and EA 1996 s 579(1)) 'education provided by means of a course of any description mentioned in Sch 6 to the Education Reform Act 1988'.

2.95   In addition to revenue from central government, an LEA may in certain circumstances obtain revenue from the levying of charges. However, for that to be lawful, the LEA must be able to show that it has the power to make the charge in question. Such power can only arise either expressly or by necessary implication from statutory provisions.[1]

2.96   It is noted that a local authority's revenue support grant[2] is by far the largest source of its income, that it is calculated by reference to the standard spending assessment made by the Secretary of State in relation to the authority,[3] and that an LEA is not obliged to spend its revenue support grant in accordance with the standard spending assessment relating to it. It is also noted that the Secretary of State has power to cap the spending of a local authority by preventing it from raising more by way of council tax than an amount specified by him.[4] Seemingly, these factors do not affect the application of ss 14–17 of the EA 2002.

Other education-related funding

2.97   In addition to the revenue support grant there are a number of specific grants which are payable by central government to LEAs in connection with their functions as such authorities. The main ones are as follows.

Grants for education support and training

2.98   Education standards grants may be made by the National Assembly for Wales to LEAs, under s 484 of the EA 1996.[5] They are made in respect of 'eligible expenditure', which is as specified in regulations.[6] Those regulations may require LEAs to delegate decisions about the spending of grant for education support and training and any amounts allocated by the authority to meet such eligible expenditure (as defined) as is approved by the Secretary of State, to 'such persons as may be determined by or in accordance with the regulations'.[7]

---

[1]   'The rule is that a charge cannot be made unless the power to charge is given by express words or *by necessary implication*. These last words impose a rigorous test going far beyond the proposition that it would be *reasonable* or even conducive or incidental to charge for the provision of a service': *R v Richmond upon Thames LBC, ex parte McCarthy & Stone Ltd* [1992] 2 AC 48, at 70H–71A, per Lord Lowry. The reference to what is conducive or incidental was made because reliance was sought to be placed by the local authority in that case on s 111(1) of the Local Government Act 1972 to justify the making of the charge in question. The reference made in the text to this note to find a power in statutory provisions is based also on the approach taken by Laws J at first instance in *R v Somerset County Council, ex parte Fewings* [1995] 1 All ER 513, at 524f and 525f. (The passage at p 524f was expressly approved by Sir Thomas Bingham MR in the Court of Appeal decision in that case, at [1995] 1 WLR 1037, at 1042H.)

[2]   Revenue support grant is paid under ss 78–84 (as amended) of the Local Government Finance Act 1988.

[3]   There is no statutory basis for this term, but the statutory authority for the process is to be found in ss 78–81 and s 139A of the Local Government Finance Act 1988 (as amended).

[4]   Local Government Finance Act 1992, Part I, Chapter IVA, as inserted by the Local Government Act 1999.

[5]   Section 484 was repealed by s 18 of the EA 2002 in relation to England only.

[6]   EA 1996, s 484(2). Recent regulations in relation to Wales include the Education (Education Standards Grants) (Wales) Regulations 2002, SI 2002/438.

[7]   Ibid, s 489(2).

Grants to meet liabilities to former employees in higher and further education

2.99   Payments to meet certain liabilities to former employees in institutions which provide or (if no longer in existence) have ceased to provide higher or further education (or both) may be made by a higher education funding council to a local authority (and to certain other bodies) under s 133 of the 1988 Act.[1] The liabilities are those prescribed in the Education (Polytechnics and Colleges Funding Council) (Prescribed Expenditure) Regulations 1991.[2]

Grants for expenditure due to ethnic population

2.100   Under s 11 of the Local Government Act 1966 (as substituted by s 1(1) of the Local Government (Amendment) Act 1993), the Secretary of State (in this instance the Home Secretary) may pay grants to local authorities who, in his opinion, are required to make special provision in the exercise of any of their functions in consequence of the presence within their areas of persons belonging to ethnic minorities whose language or customs differ from those of the rest of the community.[3] The grants must be paid with the consent of the Treasury, must be in respect of expenditure of a description determined by the Secretary of State, and in any event must be in respect of the employment of staff. Apparently, in practice, a high proportion of the expenditure under the original provisions of s 11 of the 1966 Act was spent on the education service.[4]

Recoupment of expenditure on pupils from other areas

2.101   Mention needs to be made here of certain statutory provisions for the recoupment of funding where one LEA provides education to a pupil whose home is in the area of another LEA. Section 207 of the EA 2002 empowers the making of regulations providing for the recoupment of expenditure by one LEA on the education of a pupil who 'belongs to the area of another' LEA. The regulations may empower or require the other LEA to pay either such amount as the LEAs agree, or, failing such agreement, such amount as is determined by or under the regulations.

2.102   Relevant regulations were made under the predecessor to s 207 of the EA 2002,[5] and they provide for the compulsory recoupment of costs incurred in the education of the following: (1) a child for whom a statement of SEN is maintained under (now) Chapter I of Part IV of the EA 1996; (2) a person attending a special school; and (3) a person under the age of 19 years who (a) is a patient in hospital, and (b) receives education in a special school established in a hospital or education otherwise than at school pursuant to s 19 of the EA 1996 (which includes education in a pupil referral unit). The regulations provide that an LEA may make payments to another LEA in whose area primary, secondary or further education, or part-time education for those who have not attained the age of 5 is provided for persons who

---

[1]   As substituted by s 67(1) of the FHEA 1992. See further, para **17.19**.

[2]   SI 1991/2307.

[3]   Section 11 of the 1966 Act originally related to 'commonwealth immigrants'.

[4]   See KP Poole, *Education Law* (Sweet & Maxwell, 1988), para 1.128.

[5]   The predecessor was EA 1996, s 492. The current regulations are the Education (Inter-authority Recoupment) Regulations 1994, SI 1994/3251, made under s 51(1) of the 1986 Act (which was consolidated as s 492 of the EA 1996).

belong to the area of the paying LEA.[1] The amounts to be paid are such as may be agreed between the two authorities.[2] There are time-limits contained in the regulations for the making of claims for recoupment.[3]

2.103 As can be seen, the question whether a pupil 'belongs to the area' of an LEA is important. Section 579(4) of the EA 1996 provides that this question is to be determined in accordance with regulations. That section also provides that any question under the regulations shall, in the case of a dispute, be determined by the Secretary of State. The Education (Areas to which Pupils and Students Belong) Regulations 1996[4] make the necessary provision. The general principle in those regulations is that a person other than a further education student is treated as belonging to the area of the LEA in which he is ordinarily resident.[5] However, if he has no ordinary residence, then he belongs to the area of the authority in which he is for the time being resident.[6] A further education student is treated as belonging to the area of the education authority in which he is for the time being resident.[7] Specific provision is made for several cases which would otherwise be difficult. Regulation 4 provides for boarding school pupils with statements of SEN maintained under Chapter I of Part IV of the EA 1996 and pupils with such statements who, under arrangements made pursuant to s 514 of the EA 1996, board elsewhere than at the schools which they attend, and (in both cases) who do not spend their holidays with the person responsible for them.[8] In addition, provision is made for pupils who, while they are hospital patients, receive education in a special school established in a hospital or education otherwise than at school under s 19 of the EA 1996,[9] pupils who are 'looked after by a local authority',[10] and several categories of further education students.[11]

2.104 Section 493 of the EA 1996[12] empowers the making of regulations requiring or authorising payments by an LEA in England to an education authority in Scotland and vice versa for the education of persons having a specified connection with the paying authority. No such regulations have been made under s 493.

---

[1]   Regulation 4. It is noted that s 207(2) does not empower regulations relating to further education.
[2]   Ibid.
[3]   Regulation 5. Claims must be submitted within 12 months from the end of the financial year in which the provision for education to which the claim relates was made.
[4]   SI 1996/615, as amended by SI 1997/597.
[5]   Regulation 3(a). See reg 2(2) for the definition of ordinary residence.
[6]   Regulation 3(a).
[7]   Regulation 3(b).
[8]   The definition of 'the person responsible for a school pupil' is contained in reg 2(3). See paras **4.39– 4.40** regarding s 514.
[9]   Regulation 6.
[10] Regulation 7, the terms of which apply 'to the exclusion of any other regulation which would otherwise apply to such a person'.
[11] Regulations 8–10.
[12] As amended by s 208 of the EA 2002.

THE QUALIFICATIONS AND CURRICULUM AUTHORITY AND THE QUALIFICATIONS, CURRICULUM AND ASSESSMENT AUTHORITY FOR WALES

2.105 The Qualifications and Curriculum Authority was established under s 21 of the EA 1997. Its Welsh equivalent, the Qualifications, Curriculum and Assessment Authority for Wales, was established earlier, but was continued by s 27 of the EA 1997. Their functions are (among other things) to advise, pursuant to ss 98 and 99 of the LSA 2000, the Secretary of State (or the National Assembly) or a designated body on any approval given by him or it of an external qualification within the meaning of ss 96(5)–(7) and 97(4)–(6) of the LSA 2000.[1] They are exempt charities.[2]

THE LEARNING AND SKILLS COUNCIL AND THE NATIONAL COUNCIL FOR EDUCATION AND TRAINING FOR WALES

2.106 The role of the LSC and the CETW in relation to the further education sector is discussed in detail in Chapter 16. The reason for referring to these two councils here is to place them in the national framework of organisations responsible for the provision of education, and to show how their roles link with those of the other bodies referred to in this chapter. Reference is made first to their responsibility for the provision of further education generally and the interlocking of their responsibilities with those of LEAs. Reference is then made to the division of responsibility between (1) the LSC and the CETW, and (2) LEAs in regard to persons who have SEN.

The responsibility of the Learning and Skills Council and the National Council for Education and Training for Wales for the provision of further education[3]

2.107 The LSC and the CETW have primary responsibility for the funding of full-time and part-time education (other than higher education[4]) which is 'suitable to the requirements of persons who are above compulsory school age but have not attained the age of 19'.[5] They also have primary responsibility for the funding of full-time and part-time training[6] suitable to the requirements of such persons,[7] organised leisure-time occupation connected with such education,[8] and organised leisure-time

---

[1] Regarding which see paras **11.14** and **11.15**.
[2] See Charities Act 1993, Sch 2, para 1(da) and (f).
[3] The following paragraphs need to be considered in conjunction with paras **2.81–2.83**, regarding the responsibilities of LEAs concerning further education.
[4] That is, 'education provided by means of a course of any description mentioned in Sch 6 to the Education Reform Act 1988': LSA 2000, ss 2(5)(d) and 31(5)(d).
[5] LSA 2000, ss 2(1)(a) and (5)(a) and 31(1)(a) and (5)(a).
[6] Which for this purpose 'includes vocational, social, physical and recreational training': LSA 2000, ss 2(5)(c) and 31(5)(c).
[7] LSA 2000, ss 2(1)(b) and (5)(b) and 31(1)(b) and (5)(b).
[8] Ibid, ss 2(1)(c) and 31(1)(c).

occupation connected with such training.[1] The LSC and the CETW owe similar duties in relation to the provision of 'reasonable facilities for ... education (other than higher education) suitable to the requirements of persons who have attained the age of 19'.[2]

2.108 The LSC and the CETW must each 'formulate a strategy in relation to its functions and keep it under review'.[3] The LSC may be given binding directions by the Secretary of State under s 25 of the LSA 2000, and the CETW may be given binding directions by the National Assembly under s 47 of that Act. Such directions may contain (a) 'objectives which the Council should achieve in seeking to carry out its functions', and (b) 'time limits within which the Council should achieve the objectives'. However, such directions 'may not concern the provision of financial resources in respect of activities carried on by a particular person or persons'.[4]

2.109 Under Sch 7 to the LSA 2000, the LSC and the CETW may intervene in relation to what is deemed to be 'inadequate' sixth-form provision made by a school. This power of intervention is referred to further in paras **7.54** et seq.

The responsibility of the Learning and Skills Council and the National Council for Education and Training for Wales for persons who have special educational needs

2.110 The LSC and the CETW have responsibility for special education in the further education sector, as a result of ss 13 and 41 the LSA 2000 respectively. For example, as a result of s 13(1), in discharging its functions under ss 2, 3, 5(1)(a)–(d) and (g) and 8, the LSC must 'have regard: (a) to the needs of persons with learning difficulties,[5] and (b) in particular, to any report of an assessment conducted under section 140'.[6] In addition, the LSC must in certain circumstances secure the provision of boarding accommodation for persons with learning difficulties.[7] The overlap between the LSC's and the CETW's duties in ss 13 and 41 respectively and the duties of an LEA in relation to pupils with SEN can be problematic. That overlap is considered in Chapter 6.[8]

THE HIGHER EDUCATION FUNDING COUNCILS

2.111 The higher education funding councils (one for England, one for Wales) were established under s 62 of the FHEA 1992. The place of the higher education funding councils in the framework for the public funding of education can be seen most clearly in s 65 of that Act. Section 65(1) makes those councils responsible for the administration of funds made available to them by the Secretary of State (or, in Wales,

---

[1]   LSA 2000, ss 2(1)(d) and 31(1)(d).
[2]   See ibid, ss 3 and 32 respectively.
[3]   Ibid, ss 16(1) and 44(1).
[4]   Ibid, ss 25(6) and 47(6).
[5]   Defined by s 13(5).
[6]   See paras **6.186–6.188** regarding s 140.
[7]   See s 13(2)–(4).
[8]   See paras **6.189–6.192**.

the National Assembly[1]) and others for the purpose of providing financial support for various activities. Those activities include the provision of education and the undertaking of research by higher education institutions in each council's area, and activities which are ancillary to such provision and research.[2] In addition, those activities include:

'the provision –
(i) by institutions in their area maintained or assisted by local education authorities,[3] or
(ii) by such institutions in their area as are within the further education sector,[4]
of prescribed courses of higher education.'[5]

2.112 Further, under s 69 of the FHEA 1992, for example the Secretary of State may confer or impose on the Higher Education Funding Council for England certain 'supplementary' functions in relation to institutions within the higher education sector,[6] institutions within the further education sector, or institutions maintained or assisted by LEAs at which prescribed courses of higher education are provided.[7] In addition, the higher education funding councils are responsible for the assessment of the quality of the teaching in such institutions (presumably where that teaching is funded by one of the councils).[8]

2.113 There is the possibility of the voluntary joint exercise of functions by any two or more of the LSC, the CETW, the higher education funding councils and the Scottish Higher Education Funding Council.[9] There is also the possibility of the mandatory making of joint provision by two or more of the same bodies 'for the assessment by a person appointed by them of matters relating to the arrangements made by each institution in Great Britain which is within the higher education sector for maintaining academic standards in the institution'. This occurs when the Secretary of State has given a direction to the councils in question under s 82(2) of the FHEA 1992. It is assumed that neither the LSC nor the CETW are likely in practice to be subject to such a direction.

---

[1] See the National Assembly for Wales (Transfer of Functions) Order 1999, SI 1999/672.
[2] See s 65(2)(a), (b) and (d).
[3] An institution is assisted for this purpose if it is not an institution in the further or higher education sectors (regarding which see the following footnotes), and an LEA 'make to the persons responsible for its maintenance any grant in respect of the institution or any payment in consideration of the provision of educational facilities there': see s 90(5) of the FHEA 1992 and s 579(6) of the EA 1996.
[4] Such institutions are institutions conducted by further education corporations and designated institutions as defined in s 28(4) of the FHEA 1992: s 91(3) of the FHEA 1992.
[5] FHEA 1992, s 65(2)(c).
[6] Such institutions are universities receiving financial support under s 65 of the FHEA 1992, institutions conducted by higher education corporations, and designated institutions as defined by s 72(3) of that Act: s 91(5) of the 1992 Act.
[7] FHEA 1992, s 69(5)–(7).
[8] See ibid, s 70. There is no limit on the kind of education whose quality is to be assessed under s 70: it merely has to be provided in institutions for whose activities a higher education funding council provides, or is considering providing, support. It is of note that the LSC and the CETW may 'develop schemes for the assessment of the performance of persons in providing post-16 education and training' (see ss 9(1) and 37(1) of the LSA 2000), and that post-16 education and training is defined by ss 3(6) and (7) and 32(6) and (7) in such a way as to exclude higher education.
[9] Ibid, ss 82(1) and (3) and 90(2A).

2.114   Finally in this section, it is noted that s 79 of the FHEA 1992 not only requires the governing bodies of institutions within the higher education sector to give a higher education funding council 'such information as they may require for the purposes of the exercise of any of their functions[1] under the Education Acts', but it also requires LEAs and the governing bodies of institutions at which prescribed courses of higher education are currently being, or have at any time been, provided, to do the same.

THE GENERAL STATUTORY PRINCIPLES APPLYING TO SCHOOL EDUCATION

2.115   There are some general statutory principles which apply to education in maintained schools, and which will now be considered. These are that (1) (subject to important qualifications) pupils are to be educated in accordance with the wishes of their parents, (2) it is the (absolute) duty of a parent of a child of compulsory school age to secure that he receives 'efficient full-time education suitable' to him, and that (3) (subject to exceptions) no charges may be made in respect of the education of pupils in maintained schools.

Section 9 of the Education Act 1996: duty to educate in accordance with parents' wishes

2.116   Section 9 of the EA 1996 (as amended) provides as follows:

> 'In exercising or performing all their respective powers and duties under the Education Acts,[2] the Secretary of State and local education authorities shall have regard to the general principle that pupils are to be educated in accordance with the wishes of their parents, so far as that is compatible with the provision of efficient instruction and training and the avoidance of unreasonable public expenditure.'[3]

2.117   It has been held that the expenditure referred to in s 9 is that of the LEA only, and not also that of the same corporate body, acting as (for example) the local social services authority.[4]

2.118   The duty imposed by s 9 has, however, been superseded in relation to admissions to maintained schools by the provisions which are now in Part III of the

---

1   According to s 61(1), 'In this Part of this Act – "functions" includes duties and powers'. By implication, this definition does not extend to the rest of the Act, including Parts II and III. This may be an oversight. However, s 579(1) of the EA 1996 contains the same definition for the purposes of that Act ('unless the context otherwise requires'), and according to s 90(5) of the FHEA 1992 Act (as amended by EA 1996, Sch 37, para 115(3)), 'Subject to the provisions of this Act, expressions used in this Act and in the Education Act 1996 have the same meaning in this Act as in that Act'. The question is, therefore, whether the application of the definition of 'functions' in s 61(1) of the FHEA 1992 to Part I only of that Act means that by implication the definition of 'functions' in s 579(1) of the EA 1996 does not apply to Parts II and III. It is suggested here that the simple and sensible solution is to construe s 61(1) as not having that implied effect.

2   For the definition of 'the Education Acts', see s 578 of the EA 1996.

3   EA 1996, s 9 originated in s 76 of the Education Act 1944, which was in materially the same terms.

4   *S v Somerset County Council* [2003] ELR 78, at paras 30–32.

SSFA 1998[1] and in relation to children with SEN by the right (under para 3 of Sch 27 to the EA 1996[2]) to state a preference for a maintained school for a child to whom a statement of SEN relates. No more needs to be said here about the former, but there is still room for the application of s 9 in relation to the naming of a school in a statement of SEN, as was confirmed by Sedley LJ (with whom the other Lord Justices agreed) in *C v Buckinghamshire County Council*.[3] If para 3(3) of Sch 27 applies then there is no room for the application of s 9, but if the school preferred by a parent is an independent school, then s 9 applies.[4] However, *C v Buckinghamshire County Council* was distinguished by Richards J in *T v Special Educational Needs Tribunal*[5] where the dispute between the parents and the LEA concerned whether the LEA should pay for non-school provision where appropriate school provision was available, even though the cost of the non-school provision was similar to that of the school provision.[6]

2.119 The principle in s 9 of the EA 1996 is a general one only, to which the Secretary of State and LEAs must have regard when exercising particular functions under the EA 1996 (and the other Acts which are to be construed as one with that Act) but they are not prevented by it from having regard in addition to other matters: *Watt v Kesteven County Council*.[7] The facts in *Watt* are instructive. The LEA (the county council) had insufficient places in schools maintained by it to educate the claimant's twin sons. The LEA therefore made arrangements[8] for the education of the boys at an independent secondary grammar school, in respect of which it was willing to pay the tuition fees. However, the claimant was a Roman Catholic and declined on religious grounds to send his sons there. Instead, he sent them to a Roman Catholic boarding school, the tuition fees for which were lower than those for the school with which the LEA had made arrangements for the boys' education. He claimed from the LEA repayment in full of the tuition fees which he had paid. The LEA was willing to pay a grant towards the fees on a means-tested basis under regulations made under s 81 of the Education Act 1944,[9] but declined to do more. The claimant claimed the fees in full, basing his claim on s 76 of the 1944 Act. The court held that he was mistaken, because s 76 gave rise to no independent legal right. Rather, it merely affected the exercise of any power or the carrying out of any duty under the 1944 Act, by making the exercise of the function in question subject to the principle in s 76. The duty in issue in *Watt* was that contained in s 8 of the 1944 Act, and the relevant power was

---

[1]   As to which, see paras **9.1** et seq.

[2]   Regarding which, see para **6.60**.

[3]   [1999] ELR 179, at 185, [1999] EdCR 690, at 696F–697F.

[4]   See further, paras **6.36** and **6.61**.

[5]   [2002] ELR 704, at para 38(iii).

[6]   See ibid, para 10.

[7]   [1955] 1 QB 408, CA. See also *T v Special Educational Needs Tribunal* [2002] ELR 704, para 38(ii), per Richards J: 'What is laid down by s 9 remains a general principle to be taken into account, rather than having any greater force. I reject the suggestion by Mr Friel in reply that *Watt v Kesteven County Council* [1955] QB 408 and *Cumings and Others v Birkenhead Corporation* [1972] Ch 12, since they predated the substantial reforms reflected in the 1996 Act, are outdated.'

[8]   Under ss 8 and 9 of the 1944 Act (see now ss 14(1) and 18 of the EA 1996). An obligation therefore arose to pay the fees charged by the school at which the LEA had made the arrangements, as a result of s 6 of the Education (Miscellaneous Provisions) Act 1953 (see now s 517 of the EA 1996, discussed at paras **4.59** et seq).

[9]   See now s 518 of the EA 1996, as to which see paras **4.57–4.58**.

contained in s 9 of that Act. There was no duty to provide free education at any independent school other than one with which the LEA had made relevant arrangements. Denning LJ said that s 76 left it:

'open to the county council to have regard to other things as well [as the general principle contained in section 76], and also to make exceptions to the general principle if it thinks fit to do so ... If they paid the full fees in this case, it would mean that every parent in the county, who sent his boys to boarding school, could come and ask the county council to pay the tuition fees, no matter how rich he was.'[1]

2.120 It could be said that this was not correct, since the LEA had been willing to pay the fees for the education of the boys at an independent school only because there were insufficient places in maintained schools in the area, with the result that a ruling could have been made in favour of the parent on the basis that it would not have been made if there had been sufficient such places. Nevertheless, it was held that (1) there was no evidence of a failure to have regard to the principle in s 76, and (2) the evidence indicated that the LEA had in fact had regard to that principle.[2] The claim was therefore unsuccessful.

2.121 Denning LJ said in addition that the fact that the claimant was a Roman Catholic was irrelevant: the ruling would have been the same if he had been a member of the Church of England and had declined for any reason to send his child to the school nominated by the LEA, and had instead sent him elsewhere.[3]

2.122 In *Wood v Ealing London Borough Council*,[4] where the LEA had proposed a scheme for the replacement of selective schools with comprehensive schools, parents claimed that the authority was in breach of s 76 of the 1944 Act in that it had failed to pay any, or any proper, regard to the wishes of parents in formulating the proposed scheme. Mr Justice Goff ruled that the general principle in s 76 was 'confined to the wishes of particular parents in respect of their own particular children and does not refer to the wishes of parents generally'.[5] Further, he held that 'education in section 76 must refer to the curriculum, and whether it includes any, and if so what, religious instruction, and whether co-educational or single-sex, and matters of that sort, and not to the size of the school or the conditions of entry'.[6] KP Poole refers in his book *Education Law*[7] to a subsequent case, in which it was reported[8] that s 76 did not help 'particular parents' who complained that they had not been consulted about a change in the curriculum involving the adoption of a particular system of options before that change was adopted. Apparently, the court held there that the school and the LEA had not acted unreasonably in adopting the new system of options without prior consultation. This is inconsistent with *Wood*, and seems mistaken in principle. It has to be said that the curriculum is now subject to a different regime, discussed in

---

1   [1955] 1 QB 408, at 424.
2   Ibid, at 424, 429.
3   Ibid, at 422.
4   [1967] 1 Ch 364.
5   Ibid, at 383.
6   Ibid, at 384.
7   Sweet & Maxwell, 1988, at para 1.75 (text and n 29).
8   In the *Times Educational Supplement*, 2 May 1980.

Chapter 11, but that nevertheless, where there is a discretion in regard to the curriculum, as there remains under ss 78 and 99 of the EA 2002,[1] s 9 of the EA 1996 appears to continue at least in theory to have a role.

2.123 In *Cumings v Birkenhead Corporation*,[2] the LEA sent parents a circular letter informing them that except in exceptional circumstances, pupils from Roman Catholic primary schools would be sent to Roman Catholic secondary schools. The reason for this policy was that in the long term the demand for places in non-Roman Catholic secondary schools was expected to be such that there would be room in those schools only for pupils from county primary schools (the predecessors to community primary schools) and Church of England primary schools. Several parents applied to the High Court for an injunction to prevent this policy from being applied, on the basis that s 76 had been breached. The claim was rejected. According to Lord Denning MR:[3]

> 'There are many things to which the education authority may have regard and which may outweigh the wishes of the parents. They must have regard, for instance, not only to the wishes of the parents of one particular child, but also to the wishes of the parents of other children and of other groups of children. In this particular case the education authority were having regard to the wishes of those parents who had had their children at Roman Catholic primary schools, and also the wishes of those whose children had been at other schools. The education authority were doing the best they could to allocate places as between the various groups of parents for whom they had to cater. That is quite legitimate. There is no warrant for the suggestion of a breach of section 76.'

2.124 In *Lee v Enfield London Borough Council*,[4] an LEA intended to transfer pupils to what was at the time a grammar school, but on the basis that the school was now to be a secondary school. The authority gave the parents of the pupils no opportunity to express their wishes in regard to the matter. Some of the parents applied to the High Court for an injunction to prevent this. The basis for the action was that it was contrary to s 76 and to one of the articles of government of the school to put the proposal into effect. The court ruled that both s 76 and that article had indeed been breached.

2.125 In *Winward v Cheshire County Council*[5] the LEA determined that the local primary school was not suitable for a child. (The child had what would now be referred to as SEN and had begun to be educated at the school.) The authority therefore decided that the child should instead be educated at another school 2 miles away, which had a special class for children with SEN. They therefore excluded the child from the local primary school and offered his parents a place for him at the other school. The parents claimed that the authority was obliged by s 76 to comply with their wish that their child be educated at the local school, and sought an injunction to restrain the LEA from excluding their son from the local school. The court rejected their claim, partly on the basis that the local school was not, and could not reasonably become,

---

[1]   See para **11.3**.
[2]   [1972] Ch 12.
[3]   Ibid, at 36–37.
[4]   (1967) 66 LGR 195.
[5]   (1979) 77 LGR 172.

suitable to the child's age, ability and aptitude within the meaning of s 8 of the Education Act 1944 (now, in altered form, s 14 of the EA 1996), and partly on the basis that there was no scope for the operation of s 76 in the circumstances.[1]

2.126 It may be seen, therefore, that s 76 has rarely been of practical value to parents. That it (in the guise of s 9 of the EA 1996) is likely to continue to be of little practical value was confirmed in a Scottish case concerning s 28(1) of the Education (Scotland) Act 1980 (which is in almost identical terms to those of s 9 of the EA 1996), *Harvey v Strathclyde Regional Council*.[2] In the court at first instance the parents of children at a school which the regional council proposed to amalgamate with a neighbouring school led evidence to the effect that the overwhelming majority of the parents of those children opposed the proposal. The judge (the Lord Ordinary, Lord Dervaird) held that as a matter of law, where such evidence was led by parents in relation to a claim made under s 28(1), then, in the absence of evidence from the LEA with regard to the provisos in s 28(1) (concerning compatibility with the provision of efficient instruction and training and the avoidance of unreasonable public expenditure), a prima facie inference was raised that the LEA had failed to have regard to the principle in s 28(1) of compliance with the wishes of parents. It was therefore necessary for the regional council to lead evidence to show that they *had* had regard to that principle. The judge held that the regional council had not displaced the inference that they had failed to have regard to that principle.

2.127 The regional council appealed to the Scottish Court of Appeal, the Inner House of the Court of Session. The court unanimously allowed the appeal, on the ground that there was no basis for the proposition of law referred to above. The parents appealed to the House of Lords, which dismissed the appeal and affirmed the ruling of the Inner House. Lord Keith said that:

> 'In order to succeed in securing judicial review the applicant must show either that the respondents paid no regard at all to the general principle embodied in section 28(1), or that they paid to it a degree of regard lesser than any reasonable education authority would have paid.'[3]

2.128 This appeared to mean that in any future case, unless parents could show what could best be described as narrow *Wednesbury* unreasonableness,[4] or what could be termed simply irrationality, in the context, or total disregard of their wishes, any claim based on s 28(1) or what is now s 9 of the EA 1996 would have to fail. In *Harvey*, Lord Keith said that the mere fact that the regional council's proposal to close the school in question was in conflict with the wishes of the majority of the parents of children at the school, went 'no distance at all to establish the applicant's case'.[5]

---

1. (1979) 77 LGR 172, at 182. The situation would now be governed by the regime regarding SEN contained in Ch I of Pt IV of the EA 1996.
2. [1989] SLT 612. The case is described in some detail in P Meredith, *Government, Schools and the Law* (Routledge, 1992) at pp 141–143. See also [1989] Public Law 160.
3. Ibid, p 615.
4. That is, within the meaning of *Associated Provincial Picture Houses Ltd v Wednesbury Corporation* [1948] 1 KB 223, CA.
5. [1989] SLT 612, at 615. See also *R v Secretary of State for Education, ex parte Skitt* [1995] ELR 388, at 398F.

Further, it raised no presumption at all regarding the extent to which the LEA had had regard to the general principle in s 28(1).

2.129 However, since the decision in *Harvey*, s 76 has nevertheless had an effect in several circumstances. In *R v Rochdale Metropolitan Borough Council, ex parte Schemet*,[1] the question arose whether an LEA was liable to provide free transport for a child to a school which was (a) further away than a school nearer to his or her home, and (b) outside the area of the LEA in which the child lived. The existing provision of free transport was withdrawn as a result of a change of policy by the LEA, the new policy being to the following effect:

> 'If a parent arranges for a child to attend a school which is not maintained by this authority the authority will not pay travelling expenses, even if the school is the nearest suitable school.'[2]

2.130 The reference in that policy to 'the nearest suitable school' was made because it was a defence to a prosecution brought under s 39 of the Education Act 1944 (which was re-enacted so far as relevant in s 444 of the EA 1996) in respect of a failure to secure the attendance of a child at the school at which he or she was a registered pupil, that the school was not within 'walking distance' of the child's home and that no suitable arrangements had been made by the LEA for his or her transport to and from the school or for enabling him to become a registered pupil at a school nearer to his home.[3] Roch J, having referred to case-law concerning s 6 of the 1980 Act[4] relating to the refusal of a place at a school simply because the applicant for the place lived in the area of a different LEA from that in whose area the school was situated,[5] ruled that the policy set out above was unlawful if only because it discriminated against schools maintained by other LEAs.[6]

2.131 However, that did not dispose of the case, and in order to do so it was necessary to consider whether the word 'suitable' in this context related to the school or to the arrangements made with regard to transport to the school. Roch J expressly ruled that:

> 'The proper construction of s 39(2)(c)[7] is that arrangements will not be suitable unless the school is suitable for the particular pupil.'[8]

2.132 In addition, he posed the following question:

---

[1]   [1994] ELR 89, (1992) 91 LGR 425.

[2]   Ibid, at 98G.

[3]   'Walking distance' in the case of the relevant child in *ex parte Schemet* was 3 miles. The interlinking of the provisions regarding the compulsory attendance at school of children registered as pupils at the school and the duty (contained now in s 509 of the EA 1996) to provide free transport, is considered in detail in paras **4.12** et seq.

[4]   Replaced by s 86 of the SSFA 1998; see s 86(8) so far as relevant.

[5]   Principally, *R v Greenwich LBC, ex parte Governors of the John Ball Primary School* (1989) 88 LGR 589, CA.

[6]   [1994] ELR 89, at 104B–C.

[7]   See now s 444(4) of the EA 1996.

[8]   [1994] ELR 89, at 105C–D. It must be assumed that Roch J did not mean by this to rule that the arrangements for transport did not also need to be suitable, so the ruling must be regarded as having been that both the arrangements for transport and the school had to be suitable.

'In deciding whether they are able to make suitable arrangements for the child to become a registered pupil at a school nearer to his home than the school at which the child is a registered pupil, has the LEA to take account of the parent's preferences?'[1]

He then answered it by saying: 'In my judgment, they must do so',[2] and he referred to s 76 of the 1944 Act in support of that answer. Furthermore, he made it clear that he saw s 76 as having been extended by s 6 of the Education Act 1980, since, having set out the terms of s 76, he said:

'That provision has been strengthened by s 6 of the 1980 Act.'[3]

He accordingly ruled in favour of the parents' application for judicial review.

2.133 However, the ruling in *ex parte Schemet* that not only must the arrangements for transport to school be suitable but also the school must be suitable, was overruled by the decision of the Court of Appeal in the case of *Re S (Minors)*,[4] although in overruling *ex parte Schemet*, the Court of Appeal did not refer expressly to the reliance by Roch J on s 76.[5] Nevertheless, Butler-Sloss LJ, with whom McCowan LJ and Sir Ralph Gibson agreed, referred to the argument that s 6 of the 1980 Act had the effect that the school must be suitable, and rejected that argument.[6] Accordingly, it seems that the reliance by Roch J on s 76 in the context of the provision of transport to a particular school must now be regarded as also overruled.

2.134 In *R v London Borough of Lambeth ex parte G*,[7] however, Potts J ruled that s 6 of the 1980 Act and s 76 of the 1944 Act obliged an LEA to take into account a parent's wishes with regard to the education of his child when deciding whether or not to make a grant under regulations made under s 81 of the 1944 Act.[8] In *ex parte G*, as in the case of *ex parte Schemet*, the benefit in question was denied (as a matter of policy) because the child to whom it related was attending a school in the area of an LEA other than that in whose area the child lived. Although Potts J based his decision in part on *ex parte Schemet*, he said that if he was wrong in thinking that the policy in question was *ultra vires*, and that the policy 'was made within the powers of [the LEA] in the exercise of a discretion', then nevertheless 'for the reasons given that discretion was not exercised consistently with the statutory provisions which give effect to the principle of parental choice'.[9] The 'reasons given' included that Potts J was:

---

[1]   [1994] ELR 89, at 105E.

[2]   Ibid, at 105E–F.

[3]   Ibid, at 105G. The terms and effect of the replacement of s 6 of the 1980 Act, s 86 of the SSFA 1998, are considered in detail in Chapter 9.

[4]   [1995] ELR 98; reported also under the name of *R v Dyfed County Council, ex parte S* at [1995] 1 FCR 113. See further, para **5.44**.

[5]   See [1995] ELR 98, at 104D.

[6]   [1995] ELR 98, at 104G–H.

[7]   [1994] ELR 207.

[8]   EA 1944, s 81 was replaced by s 518 of the EA 1996, regarding which, see paras **4.57–4.58**.

[9]   [1994] ELR 207, at 218D. The statutory provisions which Potts J had in mind were ss 76 and 81 of the 1944 Act and s 6 of the 1980 Act: see 218C–D.

'unable to accept that the respondent [had] taken into account the wishes of the applicant's parents'.[1]

2.135 It is possible to conclude from *ex parte G* that an application on identical facts would even now be successful on the basis that the LEA had failed to take account of the wishes of the applicant's parents. It also possible to conclude from *ex parte G* that s 9 of the EA 1996 is relevant to an application for a grant under regulations made under s 518 of the EA 1996.

Fees and charges

2.136 A general principle in relation to the provision of education in maintained schools is that such provision must be free. However, this principle is subject to a number of exceptions, not the least of which is that if the school provides part-time education suitable to the requirements of persons of any age over compulsory school age, full-time education suitable to the requirements of persons who have attained the age of 19 years, or teacher training, then in general a charge may be made in connection with the provision in question.[2]

Prohibition on charges for admission to maintained schools and for the provision of education

2.137 The general principle that (subject to the exception indicated in the preceding paragraph) education in maintained schools must be provided free of charge, is implemented by means of a prohibition on charges for admission to maintained schools of any kind (which for this purpose means any school maintained by an LEA[3] and a pupil referral unit[4])[5] and a prohibition (with exceptions) on charging for the education provided for registered pupils during school hours.[6] The exceptions relating to charging for the provision of such education are as follows:

(a) a charge may be made for tuition in playing a musical instrument where the tuition is provided either individually or to a group of no more than four pupils (but see para **2.138**);[7] and

(b) education which is provided partly during and partly outside school hours and which, by virtue of s 452 of the EA 1996, is to be regarded as provided outside school hours (as to which, see below).

---

[1] [1994] ELR 207, at 214D.

[2] This is the product of s 450(2) of the EA 1996 and the restriction of the provisions of s 451 of that Act to education provided to 'registered pupils' (as to which see para **5.8**), together with the definition of 'pupil' in s 3 of the EA 1996 (as amended).

[3] EA 1996, s 449(a); see s 20(7) of the SSFA 1998 for the precise kinds of school which this means (since the SSFA 1998 must, as a result of s 142(8) of the SSFA 1998, be read as one with the EA 1996).

[4] EA 1996, Sch 1, para 9, which applies the provisions in question to pupil referral units as if the references to governing bodies were omitted.

[5] EA 1996, s 450(1).

[6] Ibid, s 451(2). The school hours at a maintained school must be made known for this purpose, in Wales in accordance with the Education (School Hours and Policies) (Information) Regulations 1989, SI 1989/398, and in England in accordance with the Education (School Sessions and Charges and Remissions Policies) (Information) (England) Regulations 1999, SI 1999/2255.

[7] Ibid, s 451(3)(a).

2.138 If, however, the individual or group tuition in the playing of a musical instrument in respect of which a charge may prima facie be made is required as part of any syllabus for a prescribed public examination[1] for which the pupil is being prepared at the school, or if the tuition is provided as part of the National Curriculum or as part of the provision of religious education forming part of the school's basic curriculum, then no charge may be made for the tuition.[2]

2.139 In addition to the above prohibitions, s 451(4) of the EA 1996 provides that if education is provided for a registered pupil outside school hours, then no charge is to be made for it if it is required as part of any syllabus for a prescribed public examination[3] for which the pupil is being prepared at the school, or if it is religious education provided as part of the basic curriculum for the school, or if the education is provided as part of the National Curriculum.

2.140 As one would expect, a relevant body cannot avoid these prohibitions on charging by charging the parent of a registered pupil or the pupil for, or requiring from either of them the supply of, any materials, books, instruments or other equipment for use for the purposes of or in connection with education or a syllabus for a prescribed public examination in respect of which no charge may be made.[4] This, however, is subject to two exceptions, which are as follows. First, 'equipment' does not include clothing.[5] Secondly, a parent of a registered pupil may be:

> 'required to pay for or supply any materials for use for the purposes of the production, in the course of the provision of education for the pupil at the school, of any article incorporating those materials, where the parent has indicated before that requirement is made that he wishes the article to be owned by him or by the pupil.'[6]

Prohibition (with an exception) on charges for examinations

2.141 Subject to the exception indicated in the next sentence, no charge may be made in respect of the entry of a registered pupil at a maintained school for any prescribed public examination[7] in any syllabus for that examination for which the pupil has been prepared at the school.[8] However, the fees paid or payable by an LEA or the governing body of any maintained school for a registered pupil for a public examination in any syllabus for that examination may be recovered from the parent of the pupil if the pupil fails 'without good reason to meet any examination requirement

---

[1] Prescribed under the Education (Prescribed Public Examinations) Regulations 1989, SI 1989/377. See also EA 1996, s 462(4) and (5).

[2] EA 1996, s 451(3).

[3] See footnote 1 above.

[4] EA 1996, s 454(1).

[5] Ibid, s 462(1).

[6] Ibid, s 454(2).

[7] As to which, see footnote 1 above.

[8] EA 1996, s 453(1). See s 462(3) for clarification of when a pupil is to be regarded as having been prepared at a school for a syllabus for a prescribed public examination.

for that syllabus'.[1] Whether there is such a reason is determinable by the relevant authority or governing body.[2]

Prohibition on charging for transport

2.142 No charge may be made for the provision of transport for a registered pupil at a maintained school where the transport is incidental to education provided for the pupil at the school in respect of which as a result of s 451 no charge may be made.[3] In addition, no charge for such transport may be made where the transport is:

> 'provided for the purpose of enabling [the pupil] to meet any examination requirement for any syllabus for a prescribed public examination which is a syllabus for which he has been prepared at the school.'[4]

Education provided partly during and partly outside school hours; residential trips

2.143 Section 452 of the EA 1996 makes specific provision for cases where education is provided partly during and partly outside school hours,[5] and for when education provided on residential trips (in other words involving at least one overnight stay[6]) is to be regarded as provided during school hours.

2.144 If half or more of the time occupied by any educational activity together with any connected school travelling time[7] falls during school hours, then so much of the education provided during that period as is provided outside school hours is to be treated for the purposes of s 451 of the EA 1996 as provided during school hours.[8] If, on the other hand, more than half the period spent on the activity together with the connected school travelling time falls outside school hours, then so much of the education provided during that period as is provided during school hours is treated as provided outside school hours.[9]

2.145 The question whether education provided on residential trips is to be regarded (for the purposes of charging) as provided during or outside school hours is determined in the following manner. Days are divided into two half days of 12 hours, each ending at noon and midnight respectively.[10] If the number of school sessions taken up by the trip is equal to or greater than half the number of half days spent on

---

[1] EA 1996, s 453(2).

[2] Ibid, s 453(3).

[3] Ibid, s 454(3)(a). See s 454(4) for the determination of whether transport is incidental for this purpose.

[4] Ibid, s 454(3)(b). See footnote 1 at p 53 with regard to prescribed public examinations.

[5] The school hours must be publicised in Wales in the manner required by the Education (School Hours and Policies) Information Regulations 1989, SI 1989/398 and in England in the manner required by the Education (School Sessions and Charges and Remissions Policies) (Information) (England) Regulations 1999, SI 1999/2255.

[6] See EA 1996, s 462(2).

[7] 'Connected school travelling time' is defined by s 452(2) as 'time spent during school hours by the pupils taking part in the educational activity concerned in getting to or from the place where the activity takes place'.

[8] EA 1996, s 452(1)(a).

[9] Ibid, s 452(1)(b).

[10] Ibid, s 452(4).

the trip, then any education provided on the trip which is provided outside school hours is treated for the purposes of s 451 as provided during school hours.[1] If the number of school sessions taken up by the trip is less than half the number of half days spent on the trip, then any education provided on the trip which is provided during school hours is treated as provided outside school hours.[2] Where half or more of a half day is spent on a residential trip, then the whole of that half day is regarded as spent on the trip.[3] In addition, a school session is treated as taken up by a residential trip if the time spent on the trip occupies half or more of the time allowed for the session at the school.[4]

Permitted charges in respect of education

2.146 Section 455(1) of the EA 1996 makes explicit what would otherwise have been implicit – that charges may be made for those things in respect of which a charge is not prohibited. Section 455(1) can be regarded as limiting any power to charge which would otherwise have existed by implication.[5] However, the power to charge for a discretionary service under s 93 of the Local Government Act 2003 has altered the situation considerably. In any event, charges may be made under s 455(1) for the following:

(a)   education for a registered pupil at a maintained school[6] other than education in respect of which no charge may be made because of section 451;[7]

(b)   the entry of such a pupil for a public examination in any syllabus for that examination other than one in respect of which no charge may be made because of s 453(1);[8]

(c)   transport for such a pupil other than transport for which, as a result of s 454(3)[9] or s 509(2) of the EA 1996,[10] no charge may be made; and

(d)   board and lodging for any such pupil on a residential trip.[11]

2.147 However, a charge of the first three sorts can only be made with the agreement

---

[1]   EA 1996, s 452(3)(a). There is no definition in the EA 1996 of 'school session'. However, reg 3(1) of the Education (School Day and School Year) Regulations 1999, SI 1999/3181 and reg 4(1) of the Education (School Day and School Year) (Wales) Regulations 2003, SI 2003/3231, provide (with slightly different wording – that which is given is in reg 3(1)) that subject to several exceptions, 'every day on which a school meets shall be divided into two sessions which shall be separated by a break in the middle of the day unless exceptional circumstances make this undesirable'. It therefore seems (although it is true that it is only in certain cases that a statutory instrument can be used as an aid to the construction of primary legislation: see *Hanlon v The Law Society* [1981] AC 124, at 193–194) that 'school session' in s 452(3) of the EA 1996 means either a morning or an afternoon session.

[2]   Ibid, s 452(3)(b).

[3]   Ibid, s 452(5)(a).

[4]   Ibid, s 452(5)(b).

[5]   Cf *R v Richmond upon Thames LBC, ex parte McCarthy & Stone* [1992] 2 AC 48, regarding which see para **2.95**, at footnote 1.

[6]   For the definition of which, see para **2.137**.

[7]   As to which, see paras **2.137–2.140**.

[8]   As to which, see para **2.141**.

[9]   As to which, see para **2.142**.

[10]   As to which, see para **4.12**.

[11]   For the definition of a residential trip, see EA 1996, s 462(2).

of a parent of the pupil.[1] When such a charge is made, the matter to which it relates is referred to as an 'optional extra'.[2]

2.148 A charge which is permitted by s 455 is referred to as a 'regulated charge'.[3] Such a charge is payable by the parent of the pupil to whom it relates,[4] and must not exceed the cost of the optional extra or the board and lodging in question.[5] Section 456(4)–(6) of the EA 1996 contain supplementary provisions regarding what is or is not to be regarded as included in optional extras.

2.149 If the governing body of a school is to bear, or to meet from funds at its disposal, the cost of provision in respect of which a regulated charge may be made, then it decides whether a charge for it should be made.[6] If it is the LEA which is to bear such cost, then it is the LEA which decides whether a charge should be made.[7] If in those latter circumstances the LEA decides to make a charge, then the governing body may meet the charge (either partly or fully) itself or from funds at its disposal.[8] The charge then cannot, to the extent that it is so met, be recovered from the parent of the pupil concerned.[9]

2.150 Charges may be made under s 455 of the EA 1996 only if the body making the charge in question has determined and kept under review a policy with regard to the provision of optional extras (as defined in s 455(3)) and the classes or descriptions of case in which it proposes to make charges for such extras.[10] Further, in order to be able to make a charge under s 455, the body must also have determined a remissions policy.[11] The remissions policy of the governing body of a maintained school must set out any circumstances in which the governing body proposes to meet (either partly or fully) any charge payable to the LEA as a result of s 455.[12] These policies must be publicised in such manner as may be prescribed by regulations.[13] Full remission must be made of charges in respect of board and lodging provided for a pupil on a residential trip if education provided on the trip is education in respect of which by virtue of s 451 no charge may be made and the pupil's parent is for any part of the period during which the trip takes place (i) in receipt of income support, (ii) in receipt of an income-based jobseeker's allowance payable under the Jobseekers Act 1995, or

---

[1]   EA 1996, s 455(2).

[2]   Ibid, s 455(3). Presumably, pupils will not go on residential trips unless their parents consent, with the result that it was not thought necessary to include a residential trip within the definition of 'optional extra'.

[3]   Ibid, s 456(1).

[4]   Ibid, s 456(2).

[5]   Ibid, s 456(3).

[6]   Ibid, s 456(7)(a).

[7]   Ibid, s 456(7)(b).

[8]   Ibid, s 456(8)(a).

[9]   Ibid, s 456(8)(b).

[10] Ibid, s 457(1) and (2).

[11] Ibid. As a result of s 457(5), the remissions policy must be kept under review by the body by which it was determined.

[12] Ibid, s 457(3).

[13] Ibid, s 459(b). The current regulations are, in Wales, the Education (School Hours and Policies) (Information) Regulations 1989, SI 1989/398, and, in England, the Education (School Sessions and Charges and Remissions Policies) (Information) (England) Regulations 1999, SI 1999/2255.

(iii) in receipt of any other benefit or allowance prescribed for this purpose, or is entitled to any tax credit under the Tax Credits Act 2002 or element of such a tax credit prescribed for this purpose, in such circumstances as may be prescribed for this purpose.[1]

Charges for board and lodging at boarding schools

2.151 Section 458 of the EA 1996 allows charges to be made for board and lodging for pupils at maintained boarding schools.[2] However, if the LEA for a pupil's area is of the opinion that suitable education cannot otherwise be provided for him, then the LEA must pay (or, if it maintains the school, remit) the charges.[3] If the LEA is not of such opinion, though, it must nevertheless pay or remit part or all of the charges if requiring their payment by the pupil's parent would cause financial hardship to the parent.[4]

Supplementary matters

2.152 Section 460 of the EA 1996 contains some supplementary provisions, including that governing bodies and LEAs may nevertheless request or invite voluntary contributions for the benefit of the school or any school activities.[5] However, such a request or invitation must make it clear that there is no obligation to make the contribution and that registered pupils at the school will not be treated differently according to whether or not their parents have made any contribution in response to the request or invitation.[6] In addition, charges may be made by persons other than the governing body or the LEA (such as the parent-teacher association).[7] Furthermore, charges may be made of persons other than the parent of a pupil or the pupil.[8]

THE GENERAL PRINCIPLES APPLYING TO THE NEW STATUTORY EDUCATION CORPORATIONS

2.153 The new statutory education corporations set up from 1979 onwards – to conduct grant-maintained schools (which no longer exist), education associations (which also no longer exist), higher education corporations,[9] further education corporations,[10] and, most recently, foundation bodies[11] – involved the creation of a

---

1   EA 1996, s 457(4), as substituted by EA 2002, s 200. The current relevant regulations are the Education (Residential Trips) (Prescribed Tax Credits) (England) Regulations 2003, SI 2003/381 in relation to England, and the Education (Remission of Charges Relating to Residential Trips) (Wales) Regulations 2003, SI 2003/860 in relation to Wales.

2   For the meaning of the term 'maintained school', see para **2.137**.

3   EA 1996, s 458(2).

4   Ibid, s 458(4) and (5).

5   Ibid, s 460(1).

6   Ibid, s 460(2).

7   Ibid, s 460(3)(a).

8   Ibid, s 460(3)(b).

9   Established under ERA 1988, ss 121 and 122.

10   Established under FHEA 1992 ss 15 and 16.

11   See SSFA 1998, s 21(4)(a).

new type of corporation.[1] It seems clear that Parliament's aim was to set up autonomous organisations which were to be fully responsible for the conduct of the institutions which they were to conduct, free from party political influence, and with a more business-like approach than had (in Parliament's view) been taken by those responsible for the conduct of those institutions in the past. However, it appears that there have been considerable teething troubles in relation to the institutions.[2] Those teething troubles may well have resulted in part from the new structure of the institutions. The institutions are now run by corporate bodies which are in some respects not unlike registered companies set up under the Companies Act 1985. However, since many charitable activities are carried out by limited companies whose purposes are exclusively charitable, that in itself is unlikely to be the cause of the difficulties which have been encountered. Rather, it is possible that the difficulties have arisen because of the need for some sort of accountability in an academic institution.[3]

2.154 Only further education corporations (FECs) and higher education corporations (HECs) are considered here (although much of what is said in this section of this chapter may apply also to the incorporated governing bodies of maintained schools and to foundation bodies). Both types of body are exempt charities for the purposes of the Charities Act 1993 (CA 1993).[4] Although this is not the sole determinant of charitable status, since any body the purposes of which are exclusively charitable is a charity within the meaning of the CA 1993,[5] it does indicate that the purposes of the corporations in question are exclusively charitable and that their powers are accordingly limited. It is of note that an FEC is nevertheless empowered to sell goods and services in the limited circumstances referred to in s 18 of the FHEA 1992.[6] However, those circumstances are ones in which a charity might in normal circumstances be able to claim that what was done was properly classifiable as part of the activities of the charity, or was related to the primary purpose of the provision of education (which clearly *is* exclusively charitable) and therefore was not

---

[1]   The incorporation of the governing bodies of maintained schools under s 238 of the Education Act 1993 (see now SSFA 1998, s 36 and Schs 9 and 10, and EA 2002, s 19 and Sch 1) did not make them statutory corporations of the same sorts as the others mentioned in the text to this note. However, some issues which arise in relation to the latter corporations apply also to the incorporated governing bodies of maintained schools, and reference is accordingly made to them at appropriate places in Chapter 7.

[2]   See, for example, D Charter, *The battle for a university's soul*, *The Times*, 5 July 1996, at p 39 (an article about the situation of Portsmouth University). See also the report by the Comptroller and Auditor General concerning that university, HC4 Session 1997–98.

[3]   This seems to be the view of the governing body of Portsmouth University, where, according to Charter (ibid), more influence has now been given to the academic council than it seems originally to have had. This has been brought about by the setting up of a 'Chancellor's Court', composed of the Chancellor and two others appointed by him, to consider complaints presented by a minimum of four governors. Apparently, the Chancellor's Court is able to call on the governing body to review decisions. This is said to be 'enough to ensure that staff can raise issues through their representatives'.

[4]   See s 22A of the FHEA 1992 in relation to further education corporations and s 125A of the ERA 1988 in relation to higher education corporations.

[5]   See ss 96 and 97 of that Act.

[6]   See para **16.64** regarding s 18.

properly classifiable as trading.[1] On this basis, there would be no doubt about the status of an FEC in this regard, just as there can be no real doubt about the status of the other kinds of corporation under consideration here. On the other hand, s 18 could simply be interpreted as giving FECs power, as charities, to do what would otherwise not be regarded as charitable, but that does not appear to be the best view.

Can a relevant statutory education corporation establish subsidiary companies?

2.155 There is a lengthy discussion in the first edition of this book about the question whether a statutory education corporation could lawfully establish or own subsidiary companies.[2] That discussion appears now to be of largely historical interest only (albeit that the questions discussed there may continue to be relevant in some circumstances for some time), given the enactment of (1) para 15 of Sch 9 to the LSA 2000, which substituted a new s 124(2)(f) of the ERA 1988, and (2) para 22 of that Schedule, which inserted new provisions into s 19 of the FHEA 1992 concerning FECs, and given the abolition of the other kinds of corporation whose powers were in issue in that discussion. Both of the amendments made by the LSA 2000 empower the corporation in question to 'subscribe for or otherwise acquire shares in or securities of a company'. However, there are differences between the two provisions, in that the power is less wide in the case of an FEC.[3]

2.156 It is noted here, however, that in order to be lawful, the establishment of a subsidiary company would in most cases require the dedication by the education corporation of financial resources to the company. In line with the general position regarding charities, the corporation would have to consider whether the investment was a sound one. If it was not, then it would probably be unlawful to make the investment. If the only investment consisted in the purchase of shares, then it would be possible to avoid that problem by establishing a company limited by guarantee, with the memorandum of association providing for the distribution of profits.[4]

Relevant principles applicable to corporations

2.157 Apparently, the law of corporations originally developed most in the context of local authorities and of ecclesiastical bodies.[5] In addition, 'universities ... were assimilated to local authorities, which in those times had considerably more power over local inhabitants than they do now'.[6] Be that as it may, until the coming into existence of the plethora of new types of statutory corporations introduced during the period of the Conservative governments from 1979 to 1997, it seems that the law of

---

[1]   Although it is not directly relevant, it is helpful to know that the Inland Revenue Commissioners' booklet *Clubs and Charity series IR2001: Trading by Charities*, contains an indication that this might be how the Inland Revenue would view the matter.

[2]   See paras 2.179–2.188 of the first edition.

[3]   See para **16.68** for the restrictions on the power applicable to an FEC.

[4]   In order to avoid paying corporation tax, the company could covenant any profits made by it to the corporation (the corporation's purposes being, as indicated above, exclusively charitable).

[5]   See DJ Farrington, *The Law of Higher Education* (Butterworths, London, 2nd edn, 1998), at pp 18–19, para 1.33.

[6]   Ibid, p 19, para 1.35. The times in question appear to have extended to at least as late as 1670: ibid, p 20.

corporations at least in some respects came to be seen largely as a part of local government law and of the law relating to companies. However, there was a common thread in relation to corporations, although it is suggested here that the context of each may have affected the view of the courts which have had to decide issues of general importance in the law of corporations. In the meantime it is noted that the only modern textbook on the law relating to corporations as such appears to be the relevant part of *Halsbury's Laws of England*.[1]

2.158 The key relevant elements of the law relating to corporations[2] are as follows.[3] The identity of a corporation is continuous; in other words, a change in the membership of the corporation does not affect the corporation's legal identity. Accordingly, a legal right or obligation accruing to or affecting a corporation while it subsists binds the corporation despite a change in its membership. The corporation is a distinct entity, different in law from its members. It is a legal as opposed to a natural person, and is accordingly bound by the law so far as it is capable, as a corporation, of being so bound.[4]

2.159 Unlike a chartered corporation,[5] a statutory corporation can do only that which is expressly or impliedly authorised by the statutes which created it.[6]

2.160 The common law rule that a corporation aggregate needs a common seal for the execution of deeds[7] continues to apply unless there is specific legislative provision to the contrary. It therefore applies to relevant education corporations.[8] However, a seal is not necessary for entering into a contract, the former requirement in this regard having been removed by the Corporate Bodies' Contracts Act 1960.

2.161 If a corporation is liable in the law of contract, then its members cannot without more also be liable under that contract.[9] In addition, it has been said that:

---

[1] Volume 9(2), 4th edn, reissue, 1998.

[2] That is, corporations aggregate as opposed to corporations sole.

[3] Except where otherwise indicated, the principles are drawn from vol 9(2) of *Halsbury's Laws* (4th edn, reissue, 1998), at paras 1009–1010.

[4] For example, a corporation is incapable of acts of worship: *Rolloswin Investments Ltd v Chromolit Portugal* [1970] 1 WLR 912, at 915G–H.

[5] As to which, see paras **12.47** et seq.

[6] *Halsbury's Laws*, vol 9(2), paras 1130 and 1137. See now also, *R v Somerset County Council, ex parte Fewings* [1995] 1 WLR 1037. See further, paras **17.75** and **17.76** regarding the potential impact of public law on even chartered corporations.

[7] See para 1018 of vol 9(2) of *Halsbury's Laws*.

[8] This rule has survived s 1 of the Law of Property (Miscellaneous Provisions) Act 1989 (which applies only to individuals). It also remains of application to relevant education corporations despite ss 36 and 36A of the Companies Act 1985 (inserted by s 130 of the Companies Act 1989), which apply only to companies registered under the Companies Act 1985. (The Companies (Unregistered Companies) Regulations 1985, SI 1985/680, as amended, do not apply in this context, since as a result of reg 2, they do not apply to a 'body corporate mentioned in s 718(2) of the [Companies Act 1985]' which includes 'any body incorporated by or registered under any public general Act of Parliament' and 'any body not formed for the purpose of carrying on a business which has for its object the acquisition of gain by the body or its individual members'.)

[9] *Re Sheffield and South Yorkshire Permanent Building Society* (1889) 22 QBD 470, at 476, per Cave J. As it is stated in para 1010 of vol 9(2) of *Halsbury's Laws*, 'If an individual trusts a corporation, he trusts that

'Where a corporation has been dissolved, its members, in their natural capacities, can neither recover debts which were due to the corporation nor be charged with debts contracted by it.'[1]

Would the Insolvency Act 1986 apply on a relevant corporation's dissolution?

2.162 According to *Halsbury's Laws*, Part V of the Insolvency Act 1986 (which applies to the winding up of 'unregistered companies') would not apply to a statutory corporation.[2] However, whether it would apply to the education corporations under consideration here cannot be regarded as completely beyond doubt. This is because although there is an authority which would support the proposition that such corporations are not subject to Part V of the Insolvency Act 1986 – *Tamlin v Hannaford*[3] – that case concerned a statutory corporation (the British Transport Commission) the funding of which was slightly different from that of those in issue here. Yet on a closer analysis, the differences may not be substantial. Although Denning LJ said in *Tamlin v Hannaford* that borrowings of the British Transport Commission were 'guaranteed by the Treasury',[4] that was not strictly true. Only borrowings to meet liabilities to pay compensation arising out of the nationalisation of the transport operations which the Commission took over under the Transport Act 1947, had to be guaranteed by the Treasury. Other borrowings could be, but were not obliged to be, guaranteed by the Treasury.[5] Accordingly, there is no material difference between the situation regarding funding in *Tamlin v Hannaford* and that of relevant statutory education corporations.[6] Yet that does not mean that there is no room for doubt about the applicability here of the statement by Denning LJ in *Tamlin v Hannaford* that the British Transport Commission was 'not liable to be wound up at the suit of any creditor',[7] since the case did not actually concern an application to wind up the Commission.[8] It is, however, suggested here that relevant statutory education

---

legal person, and must look to its assets for payment; he may call on individual members to contribute if the Act or charter creating the corporation has so provided'.

[1] Paragraph 1204 of vol 9(2) of *Halsbury's Laws*. The authority given for this proposition – *Naylor v Cornish* (1684) 1 Vern 311n(1) and *Edmunds v Brown and Tillard* (1668) 1 Lev 237 - is rather old, but it fully supports it, and there is no reason to doubt the correctness of the proposition from the point of view of principle.

[2] Volume 7(3) *Halsbury's Laws* (4th edn, reissue 1996), para 2902 (text to n 7).

[3] [1950] 1 KB 18, at 23, where Denning LJ said that the British Transport Commission was 'not liable to be wound up at the suit of any creditor'. The proposition in *Halsbury's* stated in the text to footnote 2 above is based on *Tamlin v Hannaford* and is that 'statutory corporations' (and not just some statutory corporations) are not subject to Part V of the Insolvency Act 1986.

[4] Ibid, at 23.

[5] See s 90(1) of the Transport Act 1947.

[6] As for the relevant provisions regarding each, see paras **16.79** and **16.80** in relation to further education corporations, and s 128 of the ERA 1988 in relation to higher education corporations. The essence of each set of provisions is that in the event of the dissolution of the corporation, the liabilities of the corporation may, but must not, be met by the Secretary of State or some other body, as determined by the Secretary of State under the relevant provisions.

[7] See footnote 4 above.

[8] The question in the case was whether or not a dwelling-house owned by the Commission was subject to the Rent Restriction Acts. If property owned by the Commission was properly to be regarded as owned by the Crown, then those Acts did not apply. (The Court of Appeal in fact ruled that the property of the Commission was *not* owned by the Crown.)

corporations are not properly to be regarded as subject to Part V of the Insolvency Act 1986, and are therefore not liable to be wound up as unregistered companies.

Distinguishing a corporation from the institution it conducts

2.163 Finally here, it is noted that a statutory corporation of the relevant sorts should be regarded for some purposes as distinct from the institution which it was incorporated to conduct. That this is so can be seen from several sources in the Education Acts. For example, according to s 4(1) of the EA 1996, ' "school" means an educational institution which is outside the further education sector and the higher education sector and is an institution for providing: (a) primary education [...]'.[1] Further, in s 129B of the ERA 1988, there is a reference to 'any designated institution conducted by a company'. Moreover, s 20(1)(b) of the FHEA 1992 requires there to be 'an instrument in accordance with which the corporation, and the institution, are to be conducted (to be known as articles of government)'. Similarly, in s 23(2) of the FHEA 1992, reference is made to 'property ... used or held for the purposes of the institution the corporation is established to conduct'. These provisions therefore suggest that the word 'institution' should at least for some purposes be regarded as distinct from the corporation which conducts it.

What is an 'institution' in this context?

2.164 It is accordingly necessary to ask what is the 'institution' in this context. A distinction is made in ss 23 and 32 of the FHEA 1992 between an institution and the property 'used or held for the purposes of the institution'. Similarly, in s 126(4) of the ERA 1988, there is a reference to property 'used or held for the purposes of the transferred institution', and in s 201(2) of the EA 1996, there was a reference to property 'used or held by the authority for the purposes of the school'. Furthermore, in s 274(4) of the EA 1996, the definition of 'school property' included 'the premises used or formerly used for the purposes of the school'. All these provisions suggest that the word 'institution' in this context should be interpreted as meaning something separate from the property held for the purposes of the institution. This was in fact the conclusion of Lord Denning in *Bradbury v Enfield London Borough Council*.[2] There, the question was whether what was proposed was a change to a school or, rather, whether the proposed changes were so wholesale that it was proposed to cease to maintain the school. Lord Denning said:

> '[I]t appears to me that a "school" is an institution which exists independently of the buildings in which it is housed for the time being. Many a school retained its identity during the war even though it was evacuated to a place 200 miles away. A school is an institution with a character of its own.'[3]

Corporation as the institution

2.165 As a matter of general principle, it seems that the word 'institution' should be regarded in this context as meaning the administrative or conceptual structure of the

---

[1]   The definition of 'school' in s 114(1) of the EA 1944 also referred to a school as an 'institution'.

[2]   [1967] 1 WLR 1311.

[3]   Ibid, at 1320H.

provider of education. This is consistent with the relevant definition of the word 'institution' in the *Oxford English Dictionary*.[1] In the case of the statutory corporations in question here, that structure must mean the corporation, except where it is necessary to distinguish between the corporation and the institution which it was formed to conduct. However, it can be concluded that the buildings housing the institution are not to be regarded as the institution, despite that being (according to the *Oxford English Dictionary*) a popular conception.[2]

---

[1]   2nd edn, 1991. The relevant definition is number 7 **a**.

[2]   This proposition is supported not only by *Bradbury v Enfield London Borough Council* but also by the case of *Bunt v Kent* [1914] 1 KB 207. That case concerned a failure by a parent to cause his child to attend school where she failed to attend a cookery class which her school had arranged to be taught at a different school. At p 212, Darling J said: 'I think confusion has arisen through the use of the word "school". The word has a wider meaning that that of a school building'. There is also some support for the proposition stated in the text from a case cited in DJ Farrington, *The Law of Higher Education*, (Butterworths, 2nd edn, 1998). At para 1.38 on p 21, reference is made to the case of *The University of Glasgow v Kirkwood* (1872) 10 M 1000, where on the facts the court held that exemption from local taxes was conferred on the property of the corporation at the date of the grant (and not to its subsequently acquired property), rather than on the corporation itself.

Chapter 3

SUPPLEMENTARY FUNCTIONS OF THE SECRETARY OF STATE AND THE NATIONAL ASSEMBLY FOR WALES

3.1   As discussed in Chapter 2, the Secretary of State, and, in Wales, the National Assembly for Wales,[1] have a significant number of functions in relation to a number of specific areas of education, such as the National Curriculum. There are other areas in which the Secretary of State has specific functions, and reference is made to them elsewhere in this book. This chapter is concerned only with independent supplementary functions of the Secretary of State.

SUPERVISION

3.2   In one sense, whenever the Secretary of State has a function in regard to a matter, he has a supervisory role in relation to that matter. An example is provided by the supervisory role of the Secretary of State exercised in relation to independent schools.[2] However, this section is concerned only with the powers of the Secretary of State under s 495 of the EA 1996 (and related provisions elsewhere in the Education Acts), and ss 496, 497, 497A, 497AA and 497B of the EA 1996.

Section 495(1) and (2) of the Education Act 1996

3.3   Section 495(1) and (2) of the EA 1996 provide:

'(1) Except where this Act expressly provides otherwise, any dispute between a local education authority and the governing body of a school as to the exercise of any power conferred or the performance of any duty imposed by or under this Act may be referred to the Secretary of State (despite any enactment which makes the exercise of the power or the performance of the duty contingent upon the opinion of the authority or of the governing body).

(2) The Secretary of State shall determine any dispute referred to him under sub-section (1).'[3]

---

[1]   Except where otherwise stated, for the sake of simplicity, references in this chapter to the Secretary of State are to be read as references also to the National Assembly for Wales.

[2]   As to which, see Chapter 13. That role has in fact been diminished as a result of the involvement of Her Majesty's Chief Inspector of Schools in England and Her Majesty's Chief Inspector of Education and Training in Wales, but it is nevertheless significant.

[3]   Section 495(1) applies also in relation to the governing body of any institution which is maintained by an LEA and provides higher education or further education (or both): ERA 1988, s 219(2). The power to order a medical examination under s 506 when in the opinion of the Secretary of State such examination would assist the determination of a question under s 495 (see para **3.50**) should be borne in mind.

3.4   This potentially very useful provision has tended not to be used in practice. However, in *Board of Education v Rice*,[1] the House of Lords determined the proper approach to take to a provision which could be regarded as the predecessor to s 495, s 7(3) of the Education Act 1902. Section 7(3) provided:

> 'If any question arises under this section between the local education authority and the managers of a school not provided by the authority, that question shall be determined by the Board of Education.'

3.5   Section 7 imposed on an LEA the duty of maintaining and keeping 'efficient' all 'public elementary schools' in their area. It also provided for the essential division of functions between the LEA and the governing body of a non-provided school.[2] In *Board of Education v Rice*, the LEA had decided to pay salaries to teachers in non-provided schools which were lower than those paid to teachers in provided schools.[3] The managers (who would now be called the governors) of the school complained to the Board under s 7(3). An inquiry was held, and the inquirer reported to the Board that the LEA had failed to keep the school efficient. The Board nevertheless decided the matter in favour of the local authority and did so without determining the main question which arose under the 1902 Act. That was whether or not the LEA had 'in fixing and paying the salaries of the teachers fulfilled their duty under' s 7(1) of the 1902 Act.[4] The House of Lords quashed the Board's decision and ordered it to determine the dispute properly.

3.6   From this it can be inferred that if an LEA or the governing body of a maintained school properly sought the determination of a relevant dispute by the Secretary of State under s 495, then the Secretary of State could if necessary be ordered by the High Court (by means of a mandatory order) to determine the dispute. This is indeed in accordance with the outcomes of a series of cases determined at about the same time as *Board of Education v Rice*, concerning the question whether or not the matters in regard to which questions had arisen between the governors of non-provided schools and local education authorities were ones which were to be determined by the Secretary of State alone or by the courts.[5] Wherever it was held in these cases that a matter was determinable by the Board of Education, the jurisdiction of the court was held to be ousted. Although that aspect of the cases must now be regarded in the light of R *v Inner London Education Authority, ex parte Ali*,[6] it is clear that the jurisdiction of the courts in relation to the Board of Education's decisions was nevertheless not ousted entirely by s 7(3). This was because, for example, if a determination of the Board of Education was carried out in an improper manner then the courts could intervene. This is the implication of the approach taken by the House of Lords in *Board of Education v Rice*, where Lord Loreburn LC set out a classic statement of the proper approach of a relevant fact-finder. This is that 'they must act

---

1   [1911] AC 179.

2   That is, the predecessor to what is today called a voluntary school.

3   That is, the predecessors to what are now called community schools.

4   See [1911] AC 179, at 185, per Lord Loreburn, and at 187, per Lord Shaw.

5   *Blencowe v Northamptonshire County Council* [1907] 1 Ch 504, *Wilford v West Riding County Council* [1908] 1 KB 685, *Gillow v Durham County Council* [1913] AC 54, *West Suffolk County Council v Olorenshaw* [1918] 2 KB 687, and *Martin v Eccles Corporation* [1919] 1 Ch 387.

6   [1990] 2 Admin LR 822; (1990) *The Times*, February 20; [1990] COD 317. See paras **3.27** and **3.28**.

in good faith and fairly listen to both sides'.[1] Lord Loreburn also said that if the court was satisfied that the Board of Education had not done this or had not determined the question which they were required by s 7(3) to determine, then the court could intervene.[2] The same seems to be true of a reference to the Secretary of State under s 495.[3]

Relationship between section 495(1) and a specific provision elsewhere in the Education Acts

3.7   The opening words of s 495(1) make it clear that if there is a specific provision elsewhere in the EA 1996 or any of the Education Acts which are to be read as one with the EA 1996 for the determination of a particular dispute, then that provision excludes the operation of s 495(1). Examples are to be found in ss 496 and 497 (which are considered below), and s 560(6) (concerning work experience). A further example is provided by the situation where there is a compulsory scheme of delegation entered into pursuant to Chapter IV of Part II of the SSFA 1998, and the LEA determines to suspend the right of the governing body of a maintained school covered by the scheme to a delegated budget. In that situation, Sch 15 to the SSFA 1998 applies in relation to that determination. However, it is not clear whether the existence of Sch 15 precludes the use of s 495(1) where the provisions of Sch 15 themselves provide no remedy, and the answer to that question is likely to be relevant to other situations where s 495 is ousted to any extent by another statutory provision. It will accordingly now be considered.

3.8   Schedule 15 allows the LEA to suspend the right of a relevant governing body to a delegated budget in the circumstances described in Chapter 7.[4] The LEA can do so either on one month's notice or, as long as it has given such notice, before the expiry of that period of notice if:

> 'by reason of any gross incompetence or mismanagement on the part of the governing body or other emergency it appears to the authority to be necessary –
> (a) to give the governing body a shorter period of notice, or
> (b) to give the governing body a notice suspending their right to such a budget with immediate effect.'[5]

3.9   The governing body has the right to appeal to the Secretary of State under para 3 of Sch 15 to the SSFA 1998, but that would not provide an effective remedy in some circumstances, for example if the LEA suspended the right to a delegated budget for only a short period of time solely in order to settle an industrial tribunal

---

[1]   [1911] AC 179, at 182. This statement 'must nevertheless be viewed with caution' according to *de Smith, Woolf and Jowell, Judicial Review of Administrative Action* (Sweet & Maxwell, 5th edn, 1995), at para 7.15, for the reasons set out there.

[2]   Ibid.

[3]   Any challenge to a determination of the Secretary of State under s 495 would presumably have to be made by way of an application for judicial review on the same basis as that on which a determination by the Secretary of State made under s 496 of the EA 1996 could be judicially reviewed. That basis is considered below.

[4]   See paras **7.144** et seq.

[5]   Schedule 15, para 1(2).

claim to which the governing body was the respondent.[1] In that situation, the governing body would be likely to be unable to prevent the action in question by appealing to the Secretary of State under para 3 of Sch 15. The application of s 495(1) of the EA 1996 would then fill that gap. It remains to be seen, however, whether a court would accept that s 495(1) has a role to play in that situation. The court might decide that since there is already a régime in place, that régime displaces s 495(1) entirely. It is suggested here, though, that s 495(1) should not be regarded as having been displaced entirely in such a situation since if it were displaced, a complainant of the relevant sort would be without a remedy unless he or she made a successful application for judicial review. Further, it seems clear that s 495(1) was intended to remove the need to make such an application by giving the claimant the power to request the intervention of the Secretary of State. It also seems clear that another purpose in providing such a route for a claimant was to avoid 'the courts getting involved in education matters, which they are much less well equipped to deal with than the Secretary of State' – a statement contained in the judgment of Woolf J in *R v Secretary of State for Education and Science, ex parte Chance*.[2] Although Woolf J's comments were directed only at ss 68 and 99 of the 1944 Act (which are now consolidated as ss 496 and 497 of the EA 1996),[3] the rationale of the dictum and the approach taken by Woolf J in that case apply equally to what is now s 495(1) of the EA 1996. There is, however, one caveat which needs to be expressed. That is, that where the referral is in respect of a pure question of law, an application for judicial review would not involve the courts 'getting involved in education matters' in the manner envisaged by Woolf LJ in *ex parte Chance*. Furthermore, such an application could, if successful, lead directly to an order of the court, which is something to which a determination by the Secretary of State under s 495 could not lead directly.[4]

Section 495(3) of the Education Act 1996

3.10   Section 495(3) of the EA 1996 obliges the Secretary of State to determine:

> 'Any dispute between two or more local education authorities as to which of them is responsible for the provision of education for any pupil.'

3.11   However, as indicated above, disputes with regard to the payment by one LEA for the education of a pupil by another LEA are determinable under the Education (Areas to which Pupils and Students Belong) Regulations 1996.[5] Accordingly, the number of occasions when s 495(3) will need to be utilised may, in practice, be few.

---

[1]   See further, paras **15.74** et seq regarding the relevant responsibilities of the governing body and the LEA.

[2]   26 July 1982. The case was unreported, but the part of the judgment from which this quotation is taken is set out in *R v Secretary of State for Education, ex parte Prior* [1994] ICR 877, at 892B–893A. The passage was enthusiastically endorsed by Tucker J in *R v London Borough of Brent, ex parte F* [1999] ELR 32, at 36–37.

[3]   'Section 99 and section 68 are designed to give a person in the position of Mrs Chance a remedy through the officers of the Secretary of State': [1994] ICR 877, at 892F.

[4]   See further, para **3.12**.

[5]   SI 1996/615, as to which, see para **2.103**.

Enforcement of a section 495 or similar determination

3.12 Although there is no indication of the manner in which a determination of a relevant dispute by the Secretary of State could be enforced by the party in whose favour the dispute had been determined, it seems reasonably clear that it would be enforceable by a mandatory order in the same manner as would be a determination under s 496 of the EA 1996.[1] Presumably, however, the party against whom the order was sought could argue that the determination was mistaken in law, and if the court agreed then the order would not be enforced.

Section 496 of the Education Act 1996

3.13 Section 496 of the 1996 Act provides:

'(1) If the Secretary of State is satisfied (either on a complaint by any person or otherwise) that a body to which this section applies have acted or are proposing to act unreasonably with respect to the exercise of any power conferred or the performance of any duty imposed by or under this Act,[2] he may give such directions as to the exercise of the power or the performance of the duty as appear to him to be expedient (and may do so despite any enactment which makes the exercise of the power or the performance of the duty contingent upon the opinion of the body).

(2) The bodies to which this section applies are –
    (a) any local education authority, and
    (b) the governing body of any community, foundation or voluntary school or any community or foundation special school.'

3.14 Section 496 applies also to the governing body of an institution which is maintained by an LEA and which provides higher education or further education (or both),[3] and to a school organisation committee.[4] Section 496 applies in addition to the proprietors of a city technology college, a city college for the technology of the arts, or an Academy, in relation to the duties regarding careers advice imposed by s 43(3) of the EA 1997,[5] also ss 44(1), (4) and (6),[6] and s 45(1).[7] Section 496 applies also to an LEA, a school organisation committee and the governing body of a maintained school in relation to the powers and duties imposed by Sch 7 to the LSA 2000 regarding inadequate sixth-forms.[8] Provisions which are similar to s 496 apply to (1) the LSC or (as the case may be) the CETW,[9] and (2) the governing body of an institution within the further education sector.[10]

---

1   Regarding which, see para **3.26**.
2   This will include any Act with which the EA 1996 has to be read as one. See *Canada Southern Railway Co v International Bridge Company* (1883) 8 App Cas 723, at 727 regarding the effect of a statute being stated to be read as one with another statute.
3   ERA 1988, s 219 (as substituted by EA 1996, Sch 37, para 77).
4   SSFA 1998, Sch 4, para 10.
5   EA 1997, s 43(4).
6   Ibid, s 44(9).
7   Ibid, s 45(3).
8   See LSA 2000, s 113(3).
9   See EA 1997, ss 25(3)(b) and (4) and 47(3)(b) and (4).
10 FHEA 1992, s 57(2)(c), as substituted by LSA 2000, Sch 9, para 34. See para **16.90** regarding s 57.

When section 496 does not apply

3.15   The Secretary of State, however, cannot entertain a complaint made under s 496 where a complaint could be made to the LEA under s 409 of the EA 1996 until a complaint to the LEA under s 409 has been 'made and disposed of' under the arrangements made under that section.[1] Similarly, if a complaint could be made under para 6(3) of Sch 1 to the EA 1996 in relation to the curriculum of a pupil referral unit,[2] then no complaint may be entertained by the Secretary of State under s 496 in relation to the matter.[3] In addition, s 496 does not apply to any power conferred on an LEA by s 560(1) of the EA 1996 (which concerns work experience in the last year of compulsory schooling).[4]

The **Tameside** *case*

3.16   In *Secretary of State for Education and Science v Tameside MBC*,[5] the House of Lords decided that the word 'unreasonably' as used in the predecessor to s 496(1) meant in effect '*Wednesbury* unreasonably' in the narrow sense, a sense which is helpfully illustrated by the following extract from the speech of Lord Diplock:

> 'My Lords, in public law "unreasonable" as descriptive of the way in which a public authority has purported to exercise a discretion vested in it by statute has become a term of legal art. To fall within this expression it must be conduct which no sensible authority acting with due appreciation of its responsibilities would have decided to adopt.'[6]

3.17   However, both Lord Diplock[7] and Lord Wilberforce indicated that there was a need for an inquiry by a reviewing court as to whether there was a factual basis for the Secretary of State's intervention. Lord Wilberforce's approach was more forthright in this regard. Among other things, he said:

> 'If a judgment requires, before it can be made, the existence of some facts, then, although the evaluation of those facts is for the Secretary of State alone, the court must inquire whether those facts exist, and have been taken into account, whether the judgment has been made upon a proper self-direction as to those facts, whether the judgment has not been made upon other facts which ought not to have been taken into account.'[8]

3.18   This approach of Lord Diplock and Lord Wilberforce was at variance with that taken on occasion in different contexts.[9] It was also not followed by the

---

1   Section 409(4) concerns in the main complaints relating to the curriculum. See further, paras **4.9** et seq.
2   See paras **4.2–4.5** regarding pupil referral units.
3   EA 1996, Sch 1, para 6(4).
4   Ibid, s 560(6).
5   [1977] AC 1014. The case has given rise to much comment in textbooks on administrative law and articles in learned journals. For examples of the latter, see (1977) 93 LQR 4 and [1977] CLJ 1. The most instructive discussions in the textbooks are considered below.
6   Ibid, at 1064E. See also per Viscount Dilhorne, at 1054C, per Lord Wilberforce at 1052A and C–D, per Lord Salmon at 1070F–G, and per Lord Russell at 1074E.
7   Ibid, at 1065A–B.
8   Ibid, at 1047D. See also 1047F.
9   See *de Smith, Woolf and Jowell, Judicial Review of Administrative Action* (Sweet & Maxwell, 5th edn, 1995), at paras 5.92 et seq.

Divisional Court in R *v London Residuary Body, ex parte Inner London Education Authority*.[1] Be that as it may, it seems clear that the approach of the Secretary of State under s 496(1) is an unusual, hybrid, one. This is because he must act lawfully in deciding whether or not the body in question acted unlawfully in the narrow *Wednesbury* sense. In effect, in order to be able lawfully to intervene under s 496(1), the Secretary of State must lawfully come to the view (which must be correct in law) that the body in question has acted *Wednesbury* unreasonably in a narrow sense.[2]

3.19   P Craig, in *Administrative Law*,[3] expresses the view that:

'The natural meaning of [the term "unreasonably" in what is now section 496(1)] is "not acting as a reasonable local authority would act", as opposed to "behaviour so unreasonable that no reasonable authority would countenance it". There is no reason why the natural meaning should not apply. None of the constitutional reasons which are the basis for the artificial *Wednesbury* meaning are relevant. If the interpretation given to the term unreasonable in *Tameside* is to mean that the Secretary of State must find behaviour akin to the "red haired school teacher case", then this emasculates the one control mechanism which he possesses.'

3.20   In *de Smith, Woolf and Jowell, Judicial Review of Administrative Action*,[4] the following comment on this view is made:

'The matter surely, however, depends upon the administrative scheme established by a particular statute. It could be argued that the Education Act 1944 has as an important purpose the placing of education policy primarily with the local authority, with the Minister having power to intervene only in extreme cases. In the case of other administrative schemes, however, the statute may pose the Minister with fewer obstacles to intervention.'

3.21   The example is then given of the default power contained in the Housing Act 1980, which applied even where there was no unreasonable behaviour on the part of a local authority. Reference is then made to what is described also as an example of a situation in which there are fewer obstacles to intervention by a Minister, R *v Hampshire CC, ex parte W*.[5] There, Sedley J indicated that the 'public law test' of reasonableness was intended to protect the local authority against interference by the Secretary of State on the ground of mere disagreement.[6] He also held that that test did

---

[1]   (1987) *The Times*, July 24. The relevant passage from the judgment is set out in R *v Secretary of State for Education, ex parte Skitt* [1995] ELR 388, at 396H–397E, and is commented on by Carnwath J in *South Glamorgan County Council v L and M* [1996] ELR 400, at 411G–413A.

[2]   Sedley J in R *v London Borough of Islington, ex parte Rixon* [1997] ELR 66, at 83C–D expressed the view that what is now s 496 'by applying a test of unreasonableness, gives the Secretary of State the equivalent of a judicial review function'. It is suggested here that that oversimplifies the matter, because the Secretary of State is not a court.

[3]   3rd edn, 1994, at p 435, in the course of discussing the *Tameside* case. This passage does not appear in the current (4th) edition of that book.

[4]   Sweet & Maxwell, London, 5th edn, 1995, at para 13.069.

[5]   [1994] ELR 460; (1994) *The Times*, June 9.

[6]   See [1994] ELR 460, at 469E.

not apply to s 9 of the EA 1981.[1] Rather, Sedley J decided that s 9 required only a 'straightforward factual test' to be applied by the authority when deciding whether or not the request was unreasonable.[2] However, whether this is a true example of a situation in which there are fewer obstacles in the way of intervention by a Minister is questionable, for the following reasons. The régime under s 9 of EA 1981 allowed an LEA to decide that a relevant request made by a parent was unreasonable. The only course of action for a dissatisfied parent to take was either an application for judicial review, as occurred in *ex parte W*, or a complaint to the Secretary of State under s 68 of the Education Act 1944, the predecessor to s 496(1).[3] In the event of a complaint under s 68, the Secretary of State would have had to decide whether the LEA had acted in a *Wednesbury* unreasonable manner (in the narrow sense) in deciding that the parent's request was unreasonable. The case does not therefore support the proposition in relation to which it is cited. In fact, in the circumstances, Sedley J's interpretation of the word 'unreasonable' as used in s 9 provided the authority with more, rather than less, protection (albeit from parents rather than the Minister) than if the 'public law test' of reasonableness had applied to that word.[4] (It should be borne in mind that the reasonableness test in s 9 applied to the request by the parent, and not to the decision of the local authority.)

3.22   However, it is clear that the application of the 'public law test' to the word 'unreasonably' in s 496 is indeed helpful to local education authorities, and it seems that the view expressed in *de Smith, Woolf and Jowell* that 'the Education Act 1944 has as an important purpose the placing of education policy primarily with the local authority, with the Minister having power to intervene only in extreme cases' is correct. It is noted that the view expressed in the same place that '[t]he matter ... depends upon the administrative scheme established by a particular statute' is in fact supported by a dictum of Lord Wilberforce in *Tameside*, which was that 'there is no universal rule as to the principles on which the exercise of a discretion may be reviewed: each statute or type of statute must be individually looked at'.[5] However, it is also noted that it seems that it was only in the *Tameside* case that the courts have actually determined that the word 'unreasonably' as contained in a statute should be interpreted in the narrow *Wednesbury* sense.[6]

3.23   There is a possibility that the word 'unreasonably' in s 496 could be interpreted differently according to the context in which it applies, since only local education authorities among those bodies to which s 496 applies are democratically elected.

---

[1]   Section 9 of the EA 1981 has now been repealed and replaced by a different regime; it placed an LEA under a duty to comply with a request from a parent for an assessment of his child's special educational needs unless the request of the parent was in the opinion of the authority 'unreasonable'.

[2]   [1994] ELR 460, at 470A.

[3]   The availability of this route would have justified a decision by the court in *ex parte W* to decline to hear the application for judicial review: see para **3.28**.

[4]   This was acknowledged by Sedley J in *ex parte W*, at 470A–F.

[5]   [1977] AC 1014, at 1047G.

[6]   Cf G Aldous and G Alder, *Applications for Judicial Review* (Butterworths, London, 2nd edn, 1993), where, at p 125, it is said in relation to the *Tameside* case that, 'It has been held, perhaps surprisingly, that unreasonableness in this context is the very low standard of *Wednesbury* unreasonableness, thus making the minister's power analogous to that of a reviewing court. In other cases the scope of the power to intervene does not depend upon any finding of wrongdoing (eg *R v Secretary of State for the Environment, ex parte Norwich City Council* [1982] QB 808).'

However, this is not a strong possibility given the likelihood of the circumstances that Parliament will have intended to use the word in the sense given it by the *Tameside* case.[1]

The procedure to be followed by the Secretary of State in relation to a complaint under section 496

3.24 In R *v Secretary of State for Education and Science, ex parte Chance,*[2] Woolf LJ decided that although the Secretary of State is under an obligation to:

> 'give a fair opportunity to a complainant to put before him all the information that he or she thinks is relevant for the purposes of investigating that matter ... the obligations that are upon him are not the same as those which would be incumbent upon him if he was adjudicating between two parties in a judicial or quasi-judicial capacity. When exercising his obligations under section 68 and section 99, the Secretary of State is quite clearly acting in a purely administrative capacity. He is under an obligation to find out the facts He has to make his judgment on those facts, but in order to do that he does not need to make available to someone such as Mrs Chance all the material which is put before him by the body against whom complaint is made.'[3]

3.25 This, however, must be read in the light of R *v Secretary of State, ex parte S,*[4] which indicates that a slightly different approach would now be taken in regard to the amount of material which the Secretary of State should put before a complainant before making his decision. According to that case, if a new point or new material is in issue, then the Secretary of State must put it to the complainant before making his final decision.[5]

Enforcement of a determination of the Secretary of State made under section 496

3.26 In *Tameside*, Lord Wilberforce said in relation to the predecessor to s 496(1):

> 'This section does not say what the consequences of the giving of directions are to be, but I accept, for the purposes of the appeal, that the consequences are to impose on the authority a statutory duty to comply with them which can be enforced by an order of mandamus.'[6]

---

1   See vol 44(1) of *Halsbury's Laws* (4th edn reissue, 1995), para 1416.
2   (1982) unreported, but see Liell et al, *The Law of Education*, at para F[77] and R *v Secretary of State for Education, ex parte Prior* [1994] ICR 877, at 891–893, where important parts of the judgment of Woolf LJ are set out.
3   See R *v Secretary of State for Education, ex parte Prior* [1994] ICR 877, at 892, where this passage from the judgment in *ex parte Chance* is set out.
4   [1995] ELR 71, CA.
5   See also R *v Secretary of State for Education, ex parte Skitt* [1995] ELR 388, and R *v Secretary of State for Education, ex parte E* [1996] ELR 312. But note R *v Secretary of State for Wales, ex parte Jones* [1997] ELR 100, 112–113.
6   [1977] AC 1014, at 1046G.

When section 496 ousts the jurisdiction of the court

3.27   It has been held that the jurisdiction of the court is ousted where a claimant has a potential remedy available under what is now s 496 (or s 497) in relation to an alleged breach of what are now ss 9 and 14 of the EA 1996, unless the action in respect of which complaint is made is *ultra vires*.[1] However, in *R v Inner London Education Authority, ex parte Ali*,[2] Woolf LJ said that he:

> 'would not accept that the language of the default powers contained in s 68 and s 99 of the Act indicate that Parliament intended the jurisdiction of the courts to be ousted from considering the issues which can be considered by the Secretary of State under those sections.'[3]

3.28   However, this was obiter, since *ex parte Ali* concerned a situation in which a complaint had been made to the Secretary of State under s 99. Indeed, although there was an extensive discussion of relevant case-law (most of which was in fact relevant to s 99 of the 1944 Act rather than s 68), no mention was made of *Cumings v Birkenhead Corporation*.[4] In addition, the question of the impact of a statutory complaints procedure on an application for judicial review is one of general application, and there are a number of cases in which that question has been addressed. In *R (Rhodes) v Kingston upon Hull City Council*,[5] Goldring J accepted an analysis to this effect but concluded that an applicant cannot 'effectively ignore the outcome of the application to the Secretary of State and seek judicial review against the body in respect of whose decision it was appealing to the Secretary of State'. He also said: 'The remedy, of course, would be to seek to review the decision of the Secretary of State'.

3.29   In any event, the approach in *Cumings* must be regarded as of less importance in the light of the *Tameside* case,[6] since as a result of *Tameside* it will now only be where a complainant alleges *Wednesbury* unreasonableness in the narrow sense that a complaint could be made to the Secretary of State under s 496. Accordingly, there will now on any view be more scope for applications for judicial reviews of the decisions of relevant bodies than may have appeared to be the case at the time when *Cumings* was decided.

Section 497 of the Education Act 1996

3.30   Section 497 contains the default power exercisable by the Secretary of State in the event of a failure by an LEA or the governing body of a community, foundation or voluntary school or of a community or foundation special school, to discharge any

---

[1]   *Cumings v Birkenhead Corporation* [1972] Ch 12, 36C–D. A parallel can be drawn with *Herring v Templeman* [1973] 3 All ER 569. There, the argument that a provision in a trust deed for a higher education institution that any question as to its construction or the validity of any act done or about to be done under it 'shall be determined conclusively by the Secretary of State for Education and Science' excluded the jurisdiction of the court in a private law action to enforce a student's rights, was rejected by the court at first instance and abandoned on appeal: see ibid, at 572a–d and 574c–e.

[2]   [1990] 2 Admin LR 822; (1990) *The Times*, February 20; [1990] COD 317.

[3]   [1990] 2 Admin LR 822, at 831B. This is the most direct statement to the effect that ss 496 and 497 do not oust the jurisdiction of the court. See also ibid, at 835G.

[4]   See footnote 1 above.

[5]   [2001] ELR 230, at para 47.

[6]   [1977] AC 1014; see para **3.16**.

duty imposed on it by or for the purposes of the EA 1996 and any Act which is to be read as one with that Act. Section 497 also applies to the governing body of any institution which is maintained by an LEA and provides higher education or further education (or both),[1] to a school organisation committee,[2] and to the proprietors of a city technology college, a city college for the technology of the arts or an Academy in relation to the duties regarding careers advice imposed by s 43(3) of the EA 1997,[3] also ss 44(1), (4) and (6),[4] and s 45(1).[5] Section 497 applies also to an LEA, a school organisation committee and the governing body of a maintained school in relation to the powers and duties imposed by Sch 7 to the LSA 2000 regarding inadequate sixth-forms.[6] A similar provision (which is wider, since it concerns a failure to discharge 'any duty imposed ... by or for the purposes of any Act') applies to: (1) the LSC or (as the case may be) the CETW;[7] and (2) the governing body of an institution within the further education sector.[8]

3.31   If the Secretary of State is 'satisfied' (and, as with s 496, there is no need for a complaint to have been made for him to be so) that the relevant body has failed to discharge the relevant duty, then he may make an order declaring the body to be in default in respect of the duty in question. He may also give such directions for the purpose of enforcing the performance of the duty as appear to him to be expedient. Any such directions are enforceable, on an application made on behalf of the Secretary of State, 'by an order of mandamus'.[9]

3.32   As with s 496 of the EA 1996, no complaint may be made to the Secretary of State under s 497 where a complaint could be made to the LEA under s 409 of, or para 6(3) of Sch 1 to, the EA 1996.[10]

Does section 497 oust the jurisdiction of the court?

3.33   The predecessor to s 497, s 99(1) of the EA 1944, gave rise to little reported case-law. As indicated above, however,[11] it has been said that if a remedy was available under what is now s 497 in relation to an alleged breach of what is now s 9 or s 14 of the EA 1996, then court action was precluded until that remedy had been sought unless the matter in respect of which complaint could be made was *ultra vires*.[12] However, the comments of Woolf LJ in *R v Inner London Education Authority, ex parte Ali*,[13] set out in para **3.27** indicate that this may no longer be so. Yet, in *R v Islington*

---

1   See s 219(1) and (3) of the ERA 1988, as substituted by para 77 of Sch 37 to the EA 1996.

2   SSFA 1998, Sch 4, para 10.

3   EA 1997, s 43(4).

4   Ibid, s 44(9).

5   Ibid, s 45(3).

6   See LSA 2000, s 113(3).

7   Ibid, ss 25(3)(a) and (4) and 47(3)(a) and (4).

8   FHEA 1992, s 57(2)(b), as substituted by LSA 2000, Sch 9, para 34. See para **16.90** concerning s 57.

9   EA 1996, s 497(3). This would now be called a mandatory order. The enforcement mechanism for an order made under s 57 of the FHEA 1992 is a little more involved, but such an order could equally be enforced by means of a mandatory order: see para **16.90**.

10   See EA 1996, s 409(4) and Sch 1, para 6(4) respectively.

11   See para **3.27**.

12   *Cumings v Birkenhead Corporation* [1972] Ch 12, 36C–D; *Watt v Kesteven County Council* [1955] 1 QB 408, at 425, 430.

13   [1990] 2 Admin LR 822; (1990) *The Times*, February 20; [1990] COD 317.

London Borough Council, ex parte Rixon,[1] Sedley J referred to s 41 of the EA 1944 (which was subsequently re-enacted as s 15 of the EA 1996 but which has now been repealed[2]) as containing only a 'target duty' (adopting that term from the judgment of Woolf LJ in *ex parte Ali*, where Woolf LJ applied it to what is now s 14 of the EA 1996) and then said that in the event of an alleged breach of s 41, the proper recourse was an appeal to the Secretary of State.[3] In contrast, in *Catchpole v Buckinghamshire County Council*,[4] Laws J, (obiter) said:

> 'There might nowadays well be arguments to the effect that ss 496 and 497 do not oust the judicial review court's jurisdiction, and it is to be noted that *Cumings* and *Watt* were writ actions decided before the reforms of Ord 53 in 1977 and the growth of judicial review since.'[5]

3.34   However, if a complaint is made to the Secretary of State and he decides not to intervene, then that will be a factor which could persuade the court not to intervene.[6]

3.35   There is, however, a complication in relation to s 497 as compared with s 496, in that s 497 is a default power. The availability of an alternative route for the obtaining of redress may cause the court to decline to hear an application for judicial review. It has been held that there is a further factor to bear in mind where there is a statutory complaints procedure which could lead to the use of a default power. That factor is whether or not what has occurred constitutes a failure to act, or a positive step. If there is a failure to act, it has been held, then the complainant should seek the use of the default power. If, on the other hand, what has occurred is a positive step, then it can be classified as an *ultra vires* act, and therefore the court can intervene. This approach was taken in *Wood v Ealing London Borough Council*,[7] and *Lee v Enfield London Borough Council*[8] (where the distinction was described as one between nonfeasances and misfeasances). In each case the High Court ruled that it had power to act despite the existence of s 99 of the EA 1944, where the matter in respect of which complaint was made consisted of a failure to take account of parents' wishes (which, if proved, amounted to a breach of the predecessor to s 9 of the EA 1996). This was on the basis that what had happened could in each case properly be regarded as an *ultra vires* act, as opposed to a mere failure to act. However, it could instead have been decided that in reality there was a failure to take account of a relevant factor – parents' wishes – and that therefore there was a nonfeasance or a failure to act, which should have been the subject of a complaint to the Secretary of State.[9] Similarly, in *Bradbury v*

---

1   [1997] ELR 66.

2   See now Chapter 16 concerning the duty to fund further education.

3   [1997] ELR 66, at 83C–E.

4   [1998] ELR 463, 471D–E.

5   In the Court of Appeal, at [1999] ELR 179, 185H, Sedley LJ said: 'A further line of argument, relating to justiciability, found no favour with Laws J and (wisely) has not been repeated before us'.

6   See *ex parte Ali*, above at 837D; *R v Secretary of State for Education and Employment and the Governors of Southlands Community Comprehensive School, ex parte W* [1998] ELR 413, at 422H–423A; and *R v London Borough of Brent, ex parte F* [1999] ELR 32, at 37.

7   [1967] 1 Ch 364, 386.

8   (1967) 66 LGR 195.

9   Cf Aldous and Alder, op cit (footnote 6 at p 72), at pp 126–127, where it is said that the distinction between malfeasance and nonfeasance 'sometimes seems to be merely semantic. For example, a school closure can be classified under either head'. See also the two sentences following that passage.

Enfield London Borough Council,[1] the Court of Appeal decided that the court could intervene despite the existence of s 99 of the EA 1944 if there had been a direct contravention of a specific duty contained in that Act. In that case a failure to comply with the notice procedure regarding ceasing to maintain schools[2] meant that the public notice to close certain schools and establish new ones was defective and hence *ultra vires*.[3] The court was therefore able to intervene. In contrast, however, the court decided that a failure to ensure that certain school premises were of the requisite standard (as prescribed by regulations) was a matter in regard to which a remedy could be sought only under s 99 of the EA 1944.[4] (In *Coney v Choice*,[5] Megarry J suggested that s 99 did not apply so far as relevant in *Bradbury*. This was because, he said, the duty in question arose from s 31(5) of the London Government Act 1963, and because s 99 of the EA 1944 did not apply to the London Government Act 1963.[6] This, however, was misleading, since s 13 of the EA 1944 imposed the relevant duty, and s 31(5) of the 1963 Act added nothing material to s 13.[7])

3.36   Perhaps the best view is that the principles of public law have developed so much since 1967 that the matter should be regarded afresh, and that the best approach to apply is that taken by the courts in other cases where there is an alternative route for the satisfactory remedying of a complaint. That approach is to decline to allow applications for permission to apply for judicial review where a complaint could most conveniently be made under the alternative procedure.[8] This was in fact the approach taken in *R v Northamptonshire County Council, ex parte Gray* (although there the court declined to allow the application for judicial review, since in the circumstances the most appropriate and constructive remedy was provided by what is now s 497).[9] It was also the approach taken by Woolf LJ in *R v Inner London Education Authority, ex parte Ali*,[10] where (after considering the impact of cases such as *Bradbury v Enfield London Borough Council*) he said:

> 'On an application for judicial review the existence of a default power certainly does not exclude the jurisdiction of the court and may not, even where (as here) the breach of duty can be described as nonfeasance, deprive the court of the ability to provide a remedy. The default power will, however, still be highly relevant as to whether or not the court should grant relief as a matter of discretion.'[11]

---

[1] [1967] 1 WLR 1311.

[2] As to which, in its current guise, see now paras **7.21** et seq.

[3] [1967] 1 WLR 1311, at 1323A–E, and 1332H–1333A.

[4] Ibid, at 1324B–D and 1334F–G.

[5] [1975] 1 WLR 422.

[6] See [1975] 1 WLR 422, at 435D–E.

[7] This is despite what Diplock LJ said in *Bradbury* at [1967] 1 WLR 1330A–1331B: see per Lord Denning (with whom Danckwerts LJ agreed) at 1323A–E and 1324B–F.

[8] This practice is very clearly described in *Re M (A Minor)* [1996] ELR 135, at 140. See also *de Smith, Woolf and Jowell* op cit, at paras 20.18–20.21.

[9] (1986) *The Times*, June 10.

[10] [1990] 2 Admin LR 822; (1990) *The Times*, February 20; [1990] COD 317.

[11] Ibid, at 835G–836A. At 835F, Woolf LJ said that a declaration clarifying the legal position where a relevant body was not acting because it was under a misapprehension as to the relevant law, could be of considerable value.

Woolf LJ also considered the impact of *Meade v Haringey London Borough Council*,[1] and concluded that although dicta of Lord Denning's in it could be regarded as supporting the conclusion that the existence of a default power does not exclude any other remedy, those dicta were not in line with those of the other two members of the Court of Appeal.[2]

The procedure to follow in relation to a complaint under section 497

3.37   As mentioned above, although in *R v Secretary of State for Education and Science, ex parte Chance*,[3] Woolf J indicated that the Secretary of State is not under a duty to put before the complainant all the information put before him by the body against which complaint has been made before making a decision on a complaint made under what is now s 497 of the EA 1996, that decision has to be read in the light of that in *R v Secretary of State for Education, ex parte S*.[4] The result is that the Secretary of State is under a duty to put before a complainant any new point or material put before him by the body about which complaint has been made.

Is there an obligation on the Secretary of State to make a declaration under section 497 where a relevant body is in default?

3.38   It was held in *Bradbury v Enfield London Borough Council*[5] that even if the Secretary of State lawfully decides that a relevant body is in default, he is not obliged to declare that it is in default. Indeed, according to Harris,[6] up to 1993 there had been only one case in which a failure to intervene under the predecessor to s 497 (or, indeed, the predecessor to s 496) had been successfully challenged, and that was *R v Secretary of State for Education and Science, ex parte Chance* (as to which see para **3.24**). Since then there has been at least one case where the court has ordered the Secretary of State to reconsider his decision, and that is *R v Secretary of State for Education, ex parte Prior*.[7] However, in any event, as suggested above, the matter may require to be reconsidered in the light of the changes in the approach of the courts to public law matters since 1967.[8] Yet one thing which is clear is that the Secretary of State would be under no duty to give a direction under s 497 if there would be no point in doing so.[9]

---

[1]   [1979] 1 WLR 637.

[2]   See [1990] 2 Admin LR 822, at 834F–835B. This aspect of the judgment in *Meade* may have been overlooked in *de Smith, Woolf and Jowell*, op cit, at para 20.18, n 34. The question whether to intervene in an application for judicial review where there is a default power which could be exercised is discussed helpfully in Aldous and Alder, op cit (footnote 6 at p 72), at pp 125–127.

[3]   See para **3.24**.

[4]   [1995] ELR 71. See also para **3.25**.

[5]   [1967] 1 WLR 1311, at 1324C–D, by Lord Denning, with whom Danckwerts LJ agreed.

[6]   NS Harris, *Law and Education: Regulation, Consumerism and the Education System* (Sweet & Maxwell, London, 1993), at p 36.

[7]   [1994] ICR 877.

[8]   See para **3.36**.

[9]   In *R v Secretary of State for Education, ex parte R and D* [1994] ELR 495, McCullough J declined to allow an application for leave to move for judicial review in part on the ground that a direction under s 68 or s 99 of the EA 1944 would be of no use to the complainants since they had already left the school about whose curriculum their parents had complained. See also *R v South Tyneside Education Department and the Governors of Hebburn Comprehensive School, ex parte Cram* [1998] ELR 508. There it was submitted

Must a direction be given where a declaration is made?

3.39   In R *v Secretary of State for Education and Science, ex parte Gray*,[1] Henry J held that there is no obligation on the Secretary of State to give a direction when he makes a declaration under s 497. He said:

> 'It seems to me that it is open to the Secretary of State to make a declaration *simpliciter*, though if he thinks it expedient, having made such a declaration, he can then give directions on top of it.'

3.40   A decision by the Secretary of State to decline to seek what would now be called a mandatory order under s 497, and instead to revoke (under s 570 of the EA 1996) a direction made under s 497, was unsuccessfully challenged in R *v Secretary of State for Education and Employment and the Governors of Southlands Community Comprehensive School, ex parte W*.[2] The direction made under s 497 was revoked in the light of a significant change in the circumstances. Although the court was not referred to *ex parte Gray*, the attention of the court was drawn to the approach taken in R *v Inner London Education Authority, ex parte Ali*[3] regarding the relevance of the stance adopted by the Secretary of State under s 497 in respect of a breach of duty. The applicant's sister was already a pupil at the respondent grant-maintained school. The governing body had refused to admit the applicant to the school because of her parent's past behaviour towards the staff of the school. The refusal was contrary to the school's articles of government and therefore unlawful. Among other things, the governing body feared industrial action by the teachers if the applicant was admitted. The fact that a refusal by the court to issue an order of mandamus, requiring the governing body to admit the pupil, would appear to condone the school's unlawful act, was not decisive.

Power to intervene in respect of perceived underperformance

3.41   Several new powers of intervention have been granted by Parliament to the Secretary of State in recent years. One is a new s 497A of the EA 1996. It applies in its original form to Wales only, since it has been amended by s 60 of the EA 2002, and since s 60 is in force only in relation to England.[4]

Power to intervene in Wales under sections 497A and 497B of the Education Act 1996

3.42   In its original form, s 497A concerns an LEA's functions (of whatever nature) which relate to the provision of education (a) for persons of compulsory school age

---

(see p 510D) that 'industrial might would become in the context legal right'. Ognall J's response is at pp 511–512. *R(L) v Governors of J School* [2003] UKHL 9, [2003] 2 AC 633 can be taken not to have affected the validity of Ognall J's approach in principle, although (see para **10.35**) the approach to be taken in relation to the question in issue (the legality of the governing body's approach where the teaching staff were refusing to teach a pupil whose reinstatement had been ordered by an independent appeal panel) is now determinable by reference to *Re L*, concerning which, see para **10.35**.

1   20 July 1988, unreported, but see Liell et al, *The Law of Education* (Butterworths), at para B[3987].
2   [1998] ELR 413; [1998] Ed CR 135.
3   [1990] 2 Admin LR 822; (1990) *The Times*, February 20; [1990] COD 317.
4   See SI 2002/2002.

(whether at school or otherwise), or (b) for persons of any age above or below that age who are registered as pupils at schools maintained by the LEA. It empowers the Secretary of State (and of course in this paragraph and the following paragraph this means the National Assembly for Wales), if he is 'satisfied (either on a complaint by any person interested or otherwise)' that the LEA are 'failing in any respect to perform any function to which this section applies to an adequate standard (or at all)', to exercise his powers under subs (3) or (4). These are to 'direct an officer of the authority to secure that that function is performed in such a way as to achieve such objectives as are specified in the direction'[1] or to 'give an officer of the authority such directions as the Secretary of State thinks expedient for the purpose of securing that the function: (a) is performed, on behalf of the authority and at their expense, by such person as is specified in the direction; and (b) is so performed in such a way as to achieve such objectives as are so specified'.[2] Any such directions 'may require that any contract or other arrangement made by the authority with that person contains such terms and conditions as may be so specified'.[3] The Secretary of State may also direct that the specified person is to perform other functions to which s 497A applies.[4] Any direction made under the section may have effect indefinitely (until its revocation by the Secretary of State), or until any objectives specified in the direction have been achieved (which is to be determined in the manner specified in the direction).[5] Any direction made under s 497A may be enforced, on an application made on behalf of the Secretary of State, by a mandatory order.[6]

3.43 Where an officer of an LEA is given a direction under s 497A(4), the person specified in those directions (and any person assisting him in the performance of the specified function of the EA 1996[7]) may exercise the powers conferred by s 497B of the EA 1996.[8] Those powers include a right at all reasonable times of entry to the premises of the LEA and to inspect, and take copies of, documents and records (in each case including information recorded in any form[9]) which he considers relevant to the performance of the specified function or functions.[10] They may also do the same thing in relation to any school maintained by the LEA.[11] The LEA and the governing body of any such school are under an obligation to give the specified person 'all assistance in connection with the performance of the specified function or functions which they are reasonably able to give',[12] and to 'secure that all such assistance is also given by persons who work at the school'.[13]

---

1   EA 1996, s 497A(3).
2   Ibid, s 497A(4).
3   Ibid, s 497A(4).
4   Ibid, s 497A(5).
5   Ibid, s 497A(6).
6   Ibid, s 497A(7).
7   Ibid, s 497B(6).
8   Ibid, s 497B(1).
9   Ibid, s 497B(7).
10 Ibid, s 497B(2). See s 497B(3) regarding computer records.
11 Ibid, s 497B(5).
12 Ibid, s 497B(4) and (5)(a).
13 Ibid, s 497B(5)(b).

Power to intervene in England under sections 497A, 497AA and 497B of the Education Act 1996

3.44   Section 60 of the EA 2002 amended s 497A by widening its scope, so that it applies now also to 'a local education authority's functions under this Act and to other functions (of whatever nature) which are conferred on [the LEA] in their capacity as a local education authority'.[1] The powers of intervention are also increased in that s 60(4) inserts a new s 497A(2A) empowering the exercise by the Secretary of State of his powers of intervention under s 497A also where he has given a previous direction under the section and:

> 'he is satisfied that it is likely that if no further direction were given under [the section] on the expiry or revocation of the previous direction the authority would fail in any respect to perform that function to an adequate standard (or at all).'

3.45   Section 60 also simplifies the existing powers, by repealing s 497A(3) and replacing it and the existing s 497A(4) by new subsections 497A(4), 497A(4A) and 497A(4B). Under the new provisions, the Secretary of State can direct that a relevant function is to be carried out by 'the Secretary of State or a person nominated by him'. A new s 497A(5) is substituted, the changes in which are consequential. Finally, s 497A(6) is amended so that a direction can now be made for a fixed period (subject to revocation before the end of that period) instead of until objectives specified in the direction have been achieved.

3.46   Section 61 of the EA 2002 has also been brought into force in England only. It inserts a new s 497AA into the EA 1996, which obliges an LEA to give the Secretary of State and any person authorised by him for the purposes of s 497AA 'all such assistance, in connection with the proposed exercise of the function by the Secretary of State or another person in pursuance of directions, as they are reasonably able to give'.

3.47   Section 497B is amended (currently in relation to England only) by s 62 of the EA 2002, in ways which are purely consequential on the amendments made by s 60 to s 497A.

Power to intervene in England under sections 63 and 64 of the Education Act 2002

3.48   Under s 63 of the EA 2002 (which is in force in relation to England only), the Secretary of State may direct an LEA to obtain advisory services (whether under a contract or 'some other arrangement') to be given to either or both of the LEA and any of the schools maintained by the LEA. The power arises only where one or more of the schools which are maintained by the LEA has been the subject of an inspection carried out under Part 1 of the SIA 1996 and the Chief Inspector has given the Secretary of State a notice under s 16A(2) of that Act[2] stating that the inspector is of the view that the school has serious weaknesses or that special measures are required

---

[1]   EA 1996, s 497A(1), as substituted by EA 2002, s 60(2).

[2]   Section 16A was inserted into the SIA 1996 by s 55 of the EA 2002.

to be taken in relation to the school. Further, the power cannot be exercised unless it appears to the Secretary of State that the LEA:

'(i)   have not been effective or are unlikely to be effective in eliminating deficiencies in the conduct of that school or those schools,

(ii)   are unlikely to be effective in eliminating deficiencies in the conduct of other schools which may in the future [satisfy the condition set out in the preceding sentence above], or

(iii) maintain a disproportionate number of schools [satisfying that condition]'.[1]

A direction given under s 63 is enforceable by means of a mandatory order on the application of the Secretary of State.[2]

3.49   Before giving such a direction, the Secretary of State may notify the LEA that he is contemplating doing so. If he does, then the LEA come under a duty to give such assistance as they are reasonably able to give in connection with the proposed contract or other arrangement.[3] Where a direction has been given under s 63, the relevant person[4] is then entitled for example to enter the LEA's premises for the purpose of providing the advisory services.[5]

POWER TO REQUIRE MEDICAL EXAMINATION OF PUPILS

3.50   The Secretary of State has power under s 506 of the EA 1996 to require the parent of a pupil to present the pupil for examination by a registered medical practitioner. This power may be exercised only where a question is referred to the Secretary of State under s 442(3) (concerning a refusal by an LEA to comply with a parent's request to revoke a school attendance order on the ground that the child in question is receiving suitable education otherwise than at school[6]) or s 495 of the EA 1996,[7] and in the opinion of the Secretary of State the examination would assist in determining the question.[8] A failure by a parent without reasonable excuse to comply with such a requirement is an offence, punishable by a fine to a maximum of level 1 on the standard scale.[9]

DUTY TO PROVIDE CERTAIN SERVICES TO SCHOOLS IN OTHER MEMBER STATES

3.51   Under s 226(2) of the ERA 1988, the Secretary of State is under a duty:

---

[1]   EA 2002, s 63(1)(b).
[2]   Ibid, s 63(5).
[3]   Ibid, s 64(1).
[4]   Defined by s 64(7) to include any person assisting the person who is providing the advisory services.
[5]   See EA 2002, s 64(2)–(6).
[6]   See para **5.28**.
[7]   Regarding which, see paras **3.3** et seq.
[8]   EA 1996, s 506(1).
[9]   Ibid, s 506(2) and (3). Currently, level 1 is £200.

'(a)   on a regular basis [to] provide the persons responsible for the management of [a school to which section 226 applies[1]] with such information relating to educational developments in England and Wales as he thinks appropriate; and

(b)   if those persons so request, make arrangements for inspections to be made of the school by, or under the direction of, one or more of Her Majesty's Inspectors of Schools for England.'[2]

3.52   The schools to which s 226 applies are those situated in member states of the European Community other than the United Kingdom, which provide education for pupils who (a) are British citizens, (b) have attained the age of 5 years but not the age of 19 and (c) are residing in that member state.[3] The schools must also have a curriculum which in the case of any pupil at the school is broadly similar to that which he would follow if he were a pupil at a community, foundation or voluntary school in England and Wales and has 'such other characteristics as may be prescribed'.[4]

INQUIRIES

3.53   The Secretary of State has power under s 507 of the EA 1996 to 'cause a local inquiry to be held for the purpose of the exercise of any of his functions under this Act'. The power extends to any function under any other enactment which is to be read as one with the EA 1996.[5] It also extends to the Secretary of State's functions under s 57 of the FHEA 1992.[6] It appears to be a little-used power.[7]

3.54   The provisions of s 250 of the Local Government Act 1972 apply with regard to the giving of evidence and the payment of the costs of an inquiry under s 507.[8] One result of this is that either the LEA in whose area the inquiry is held or a party to the inquiry may be ordered by the relevant Minister to pay the costs of the inquiry.

PUBLICATION OF GUIDANCE

3.55   Section 571 of the EA 1996 provides that when the Secretary of State gives guidance for the purposes of any provision of the EA 1996 (which will include any other enactment with which the EA 1996 is to be read as one[9]), he may do so in such manner as he thinks fit.

---

[1]   Regarding which, see para **3.52**.

[2]   If such an inspection is made, then the Secretary of State must charge 'such fees as will cover the full cost of the inspection': s 226(3).

[3]   ERA 1988, s 226(1).

[4]   Ibid, s 226(1) and (4). No such characteristics have been prescribed.

[5]   See *Canada Southern Railway Co v International Bridge Company* (1883) 8 App Cas 723, at 727 regarding the effect of a statute being stated to be read as one with another statute.

[6]   FHEA 1992, s 57(9). See para **16.90** regarding s 57.

[7]   According to P Meredith, *Individual Challenge to Expenditure Cuts in the Provision of Schools* (1982) JSWL 344, the power in s 93 of the EA 1944, which was the predecessor to s 507, had been used only once before the time of the writing of that article. The inquiry apparently concerned the establishment of a Roman Catholic primary school in Haverfordwest.

[8]   EA 1996, s 507(2).

[9]   See footnote 5 above concerning the reading of Acts as one.

GRANTS

3.56   As mentioned in Chapter 2,[1] certain grants are payable by the Secretary of State to LEAs. The powers mentioned in Chapter 2 extend also to the giving by the Secretary of State of financial assistance to persons other than LEAs (in the case of s 14 of the EA 2002, to 'any person'). The Secretary of State's other grant-making powers are as follows.[2]

Teacher training bursaries

3.57   The Secretary of State is authorised by regulations made under s 50(1)(a) of the EA 1986[3] to make grants to persons other than LEAs to facilitate and encourage the training of teachers. The current regulations include the Teacher Training Incentive (Wales) Regulations 2000,[4] the Teaching Training Incentive (Further Education) (Wales) Regulations 2001,[5] the Education (Teacher Training Hardship Grants) (England) (No 2) Regulations 2001,[6] the Education (Fast Track Bursaries and Grants) (England) Regulations 2001,[7] and the Education (Teacher Training Bursaries) (England) Regulations 2002.[8]

Grant-making powers in regulations

3.58   Grants may be made by the Secretary of State under regulations made under s 485 of the EA 1996 to 'persons other than local education authorities'. The grants must be in respect of expenditure incurred or to be incurred by such persons for the purposes of, or in connection with, the provision or proposed provision of educational services, or for the purposes of educational research. A notable example of regulations made (partly) under the predecessor to s 485, s 100 of the EA 1944, is the Education (Grant) Regulations 1990.[9] Under those regulations, the Secretary of State may make grants in respect of the following: education in special schools,[10] education in non-maintained, non-profit-making further or higher education institutions which are neither in the higher education sector nor further education corporations,[11] approved courses of adult education provided by national associations whose principal object (or one of whose principal objects) is the provision of adult education,[12] other educational services provided by such associations,[13] vocational, social, physical and recreational training provided otherwise than in educational

---

[1]   Paragraphs **2.98**, **2.102** and **2.104**.
[2]   The power of the Secretary of State to make grants to the governing bodies of voluntary aided schools under paras 5 and 6 of Sch 3 to the SSFA 1998 is referred to in paras **7.126** et seq.
[3]   EA 1986, s 50(1)(b) was repealed by EA 2002, s 18(1)(c).
[4]   SI 2000/2560.
[5]   SI 2001/2536.
[6]   SI 2001/2621.
[7]   SI 2001/3071, as amended by SI 2003/2039.
[8]   SI 2002/508, amended by SI 2003/3094. The Education (Bursaries for School Teacher Training) (England) Regulations 2002, SI 2002/509, were revoked, with savings, by SI 2002/3005.
[9]   SI 1990/1989.
[10]   Regulation 6.
[11]   Regulation 7.
[12]   Regulation 10.
[13]   Regulation 11.

institutions and otherwise than for profit,[1] the training of youth leaders and community centre wardens,[2] certain educational services and research,[3] and the training of teachers and others abroad.[4] The regulations also empower the making of payments to certain learned societies whose object (or main object) is, in the opinion of the Secretary of State the promotion of learning or research,[5] and to the Engineering Council in respect of the payment of bursaries for students attending courses leading to a degree in engineering.[6] Conditions may be specified by the Secretary of State when making a grant under the 1990 regulations,[7] and certain requirements must be observed by the recipients of those payments.[8]

3.59   The following regulations should also be borne in mind: the Grants for Welsh Language Education Regulations 1980,[9] the Education (Grants) (City Technology Colleges) Regulations 1987,[10] the Education (Grants) (Voluntary Aided Sixth Form Colleges) Regulations 1992,[11] the Education (Grants) (Higher Education Corporations) Regulations 1992,[12] the Education (Grants) (Travellers and Displaced Persons) Regulations 1993,[13] the Education (Grants) (Music, Ballet and Choir Schools) Regulations 1995,[14] the Education (Grants for Early Excellence Centres) (England) Regulations 1998,[15] the Education (Post-16 Partnership Grant) (England) Regulations 1999,[16] the Education (Grants) (Music, Ballet and Choir Schools) (England) Regulations 2001,[17] the Education (Grants etc) (Dance and Drama) (England) Regulations 2001,[18] the Education (Grant) (Financial Support for Students) Regulations 2001,[19] and the Education (Standards Fund) (England) Regulations 2002.[20]

Partnership grants

3.60   One set of regulations made under s 485 of the EA 1996 which merits more consideration here is the Education (Partnership Grant) Regulations 1998.[21] Those regulations empower the making of grants (defined as 'partnership grants'[22]) to any

---

[1]   Regulation 12.
[2]   Regulation 13.
[3]   Regulation 15.
[4]   Regulation 16.
[5]   Regulation 14.
[6]   Regulation 16A.
[7]   Regulation 17.
[8]   Regulation 18.
[9]   SI 1980/1011.
[10]   SI 1987/1138.
[11]   SI 1992/2181.
[12]   SI 1992/3237.
[13]   SI 1993/569, as amended, most recently by SI 1999/606 so that they apply only to Wales after 31 March 1999.
[14]   SI 1995/2018 (as amended, including that they now apply only to Wales).
[15]   SI 1998/1877.
[16]   SI 1999/605.
[17]   SI 2001/2743.
[18]   SI 2001/2859.
[19]   SI 2001/2894.
[20]   SI 2002/510.
[21]   SI 1998/1222.
[22]   See regs 2 and 3(2).

person (other than the governing bodies of maintained schools) (defined as 'project organisers'[1]) in respect of 'partnership projects'.[2] The regulations also empower the making of grants (defined as 'research grants'[3]) in respect of research into partnership projects.[4] A partnership project is defined by regulation 3(1) as:

> 'a scheme in which a group of schools, which must include at least one independent and one maintained school, agree to co-operate with each other and, where the schools in the group so agree, with other persons (who may include a LEA) for the purpose of taking measures designed –
> (a) to widen the educational opportunities of pupils attending one or more of the schools in that group, and
> (b) to contribute towards the raising of standards of education provided for such pupils.'

3.61   Partnership grants are payable only in respect of expenditure which is approved by the Secretary of State under reg 3(2). Research grants are payable only in respect of expenditure which is approved by the Secretary of State under reg 5(2). A grant of either sort 'may be of an amount constituting reimbursement of the approved expenditure to which it relates, or of a lesser sum determined by the Secretary of State'.[5] However, if the project organiser is an LEA, then a partnership grant is payable at the rate of 100 per cent of approved expenditure.[6] Conditions may be attached to grants of both kinds, under reg 9.[7]

Grants in respect of provision for ethnic minorities

3.62   Section 490 of the EA 1996 extended the power of the Secretary of State contained in s 11 of the Local Government Act 1966 (as substituted)[8] to make payments to local authorities in consequence of the presence within their areas of persons belonging to ethnic minorities whose language or customs differ from those of the rest of the community. That power was so extended in order to allow the Secretary of State to make payments to persons who, in pursuance of undertakings under agreements under s 482 of the EA 1996, maintain and carry on, or provide for the carrying on of, a city technology college, a city college for the technology of the arts, or a city academy. Such payments were enabled if, in the Secretary of State's opinion, special provision was made by the person in question in consequence of the presence within the locality of the institution in question of such persons as are referred to in s 11 of the 1966 Act. Section 490 was repealed in relation to England only by s 18(1)(g) of the EA 2002, and replaced by the rather more general powers in s 14 of that Act.

---

[1]   See reg 2.
[2]   Regulation 3(2).
[3]   See reg 2.
[4]   Regulation 5.
[5]   Regulation 6(1).
[6]   Regulation 6(2).
[7]   See regs 8 and 9.
[8]   See para **2.100**.

Individual learning accounts

3.63   The Secretary of State's power to make regulations under ss 104[1] and 105 of the LSA 2000 concerning grants, known as individual learning accounts, made under s 108 of that Act, needs to be mentioned here. The current regulations are the Individual Learning Accounts (England) Regulations 2000[2] and the Individual Learning Account Wales Regulations 2003.[3]

EDUCATION (FEES AND AWARDS) ACT 1983

3.64   Under the Education (Fees and Awards) Act 1983,[4] the Secretary of State is empowered to make regulations requiring or authorising the charging by educational institutions[5] of certain sorts of fees which are higher in the case of students not having such a connection as may be specified in the regulations with the United Kingdom than in the case of students who have such a connection.[6] He is also empowered to make regulations authorising the adoption of rules of eligibility for discretionary awards which confine the awards to persons having such a connection with the United Kingdom or part of it as may be specified in the regulations.[7] The current regulations are the Education (Fees and Awards) Regulations 1997.[8]

STUDENT LOANS

3.65   Under s 22 of the THEA 1998, regulations must make provision authorising or requiring the Secretary of State (and not the National Assembly for Wales) to make grants or loans, 'for any prescribed purposes', to eligible students in connection with their attending (a) higher education courses, or (b) further education courses which (in both cases) are designated for the purposes of s 22 by or under the regulations. The main current regulations are the Education (Student Support) (No 2) Regulations 2002.[9] Their salient features include that they make provision for grants as well as loans, but that eligibility for grants for living costs is explicitly not extended to European Community students.[10] The regulations have echoes of former regulations concerned with the same subject-matter, including those under which mandatory

---

[1]   Only the Secretary of State may make regulations under s 104: see LSA 2000, s 150(1) and (4).

[2]   SI 2000/2146. It is of note that the scope and manner of exercise of the Secretary of State's power, under reg 7, to determine the size of the grant made was in issue in R *(Amraf Training plc) v Secretary of State* [2001] EWCA Civ 914, *The Times*, June 28 (reported at first instance only in the ELR, at [2001] ELR 125).

[3]   SI 2003/918.

[4]   The Act was enacted in response to the decision in R v *Barnet London Borough Council, ex parte Shah* [1983] 2 AC 309. It has subsequently been amended, but merely to take account of the introduction of new funding regimes under subsequent enactments, most recently the LSA 2000.

[5]   The relevant institutions are referred to in s 1 of the Act, and are funded mainly by public bodies.

[6]   See s 1.

[7]   Ibid, s 2.

[8]   SI 1997/1972, as amended by SI 1998/1965, SI 1999/229, SI 2000/2192 and SI 2000/2945.

[9]   SI 2002/3200, as amended, including by SI 2003/1065, SI 2003/3280, SI 2004/161, SI 2004/1602 and SI 2004/2041.

[10]   See reg 12(1), read with Sch 1.

awards used to be made.[1] It is of note, however, that ordinary residence falls to be determined only in accordance with the terms of the regulations, since (unlike in relation to the mandatory awards regulations) it is irrelevant in which LEA's area a student lives.[2] In addition, the Education (Grants for Disabled Postgraduate Students) Regulations 2000[3] should be noted.

3.66   The interest rates payable by ex-students for loans made under regulations made under s 22 may be: '(i) no higher than those which the Secretary of State is satisfied are required to maintain the value in real terms of the outstanding amounts of such loans, and (ii) shall at no time exceed the specified rate for low interest loans'.[4] Further, among other things regulations made under s 22 may impose on 'employers, any government department, or (as the case may be) such other persons or bodies as may be prescribed', requirements with respect to (i) the making of deductions of amounts due from borrowers under loans made under s 22 from emoluments payable to borrowers, (ii) 'the collection by other means of such amounts' and (iii) the transmission of such amounts to the Secretary of State.[5] The current regulations made under the powers referred to in the preceding sentence are the Education (Student Loans) (Repayment) Regulations 2000.[6] Under s 22(3) of the THEA 1998 (as inserted by s 42 of the HEA 2004), regulations may be made with respect to the effect of bankruptcy on a borrower's liability to make repayments in respect of a loan made pursuant to s 22.

3.67   Under s 23(1) of the THEA 1998, the Secretary of State may transfer any of his functions under regulations made under s 22, either to an LEA or to the governing body of an institution at which eligible students (within the meaning of the regulations) are attending courses. The body to which any such function is delegated is obliged by s 23(2) to comply with any directions given by the Secretary of State as to the exercise of the function. Under s 23(4), the Secretary of State may delegate any function of his under regulations made under s 22, but if he does so then he is nevertheless able to continue to exercise the function himself.[7] The supply of information which is held by the Commissioners of Inland Revenue or by a person providing services to those Commissioners and in connection with the provision of those services, is authorised by s 24(2), but only for the purpose of enabling or assisting the recipient of the information to exercise any function in connection with the operation of the regulations made under s 22 and governing the student loans scheme.[8]

---

[1]   Currently, such awards are still the subject of regulations, the most recent of which are the Education (Mandatory Awards) Regulations 2003, SI 2003/1994, as amended by SI 2004/1038 and SI 2004/1792.

[2]   The ordinary residence requirement is in para 8(a) and (b) of Sch 1 to the regulations. In relation to whether a student's residence has been 'wholly or mainly for the purpose of receiving full-time education', within the meaning of para 8(c) of Sch 1, see *R (Haracoglou) v Department for Education and Skills* [2001] EWHC Admin 678, [2002] ELR 177.

[3]   SI 2000/2330, amended by SI 2000/3087, SI 2001/2300, SI 2002/2104, SI 2003/1588, SI 2003/3280 and SI 2004/1658.

[4]   THEA 1998, s 22(4). The specified rate for low interest loans is defined in s 22(9).

[5]   Ibid, s 22(5).

[6]   SI 2000/944, as amended by SI 2001/971 and SI 2002/2087.

[7]   THEA 1998, s 23(5).

[8]   Ibid, s 24(2) and (6). See also s 24(3).

ACADEMIES

3.68   The Secretary of State (but not the National Assembly for Wales[1]) has power under s 482 of the EA 1996 to enter into agreements with persons under which those persons undertake to establish and maintain, and to carry on or provide for the carrying on of, what are now known (under s 482 as inserted by s 65 of the EA 2002) as Academies. The section as originally enacted (its first form was as s 105 of the ERA 1988) called the institutions established under it 'city technology colleges' and 'city colleges for the technology of the arts'. Section 105 was consolidated as s 482 of the EA 1996, and the latter was amended by s 130 of the LSA 2000 in relation to England to empower the establishment of a third kind of institution, a city academy. Sections 67 and 68 of the EA 2002 relate to these earlier institutions. Section 67 provides that a city academy is now to be known as an Academy and to be treated as having been established under the substituted s 482 as an Academy. Section 68, however, provides that if (1) the proprietor of a city technology college or a city college for the technology of the arts, and (2) the Secretary of State agree that the college should now be regarded as an Academy established under s 482 as substituted by s 65 of the EA 2002, then the college is to be so known and regarded as so established.

3.69   All of these institutions (whether a 'college' or an 'academy') are in reality schools, as is made clear by s 482(1)(a), which refers to them as 'independent school[s]'. Further, in reality they are state schools, since despite being called 'independent' schools, they are funded by the state and are subject to public law principles and hence the possibility of judicial review.[2] However, since their funding and organisation do not fit into the framework for the rest of the state school system, they are considered here, rather than in Chapter 7.

3.70   The 'independent' schools to which the agreements under s 482 relate must: (a) have 'a curriculum satisfying the requirements of s 78 of the Education Act 2002, but with an emphasis on a particular subject area, or particular subject areas, specified in the agreement'; and (b) provide 'education for pupils of different abilities who are wholly or mainly drawn from the area in which the school is situated'.[3]

3.71   No charge may be made for admission to an Academy, or, subject to whatever the agreement in relation to an Academy may provide, for education provided at the Academy.[4] The agreements entered into under s 482 may not be for a period of less

---

1   This is the effect of the words 'an independent school in England' in s 482(1)(a) as substituted by s 65 of the EA 2002.

2   See *R v Governors of Haberdashers' Aske's Hatcham College Trust, ex parte T* [1995] ELR 350, where Dyson J held that a city technology college was subject to judicial review in respect of its admission arrangements. The application failed on its facts, which is apparent only from the reports in (1994) *The Independent*, October 12 (under the name of *R v Governors of Haberdashers' Aske's Hatcham College Trust, ex parte Tyrell*) and (1994) *The Times*, October 19. The challenge was that the governors had applied admission criteria which were different from those which they had published: see [1995] ELR 350, at 357B–D.

3   EA 1996, s 482(2) as substituted.

4   Ibid, s 482(4).

than 7 years.[1] The effect of the provisions of s 483 of the EA 1996 is in general that the Secretary of State may take on the full financial burden of the risk of failure of the Academy, subject to the possibility of the repayment to the Secretary of State of sums relating to capital expenditure.[2]

3.72 The proprietors of city technology colleges, city colleges for the technology of the arts and Academies must comply with the duty imposed on the governing body of any maintained community, foundation or voluntary school or any community or foundation special school which is not established in a hospital, to distribute information provided to them by the governing bodies of institutions in the further education sector.[3] In addition, ss 43–45 of the EA 1997 (which concern careers guidance) apply to the proprietors and head teacher of: (a) a city technology college; (b) a city college for the technology of the arts; or (c) an Academy, in the same way that they apply to the head teacher and the governing body of a maintained school.[4]

3.73 The governing body of a city technology college, a city college for the technology of the arts, and an Academy must comply with s 110 of the SSFA 1998 and therefore must adopt a home–school agreement under that section, together with a parental declaration to be used in connection with the agreement.[5]

SUPPORT FOR 13–19-YEAR-OLDS IN ENGLAND; SUPPORT FOR 11–25-YEAR-OLDS IN WALES

England

3.74 Section 114(1) of the LSA 2000 empowers the Secretary of State to 'provide or secure the provision of services which he thinks will encourage, enable or assist (directly or indirectly) effective participation by young persons in education or training'. In doing so, the Secretary of State may make arrangements with LEAs for the provision of services, or direct them to (1) provide services, (2) secure the provision of services, or (3) participate in the provision of services.[6] He may also make arrangements with other persons for the provision of such services.[7] Such arrangements and directions may include provision for grants, loans and other kinds of financial assistance by the Secretary of State,[8] who may give guidance to which the

---

[1] EA 1996, s 483(2). The agreements may be for an indefinite period, and if they are then they must not be capable of being terminated on less than 7 years' written notice: ibid.

[2] See ibid, s 483(3), which sets out the factors to be taken into account in determining the amount of any repayment. In relation to England, s 483(3) may be applied to an Academy with such modifications as the Secretary of State may by order specify: s 483(3A).

[3] See para **7.184**. The obligation is imposed by s 541 and the Further Education Institutions Information (Wales) Regulations 1994, SI 1994/1321. (The Further Education Institutions Information) (England) Regulations 1995, SI 1995/2065 were revoked by SI 2003/51.)

[4] See paras **11.25–11.30** regarding ss 43–45.

[5] See paras **7.177–7.179** concerning home–school agreements and parental declarations.

[6] LSA 2000, s 114(2).

[7] Ibid, s 114(2)(a).

[8] Ibid, s 114(3)(a).

persons with whom arrangements are made or to whom directions are given must have regard.[1]

3.75   Before exercising the power in s 114(1), the Secretary of State must consult as required by s 115 of the LSA 2000. The bodies referred to in s 115(1) (which are a Health Authority, a Primary Care Trust, a local authority, a chief officer of police, a youth offending team and a probation committee) must 'exercise their functions so as to support and assist the services provided, secured or proposed by the Secretary of State'.[2] They must also 'coordinate the exercise of their functions, so far as seems reasonable, with persons providing those services'.[3]

3.76   LEAs are empowered by s 116(1)(a) to enter into arrangments of the sort referred to in s 114, and are required by s 116(1)(b) to comply with any relevant direction given under s 114. They are, in addition, empowered by s 116(1)(c) to make provision of the sort referred to in s 114(1) otherwise than as so empowered or directed. In all three connections, LEAs may among other things form companies and employ officers.[4] They are enabled by s 116(2) to act under s 116(1) in relation to persons from areas other than their own. None of these powers is to be taken in any way as restricting LEAs' other powers to provide services or incur expenditure.[5]

3.77   All maintained schools (other than special schools established in hospitals), city technology colleges, city colleges for the technology of the arts, Academies, pupil referral units, institutions within the further education sector, and institutions in receipt of funding from the LSC, must provide any person providing services pursuant to s 114(1) with information about pupils and students at the institutions, unless the pupil, or if he is below the age of 16, his parent, has instructed the institution not to provide the information.[6] Those schools and other institutions must also permit access to a pupil or student on the school or institution's premises at any reasonable time,[7] and must make available, 'so far as is reasonably convenient', facilities on the premises for providing the relevant services.[8]

3.78   The provision and receipt of information about young persons by relevant public bodies is empowered by s 120, which empowers the provision of information to the Secretary of State, but not by him. He, however, is empowered by s 119 to supply information to any person for the purpose of the provision of services of the sort referred to in s 114(1), including 'social security information'. Such a person may not disclose such information except in certain circumstances, which include that the

---

[1]   LSA 2000, s 114(3)(b).
[2]   Ibid, s 115(4)(a).
[3]   Ibid, s 115(4)(b).
[4]   Ibid, s 116(3).
[5]   Ibid, s 116(4).
[6]   Ibid, s 117. Certain of the definitions of these institutions are set out in s 121 of that Act. An institution in the further education sector is not so defined, and accordingly should (although there is no specific provision requiring this) be taken to be defined by s 91(3) of the FHEA 1992; that is, it is an institution conducted by a further education corporation or an institution designated under s 28(4) of the FHEA 1992. It is odd that all of these institutins themselves, rather than their governing bodies, are under the relevant obligations.
[7]   Ibid, s 117(1)(d).
[8]   Ibid, s 117(1)(e).

disclosure is made for the purpose of the provision of services under s 114(1), and a disclosure made otherwise than in those circumstances is an offence.[1] However, it is a defence to a prosecution for the offence to show that the accused 'reasonably believed that his dislosure was lawful'.[2] The maximum penalty for the offence is a term of imprisonment for 2 years and a fine.[3]

3.79   The Chief Inspector of Schools in England must advise the Secretary of State on request about 'matters relating to services provided in pursuance of section 114(1)',[4] and must, when requested to do so by the Secretary of State, inspect and report on the provision of those services.[5] The latter request 'may be general or in relation to specific matters', and may relate not only to a specific class of person or institution providing services, but also to a specific such person or institution.[6]

Wales

3.80   Section 123(1) of the LSA 2000 confers on the National Assembly for Wales similar powers to those conferred by s 114 on the Secretary of State, and the subsequent sections of that Act are also similar to the sections following s 114. However, there are some material differences. For example, the powers in Wales extend to persons aged 11–25 rather than 13–19. The wording of the relevant powers and duties is also different in several material respects. Nevertheless, the substance of the functions is largely the same, albeit that they are worded differently.

EDUCATIONAL TRUSTS

3.81   Until the Education Act 1973, under s 2 of the Charities Act 1960 the Secretary of State had concurrent jurisdiction with the Charity Commissioners regarding charitable trusts and had power to make educational endowment schemes under the Endowed Schools Acts 1869–1948. However, s 1(1) of the 1973 Act repealed those provisions. Similarly, the Secretary of State's approval for the appointment of new trustees of an educational charity regulated by a scheme made before the Education Act 1918 was enacted, ceased to be required as a result of the amendments made by the 1973 Act to s 47 of the 1918 Act.[7] The Secretary of State's

---

[1]   LSA 2000, s 119(4).

[2]   Ibid, s 119(5).

[3]   Ibid, s 119(6).

[4]   Ibid, s 118(1).

[5]   Ibid, s 118(2). Such provision includes the management and use of resources in providing services: s 118(3). See s 118(5)–(7) for the rights of the inspector and the obligation, which is enforceable by criminal proceedings, the maximum penalty being a fine at level 4 on the standard scale (currently £2,500), not wilfully to obstruct a person carrying out or participating in the inspection.

[6]   Ibid, s 118(2).

[7]   It is noted here that although the Technical and Industrial Institutions Act 1892 is still in force, s 9 of that Act (under which land held for the purposes of an institution within the meaning of s 2 of that Act cannot be sold or exchanged unless the Charity Commissioners give their consent) may have been impliedly repealed by s 36 of the Charities Act 1993. In any event, it is unlikely that the 1892 Act continues to have much application.

main powers in relation to educational (and hence charitable) trusts are now to be found in ss 553–556 of the EA 1996.[1]

Schemes under the Endowed Schools Acts 1869–1948

3.82　Section 553(1) of the EA 1996[2] waives the requirement for the trustees of any charity under a scheme made under the Endowed Schools Acts 1869–1948 to obtain the approval or order of any other person for the application of property for the purposes of the scheme. Section 553(2), however, provides that the Secretary of State may, on the application of such other person, direct that the requirement is to continue to have effect.[3]

Religious educational trusts

3.83　Section 554 of the EA 1996[4] empowers the Secretary of State to make new provision in certain circumstances as to the use of any endowment[5] of a voluntary, foundation or (where the school was on its closure a grant-maintained school) grant-maintained school where the premises of the school have ceased to be used for the purposes of the school or where it is in the opinion of the Secretary of State likely that they will cease to be so used. The circumstances are of two sorts. The first set of circumstances is relatively simple and is that the Secretary of State is satisfied that the endowment either is or has been held wholly or partly for or in connection with the provision at the school of religious education in accordance with the tenets of a particular religion or religious denomination. The second set of circumstances is that the endowment either is or has been used wholly or partly for or in connection with the provision at the school of such religious education, and the school was or has been maintained since 1 April 1945 (the date when the EA 1944 came into force) as a voluntary, grant-maintained school or foundation school. Further, the religious education in question must have been provided at the school from 1 April 1945, or, where the premises have ceased to be used for the purposes of the school, must have been provided (pursuant to s 377 or s 378, or s 380 or s 381 of the EA 1996 or the predecessors to those provisions) at the school since that date to the date when the premises ceased to be so used.[6] Finally, s 554(6) applies the other provisions of s 554 to premises which before 1 April 1945 ceased to be used for a non-provided public elementary school, the predecessor to what is now called a voluntary school.

---

[1]　See also: (1) s 489(3) and (4) of the EA 1996 regarding grants made under regulations made under s 485 of that Act; and (2) s 82 of the SSFA 1998. See para **3.88** regarding the latter.

[2]　ERA 1988, s 113 is the place where this provision first appeared.

[3]　With the proviso that no liability is to be incurred in respect of a failure to obtain the relevant approval or order before the making of the direction.

[4]　EA 1996, ss 554–556 (as amended by the SSFA 1998) replace s 2 of the Education Act 1973.

[5]　By virtue of s 554(5), '"endowment" includes property not subject to any restriction on the expenditure of capital'. The necessity for this definition becomes apparent when the definition of 'permanent endowment' in s 96(3) of the Charities Act 1993 is considered.

[6]　Sections 377, 378, 380 and 381 of the EA 1996 were repealed and replaced by provisions in the SSFA 1998 (see s 69 and Sch 19 to that Act for the replacement provisions). By virtue of s 17 of the Interpretation Act 1978, the references in s 554 to ss 377, 378, 380 and 381 of the EA 1996 are to be read as references to their replacement provisions in the SSFA 1998. It should be noted also that EA 1996, s 554(4) enacts two rebuttable presumptions which apply to the matters in question.

3.84   Section 555(1) of the EA 1996 provides that an order can be made under s 554 only where the Secretary of State has been requested to make the order by what appears to the Secretary of State to be the 'appropriate authority of the religion or denomination concerned'. Further, there are certain procedural requirements in s 555(2) which apply in relation to orders under s 554.

3.85   Section 556 makes provision with regard to the content of orders made under s 554. An order under s 554 may require or authorise the sale of the relevant property and may consolidate any endowments to be dealt with by the scheme.[1] Subject to this and to any provision of a public general Act of Parliament affecting the endowments, an order under s 554 must establish and, with a view to enabling the religion or denomination concerned to participate more effectively in the administration of the statutory system of public education, give effect to a scheme or schemes for the endowments to be used for 'appropriate educational purposes'.[2] These purposes must be either in connection with foundation or voluntary schools or partly in connection with such schools and partly in other ways related to the locality served by the school in question.[3] 'Appropriate educational purposes' means 'educational purposes in connection with the provision of religious education in accordance with the tenets of the religion or denomination concerned', including any of the purposes set out in Sch 36 to the EA 1996 (which contain the 'uniform statutory trusts for educational purposes').[4]

3.86   An order under s 554 may extinguish any rights to which a person is or may become entitled as a beneficiary under a trust arising under s 1 of the Reverter of Sites Act 1987.[5]

3.87   Finally in this section, it is noted that the trustees of certain endowments may by a simple majority resolution adopt the 'uniform statutory trusts' set out in Sch 36 to the EA 1996. The endowments are those which are regulated by a qualifying scheme under the Endowed Schools Acts 1869–1948 or by an order under s 2 of the 1973 Act or s 554 of the EA 1996, and which are held for the purpose of: (a) providing religious education at foundation and/or voluntary schools in a diocese or other geographical area (but not only at a particular school or schools); or (b) providing premises for such schools at which religious education is, or is to be, provided in a diocese or other geographical area (but not only at a particular school or schools).[6] The rights of those entitled under the third proviso to s 2 of the School sites Act 1841[7] and the rights of LEAs under para 7 or 8 of the First Schedule to the Education Act 1946 or ss 60(4) and 62(2) of the EA 1996[8] are, however (subject to

---

[1]   EA 1996, s 556(1).

[2]   Ibid, s 556(2).

[3]   Ibid.

[4]   Ibid, s 556(3).

[5]   See s 5 of the Reverter of Sites Act 1987, as to which, see para **8.39**.

[6]   EA 1996, s 557(1) and (3), the provisions of which do not apply to an endowment if or in so far as it constitutes a religious education fund: s 557(1).

[7]   As to which, see paras **8.25** et seq.

[8]   EA 1996, ss 60 and 62 were repealed by the SSFA 1998, but rights which had previously arisen under s 60(4) were preserved by Art 14 of SI 1999/2323. The replacement provisions in the SSFA 1998 for s 60(4) of the EA 1996 are para 2(6) of Sch 3 to the SSFA 1998 and para 16(5) of Sch 6 to that Act,

one qualification), protected by the adoption by the trustees of the uniform statutory trusts.[1] The qualification is that an order under s 554 of the EA 1996 or s 2 of the Education Act 1973 made by virtue of s 5 of the Reverter of Sites Act 1987, may provide otherwise.[2]

Variation of trust deeds and instruments

3.88   Under s 82(1) of the SSFA 1998, the Secretary of State may by order modify the provisions of any trust deed or other instrument relating to a school in such manner as appears to him to be 'necessary or expedient in connection with the operation of any provision of this Act or anything done under or for the purposes of any such provision'. Before making any such modification, the Secretary of State must consult (1) the governing body of the school in question, (2) any trustees holding property on trust for the purposes of the school, (3) in the case of a Church of England, Church in Wales or Roman Catholic School, the appropriate diocesan authority;[3] and (4) 'such other persons as he considers appropriate'.[4] Any modification so made may be of either temporary or permanent duration.[5]

3.89   Finally, the Secretary of State also has power (under s 349 of the EA 1996[6]) by order[7] to make such modifications of any trust deed or other instrument relating to a school as appear to him, after consultation with the governing body or other proprietor of the school, to be necessary to enable the governing body or other proprietor to meet any requirement imposed by regulations made under s 342 or s 347 of the EA 1996. (Those sections relate to the approval of special schools and independent schools for the purpose of allowing them to admit pupils with special educational needs.)

---

and as a result of s 17 of the Interpretation Act 1978, the reference to s 60(4) of the EA 1996 is to be read as a reference to para 2(6) of Sch 3 and para 16(5) of Sch 6. The replacement provisions in the SSFA 1998 for s 62(2) of the EA 1996 are contained in Sch 22 to the SSFA 1998 (principally paras 3(3) and (4)), and s 17 applies in the same manner to the reference in s 557(8)(b) to s 62(2).

[1]   EA 1996, s 557(8).
[2]   Ibid.
[3]   Defined by SSFA 1998, s 142(1).
[4]   Ibid, s 82(2).
[5]   Ibid, s 82(3).
[6]   Which replaced s 191 of the 1993 Act, which itself replaced s 1(2)(b) of the 1973 Act.
[7]   Which need not be made by statutory instrument: s 568(2) of the EA 1996.

Chapter 4

SUPPLEMENTARY FUNCTIONS OF LOCAL EDUCATION AUTHORITIES

4.1　A number of functions of LEAs are examined in this chapter. They are referred to in the title of the chapter as 'supplementary' functions, but they are no less important than the primary functions of LEAs with regard to education. Rather, they are functions which are complementary to those of the Secretary of State (and therefore in Wales the National Assembly) referred to in Chapter 2.[1]

EDUCATION OUTSIDE SCHOOL; PUPIL REFERRAL UNITS

4.2　An LEA is obliged by s 19(1) of the EA 1996 to:

> 'make arrangements for the provision of suitable education at school or otherwise than at school for those children of compulsory school age who, by reason of illness, exclusion from school or otherwise, may not for any period receive suitable education unless such arrangements are made for them.'[2]

4.3　This obligation does not apply where a parent unreasonably withdraws his child from a suitable school which it is reasonably practicable for the child to attend.[3]

4.4　It was decided by the House of Lords in R v East Sussex County Council, ex parte Tandy[4] that an LEA's resources are not relevant in determining what is suitable education for the purposes of s 19. This was despite the decision (also of the House of Lords) in R v Gloucestershire County Council, ex parte Barry.[5] However, where there is more than one way of providing suitable education, the LEA can have regard to financial resources.[6] Further, as a result of s 19(4A) of the EA 1996, the LEA must 'have regard to any guidance given from time to time by the Secretary of State'.[7]

4.5　A school established for the purpose of carrying out an LEA's duty under s 19(1) which is 'not a county or a special school' [sic] is known as a 'pupil referral

---

[1]　As elsewhere in this book, references to the Secretary of State are to be read also as references to the National Assembly for Wales unless otherwise indicated.

[2]　'Suitable education' for this purpose means 'efficient education suitable to his age, ability and aptitude and to any special educational needs he may have': s 19(6).

[3]　R(G) v Westminster City Council [2004] EWCA Civ 45, [2004] ELR 135 .

[4]　[1998] AC 714, [1998] ELR 251.

[5]　[1997] AC 584.

[6]　Ex parte Tandy, above.

[7]　Subsection (4A) was inserted by s 47 of the EA 1997. For the impact of the requirement to 'have regard' to such guidance, see paras **2.34–2.36** et seq.

unit',[1] and may be named as the school at which a child is to attend in a school attendance order made under s 437 of the EA 1996.[2] Boarding provision may be made at any such unit.[3] Regulations may be made requiring management committees to be established for such units and providing for (among other things) the proceedings of such committees.[4]

4.6 Section 19(4) of the EA 1996 empowers LEAs to do that which they are obliged to do under s 19(1) for children of compulsory school age also for 'young persons'.[5] Children and young persons for whom education is provided otherwise than at school under s 19 are treated for the purposes of the EA 1996 (and therefore other Acts which are to be read as one with that Act) as pupils.[6]

4.7 There are a number of provisions relating to pupil referral units contained in Sch 1 to the EA 1996 and those provisions apply a number of provisions in the Education Acts to pupil referral units, in some cases with modifications.[7]

COMPLAINTS ABOUT THE CURRICULUM: SECTION 409 OF THE EDUCATION ACT 1996

4.8 Local education authorities are required by s 409(1) of the EA 1996 to make arrangements for the consideration and disposal of certain kinds of complaint.[8] These include complaints to the effect that the LEA or the governing body of any community, foundation, or voluntary school maintained by them, or of any community or foundation special school maintained by them which is not established in a hospital, has acted or is proposing to act unreasonably in relation to the exercise of a power conferred on it by or under various provisions in Part V of the EA 1996 or in the EA 2002 regarding the curriculum[9] or of any other enactment relating to the curriculum for, or religious worship in, maintained schools.[10] In addition, complaints that the LEA or any governing body of the relevant sort has acted or is proposing to act unreasonably in relation to the performance of, or have failed to discharge, any duty of the same sort are to be determined under the arrangements in question.[11]

---

[1] EA 1996, s 19(2). Curiously, the reference in the subsection to a county school was not amended by the SSFA 1998.

[2] See further, paras **5.20** et seq.

[3] EA 1996, s 19(3).

[4] Ibid, Sch 1, para 15, as inserted by s 48 of the EA 1997.

[5] EA 1996, s 19(4). A 'young person' in this context is a person who is over compulsory school age but under the age of 18: s 579(1) of the EA 1996.

[6] EA 1996, s 19(5). See footnote 2 on p 69 regarding the reading of Acts as one.

[7] See the Education (Pupil Referral Units) (Application of Enactments) Regulations 1994, SI 1994/2103, as amended by SI 1995/602, SI 1996/2087 and SI 1997/1966.

[8] This provision first appeared as s 23(1) of the 1988 Act.

[9] The specific provisions are referred to in s 408(4) (as amended, including by the EA 2002) and s 408(4A): see s 409(2)(a), (3)(a) and (3)(aa).

[10] EA 1996, s 409(2)(a) and (3)(b).

[11] Ibid, s 409(2)(b).

4.9   Section 409(4) of the EA 1996 provides that the Secretary of State cannot entertain a complaint made to him under s 496 or s 497 of the EA 1996[1] in respect of a matter in regard to which arrangements are required to be made by the LEA under s 409(1) of the EA 1996, 'unless a complaint concerning the same matter has been made and disposed of in accordance with arrangements made under subsection (1)'.

4.10   The arrangements made under s 409(1) must be preceded by consultation with the governing bodies of foundation and voluntary aided schools. Presumably, this duty to consult extends only to the governing bodies of such schools in the LEA's area. The Secretary of State issued relevant guidance in DES Circular 1/89, according to which LEAs should consult in addition with the governing bodies of all other schools maintained by them, and the head teachers of all schools maintained by them.[2]

4.11   The complaints procedure is intended to be available in respect of complaints about the acts of the LEA and of a relevant governing body in respect of, for example, the National Curriculum. Since the duties of such bodies are general while those of the head teacher are specific,[3] it might well be thought that the complaints procedure in s 409(1) should not apply to complaints about the practices of individual teachers. However, since the power to enforce the wishes of the governing body where it has a delegated budget under Chapter IV of Part II of the SSFA 1998, and the power to enforce the wishes of the LEA where there is no such delegated budget, is in the hands of the governing body and the LEA respectively,[4] it is likely that a complaint about the practices of individual teachers would have to be made under the arrangements required by s 409(1).[5] There may, however, be exceptional situations where the complaint could be brought under s 496 or s 497 of the EA 1996 without first using the s 409(1) procedure.

TRANSPORT

Section 509 of the Education Act 1996

4.12   The statutory functions of an LEA in regard to the provision of transport are now contained primarily in s 509 of the EA 1996. Under s 509(1) and (1A), an LEA is under a duty to:

---

[1]   See Chapter 3 regarding ss 496 and 497.
[2]   Paragraph 1 of Annex A to the Circular.
[3]   EA 1996, s 357(1).
[4]   See paras **15.74** and **15.75**.
[5]   Harris, op cit (see footnote 1 at para **2.85**), at p 247, suggests otherwise. This is on the basis that the determination and organisation of the school curriculum is the responsibility of the head teacher. However, the head teacher is also subject to the possibility of disciplinary action by either the governing body of the school or (where there is no delegated budget) the LEA, with the result that in reality it will be the acts or omissions of the governing body or the LEA which will be responsible for the continuation of a state of affairs concerning the curriculum which results from the acts of individual teachers.

'make such arrangements for the provision of transport and otherwise as they consider necessary, or as the Secretary of State may direct, for the purpose of facilitating the attendance of persons receiving education'

at four types of institution. The four types of institutions are (a) schools, (b) any institution which is maintained or assisted[1] by the LEA which provides further education or higher education (or both), (c) institutions within the further education sector and (d) in certain circumstances institutions outside both the further education and higher education sectors. Those circumstances are where the LSC or (as the case may be) the CETW has secured for the person in question the provision of education or training at the institution and the provision of boarding accommodation under s 13 or s 41 of the LSA 2000. Where such arrangements are made, then any transport must be provided free of charge.[2] Provision 'otherwise' includes guides and other persons to take care of pupils on their journey.[3] Where transport is provided under s 509(1), then it must be 'non-stressful'.[4] However, any stress which is induced by an irrational dislike of the school to which transport is provided communicated by a child's parent to the child, is irrelevant.[5]

4.13   By far the greatest provision made under s 509(1)–(2) of free transport is made for children of compulsory school age who live further away than walking distance (as defined in s 444(5) of the EA 1996) from school and neither s 444(4)(b)(ii) nor s 444(4)(b)(iii) applies.[6] An LEA is obliged to consider it necessary to provide free transport to school for such children because, if it did not do so, a parent of such a child would have a good defence to a prosecution brought under s 444 for failing to ensure the regular attendance of his child at school. This was expressly held by the House of Lords in *Devon County Council v George*.[7]

4.14   In considering whether or not they are required to provide free transport under s 509(1) or (1A), as a result of s 509(4)(a), an LEA must have regard to (among other things) the age of the person and the nature of the route, or alternative routes, which he could reasonably be expected to take. It is worthy of note in this context

---

[1]   For the meaning of 'assisted', see s 579(6)–(7) of the EA 1996.

[2]   EA 1996, s 509(2). Where an LEA decides to give a child a season ticket (or 'bus pass') in the mistaken belief that the child lives further away than walking distance, then they are entitled to rescind that determination: *Rootkin v Kent County Council* [1981] 1 WLR 1186.

[3]   In *Jacques v Oxfordshire County Council* (1967) 66 LGR 440, it was held that supervision of pupils by prefects on a journey to or from school may be sufficient. See further, para **14.47**.

[4]   *R v Hereford and Worcester County Council, ex parte P* [1992] 2 FLR 207, at 216A. McCullough J in that case referred to and relied upon dicta of Lord Donaldson in the Court of Appeal in *Devon County Council v George* [1989] AC 573, at 581F–G, dicta which (as stated by McCullough J at p 213B) can be taken not to have been over-ruled by the reversal by the House of Lords of the decision of the Court of Appeal.

[5]   *R v Carmarthenshire County Council, ex parte White* [2001] ELR 172, where Tomlinson J held that Art 1 of Protocol 1 to the European Convention on Human Rights was not contravened in the circumstances.

[6]   See further, paras **5.39** et seq.

[7]   'In the case of such pupils, an LEA would be acting unreasonably if it decided that free transport was unnecessary for the purpose of promoting their attendance at school, because if it were not provided the parents of these pupils would be under no legal obligation to secure their attendance' [1989] AC 573, at 604B, per Lord Keith. In effect, the same had been held by Lynskey J in *Surrey County Council v Ministry of Education* [1953] 1 WLR 516, but the matter was helpfully clarified in *Devon County Council v George*. Collins J in *R (Jones) v Ceredigon County Council* [2004] EWHC 1376, (2004) *The Times*, July 8, rejected an argument that this statement was wrong.

that the defence which is now contained in s 444(4) originated in s 74 of the Elementary Education Act 1870, where the following was provided:

> 'Any of the following reasons shall be a reasonable excuse [for a failure by a parent to ensure the attendance at school of his child]; namely ... (3) That there is no public elementary school open which the child can attend within such distance, not exceeding three miles, measured according to the nearest road from the residence of such child, as the byelaws may prescribe.'

4.15 Conditions have changed since 1870, so it may be that a route which a child could reasonably have been expected to take in 1870 would no longer be a route which a child of the same age could reasonably be expected to take, even if accompanied by an adult, for example because of modern traffic conditions.

4.16 The requirement in s 509(4)(a) was added to the predecessor to s 509 (s 55 of the Education Act 1944) after the decision of the House of Lords in *Rogers v Essex County Council*.[1] It seems, however, that it has not affected the position as determined by the House of Lords in that case. Rather, it has simply made explicit what was there decided.[2] The decision of the House of Lords in *Devon County Council v George*[3] is to a similar effect. In that case, the House of Lords ruled that the mere fact that a route is too dangerous for a child to walk along it alone is not sufficient to place the LEA under an obligation to consider it necessary to provide free transport for the child.[4] However, the House of Lords ruled, even if a parent is not readily able to accompany the child, that may not affect the matter.[5]

4.17 It may be that as a result of the decision in *R v Gloucestershire County Council, ex parte Barry*,[6] financial considerations are relevant to the question whether transport is 'necessary' in any relevant situation.[7] However, financial considerations may not be so relevant in every situation.[8] Indeed, it may be that as a result of *R v East Sussex County Council, ex parte Tandy*,[9] resources would not be relevant in determining whether transport is necessary. The fact that an LEA must 'consider' it necessary to provide transport under s 509 of the EA 1996, might tip the balance in favour of the ruling in *ex parte Barry*, although since safety is an objective matter, it should not do so.

4.18 When considering whether or not they are required to provide free transport under s 509(1), as a result of s 509(4)(b), an LEA must also have regard to any wish of a child's parent for the child to be provided with education or training at a school or

---

1   [1987] AC 66. See para **5.39**.
2   This includes that it must be 'reasonably practicable for a child to walk along [the route in question] to school': ibid., p 77E, per Lord Ackner. Lord Ackner also said, at p 78E: 'In my judgment a route to be "available" within the meaning of section 39(5) [of the EA 1944] must be a route along which a child accompanied as necessary can walk and walk with reasonable safety to school'.
3   [1989] AC 573.
4   Ibid, at 607A.
5   Ibid.
6   [1997] AC 584. See also *R v Norfolk County Council, ex parte Thorpe*, (1998) *The Times*, February 9; [1998] COD 208; [1998] NPC 11, on an analogous provision.
7   See further, para **6.40** regarding *ex parte Barry*.
8   Cf *ex parte Barry* [1997] AC 548, at 611 A–B.
9   [1998] AC 714, [1998] ELR 251.

institution in which the religious education or training provided is that of the religion or denomination to which the parent adheres. This requirement was added to s 55 of the 1944 Act after the decision in the case of *R v Rochdale Metropolitan Borough Council, ex parte Schemet*.[1] It was held by Turner J in *R(T) v Leeds City Council*[2] that (as one might expect) s 509(4)(b) does not impose a duty to comply with a parent's wishes concerning religious education. The requirement in s 509(4)(b) nevertheless does not resolve the difficulties which can arise where a parent's preferred school is not the nearest school which is otherwise suitable for his child of compulsory school age; rather, s 509(4)(b) has simply added a factor which the LEA are obliged to take into account, but which they can (unless their decision is irrational) lawfully decide is outweighed by other factors. As McCullough J put it in *R v Kent County Council, ex parte C*:[3]

> 'In my judgment: (1) a LEA cannot properly refuse to provide free transport on the basis that there is a nearer school which a child could attend unless it is of the view that the nearer school would be a suitable school for that child to attend, and (2) when considering a challenge to a local authority's refusal to provide free transport, if the refusal was based on the authority's view that there was a nearer suitable school, the function of the court is to see whether it has been shown that the authority's view about that school's suitability was lawfully reached, which in most cases will require no more than a consideration of the rationality of its conclusion.'[4]

4.19   In general terms, once a school has been specified in a statement of SEN under s 324 of the EA 1996, it is not open to the LEA when considering whether to provide free school transport under s 509, to take the view that the child's needs would be met at other, nearer schools. This can be stated with some confidence as a result of *R v Havering London Borough Council, ex parte K*.[5] The judgment of Sedley J in that case was, to his regret, not reserved, and the facts of the case were in some respects unusual. Nevertheless, the proposition stated at the beginning of this paragraph is in principle sound.

4.20   In *R v Islington London Borough Council, ex parte A (A Child)*,[6] Mr Jack Beatson QC, sitting as a deputy judge of the Queen's Bench Division, said that where a school is named in a statement of SEN on the basis that the parent of the child to whom the statement relates will make the necessary arrangements for the provision of transport to the school and there is a nearer school which the LEA considers to be suitable for

---

[1]   [1994] ELR 89, (1992) 91 LGR 425. The part of the judgment from which s 509(4)(b) was derived was not affected by the decision of the Court of Appeal in *Re S (Minors)* [1995] ELR 98 (as to which, see paras **5.44** et seq).

[2]   [2002] ELR 91, at 97.

[3]   [1998] ELR 108, at 114A–B.

[4]   See further, paras **5.45** and **5.46** regarding McCullough's view of the *ratio* of *Re S (Minors)*, and why he felt that it was open to him to rule as he did in *R v Kent County Council, ex parte C*. McCullough J's analysis of the policy regarding the provision of free transport of the LEA in the latter case could be instructive for other LEAs: see in particular [1998] ELR 108, at 118E–119D. In *R (Jones) v Ceredigion County Council* [2004] EWHC 1376, (2004) *The Times*, July 8, Collins J in para 18 concluded that the approach of McCulloch J in relation to *Re S (Minors)* was approved by the Court of Appeal in *R v Vale of Glamorgan County Council, ex parte J* [2001] ELR 758.

[5]   [1998] ELR 402.

[6]   (2000) *The Times*, October 20; CO 2559/2000. The text of the judgment is available on the Internet at www.bailii.org.

the child, the LEA can protect its position by naming both schools in the statement of SEN on the basis that if the parent provides transport to one school, then the LEA will pay for the child to attend that school, but if the parents are unable to do so, or to continue to do so, then the child will attend another school, which is closer to the child's home. In doing so, Mr Beatson QC relied upon the decision of the Court of Appeal in *Re C (A Minor)*,[1] which clearly supported the proposition. Further, Mr Beatson QC stated[2] that if the parent of the child in such a situation wished the preferred school to be the only school named, then the parent could appeal to the Special Educational Needs and Disability Tribunal (or, in Wales, the Special Educational Needs Tribunal for Wales) against the naming of the school which was not preferred, and that the suitability of the other (nearer) school was not a matter for the High Court. Mr Beatson QC stated, however, that it would be necessary to consider fresh applications for the provision of transport to school where the circumstances had changed since the initial decision not to provide such transport was made.

4.21 *R v Islington London Borough Council, ex parte A (A Child)* and *R v Havering London Borough Council, ex parte K* were applied by Mr Michael Supperstone QC, sitting as a deputy High Court judge, in *R(H) v London Borough of Brent*.[3] The effect of his ruling was that since the LEA had named a school in Part 4 of a statement of SEN without any qualification as to the provision of transport, and only that school, and that school was more than 3 miles from the child's home, the LEA was under a duty to pay the relevant transport costs.[4]

4.22 Section 509(5) of the EA 1996 contains some provisions which are designed to ensure that an LEA does not, when exercising its functions under s 509(1), discriminate against (a) persons receiving full-time education at institutions within the further education sector, or (b) persons receiving full-time education or training at institutions outside both the further and higher education sectors where the LSC or (as the case may be) the CETW has secured for the person in question the provision of education or training at the institution and the provision of boarding accommodation under s 13 or s 41 of the LSA 2000. In the first of these two situations, the provision made for the persons in question by the LEA must be no less favourable than that made by them for relevant persons of the same age at schools maintained by an LEA.[5] In the second of these two situations, the provision must be no less favourable than that made for persons of the same age with learning difficulties (within the meaning of s 13 of the LSA 2000) at schools maintained by an LEA or (where there is no such provision) than that made for such persons 'for whom the authority secures the provision of education at any other institution'.[6]

4.23 Section 509(3) allows an LEA to pay the whole or part of the reasonable travelling expenses of any person receiving education or training at the same types of

---

[1]   [1994] ELR 273.
[2]   In para 27 of his judgment.
[3]   [2002] ELR 509.
[4]   See, in particular, paras 31 and 33 of the judgment.
[5]   EA 1996, s 509(5)(b).
[6]   Ibid, s 509(5)(c).

institutions as those to which the duties imposed by s 509(1) and (1A) relate and for whom no transport arrangements have been made under those subsections. This does not appear to allow an LEA to provide partly or wholly funded transport for persons who do not qualify for free transport under s 509(1). However, because of the existence of the power to charge for the provision of transport for a registered pupil at a maintained school other than transport in respect of which, by virtue of s 454(3) or 509(2), no charge may be made,[1] it seems that there is a power to provide transport for these pupils and to charge for it. Bearing this in mind, it seems clear that it is possible to provide (under s 111(1) of the Local Government Act 1972[2]) transport instead of paying expenses only under s 509(3).

4.24   It might be thought that an LEA may not pay for free travel to (for example) school for those to whom they owe a duty under s 509(1) to provide free transport. However, as McCullough J pointed out in *R v Kent County Council, ex parte C*:[3]

> 'Suffice it to say, without having heard argument about it, that, in considering its duty under s 55(1) [now s 504(1) and (2)] one material consideration would be the fact that it had used its power under s 55(2) [now s 504(3)] to pay for children to use public transport.'

Manner of providing transport under section 509 of the Education Act 1996

4.25   An LEA which arranges free transport under s 509(1) of the EA 1996 may do so in a number of ways. An LEA may provide the transport itself, or it may contract with private transport operators for the relevant services. There are some useful provisions which may help LEAs in this context. First, an LEA may use a school bus when it is being used to provide free school transport under s 509(1) to carry, in addition, fare-paying passengers.[4] Secondly, if a permit is granted under ss 18–21 of the Transport Act 1985 to, and is being used by (a) an LEA, (b) a school or other body which fulfils the duty of the LEA under the EA 1996 with respect to the provision of education, or (c) a body connected with such a school or body,[5] in respect of a bus (meaning a vehicle which is adapted to carry more than eight passengers[6]) which is to be used otherwise than for profit (or incidentally to an

---

[1]   See EA 1996, s 455(1)(c), as to which, see para **2.146**.

[2]   Which is the general power for a local authority to do that which is 'calculated to facilitate, or is conducive or incidental to, the exercise of any of their functions'.

[3]   [1998] ELR 108, at 110E–F.

[4]   Public Passenger Vehicles Act 1981, s 46. This provision may not apply to buses provided by private operators, since the definition of 'school bus' in this context is 'in relation to a local education authority, ... a motor vehicle which is used by that authority to provide free school transport'. When that occurs, ss 6 (certificates of initial fitness for use as public service vehicles), 8 (powers of inspection), 9 (prohibition of driving unfit public service vehicles) and 12(1) (operators' licences) of that Act do not apply to the bus: 46(1). However, a service on which fare-paying passengers are carried is nevertheless subject to registration under s 6 of the Transport Act 1985.

[5]   See the Section 19 Minibus (Designated Bodies) Order 1987, SI 1987/1229, as amended by SI 1990/1708, SI 1995/1540 and SI 1997/535.

[6]   Transport Act 1985, s 19(1).

activity which is itself carried on with a view to a profit[1]) and on which members of the public are not to be carried, then the ordinary licensing requirements for public service vehicles do not apply.[2] Permits of this kind for small buses (minibuses), which carry nine to 16 passengers, may be granted by LEAs as well as by a traffic commissioner; permits for large busus may only be granted by a traffic commissioner.[3] Conditions of fitness for such buses nevertheless apply; those for minibuses are contained in the Minibus and Other Section 19 Permit Buses Regulations 1987,[4] and those for large buses are contained in the Public Service Vehicles (Conditions of Fitness, Equipment, Use and Certification) Regulations 1981.[5]

Provision of assistance in relation to transport to place where nursery education is provided

4.26   Section 509A of the EA 1996 confers a power on an LEA to provide a child with assistance in relation to transport if it is satisfied that, without such assistance, the child would be prevented from attending at any premises which are not a school or part of a school but at which nursery education is provided (broadly) at public expense. The assistance may take the form of either the making of 'arrangements (whether for the provision of transport or otherwise) for the purpose of facilitating the child's attendance at the premises concerned', or the payment of the whole or any part of the child's reasonable travel expenses.[6] The assistance must be for the purpose of receiving the relevant nursery education at the premises in question.[7]

4.27   When considering whether to provide a child with assistance under s 509A, the LEA must have regard '(among other things) to whether it would be reasonable to expect alternative arrangements to be made for him to receive relevant nursery education at any other premises (whether nearer to his home or otherwise)'.[8] The LEA may charge either the child's parent or the person providing the relevant education for the provision of the relevant transport.[9]

SCHOOL CROSSING PATROLS

4.28   Under s 26 of the Road Traffic Regulation Act 1984,[10] county and metropolitan district councils, the Common Council of the City of London and London borough councils, may make arrangements for patrolling, at such times as the

---

[1]   Thus an independent school which is carried on with a view to a profit cannot properly be granted a permit under s 19: *R v Secretary of State for the Environment, Transport and the Regions, ex parte Thomas's London Day Schools (Transport) Limited* [2000] Ed CR 283.

[2]   See Transport Act 1985, ss 18 and 19 and the Section 19 Minibus (Designated Bodies) Order 1987, SI 1987/1229, as amended.

[3]   See Transport Act 1985, s 19(3) and (4), and the Section 19 Minibus (Designated Bodies) Order 1987 (as amended) (which applies to small buses only).

[4]   SI 1987/1230, as amended, made under s 21 of the Transport Act 1985.

[5]   SI 1981/257 (as amended).

[6]   EA 1996, s 509A(2).

[7]   Ibid, s 509A(1).

[8]   Ibid, s 509A(3).

[9]   Ibid, s 509A(4).

[10]   As amended by s 288 of the Greater London Authority Act 1999 and s 270 of the Transport Act 2000.

council thinks fit, places where children cross roads on their way to or from school or from one part of a school to another. In deciding whether to make such arrangements, all such councils except the Council of the City of London must have regard to representations made by local authorities within their area.[1] Before deciding whether to make arrangements for the patrolling of places where children cross Greater London Authority roads, a London borough council or the Common Council of the City of London must consult Transport for London and take account of any representations made by the latter.[2] The appointing councils must be satisfied that the persons appointed as school crossing patrols are adequately qualified and must give those persons 'requisite' training.[3] The arrangements made under s 26 may (except in the case of the Common Council of the City of London) include an agreement with the local police authority[4] for the performance of specified functions by that authority (acting through a police officer or a traffic warden[5]).

4.29 A uniformed school crossing patrol has the power, by exhibiting a prescribed sign, to require the person driving or propelling a vehicle (a) to stop it before it reaches the crossing place, (b) not to start it again while the sign is displayed, and (c) not to impede the person who is crossing or seeking to cross the road.[6] A failure to comply with the requirements is an offence.[7] There is a rebuttable presumption that the patrol's uniform and sign are of the appropriate type.[8] When the sign is exhibited, drivers must stop, whether or not any children are impeded in their crossing of the road.[9] The sign must, however, be exhibited so that oncoming traffic can see the word 'stop'.[10]

MEALS AND MILK

Duties and powers of local education authorities

4.30 Local education authorities may provide (a) registered pupils at any school maintained by them, (b) 'other persons who receive education at such a school', and (c) 'children who receive relevant funded nursery education' with 'milk, meals and other refreshments', either on the school premises or at any place other than the

---

[1] Road Traffic Regulation Act 1984, s 26(4)(a).

[2] Ibid, s 26(4A).

[3] Ibid, s 26(3).

[4] As to which, see ss 1–3 of the Police Act 1964, as substituted by the Police and Magistrates' Courts Act 1994.

[5] See Road Traffic Regulation Act 1984, s 95(4)(a) regarding traffic wardens.

[6] Road Traffic Regulation Act 1984, s 28. The uniform must be 'approved by the Secretary of State': s 28(1). As to the sign, see the Traffic Signs Regulations and General Directions 2002, SI 2002/3113 and (for Wales) the Traffic Signs (Welsh and English Language Provisions) Regulations and General Directions 1985, SI 1985/713, reg 4 and Sch 1.

[7] Road Traffic Regulation Act 1984, s 28(3); and see s 9 of and Part 1 of Sch 2 to the Road Traffic Offenders Act 1988.

[8] Ibid, s 28(5).

[9] See *Franklin v Langdown* [1971] 3 All ER 662 and *Wall v Walwyn* [1974] RTR 24.

[10] *Hoy v Smith* [1964] 1 WLR 1377.

school premises where education is being provided.[1] Local education authorities must, however, provide school lunches[2] for any such person if (a) any requirements prescribed by an order of the Secretary of State (or, in Wales, the National Assembly[3]) are met, (b) a request for the provision of school lunches has been made by or on behalf of that person to the LEA, and (c) either the person is eligible for free school lunches (within the meaning of EA 1996, s 512ZB, as substituted by EA 2002, s 201 – regarding which see para **4.31**) or the person is a registered pupil at a school maintained by the LEA and 'it would not be unreasonable for the authority to provide the lunches'.[4] These lunches may take such form as the LEA thinks fit, except that it must comply with any nutritional standards imposed by regulations made under s 114(1) of the SSFA 1998 (regarding which, see para **4.38**).[5]

4.31   The LEA must charge for everything provided by it under s 512(1) and (3), and must charge every person the same price for the same quantity of the same item, unless the provision must, as a result of s 512ZB of the EA 1996, be made free of charge.[6] Section 512ZB(1) provides that an LEA must provide free school lunches under s 512(3) to a person who is eligible for free school lunches as defined by s 512ZB(4) and who has made a request to the LEA that such lunches be provided free of charge, or on whose behalf such a request has been made. Section 512ZB(3) makes equivalent provision in relation to milk provided under s 512(1)(a) or (c).

4.32   A person is eligible for free school lunches if his parent is in receipt of (a) income support, (b) an income-based jobseekers' allowance (payable under the Jobseekers Act 1995), (c) support provided under Part 6 of the Immigration and Asylum Act 1999, or (d) any other benefit or allowance, or is entitled to any tax credit under the Tax Credits Act 2002 or any element of such a tax credit, which is prescribed for this purpose and in such circumstances as may be so prescribed.[7] A person is also eligible for free support if he himself is in receipt of (a) income support, (b) an income-based jobseekers' allowance, or (c) any another benefit or allowance, or is entitled to any tax credit under the Tax Credits Act 2002 or any element of such a tax credit, which is prescribed for this purpose and in such circumstances as may be so prescribed.[8]

---

[1]   EA 1996, s 512(1) and (2) as substituted by EA 2002, s 201. References below to s 512 are to the substituted provision. Currently, s 201 is in force with the exception that s 512(1)(c) and related provisions in the provisions substituted by s 201 are not yet in force: see SI 2003/124 and SI 2002/3185.

[2]   Defined for the purposes of ss 512, 512ZA and 512ZB as substituted by s 201 of the EA 2002, by s 512(6). It means in relation to a pupil 'food made available for consumption by the pupil as his midday meal on a school day, whether involving a set meal or the selection of items by him or otherwise'.

[3]   See EA 2002, s 211 and SI 1999/672.

[4]   EA 1996, s 512(3). Requirements have been prescribed for this purpose by the Education (School Lunches) (Prescribed Requirements) (England) Order, SI 2003/382 and the Education (School Lunches) (Prescribed Requirements) (Wales) Order, SI 2003/880.

[5]   Ibid, s 512(4).

[6]   Ibid, s 512ZA, as substituted by EA 2002, s 201.

[7]   Ibid, s 512ZB(4)(a). See the Education (Free School Lunches) (Prescribed Tax Credits) (England) Order, SI 2003/383 and the Education (Free School Lunches) (Prescribed Tax Credits) (Wales) Order, SI 2003/879 regarding the relevant prescribed tax credits and circumstances.

[8]   Ibid, s 512ZB(4)(b). No order has been made under that provision.

4.33   An LEA must also provide at any school maintained by them 'such facilities as they consider appropriate for the consumption of any meals or other refreshment brought to the school by registered pupils'.[1]

4.34   Where persons other than pupils[2] receive education at a school maintained by an LEA, then they must be treated in the same way as pupils.[3]

4.35   LEAs may make arrangements for securing the provision (which appears to include making the provision themselves) of milk, meals and other refreshment for pupils in attendance at a school in their area which is not maintained by them, but only with the consent of the proprietor of the school.[4] Section 513(2) of the EA 1996 requires that the arrangements must be on such financial and other terms (if any) as may be agreed between the LEA and the proprietor of the school, but must so far as practicable be such that the expense incurred by the LEA in connection with the provision of any service or item under the arrangements does not exceed the expense which the LEA would have incurred in providing the same thing if the pupil had been a pupil at a school maintained by it. However, s 513(2) will not apply to an LEA, or to any pupils of any age or ages specified in the order, where an order made by the Secretary of State under s 512A(1) of the EA 1996 as inserted by s 116 of the SSFA 1998 is in force and the order so provides.[5]

Duties of the governing bodies of maintained schools

4.36   Under s 512A of the EA 1996, the Secretary of State may order that the governing body of a maintained school to which the order applies is (unless it does not have a delegated budget) subject to (a) the duty to provide school lunches in accordance with s 512(3) and (4) of the EA 1996, (b) the duty to provide school lunches free of charge in accordance with s 512ZB(1) and (c) the duty to provide free milk in accordance with s 512ZB(3).[6] Such an order may be made in relation to (a) all maintained schools, (b) any class of maintained schools specified in the order, or (c) all schools maintained by specified LEAs, or any specified class of such schools.[7] One result of any such order is that the corresponding duty no longer falls to be performed by the LEA in relation to a relevant school, unless the school does not have a delegated budget.[8]

4.37   Orders have been made under s 512A. The current orders are the Education (Transfer of Functions Concerning School Lunches) (Wales) Order 1999,[9] the Education (Transfer of Functions Concerning School Lunches) (Wales) (No 2) Order

---

[1]   EA 1996, s 512(5).

[2]   As defined in s 3(1) of the EA 1996.

[3]   EA 1996, s 533(3).

[4]   Ibid, s 513(1). See s 579(1) of the EA 1996 for the definition of 'proprietor'.

[5]   Ibid, s 512A(5) and (7).

[6]   Ibid, s 512A(1) and (2) as amended by EA 2002, s 201(2).

[7]   Ibid, s 512A(3). For this purpose 'specified' means 'specified in an order under [s 512A]': s 512A(7).

[8]   Ibid, s 512A(4)(a) and (6), as inserted by SSFA 1998, s 116 and amended by EA 2002, s 201(2).

[9]   SI 1999/610.

1999,[1] and the Education (Transfer of Functions Concerning School Lunches etc) (England) (No 2) Order 1999.[2]

Nutritional standards

4.38   Regulations may be made under s 114(1) of the SSFA 1998 prescribing 'nutritional standards, or other nutritional requirements, which (subject to such exceptions as may be provided for by or under the regulations) are to be complied with in connection with the provision of school lunches[3] for registered pupils at schools maintained by local education authorities'.[4] Where an LEA or the governing body provide school lunches for registered pupils at such a school, it must 'secure that any applicable provisions of regulations under this section are complied with'.[5] This is so: '(a) whether the lunches are provided on school premises or at any other place where education is being provided; and (b) whether they are being provided in pursuance of any statutory requirement or otherwise'.[6]

BOARD AND LODGING OTHERWISE THAN AT SCHOOL

4.39   Section 514 of the EA 1996 empowers the provision by an LEA of board and lodging for a pupil otherwise than at school in two situations. The first is where the LEA is satisfied that (a) education suitable to the pupil's age, ability and aptitude and to any SEN he may have can best be provided for him at a particular community, foundation or voluntary or community or foundation special school, but (b) such education cannot be so provided unless boarding accommodation is provided for him otherwise than at the school.[7] The second situation is where the LEA is satisfied that the provision of board and lodging is necessary for a pupil with SEN in order to enable him to receive the required special educational provision.[8] In each case, the LEA must, so far as practicable, give effect to the wishes of the pupil's parent as to the religion or religious denomination of the person with whom the pupil will reside.[9]

4.40   An LEA must charge the parents of a pupil for whom they have provided board and lodging under s 514 such sums (not exceeding the cost to the LEA of the board and lodging) as the parents can in the opinion of the LEA pay without financial hardship, unless the LEA are of the view that education suitable to the pupil's age,

---

[1]   SI 1999/1779.

[2]   SI 1999/2164, which must be read with the Education Act 2002 (School Meals) (Consequential Amendments) (England) Regulations 2003, SI 2003/689.

[3]   'School lunch' is defined by s 114(5) to mean in relation to a pupil 'food made available for consumption by the pupil as his midday meal on a school day, whether involving a set meal or the selection of items by him or otherwise'. This is the same as the definition in s 512(6) of the EA 1996, as substituted.

[4]   The current regulations are the Education (Nutritional Standards for School Lunches) (England) Regulations 2000, SI 2000/1777 and the Education (Nutritional Standards for School Lunches) (Wales) Regulations 2001, SI 2001/1784.

[5]   SSFA 1998, s 114(2).

[6]   Ibid, s 114(3).

[7]   EA 1996, s 514(1).

[8]   Ibid, s 514(2).

[9]   Ibid, s 514(3).

ability and aptitude or SEN could not otherwise be provided for him.[1] Any such sum is recoverable summarily as a civil debt (in other words, it may be recovered in a magistrates' court under s 58 of the Magistrates' Courts Act 1980).[2]

HEALTH

4.41   Under s 520(1) of the EA 1996, an LEA is under a duty to make arrangements for 'encouraging and assisting' pupils (other than pupils whose parents give notice that they object to such encouragement or assistance[3]) at maintained schools to take advantage of the provision for them of medical and dental inspection and treatment under s 5(1) or (1A) of the National Health Service Act 1977 or para 1(a)(i) of Sch 1 to that Act.[4] LEAs must, in addition, make available appropriate accommodation for this purpose.[5]

4.42   Under s 21 of the Public Health (Control of Disease) Act 1984, if the 'proper officer'[6] of the relevant local authority gives notice to a person having care of a child that the child is or has been suffering from a notifiable disease,[7] or has been exposed to infection from such a disease, then that person must not permit the child to attend school (which includes for this purpose a Sunday or sabbath school[8]) until a certificate permitting attendance has been given by such officer. A failure by the person having care of the child to comply with this prohibition amounts to an offence.[9] Under s 22 of Public Health (Control of Disease) Act 1984, the principal[10] of a school in which any pupil is suffering from a notifiable disease must, if required to do so by the proper officer of the relevant local authority, provide a list of the names and addresses of day pupils. A failure to do so also amounts to an offence.[11]

4.43   Under s 26(3) of the National Health Service Act 1977, the Secretary of State must make available to local authorities (among other things) the use of premises and the services of (1) medical practitioners, (2) dental practitioners, (3) nurses in the health service, and (4) other staff, so far as is reasonably necessary and practicable to

---

[1]   EA 1996, s 514(4)–(6).

[2]   Ibid, s 514(7).

[3]   Ibid, s 520(2).

[4]   The restriction of the duty in s 520(1) of the LEA to pupils at maintained schools results from the terms of s 5(1) and (1A) of the 1977 Act. The services in question may be provided for junior and senior pupils at a non-maintained establishment by agreement with the proprietor, and the proprietor may be obliged by the agreement to pay for the services: 1977 Act, Sch 1, paras 1(b) and 2.

[5]   1977 Act, Sch 1, para 3. This duty is imposed by that paragraph also on the governing bodies of foundation, voluntary and foundation special schools in respect of those schools.

[6]   Defined in s 74 of that Act.

[7]   As to which, see s 10 of the 1984 Act and regulations made under s 13 of that Act, including the Public Health (Infectious Diseases) Regulations 1988, SI 1988/1546 (which specify among other things measles, meningitis, scarlet fever and whooping cough). The local authority may specify more diseases as notifiable, under s 16 of the 1984 Act.

[8]   Public Health (Control of Disease) Act 1984, s 74.

[9]   Ibid, s 21(3). The maximum penalty is a fine at level 1 on the standard scale, which is £200.

[10]   This means the person in charge of a school, but if there is no such person then it includes the head of any department: s 22(4).

[11]   Ibid, s 22(3). The maximum penalty is a fine at level 1 on the standard scale, which is £200.

enable local authorities to discharge their functions relating to education. The LEA may be required to pay for these services or facilities.[1]

CLEANLINESS

4.44　An LEA may give its medical officer[2] directions in writing authorising him to have the persons and clothing of pupils in attendance at schools maintained by the LEA examined whenever in his opinion such examination is necessary in the interests of cleanliness.[3] The directions may relate to some or all of such schools.[4] Such an examination must be made by a person authorised by the LEA for the purpose, and, if the examination is of a girl, then it must not be made by a man unless the man is a registered medical practitioner.[5]

4.45　If such an examination reveals that either the person or the clothing of the pupil is found to be 'infested with vermin or in a foul condition', then any officer of the LEA may serve a notice on the pupil's parent, requiring the parent to cause the pupil's person or clothing to be cleansed.[6] The notice must inform the parent that if the pupil's person and clothing are not by the end of the period specified in the notice (which must be not less than 24 hours) cleansed to the satisfaction of the person specified in the notice, then the cleansing will be carried out under arrangements made by the LEA.[7] If a medical officer of the LEA is not satisfied, on a report made to him by the person specified in the notice after the relevant period, that the pupil's person and clothing have been properly cleansed, then he may by order direct that they are to be cleansed under arrangements made by the LEA under s 523 of the EA 1996.[8] Such an order will empower an officer of the LEA to convey the pupil to, and detain him at, any premises provided in accordance with such arrangements, and to cause the cleansing to be carried out under the relevant arrangements.[9] District councils in England may (on such terms as may be agreed or if necessary determined by the Secretary of State) be required by the LEA to make available for the use of the latter any facilities at which the district council have the persons or clothing of persons infested with vermin cleansed.[10]

4.46　If, after cleansing under s 522, a pupil's person or clothing are as a result of neglect on the part of his parent again infested with vermin or in a foul condition

---

1　National Health Service Act 1977, s 27(4).
2　Which means 'a registered medical practitioner who is employed or engaged (whether regularly or for the purposes of any particular case) by the authority or whose services are made available to the authority by the Secretary of State': EA 1996, s 579(1).
3　EA 1996, s 521(1) and (4).
4　Ibid, s 521(2).
5　Ibid, s 521(3).
6　Ibid, s 522(1).
7　Ibid, s 522(2) and (3).
8　Ibid, s 522(4).
9　Ibid, s 522(5). A girl may only be cleansed by a woman authorised for the purpose by the LEA, or by a registered medical practitioner: s 523(4).
10　Ibid, s 523(2) and (3).

while he is in attendance at a maintained school, then the parent[1] is guilty of an offence under s 525(1), and may be fined up to a maximum of level 1 on the standard scale.[2]

CLOTHING

4.47   An LEA may provide clothing[3] (1) to any pupil who is a boarder at an educational institution maintained by it, (2) any pupil at a nursery school maintained by it, or (3) any pupil in a nursery class at a school maintained by it.[4] Further, an LEA may provide clothing to a pupil for whom it provides board and lodging elsewhere than at an educational institution maintained by it and for whom special educational provision is made under arrangements made by it.[5] An LEA may in addition provide clothing to pupils, other than the ones just mentioned, who are at a school maintained by it or at a special school (whether maintained by it or not) where it appears to the LEA that the pupil in question is unable 'by reason of the inadequacy or unsuitability of his clothing to take full advantage of the education provided at the school'.[6] The clothing must be such as in the opinion of the LEA is necessary for the purpose of ensuring that the pupil is sufficiently and suitably clad while he remains a pupil at the school.[7]

4.48   Furthermore, an LEA may make arrangements with the consent of the proprietor of a school which is not maintained by it (other than a special school), on such financial and other terms (if any) as may be agreed between it and the proprietor, for securing the provision of clothing in the same circumstances as those mentioned in s 510(3).[8] The cost to the LEA of clothing so provided must, so far as is practicable, not exceed the cost which would have been incurred by the LEA if the pupil had been a pupil at a school maintained by it.[9]

4.49   An LEA may also provide for pupils at any maintained school in its area, or at an institution maintained by it which provides further education or higher education (or both), clothing which is suitable for the physical training provided at the relevant school or institution.[10] It may also provide such clothing to persons who have not yet attained the age of 19 and who are receiving education at an institution within the

---

[1]   If a child lives with his mother and father, and the neglect is the fault of only one of them, then he or she alone may properly be convicted: *Plunkett v Alker* [1954] 1 QB 420.

[2]   Level 1 is currently £200.

[3]   Which includes footwear: EA 1996, s 579(1).

[4]   Ibid, s 510(1).

[5]   Ibid, s 510(2).

[6]   Ibid, s 510(3).

[7]   Ibid.

[8]   Ibid, s 510(5).

[9]   Ibid, s 510(6).

[10]   Ibid, s 510(4)(a).

further education sector,[1] and to persons who make use of facilities for physical training provided by the LEA under s 508(2) of the EA 1996.[2]

4.50   In all of these cases, the LEA may either confer a right of property in the clothing or a right only to use it, unless regulations prescribe otherwise.[3] The LEA must then require the parent of the pupil (unless the person is over the age of 18 and is not a registered pupil at a school, in which case the requirement will apply to the person and not his parent[4]) to whom clothing has been provided under s 510 to pay the LEA such sum (not exceeding the cost to the LEA of the provision) as he is in its opinion able without financial hardship to pay, or, alternatively, a lesser sum.[5] Such a sum is by virtue of s 511(3) recoverable summarily as a civil debt.[6]

PUBLICATION AND PROVISION OF INFORMATION

4.51   Local education authorities are now required to publish a significant amount of information, of which the following is a summary.

School admissions and other information relating to maintained schools

4.52   Section 92 of the SSFA 1998[7] empowers the making of regulations:

(a)   requiring the publication by an LEA of information relating to admissions;
(b)   requiring the publication by the governing body of a foundation or voluntary aided school of information relating to admissions;
(c)   requiring or allowing the publication (i) by the governing body of any maintained school or (ii) by the LEA on behalf of such governing body, of information relating to the school; and
(d)   making provision as to the time by which, and the manner in which, information which the section requires to be published, is to be published.

4.53   Section 408 of the EA 1996 provides that regulations may require, in relation to every maintained school, the LEA, the governing body or the head teacher, to make available (either generally or to prescribed persons) information with regard to:

(a)   the curriculum for maintained schools;
(b)   the educational provision made by the school for pupils at the school and any syllabuses to be followed by those pupils;

---

[1]   EA 1996, s 510(4)(b).
[2]   Ibid, s 510(4)(c). See para **4.64** regarding s 508(1).
[3]   Ibid, s 511(1). No regulations so prescribe: the Education (Provision of Clothing) Regulations 1980, SI 1980/545, are the only relevant regulations, and they make no relevant provision.
[4]   EA 1996, s 511(4) and reg 3(2) of SI 1980/545.
[5]   Ibid, s 511(2) and reg 3(1) of SI 1980/545.
[6]   As to which, see para **4.40**.
[7]   As substituted by EA 2002, Sch 4, para 7.

(c)   the educational achievements of the pupils at the school, including the results
        of any assessments of those pupils made for the purpose of ascertaining their
        achievements;

(d)   the educational achievements of such classes or descriptions of pupils as may
        be prescribed; and

(e)   arrangements relating to external qualifications within the meaning of s 96(5)
        of the LSA 2000,[1] and to courses leading to such qualifications.[2]

4.54   Under s 29 of the EA 1996, an LEA is obliged (among other things) to
provide reports and returns to the Secretary of State,[3] and to publish in the manner
required by regulations information of the sort required by the regulations with
respect to its policy and arrangements in respect of any matter relating to primary or
secondary education.[4]

4.55   Before the substitution of the current s 92 of the SSFA 1998, various sets of
regulations had been made under several predecessor provisions and the other
provisions mentioned in the preceding paragraphs above. These included the
Education (School Hours and Policies) (Information) Regulations 1989.[5] In relation to
England, these also included the Education (School Curriculum and Related
Information) Regulations 1989,[6] the Education (School Sessions and Charges and
Remissions Policies) (Information) (England) Regulations 1999,[7] the Education
(Special Educational Needs) (Information) (England) Regulations 1999,[8] the
Education (Information as to Provision of Education) (England) Regulations 1999,[9]
and the Special Educational Needs (Provision of Information by Local Education
Authorities) (England) Regulations 2001.[10] The Education (School Information)
(England) Regulations 2002[11] were made in part under the substituted s 92. In relation
to Wales, the regulations included the Education (Special Educational Needs)
(Information) (Wales) Regulations 1999,[12] the Education (School Information)
(Wales) Regulations 1999,[13] and the Special Educational Needs (Provision of
Information by Local Education Authorities) (Wales) Regulations 2002.[14]

---

[1]   See para **11.14** regarding s 96 of the LSA 2000.
[2]   EA 1996, s 408(1) and (2).
[3]   Ibid, s 29(1). See the Education (Information as to Provision of Education) (England) Regulations
      1999, SI 1999/1066, as amended by SI 2003/190.
[4]   Ibid, s 29(5). An LEA is not required to publish information under EA 1996, s 29(5) in relation to
      nursery schools or children who will be under compulsory school age at the time of their proposed
      admission: ibid, s 29(6).
[5]   SI 1989/398.
[6]   SI 1989/954, as amended.
[7]   SI 1999/2255.
[8]   SI 1999/2506, as amended by SI 2002/2469.
[9]   SI 1999/1066, as amended by SI 2003/190.
[10] SI 2001/2218, as amended by SI 2002/2469.
[11] SI 2002/2897, as amended by SI 2004/1076.
[12] SI 1999/1442.
[13] SI 1999/1812, as amended by SI 2001/1111, SI 2001/3710 and SI 2002/1400.
[14] SI 2002/157.

PAYMENT OF SCHOOL FEES AND EXPENSES

4.56   Local education authorities have the power in certain circumstances to: (1) defray certain school expenses; (2) pay school fees; and (3) grant various allowances to persons over compulsory school age, and a duty in other circumstances to pay school fees. The situation is complicated by the fact that certain provisions in the SSFA 1998 which have not yet been brought into force will, as described below, when they are in force, repeal and replace relevant parts of the EA 1996.

Power to pay school fees and expenses and to make certain allowances

4.57   An LEA's power to pay school fees and expenses is derived from s 518 of the EA 1996, as substituted by s 129 of the SSFA 1998.[1] Section 518 now provides:

'(1)   A local education authority, for the purpose of enabling persons to take advantage of any educational facilities available to them, may in such circumstances as may be specified in or determined in accordance with regulations –

 (a)   pay such expenses of children attending community, foundation, voluntary or special schools as may be necessary to enable them to take part in any school activities,

 (b)   grant scholarships, exhibitions, bursaries and other allowances in respect of persons over compulsory school age.

(2)   Regulations may make provision –

 (a)   for requiring a local education authority to make, in relation to each financial year, a determination relating to the extent to which they propose to exercise their power under subsection (1)(b) in that year; and

 (b)   for authorising an authority to determine not to exercise that power in a financial year –

   (i)   generally,

   (ii)   in such cases as may be prescribed, or

   (iii)   in such cases as may be determined by the authority.'

4.58   It is of note that the power to determine not to exercise the power to make grants under regulations made under the section, was new. The current regulations made under s 518(1)(a) are the Local Education Authority (Payment of School Expenses) Regulations 1999,[2] and the Education Maintenance Allowance (Pilot Areas) Regulations 2001.[3] The current regulations made under s 518(1)(b) are the Local Education Authority (Post-Compulsory Education Awards) Regulations 1999,[4] and, in

---

[1]   The Scholarships and Other Benefits Regulations 1977, SI 1977/1443, made under the predecessor to s 518, remain in force for certain purposes: see Art 3 of SI 1999/120.

[2]   SI 1999/1727. Note that reg 4(a) of the Scholarship and Other Benefits Regulations 1977, SI 1977/1443, nevertheless (see reg 3 of SI 1999/1727) continued to apply 'in connection with: (a) the payment of expenses; or (b) a decision to pay expenses, under that provision in relation to educational facilities made available before 1st September 1999'. Presumably those conditions were satisfied in the circumstances which were under consideration in *R (Southern) v Oxfordshire County Council* (2004) *The Times*, March 3.

[3]   SI 2001/2750, as amended by SI 2002/1841 and 2003/553, and revoked with effect from 1 September 2004 by SI 2004/1006.

[4]   SI 1999/229.

relation to Wales, the Local Education Authority (Post-Compulsory Education Awards) (Wales) Regulations 2002.[1]

Duty to pay school and related fees

Section 517 of the Education Act 1996

4.59   Section 517(1) of the EA 1996[2] obliges an LEA to pay school and related fees in certain circumstances.[3] There are two (alternative) primary conditions for the duty to arise (set out in s 517(1)), and several secondary ones. The primary conditions are that the LEA has made arrangements either under s 18 of the EA 1996[4] or under Part IV of the EA 1996 (concerning SEN)[5] for the provision of primary or secondary education for a pupil at a school which is not maintained by an LEA. The secondary conditions are contained in s 517(2), (3) and (5).

4.60   Section 517(2) applies where the pupil fills a place in a school which the proprietor of the school has put at the disposal of the LEA and the school is in receipt of grants made by the Secretary of State under s 485 of the EA 1996.[6] Section 517(3) applies where an LEA is satisfied that, because of a shortage of places in every maintained school to which a pupil could be sent with reasonable convenience, education which is suitable to his age, ability, aptitude and to any SEN which he may have cannot be provided for him except at a school which is not maintained by an LEA.[7] In both of these cases, the LEA must in the circumstances where s 517(1) applies, pay the whole of the fees for the education provided under the relevant arrangements.[8]

4.61   Section 517(5) (as amended by s 517(6) as from 1 September 1997) applies where s 348(2) does not apply,[9] and the LEA is satisfied that education which is suitable to a pupil's age, ability, aptitude and to any SEN which he may have cannot be provided for him at any school unless board and lodging are also provided for him (whether at school or elsewhere). In that situation, where the circumstances referred to in s 517(1) exist, the LEA is under a duty to pay the whole of the fees payable in respect of the pupil's board and lodging.[10]

---

[1] SI 2002/1856.

[2] As amended by SI 1999/2260 from 1 September 1999 until the repeal of s 517, regarding which, see below.

[3] Section 517 applies in circumstances in which s 348 would, if it were in force, also apply. It was accordingly provided by s 517(6)(d) and (e) as originally enacted that, once s 348 was brought into force, s 517 would cease to apply to those circumstances. Section 348 was brought into force on 1 September 1997 by SI 1997/1623.

[4] As to which, see paras **2.46–2.48**.

[5] As to which, see Chapter 6.

[6] As to which, see para **3.58**.

[7] The predecessor to s 517(3) was s 6(2)(a)(ii) of the Education (Miscellaneous Provisions) Act 1953, in connection with which the decision in *Watt v Kesteven County Council* [1955] 1 QB 408 (as to which see paras **2.119–2.121**) should be noted.

[8] EA 1996, s 517(1)(a).

[9] Ibid, s 517(7), as substituted by s 517(6) by virtue of Art 3 of SI 1997/1623 and amended by SI 1999/2260. See para **4.63** regarding s 348.

[10] Ibid, s 517(1)(b).

Repeal of section 517 of the Education Act 1996

4.62 Section 517 of the EA 1996 will be repealed by the SSFA 1998.[1] Once that has occurred and places originally made available under the assisted places scheme[2] no longer need to be funded, LEAs will be under a duty to pay fees for children attending non-maintained schools only where s 348 of the EA 1996 applies. Their only power to pay such fees (as opposed to expenses) will reside in s 18 of the EA 1996, as substituted by s 128 of the SSFA 1998.[3]

Section 348 of the Education Act 1996

4.63 Section 348 of the EA 1996 was brought into force on 1 September 1997.[4] It is self-explanatory, and provides as follows.

   '(1)   This section applies where –
        (a)   special educational provision in respect of a child with special educational needs is made at a school which is not a maintained school,[5] and
        (b)   either the name of the school is specified in a statement in respect of a child under section 324 or the local education authority are satisfied –
           (i)   that his interests require the necessary special educational provision to be made for him at a school which is not a maintained school, and
           (ii)   that it is appropriate for the child to be provided with education at the particular school.
   (2)   Where this section applies, the local education authority shall pay the whole of the fees payable in respect of the education provided for the child at the school, and if –
        (a)   board and lodging are provided for him at the school, and
        (b)   the authority are satisfied that the necessary special educational provision cannot be provided for him at the school unless the board and lodging are also so provided,
the authority shall pay the whole of the fees payable in respect of the board and lodging.'

THE YOUTH SERVICE; RECREATION AND SOCIAL AND PHYSICAL TRAINING

4.64 There is no specific reference in the Education Acts to a 'youth service'. What LEAs do in connection with what is known as the youth service is in the main authorised by s 508 of the EA 1996, the successor to s 53 of the EA 1944, albeit that it has now been amended by the LSA 2000. Section 508(1) places LEAs under a duty to 'secure that the facilities for primary and secondary education provided for their area include adequate facilities for recreation and social and physical training'. Section 508(1A), as inserted by the LSA 2000, empowers the provision by an LEA of 'facilities for recreation and social and physical training as part of the facilities for further education provided (whether or not by them) for their area'. Section 508(2)

---

1   SSFA 1998, Sch 30, para 138.
2   See para **13.30** regarding the assisted places scheme.
3   Regarding which, see paras **2.47–2.48**.
4   SI 1997/1623.
5   That is, a school which is maintained by an LEA: s 348(3) as substituted by SSFA 1998, Sch 30, paras 57 and 84.

provides that for both such purposes an LEA may establish, maintain and manage, or assist the establishment, maintenance and management of, camps, holiday classes, playing fields, play centres, and other places (including playgrounds, gymnasiums and swimming baths not appropriated to any school or other educational institution) at which facilities for recreation and social and physical training are available for persons receiving primary, secondary or further education. They may also under s 508(2) organise games, expeditions and other activities for such persons, and defray or contribute towards the expenses of such games, expeditions and other activities.[1]

4.65   As is implicit in this, it is open to an LEA to co-operate with other organisations in regard to its functions under s 508(1)–(2). Section 508(3) indeed explicitly provides that when making arrangements for the provision of facilities or the organisation of activities in the exercise of their powers under s 508(2), an LEA must, in particular, have regard to the expediency of co-operating with any voluntary societies or bodies whose objects include the provision of facilities or the organisation of activities of a similar nature.

4.66   Problems can occur in this context when an LEA seeks to co-operate with a voluntary organisation by allocating funds to the organisation to spend in consultation with (for example) an officer of the LEA. Such an allocation could amount to an outright gift of the funds to the organisation (which in all probability will be a charity,[2] but may not be). It could, however, amount in the alternative to an unlawful delegation of power (s 101 of the Local Government Act 1972 not authorising such a delegation).[3] The solution is to make it clear to all concerned that a gift is occurring, if that is what is desired, and to make it clear that if no gift is occurring, then the power to determine how the money is to be spent is to remain in the hands of the LEA.

4.67   There are two matters relating to youth and community workers to which reference can usefully be made here. The first is that, as noted above,[4] under the Education (Grant) Regulations 1990,[5] the Secretary of State may make grants in respect of the training of youth leaders and community centre wardens.[6] The second relevant matter is that the Education (Prohibition from Teaching or Working with Children) Regulations 2003[7] apply to youth and community workers employed by LEAs or by others at schools or further education institutions.[8]

---

1   The Secretary of State's power to make grants to persons other than local education authorities in respect of vocational, social, physical and recreational training, under reg 12 of the Education (Grant) Regulations 1990, SI 1990/1989 (as amended), has already been noted, at para **3.58**.
2   As for the meaning of which, see paras **7.201–7.202**.
3   This is on the assumption that it is correct to say that delegating to a voluntary organisation the power to spend LEA money goes further than merely co-operating with such an organisation under s 508(3).
4   See para **3.58**.
5   SI 1990/1989 (as amended).
6   Ibid, reg 13.
7   SI 2003/1184.
8   This is because those regulations apply to the Secretary of State's powers under s 142 of the EA 2002 (regarding which, see paras **15.36** et seq), and since such workers are clearly covered by s 142.

REGULATION OF THE EMPLOYMENT OF CHILDREN

4.68   Section 559(1) of the EA 1996 empowers an LEA, if it appears to them that a child[1] who is a registered pupil at a community, foundation, voluntary or special school or a pupil referral unit[2] (but not an independent school) is being employed in such a manner as to be prejudicial to his health, or otherwise to render him unfit to obtain the full benefit of the education provided for him, to serve a notice in writing on his employer. The notice may either prohibit the employer from employing the child or impose restrictions on the employment of the child. The LEA may also serve a notice on the parent or employer of a child who is a registered pupil at a community, foundation, voluntary or special school or a pupil referral unit[3] requiring the parent or employer to provide the LEA with such information as appears to it to be necessary to enable it to ascertain whether the child is being employed in such a manner as to render him unfit to obtain the full benefit of the education provided for him.[4]

4.69   It is an offence to fail to comply with either such kind of notice,[5] the penalty for which is either a fine up to a maximum of level 1 on the standard scale,[6] or a maximum of one month's imprisonment, or both.[7] However, before convicting, the magistrates' court must be satisfied that the LEA in question was 'reasonably satisfied by a report of the medical officer or other evidence that the child is being employed in a manner prejudicial to his health or otherwise [to render him unfit to obtain the full benefit of the education provided for him]'.[8] When s 2 of the Employment of Children Act 1973 is brought into force, s 559 of the EA 1996 will cease to have effect.[9]

4.70   Other functions with regard to LEAs and the employment of children need to be mentioned here. The restrictions contained in s 18 of the Children and Young Persons Act 1933 (as amended) may be modified by byelaws made by the LEA.[10] The byelaws may enable children under the age of 14 but of at least 13 years to be employed on an occasional basis by their parents or guardians in light agricultural or horticultural work and by any employer for not more than one hour before school begins.[11] Further, the performance of children in various kinds of entertainment is normally prohibited by s 37(1) of the Children and Young Persons Act 1963 (as

---

[1]   Who is not over compulsory school age: EA 1996, s 558.
[2]   Education (Pupil Referral Units) (Application of Enactments) Regulations 1994, SI 1994/2103, reg 2, Sch 1, para 1.
[3]   Education (Pupil Referral Units) (Application of Enactments) Regulations 1994, SI 1994/2103, reg 2, Sch 1, para 1.
[4]   EA 1996, s 559(2).
[5]   Ibid, s 559(3).
[6]   £200.
[7]   EA 1996, s 559(4).
[8]   *Margerison v Hind* [1922] 1 KB 214, at 220.
[9]   EA 1996, s 559(6). Section 2 of the 1973 Act apparently may never be brought into force.
[10]   Children and Young Persons Act 1933, s 18(2). As for the local authority for this purpose, see ss 96 and 97 of the 1933 Act. The 1933 Act was amended by SI 1998/276 in order to implement the 1994 Community Directive on the protection of young people at work (94/33/EC), by SI 2000/1333 and by SI 2000/2548.
[11]   Ibid, s 18(2), as amended.

amended) unless a licence for the purpose is granted by the LEA.[1] The LEA can only grant such a licence if it is satisfied with regard to the child's fitness to do what it is allowing him to do, that the child's health and kind treatment will be secured, and that his education will not suffer; but if they are so satisfied, then they must grant the licence.[2] The licences must comply with the Children (Performances) Regulations 1968,[3] which include requirements with regard to the child's education. Under s 38 of the 1963 Act, there are some specific restrictions with regard to the granting of licences for performances by children aged under 14. Furthermore, children who are not over compulsory school age are prohibited from taking part in performances which endanger life or limb,[4] and there are restrictions on training for performances of a dangerous nature.[5] Powers of entry in relation to the enforcement of these provisions are contained in s 28(1) and (3) of the Children and Young Persons Act 1933, and they apply in part also to the provisions of s 559 of the EA 1996.[6]

Work experience under section 560 of the Education Act 1996

4.71   As a result of s 560 of the EA 1996,[7] work experience pursuant to arrangements made by (1) an LEA, or (2) the governing body of a school on behalf of an LEA, for children in the last 2 years of their compulsory schooling with a view to providing them with such experience as part of their education, is not affected by these (or any other relevant) prohibitions.[8] The last 2 years of a child's compulsory schooling are taken for this purpose to begin at the beginning of the last 2 school years at his school during the whole or part of which he is of compulsory school age.

4.72   However, s 560(1) does not permit a person to be employed in any way contrary to an enactment (which for the purposes of s 560 includes a byelaw, regulation or any other provision having effect under an enactment[9]) which in terms applies to persons of less than, or not over, a specified age expressed as a number of years.[10] Section 560(1) also does not permit a person to be employed in any way contrary to s 1(2) of the Employment of Women, Young Persons and Children Act 1920 or s 55(1) of the Merchant Shipping Act 1995 (which prohibit the employment of children on ships).[11] Furthermore, the arrangements made under s 560(1) must not allow a child to be employed in a manner which would contravene any enactment

---

1   The exceptions are that the child has not performed on more than 3 days over the preceding period of 6 months, or that the performance is given under arrangements made by a school or body approved by the Secretary of State or the LEA in whose area the performance takes place, and (in both cases) no payments are made in respect of the child's taking part in the performance except for defraying expenses: s 37(3), as amended by SI 1998/276.
2   Children and Young Persons Act 1963, s 37(4), as amended by SI 1998/276.
3   SI 1968/1728, as amended by SI 1998/1678.
4   Children and Young Persons Act 1933, s 23 (as amended).
5   See s 24 of the 1933 Act and s 41 of the 1963 Act (as amended).
6   EA 1996, s 559(5).
7   As amended by the SSFA 1998.
8   EA 1996, s 560(1).
9   Ibid, s 560(7).
10   Ibid, s 560(3)(a).
11   Ibid, s 560(3)(b).

prohibiting or regulating the employment of young persons if the child were a young person (within the meaning of the relevant enactment), and not a child.[1]

EDUCATIONAL RESEARCH AND CONFERENCES

4.73 Under s 526 of the EA 1996, an LEA may conduct, or assist the conduct of, such research as appears to it to be desirable for the purpose of improving the educational facilities provided for its area. Under s 527, an LEA may organise or participate in the organisation of conferences for the discussion of questions relating to education, and may spend reasonable sums in paying or contributing towards any expenditure incurred in connection with such conferences (including expenses incurred by any person authorised by it to attend such a conference).

MAKING AND PUBLICATION OF PLANS RELATING TO CHILDREN WITH BEHAVIOURAL DIFFICULTIES

4.74 Under s 527A of the EA 1996,[2] an LEA is required to prepare, and from time to time to review, a statement setting out, in accordance with the provisions of s 527A, the arrangements made or proposed to be made by the LEA in connection with the education of children with behavioural difficulties. The statement must set out the arrangements made or to be made by the LEA for the provision of advice and resources to schools maintained by the LEA, and other arrangements made or to be made by them, with a view to doing two things.[3] Those are (i) 'meeting requests by such schools for support and assistance in connection with the promotion of good behaviour and discipline on the part of their pupils', and (ii) 'assisting such schools to deal with general behavioural problems and the behavioural difficulties of individual pupils'.[4] The statement must also set out the arrangements made or to be made by the LEA in pursuance of s 19(1) of the EA 1996,[5] and any other arrangements made or to be made by them for assisting children with behavioural difficulties to find places at suitable schools.[6] In addition, the statement must deal with the interaction between such arrangements and those made by the LEA in relation to pupils with behavioural difficulties who have SEN.[7] Section 527A(4) requires the LEA to carry out 'such consultation as may be prescribed', and s 527A(5) requires the LEA to publish, revise and provide copies of any statement or revised statement made under s 527A in 'such manner ... as may be prescribed'. The relevant regulations for both purposes are the Local Education Authority (Behaviour Support Plans) Regulations 1998.[8] In

---

1   EA 1996, s 560(4) and (5).
2   Ibid, s 527A was inserted by s 9 of the EA 1997.
3   Ibid, s 527A(2)(a) and (7).
4   Ibid, s 527A(2)(a).
5   See paras **4.2** et seq regarding s 19(1).
6   EA 1996, s 527A(2)(b) and (c).
7   Ibid, s 527A(3).
8   SI 1998/644, as amended in relation to Wales by SI 2001/606 and in relation to England by SI 2001/828; see also SI 2003/3082 in relation to England, excepting certain authorities from reg 5(3)(b) of SI 1998/644.

discharging their functions under s 527A, an LEA must 'have regard to any guidance given from time to time by the Secretary of State'.[1]

THE SUPPLY OF GOODS AND SERVICES

4.75   Local authorities' powers to supply goods and services are conferred mainly by the provisions of the Local Authorities (Goods and Services) Act 1970. In addition, however, s 318 of the EA 1996 confers several powers to supply goods and services in connection with the provision of education. Its co-existence with the 1970 Act could be regarded as problematic, but for the reasons set out below it need not be so regarded.

Section 318 of the Education Act 1996

4.76   Section 318(1)[2] provides that an LEA:

'may, for the purpose only of assisting
(a)   the governing bodies of community, foundation or voluntary schools or maintained nursery schools (in their or any other area) in the performance of the governing bodies' duties under section 317(1)(a),[3] or
(b)   the governing bodies of community or foundation special schools or maintained nursery schools (in their or any other area) in the performance of the governing bodies' duties,
supply goods or services to those bodies.'

4.77   Section 318(3) and (3A) (as inserted by the SSFA 1998) empower the supply by an LEA of goods and services to 'any authority or other person (other than a governing body within subsection (1)) for the purpose only of assisting them in making for any child [who is receiving publicly-funded nursery education as stated in s 318(3A)] any special educational provision which any learning difficulty of the child calls for'. Section 318(4) provides that s 318 is 'without prejudice to the generality of any other power of local education authorities to supply goods or services'. Section 318(2) allows an LEA to charge for the supply in question in accordance with regulations.[4]

4.78   The difficulty caused by s 318 is probably not in practice likely to be significant, and it is mentioned here only for the sake of completeness. The difficulty is that s 318(1) refers to the supply by an LEA of goods and services to the governing bodies of maintained schools in its area. This in turn implies that there is a need to make specific legislative provision for the supply by an LEA of goods and services to the governing bodies of schools maintained by it. However, in the past it had not been thought necessary to make such provision, and it appears that it was not

---

[1]   EA 1996, s 527A(6). See paras **2.34–2.36** as to the impact of a requirement to 'have regard' to such guidance.

[2]   As amended by EA 2002, Sch 21, para 41. Section 318 is applied to pupil referral units by EA 1996, Sch 1, para 13.

[3]   As to which, see para **6.24**.

[4]   See the Education (Payment for Special Educational Needs Supplies) Regulations 1999, SI 1999/710.

questioned that an LEA had the power to supply goods and services to a school which it maintained. It seems simply to have been accepted that it could do so pursuant to its duty to maintain the school,[1] presumably under s 111(1) of the Local Government Act 1972.[2] Apparently, as a result, what were county and controlled schools (now community and voluntary controlled schools) were never designated as public bodies to which an LEA could supply goods and services under the Local Authorities (Goods and Services) Act 1970.[3] Accordingly, the enactment of the provision which s 318(1) replaced (s 162(1) of the Education Act 1993) might be regarded by a court as having made doubtful the lawfulness of the supply by an LEA of goods and services to community and voluntary controlled schools except under s 318(1). It is suggested here that this may simply have been an oversight, and that s 318(4) should in any event be regarded as preserving the existing power to rely upon s 111(1) of the 1972 Act in relation to the supply of goods and services to what are now community and voluntary controlled schools.[4]

THE PAYMENT OF ALLOWANCES FOR GOVERNORS

4.79   Section 519(1) of the EA 1996 (as amended) empowers LEAs to pay such allowances as may be prescribed (and no other kind of allowance[5]) to governors of any community, foundation or voluntary school or community or foundation special school which does not have a delegated budget within the meaning of Part II of the SSFA 1998[6] and to governors of any institution maintained by an LEA which provides higher education or further education (or both). However, the power exists only once the LEA has made a scheme under s 519(1) for the purpose.[7] Such a scheme may make different provision for different categories of governors, but not so that the governors of a particular school or institution may be treated differently.[8] If a scheme has been made under s 519(1), then the LEA (subject to exceptions) may pay travelling and subsistence allowances to any person appointed by them to represent them on the governing body of any institution providing higher education or further education (or both) which is not maintained by them, or on the governing body of an

---

[1]   That duty is now to be found in SSFA 1998, s 22, regarding the relevant aspect of which, see paras **7.8**, **7.9**, **7.12**, **7.14** and **7.16**.

[2]   Section 111(1) empowers a local authority to do anything which is 'calculated to facilitate, or is conducive or incidental to, the discharge of any of their functions'.

[3]   The governing bodies of aided and special agreement schools were so designated, under SI 1975/193, presumably so that local authorities could supply goods and services to them when the governing bodies were acting pursuant to their duty to maintain their school buildings under s 15(3) of the 1944 Act and (subsequently) s 59(3) of the EA 1996, and in relation to their functions as employer of (at least some of) their staff.

[4]   *R v Yorkshire Purchasing Organisation, ex parte British Educational Suppliers Ltd* [1998] ELR 195, at 202D–E provides strong support for this view, albeit that that passage was addressed to a different argument from that envisaged in the text to this note.

[5]   EA 1996, s 519(6).

[6]   The governing body in that situation has the power to pay travelling and subsistence allowances to governors under regulations made under SSFA 1998, Sch 11, para 6. The current regulations are the Education (Governors' Allowances) Regulations 1999, SI 1999/703 and the Education (Governors' Allowances) (England) Regulations 2003, SI 2003/523.

[7]   EA 1996, s 519(5) and (6).

[8]   Ibid, s 519(2).

independent school or a special school which is not maintained by them.[1] The exceptions are that no allowances may be made if (1) the person in question is entitled to reimbursement of the relevant expenses from some other person,[2] or (2) the arrangements under which the expenses are to be paid allow for more generous allowances than the most generous payable under any scheme made by the LEA under s 519(1),[3] or contain any provision which the LEA would not have power to include in such a scheme.[4]

1   EA 1996, s 519(3).
2   Ibid, s 519(4).
3   Ibid, s 519(5)(a).
4   Ibid, s 519(5)(b).

Chapter 5

SCHOOL ATTENDANCE

INTRODUCTION

5.1   A parent is under a duty as a result of s 7 of the EA 1996 to cause his child to receive 'efficient full-time education suitable ... to his age, ability, and aptitude, and ... to any special educational needs he may have, either by regular attendance at school or otherwise' while the child is of compulsory school age. This duty is now enforced by LEAs under provisions in the EA 1996 relating to school attendance orders and prosecutions for failures to ensure the regular attendance at school of registered pupils. The duty is enforced in England also by fixed penalty notices (to be used instead of such a prosecution, unless the penalty is not paid) and parenting contracts, both of which measures were introduced by the Anti-social Behaviour Act 2003. The duty in s 7 may in addition be enforced by means of education supervision orders under s 36 of the CA 1989.

PARENTAL DUTY TO SECURE EDUCATION UNDER SECTION 7 OF THE EDUCATION ACT 1996

5.2   Section 7 of the EA 1996 provides:

> 'The parent of every child of compulsory school age shall cause him to receive efficient full-time education suitable –
> (a) to his age, ability, and aptitude, and
> (b) to any special educational needs he may have,
> either by regular attendance at school or otherwise.'

This seemingly simple provision requires careful analysis.

Parent

5.3   The definition of 'parent' is now contained in s 576 of the EA 1996, and is as follows:

> '(1)   In this Act, unless the context otherwise requires, "parent", in relation to a child or young person, includes any person –
> (a)   who is not a parent of his but has parental responsibility for him, or
> (b)   who has care of him,
> except that in section 499(8)[1] it only includes such a person if he is an individual
> ...

---

[1]   See paras **2.87–2.88** regarding s 499.

(3)   In subsection (1) "parental responsibility" has the same meaning as in the Children Act 1989.

(4)   In determining for the purposes of subsection (1) whether an individual has care of a child or young person, any absence of the child or young person at a hospital or boarding school and any other temporary absence shall be disregarded.'

5.4   One question which may need answering is whether this definition includes the father of an illegitimate child where the father does not have parental responsibility within the meaning of that term as used in the CA 1989.[1] However, it seems clear that the natural father of an illegitimate child *is* within the definition of parent in s 576 whether or not he has parental responsibility within the meaning of the CA 1989. This is because if the opposite had been meant by Parliament, then the words 'is not a parent of his but' in s 576(1)(a) would have been otiose.[2]

5.5   It is suggested here that if an intractable dispute between the parents of a pupil arises in relation to the proposed exercise by one parent of any relevant power under the Education Acts (whether or not the child is illegitimate, and, if the child is illegitimate, whether or not the father has acquired parental responsibility under s 4 of the CA 1989), then that is a problem which would be likely to be determined most satisfactorily by the making of an application to a court for a 'specific issue order' under ss 8 and 10 of the CA 1989.[3]

5.6   That there can be more than one type of person coming within the definition of 'parent' at the same time was confirmed by Laws J in *Fairpo v Humberside County Council*,[4] where he held that a local authority foster parent came within the definition in what is now s 576 of the EA 1996. Further, it was submitted to him that the potential for conflict between 'parents' within the meaning of s 576(1) meant that the definition should be construed restrictively.[5] He rejected that submission.[6]

---

[1]   'Parental responsibility' is defined in s 3 of the CA 1989. Such responsibility is given only to the natural mother of a child where she and the child's father were not married at birth: s 4(1) of that Act. Such a father may acquire parental responsibility either by means of a court order, for which he must apply, or by means of an agreement for the purpose with the child's mother: s 4(1). If a court makes a residence order in favour of the father of a child in relation to whom the father does not have parental responsibility, then the court must also make an order under s 4 giving him parental responsibility: s 12(1) of the 1989 Act. If the court makes a residence order in favour of any person who is not the parent or guardian of a child, then that person has parental responsibility for the child while the order remains in force: s 12(2).

[2]   It is noted in addition that in some cases there may be difficulty in determining whether or not a particular person is a natural parent (for example because a child may have been born as a result of artificial insemination), as noted by C Piper in *Parental Responsibility and the Education Acts* [1994] Fam Law 146, and as discussed by G Douglas and NV Lowe in *Becoming a Parent in English Law* (1992) 102 LQR 414.

[3]   This is what occurred in *A (Children) (Specific Issue Order: Parental Dispute)* [2001] 1 FLR 121, [2001] 1 FCR 210, [2001] Fam Law 22, CA.

[4]   [1997] 1 All ER 183, [1997] ELR 12.

[5]   [1997] ELR 17E–G.

[6]   Ibid, at 18E, 20C and 21B.

Child

5.7   The definition of a 'child' for the purposes of the EA 1996 is contained in s 579(1) of that Act, and is 'a person who is not over compulsory school age'. This adds nothing to the meaning of s 7 of the EA 1996, but it leads on to a consideration of the meaning of the phrase 'compulsory school age' in this context.

Compulsory school age in this context

5.8   The definition of 'compulsory school age' is contained in s 8 of the EA 1996.[1] However, both the beginning and the ending of a child's being of compulsory school age may not coincide with the beginning and ending of school terms. Accordingly, as one might expect, provision has been made to cater for this. As far as the commencement of a term is concerned, in the case of maintained schools, subject to two exceptions there is no obligation on the proprietor of a school to admit a child as a registered pupil[2] except at the beginning of a school term.[3] The exceptions are that the child was prevented from entering a school at the beginning of a term:

> '(a) by his being ill or by other circumstances beyond his parent's control, or
> (b) by his parent's having been then resident at a place from which the school was not accessible with reasonable facility.'[4]

5.9   In any event, LEAs may give to the governing bodies of schools maintained by them general directions with regard to the time of admission of children as pupils, and the governing bodies must comply with such directions unless the circumstances in either s 433(2)(a) or (b) exist.[5] A parent will not be in breach of s 7 of the EA 1996 where he fails to send his child to a school between the child's fifth birthday and the beginning of the following term or, if appropriate, such different date as contained in a relevant direction made by the LEA, if as a result of s 433(1)–(3) of that Act, it was not practicable for him to arrange for the child to be admitted as a pupil at a school.[6]

---

[1]   Regarding which, see paras **2.40** and **2.41**.

[2]   The definition of 'registered pupil' for the purposes of the EA 1996 is contained in s 434(5) of that Act, and is 'a person registered as a pupil at the school in the register kept under this section'. Section 434(1) requires the keeping by the proprietor of a school of a register 'in accordance with regulations, ... containing the prescribed particulars in respect of all persons who are pupils at the school'. The current regulations are the Education (Pupil Registration) Regulations 1995, SI 1995/2089, as amended by SI 1997/2624 and reg 8 of SI 1999/2267, and, in relation to England, by SI 2001/2802, and, in relation to Wales, by SI 2001/1109. The definition of 'pupil' for this purpose is contained in s 3(1) of the EA 1996.

[3]   EA 1996, s 433(1). There is no definition of a school term, but see para **7.157** regarding the determination of the beginning and end of a school term. The word 'proprietor' is defined by s 579(1) of the EA 1996 to mean 'the person or body of persons responsible for the management of the school (so that, in relation to a community, foundation or voluntary or community or foundation special school, it means the governing body)'.

[4]   EA 1996, s 433(2).

[5]   Ibid, s 433(3).

[6]   Ibid, s 433(5).

Regular attendance at school

5.10   Regular attendance at school does not include attendance at school after the time prescribed for the school.[1] Nor does it include attendance at school in breach of the school's disciplinary requirements.[2] There is a tension between this line of authority and the current statutory regime concerning exclusions from maintained schools (concerning which, see Chapter 10), in that it could be said that a refusal to admit a pupil who is in breach of the school's disciplinary requirements amounts to an exclusion. However, the best view appears to be that a refusal to admit a child who is, to the knowledge of the child's parent, in breach of a school's rules will not amount to an exclusion for the purposes of that regime. Further difficulty arises, however, if the breach of the rule is not immediately obvious and is discovered only after the child has been admitted to the school for a period of time, and the child is then sent home (presumably into the care of an appropriate person if the pupil would normally be met at the school gate). Nevertheless, given that the breach of the rule will have resulted from conduct of the parent which occurred before the pupil went to school on that day, it would be credible to argue that there is no justification for regarding the situation as involving an exclusion. The approach of Bennett J in R *(Begum)* v *Headteacher and Governors of Denbigh High School*[3] is consistent with the analysis in this paragraph.

Full-time education

5.11   There is no definition in the Education Acts of 'full-time' education for this purpose, but it is noted that the Education (Schools and Further Education) Regulations 1981[4] used to provide that pupils in classes for children under the age of 8 years had to receive at least 3 hours of secular instruction, and that classes for pupils over the age of 8 years had to receive a minimum of 4 such hours of instruction.[5]

Efficient education

5.12   In practice, the question whether the education provided for a child has been efficient (within the meaning of s 7 of the EA 1996) has arisen only when the education has been provided otherwise than at school, usually when parents have provided the education themselves. The meaning of 'efficient education' is accordingly considered below, where school attendance orders are considered.[6]

---

[1]   *Hinchley v Rankin* [1961] 1 WLR 421.

[2]   *Spiers v Warrington Corporation* [1954] 1 QB 61. In that case, a father persistently sent his daughter to school in trousers in the circumstances that there was no medical reason to do so and that it was against the school's rules for girls to wear trousers. It seems likely that the same decision on the same facts could now be reached, despite the application of the Sex Discrimination Act 1975 to schools (as to which generally, see further Chapter 18); cf *Smith v Safeway plc* [1996] ICR 868.

[3]   [2004] EWHC 1389 (Admin), (2004) *The Times*, June 18.

[4]   SI 1981/1086.

[5]   The regulations were amended in this regard by the Education (Schools and Further Education) (Amendment) Regulations 1990, SI 1990/2259.

[6]   See paras **5.16–5.18** regarding efficient education otherwise than at school.

5.13 The enforcement mechanism for a failure to comply with s 7 of the EA 1996 will in most cases be the service of a school attendance order[1] and, if necessary, proceedings to enforce that order,[2] or proceedings for failing to ensure that a child who is registered as a pupil at a school attends regularly at the school.[3]

SCHOOL ATTENDANCE ORDERS

5.14 Section 437(1) of the EA 1996 provides that:

'If it appears to a local education authority that a child of compulsory school age in their area is not receiving suitable education, either by regular attendance at school or otherwise, they shall serve a notice in writing on the parent requiring him to satisfy them within the period specified in the notice that the child is receiving such education.'[4]

5.15 In theory, the question whether the education provided for a child is 'efficient' could arise in relation to the school at which the child is registered as a pupil, but in practice the action taken against such a school would be taken either under s 165 of the EA 2002[5] or under ss 14–19 of the SSFA 1998.[6] In practice, the question whether education is efficient arises where the parents of a child are educating the child otherwise than at school.

Efficient education otherwise than at school

5.16 In order to determine whether education provided by a parent otherwise than at school is efficient, reference may be made to the standard of achievement attained by pupils who are of the same age as that of the relevant child and who are educated at a maintained school.[7] However, the best view is that such evidence is not conclusive. This is the result of *Bevan v Shears*.[8] It should be noted that in *Osborne v Martin*,[9] Avery J said: 'I think that "efficient instruction in some other manner" means efficient instruction in the curriculum approved for elementary schools' (which, in the context, meant schools at which children could be required to attend). *Bevan*, however, was not cited to the court in *Osborne*. In any event, *Osborne* can be distinguished from the other cases concerning what amounts to efficient education otherwise than at school, since the parent in that case withdrew his child from school on only one day a week, and for part only of that day. He did so because that was the only day when he could obtain for his daughter the services of a music teacher (the area in which he lived being at that time relatively remote). He had, indeed, tried but failed to obtain music lessons for her outside school hours. The principle for which the case is an

---

[1] Under s 437 of the EA 1996, as to which, see paras **5.14** et seq.
[2] Under s 443 of the EA 1996; see paras **5.29** and **5.50–5.53**.
[3] Under s 444 of the EA 1996; see paras **5.30–5.53**.
[4] 'Suitable education' for this purpose means 'efficient full-time education suitable to his age, ability and aptitude and to any special educational needs he may have': s 437(8). This definition is the same as that in s 19 of the EA 1996, and is consistent with the terms of s 7 of that Act.
[5] As to which, see para **13.14**.
[6] As to which, see paras **12.33** et seq.
[7] *R v Walton and Other Justices, ex parte Dutton* (1911) 75 JP 558.
[8] [1911] 2 KB 936.
[9] (1927) 91 JP 197.

authority is accordingly as indicated by the judgment of Salter J, who said: 'A parent is not obliged to avail himself of the free education provided by the State, if he prefers to provide privately for his child's education; but if he does avail himself of it, he must take it as a whole'. The words of Avery J set out above were accordingly obiter.

5.17 Nevertheless, it seems clear that there must be some sort of systematic full-time study.[1] Further, although 'as a general rule', an LEA should not insist on inspection as the only method of satisfying itself that children are receiving an efficient full-time education,[2] a parent must in some circumstances allow the LEA to inspect the relevant educational provision.[3] However, before determining that a parent is failing to provide efficient education otherwise than at school, the local authority is under a duty to 'make it clear [to the parent] in relation to what matters it requires to be satisfied'.[4] Furthermore, the LEA may 'in some special circumstances ... [be under a duty to] draw specific matters to the [parent's] attention and invite further information or comment'.[5] However, there is no general duty following a home visit to 'bring to the attention of the parents all the specific matters or impressions which [point] towards the conclusion that the child [is] not receiving education of the nature required'.[6]

5.18 It is suggested here that a parent would not need to follow the National Curriculum when educating his child otherwise than at school, although no doubt it would be relevant to the question whether the education was efficient. This is because independent schools are not obliged to follow the National Curriculum, and because it would be odd if a parent could avoid both a breach of s 7 of the EA 1996 and a school attendance order by sending his child to such a school but nevertheless be in breach of s 7 and liable to be the subject of a school attendance order as a result of failing to follow the National Curriculum when providing the child's education otherwise than at school.

Procedure for serving school attendance order

5.19 The period specified in the notice referred to in s 437(1) may not be less than 15 days beginning with the day on which the notice is served.[7] If the parent fails within the period specified in the notice to 'satisfy' the LEA that the child is receiving

---

1   *Baker v Earl* [1960] Crim LR 363. See also the cases referred to by AJ Petrie in 'Education at home and the law' (1993) 5 *Education and the Law* 139. *Philips v Brown* is there referred to as unreported, but there is an extract from the judgment in Butterworths' *The Law of Education*, at para F[82].

2   *R v Surrey Quarter Sessions Appeals Committee, ex parte Tweedie* (1963) 61 LGR 464, at 467. (Reported also, under the name of *Tweedie v Pritchard* at [1963] Crim LR 270.)

3   Ibid.

4   *R v Gwent County Council, ex parte Perry* (1985) 129 SJ 737, per Slade LJ. The case concerned the withdrawal by a parent of his child from school and the impact of that on the registration of the child as a pupil at the school under the Pupils' Registration Regulations 1956, but the principles in that case seem clearly to apply as indicated in the text. At the time when *ex parte Perry* was decided, there was no equivalent in the 1956 Regulations of reg 9(1)(c) of the Education (Pupil Registration) Regulations 1995, SI 1995/2089, which provides for the deletion from the admission register of the name of a pupil whose parent notifies the proprietor of the school in writing that the pupil is receiving education otherwise than at school.

5   Ibid.

6   Ibid.

7   EA 1996, s 437(2).

suitable education, and it is in the opinion of the LEA expedient that the child should attend school, then the LEA is under a duty to serve a school attendance order[1] on the parent. Such an order requires the parent to cause the child to become a registered pupil at a school named in the order.[2] The procedure which needs to be followed differs according to whether or not the child is the subject of a statement of SEN.

Children for whom no statement of special educational needs is maintained

5.20 The following paragraphs describe the situation where no statement of SEN is maintained in respect of a child under s 324 of the EA 1996. In that situation, where the LEA intend to serve a school attendance order on a parent, they must first serve a notice in writing on the parent informing him of its intention to do so.[3] The notice must in addition specify both the school (which may be a pupil referral unit[4]) which is intended to be named in the order and (if the LEA thinks fit) one or more other schools which the LEA regard as alternatives. Paragraph 14 of Sch 1 to the EA 1996 makes specific provision in relation to school attendance orders where it is proposed to name a pupil referral unit as the school at which a child must attend. That provision is slightly different from that relating to schools as such, and what follows is not intended to be read as applying to a pupil referral unit, although some of the provisions described below do apply where a school attendance order is proposed or made naming a pupil referral unit as the school in question.

5.21 A school cannot be specified in a notice served under s 438(2) if the child to which the order relates has been permanently excluded from it.[5] Further, a school cannot normally be specified in such a notice if the admission of the child would take the number of pupils in the child's age group above the admission number,[6] unless the LEA is 'responsible for determining the arrangements for the admission of pupils to the school'.[7] However, subject to an exception, an LEA may nevertheless specify a school in a notice under s 438(2) where, if the child were admitted, the number of pupils in the relevant age group would exceed the admission number or the approved admission number, if in the opinion of the LEA there is no maintained school within a reasonable distance from the home of the child concerned, other than the school in question.[8] The exception is that an LEA may not specify a school in a notice under s 438(2) if the admission of the child concerned would result in prejudice of the kind referred to in s 86(3)(a) of the SSFA 1998 by reason of measures required to be taken

---

[1] Which must be in the form prescribed by the Education (School Attendance Order) Regulations 1995, SI 1995/2090.

[2] EA 1996, s 437(3).

[3] Ibid, s 438(2).

[4] This is the result of the definition of 'school' in s 4(1) and (2) of the EA 1996.

[5] EA 1996, s 439(4).

[6] As determined under s 93 of the SSFA 1998, which applies only to maintained schools.

[7] EA 1996, s 439(1) and (2). The LEA will be 'responsible for determining the arrangements for the admission of pupils to the school' where the school is a community or voluntary controlled school, unless the LEA has, with the school's governing body's agreement, delegated that responsibility to the governing body: see s 88 of the SSFA 1998.

[8] EA 1996, s 439(3).

of the sort referred to in s 86(4) of that Act (in other words measures to do with limiting class sizes in infant schools).[1]

5.22 Before deciding to specify a particular maintained school in a notice under s 438(2), the LEA must consult the governing body and, if another LEA is responsible for determining the admission arrangements for the school,[2] that LEA.[3] Furthermore, if, after such consultation, the LEA determines to specify the school in the notice to be served under s 438(2), then the LEA must serve notice in writing to that effect both on those parties and on the head teacher of the school.[4] The governing body or LEA in question may then within the period of 15 days beginning with the day on which the notice was served under s 439(6), under s 439(7) apply to the Secretary of State for a direction under s 439. If they do so, then they must inform the LEA by which the notice was served accordingly.[5] The Secretary of State may then direct which school or schools are to be named in the s 438(2) notice.[6]

5.23 Once a notice is served under s 438(2), the parent on whom it has been served has the right within the next 15 days to choose one of any of the schools which the LEA has named in the notice as alternatives.[7] In addition, the parent may within that period obtain a place for the child at a suitable school, whether maintained or independent,[8] but not a pupil referral unit.[9] When that occurs, then the school in question is to be named in the order.[10] It is implicit that if the parent has done none of these things once the 15 days have elapsed, then the LEA is, as a result of s 437(3), under a duty to serve on the parent a school attendance order specifying a school named in the s 438(2) notice.

Children for whom statements of special educational needs are maintained

5.24 The process just described has no parallel in the case of a child for whom a statement of SEN is maintained under s 324 of the EA 1996. Where a school is specified in such a statement, any school attendance order served in respect of the child to whom the statement relates must specify the school named in the statement.[11] If no school is specified in the statement, then the LEA must amend the statement so that it specifies the name of a school.[12] That school is then named in the school attendance order.[13] If at any time a child is the subject of both a school attendance

---

1   EA 1996, s 439(4A).
2   See footnote 7 at para **5.21**.
3   EA 1996, s 439(5).
4   Ibid, s 439(6).
5   Ibid, s 439(7).
6   Ibid, s 439(8).
7   Ibid, s 438(3).
8   Ibid, s 438(4)–(6).
9   Ibid, Sch 1, para 14(2)
10   Ibid, ss 438(3)–(6).
11   Ibid, s 441(1) and (2).
12   Ibid, s 441(3)(a). Such an amendment is treated for the purposes of EA 1996, Sch 27 as if it were an amendment proposed following a periodic review within the meaning of that Schedule: s 441(3A). Such a periodic review is a review conducted in accordance with EA 1996, s 328(5)(b): Sch 27, para 1. See paras **6.94** et seq regarding such a review.
13   EA 1996, s 441(3)(b).

order and a statement of SEN maintained under s 324, and the school named in the statement is changed, then the order must be amended accordingly.[1]

Effect of a school attendance order on parties other than the parent

5.25 Where a maintained school is named in a school attendance order, the LEA is under a duty to inform the governing body and the head teacher of the school.[2] The governing body named in the order and (if the school is a maintained one) the LEA is placed under a duty to admit the child to the school.[3] However, a pupil who is already a registered pupil at the school may nevertheless be excluded from the school.[4]

Duration of school attendance orders

5.26 A school attendance order continues in force (subject to any amendment made by the LEA) until the child ceases to be of compulsory school age, unless either the order is revoked by the LEA or a court directs under s 443(2)[5] or s 447(5)[6] that it is to cease to be in force.[7]

Amendment of school attendance order

5.27 In the case of a child to whom a school attendance order relates and in relation to whom no statement of SEN is maintained under s 324 of the EA 1996, the child's parent may in some situations require the LEA to name a different school in the order. As one would expect, this occurs where the parent arranges for his child to be admitted to a different (suitable) school and then requests the LEA to amend the order by substituting the new school for the original or previous one in the order.[8]

Revocation of school attendance order

5.28 A parent of a child to whom a school attendance order relates may (unless a statement of SEN is maintained in respect of the child under s 324 and a school or other institution is named in Part 4 of the statement) at any time request that the LEA revokes the order on the ground that arrangements have been made for the child to receive suitable education otherwise than at school.[9] The LEA then comes under a duty to revoke the order unless it is of the opinion that no satisfactory arrangements

---

[1]   EA 1996, s 441(4).

[2]   Ibid, s 437(5).

[3]   Ibid, s 437(6).

[4]   Ibid, s 437(7).

[5]   Which applies where a parent is prosecuted pursuant to s 443(1) for failing to comply with the order: see para **5.29**.

[6]   Which applies where an LEA applies for an education supervision order under s 36 of the CA 1989, and the court decides that s 36(3) of that Act prevents it from making the order. Section 36(3) provides that a court may only make such an order if it is satisfied that the child is of compulsory school age and is not being properly educated.

[7]   EA 1996, s 437(4).

[8]   Ibid, s 440. The LEA is then under an obligation to comply with the request; ibid.

[9]   Ibid, s 442(1), (2) and (5)(a).

of the relevant sort have been made.[1] If the parent is aggrieved by the LEA's refusal in such circumstances to revoke the school attendance order, then he may 'refer the question to the Secretary of State',[2] who 'shall give such direction determining the question as he thinks fit'.[3] In the case of a pupil for whom a statement of SEN (which does not name a school or other institution) is maintained under s 324, such a direction may require the LEA to make 'such amendments in the statement as the Secretary of State considers necessary or expedient in consequence of his determination'.[4]

Offence of failing to comply with school attendance order

5.29   It is an offence for a parent to fail to comply with the requirements of a school attendance order unless he proves that he is causing the child to receive suitable education otherwise than at school.[5] If a parent is prosecuted for the offence in s 443(1) but is acquitted, then the court may direct that the school attendance order is to cease to have effect.[6] However, such a direction does not prevent the LEA from recommencing the procedure under s 437 if the circumstances change; rather, the LEA remains under a duty to take further action under s 437 if it is of the opinion that, as a result of a change of circumstances, it is expedient to do so.[7] It has been held that if a parent is prosecuted for the offence in s 443(1) and is convicted, then the order is spent, and if the parent again fails to comply with s 7 of the EA 1996, it will be necessary to serve a new order under s 437 before the parent could again be convicted of the offence in (now) s 443(1).[8] It has also been held that if an attendance order is made against one parent only, and he or she dies, then the order cannot be enforced against another parent.[9]

Offence of failing to ensure regular attendance at school of a registered pupil

5.30   If a child of compulsory school age who is a registered pupil at a school fails to attend regularly at the school,[10] then his parent is guilty of an offence contrary to

---

[1]   EA 1996, s 442(2).

[2]   Ibid, s 442(3).

[3]   Ibid, s 442(4). The Secretary of State has power under s 506 of the EA 1996 (as to which see further, para **3.50**) to require the parent to present the pupil for examination by a medical practitioner where in the Secretary of State's opinion such examination would assist in determining the question.

[4]   Ibid, s 442(5)(b).

[5]   Ibid, s 443(1). The maximum penalty is a fine at level 3 on the standard scale (which is currently £1,000): s 443(4).

[6]   Ibid, s 443(2).

[7]   Ibid, s 443(3).

[8]   *Enfield London Borough Council v Forsyth and Forsyth* [1987] 2 FLR 126, 85 LGR 526, a decision of a three-judge Divisional Court. There was in that case full consideration of the meaning and effect of the provision in what is now s 437(4) that a school attendance order continues in force for so long as a child is of compulsory school age, unless it is either revoked by the LEA or a court directs that it ceases to be in force. The court decided that that provision did not compel the conclusion that a continuing failure by a parent to comply with a school attendance order could be prosecuted twice (that is, with no need for a further notice to be served under what is now s 437).

[9]   *Hance v Fairhurst* (1882) 47 JP 53.

[10]   A registered pupil means a person who is registered as a pupil at the school in the register kept under s 434 of the EA 1996: s 434(5).

s 444(1) of the EA 1996 unless he is able to rely upon one of a number of possible defences contained in the rest of that section, to which reference is made.[1] The maximum penalty for the offence is a fine at level 3 on the standard scale.[2] If the parent knows that his child is failing to attend regularly at the school and fails without reasonable justification to cause him to do so, he is guilty of an offence contrary to s 444(1A) of the EA 1996. The maximum penalty for a breach of s 444(1A) is greater than that for a breach of s 444(1): it is a fine at level 4 on the standard scale or imprisonment for a maximum of 3 months.[3]

5.31 Regular attendance at school for the purposes of s 444 means regular attendance at the times determined upon by the governing body of the school for the commencement of school sessions.[4] Whether regular attendance has occurred is a question of fact, but guidance with regard to this question may be found in the case of *Crump v Gilmore*.[5] There, a magistrates' court found parents not guilty of the offence in the predecessor provision (s 39 of the EA 1944) where their daughter failed without a proper excuse to attend on 12 out of 114 sessions, but only because they felt that the parents were not at fault. Having determined that the offence was one of strict liability (see further below), the Divisional Court remitted the case to the justices with a direction to convict the defendants. This was because the justices had implicitly determined that a failure to attend without a proper excuse on 12 out of 114 sessions was not regular attendance. However, Lord Parker CJ, with whom the other two members of the court agreed, stated that although what was important was what the justices had implicitly determined, in his judgment the child in question had indeed not attended regularly.

5.32 Boarding school pupils are to be taken to have failed to attend regularly if they have been absent from school without leave during any part of the school term when they were not prevented from being present by reason of sickness or any unavoidable cause.[6] The fact that a child's parent finds it impossible because of business problems to take the child to and from school will not normally amount to an unavoidable cause for this purpose, although want of transport is capable of being such an unavoidable cause.[7]

---

1   It was held in *Barnfather v London Borough of Islington and the Secretary of State* [2003] EWHC 418 (Admin); [2003] ELR 263, that s 444(1) is not contrary to Art 6 of the European Convention on Human Rights, simply because Art 6 was not engaged. Had it been, one member of the court (Maurice Kay J) would have said that it was in any event justified. The other (Elias J) would have said that the Secretary of State had given insufficient reasons for the justification of imposing criminal liability without proof of fault and that the strict liability offence in s 444(1) is disproportionate to the objective to be achieved.
2   Section 444(8). Level 3 is currently £1,000.
3   Section 444(8A); level 4 on the standard scale is currently £2,500.
4   *Hinchley v Rankin* [1961] 1 WLR 421. The times of a maintained school's sessions are determined by the governing body of the school: see EA 2002, s 32(1)(b) and (2)(b), concerning which, see further para **7.157**.
5   (1969) 68 LGR 56.
6   EA 1996, s 444(7).
7   *R v Havering London Borough Council, ex parte K* [1998] ELR 402. See further para **5.35** with regard to what is an 'unavoidable cause' for this purpose.

5.33   The offence is one of strict liability, so if the parent does not know that his child is absent from school on the relevant occasions, that is no excuse;[1] the same is true if the parent was not guilty of any neglect in seeking to ensure that the child attended regularly.[2] Rather, those are merely matters in mitigation.[3]

Defences

Leave

5.34   It is a good defence to a prosecution under s 444(1) that the child was absent with leave,[4] although only in exceptional circumstances may a pupil be granted more than 10 school days' leave of absence in any school year.[5] Further, leave cannot lawfully be granted to a pupil to enable the pupil to undertake employment (whether paid or unpaid) except employment for the purposes of taking part in a performance within the meaning of s 37 of the Children and Young Persons Act 1963 under a licence granted by the local authority under that section, or employment abroad authorised by a licence granted by a justice of the peace under s 25 of the Children and Young Persons Act 1933.[6] Suspension does not equate to 'leave' for this purpose.[7] Nor does a refusal to admit to a state school a child whose parent refused to allow the school to administer corporal punishment to the child (at a time when it was still lawful to administer such punishment in state schools).[8]

Sickness or unavoidable cause

5.35   It is a good defence to a prosecution under s 444(1) that the pupil's attendance was 'prevented ... by reason of sickness or any unavoidable cause'.[9] The unavoidable cause must, however, relate to and actually affect the child.[10] Similarly, the sickness must be of the child, and not of the child's parent.[11] An example of an 'unavoidable cause' would be the burning down of the parent's house, but that would operate only for a day or two.[12] An 'unavoidable cause' is something in the nature of an

[1]   *Crump v Gilmore*, ibid; *Bath and North East Somerset District Council v Warman* [1999] ELR 81; [1999] EdCR 517.
[2]   *Crump v Gilmore*, ibid.
[3]   Ibid.
[4]   EA 1996, s 444(3)(a). The leave must for this purpose be granted by any person authorised to do so by the governing body or proprietor of the school: s 444(9).
[5]   Education (Pupil Registration) Regulations 1995, SI 1995/2089, reg 8(4). See *R v Governing Body of Gateway Primary School, ex parte X* [2001] ELR 321 in relation to the permissible (and the impermissible) conclusions that may be drawn by the head teacher of a maintained school (pursuant to reg 9) from the fact that a parent takes his child on holiday for longer than 10 days.
[6]   Education (Pupil Registration) Regulations 1995, SI 1995/2089, reg 8(2).
[7]   *Happe v Lay* (1977) 76 LGR 313. In that case, the pupil was suspended indefinitely. That is no longer possible in a state school: see para **10.30**.
[8]   *Jarman v Mid-Glamorgan Education Authority* (1985) *The Times* February 11, 82 LS Gaz 1249.
[9]   EA 1996, s 444(3)(b). With regard to the potential problems which may arise in attempting to prove that a child was 'sick', see Maureen Grenville, *Sickness and compulsory school attendance* (1989) 1 *Education and the Law* 113.
[10]   *Jenkins v Howells* [1949] 2 KB 218, at 220. See also *R v London Borough of Havering, ex parte K* [1998] ELR 402, at 411C–D.
[11]   *Jenkins v Howells*, ibid.
[12]   Ibid.

emergency.[1] A lawful refusal by a school to admit a registered pupil because the pupil's class is being educated elsewhere is not an 'unavoidable cause' for these purposes.[2]

5.36 It is a separate defence to a prosecution under s 444(1) that a direction under s 524(1) of the EA 1996 has been given by a medical officer of an LEA,[3] unless the giving of the direction was necessitated by the wilful default of the pupil or his parent.[4] Section 524(1) authorises such an officer to direct that a pupil is to be excluded from a school maintained by the LEA where the officer suspects that the person or clothing of the pupil is infested with vermin or in a foul condition, but action for the examination or cleansing of the pupil's person and clothing cannot be taken immediately. The direction may be made only if the officer considers such action to be necessary in the interests either of the pupil or of other pupils in attendance at the school. The direction has effect only until the relevant action has been taken.

5.37 There is neither 'sickness' nor an 'unavoidable cause' for these purposes if the school in question refuses to allow the relevant pupil to attend because he is in a verminous condition and the parent is aware that the child will be refused admission as a result.[5] Nor would it be an 'unavoidable cause' and therefore a defence to a prosecution under s 444(1) if a child has been excluded from school because of a refusal to submit to a medical examination under (now) s 521 of the EA 1996,[6] and the parent has sent the child to school having instructed him to refuse to submit to such an examination, knowing at the same time that if the child does so then he will be excluded as a result.[7] However, it may be lawful for a parent to refuse to send his child to school because there are other children attending who are in a dirty or verminous condition.[8]

Religious observance

5.38 It would be a good defence to a prosecution under s 444(1) that the child was absent from school 'on any day exclusively set apart for religious observance by the

---

[1] *Jenkins v Howells* [1949] 2 KB 218, at 220.

[2] *Bunt v Kent* [1914] 1 KB 207; cf *Saunders v Richardson* (1881) 7 QBD 388. Section 29(3) of the EA 2002 now specifically authorises the governing body of a maintained school to require pupils to attend elsewhere than at the school in certain circumstances; as to which see para **7.194**.

[3] For the meaning of the phrase 'medical officer of a local education authority', see para **4.44**.

[4] EA 1996, s 524(2).

[5] *Walker v Cummings* (1912) 107 LT 304.

[6] As to which, see para **4.44**.

[7] *Fox v Burgess* [1922] 1 KB 623. The same principle was applied in *Spiers v Warrington Corporation* [1954] 1 KB 61, as to which, see para **5.10**.

[8] *Symes v Brown* (1913) 109 LT 232. The case of *Bowen v Hodgson* (1923) 93 LJKB 76 is analogous. There it was held by the Divisional Court not to have been unlawful for a magistrates' court to have held that a parent had a reasonable excuse for refusing to submit his daughter to a medical examination by a dermatologist which the LEA had demanded. The father's refusal was on the basis that his daughter would be in danger of being reinfected if she went to the clinic at which the LEA had directed the examination to take place. The father had, however, agreed to allow the dermatologist to examine his daughter at her home.

religious body to which his parent belongs'.[1] An example of such a day is Ascension Day for Church of England adherents.[2]

School further away than walking distance

5.39 If the parent of the child in question proves that the school at which the child is a registered pupil is not within 'walking distance' of the child's home, and that no suitable arrangements have been made by the LEA either for his transport to and from the school,[3] for boarding accommodation for him at or near the school,[4] or for enabling him to become a registered pupil at a school nearer to his home,[5] then the parent will not be guilty of the offence in s 444(1).[6] 'Walking distance' means 3.218688 kilometres (2 miles) in relation to a child who is below the age of eight, and 4.828032 kilometres (3 miles) in relation to a child who is 8 or more years of age, in each case measured by the 'nearest available route'.[7] The mere fact that a route is dangerous for an unaccompanied child does not mean that it is unavailable.[8] However, it must be 'reasonably practicable for a child to walk along it to school'.[9] The question whether a particular route is 'available' within the meaning of s 444(5) is one which should normally be expressed first by making a complaint to the Secretary of State under s 496 or s 497 of the EA 1996,[10] rather than by making an application for judicial review.[11] This is for the following reasons:

> 'It is not for the court to judge safety. The court would not go to the route and look at it for itself. The Secretary of State, on the other hand, through his officials, could do exactly that and, if need be, on different occasions. He is in a far better position to assess safety by watching the traffic, considering visibility, taking account of the width, and perhaps the absence of verges and so on – all matters more suitable for decision by the Secretary of State.'[12]

5.40 The question of the availability of the route is one which in most cases needs to be considered in relation to the question whether or not the LEA is under a duty to provide free transport, and it is accordingly referred to in Chapter 4, where that matter is considered.[13]

---

[1] EA 1996, s 444(3)(c).
[2] See *Marshall v Graham* [1907] 2 KB 112, where it was held that it was not necessary that the whole of the day, or even the whole of the school day, in question be set aside for religious observance. This was despite the existence also in the relevant provision (the predecessor to s 444(3)(c)) of the word 'exclusively'.
[3] EA 1996, s 444(4)(b)(i).
[4] Ibid, s 444(4)(b)(ii).
[5] Ibid, s 444(4)(b)(iii).
[6] Ibid, s 444(4).
[7] Ibid, s 444(5).
[8] *Essex County Council v Rogers* [1987] AC 66.
[9] Ibid, at 77E, per Lord Ackner.
[10] See Chapter 3 regarding those provisions.
[11] *R v Essex County Council, ex parte EB* [1997] ELR 327.
[12] Ibid, at 329D–E.
[13] See paras **5.13–5.16**.

Suitable arrangements for transport

5.41   Where arrangements for transport are made, then in order for them to be 'suitable', they must be made from a point which is reasonably near to the child's home to a point which is reasonably near to the school door.[1] So, for example, merely providing transport to a point 3 miles away from the school would not be a suitable arrangement for this purpose: rather, it would consist of the provision of transport for only part of the way to the school.[2]

5.42   Where a child has no fixed abode, then the defence that the school is further than walking distance from his home cannot apply.[3] However, the parent is nevertheless entitled to be acquitted if he proves (a) that he is engaged in a trade or business of such a nature that he is required to travel from place to place, (b) that the child has attended at a school as a registered pupil as regularly as the nature of that trade or business permits, and (c) if the child is 6 or more years old, that the child has made at least 200 attendances during the period of 12 months ending with the date on which the proceedings were instituted.[4]

Suitable arrangements for enabling pupil to attend school nearer home

5.43   In *R v Rochdale Metropolitan Borough Council, ex parte Schemet*,[5] Roch J expressly ruled that:

> 'The proper construction of s 39(2)(c)[6] is that arrangements will not be suitable unless the school is suitable for the particular pupil.'[7]

5.44   However, as indicated above,[8] the Court of Appeal in the case of *Re S (Minors)*[9] overruled *ex parte Schemet* in this regard. The arguments in both cases concerned the question whether or not the enactment of s 6 of the Education Act 1980 and the consequent right of a parent to express a preference with regard to the school at which his child should be educated,[10] meant that suitable arrangements within the meaning of s 444(4) could be made for enabling the child to become a registered pupil at a school which was nearer to his home but which the parent had not chosen and did not wish to choose. The answer, according to the Court of Appeal, was that the nearer school did not need to be one with which the parent was content. It did not even need to be proved by the LEA that the school was objectively suitable. Lady Justice Butler-Sloss said this:

---

1   *Surrey County Council v Minister of Education* [1953] 1 WLR 516. In *Hares v Curtin* [1913] 2 KB 328, the distance was measured from inside the porch of the parent's residence to inside the porch of the school.
2   *Surrey County Council v Minister of Education* [1953] 1 WLR 516.
3   EA 1996, s 444(6).
4   Ibid.
5   [1994] ELR 89, (1992) 91 LGR 425. See also paras **2.129** et seq.
6   Now s 444(4)(b)(iii) of the EA 1996.
7   [1994] ELR 89, at 105D.
8   At para **2.133**.
9   [1995] ELR 98.
10   See now s 86 of the SSFA 1998, which is discussed in Chapter 6.

'It is inconceivable to my mind that Parliament intended the objective suitability of a school to be a defence in a subsection dealing with the lack of suitable arrangements for ensuring the attendance of a pupil. The requirement of considering objective suitability has to be inferred from the subsection and it is a construction which I do not consider it is capable of bearing.'[1]

5.45   The problem with this approach is that although it is possible to envisage the making of unsuitable arrangements for transport to school, or for boarding accommodation for a pupil at or near a school, it is difficult to see what Parliament can have meant by the word 'suitable' in relation to arrangements made for enabling a child to become a registered pupil at a school nearer to his home, unless Parliament meant to refer to the suitability of the school. For example, it could not reasonably be said to involve the making of suitable arrangements for enabling a child to become a registered pupil at a special school which is nearer to a child's home where the child does not have SEN. Indeed, McCullough J went so far as to say in *R v Kent County Council, ex parte C*:[2]

> 'I have not found it easy to know what is the effect of this judgment and in particular to know what meaning the Court of Appeal was saying should be given to the words "suitable arrangements ... for enabling him to become a registered pupil at a school nearer to his home". Despite the court's express disagreement with what Staughton LJ had said [in *R v Essex County Council, ex parte C*[3]], I can hardly think that the court meant that the decision of a LEA that a school was suitable when it was obviously not would be beyond challenge. Suppose, to take an extreme and improbable example for the purpose of testing the point, that the nearer school which the LEA regarded as suitable was a boy's school and the child in question was a girl, or it was a special school and the child was of normal intelligence.'

5.46   He accordingly deduced that the decision of the court in *Re S* was that:

> 'the objective suitability of the nearer school was not a matter for the court to determine. Either that was all it decided, or, additionally, which I think more likely, it decided that the relevant question was whether the authority's view that the nearer school was suitable had been shown to have been reached unlawfully.'

In most cases, he said, the function of the court in determining whether such a view was lawfully reached 'will require no more than a consideration of the rationality of its conclusion'.[4] Accordingly, he decided that an LEA 'cannot properly refuse to provide free transport on the basis that there is a nearer school which a child could attend unless it is of the view that the nearer school would be a suitable school for that child to attend',[5] and that view was reached lawfully.[6]

---

1   [1995] ELR 98, at 104G–H.
2   [1998] ELR 108, at 113D–F.
3   (1993) 93 LGR 10, at 14, [1994] ELR 273, at 276F.
4   [1998] ELR 108, at 114B.
5   Ibid, at 114A.
6   This formulation was approved by Schiemann LJ (with whose judgment the other two Lords Justices agreed in this respect) in *R(J) v Vale of Glamorgan County Council* [2001] EWCA Civ 593, [2002] ELR 758, at para 2.

5.47   *R v Kent County Council, ex parte C* was not cited in *R(T) v Leeds City Council.*[1] However, it is unlikely that its citation would have altered the outcome. In that case, Turner J held that it was not unlawful to decline to provide free transport to school for pupils who had moved to the area of an LEA from that of an LEA in which there was a school for members of the Orthodox Jewish faith and which the claimants attended. He also held that there was no discrimination contrary to the European Convention on Human Rights ('the Convention') in the circumstances.

5.48   The making of a school attendance order naming a school which is further than walking distance away from a child's home, would not necessarily enable the child's parent to claim successfully that no offence had been committed under s 444 if the parent failed to ensure the regular attendance of the child at school merely because the LEA had not provided free transport to the school. This is because it may still be open to the LEA to make suitable arrangements for enabling the child to become a registered pupil at a school nearer to his home.[2]

Boarding accommodation

5.49   If boarding accommodation is made available for a pupil at or near the school, then only that accommodation – and not the school at which the pupil attends – would have to be suitable for the purposes of s 444(4)(b)(ii).[3]

PROSECUTIONS FOR OFFENCES UNDER SECTIONS 443 AND 444

5.50   Prosecutions may[4] be brought against parents for breaches of ss 443(1), 444(1) and 444(1A) of the EA 1996 only by LEAs.[5] Which parent or parents (and, as indicated above,[6] there may be more than two people who can properly be described as parents in some cases) should be prosecuted would be a matter of discretion for the LEA concerned, just as the LEA would have a discretion as to whether or not to initiate a prosecution at all. However, some rather old authorities may provide guidance. For example, as one would expect, it would not be right to prosecute a parent who did not have actual custody of a child because he was in prison or at sea and consequently could not do anything about the matter, but it would be right to prosecute the parent who had custody of the child.[7] Further, it is clear from *The School Board for London v Jackson*[8] that the fact that another party has care of a child (and is

[1]   [2002] ELR 91.
[2]   *Re C (A Minor)* [1994] ELR 273, CA.
[3]   This is implicit; see further the discussion at paras **5.43–5.46**.
[4]   Before instituting a prosecution, the LEA must first consider whether to apply for an education supervision order in relation to the child, either as well as or instead of instituting the prosecution: see para **5.54**. However, it is not an abuse of process to prosecute a parent in respect of failures to attend which were the basis for the granting of a supervision order, although it might be an abuse of process to do so in respect of failures to attend after the supervision order commenced: *Graves v London Borough of Islington* [2003] EWHC 2817; [2004] ELR 1.
[5]   EA 1996, s 446.
[6]   See para **5.6**.
[7]   *Hance v Burnett* (1880) 45 JP 54, followed in *Woodward v Oldfield* [1928] 1 KB 204.
[8]   (1881) 7 QBD 502.

therefore within the definition of parent for these purposes) does not mean that the natural parent may not also be prosecuted. It also seems clear that, contrary to *London County Council v Stansell*,[1] it would no longer be right to regard the father as the prime candidate for a prosecution where a child is not attending school. Rather, the circumstances of each case and the culpability of the various potential defendants should be considered.[2]

5.51   The question whether a prosecution should have been brought is one which could be raised in several ways. An application for judicial review would in theory be possible, but only if the applicant could properly challenge the decision to prosecute 'on the normal grounds of reasonableness'.[3] That would probably be possible only on facts similar to those of the case in which that statement was made. In that case, which concerned a decision to enforce an obligation in planning law, it was alleged that the local authority had an ulterior motive for bringing the prosecution, so that although technically the prosecution was bound to be successful, that ulterior motive made the decision to prosecute unlawful. However, the normal manner in which the decision to prosecute would be raised is by arguing at the hearing of the prosecution itself that the prosecution should fail because the offence has not been committed. Yet a public law defence could in theory be raised at that hearing also.[4]

5.52   Where a prosecution is brought under s 443 or s 444, the child in question is presumed to have been of compulsory school age at the material time unless the parent proves the contrary.[5] The 'registrar having the custody of the register of birth and deaths[6] containing the entry relating to the birth of' any person whose age is required to be proved for the purposes of the EA 1996, must provide an applicant who presents a written requisition in the appropriate form and who pays a fee of £2 with 'a copy of the entry certified under his hand'.[7] The registrar must, however, supply (free of charge) to an LEA such particulars of the entries contained in the register in his custody as they may from time to time require.[8]

5.53   There are some provisions which may in certain cases be helpful to LEAs when prosecuting parents for breaches of s 443 or s 444. These are contained in s 566(1) of the EA 1996. For example, a document purporting to be issued by an LEA and to be signed by the clerk of the LEA or by the chief education officer of the LEA or by any other officer of the LEA authorised to sign it, 'shall be received in evidence and shall be treated, without further proof, as the document which it purports to be and as having been signed by the person by whom it purports to have been signed, unless the contrary is proved'.[9] The same is true of 'a document purporting to be a certificate giving particulars of the attendance of a child or young

---

[1]   (1935) 154 LT 241. The decision was doubted in *Plunkett v Alker* [1954] 1 QB 420, at p 426, by Lord Goddard CJ, who was in fact a member of the court in *Stansell*.
[2]   This was indeed the conclusion of Lord Goddard in *Plunkett v Alker*, ibid, at 427.
[3]   *R v Elmbridge Borough Council, ex parte Activeoffice Ltd* (1998) 10 Admin LR 561; (1998) 162 JPN 828.
[4]   See *Boddington v British Transport Police* [1999] 2 AC 143.
[5]   EA 1996, s 445(2).
[6]   Kept under the Births and Deaths Registration Act 1953: s 564(4) of the EA 1996.
[7]   EA 1996, s 564(1).
[8]   Ibid, s 564(3).
[9]   Ibid, s 566(1)(a) and the closing words to s 566(1).

person at a school, and to be signed by the head teacher of the school',[1] as it is of a document purporting to be a certificate issued by a medical officer of an LEA, and to be signed by such an officer.[2] Furthermore, and perhaps most helpfully:

'In any legal proceedings, any such extract or certificate as is mentioned in subsection (1)(b), (c) or (d) shall be evidence of the matters stated in it.'[3]

EDUCATION SUPERVISION ORDERS

5.54   Before instituting proceedings for an offence under s 443 or s 444, an LEA must consider:

'whether it would be appropriate (instead of or as well as instituting the proceedings) to apply for an education supervision order with respect to the child.'[4]

5.55   In addition, if a parent is convicted of the offence in s 443 or is charged with an offence under s 444, then the court before which the proceedings are brought may direct the LEA which instituted the proceedings to apply for an education supervision order with respect to the child unless that authority, having consulted the 'appropriate local authority'[5] (which will presumably involve consulting the social services department of the relevant authority), decide that the child's welfare will be satisfactorily safeguarded even though no education supervision order is made.[6]

5.56   Where, following such a direction, the LEA decide not to apply for an education supervision order, they must inform the court of the reasons for so deciding.[7] They must do this within 8 weeks of the day when the direction was given, unless the court directs otherwise.[8]

5.57   The regime governing education supervision orders is contained in the CA 1989. Section 36 of that Act provides that on the application of an LEA, a court may, where a child is not in the care of a local authority,[9] in certain circumstances make an order 'putting the child with respect to whom the application is made under the supervision of a designated local education authority'. Such an order may be made where the child is of compulsory school age and is not being 'properly educated', which means 'receiving efficient full-time education suitable to his age, ability and aptitude and any special educational needs he may have'[10] – which is the condition for

---

[1]   EA 1996, s 566(1)(c).
[2]   Ibid, s 566(1)(d) (and see para **4.44** for the meaning of 'a medical officer of a local education authority'). Section 566(1)(b) is in the same vein, and refers to documents purporting to be extracts from the minutes of proceedings of the governing body of a maintained school, and to be signed by the chairman of such body or its clerk.
[3]   Ibid, s 566(2).
[4]   Ibid, s 447(1).
[5]   As determined in accordance with s 36(9) of the CA 1989.
[6]   EA 1996, s 447(2).
[7]   Ibid, s 447(3).
[8]   Ibid, s 447(4).
[9]   CA 1989, s 36(6).
[10]   Ibid, s 36(3) and (4).

the service of a school attendance order under s 437 of the EA 1996. It is therefore not surprising that if a child is the subject of a school attendance order which is in force under s 437 and the order has not been complied with, or if a child is a registered pupil at a school which he is not attending regularly within the meaning of s 444 of the EA 1996, then, unless it is proved that he is being properly educated, it is to be assumed that he is not being so educated.[1]

5.58   Where an LEA proposes to make an application for an education supervision order, it must first consult the appropriate local (that is, social services) authority.[2] The welfare of the child will be the paramount consideration when a court is determining whether to grant an application for an education supervision order.[3] However, no such order may be made unless the court considers that making an order would be better for the child than making no order at all.[4] There is a right of appeal to the High Court against the granting of an order by a magistrates' court.[5]

5.59   The effect of an education supervision order is that a supervisor is under a duty to 'advise, assist and befriend, and give directions to' the child to whom the order relates and his parents,[6] 'in such a way as will, in the opinion of the supervisor, secure that [the child] is properly educated'.[7] The supervisor is also under a duty to consider what further steps to take in the exercise of his powers under the CA 1989 if the child or his parent does not comply with the directions.[8] Before giving directions,[9] however, the supervisor must, so far as is reasonably practicable, ascertain the wishes and feelings of the child and his parents, including in particular their wishes as to the place at which the child should be educated.[10]

5.60   An education supervision order initially has effect for one year beginning with the date when it was made.[11] It may, however, be extended if, during the period of 3 months before the date when the order would otherwise have ceased to have effect, an application for an extension is made by the LEA in whose favour the order was made.[12] There may be more than one extension, but no single extension may be for a period of more than 3 years.[13] An education supervision order ceases to have effect if during the time the order is in force (a) the child ceases to be of compulsory school age, (b) a care order is made with respect to the child, or (c) the order is discharged by

---

[1]   CA 1989, s 36(5).
[2]   Ibid, s 36(8).
[3]   Ibid, s 1(1).
[4]   Ibid, s 1(5). Note also s 1(2) and (3).
[5]   Ibid, s 94.
[6]   The word 'parent' has the same meaning as in the EA 1996: para 21 of Sch 3 to the CA 1989 (as amended).
[7]   Ibid, Sch 3, para 12(1)(a).
[8]   Ibid, para 12(1)(b).
[9]   Which may be given at any time while the supervision order is in force: ibid, para 12(4).
[10]   Ibid, para 12(2). See also para 12(3).
[11]   Ibid, para 15(1).
[12]   Ibid, para 15(2) and (3).
[13]   Ibid, para 15(4) and (5).

the court on the application of either the child, a parent of the child, or the LEA concerned.[1]

5.61 During the period when the supervision order has effect, the parent of the child in question does not need to comply with the duty contained in s 7 of the EA 1996, nor may he be prosecuted for the offences in s 443 or s 444.[2] Furthermore, any school attendance order which was in force immediately before the education supervision order was made ceases to have effect when the education supervision order is made.[3] On the other hand, the general duty of the LEA to educate children in accordance with their parents' wishes (contained in s 9 of the EA 1996), the limited duty to comply with a parental preference with regard to the school at which they wish their children to be educated (contained in s 86 of the SSFA 1998), and the duty to make arrangements to enable a parent to appeal against a refusal to admit his child to the school of his choice (contained in s 89 of the SSFA 1998), do not apply while an education supervision order is in force.[4]

5.62 Instead, both the child to whom an education supervision order relates and the parent of that child are under a duty to comply with directions made by the supervisor under the order. The sanction for the parent of persistently failing to do so is the possibility of being prosecuted[5] for failing to comply with a direction under the order.[6] The sanction for the child is that the LEA must notify the relevant local (that is, social services) authority,[7] and the latter must then 'investigate the circumstances of the child',[8] presumably in order to enable it to consider whether to provide support for the child or his family under Part III of the CA 1989, or whether to apply for a care order in relation to the child under Part IV of that Act.

CARE ORDERS

5.63 It used to be a potential ground for the making of a care order that a child was not receiving education, as long as certain other conditions were satisfied, but that is no longer so.[9] However, it is still possible that a child may, because he is not receiving education, lawfully become the subject of a care order under s 31 of the CA 1989.[10] The fact that the LEA has not made an application for an education supervision order will not preclude the making of an application by the local social services authority for

---

[1]   CA 1989, paras 15(6) and 17(1).

[2]   Ibid, paras 13(1) and (2)(b)(i).

[3]   Ibid, Sch 3, para 13(2)(a).

[4]   Ibid, para 13(2)(b)(ii) and (iii), read in the light of s 17(2) of the Interpretation Act 1978.

[5]   Under CA 1989, Sch 3, para 18.

[6]   The maximum penalty is a fine on level 3 on the standard scale (which is currently £1,000): ibid, para 18(3).

[7]   Ibid, para 19(1) and (3).

[8]   Ibid, para 19(2).

[9]   Section 1(2)(e) of the Children and Young Persons Act 1969, which so provided, was repealed by the CA 1989.

[10]   See *In Re O (A Minor) (Care Proceedings: Education)* [1992] 1 WLR 912.

a care order, as long as all measures that could be taken under an education supervision order have been taken.[1]

MEASURES INTRODUCED BY THE ANTI-SOCIAL BEHAVIOUR ACT 2003

5.64   The Anti-social Behaviour Act 2003 introduced two new tools for LEAs to use in combatting truancy. These are: (1) parenting contracts, empowered by s 19 (which apply also in relation to pupils who have been excluded from what might be called a state school); and (2) penalty notices, empowered by new ss 444A and 444B of the EA 1996, inserted by s 23 of the Anti-social Behaviour Act 2003.

Parenting contracts

5.65   If a pupil has been excluded either for a fixed period or permanently on disciplinary grounds from (1) a community, foundation or voluntary school, (2) a community or foundation special school, (3) a maintained nursery school, (4) a city technology college, (5) a city college for the technology of the arts, (6) an Academy; or (7) a pupil referral unit (each of which is in this context a 'relevant school'), or if a child who is of compulsory school age and is a registered pupil at a relevant school has failed to attend regularly at the school, the LEA or the governing body of the school may enter into a parenting contract within the meaning of s 19 of the Anti-social Behaviour Act 2003.[2] Such a contract is a document which contains:

'(a)   a statement by the parent[3] that he agrees to comply with such requirements as may be specified in the document for such period as may be so specified, and

(b)   a statement by the local education authority or governing body that it agrees to provide support to the parent for the purpose of complying with those requirements.'[4]

5.66   These requirements may include 'a requirement to attend a counselling or guidance programme', and the purpose of the requirements must be to improve the behaviour of the pupil or (as the case may be) to ensure that the child attends regularly at the school in question.[5] In exercising their functions in relation to parenting contracts, LEAs and the governing bodies of relevant schools must have regard to any guidance which is issued by the Secretary of State in relation to England or the National Assembly for Wales in relation to Wales.[6]

---

[1]   See *In Re O (A Minor) (Care Proceedings: Education)* [1992] 1 WLR 912.

[2]   Anti-social Behaviour Act 2003, ss 19(1)–(3) and 24. The term 'pupil' in this context is to be construed in accordance with s 3(1) and (1A) of the EA 1996, and the term 'registered pupil' has the meaning given by s 434(5) of the EA 1996: Anti-social Behaviour Act 2003, s 24.

[3]   The term 'parent' is to be construed in accordance with s 576 of the EA 1996, except that it does not include a person who is not an individual: Anti-social Behaviour Act 2003, s 24.

[4]   Anti-social Behaviour Act 2003, s 19(4).

[5]   Ibid, s 19(5) and (6).

[6]   Ibid, ss 19(9) and 24.

5.67   A parenting contract must be signed by the parent and signed on behalf of the LEA or governing body.[1] It does not create any obligations in respect of whose breach any liability arises in contract or tort.[2]

Penalty notices

5.68   Section 23 of the Anti-social Behaviour Act 2003 inserted ss 444A and 444B into the EA 1996, empowering in England (although the National Assembly for Wales is given power by s 23(9) to apply those sections to Wales) the issuing of a penalty notice instead of the instigation of a prosecution for the offence, contrary to s 444(1) of the EA 1996, of failing to ensure the regular attendance at a school of a child who is of compulsory school age and is a registered pupil at the school. The notice must be issued by an 'authorised officer', who must have reason to believe that that offence has been committed in relation to 'a relevant school' in England.[3] Where there is more than one person liable for the offence, a separate notice may be issued to each person.[4] The form and content of penalty notices must be as prescribed by reg 2 of the Education (Penalty Notices) (England) Regulations 2004.[5] Service of a penalty notice may be effected by sending it by first-class post to the recipient at the recipient's usual or last-known address, and the notice is deemed to have been served on the second working day after its posting, unless the contrary is proved.[6]

5.69   A 'relevant school' for the purposes of ss 444A and 444B means (a) a maintained school,[7] (b) a pupil referral unit, (c) an Academy, (d) a city technology college, or (e) a city college for the technology of the arts.[8] An 'authorised officer' in this context means (1) a constable, (2) an officer of an LEA in England who is authorised by the LEA to give penalty notices, (3) a head teacher of a relevant school in England, or (4) a member of the staff of a relevant school in England who is authorised by the head teacher of the school to give penalty notices.[9] Such a head teacher may, however, only authorise a deputy or assistant head teacher to issue penalty notices.[10] A head teacher, deputy head teacher and assistant head teacher may issue a penalty notice only in respect of a child who is a registered pupil at his school.[11] An officer of an LEA may issue a penalty notice only in respect of a child who is a registered pupil at a school in the area of that LEA or any other LEA which has an agreement to that effect with his LEA.[12]

---

[1]   Anti-social Behaviour Act 2003, s 19(7).

[2]   Ibid, s 19(8).

[3]   EA 1996, s 444A(1). For the meaning of 'authorised officer' and 'relevant school', see the next para below.

[4]   Education (Penalty Notices) (England) Regulations 2004, SI 2004/181, reg 11.

[5]   SI 2004/181.

[6]   Ibid, reg 20, as amended by SI 2004/920.

[7]   Meaning a community, voluntary or foundation school, or a community or foundation special school: SSFA 1998, s 20(7) and 142(8).

[8]   EA 1996, s 444B(4).

[9]   Ibid.

[10]   Education (Penalty Notices) (England) Regulations 2004, SI 2004/181, reg 8.

[11]   See reg 9 of SI 2004/181 read with EA 1996, s 444B(4).

[12]   SI 2004/181, reg 10.

5.70   A penalty notice for this purpose is 'a notice offering a person the opportunity of discharging any liability to conviction for the offence under s 444(1) to which the notice relates by payment of a penalty in accordance with the notice'.[1] The penalty is payable to the LEA,[2] which must use sums received by way of such penalties in meeting the cost of issuing and enforcing penalty notices, or the cost of prosecuting recipients who do not pay the penalties.[3] Where a person is given a penalty notice, proceedings for the offence to which the notice relates (or an offence under s 444(1A) arising out of the same circumstances) may not be instituted before 42 days have passed.[4] If the person pays the penalty in accordance with the notice, then he cannot be convicted of the offence to which the notice relates (or an offence under s 444(1A) arising out of the same circumstances).[5]

5.71   The penalty is either £50 or £100, depending on the time by which it is paid. If it is paid within 28 days of receipt of the notice, then it is £50.[6] If it is paid within 42 days of receipt of the notice, then it is £100.[7] If the penalty is not paid within 42 days, then the LEA named in the notice must either institute proceedings against the recipient for the offence to which the notice relates or withdraw the notice either because it ought not to have been issued or because it ought not to have been issued to the person named as the recipient.[8]

5.72   LEAs must keep records of penalty notices, including whether the recipient was prosecuted for the offence for which the notice was issued.[9] Every person who issues a penalty notice must forthwith provide a copy to the LEA which is named in the notice.[10]

Secretary of State's guidance and LEAs' codes

5.73   LEAs, head teachers and authorised officers must, in carrying out their functions in relation to penalty notices, have regard to any guidance issued by the Secretary of State under s 444B(3) of the EA 1996 in relation to such notices. Every LEA must also draw up a code of conduct which sets out measures to ensure consistency in the issuing of penalty notices, including (1) means of avoiding the issue of duplicate notices, (2) measures to ensure that a notice is not issued when proceedings for an offence under s 444 are contemplated or have been commenced by the LEA, (3) the occasions when it will be appropriate to issue a penalty notice for an offence, (4) a maximum number of penalty notices which may be issued to one parent in any 12-month period, and (5) arrangements for co-ordination between the LEA, neighbouring LEAs where appropriate, the police and authorised officers.[11] In

---

[1]   EA 1996, s 444A(2).

[2]   Ibid, s 444A(5).

[3]   Ibid, s 444A(6) and reg 21 of the Education (Penalty Notices) (England) Regulations 2004, SI 2004/181.

[4]   EA 1996, s 444A(3) and reg 5 of the Education (Penalty Notices) (England) Regulations 2004.

[5]   Ibid, s 444A(4).

[6]   Education (Penalty Notices) (England) Regulations 2004, reg 3(a).

[7]   Ibid, reg 3(b).

[8]   Ibid, regs 6 and 7(1).

[9]   Ibid, reg 18.

[10]   Ibid, reg 17.

[11]   Ibid, reg 12.

preparing the code, the LEA must consult governing bodies (presumably of relevant schools), head teachers and the chief officer of police for a police area which includes all or part of the area of the LEA, and must have regard to any guidance issued by the Secretary of State.[1] Any person issuing a penalty notice must do so in accordance with the code.[2] The Secretary of State may at any time direct an LEA either to prepare a draft code for his approval or, if it has already drawn up a code under reg 12 of the Education (Penalty Notices) (England) Regulations 2004, to prepare draft revisions to that code for his approval.[3]

---

[1] Education (Penalty Notices) (England) Regulations 2004, reg 13.
[2] Ibid, reg 14.
[3] See ibid, regs 15 and 16.

Chapter 6

SPECIAL EDUCATIONAL NEEDS

6.1   The law relating to persons with SEN applies in the main to those who are being educated in school or who are below school age. However, there are in addition some significant provisions concerning the further education of persons with SEN. There are no significant provisions affecting the higher education of persons with SEN as such, and although the provisions of the Disability Discrimination Act 1995 (DDA 1995), as amended by the Special Educational Needs and Disability Act 2001 (SENDA 2001), apply to the provision of higher education, the DDA 1995 does not affect higher education students who have SEN in relation to those needs.[1] This chapter accordingly concerns only the law relating to SEN, and not disability discrimination (which is considered in Chapter 18), although it is noted that claims of discrimination contrary to the new Part 4 of the DDA 1995 may now be made in the Special Educational Needs and Disability Tribunal in England and its Welsh equivalent, the Special Educational Needs Tribunal for Wales, and that such claims may, where appropriate, be joined with claims under Part IV of the EA 1996 relating to SEN.

HISTORY

6.2   Schools which were specially organised for the provision of what is now called special education seem to have been mentioned first in legislation affecting England and Wales in the Elementary Education (Blind and Deaf Children) Act 1893.[2] Every school authority (as defined in s 4 of the Act) was placed under a duty to secure the provision of education for blind and deaf children, and for that purpose was given the power to establish, acquire and maintain schools. Certification by the Education Department[3] of schools for the education of blind and deaf children was introduced by s 2(1) of that Act. However, the Act placed no duty on a school authority in respect of 'idiots or imbeciles'.[4] The Elementary Education (Defective and Epileptic Children) Act 1899 subsequently empowered the making of specific provision for 'defective and epileptic' children (excluding 'idiots', 'imbeciles' and children who were

---

[1]   The only way in which a person with SEN could rely on the DDA 1995 in relation to the provision of higher education (as such) is by being able to show that he or she has a mental impairment which affects normal day-to-day activities (see s 1 of the DDA 1995, and note in relation to a mental illness para 1 of Sch 1 to that Act), and even then, a higher education institution is entitled to discriminate against such a person where that is necessary in order to maintain academic standards: see para **18.67**.

[2]   Mention of children with what are now called special educational needs seems first to have been made in legislation affecting Scotland in the Education of Blind and Deaf-mute Children (Scotland) Act 1890, although reference was first made in s 69 of the Education (Scotland) Act 1872 to the education of blind children.

[3]   As to which, see para **1.7**.

[4]   Elementary Education (Blind and Deaf Children) Act 1893, s 2(2)(a).

'merely dull or backward'[1]) in England and Wales. Certification of schools for defective and epileptic children was provided for in s 2 of that Act. By the Elementary Education (Defective and Epileptic Children) Act 1914, the power in the 1899 Act was converted into a duty. The next major change came with the EA 1944, but the foundation of the modern law is to be found in the EA 1981. Many of the provisions of that Act are now reproduced, albeit in some cases with significant amendments made by the EA 1993, in the EA 1996. However, in addition to amending the 1981 Act regime, the 1993 Act contained some significant new provisions which are also now contained in the EA 1996. The EA 1997 made minor changes to those in the EA 1996 concerning SEN, and the provisions in the EA 1996 relating to children with SEN were amended so that they reflected the new types of maintained schools which came into existence with the coming into force of the SSFA 1998, but otherwise the SSFA made relatively little change to the law relating to SEN. However, the SENDA 2001 made significant changes to the part of the EA which contains the current statutory regime relating to the meeting of SEN in schools or in relation to school-age children (Chapter 1 of Part IV of the EA 1996). The SENDA 2001 of course also applied the DDA 1995, with modifications, to the provision of education. The EA 2002 altered the law relating to SEN mainly by empowering the National Assembly to direct two or more LEAs in Wales to make regional provision for SEN and by providing for a Special Educational Needs Tribunal for Wales.[2]

ASSESSMENTS AND STATEMENTS OF SPECIAL EDUCATIONAL NEEDS: AN OVERVIEW

Definition of 'special educational needs'

6.3   The starting-point for an analysis of the law relating to special educational needs must be the statutory definition of that phrase. That definition is contained in the first section of Chapter 1 of Part IV of the EA 1996, s 312. Section 312(1) provides that a child has 'special educational needs' for the purposes of the EA 1996 'if he has a learning difficulty which calls for special educational provision to be made for him'. Section 312(2) provides:

> 'Subject to subsection (3) (and except for the purposes of section 15A or 15B)[3] a child has a "learning difficulty" for the purposes of this Act if –
> (a)   he has a significantly greater difficulty in learning than the majority of children of his age,

---

[1]   See Elementary Education (Defective and Epileptic Children) Act 1899, s 1(1).

[2]   See ss 191–194 of the EA 2002, concerning which see para **2.38** and s 195 of the EA 2002, concerning which, see footnote 2 at para **6.116**.

[3]   EA 1996, ss 15A and 15B concern part-time education for 16–18-year-olds and education other than higher education provided to persons above the age of 19 respectively. Subsection (3) of both those sections requires LEAs when exercising their functions under the section to have regard to the needs of persons with learning difficulties within the meaning of s 13(5) and (6) of the LSA 2000. Sections 15A and 15B are discussed further in paras **2.81–2.82**, **6.184**, **16.53** and **16.54**.

(b)   he has a disability which either prevents or hinders him from making use of educational facilities of a kind generally provided for children of his age in schools within the area of the local education authority, or

(c)   he is under compulsory school age and is, or would be if special educational provision were not made for him, likely to fall within paragraph (a) or (b) when of that age.'

6.4   Section 312(3) provides:

'A child is not to be taken as having a learning difficulty solely because the language (or form of the language) in which he is, or will be, taught is different from a language (or form of a language) which has at any time been spoken in his home.'

6.5   As can be seen, it is necessary also to know what is meant by the phrase 'special educational provision'. Section 312(4) provides that:

'In this Act, "special educational provision" means –
(a)   in relation to a child who has attained the age of two, educational provision which is additional to, or otherwise different from, the educational provision made generally for children of his age in schools maintained by the local education authority (other than special schools) in their area; and
(b)   in relation to a child under that age, educational provision of any kind.'[1]

6.6   The final part of s 312 is equally important, as it contains a provision which governs the division of responsibility between an LEA and the LSC or (as the case may be) the CETW in relation to a person who has special educational needs and who is either approaching or has attained the age of 16.[2] It is also important for setting a limit on the potential liability of an LEA for funding a young person's special education. Section 312(5) provides (among other things) that:

'In this Part –

"child" includes any person who has not attained the age of 19 and is a registered pupil at a school.'

6.7   Although the use of the word 'includes' in this definition could have been for the purpose of 'clarification and the avoidance of doubt',[3] it is suggested here that, given that the natural meaning of the word 'child' is a person below the age of 18, the result of the use of the word 'includes' in this definition rather than 'means' is that the word 'child' is to be taken to be extended by the definition. Lord Watson's description in *Dilworth v Commissioner of Stamps*[4] of the effect of the use of the word 'includes' in a statutory definition is instructive:

'The word "include" is very generally used in interpretation clauses in order to enlarge the meaning of words or phrases occurring in the body of the statute; and when it is so used these words or phrases must be construed as comprehending, not only such things as

---

[1]   The significance of this definition is considered below, in particular in relation to the duty to make and maintain a statement of special educational needs.
[2]   As to which, see paras **6.189** et seq.
[3]   To use the words of Lord Oliver in *Coltman v Bibby Tankers Ltd* [1988] AC 276, at 298G.
[4]   [1899] AC 99, at 105–106.

they signify according to their natural import, but also those things which the interpretation clause declares that they shall include. But the word "include" is susceptible of another construction, which may become imperative, if the context of the Act is sufficient to shew that it was not merely employed for the purpose of adding to the natural significance of the words or expressions defined. It may be equivalent to "mean and include," and in that case it may afford an exhaustive explanation of the meaning which, for the purposes of the Act, must invariably be attached to these words or expressions.'

6.8   However, definitions cannot be applied in a vacuum. Here, the context is the framework for the provision of education in schools. Given that context, it suggested here that there are good reasons for interpreting s 312(5) as applying (with one possible exception) only to pupils who are in the first or second school year after their final year of compulsory schooling. This is because of the definition of the word 'pupil' in s 3 of the EA 1996 and the related definitions of 'school' and 'secondary education' in ss 4 and 2 of that Act respectively, and because the oldest pupil in a school year will attain the age of 19 on the first day of the third academic year after the school year in which he ceases to be of compulsory school age. The possible exception would result from the fact that s 2(5) of the EA 1996 provides that where a person has begun a particular course of secondary education before attaining the age of 18 and continues to attend that course, the education remains secondary education despite him reaching the age of 19. Thus, applying the inclusive approach taken by the House of Lords in *Coltman v Bibby Tankers Ltd*,[1] the best view may be that the definition in s 312(5) extends to include not only a person who is below the age of 19 and is a registered pupil at a school, but also a person who has begun a particular course of secondary education before attaining the age of 18 and has not yet finished that course (even though he has attained the age of 19).

6.9   For another reason, the definitions of the word 'school' in s 4 of the EA 1996 and 'secondary education' in s 2 of that Act are of particular importance in determining whether a person is a child within the meaning of s 312 where he is over the age of 16. This is because the definition of 'secondary education' includes education which is provided, for example, at a further education institution where the person is a registered pupil at a school.[2]

6.10   Although at first sight it may seem surprising, a child who is of exceptionally high intelligence may nevertheless have special educational needs[3] (although being especially gifted is not a learning difficulty[4]). It is rather more obvious that a child may have more than one learning difficulty,[5] and that it is necessary to look at the whole child.[6] It was certainly 'obvious [to Laws J in *G v Wakefield City Metropolitan District*

---

[1]   [1988] AC 276.
[2]   See EA 1996, s 2(2B), concerning which, see para **7.4**; see also *Wakefield Metropolitan District Council v E* [2002] ELR 203. See further, paras **6.189** et seq.
[3]   *R v Secretary of State for Education, ex parte C* [1996] ELR 93.
[4]   *R v Portsmouth City Council, ex parte Faludy* [1998] ELR 619, at 622F; [1999] EdCR 462, at 471B. The point was not argued on appeal: see [1999] ELR 115.
[5]   *R v Secretary of State for Education and Science, ex parte E* [1992] 1 FLR 377, at 388E.
[6]   Ibid, at 388F.

Council[1]] that the concepts of "learning difficulty" and "special educational provision" are not tightly defined'.

RESPONSIBILITY FOR PUPILS AND THOSE BELOW SCHOOL AGE WHO HAVE SPECIAL EDUCATIONAL NEEDS

6.11   In this section, an overview is given of the responsibilities of the various bodies concerned with children who have or may have SEN. Particular responsibilities in relation to the carrying out of assessments of educational needs and the making of statements of SEN are considered later in this chapter, and are therefore not considered comprehensively here. Further, the role of the Special Educational Needs and Disability Tribunal or the Special Educational Needs Tribunal for Wales (referred to below compendiously as 'the Tribunal') is considered separately (albeit not exclusively, since where relevant the right of appeal to that Tribunal is referred to throughout this chapter), after the sections concerning such assessments and statements.

Local education authorities[2]

6.12   The sole responsibility for ensuring that the special educational needs of children in the area of an LEA are met, lies with that authority. This is the product of (in particular) ss 14(6)(b), 321, 323 and 324 of the EA 1996. As a result of s 14(6)(b), an LEA is under a duty when exercising its functions under s 14[3] to 'have regard to ... the need for securing that special educational provision is made for pupils who have special educational needs'. As a result of s 321(1) and (2), LEAs have a duty to exercise their powers with a view to securing that they identify the children for whom they are responsible and who have special educational needs for which it is necessary that they determine special educational provision in a statement of special educational needs. The children for whom an LEA is responsible are those:

(a)   who are registered pupils at maintained schools[4] or maintained nursery schools,

(b)   for whom education is provided, at the expense of the LEA, at a school which is neither a maintained school nor a maintained nursery school,

(c)   who, not falling within (a) or (b) above, are registered pupils at a school and who have been brought to the attention of the LEA as having (or probably having) special educational needs, or

(d)   who are not registered pupils at a school but are not under the age of two or

---

1   [1998] 2 FCR 597, (1998) 96 LGR 69 at 80g, [1998] COD 288.

2   The functions of an LEA in regard to special educational needs do not extend to higher education: *R v Portsmouth City Council, ex parte Faludy* [1999] ELR 115, at 117; [1999] EdCR 462, at 473.

3   Regarding which, see paras **2.39** et seq.

4   In Part IV of the 1996 Act, 'maintained school' means any community, foundation or voluntary school or foundation special school not established in a hospital: s 312(5).

over compulsory school age and have been brought to the attention of the LEA as having (or probably having) SEN.[1]

6.13   Having identified a pupil for whom it is responsible who in its opinion has SEN which require a statement of SEN, an LEA is under a duty to serve notice on the parent of the child that it intends to assess the child's SEN.[2] If, having followed the proper procedure,[3] the authority remains of the view that the child has educational needs which require a statement of SEN then it must carry out an assessment of his educational needs.[4] The LEA must then follow the proper procedure with regard to the making of statements of SEN.[5] If, having done so, it is necessary to determine the special educational provision which any learning difficulty a child has calls for, the LEA must make and maintain a statement of his SEN.[6] Maintenance of such a statement involves paying for the special educational provision which the statement specifies, unless the parent makes alternative arrangements for the child.[7]

6.14   An LEA is also under a duty in certain circumstances to carry out an assessment under s 323 of the EA 1996 at the request of (1) the head teacher of a maintained nursery school or pupil referral unit, (2) the governing body of a maintained school,[8] or (3) the proprietor of an independent school or a school approved under s 342 of the EA 1996. The circumstances are that (1) the request is made in relation to a registered pupil at the institution in question, (2) no assessment under s 323 has been made in respect of that pupil within the period of 6 months ending with the date when the request was made, and (3) 'it is necessary for the authority to make an assessment or further assessment under s 323'.[9]

6.15   An LEA is under a duty to review a statement of SEN if it makes a further assessment of the child's educational needs under s 323,[10] and in any event every 12 months from either the making of the statement, or, as the case may be, the previous review.[11]

6.16   An LEA must arrange for the provision to the parent of any child with SEN in the LEA's area of advice and information about 'matters relating to those needs'.[12] An LEA must also make arrangements 'with a view to avoiding or resolving disagreements' between (a) themselves and the governing bodies of maintained schools in their area, and (b) parents of children in their area, about the exercise by

---

[1]   EA 1996, s 321(3), as amended, including by EA 2002, Sch 21, para 42. It is noted that children of illegal immigrants are theoretically within the definition of a child for whom an LEA is responsible. The amendments made by EA 2002, Sch 21, paras 36–44 to the EA 1996 are not yet in force. Those paragraphs refer to maintained nursery schools.

[2]   EA 1996, s 323(1).

[3]   The procedure which needs to be followed is considered at paras **6.47** et seq.

[4]   EA 1996, s 323(3).

[5]   As to which, see paras **6.57** et seq.

[6]   EA 1996, s 324(1).

[7]   Ibid, s 324(5)(a), as to which, see further, paras **6.87** and **6.88**.

[8]   Defined for this purpose by s 312(5).

[9]   EA 1996, s 329A(1) and (2), added by s 8 of SENDA 2001.

[10]   Ibid, s 328(5)(a). This is called for the purposes of Sch 27 a 're-assessment review': Sch 27, para 1.

[11]   Ibid, s 328(5)(b). This is called a 'periodic review': Sch 27, para 1.

[12]   Ibid, s 332A(1), inserted by s 2 of SENDA 2001.

themselves and such governing bodies of functions in relation to SEN under Part IV of the EA 1996.[1] Furthermore, an LEA must make arrangements with a view to avoiding or resolving disagreements between (1) the proprietors of (a) maintained schools, (b) maintained nursery schools, (c) city technology colleges, (d) city colleges for the technology of the arts, (e) city academies,[2] (f) independent schools named in statements of SEN maintained under s 324 of the EA 1996, and (g) schools approved under s 342 of that Act,[3] and (2) the parents of children who are registered pupils at such institutions and have SEN.[4] In both situations, the arrangements must include the appointment of 'independent persons with the function of facilitating the avoidance or resolution of such disagreements'.[5] In making these arrangements, LEAs must have regard to guidance given by the Secretary of State or the National Assembly,[6] and must publicise the arrangements.[7] Parents' entitlements to appeal to the Tribunal are not affected by these arrangements.[8]

6.17 An LEA must also inform the parent of a child (1) for whom a statement of SEN is not maintained under s 324 of the EA 1996, (2) who is a registered pupil at a community, foundation or voluntary school, or a pupil referral unit, or to whom the LEA is providing nursery education, (3) for whom the LEA is making special educational provision 'because it is considered that he has special educational needs'; and (4) his parent has not previously been informed that the child is receiving such special educational provision, or that provision for that reason.[9]

6.18 Finally, an LEA is under a duty to keep under review the arrangements made by it for special educational provision.[10] In doing so, it must, to the extent that it appears necessary or desirable for the purpose of co-ordinating provision for children with SEN, consult the governing bodies of community, foundation and voluntary schools, community and foundation special schools, and maintained nursery schools, in its area.[11]

The Secretary of State[12]

Code of practice

6.19 Apart from the important function of approving (1) special schools under s 342 of the EA 1996,[1] and (2) placements at non-maintained special schools under

---

1   EA 1996, s 332B(1), inserted by s 3 of SENDA 2001.
2   But not Academies, the drafters of the EA 2002 having overlooked this situation.
3   See para **6.181** regarding s 342.
4   EA 1996, s 332B(2).
5   Ibid, s 332B(3).
6   Ibid, s 332B(4).
7   Ibid, s 332B(5)
8   Ibid, s 332B(6).
9   Ibid, s 317A and SSFA 1998, s 123(3A) and (3B), all of which were inserted by s 7 of SENDA 2001.
10   Ibid s 315(1). It was held in *P v Harrow London Borough Council* [1993] 1 FLR 723, at 733D, that the predecessor of this provision, s 2 of the EA 1981, which was in similar terms, applies generally only; it does not apply to individual pupils. That ruling was applied in *R(C) v Special Educational Needs and Disability Tribunal* [2003] EWHC 1590 (Admin), [2004] ELR 111.
11   EA 1996, s 315(2) as amended by EA 2002, Sch 21, para 37 (which, as noted above, is not yet in force).
12   In relation to Wales, references to the Secretary of State should be read as references to the National Assembly for Wales, as a result of SI 1999/672.

s 347(5) of the EA 1996,[2] the Secretary of State's main role now in relation to children who have SEN is to make and 'from time to time' to revise a code of practice 'giving practical guidance in respect of the discharge by local education authorities and the governing bodies of' community, foundation and voluntary schools, community and foundation special schools which are not established in a hospital, and maintained nursery schools, of their functions under Part IV of the EA 1996 (concerning children with SEN).[3] The code may also include 'practical guidance in respect of the provision of relevant nursery education for children with special educational needs in circumstances where functions under Part IV of the Education Act 1996 do not fall to be discharged'.[4] The Secretary of State must 'publish the code as for the time being in force'.[5] Where the Secretary of State proposes to issue or revise a code of practice under s 313(1), he must prepare a draft code (or draft revised code),[6] consult such persons as he thinks fit about the draft,[7] and consider any representations made by them.[8] Where the Secretary of State determines to proceed with the draft code, either in its original form or with such modifications as he thinks fit, he must lay it before both Houses of Parliament.[9] If (and only if) both Houses by resolution approve it, he must issue the code accordingly.[10] The code then comes into force on the day appointed by the Secretary of State by order.[11]

6.20   It is convenient to consider here the effect of the code of practice. Section 313(2) provides that:

'It shall be the duty of –
(a)   local education authorities, and [the governing bodies of maintained schools[12]], exercising functions under [Part IV of the EA 1996], and
(b)   any other person exercising any function for the purpose of the discharge by local education authorities, and such governing bodies, of functions under [that] Part, to have regard to the provisions of the code.'

6.21   In addition, according to s 313(3):

'On any appeal under [Part IV of the EA 1996] to the Tribunal, the Tribunal shall have regard to any provision of the code which appears to the Tribunal to be relevant to any question arising on the appeal.'

---

1   See para **6.181** concerning s 342.
2   See para **6.183** concerning s 347.
3   EA 1996, s 313(1) as amended by SSFA 1998 and EA 2002, Sch 21, para 36 (which, as noted above, is not yet in force) and s 312(5).
4   SSFA 1998, s 123(2).
5   EA 1996, s 313(4).
6   Ibid, s 314(1).
7   Ibid, s 314(2).
8   Ibid.
9   Ibid, s 314(3).
10 Ibid, s 314(4).
11 Ibid. The current code for England came into force on 1 September 2001, under the Education (Special Educational Needs Code of Practice) (England) (Appointed Day) Order 2001, SI 2001/3943. The current code for Wales came into force on 1 April 2002, under the Education (Special Educational Needs Code of Practice) (Wales) (Appointed Day) Order 2002, SI 2002/156.
12 Defined by s 312(5), regarding which see footnote 4 at para **6.12**.

6.22 The question of the effect of a duty placed on a public body to 'have regard' to something is relevant in a number of contexts, and it is examined in Chapter 2.[1] In any event, it is possible to state that a failure to follow the provisions of the code of practice empowered now by s 313 of the EA 1996 would be likely to be subjected to close scrutiny, and that it is likely that the departure would need to be justified by cogent evidence before the Tribunal (or the court) would be likely to approve it.

Guidance under section 123(3) of the SSFA 1998

6.23 If the code of practice published under s 313 of the EA 1996 does not include 'practical guidance in respect of the provision of relevant nursery education[2] for children with special educational needs in circumstances where functions under Part IV of the Education Act 1996 do not fall to be discharged' then the Secretary of State must publish a document 'explaining how the practical guidance contained in that code applies in circumstances where functions under Part IV of the Education Act 1996 do not fall to be discharged'.[3] The current code of practice does in fact include the guidance referred to in the first sentence of this paragraph.

The governing bodies of community, foundation, voluntary and maintained nursery schools

6.24 The governing body of a community, foundation, voluntary or maintained nursery school is under a duty to use its best endeavours in exercising its functions in relation to the school to secure that provision is made for the SEN of any registered pupil at the school.[4] It must also secure that where the head teacher or appropriate governor (that is, the chairman of the governing body or, where the governing body has designated another governor for the purpose, that other governor) has been informed by the LEA that a registered pupil at the school has SEN, those needs are made known to all who are likely to teach the pupil,[5] and that the teachers in the school are aware of the importance of identifying and providing for those registered pupils who have SEN.[6] In addition, when exercising their functions relating to provision for children with SEN, such bodies must, to the extent that it appears necessary or desirable for the purpose of co-ordinating such provision, consult the LEA and the governing bodies of other such schools.[7] Although the governing bodies of maintained schools and maintained nursery schools will not themselves be concerned with actually making the special educational provision for a child who is being educated at their school and who has SEN, it is noted here that those who are so concerned must secure, so far as is reasonably practicable and is compatible with:

(a)   the child receiving the special educational provision which his learning difficulty calls for,

---

1   See paras **2.34–2.36**.
2   Defined by SSFA 1998, s 123(4).
3   Ibid, s 123(3)(a).
4   EA 1996, s 317(1)(a), as amended by EA 2002, Sch 21, para 39 (which, as noted above, is not yet in force).
5   EA 1996, s 317(1)(b) and s 317(2) as amended by EA 2002, Sch 21, para 39 (which, as noted above, is not yet in force).
6   EA 1996, s 317(1)(c).
7   Ibid, s 317(3)(a) as amended by EA 2002, Sch 21, para 39 (which, as noted above, is not yet in force).

(b)   the provision of efficient education for the children with whom he will be
         educated, and

(c)   the efficient use of resources,

that the child engages in the activities of the school together with children who do not
have SEN.[1] Since the governing bodies of such schools are almost universally the only
body with power to discipline the staff employed to work at schools conducted by
them,[2] only they will be in a position to enforce this duty. Their public accountability
(if any) for a failure to do so will be via their annual report,[3] which must include a
report containing such information as may be prescribed by regulations about the
implementation of the governing body's policy for pupils with SEN.[4] The annual
report must also include information as to the arrangements for the admission of
disabled pupils,[5] the steps taken to prevent disabled pupils from being treated less
favourably than other pupils, and the facilities provided to assist access to the school
by disabled pupils.[6]

6.25   Where a statement of SEN names a maintained school or a maintained nursery
school, the governing body of the school must admit the pupil to the school.[7] It is
irrelevant that the LEA which maintains the statement is not the LEA which
maintains the school.[8] Further, where an LEA maintains a statement of SEN for a
child under s 324 and in pursuance of the statement the child is educated at a school
maintained by another LEA, the governing body is bound by s 327(2) of the EA 1996
not to impede access at any reasonable time to the premises of the school for the
purpose of monitoring the special educational provision made in pursuance of the
statement for the child at the school.[9]

Health authorities, Primary Care Trusts and local authorities

6.26   Where it appears to an LEA that any health authority, Primary Care Trust or
any local authority could, by taking any specified action, help in the exercise of any of

---

[1]   EA 1996, s 317(4).
[2]   Only the governing body of a maintained school whose right to a delegated budget has been suspended
       will not have the power to discipline staff: see paras **15.74** and **15.75**.
[3]   That is (see s 317(7) as amended by EA 2002, Sch 21, para 39 – which, as noted above, is not yet in
       force) the annual report prepared under the articles of government for the school under s 30(1) of the
       EA 2002.
[4]   EA 1996, s 317(5). The relevant regulations are the Education (Special Educational Needs)
       (Information) (Wales) Regulations 1999, SI 1999/1442 and the Education (Special Educational Needs)
       (Information) (England) Regulations 1999, SI 1999/2506.
[5]   That is pupils who are disabled persons for the purposes of the DDA 1995: s 317(6).
[6]   EA 1996, s 317(6).
[7]   Ibid, s 324(5)(b) as amended by EA 2002, Sch 21, para 43 (which, as noted above, is not yet in force).
       This does not affect any power to exclude from a school a pupil who is already a registered pupil there:
       s 324(6).
[8]   *R v Chair of Governors and Headteacher of a School, ex parte T* [2000] ELR 274.
[9]   LEAs have the power to inspect schools maintained by them for specific purposes such as this under
       s 25 of the SIA 1996. In addition, a person authorised by an LEA which arranges for pupils to attend a
       non-maintained special school has the right to have access to the school at all reasonable times: see the
       Education (Special Schools) Regulations 1994, SI 1994/652, reg 5 and Sch, Part II, para 19 and the
       Education (Non-Maintained Special Schools) (England) Regulations 1999, SI 1999/2257, reg 4 and
       Sch, Part II, para 19.

its functions under Part IV of the EA 1996, it may request the help of the authority or trust in question in relation to the specified action.[1] The authority to which the request has been made must comply with it unless one of several exceptions applies. The first is that it considers that the help requested is not necessary 'for the purpose of the exercise by the local education authority of those functions'.[2] In R *v Staffordshire County Council, ex parte Reynolds*,[3] Kay J decided that the words had to be read literally, and that unless a request purportedly made under s 322(1) is made for the purposes of the requesting LEA's functions, the request is not a request made under s 322(1). This might be thought to render s 322(1) otiose: there appears to be no reason why the request should be made specifically for the purpose of the requesting LEA's functions, since the request will be that the other authority exercises one or more of *its* functions, which the LEA will by necessary implication be unable to exercise.

6.27 The second exception applies only in the case of a health authority or Primary Care Trust, and is that the authority or trust:

> 'consider that, having regard to the resources available to them for the purpose of the exercise of their functions under the National Health Service Act 1977, it is not reasonable for them to comply with the request.'[4]

6.28 The third exception applies only to a local authority, and is that the authority:

> 'consider that the request is not compatible with their own statutory or other duties and obligations or unduly prejudices the discharge of any of their functions.'[5]

6.29 An LEA may not request help from a health authority under s 322(1) and then, when such help is not provided, decline to make the provision required by a statement of SEN made under s 324.[6] The duty to maintain such a statement cannot be delegated to a health authority by the making of a request under s 322(1).[7]

6.30 If a health authority or a Primary Care Trust in the course of exercising any of their functions in relation to a child who is under compulsory school age, form the opinion that the child has or probably has SEN[8] then it must, after giving the child's parent an opportunity to discuss that opinion with an officer of the authority or trust, bring it to the attention of the appropriate LEA.[9] It must also inform the child's

---

1   EA 1996, s 322(1). Section 322(4) provides that regulations may prescribe the period within which a request made under s 322(1) must be complied with, and reg 12(8)–(11) of the Education (Special Educational Needs) (England) (Consolidation) Regulations 2001, SI 2001/3455 and of the Education (Special Educational Needs) (Wales) Regulations 2002, SI 2002/152 have so provided. The periods are 6 weeks unless for various reasons (see reg 12(9)–(11)) it is impracticable to do so. The help requested could consist only of the provision of information relating to a particular child.
2   EA 1996, s 322(2)(a).
3   [1998] EdCR 295.
4   EA 1996, s 322(2)(b) and (3)(a). A health authority may ration its resources available to meet requests made under s 322(1): R *v Brent and Harrow Health Authority, ex parte Harrow London Borough Council* [1997] ELR 187.
5   EA 1996, s 322(2)(b) and (3)(b).
6   R *v Harrow London Borough Council, ex parte M* [1997] ELR 62.
7   Ibid, at p 64D–E.
8   As defined in s 312; see para **6.3**.
9   EA 1996, s 332(1) and (2)(b), as amended.

parent of that opinion and of that duty.[1] If it is of the opinion that a particular voluntary organisation is likely to be able to give the parent advice or assistance in connection with any SEN which the child may have, then it must also inform the parent accordingly.[2]

SOME GENERAL PRINCIPLES AND STATUTORY POWERS REGARDING PUPILS WITH SPECIAL EDUCATIONAL NEEDS

6.31   There are some general principles contained in the EA 1996 and the case-law which apply to the education of children with SEN. The most important principle in the Act is contained in s 316, which is subject to the exceptions set out in s 316A. Both of those sections were inserted by s 1 of the SENDA 2001. Their effect is as follows. If no statement of SEN is maintained for a child under s 324 of the EA 1996 but he 'should be educated in a school', then he 'must' be educated in a mainstream school.[3] The definition of a mainstream school for the purposes of ss 316 and 316A is in s 316(4) and is any school other than a special school or an independent school which is not a city technology college, a city college for the technology of the arts, or a city academy.[4] If a statement of SEN *is* so maintained, then the child must be educated in a mainstream school unless either exception in s 316(3) applies, which is that such education is incompatible with (a) the wishes of his parent, or (b) the provision of efficient education for other children.[5] An LEA may, in relation to its mainstream schools taken as a whole, rely on the latter exception only if it shows that 'there are not reasonable steps that they could take to prevent the incompatibility'.[6] In relation to a particular mainstream school, an LEA or the governing body may rely on that exception only if it shows that there are no reasonable steps that it or another authority in relation to the school[7] could take to prevent that incompatibility.[8] The exception in s 316(3)(b) does not permit a governing body to fail to comply with s 324(5)(b) of the EA 1996.[9] The governing bodies of maintained schools and maintained nursery schools, and LEAs, must have regard to guidance issued by the Secretary of State or the National Assembly for Wales in relation to ss 316 and 316A,[1]

---

[1]   EA 1996, s 332(1) and (2)(a).
[2]   Ibid, s 332(3).
[3]   Ibid, s 316(1) and (2). A pupil referral unit is included in the definition of a school by virtue of s 4(1) and (2) of the EA 1996. This appears to have been overlooked in *R(C) v Special Educational Needs and Disability Tribunal* [2003] EWHC 1590 (Admin), [2004] ELR 111.
[4]   But not an Academy within the meaning of s 65 of the EA 2002, despite s 67 of that Act. This is an apparent oversight.
[5]   EA 1996, s 316(3).
[6]   Ibid, s 316A(5).
[7]   An authority in relation to a mainstream school is defined in s 316A(11).
[8]   EA 1996, s 316A(6) and (11). The word 'they' is used in relation to an LEA in s 316A(5), and 'it' in s 316A(6). This is despite the use of 'they' in relation to a governing body in eg s 21(4) of the EA 2002.
[9]   EA 1996, s 316A(7); see para **6.25** regarding s 324(5)(b).

316A,[1] which must relate to steps which may or may not be regarded as reasonable for these purposes.[2]

6.32   The principle in s 316 also does not prevent a child from being educated in an independent school which is not a mainstream school or a school which is approved under s 342 of the EA 1996 if the cost is met otherwise than by an LEA.[3] However, this does not affect the operation of s 348 of, or para 3 of Sch 27 to, the EA 1996.[4]

6.33   Section 316(3) does not have the effect that if a parent disagrees with the child being educated in a mainstream school then the child must be educated in a special school. Rather, it means that if the parent does not wish the child to be educated in a mainstream school then the qualified duty contained in s 316(3) does not apply. The LEA is then simply under a duty to consider what is best for the child, unless some other provision in the EA 1996 requires the authority to place the child in a special school.[5]

6.34   The most important principle concerning the education of children with SEN in the relevant case-law is probably that contained in the case of *R v Surrey County Council, ex parte H*.[6] There, it was stressed that an LEA is not under a duty to provide the best possible education for such a child. Slade LJ stated:

> '[T]here is no question of Parliament having placed the local authority under an obligation to provide a child with the best possible education. There is no duty on the authority to provide such a Utopian system, or to educate him or her to his or her maximum potential. With great respect to [the applicant's] parents, I am not sure that they have fully appreciated the constraints under which the county council themselves operate under the relevant legislation.'[7]

6.35   Sedley J put it this way in *R v Cheshire County Council, ex parte C*:[8]

> 'there is nothing in the statutory scheme which calls upon the local education authority to specify the optimum available provision and much in its general duty of husbandry to entitle it to choose the least expensive of the appropriate options.'

6.36   However, an LEA or the Tribunal is not *obliged* to choose the least expensive of the appropriate options,[9] and a school will not be appropriate merely because it is 'adequate'.[10] Further, where a parent seeks the education of his child at a non-

---

[1]   EA 1996, s 316A(8). See DfES/0074/2001, 'Inclusive Schooling – Children with Special Educational Needs'.

[2]   EA 1996, s 316A(9).

[3]   Ibid, s 316A(1).

[4]   Ibid, s 316A(3); see para **4.63** regarding s 348 and paras **6.60** et seq regarding Sch 27, para 3. In *R (MH) v Special Educational Needs and Disability Tribunal* [2004] EWCA Civ 770, (2004) *The Times*, July 8, it was held that ss 316 and 316A come into play only when the Sch 27, para 3 process has been exhausted.

[5]   *L v Worcestershire County Council* [2000] ELR 674, CA.

[6]   (1985) 83 LGR 219.

[7]   Ibid, at 235.

[8]   [1998] ELR 66, at 78D.

[9]   *South Glamorgan County Council v L and M* [1996] ELR 400, at 408E–F.

[10]   *C v Buckinghamshire County Council* [1999] ELR 179; see para **6.63**.

maintained special school, s 9 of the EA 1996 applies.[1] The proper approach to take according to Sedley LJ, giving the judgment of the Court of Appeal in *Oxfordshire County Council v GB*,[2] in this regard is as follows:

'15. ... In our judgment the chief object of the last part of s.9 is to prevent parental choice placing an undue or disproportionate burden on the education budget. When one considers that a single placement in the independent sector may well cost a ring-fenced education budget more than a teacher's salary, one can readily see why.

16. In cases like the present, the parental preference for an independent school over an available state school, while perfectly reasonable, may have difficult cost implications for the LEA. In that event it is for the LEA, or on appeal the SENT, to decide whether those cost implications make the expenditure on the independent school unreasonable. This means striking a balance between (a) the educational advantages of the placement preferred by the parents and (b) the extra cost of it to the LEA as against what it will cost the LEA to place the child in the maintained school.[3] In cases where the state system simply cannot provide for the child's needs, there will be no choice: the LEA must pay the cost. In cases where the choice is between two independent schools, it is accepted on all hands that the second criterion is simply the respective annual fees, whatever the comparative capital costs or other sources of income of the two establishments: for example, the one with lower fees may have private or charitable funding, but this will have no bearing on the quantum of public expenditure involved in a placement there.'

6.37   In *S v Somerset County Council*,[4] Sir Richard Tucker decided that the costs to be taken into account when applying s 9 are those of the LEA only, and not also those of the same corporate body acting as the local social services authority. As can be seen, the above passage could be taken to provide some mild support for that decision, given its express reference to 'the education budget', but given also that the point was clearly not in issue in that case.

6.38   The cost of the provision must be calculated over its proposed life. Thus if one proposed programme of provision will extend over a longer period than another, then the total cost of the longer period must be compared with that of the shorter proposed programme. This was expressly held by Sullivan J in *Southampton City Council v TG*[5] where the Tribunal had failed to take into account that the longer programme (of 6 years) would necessarily cost more than the shorter one (of 5 years). However, no allowance was (seemingly erroneously) made by Sullivan J for the likely cost of the

1 See paras **2.116** et seq regarding s 9.
2 [2002] ELR 8.
3 Of course, all relevant costs must be included. Even if, taking into account costs which should have been (but were not) taken into account, there is still a significant difference between the parent's proposed provision and that which is proposed by the LEA, a decision of the SENDIST may still be quashed: see *Wardle-Heron v London Borough of Newham* [2002] EWHC 2086 (Admin); [2004] ELR 68, para 16.
4 [2003] ELR 78; that case was relied on by the appellant, but determined by Gibbs J to be irrelevant on the facts, in *Oxfordshire County Council v M* [2002] EWHC 2908; [2003] ELR 718.
5 [2002] EWHC 1516 (Admin); [2002] ELR 698.

provision which would have to be made after the shorter proposed programme had expired.[1]

6.39 In *R v Cumbria County Council, ex parte NB*,[2] Schiemann J went so far as to say that 'the local education authority has the widest discretion as to whether or not to statement a child with special educational needs'.[3] This, however, appears to go too far, bearing in mind that s 324 provides as follows:

> '(1) If, in the light of an assessment under s 323 of any child's educational needs and of any representations made by the child's parent in pursuance of Schedule 27, it is necessary[4] for the local education authority to determine the special educational provision which any learning difficulty he may have calls for, the authority shall make and maintain a statement of his special educational needs.'

6.40 The discussion in *Duties and Powers: The Law Governing the Provision of Further Education to Students with Learning Difficulties and/or Disabilities*[5] at paras 26–46 and the criticism expressed there of the decision in *R v Gloucestershire County Council, ex parte Mahfood*[6] is illuminating in regard to the latitude of a public body where it is under a 'specific' duty such as that in s 324(1). However, although the *Mahfood* decision at first instance was overruled (under the name of *R v Gloucestershire County Council, ex parte Barry*) by the Court of Appeal,[7] the House of Lords in turn allowed the appeal against that decision.[8] In doing so, the House of Lords ruled that a local authority's resources were relevant in determining what was 'necessary' in a slightly different context. Given the further decision of the House of Lords in *R v East Sussex County Council, ex parte Tandy*,[9] however, the best view appears to be that a scarcity of resources would *not* affect the duty of an LEA under s 324(1).[10] In any event, it does seem that the approach of Schiemann J in *ex parte NB* went too far, and that an LEA does not have as much latitude as he suggested.

---

1   See ibid, para 18. The report contains (in paras 25–27) useful guidance regarding opposition to what is clearly a mistaken ruling of the Tribunal, although, as indicated in the text to this note, the ruling in question appears not to have been as clearly wrong as Sullivan J thought.

2   [1996] ELR 65.

3   Ibid, at 69H.

4   Guidance as to the meaning of the word 'necessary' may be provided by the decision of the House of Lords in *Devon County Council v George* [1989] AC 573, where it was said that the word 'necessary' in s 509(1) of the EA 1996 (which imposes the duty to provide free transport in certain circumstances where the local education authority consider it 'necessary' to do so: see further, paras **4.12** et seq) meant 'really needed': ibid, at 604B.

5   Attributed to Beachcroft Stanleys, the work is further subtitled 'A Report to the Learning Difficulties and/or Disabilities Committee', and was published by HMSO in 1996 in conjunction with the Further Education Funding Council.

6   (1995) *The Times*, June 21.

7   [1996] 4 All ER 421.

8   [1997] AC 584.

9   [1998] AC 714; [1998] ELR 251, as to which, see para **4.4**.

10   The approach of Collins J in *R v London Borough of Hillingdon, ex parte Governing Body of Queensmead School* [1997] ELR 331 so far as relevant was based on the Court of Appeal decision in *ex parte Barry*. In the light of the decision of the House of Lords in *ex parte Tandy*, it seems that that part of his judgment is nevertheless correct.

6.41   Several statutory powers need to be mentioned here. The first is that where an LEA is satisfied that it would be inappropriate for the special educational provision which is required to be made for a child (or any part of such provision) to be made in a school, it may under s 319(1) arrange for that provision (or that part of it) to be made otherwise than in school.[1] However, before doing so, it must consult the parent of the child.[2] Where the LEA is of the view that education in a school is appropriate, it may not exercise the power in s 319(1).[3]

6.42   An LEA also has the power to make arrangements for the education at an institution outside England and Wales of a child for whom it maintains a statement under s 324.[4] The institution must specialise in providing for children who would, if they were in England and Wales, be classified as having 'special educational needs' within the meaning of the EA 1996.[5] The arrangements may include contributing to or paying (1) fees charged by the institution, (2) expenses reasonably incurred in maintaining the child while he is at the institution or travelling to or from it, (3) the child's travelling expenses, and (4) expenses reasonably incurred by any person accompanying the child while he is travelling or staying at the institution.[6] This power to pay only part of the cost of educating a child with SEN is confined to the situation described in this paragraph. However, where it applies, and the cost of educating a child at a relevant institution abroad would, as a result of the possibility of the parents (or anyone else) paying part of the fees, be equal to the cost of the child's education in the least expensive manner, the choice with regard to the school to which the child should be sent is to be made on purely educational grounds.[7]

6.43   The power of an LEA to supply goods and services to the governing bodies of community, foundation or voluntary schools, or maintained nursery schools, under s 318 of the EA 1996, has already been mentioned.[8] Such supplies may be charged for in certain circumstances.[9]

6.44   Finally in this section, the possibility of a child with SEN not being required to follow the National Curriculum should be noted. This is the result of ss 92, 93, 113 and 114 of the EA 2002.[10]

---

[1]   This provision does not require an LEA to assess a child's special educational needs where the child wishes to be educated at a university or college: *R v Portsmouth City Council, ex parte Faludy* [1999] ELR 115.

[2]   EA 1996, s 319(2).

[3]   *T v Special Educational Needs Tribunal* [2002] EWHC 1474 (Admin); [2002] ELR 704, at para 38(i), per Richards J. At para 38(iii), which must be read with para 27 of the report, Richards J held that there was no room for the application of s 9 of the EA 1996 in the circumstances.

[4]   EA 1996, s 320(1). This is without prejudice to any other powers of an LEA: s 320(4).

[5]   Ibid, s 320(1) and (2).

[6]   Ibid, s 320(3).

[7]   *R v Cheshire County Council, ex parte C* [1998] ELR 66, at 78E–F.

[8]   See paras **4.76** et seq.

[9]   See s 318(2) and the Education (Payment for Special Needs Supplies) Regulations 1999, SI 1999/710.

[10]   See footnote 3 at para **6.74**.

THE PRINCIPLES IN THE CODE OF PRACTICE

6.45   The code of practice issued by the Secretary of State under s 313 of the EA 1996[1] (the SEN Code) contains a number of general principles which are intended to be applied by LEAs, the governing bodies of maintained schools, and 'settings in receipt of government funding to provide early education – and to those who help them, including the health services and social services'.[2] It also provides 'general practical guidance to such settings about the provision of nursery education to children with special educational needs'. The general principles are set out in paras 1:5 and 1:6 of the SEN Code. To an extent, they exhort compliance with the law – for example, in para 1:6 one of the 'Critical success factors' is that:

'LEAs make assessments and statements in accordance with prescribed time limits'.

6.46   This is the second code published under s 313. The first recommended the general adoption of a staged model of SEN. The first three stages were based in the school, and at stages 4 and 5 the LEA shared responsibility with schools. These stages have been replaced by a 'graduated approach', described by para 8 of the Foreword to the SEN Code:

'The revised Code recommends that, to help match special educational provision to children's needs, schools and LEAs should adopt a graduated approach. It sets out a model of school-based intervention for children with special educational needs within both early education and school settings: Early Years Action or School Action describes similar interventions to stage 2 in the 1994 Code, whilst Early Years Action Plus or School Action Plus corresponds largely to the previous stage 3.'

INITIATING ASSESSMENTS

Instigation by the Local Education Authority

Children under the age of 2

6.47   Where an LEA is of the opinion that a child in its area who is under the age of 2 has or probably has SEN in relation to which it is necessary to determine special educational provision, it may, but only with the consent of the child's parent, make an assessment of the child's SEN.[3]

Children aged 2 and above

6.48   Where an LEA is of the opinion that a child for whom it is responsible[4] has or probably has SEN in relation to which it is necessary to determine special educational

---

[1]   Regarding which, see para **6.19**.
[2]   SEN Code, para. 1:1.
[3]   EA 1996, s 331(1) and (2). See also para 4:48 of the SEN Code.
[4]   See EA 1996, s 321(3) and para **6.12** regarding children for whom an LEA is responsible; the definition excludes children under the age of 2.

provision, it is under a duty to serve notice on the child's parent under s 323(1).[1] The notice must inform the parent (a) that the authority proposes to make an assessment of the child's educational needs, (b) of the procedure to be followed in making the assessment, (c) of the name of the officer of the authority from whom further information may be obtained, and (d) of the parent's right to make representations and to submit written evidence to the authority within a period (which must be specified in the notice) of not less than 29 days beginning with the date of the notice.[2] A copy of the notice must be sent to (1) the social services authority, (2) the health authority, (3) if the child is registered at a school, the head teacher of the school, and (4) if the child receives education from an early education provider, the head of SEN in relation to that provider.[3] The LEA must, at the same time as serving such a copy, inform the recipient what help the authority is likely to request.[4]

6.49   Once the period specified in the notice has expired, if the LEA, having taken into account any representations made and any written evidence submitted by the parent, remain of the opinion that the child has or may have SEN in relation to which it is necessary to determine special educational provision, then it must make an assessment of his educational needs.[5] The authority must give notice in writing to the child's parent of its decision to make such an assessment, and of its reasons for the decision.[6] If, however, at any time after serving a notice under s 323(1), an LEA decides not to make an assessment of the child's educational needs after all, then it must give notice in writing of that decision to the child's parent.[7] Notice of a decision to make or, as the case may be, not to make an assessment, must normally be given to a parent within 6 weeks of the date of service of the notice served under s 323(1).[8] There is no right of appeal against a decision not to carry out an assessment in these circumstances.

---

[1]   The provisions of the SEN Code which are relevant to assessments include paras 4:41–4:47 and chapter 7.

[2]   EA 1996, s 323(1). The consent of the child's parent to the making of a medical examination or a psychological assessment will usually need to be obtained, and para 5:60 of the SEN Code recognises this.

[3]   Regulation 6(1) and (2) of the Education (Special Educational Needs) (England) (Consolidation) Regulations 2001, SI 2001/3455 and of the Education (Special Educational Needs) (Wales) Regulations 2002, SI 2002/152. Both sets of regulations are referred to below as the Special Educational Needs Regulations, and if no difference is mentioned between them, then it is because they are in identical terms.

[4]   Regulation 6(3) of the Education (Special Educational Needs) (England) (Consolidation) Regulations 2001, SI 2001/3455 and of the Education (Special Educational Needs) (Wales) Regulations 2002, SI 2002/152.

[5]   EA 1996, s 323(3).

[6]   Ibid, s 323(4).

[7]   Ibid, s 323(6). See also para 7:69 of the SEN Code which states, among other things, that 'Regardless of whether the initiative for a possible assessment came from the LEA or a request from the parents or school, the LEA should write to the school, as well as the child's parents, giving full reasons for their decision'.

[8]   Regulation 12(1)–(4) of the Special Educational Needs Regulations. The time allowed to the authority to consider any representations and evidence submitted by a parent under s 323(1)(d) may therefore be no more than 13 days. The circumstances when the time-limit of 6 weeks can be extended are set out in reg 12(5).

Instigation by a parent

Children under the age of 2

6.50   The parent of a child who is under the age of 2 may request the LEA to carry out an assessment of the child's educational needs, and the authority must comply with the request unless in its opinion the child does not have SEN in relation to which it is necessary to determine special educational provision.[1] There is no right of appeal against a decision not to comply with such a request.

Children over the age of 2

6.51   The parent of a child aged 2 or above for whom no statement is maintained under s 324 may, under s 329, ask the LEA to arrange an assessment under s 323 of the child's educational needs.[2] If no such assessment has been made within the period of 6 months ending with the date on which the request was made, then 'if it is necessary for the authority to make an assessment under that section', the authority must comply with the request.[3] Where a statement is maintained for a child under s 324, the child's parent requests an assessment under s 323, no such assessment has been made within the period of 6 months ending with the date on which the request was made, and it is necessary for the authority to make a further assessment under s 323, the authority must comply with the request.[4] In both situations, the LEA must give notice in writing to (1) the social services authority, (2) the health authority, (3) if the child is registered at a school, the head teacher of the school, and (4) if the child receives education from an early education provider, the head of SEN in relation to that provider.[5] The notice must inform the recipient that the request has been made and what help the LEA is likely to request.[6] Further, in both situations the LEA must normally within 6 weeks of the date of the parent's request give notice to the parent of its decision either to make an assessment or not to do so, and, in the latter case (1) of the availability to the parent of advice and information on matters related to the child's SEN from the 'parent partnership service' (that is the arrangements made by the LEA under s 332A[7]), (2) of the availability to the parent of arrangements for the prevention and resolution of disagreements between parents and authorities made by the LEA under s 332B,[8] (3) of the parent's right to appeal to the Tribunal against the determination not to make an assessment, (4) of the time-limit for doing so; and (5) that arrangements made under s 332B cannot affect the right to appeal, and that a parent may appeal *and* enter into such arrangements.[9]

---

[1]   EA 1996, s 331(1) and (2). See also para 4:47 of the SEN Code.
[2]   The restriction of s 329 to children aged 2 and above results from the applicability of that section only to children for whom an LEA is responsible, as to which see para **6.12**. Note also paras 3:18–3:21 of the SEN Code.
[3]   EA 1996, s 329(1). See also paras 4:39–4:47 of the SEN Code.
[4]   Ibid, s 328(2).
[5]   Regulation 6(1) and (2) of the Special Educational Needs Regulations.
[6]   Ibid, reg 6(3).
[7]   Regarding which, see para **6.16**.
[8]   Ibid.
[9]   EA 1996, s 328(3) and (3A); reg 12(2) of the Special Educational Needs Regulations. The exceptions to the duty to give notice within 6 weeks are set out in reg 12(5). Note also para 7:16 of the SEN Code.

Instigation by the head teacher or proprietor of a school or pupil referral unit, or by the person or persons responsible for the management of publicly-funded nursery education

6.52   Section 329A of the EA 1996 (inserted by s 8 of the SENDA 2001) applies where a child is a registered pupil at a maintained school, a maintained nursery school, a pupil referral unit, an independent school or a school approved under s 342 of the EA 1996. It also applies where a child is provided with nursery education within the meaning of s 123 of the SSFA 1998.[1] In all those cases, if (1) the person or body defined as the 'responsible body' by s 329A(13) asks the LEA to arrange for an assessment to be carried out under s 323 and no such assessment has been made within the period of 6 months ending with the date of the request, and (2) it is necessary for the authority to make such an assessment, then the LEA must comply with the request.[2] Before deciding whether to comply with the request, the LEA must serve notice on the child's parent in accordance with s 329A(3).[3] If the LEA decides not to carry out an assessment under s 329A, the parent has a right of appeal to the Tribunal against that decision.[4]

PROCEDURE TO BE FOLLOWED IN THE MAKING OF AN ASSESSMENT

6.53   An assessment of a child under the age of 2 may be made in any manner which the authority considers appropriate.[5] The procedure to be followed in the making of an assessment under s 323 of the educational needs of a child aged 2 or above is, however, prescribed in regulations made under s 323(5) of and Sch 26 to the EA 1996.[6] These are regs 7–12 of the Special Educational Needs Regulations. Regulation 7 prescribes the advice to be sought: advice from the child's parent, educational advice of the sort specified in reg 6, medical advice sought from the health authority as provided for in reg 9,[7] psychological advice as provided for in reg 10, advice from the social services authority[8] and 'any other advice which the authority consider appropriate for the purpose of arriving at a satisfactory assessment'.[9] The nature of

---

See paras **6.108** and **6.113** regarding the right of appeal under ss 329(2)(b) and 328(3)(b) respectively against a refusal to comply with the request.

[1]   That is, education of the sort referred to in s 123(4), regarding which see the opening sentence of para **2.73**.

[2]   EA 1996, s 329A(1) and (2).

[3]   This is in the same terms as s 323(1), regarding which see para **6.48**. The rest of the procedure required by s 329A and the Special Educational Needs Regulations is also in the same, or similar terms.

[4]   EA 1996, s 329A(8)(b).

[5]   Ibid, s 331(3). See also para 4:47 of the SEN Code.

[6]   See also paras 4:41–4:43 and chapter 7 of the SEN Code.

[7]   Such advice must be given within 6 weeks of the date when it was requested unless one of the circumstances referred to in reg 12(9) or (10) of the Special Educational Needs Regulations exists: reg 12(8) of those regulations.

[8]   The time-limit which applies to advice sought from the health authority applies also to advice sought from the social services authority: reg 12(8), (9) and (11) of the Special Educational Needs Regulations.

[9]   Regulation 7(1)(f). See generally, paras 7:78-7:84 of the SEN Code regarding the advice which is to be sought under reg 7(1). 'Any other advice' may include medical advice other than that to which reg 7(1)(C) applies: *R v Commissioner for Local Administration, ex parte S* [1999] ELR 102.

the advice is specified in reg 7(2), and the manner in which it is to be sought or given is prescribed by reg 7(3) and (4).[1] If relevant advice has been sought within the preceding 12 months, there may be no need to seek further advice of the same sort.[2] The SEN Code recommends (in para 7:85) that the views of the child are identified and taken into account by the LEA.

6.54 The assessment must normally be made within 10 weeks of the date on which the LEA gave notice to the parent of the child in question of its decision under s 323(4) to assess the child's educational needs.[3] Regulation 11 obliges the LEA to take into consideration when making an assessment not only the advice obtained under reg 7 but also any representations made by the child's parent and evidence submitted by the parent or at his request under s 323(1)(d) or 329A(3)(d). If the LEA wishes an examination of the child to be carried out for the purpose of the assessment, it may serve notice on the child's parent requiring the child's attendance for such examination.[4] The parent may be present at the examination if he so wishes,[5] and the notice must inform the parent of this right, as well as (a) the purpose of the examination, (b) the time and place at which the examination will be held, (c) the name of an officer of the authority from whom further information may be obtained, and (d) that the parent may submit such information to the authority as he may wish.[6] It is an offence to fail without reasonable excuse to comply with any requirement of such a notice if the notice relates to a child who is not over compulsory school age at the time stated in the notice as the time for holding the examination.[7] The maximum penalty for committing such offence is a fine not exceeding level 2 on the standard scale.[8]

6.55 The authority must, within 2 weeks of completion of the assessment of a child for whom no statement of SEN is maintained, either give notice under s 325(1) to the parent that it does not propose to make such a statement and that the parent may appeal against that decision to the Tribunal, or (as the case may be) serve on the parent a copy of the proposed statement and a written notice of the sort referred to below.[9]

---

1   In *R v Commissioner for Local Administration, ex parte S* [1999] ELR 102, at 111A Collins J said: 'The council, as it seems to me, quite clearly has the obligation to ensure that the advice that it has sought is properly received. Of course if the advice is given and there is no reason for the council to believe it is other than full advice, then it cannot be criticised. If, on the other hand, it is plain that the advice is not full advice and that there are gaps which ought to be filled, then, as it seems to me, the obligation is clearly upon the council to seek and obtain any further advice that is necessary to fill such gaps'.
2   Regulation 7(5).
3   Regulation 12(6) of the Special Educational Needs Regulations. The occasions when this time-limit does not need to be complied with are set out in reg 12(7).
4   EA 1996, Sch 26, para 4(1).
5   Ibid, Sch 26, para 4(2).
6   Ibid, Sch 26, para 4(3).
7   Ibid, Sch 26, para 5(1). The fact that para 5(1) refers to 'any requirements' should, it is suggested, not be regarded as requiring more than one requirement in the notice not to have been complied with for the offence to have been committed.
8   Ibid, Sch 26, para 5(2); level 2 is currently £500.
9   Regulation 17(1) of the Special Educational Needs Regulations. See para **6.66** for the form of the notice. See para 7:88 of the SEN Code regarding the situation where the LEA decides not to make a

6.56   Where an assessment is made of a child for whom a statement of SEN is maintained, the LEA must, within 2 weeks of the date when the assessment was completed (1) serve notice on the parent under paras 2A(2) and 2B(2) of Sch 27 to the EA 1996[1] and a copy of the proposed amended statement, (2) serve notice under para 11(2) of Sch 27 that it has determined to cease to maintain the statement, that the parent may appeal to the Tribunal against that determination, and the time-limit for doing so, or (3) serve notice on the parent informing him that it has determined not to amend the statement, their reasons for so determining, and giving certain other information.[2] That other information includes that the parent has the right to appeal to the Tribunal against the description in the statement of the LEA's assessment of the child's SEN, the special educational provision specified in the statement, or, if no school is named in the statement, that fact.[3]

STATEMENTS OF SPECIAL EDUCATIONAL NEEDS

Making a statement

6.57   The duty of an LEA to make and maintain a statement of SEN is imposed by s 324 of the EA 1996 as supplemented by Sch 27 to that Act. If, in the light of an assessment under s 323 of any child's educational needs and of any representations made by the parent under Sch 27, it is necessary to determine the special educational provision which any learning difficulty the child may have calls for, then the authority must make and maintain a statement of the child's SEN.[4]

6.58   An LEA needs to determine the special educational provision which a learning difficulty of a child who is aged 2 or above calls for, only when the provision in question is not made generally for children of the child's age in schools maintained by the authority (other than special schools) in its area.[5] It was held in relation to the relevant corresponding provision of the EA 1981, s 7(1), that an LEA need not necessarily make a statement for a child who had SEN.[6] Although the wording in s 324(1) of the EA 1996 is different from that of s 7(1) of the EA 1981, the effect of s 324(1) is probably in practice the same. This is because all that s 324(1) requires is that a statement be made for a child in relation to whom it is 'necessary for the LEA to determine the special educational provision which any learning difficulty he may have calls for', and even if a child has a special educational need, it may not be necessary to determine the provision to meet it. However, once an LEA has determined that it is necessary to make a statement of some of the child's SEN, it

---

statement. In such a situation, the LEA should 'preferably provide a note in lieu of a statement'. See para **6.108** regarding the right of appeal.

[1]   Regarding which, see para **6.100**.

[2]   Regulation 17(2) of the Special Educational Needs Regulations.

[3]   Ibid. See para **6.111** regarding the right of appeal.

[4]   EA 1996, s 324(1). See also paras **6.39** and **6.40**.

[5]   Ibid, s 312(4), and see R *v Hampshire Education Authority, ex parte J* (1985) 84 LGR 547, at 555–556. So, for example, provision for deaf children will be special educational provision. On statements for children below the age of 2, see paras 4:48–4:53 of the SEN Code.

[6]   R *v Secretary of State for Education and Science, ex parte Lashford* [1988] 1 FLR 72; (1988) 86 LGR 13, CA.

must make the statement in relation to all of his needs.[1] Further, once any such need is so specified, the provision to be made for it must be specified in the statement also.[2]

6.59   If an LEA believes that it is necessary to make a statement of a child's SEN then it must serve on the parent concerned a copy of the proposed statement and a notice explaining (1) the effect of paras 3 and 4 of Sch 27 (regarding which, see the following paras below) in the circumstances, and (2) the right of appeal under s 326.[3] The parent may make representations (or further representations) to the LEA about the content of the statement and may, within 15 days of service of the notice, require the authority to arrange a meeting between him and an officer of the authority, at which the statement can be discussed.[4] Where a meeting of this sort is arranged, and after it the parent disagrees with any part of the assessment, the parent may, within 15 days of the date fixed for the meeting, require the authority to arrange 'such meeting or meetings as they consider will enable him to discuss the relevant advice with the appropriate person or persons'.[5] The parent's representations must be made within 15 days of either the service of the notice or the date of the relevant meeting or (if there are more than one) last relevant meeting.[6]

6.60   The parent in addition has the right to express a preference as to the maintained school[7] at which he wishes education to be provided for his child, and to give reasons for such preference.[8] This preference must be expressed or made within the period of 15 days of either the service of the notice described in para **6.59** or the date of the meeting (or, if there are more than one, the last meeting) arranged under para 4 of Sch 27.[9] Where such a preference is expressed, and the LEA makes a statement under s 324, it must specify the school for which the preference was expressed unless one of two conditions in paragraph 3(3) of Sch 27 is satisfied. Those are that either:

'(a)   the school is unsuitable to the child's age, ability or aptitude or to his special educational needs, or

(b)   the attendance of the child at the school would be incompatible with the provision of efficient education for the children with whom he would be educated or the efficient use of resources.'[10]

---

1   *R v Secretary of State for Education and Science, ex parte E* [1992] 1 FLR 377, CA.
2   Ibid. But see *Re L* [1994] ELR 16, as to which, see further para **6.77**.
3   EA 1996, Sch 27, paras 2 and 2B. The notice must contain the information specified in Part A of Sch 1 to the Special Educational Needs Regulations. The statement may not specify the type of school, or the school, at which the LEA propose that the child is to be educated: Sch 27, para 2(4). For the time-limit for the service of the notice, see para **6.55**. For Wales, see also the Education (Special Educational Needs) (Prescribed Forms) (Welsh Forms) Regulations 1995, SI 1995/45.
4   EA 1996, Sch 27, para 4(1), (4) and (5). See also paras 8:105–8:107 of the SEN Code.
5   EA 1996, Sch 27, para 4(2) and (6).
6   Ibid, Sch 27, para 4(4).
7   This includes a maintained special school not established in a hospital: s 312(5).
8   EA 1996, Sch 27, para 3(1). See also paras 4:45, 4:55, and 8:57–8:69 of the SEN Code.
9   Ibid, Sch 27, para 3(2).
10   Note also para 4:45 of the SEN Code.

6.61   Paragraph 3(3) of Sch 27 was held by Sedley LJ (with whom the other Lord Justices agreed) in *C v Buckinghamshire County Council*[1] not to exclude the application of s 9 of the EA 1996[2] to all SEN cases: if para 3(3) applies then there is no room for the application of s 9, but if the school preferred by a parent is an independent school then s 9 applies.[3] Sedley LJ also stated that the effect of para 3(3) 'is that in special educational needs cases a duly expressed parental preference for a state-sector school is binding in the absence of a disqualifying factor'.[4]

6.62   Paragraph 3(3) of Sch 27 was determined in *C v Lancashire County Council*[5] to be identical in effect to s 316(1) and (2) of the EA 1996 in its original form.[6] Accordingly, it was there held, all three conditions in para 3(3) need to be satisfied.[7] It was held in *Surrey County Council v P*[8] that it would be wrong to consider the advantages to a child in attending the school at which his parents preferred him to be educated when considering whether these conditions are satisfied. Further, it was stated (obiter) in that case that:

> 'the use of the word "incompatible" indicates that something more than a marginal disadvantage has to be demonstrated. If the situation was that one alternative would result in significant additional expenditure, then provided both schools were appropriate for the child's special educational needs, the local authority would be entitled to justify sending the child to a school other than that of the parents' choice.'[9]

6.63   As Thorpe LJ stated in *C v Buckinghamshire County Council*:[10]

> '[T]he LEA has a duty to ensure that a child with special educational needs is placed at a school that is "appropriate". It is not enough for the school to be merely adequate. To determine if the school is appropriate, an assessment must be made both of what it offers and what the child needs. Unless what the school offers matches what the child needs, it is unlikely to be appropriate. The assessment of the child's needs necessarily imports elements of a welfare judgment. If there are two schools offering facilities and standards that exceed the test of adequacy, then I would hope that ordinarily speaking the better would be judged appropriate, assuming no mismatch between specific facilities and specific needs. Parental preference obviously has a part to play in the assessment of what is appropriate. In a case where there appears to be a parity of cost and parity of facilities, parental preference may be the decisive factor. But it would be wrong to elevate parental preference to the height that Mr Bowen appeared to contend for in his submissions [for the parent]. A bare preference might be ill-informed or capricious. In practice, parental preference may mean a fair opportunity to the parents to contend by evidence and argument for one school in preference to another. Therefore, preferences must be reasoned to enable the parent to demonstrate that they rest on a sound foundation of accurate information and wise judgment.'

[1] [1999] ELR 179, at 185; [1999] EdCR 690, at 696F–697F.
[2] Regarding which, see paras **2.116** et seq.
[3] See further, para **6.36**.
[4] [1999] ELR 179, at 185. See further the passage in the judgment of Thorpe LJ, set out in para **6.63**.
[5] [1997] ELR 377, at 380D.
[6] See paras **6.31–6.33** for the new ss 316 and 316A which replaced the original s 316.
[7] [1997] ELR 377, at 380D.
[8] [1997] ELR 516, at 523A–B.
[9] [1997] ELR 516, at 523B–C.
[10] [1999] ELR 179, at 189E; [1999] EdCR 690, at 702C.

6.64   In *F v Special Education Needs Tribunal*[1] it was said by Moses J that in determining whether the attendance of the relevant child at the school for which a preference has been expressed would be incompatible with the efficient use of resources, the authority must carry out an exercise balancing the disadvantages of an inefficient use of its resources with the advantages of compliance with the preference. That case was appealed (eventually to the House of Lords, whose decision was reported under the name of *B v London Borough of Harrow*[2]), but this statement of Moses J was not criticised either by the Court of Appeal[3] or by the House of Lords. The effect of the ruling of the House of Lords is of considerable practical importance. It is that where the school at which a parent wants his child to be educated is situated in the area of a neighbouring LEA, the resources which are to be taken into account in determining whether there would be an inefficient use of resources are only those of the LEA in whose area the child lives.

6.65   Before specifying in a statement the name of a maintained school or maintained nursery school, an LEA must serve a copy of the proposed statement on, and consult, the governing body of that school, and, if the school is maintained by another LEA, that other authority.[4]

6.66   Where an LEA has served a proposed statement on a parent under para 2 of Sch 27 and they subsequently decide to make a statement, then it must within 8 weeks of the date of service of the proposed statement (unless any relevant exception applies) serve on the parent a copy of a completed statement and a written notice of his right to appeal under s 326(1) against (a) the description in the statement of the authority's assessment of the child's SEN, (b) the special educational provision specified in the statement (including the name of a school specified in the statement), or (c) if no school is named in the statement, that fact.[5]

6.67   However, before serving the completed statement, the authority must consider any representations made to it, and the period or the last of the periods allowed by para 4 of Sch 27 for making requirements or further representations must have elapsed.[6] It is, furthermore, provided (presumably for the avoidance of doubt) that the statement may be in the form originally proposed (except as to the matters which were required by para 2 to be excluded from the proposed statement), or in a form modified in the light of the representations.[7]

---

[1]   [1998] EdCR 1, at 11D (reported also in (1997) *The Times*, December 29, under the name of *F v Harrow London Borough Council*), applying *Crane v Lancashire County Council* (1997) *The Times*, May 16. The latter was subsequently reported as *C v Lancashire County Council* [1997] ELR 377.

[2]   [2000] 1 WLR 223; [2000] ELR 109.

[3]   [1998] ELR 351; [1998] EdCR 176: see at 186G–187A and 360D–E respectively.

[4]   EA 1996, Sch 27, para 3A as amended by EA 2002, Sch 21, para 58 (which is not yet in force) so as to apply para 3A to maintained nursery schools.

[5]   See reg 17(3) and (4) of the Special Educational Needs Regulations and the EA 1996, Sch 27, para 6.

[6]   EA 1996, Sch 27, para 5(1).

[7]   Ibid, Sch 27, para 5(2).

Content of a statement

6.68   The statement must be in the form and contain the information prescribed by regulations.[1] The statement must give details of the LEA's assessment of the child's SEN and specify the special educational provision to be made for the purpose of meeting those needs.[2] The LEA will not comply with its duty under this subsection in relation to the educational provision to be made if it specifies in a child's statement directly or indirectly that the parent will make all or part of that provision himself.[3] However, to require a parent to participate in his child's educational programme during the weeks when the child is not at school, by requiring the parent:

> 'to work with the grain of the specialist treatment she receives, to liaise with the specialist providers by "adopting a constructive and compatible approach at home during times of non-educational care", to use Pitchford J's phrase [in *R(A) v Cambridgeshire County Council*[4]], does not offend against the principle that it is for the LEA and for it alone to provide for I's special educational needs.'[5]

6.69   The statement must have sufficient 'specificity', to use the term used by Laws J in *L v Clarke and Somerset County Council*,[6] where Laws J stated: 'it is plain that the statute requires a very high degree of specificity'. Since then, the extent to which it is necessary to specify the educational provision in a statement of SEN has been considered in the High Court on a number of occasions,[7] and three times in the Court of Appeal.[8] The outcome of those cases is that the degree of specificity required will depend on the circumstances, and that it may be appropriate to a certain extent to leave open the particular provision to be made in respect of a particular need, so that that provision can be 'decided upon as the child's attendance at school and progress in that school' indicates.[9] However, this is likely to be lawful only where the LEA or the Tribunal can be sure that the necessary provision will be made despite the absence of a specification of the minimum provision which is required. According to Stanley Burnton J in *E v London Borough of Newham*:

---

[1]   EA 1996, s 324(2). The current regulations are the Special Educational Needs Regulations; see further, para **6.76**.

[2]   Ibid, s 324(3).

[3]   *R(A) v Cambridgeshire County Council* [2002] EWHC 2391 (Admin), [2003] ELR 464, at para 60, applied in *DM & KC v Essex County Council* [2003] EWHC 135 (Admin), [2003] ELR 491.

[4]   [2003] ELR 464, at para 63.

[5]   *R(KW) v SENT & Rochdale Metropolitan Borough Council* [2003] EWHC 1770 (Admin); [2003] ELR 566, para 26, per Mackay J.

[6]   [1998] ELR 129, at 136H.

[7]   Including *C v Special Educational Needs Tribunal* [1999] ELR 5; *S v City and Council of Swansea and Confrey* [2000] ELR 315; *H v Leicestershire County Council* [2000] ELR 471; *S v London Borough of Hackney* [2002] ELR 45; *E v Rotherham Metropolitan Borough Council* [2002] ELR 266; *E v Flintshire County Council* [2002] ELR 378; and *E v London Borough of Newham* [2002] ELR 453.

[8]   *London Borough of Bromley v Special Educational Needs Tribunal* [1999] ELR 260; *E v Newham LBC* [2003] EWCA Civ 09; [2003] ELR 286; and *R (IPSEA Ltd) v Secretary of State* [2003] EWCA Civ 07; [2003] ELR 393.

[9]   See per Collins J in *S v London Borough of Hackney* [2002] ELR 45, at para 36. Stanley Burnton J said at para 39 of the report of *E v London Borough of Newham* [2002] ELR 453, at 471, that he shared the doubts of Richards J expressed in *C v Special Educational Needs Tribunal* [1999] ELR 5 as to the lawfulness of delegating to a school the final determination of the content of the special educational provision, but noted that the division of the Court of Appeal which decided *London Borough of Bromley v Special Educational Needs Tribunal* [1999] ELR 260 did not appear to share those doubts.

'the description in Part 3 of the statement of the provision to be made for the child must be specific, even if some flexibility is required, and even if the provision is unquantified. Normally the provision should be not only specific but also detailed and quantified. Quantification may be dispensed with "where some flexibility is required to meet the changing special needs of the child". The more natural reading of "changing special needs" refers to changes over a period of time, rather than changes from day to day, but I would be inclined to give those words a wide meaning. However, changing special needs may justify *some* flexibility, not, if the SEN Code is read literally, complete flexibility.'[1]

6.70 Similarly, Bell J in *E v Rotherham Metropolitan Borough Council*[2] overturned a decision of the Tribunal which allowed the provider of educational needs set out in a statement of SEN so much flexibility that the effect of the decision was to deprive the parent of a right of appeal to the Tribunal against an amendment to the statement. The following formulation of Newman J in *E v Flintshire County Council*[3] is helpful:

'The requirement for specificity outlaws from the scheme that which could amount to a general statement as to provision expressed in such broad terms that it could lead to specific needs being ignored or inadequately focused upon. The second purpose is that, once made in terms which are specific, the purpose of the provision can be furthered and effected by its enforceability in circumstances where non-provision occurs.'[4]

6.71 However, where the educational provision in question includes 'liaison and consistency in approach', it may be impossible to be specific about this aspect of the provision.[5]

6.72 The type of school or other institution which the authority considers would be appropriate for the child must be specified.[6] So must the name of the school as required by para 3 of Sch 27.[7] If the authority is not obliged by that paragraph to name a school, then it should specify the name of a school or institution which it considers would be appropriate for the child and which it considers should be

---

1   [2002] ELR 45, at para 34. See too the following paragraphs, up to and including para 39. These were not the subject of any comment (let alone any adverse comment) by the Court of Appeal, and that court said that it thought that 'the judge was right' and accordingly dismissed the appeal: [2003] ELR 286, at para 67.

2   [2002] ELR 266, at 275, paras 33 and 34.

3   [2002] ELR 378.

4   [2002] ELR 378, at 383, para 19. The actual decision in the case was to reject the challenge to the flexibility in the statement, and the approach taken by Newman J in doing so is instructive: see paras 37–42 inclusive at 388–389. This case was not referred to in *E v Newham LBC* [2003] ELR 286.

5   *R (Tottman) v Hertfordshire County Council* [2003] EWHC 1725 (Admin); [2003] ELR 763, para 11, per Moses J.

6   EA 1996, s 324(4)(a). It will not necessarily be (and will in most cases probably not be) contrary to Art 8 of the European Convention on Human Rights to name a boarding school in a statement of SEN as the school at which a child is to be educated: *CB v Merton London Borough Council* [2002] ELR 441, at 450, paras 19–23.

7   EA 1996, s 324(4)(b). See paras **6.60–6.64** regarding Sch 27, para 3. Where a school is specified in a statement made under s 324, it is not open to the LEA when considering whether to provide free school transport under s 509 (as to which, see paras **4.12** et seq) to conclude that the needs of the child in question could be met at other, nearer schools: *R v London Borough of Havering, ex parte K* [1998] ELR 402, at 408D.

specified in the statement.[1] Only in a few cases will a particular school be (to use the words of Pill LJ in R *v London Borough of Hackney, ex parte GC*[2]) 'necessary as part of the "special educational provision" as defined'. As Dyson J put it in *White v London Borough of Ealing*:[3]

> 'a decision by an authority whether or not to name a school involves a considerable element of judgment, both as to whether a particular school is appropriate for the child and, as to whether, having regard to the statutory duties contained in ss 9 and 316, a particular school "should" be named. ... Accordingly, the statute does not impose an absolute duty on the authority to name the school, either in the case of schools in the maintained sector or those in the non-maintained sector. ... Nor is there anything in s 326 which suggests that the tribunal is required to adopt a different approach to this issue on appeal.'[4]

6.73   An emotional need of a child may in some cases require that the child attends at a particular type of school, such as one run by the adherents of a particular religion.[5] However, a child's religious and cultural background cannot be a special educational need in its own right.[6]

6.74   In one case, it was said that where there is no modification or exclusion of the National Curriculum for a pupil with SEN,[7] a pupil referral unit in which the National Curriculum is not taught may be specified in a statement, provided that arrangements are made for the subjects not taught in the school itself to be taken at another school.[8] However, since a pupil referral unit is not obliged to apply the National Curriculum (unless the statement of SEN of a pupil who is placed there so states),[9] this appears to have been mistaken.

6.75   The statement must also specify any special educational provision for the child which the authority arranges (under s 319) to be provided outside school and which it considers should be specified in the statement.[10]

1   EA 1996, s 324(4)(b). Sedley J in R *v London Borough of Havering, ex parte K* [1998] ELR 402, at 404B said that there appeared to be 'no reason why more than one school should not be specified in a statement if, in the view of the authority or the tribunal, more than one school would equally answer the child's needs'.
2   [1996] ELR 142, at 151E.
3   [1998] ELR 203, at 211G–H and 212D. The case was appealed to the Court of Appeal, but the appeal on this point was dismissed: see [1998] ELR 319, at 330B–E; [1998] EdCR 308, at 321D–F (under the name of *Richardson v Solihull Metropolitan Borough Council*).
4   On appeal, Beldam LJ specifically approved this approach, and the other two judges gave concurring judgments.
5   R *v Secretary of State for Education, ex parte E* [1996] ELR 312.
6   G *v London Borough of Barnet and the Special Educational Needs Tribunal* [1998] ELR 480, at 483E; [1998] EdCR 30.
7   For the possibility of such modification or exclusion, see ss 92, 93, 113 and 114 of the EA 2002.
8   R *v Kingston upon Thames Council and Hunter* [1997] ELR 223, at 234E–F.
9   See EA 1996, Sch 1 and the Education (Pupil Referral Units) (Application of Enactments) Regulations 1994, SI 1994/2103.
10   EA 1996, s 324(4)(c). See para **6.41** regarding s 319.

6.76   The Special Educational Needs Regulations require[1] that a statement is divided into six parts (1) an introduction, (2) a statement of the child's SEN, (3) a statement of the special educational provision designed to meet those needs (divided into the objectives of the provision, the provision itself, and the arrangements for monitoring the provision), (4) the placement for the provision (including the type of school, and, if appropriate, the name of the school at which the special educational provision should be provided, together with any provision otherwise than at school which the authority considers appropriate), (5) the child's non-educational needs, and (6) the non-educational provision which the authority proposes to make available or which it is satisfied will be made available by a health authority, a social services authority or some other body.[2] In addition, the statement must have attached to it up to seven appendices, containing the parent's representations and written evidence (if any), the educational, medical and psychological advice, together with advice from the social services authority and any 'other advice obtained by the authority' under reg 7(1)(f).[3] The statement may exclude the application of the National Curriculum, or apply it with such modifications as are specified in the statement.[4]

6.77   In *R v Secretary of State for Education and Science, ex parte E*,[5] the Court of Appeal took a strict line in relation to the degree to which the special educational provision should be specified in a statement: if a need was specified then the provision to meet that need should be specified, even if the school in question could make that provision without further help.[6] However, in *Re L*,[7] the Court of Appeal resiled from this approach. Leggatt LJ, with whom Mann and Glidewell LJJ agreed, said:

> 'it is right to remark that the case of *ex parte E* ... must be applied in a context such as the present with caution. In explaining that the purpose of Part III[8] is to make the provision intended by a local education authority to match the needs identified in Part II, the court was not inviting a line by line examination of the parts in order to gauge the degree of correspondence between them. Inelegant or even imperfect matching, whether or not the product of poor draftsmanship, would not be enough. Only if there were a clear failure to make provision for a significant need would the court be likely to conclude that there was

---

[1]   See reg 16 of and Sch 2 to the Special Educational Needs Regulations. For Wales, see also the Education (Special Educational Needs) (Prescribed Forms) (Welsh Forms) Regulations 1995, SI 1995/45. The description in the text of the content of a statement is not exhaustive.

[2]   Only the general nature of the non-educational provision need be specified: *R v Hereford and Worcester County Council, ex parte P* [1992] 2 FLR 207, at 216E–F, per McCullough J. Furthermore, there is no need to specify any non-educational provision if the local education authority decides, after proper consideration, not to provide it: ibid, at 214E–F.

[3]   It has been held that there is no need to include in the statement the causes of the child's problems: *R v Secretary of State for Education, ex parte S* [1995] ELR 71, at 83B.

[4]   EA 2002, ss 92, 93, 113 and 114. It should be borne in mind in this connection that only maintained schools (as defined by ss 76 and 97 of that Act) are obliged to implement the National Curriculum, and that a pupil referral unit is not bound to follow the National Curriculum: see EA 1996, Sch 1 and the Education (Pupil Referral Units) (Application of Enactments) Regulations 1994, SI 1994/2103.

[5]   [1992] 1 FLR 377.

[6]   Ibid, at 389F–H. At 388H–389A, Balcombe LJ also said this: 'In my judgment, the judge's analogy with a medical diagnosis and prescription is entirely apt. It then becomes the duty of the authority to arrange that the special educational provision specified in the statement is made for the child'.

[7]   [1994] ELR 16.

[8]   Now Part 3.

such a dereliction of duty by a local education authority as called for the intervention of an appeal committee.'[1]

6.78   In *L v Salford City Council*,[2] however, Tucker J ruled that if a child's needs are such as to require the making of a statement then that statement must list and provide for all his needs, including those needs which would not of themselves require the making of a statement. The converse was also true: if a child's needs, considered as a whole, were not such as to require a statement, then cessation of the statement was appropriate even though there might be a continuing need for (for example) occupational therapy.

6.79   In *London Borough of Wandsworth v K*,[3] Newman J held that where in respect of any child, educational provision is appropriate, it should be included in part 3 of the child's statement, and that:

> 'If a qualification exists in connection with that special provision and its appropriateness, for example, that it is only appropriate by reason of the absence of special provision in a specialised unit in a mainstream school, then that should also be stated in part 3. As to part 4 there is no reason why, if it is considered necessary, it should not contain reference to the [educational provision] as the measure which is appropriate for the time being and a reference to the type of school to which a placement would be appropriate in the event one becomes available.'

6.80   In *R v London Borough of Newham, ex parte R*,[4] it was held that it was open to an LEA to have a long-term policy of seeking to provide in its own schools for all of those with SEN, by making the special educational provision in its own schools so good that there was no need to go elsewhere. However, that was subject to the qualification that the policy had to be flexible enough to allow each case to be looked at on its merits, so that if necessary a child could nevertheless where appropriate be sent to, for example, a non-maintained special school.[5] In *R v Cumbria County Council, ex parte P*,[6] the LEA had a policy of allocating pupils with SEN into various bands or categories, all but one of which had a cash figure against them, and the delegation (under a scheme of local management[7]) to individual schools of the power to spend the money in relation to any pupil so banded who attended the school. The court held that this was not unlawful, since it neither indicated any unwillingness by the authority to have regard to the need for securing that special educational provision was made for pupils with SEN, nor did it fetter the authority's discretion as to what was

---

1   [1994] ELR 16, at 22D–E. The appeal would of course now be heard by the Tribunal. It is suggested by J Friel and D Hay in *Special Educational Needs and the Law* (Sweet & Maxwell, 1996), at p 52, that this dictum of Leggatt LJ was *obiter*. This is doubtful. In any event, the approach of the court in *Re L* would undoubtedly assist a court wishing to cut down the effect of *ex parte E*.

2   [1998] ELR 28, at 36E–F. Neither *R v Secretary of State for Education, ex parte E* nor *Re L* was cited to the court.

3   [2003] EWHC 1424 (Admin); [2003] ELR 554, at para 14.

4   [1995] ELR 156.

5   Ibid, at 162.

6   [1995] ELR 337.

7   As to which, see paras **7.132** et seq.

contained in the statements of any of the authority's statemented pupils.[1] This, however, must be read as subject to the qualification that the amount allocated to a school in a delegated budget for the needs of a child in relation to whom there is a statement of SEN, must be sufficient to meet those needs.[2] Further, where there are significant changes proposed to funding levels, the LEA will almost certainly have to consult the schools to be affected.[3] 'This is not so much because of the requirements of fairness but because of the need to have regard to all material considerations'.[4]

6.81 In R v *Cumbria County Council, ex parte NB*,[5] in contrast to the situation in R v *Cumbria County Council, ex parte P*,[6] it was common ground that the authority was entitled to have policies which in general guided their decision as to whether or not to make a statement under (now) s 324.[7] Although, for reasons indicated above,[8] Schiemann J's approach in *ex parte NB* is now doubtful in some respects, the policy in issue in *ex parte NB* would probably still be regarded as lawful. The policy was to make statements only for children whose development quotient was either below 70 or at least 85, but not for those whose development quotient was in between these two bands. This was for reasons which bore (and would probably still bear) scrutiny.[9] The only caveat was (as one would expect) that the authority had to avoid shutting its ears to the possibility that it should nevertheless make a statement of SEN for the child in question.[10]

Educational and non-educational needs

6.82 It may on occasion be difficult to know whether certain types of provision are educational or non-educational (although the application of the DDA 1995 to schools may have diminished the importance of this distinction in some circumstances; see further Chapter 18). The most common example of such a type of provision appears to be speech therapy. In R v *Lancashire County Council, ex parte M*,[11] it was held that speech therapy may in some cases be special educational provision and need not be 'non-educational provision', and that it will be a question of fact in each case whether speech therapy is special educational provision. It was held in C v *Special Educational Needs Tribunal*,[12] following *ex parte M*, that where the Tribunal does not interfere with

---

1   [1995] ELR at 345D–E. See also R v *Oxfordshire County Council, ex parte P* [1996] ELR 153, where it was held (at 159E–F) that the delegation of a sum to the governing body of a locally managed maintained school to be spent on special educational provision for a particular child, did not mean that the duty of the LEA under the predecessor of what is now s 324 had been unlawfully delegated.

2   R v *London Borough of Hillingdon, ex parte Governing Body of Queensmead School* [1997] ELR 331, at 347D. This part of the judgment is unaffected by the overturning by the House of Lords of the decision of the Court of Appeal in R v *Gloucestershire County Council, ex parte Barry* [1997] AC 584.

3   R v *London Borough of Hillingdon, ex parte Governing Body of Queensmead School* [1997] ELR 331, at 348F.

4   Ibid, at 348F–G.

5   [1996] ELR 65.

6   [1995] ELR 337.

7   [1996] ELR 65, at 68B–C.

8   See paras **6.39** and **6.40**.

9   See [1996] ELR 65, at 69B–72F.

10   [1996] ELR 65, at 70C–D.

11   [1989] 2 FLR 279.

12   [1997] ELR 390, at 399D.

the LEA's classification of a particular therapy as non-educational, the High Court, on appeal, should be 'very slow to find that the tribunal has erred in law'.[1]

6.83   Children with severe disabilities may need medical and social care as well as special educational provision. These needs may overlap, as was recognised by Dyson J in *White v London Borough of Ealing*[2] in relation to educational and care needs. However, they are nevertheless separate needs. This has been confirmed in a number of recent cases. For example, in *R v London Borough of Lambeth, ex parte MBM*,[3] it was argued that the provision of a lift for a pupil who lacked mobility and who was as a result in practice unable to use her school's first floor facilities, was special educational provision. The court rejected that argument, ruling that the lift was necessary to assist the child's mobility, and not as special educational provision.[4] In *City of Bradford Metropolitan Council v A*,[5] the court, having been referred to *ex parte MBM*, held that 100 per cent nursing care could not be educational provision.[6] In *B v Isle of Wight Council*,[7] McCullough J held (apparently without having been referred to *ex parte MBM*) that:

> 'a child with bad sight or hearing may have "a disability which prevents or hinders him from making use of educational facilities of a kind generally provided", but if all he needs is a pair of spectacles or a hearing aid he has no need for any special *educational* provision and therefore has no "special *educational* needs". The same would be so of a diabetic or epileptic child who needed only drug therapy and of a child unable to walk who needed only a wheelchair.' (McCullough J's emphasis.)

6.84   McCullough J went on to say:

> 'All that anyone can do when judging whether a "provision" is "educational" or "non educational" is to recognise that there is an obvious spectrum from the clearly educational (in the ordinary "schools" sense of that word) at one end to the clearly medical at the other, take all the relevant facts into account, apply common sense and do one's best.'[8]

6.85   Sedley LJ's approach in *London Borough of Bromley v Special Educational Needs Tribunal*[9] was a little more helpful:

> 'Special educational provision is, in principle, whatever is called for by a child's learning difficulty. A learning difficulty is anything inherent in the child which makes learning significantly harder for him than for most others or which hinders him from making use of ordinary school facilities. What is special about special educational provision is that it is additional to or different from ordinary educational provision (see s 312(4)). So far the meaning is open-ended. It is when it comes to the statement under s 324 that the LEA is required to distinguish between special educational provision and non-educational

[1]   See further, paras **6.106** et seq regarding appeals to the Tribunal and paras **6.172** et seq regarding appeals to the High Court on a point of law from a decision of the Tribunal.

[2]   [1997] ELR 203, at 217A.

[3]   [1995] ELR 374.

[4]   Ibid, at 383A–B.

[5]   [1997] ELR 417.

[6]   Ibid, at 429B–D.

[7]   [1997] ELR 279, at 285F–H.

[8]   [1997] ELR 279, at 286D.

[9]   [1999] ELR 260, at 295–296. Mummery and Evans LJJ agreed with Sedley LJ's judgment.

provision; and the prescribed form is divided up accordingly. Two possibilities arise here: either the two categories share a common frontier, so that where the one stops the other begins; or there is between the unequivocally educational and the unequivocally non-educational a shared territory of provision which can be intelligibly allocated to either. It seems to me that to adopt the first approach would be to read into the legislation a sharp dichotomy for which Parliament could easily have made express provision had it wished to do so, but which finds no expression or reflection where one would expect to find it, namely in s 312. Moreover, to interpose a hard edge or a common frontier does not get rid of definitional problems: it simply makes them more acute. And this is one of the reasons why, in my judgment, the second approach is the one to be attributed to Parliament. The potentially large intermediate area of provision which is capable of ranking as educational or non-educational is not made the subject of any statutory prescription precisely because it is for the local education authority, and if necessary the [Tribunal], to exercise a case-by-case judgment which no prescriptive legislation could ever hope to anticipate. The potential breadth of what can legitimately be regarded as educational is illustrated by s 322, permitting as it does the enlistment by the LEA of other statutory providers to "help in the exercise of any of their functions under this Part". It is true that the LEA's functions (which include both powers and duties: see s 579(1)) will include the elective making of arrangements for non-educational provision as well as the mandatory making of arrangements for educational provision pursuant to s 324(5)(a); but it is the fact that health, social services and other authorities can be enlisted to help in the making of special educational provision which gives some indication of possible breadth of the duty. ... Whether a form of help needed by the child falls within [the description "special educational provision" in Part IV of the Act] is a question primarily for the LEA and secondarily for the [Tribunal]'s expert judgment. If, but only if, the [Tribunal] has gone wrong in law will the High Court overset its judgment.'

6.86   This is consistent with the approach of Leggatt LJ in *Re L*[1] towards a mistaken placing in the part of a statement concerning non-educational provision of an aspect of the special educational provision, where, on the facts of that case, he said:

'I agree with the judge that it was a matter for the authority to determine what provision should be made for the needs which they had identified, and the fact that provision for part of it was specified in Part V rather than in Part III was not of such consequence as would warrant the intervention of the court.'

Maintaining a statement

6.87   The duty of an LEA to maintain a statement of SEN under s 324(1) is described in s 324(5). It is as follows:

'(a)   unless the child's parent has made suitable arrangements, the authority –
   (i)   shall arrange that the special educational provision specified in the statement is made for the child, and
   (ii)   may arrange that any non-educational provision specified in the statement is made for him in such manner as they consider appropriate.'

---

[1]   [1994] ELR 16, at 22H.

6.88   It was confirmed in *City of Bradford Metropolitan Borough Council v A*,[1] that there is no duty placed on an LEA to arrange non-educational provision specified in a statement of SEN made under s 324. It was confirmed in *R v London Borough of Barnet, ex parte G*[2] that a statement made under s 324 is prospective only. However, if a challenge by way of an application for judicial review is made to the appropriateness of the purported implementation of the special educational provision required by such a statement, then, according to Sedley J in *R v Wandsworth London Borough Council, ex parte M*,[3] such implementation falls to be adjudged as at the date of the granting of permission to apply for judicial review. It is of note in this connection that in *R v Northamptonshire County Council, ex parte Marshall*,[4] Sedley J said:

> 'The LEA's statement of Special Educational Needs is not a pleading to which, absent an authorised amendment, it or the tribunal is tied.'

6.89   An LEA will not normally have the power to direct a school named in a statement of SEN as to the manner in which the statement is implemented (or purported to be implemented). However, a long-lasting or deliberate failure by those responsible for the conduct of the school to implement, or implement properly, the relevant requirements of the statement could mean that the authority had failed to make the arrangements required by s 324(1)(a)(i).[5]

6.90   It may sometimes not be clear whether an LEA is obliged to take over responsibility for the payment of fees at a non-maintained school where a parent has already made arrangements for the education of the child to whom a statement of SEN relates at such a school. In those circumstances, assuming that the school is a suitable school for the child, it could be said that the parent has made suitable arrangements within the meaning of the opening words of s 324(5)(a).[6] However, the parent may have made those arrangements only for a short period of time, hoping that the LEA will name the school in the child's statement. Alternatively, the parent's means may have diminished since the arrangements were made. In both those situations, as a matter of principle, it would be wrong to say that the parent has made such suitable arrangements. Some of the relevant case-law bears this out. In *R v Kent County Council, ex parte W*,[7] Turner J followed the approach of Auld J at first instance in *R v London Borough of Hackney, ex parte GC*[8] in deciding that where a parent has sent the child to whom a statement of SEN relates to a suitable non-maintained school, the LEA must nevertheless arrange for the provision of education to that child where the parents cannot pay the fees, or where they have not paid them and have sent the child to the school contingently upon the authority agreeing to pay or being required

---

1   [1997] ELR 417, at 420D–E.
2   [1998] ELR 281; [1998] EdCR 252.
3   [1998] ELR 424, at 428; [1998] EdCR 252, at 257D.
4   [1998] EdCR 262; the case is wrongly named in that report: the case was an appeal to the High Court from a decision of the SEN Tribunal.
5   *R v London Borough of Brent and Vassie (Chairman of the Special Educational Needs Tribunal), ex parte AF* [2000] ELR 550.
6   If a parent has arranged the child's education at an independent school, that school need not have been approved under s 347(5) of the EA 1996 for the arrangements to be suitable for the purposes of s 324(5): EA 1996, s 347(5A).
7   [1995] ELR 362.
8   [1995] ELR 144.

to pay the fees. The authority will only be under no duty to pay the fees where the parent has made effective arrangements, including the payment by them of school fees if required and where they can continue to pay those fees without assistance from the authority.[1] However, in the Court of Appeal in the case of *R v London Borough of Hackney, ex parte GC*,[2] Staughton LJ said (obiter) that it was possible to take another view. He said:

'It may be that arrangements can in law be suitable if they are presently operating suitably even though they may not continue to do so in the future.'

6.91   The approach taken in para 8:97 of the SEN Code is not consistent with this statement of Staughton LJ. There, the following is said:

'Parents should not be treated as having made suitable arrangements if the arrangements do not include a realistic possibility of funding those arrangements for a reasonable period of time. The LEA are, whether or not a school is named in the statement, still under a duty to maintain the child's statement and to review it annually, following the procedures set out in Chapter Nine.'

6.92   It is of note that in *White v Ealing London Borough Council*,[3] Dyson J adopted the approach taken by Turner J in *ex parte W* and by Auld J at first instance in *ex parte GC* albeit with the gloss that 'suitable arrangements must at least include arrangements for funding for a reasonable period of time'.[4] In any event, s 348 of the EA 1996 provides that:

'where ... special educational provision in respect of a child is made at a school which is not a maintained school, and ... either the name of the school is specified in a statement in respect of the child under section 324 or the local education authority are satisfied (i) that his interests require the necessary special educational provision to be made for him at a school which is not a maintained school, and (ii) that it is appropriate for the child to be provided with education at the particular school ... the local education authority shall pay the whole of the fees payable in respect of the education provided for the child at the school.'

6.93   Accordingly, in some circumstances, this provision will require the LEA to pay the fees for the education of a child at a non-maintained school even though the parents of the child have made suitable arrangements within the meaning of s 324(5)(a) for his education at the school.

Review of a statement

6.94   A statement of SEN must be reviewed by the LEA whenever it makes an assessment of the child's educational needs under s 323,[5] and must in any event be

---

[1]   See *ex parte W* [1995] ELR 362, at 370 (where the extract from *ex parte GC* contains a mistake: the word 'cannot' in the penultimate line of the quotation should be 'can').

[2]   [1996] ELR 142, at 152E.

[3]   [1998] ELR 203.

[4]   Ibid, at 225B. This aspect of Dyson J's judgment was not referred to by the Court of Appeal in that case (see [1998] ELR 319).

[5]   EA 1996, s 328(5)(a).

reviewed within the period of 12 months beginning with the making of the statement or, as the case may be, with the previous review.[1] The conduct of most such reviews is governed by the Special Educational Needs Regulations. Regulation 18 requires the taking of certain procedural steps in relation to such reviews. These include the giving by an LEA of a notice not less than 2 weeks before the first day of every school term to the head teacher of every school, defined by reg 18 as (1) a maintained school, (2) a maintained nursery school, (3) a pupil referral unit, (4) a school approved by the Secretary of State under s 342 or s 347 (or, in Wales, by the National Assembly under s 342), (5) a city technology college, (6) a city college for the technology for the arts, or (7) City Academy. The notice must list every registered pupil at the school with a statement under s 324 and for whom the LEA is responsible and whose annual reviews fall to be carried out before the commencement of the second term after the notice is given. Regulation 18(3) and (4) require the notice to require the head teacher to submit a report in connection with the forthcoming review, in accordance with reg 20 or 21 (whichever applies; see below). Regulation 18(5) and (6) require the LEA to serve notices of similar sorts on the Connexions Service[2] (or, where there is no such service, the Careers Service) for its area, the health authority and the social services authority.

6.95   Regulation 19 requires an LEA to amend the statement of SEN for each child who is 'within twelve calendar months of a transfer between phases of his schooling' by 15 February in the calendar year of the child's transfer so that the statement names the school or other institution which the child will be attending after that transfer. Regulation 20 applies to reviews of statements for children who are attending school and who are not in the tenth year of their compulsory education. Regulation 21 applies to reviews of statements for children who are in such year. Regulation 22 applies to the reviews of statements of children who are not attending school (as defined by reg 18).

6.96   The procedure followed in relation to each case is similar, but the emphasis differs. As indicated above, the procedure commences, in the case of a child at school, with the seeking by the LEA of a report from the head teacher of the school which the child attends.[3] In the case of a child who does not attend school, the procedure commences with the preparation by the authority of a report concerning, among other things, the child's progress.[4] Various parties are then to be invited to attend a meeting.

---

[1]   EA 1996, s 328(5)(b). See paras 3:2, 3:15, 3:17, 4:55, 5:68–5:73, 6:8, and 8:40, and chapter 9 of the SEN Code regarding the annual review generally. In the case of children under 5, para 4:46 of the SEN Code recommends an informal review in addition at least every 6 months.

[2]   There is no such service in Wales, and reg 18(5) of SI 2002/152 reflects this by referring only to the Careers Service. The terms 'Connexions Service' and 'Careers Service' are defined by reg 2(1). The former is 'a body established to provide careers services under sections 8–10 of the Employment and Training Act 1973' (which is specifically stated by SI 2002/152 to include a body which does not have legal personality) and the latter is 'a person of any description with whom the Secretary of State has made an arrangement under section 114(2)(a) of the Learning and Skills Act 2000 and section 10(1) of the Employment and Training Act 1973 and any person to whom he has given a direction under section 114(2)(b) of the Learning and Skills Act 2000 and section 10(2) of the Employment and Training Act 1973'.

[3]   Regulations 20(2) and 21(2).

[4]   Regulation 22(2).

The parties include the child's parent[1] and, in the case of a child at school, a member or members of staff of the school who teach the pupil or who are otherwise responsible for the education of the pupil whom the head teacher considers appropriate.[2] Where the review is of the statement of a child who is in his tenth year of compulsory schooling, a representative of the social services authority must also be invited to attend,[3] as must a representative of the Connexions Service or, if there is no such service at the date of the invitation, the Careers Service.[4] Others whose attendance the authority considers appropriate must also be invited to attend.[5] A report concerning the child's situation and (among other things) the recommendations made at the meeting must then be completed by the head teacher,[6] and the LEA must carry out the review of the child's statement of SEN in the light of (among other things) the report.[7] Under reg 20(13), it must record in writing its decisions on certain matters (including whether the statement should be amended), and, where a transition plan exists (regarding which, see para **6.97**), make written recommendations for any amendments to that plan which it considers appropriate. Under reg 21(13), the LEA need only make recommendations, but those must include recommendations as to 'the matters which [the meeting] concludes ought to be included in a transition plan'. The SEN Code states (in para 9:50) that the head teacher 'must' ensure that a transition plan is drawn up. Under reg 22(9), the LEA must prepare a transition plan, or, if one already exists, amend it as it considers appropriate. Within one week of completing the review, it must send to the child's parents and to certain other persons copies of the decisions and recommendations, or (as appropriate) the recommendations and transition plan or amended transition plan.[8]

Transition plan

6.97   A transition plan is:

'a document which sets out the appropriate arrangements for a young person during the period beginning with the commencement of his tenth year of compulsory education and ending when aged 19 years, including arrangements for special educational provision and for any other necessary provision, for suitable employment and accommodation for leisure activities, and which will facilitate a satisfactory transition from childhood to adulthood.'[9]

Change of named school[10]

6.98   Where a statement names a particular school or institution and the parent of the child to whom the statement relates asks the LEA to substitute for that name the

---

1   Regulations 20(6)(b), 21(6)(a) and 22(3)(a).
2   Regulations 20(6)(c) and 21(6)(b).
3   Regulations 21(6)(c) and 22(3)(b).
4   Regulations 21(6)(d) and 22(3)(c).
5   Regulations 20(6)(d), 21(6)(f) and 23(3)(d).
6   Regulations 20(11), 21(11) and 22(7). See also paras 9:18, 9:32 and 9:33 of the SEN Code.
7   Regulations 20(13), 21(13) and 22(9).
8   Regulations 20(14), 21(10) and 22(10).
9   Regulation 2(1). Paragraphs 3:16, 3:17, 9:45 and 9:50 to 9:62 of the SEN Code apply to the transition plan and its preparation.
10   See, generally, paras 8:58–8:69 of the SEN Code.

name of a maintained school,[1] as long as the request is made no sooner than 12 months after the date when (i) a previous such request was made, (ii) the statement (or amended statement) was originally served on the parent under para 6 of Sch 27, or (iii) if the parent has appealed to the Tribunal under s 326 or para 8 of Sch 27, the conclusion of the appeal, whichever is the later, then the authority must comply with the request unless one of two possible exceptions applies.[2] The exceptions are that (a) the school is unsuitable to the child's age, ability or aptitude or to his SEN, or (b) the attendance of the child would be incompatible with the provision of efficient education for the children with whom he would be educated, or the efficient use of resources.[3]

6.99   The LEA must within 8 weeks either comply with the request or give written notice under para 8(3) of Sch 27 that they have determined not to comply with the request and that the parent may appeal against that determination to the Tribunal.[4] Where the LEA determines not to comply with the request, it must in the notice communicating that fact inform the parent of that right of appeal,[5] and of its reasons for that decision.[6]

Amendment of a statement

6.100   An amendment to a statement of SEN may be made by an LEA only under paras 2A and 2B of Sch 27, unless one of two exceptions applies.[7] Those exceptions are that (1) the Tribunal orders the amendment, or (2) the Secretary of State directs the amendment under s 442(4) of the EA 1996 (which so far as relevant applies where a parent refers a question to the Secretary of State after a refusal by the LEA to revoke a school attendance order).[8] Before amending the statement, the authority must serve on the parent of the child concerned a copy of the proposed amended statement, a written notice explaining the effect of paras 3 and 4 of Sch 27 and of the right of appeal under s 326 (to the extent that they are applicable), and, in most cases, also a notice in writing giving details of the amendments to the statement proposed by the LEA (called an 'amendment notice').[9] The parent then has a right to make representations under para 4 of Sch 27 in the same way that such right arises where a statement is first made under s 324.[10] Where an LEA has so served a copy of a proposed amended statement on the child's parent, it must, normally within 8 weeks

---

1   A 'maintained school' is defined for this purpose by s 312(5).
2   EA 1996, Sch 27, para 8(1).
3   Ibid, Sch 27, para 8(2).
4   Regulation 17(5) of the Special Educational Needs Regulations.
5   EA 1996, Sch 27, para 3A.
6   Regulation 17(5).
7   EA 1996, Sch 27, para 2A(1). See paras 8:125–8:133 of the SEN Code regarding amendments to a statement of SEN.
8   Regarding which, see para **5.28**.
9   See EA 1996, Sch 27, paras 2A(2)–(6) and 2B. The notice must contain the information set out in Part A or Part B (whichever applies) of Sch 1 to the Special Educational Needs Regulations: see regs 14 and 15 of those regulations. The only time when an amendment notice is not required is when an amendment is proposed following a re-assessment review (as opposed to a periodic review). A re-assessment review is a review conducted in accordance with s 328(5)(a) and a periodic review is an assessment conducted in accordance with s 328(5)(b): Sch 27, para 1.
10   See para **6.59** regarding the procedure in para 4 of Sch 27.

of doing so, serve a copy of the completed amended statement and a written notice of the parent's right to appeal to the Tribunal under s 326 of the EA 1996 against the description in the statement of the LEA's assessment of the child's SEN, the special educational provision specified in the statement (including the name of a school specified in the statement), or, if no school is named in the statement, that fact.[1] The exceptions to this 8-week time-limit are set out in reg 17(4) and (7) of the Special Educational Needs Regulations. They include that the parent has indicated that he or she wishes to make representations to the LEA about the content of the statement under para 4(1) of Sch 27 after the expiry of the 15-day period for making such representations provided for in para 4(4) of Sch 27, and that the LEA has sent a written request to the Secretary of State or (as the case may be) the National Assembly seeking his (or its) consent under s 347(5) to the child being educated at an independent school which is not approved by him (or it) and such consent has not been received by the LEA within 2 weeks of the date when the request was sent.

6.101 It was held by Moses J in *R v Kent County Council, ex parte AMS*[2] that even where there is a real prospect of an appeal against the contents of a statement, the LEA are not bound to consider when amending the statement whether it would be better not to name a school than to name a school in the statement in order to avoid any delay which might arise while it is seeking to find whether a particular school is appropriate or available.

Transfer of a statement

6.102 A statement must be transferred from one LEA to another where the child to whom the statement relates moves from the area of the authority which maintains the statement (the old authority) to the area of another authority (the new authority).[3] No time-limit is specified for such a transfer, however.[4] The statement is treated as from the date of the transfer as having been made by the new authority on the date when it was made by the old authority.[5] Where the new authority carries out an assessment under s 323, any advice obtained by the old authority for the purpose of a previous such assessment is treated for the purposes of reg 7(5) of the Special Educational Needs Regulations as if it had been obtained by the new authority.[6] The new authority must, within 6 weeks of the date of the transfer, serve a notice on the parent informing him that the statement has been transferred, whether it proposes to make an assessment under s 323, and when it proposes to review the statement under

---

[1] EA 1996, Sch 27, para 6(1) and (2) and reg 17(3) and (6) of the Special Educational Needs Regulations. Paragraph 8:31 of the SEN Code states that the amended statement should also make clear which parts of the statement have been amended, so that parents and professionals can clearly see and understand the changes.

[2] [2000] EdCR 68, at 77E–F.

[3] EA 1996, Sch 27, para 7(2), and reg 23 of the Special Educational Needs Regulations. See also paras 8:113 and 8:115 of the SEN Code.

[4] See reg 23(2).

[5] Regulation 23(3)(a). This does not necessarily mean that the child can no longer attend the school named in the statement. If confirmation of this is needed, it is to be found in *R v Manchester City Council, ex parte S* [1999] ELR 414.

[6] See reg 23(3)(b) and the definition of an assessment in reg 2(1). See footnote 9 to para **6.53** regarding reg 7(5).

s 328(5).[1] If the statement names a school at which, as a result of the child's move, it is no longer practicable for the child to attend, then the authority may arrange for the child's attendance at another school appropriate for the child until such time as it is possible to amend the statement in accordance with the procedure in Sch 17.[2]

Restrictions on disclosure of statements

6.103 A statement and any representations, evidence, advice or information which is set out in the appendices to the statement, may not be disclosed without the consent of the parent except in certain circumstances.[3] The exceptions include that the authority is of the opinion that the statement should be disclosed in the interests of the child concerned.[4] The arrangements for the keeping of statements must be such as to ensure, so far as is reasonably practicable, that unauthorised persons do not have access to them.[5] A child who has sufficient age and understanding to allow him to understand the implications of doing so, may consent to the disclosure of the statement,[6] and the parent of a child who does not have such age or understanding may so consent on his behalf.[7]

Ceasing to maintain a statement

6.104 Unless one of two exceptions applies, an LEA may cease to maintain a statement of SEN 'only if it is no longer necessary to maintain it'[8] and only under para 11 of Sch 27.[9] The exceptions are that (i) the LEA ceases to maintain a statement for a child who has ceased to be a child for whom it is responsible,[10] or (ii) the LEA is ordered to cease to maintain the statement by the Tribunal under s 326(3)(c).[11] Where the LEA determines to cease to maintain a statement, it must serve on the parent notice in writing of that fact, and of the right of the parent to appeal to the Tribunal under para 11(2)(b).[12] Where the parent of the child appeals to the Tribunal under that sub-paragraph, the LEA may not then cease to maintain the statement until that appeal has been determined or withdrawn.[13] However, where a parent does not so

---

[1]   Regulation 23(4) and (5). The review must take place within 12 months of the making of the statement or, as the case may be, the previous review, or within 3 months of the date of the transfer (whichever is the later): reg 23(5).

[2]   Regulation 23(6). See also para 8:114 of the SEN Code.

[3]   EA 1996, Sch 27, para 7(1), and reg 24 of the Special Educational Needs Regulations.

[4]   Regulation 24(1)(a). There are a total of 11 exceptions, set out in reg 24(1). See also paras 8:111 and 8:112 of the SEN Code.

[5]   Regulation 24(4).

[6]   Regulation 24(2).

[7]   Regulation 24(3).

[8]   EA 1996, Sch 27, para 11(1). See also paras 8:117–8:124 of the SEN Code. The decision of Owen J in *R (Jane W) v Blaenau Gwent Borough Council* [2003] EWHC 2880 (Admin), [2004] ELR 152, is instructive in relation to the circumstances in which an LEA may not cease to maintain a statement of SEN.

[9]   EA 1996, Sch 27, para 9(1).

[10] Ibid, Sch 27, para 9(2)(a). These words do not apply to the situation where the person named in the statement 'has ceased to be a child simpliciter because of no longer being of compulsory school age': *Wakefield Metropolitan District Council v E* [2002] ELR 203, at 211, para 30, per Collins J, declining to apply the approach of Turner J in *S v Essex County Council* [2000] ELR 718. See further, para **6.189** et seq.

[11] EA 1996, Sch 27, para 9(2)(c).

[12] Ibid, Sch 27, para 11(2).

[13] Ibid, Sch 27, para 11(5), as inserted by SENDA 2001, s 6.

appeal within the prescribed period for doing so, the LEA may cease to maintain the statement.[1]

6.105 In *L v Salford City Council*,[2] it was held that an LEA did not need to comply with the requirements in para 11 of Sch 27 before ceasing to maintain a statement where an appeal to the Tribunal had been made against a refusal to amend the statement and the Tribunal had ordered the LEA to cease to maintain the statement.[3] However, the LEA had in that case previously clearly indicated to the child's parent its intention to argue at the hearing of the appeal that the statement no longer needed to be maintained, and no unfairness was held to have been caused to the parent in the circumstances by the LEA's failure to serve notice under para 11(2)(a) of Sch 27.

RIGHTS OF APPEAL TO THE TRIBUNAL IN RELATION TO SPECIAL EDUCATIONAL NEEDS MATTERS

Who may appeal

6.106 A parent[4] may appeal to the Tribunal in a number of situations. The possibility of seeking to judicially review a statement made by an LEA instead of appealing to the Tribunal was considered by Latham J in *S (A Minor) v Special Educational Needs Tribunal*.[5] Although he rejected the submission that the statement in that case was unlawful, he said that he could see that:

> 'there might be an argument in some circumstances that the failure to obtain a particular report was so fundamental that no decision could be reached as to the nature or extent of the child's special needs until it was obtained, and therefore no conclusion could be reached as to the way in which those needs were capable of being met.'[6]

6.107 Nevertheless, in most cases the proper route for challenging a decision relating to a child's SEN where there is a right of appeal to the Tribunal in respect of the decision, will be by way of an appeal to the Tribunal,[7] following one of the routes to which reference will now be made.

---

1   Special Educational Needs Regulations, reg 17(8). There is an apparent conflict between Sch 27, para 11(4) and reg 17(8), but the terms of the latter support the text to this note.

2   [1998] ELR 28.

3   The Tribunal can order an authority to cease to maintain a statement on such an appeal: see para **6.112**.

4   And only a parent: *R v Special Educational Needs Tribunal and the City of Westminster* [1996] ELR 228, CA.

5   [1995] 1 WLR 374; [1996] ELR 102.

6   [1995] 1 WLR 1627, 1639D; [1996] ELR 102, at 115D–E.

7   See *Re M (A Minor)* [1996] ELR 135, where the Court of Appeal gave a very clear indication that judicial review would be unlikely to be appropriate. In *R v Worcestershire County Council, ex parte S* [1999] ELR 46, an application for judicial review was made to quash a refusal to carry out an assessment where by the time of the hearing the Tribunal had ordered the respondent LEA to carry out an assessment and that assessment was going to be carried out by about 7 weeks from the date of the hearing. There was also an application for an interim order that the LEA pay for a Lovaas programme which had formerly been paid for by the parents of the child in question; the applicant's submission was that 'in the light of the failure by the local authority to carry out their statutory assessment, the applicant is entitled to interim relief to enable the programme to continue but now at the authority's expense' (see p 48). Both applications were unsuccessful, and the reasons why they were dismissed are instructive. In contrast, an interim injunction was ordered in *R(S) v Norfolk County Council* [2004]

Appeal against a refusal to assess a child for whom no statement is maintained

6.108 A parent of a child for whom no statement is maintained may appeal under s 329(2) of the EA 1996 to the Tribunal against a decision by the LEA not to assess the child's educational needs under s 323.[1] The Tribunal may then either dismiss the appeal or order the authority to arrange for an assessment to be made under s 323.[2] It was said in *S v Cardiff City Council*[3] that the Tribunal must believe it to be 'necessary' for a statement to be made before it can order under s 329 that an assessment be made under s 323. This ignores the impact of s 323, which provides that an LEA need only think that a child 'probably' has SEN which call for a statement before it is under a duty to carry out an assessment under s 323. The best view appears to be that the Tribunal may order under s 329 that an assessment is carried out under s 323 when the Tribunal concludes on the balance of probabilities that the child probably has SEN which are such that it is necessary that a statement under s 324 is made in relation to those needs.

6.109 A parent of a child for whom no statement is maintained may also appeal under s 329A(8) against a refusal of the LEA to carry out an assessment under s 323 after a request for such an assessment has been made under s 329A by the body or person responsible for conducting a school or nursery school. Here too, the Tribunal may either dismiss the appeal or order the authority to arrange for an assessment to be made under s 323.[4]

Appeal against refusal to make a statement

6.110 A parent may appeal against a decision by the LEA, having carried out an assessment under s 323, not to make a statement of SEN under s 324.[5] The Tribunal may in such a case dismiss the appeal, order the LEA to make and maintain a statement, or remit the case to the LEA for it to reconsider whether, having regard to any observations made by the Tribunal, it is necessary for it to determine the special educational provision which any learning difficulty the child may have calls for (ie make a statement under s 324).[6] Where the Tribunal remits the case to the LEA to reconsider the latter question and the LEA again proposes not to make a statement under s 324, a further right of appeal arises.[7] However, where the Tribunal can properly decide that the further appeal is 'scandalous, frivolous or vexatious', it may strike out the appeal.[8]

EWHC 404 (Admin), [2004] ELR 259. The possibility of the joinder of an appeal to the Tribunal with a claim made under the DDA 1995 (regarding which, see Chapter 18) should be borne in mind.

[1] EA 1996, s 329(2)(b). See para **6.51** regarding s 329.

[2] Ibid, s 329(3).

[3] [1999] EdCR 645.

[4] EA 1996, s 329A(10).

[5] Ibid, s 325(2).

[6] Ibid, s 325(3).

[7] *O v London Borough of Harrow* [2002] ELR 195, CA.

[8] Ibid, at 200, para 22, per Simon Brown LJ.

Appeal against contents of a statement

6.111 A parent may, except in certain circumstances, appeal to the Tribunal under s 326 of the EA 1996 (1) where an LEA first makes a statement of SEN, (2) when the statement is amended, or (3) against a determination by the LEA not to amend the statement after carrying out an assessment under s 323.[1] The appeal may be against either (a) the description in the statement of the LEA's assessment of the child's SEN, (b) the special educational provision specified in the statement (including the name of a school so specified), or (c) if no school is named in the statement, that fact.[2] The exceptions (that is, the circumstances in which a parent may not appeal under s 326 despite having a prima facie right to do so) include that no appeal may be made against (1) a change of a named school under para 8 of Sch 27,[3] (2) an amendment ordered by the Tribunal under para 11(3)(b) of Sch 27 (which applies on an appeal against a decision to cease to maintain a statement),[4] or (3) an amendment directed by the Secretary of State to be made under s 442 (which applies where a parent seeks the revocation of a school attendance order).[5] The final exception is that an appeal may not be made under s 326(1)(c) against a determination made following the service of a notice under para 2A of Sch 27.[6] Since (1) an amendment made under para 2A would give rise to a right of appeal under s 326(1)(b), and (2) there is no right to appeal against a refusal to amend a statement unless the refusal follows an assessment carried out under s 323, this final exception can apply only where a determination is made under para 2A not to amend a statement following an assessment under s 323.

6.112 On appeal, the Tribunal may (a) dismiss the appeal, (b) order the authority to amend (i) the description in the statement of the authority's assessment of the child's SEN, or (ii) the specification in the statement of the special educational provision and (in the case of both (i) and (ii)) make consequential amendments to the statement, or (c) order the authority to cease to maintain the statement.[7] The Tribunal may not, however, order the LEA to specify the name of any school in the statement (either in substitution for an existing name or where no school is named) unless either (a) the parent has expressed a preference for the school under arrangements made under para 3 of Sch 27,[8] or (b) in the proceedings the parent, the LEA, or both have proposed the school.[9] The Tribunal may also, before determining any appeal under s 326, correct any deficiency in the statement – but only with the agreement of the parties.[10]

---

[1]   EA 1996, s 326(1), as substituted by SENDA 2001, Sch 1, para 19.
[2]   Ibid, s 326(1A), as inserted by SENDA 2001, Sch 1, para 19.
[3]   In relation to which there is a separate right of appeal under para 8(3)(b); see para **6.114**.
[4]   Regarding which, see para **6.115**.
[5]   EA 1996, s 326(2).
[6]   Ibid.
[7]   Ibid, s 326(3).
[8]   As to which, see paras **6.60–6.64**.
[9]   EA 1996, s 326(4).
[10] Ibid, s 326(5).

Appeal against refusal to assess a child for whom a statement is maintained

6.113 Where a statement is maintained for a child and the LEA refuses the parent's request made under s 328(2) for an assessment under s 323 of the child's educational needs,[1] the parent may appeal to the Tribunal against that refusal.[2] On appeal, the Tribunal may either dismiss the appeal or order the authority to arrange for such an assessment to be made.[3]

Appeal against a refusal to change named school

6.114 If an LEA refuses to comply with a parent's request made under para 8 of Sch 27 to change the named school in the relevant statement,[4] the LEA must give the parent notice of that refusal, its reasons for it, and of the parent's right to appeal to the Tribunal against that refusal.[5] On appeal, the Tribunal may either dismiss the appeal or order the authority to substitute for the name of the school or other institution specified in the statement the name of the school specified by the parent.[6]

Appeal against a decision to cease to maintain a statement

6.115 Where an LEA determines to cease to maintain a statement of SEN,[7] the parent of the child concerned may appeal against that refusal to the Tribunal.[8] On appeal, the Tribunal may either dismiss the appeal or order the authority to continue to maintain the statement, either in its existing form or with amendments.[9] The amendments may be of the description in the statement of the authority's assessment of the child's SEN, or of the special educational provision specified in the statement, and such other consequential amendments as the Tribunal may determine.[10]

CONSTITUTION OF THE SPECIAL EDUCATIONAL NEEDS AND DISABILITY TRIBUNAL[11]

6.116 A President of the Tribunal must be appointed,[12] as must be a panel of persons who may serve as 'chairman' of the Tribunal,[13] and a panel of persons to

---

[1]   See para **6.51** regarding this situation.

[2]   EA 1996, s 328(3)(b).

[3]   Ibid, s 328(4).

[4]   As to which, see paras **6.98–6.99**.

[5]   EA 1996, Sch 27, para 8(3) and (3A); Special Educational Needs Regulations, reg 17(5).

[6]   Ibid, Sch 27, para 8(4).

[7]   As to which, see paras **6.104–6.105**.

[8]   EA 1996, Sch 27, para 11(2)(b).

[9]   Ibid, Sch 27, para 11(3).

[10] Ibid, Sch 27, para 11(3).

[11] The Special Educational Needs Tribunal for Wales came into existence on 1 September 2003, when s 195 of and Sch 18 to the EA 2002 came into force (see SI 2002/3185). Those apply ss 333–336 of the EA 1996 as modified by s 336ZA of the EA 1996 (which was inserted by para 5 of Sch 18) to that tribunal.

[12] EA 1996, s 333(2)(a).

[13] Ibid, s 333(2)(b). This is 'the chairmen's panel': ibid.

serve as the two other members of the Tribunal.[1] The President and the chairmen are appointed by the Lord Chancellor,[2] and the lay panel by the Secretary of State.[3] The latter provides the necessary staff and accommodation for the Tribunal, with the consent of the Treasury.[4] The staff include the Secretary of the Tribunal, any of whose functions may be performed by another member of the staff of the Tribunal who is authorised by the President to do so.[5]

6.117 The President and the chairmen must have a 7-year general qualification within the meaning of s 71 of the Courts and Legal Services Act 1990.[6] Persons may be appointed as members of the lay panel only if the Secretary of State is satisfied that they have knowledge and experience in respect of children with SEN or of local government and are not eligible to be appointed to the chairmen's panel.[7] The President and the other members of the Tribunal may be paid remuneration and allowances by the Secretary of State,[8] and the other expenses of the Tribunal are also to be met by the Secretary of State.[9]

6.118 The Tribunal can consist only of a chairman and two other members, except where one of the lay members is absent after the commencement of a hearing, in which case the remaining two members may continue to conduct the hearing, but only with the consent of the parties.[10] The chairman must be either the President or a person selected from the chairmen's panel by the President.[11] The lay members must be selected from the lay panel by the President.[12] The President has a number of further functions which he (or a member of the chairmen's panel authorised by the President[13]) can exercise in relation to procedural matters. (Where a relevant reference is made below to the President, it should accordingly be read as including a reference to a chairman authorised by the President.)

6.119 If, following the decision of the Tribunal, the chairman of the tribunal in question dies, becomes incapacitated, or ceases to be a member of the chairmen's panel, then the functions of the Tribunal in relation to any review of that decision may be exercised by the President or any member of the chairmen's panel.[14] If, following the decision of the Tribunal, a lay member dies, is incapacitated, or ceases to be a

---

[1]   EA 1996, s 333(2)(c). This is 'the lay panel': ibid.

[2]   Ibid, s 333(3).

[3]   Ibid, s 333(4).

[4]   Ibid, s 333(6).

[5]   Regulation 47.

[6]   EA 1996, s 334(1). See s 334(3) in relation to the period of office of the President, s 334(4) in relation to the period of office of members of the chairmen's panel and of the lay panel, and s 334(5) in relation to the resignation and possible reappointment of all members of the Tribunal.

[7]   Special Educational Needs and Disability Tribunal (General Provisions and Disability Claims Procedure) Regulations 2002, SI 2002/1985, reg 3.

[8]   EA 1996, s 335(1).

[9]   Ibid, s 335(2). The consent of the Treasury is required in relation to the amounts paid under both s 335(1) and (2).

[10] Special Educational Needs Tribunal Regulations 2001, SI 2001/600, reg 32(5) and SI 2002/1985, reg 5(1).

[11] SI 2002/1985, reg 5(2).

[12] Ibid.

[13] SI 2001/600, reg 45(1).

[14] Ibid, reg 45(3).

member of the lay panel, then, subject to two exceptions, the functions of the Tribunal in relation to any review of that decision may be undertaken by the other two members of the Tribunal.[1] The exceptions are that the Tribunal in question consists of two members in accordance with reg 32(5)[2] or that a person has been authorised to act in place of the chairman in accordance with reg 45(3).[3]

PROCEDURE OF THE SPECIAL EDUCATIONAL NEEDS AND DISABILITY TRIBUNAL IN APPEALS CONCERNING SPECIAL EDUCATIONAL NEEDS

6.120 The rules which govern the procedure in the Tribunal where appeals are brought in relation to SEN matters are the Special Educational Needs Tribunal Regulations 2001[4] (made under s 336(1)). Before their salient features are described, however, reference is made here to two provisions in the EA 1996. First, witnesses and others may be paid expenses for attending the Tribunal.[5] Secondly, according to s 336(5):

'Any person who without reasonable excuse fails to comply with –
(a)   any requirement in respect of the discovery or inspection of documents imposed by the regulations by virtue of subsection (2)(g),[6] or
(b)   any requirement imposed by the regulations by virtue of subsection (2)(h),[7] is guilty of an offence.'[8]

The first of these two possible offences is unusual.

6.121 Subject to the provisions of EA 1996 and the 2001 Regulations, the Tribunal may regulate its own procedure.[9]

Appealing to the tribunal

6.122 An appeal is made by notice to the Tribunal,[10] and the notice must both be signed by the parent and contain the grounds of appeal and certain other

---

1   Special Educational Needs Tribunal Regulations 2001, SI 2001/600, reg 46(1).
2   Regarding which, see para **6.118**.
3   Regulation 46(2) as amended by SI 2002/2787.
4   SI 2001/600 (the 2001 Regulations). Where there is a reference in the rest of this section of this chapter to a regulation without any indication of the set of regulations of which it is a member, it is a reference to one of the 2001 Regulations.
5   EA 1996, s 336(3).
6   Ibid, s 336(2)(g) empowers the making of provision 'for granting any person such discovery or inspection of documents or right to further particulars as might be granted by a county court'.
7   Ibid, s 336(2)(h) empowers the making of provision 'requiring persons to attend to give evidence and produce documents'.
8   The offence is summary, and the maximum fine is at level 3 on the standard scale (which is currently £1,000): s 336(6).
9   2001 Regulations, reg 42(1).
10   See reg 50 for the provisions regarding the sending or delivery of notices and other documents generally.

information.[1] The notice must be delivered to the Secretary of the Tribunal 'so that it is received no later than the first working day after the expiry of 2 months from the date on which the authority gave [the parent] notice, under Part IV of the 1996 Act, that he had a right of appeal'.[2] This time-limit may, however, be extended by the President 'in exceptional circumstances', either on the application of the parent or of the President's own motion.[3] The conduct of a representative might amount to exceptional circumstances for this purpose, such as sudden illness or accident, but a simple delay on the part of the representative would not suffice.[4]

6.123 The Secretary of the Tribunal must, on receipt of the appeal, enter particulars of it in the records, acknowledge it, and send the parent certain information.[5] Where the Secretary is of the opinion that, on the basis of the notice of appeal, the parent is asking the Tribunal to do something which it cannot do, the Secretary may give notice to that effect to the parent, stating the reasons for the opinion and informing the parent that the notice of appeal will not be entered in the records unless the parent notifies the Secretary that he wishes to proceed with it.[6] Further, where the Secretary is of the opinion that there is an obvious error in the notice of appeal, he may correct the error, and if he does so, he must notify the parent and inform the parent of the right to object within 5 working days to that correction.[7] If the parent objects within that time-limit (unless it is extended by the President under reg 51 of the 2001 Regulations), the notice of appeal in its original form stands, but if the parent does not so object, then the notice of appeal as corrected is treated as the notice of appeal for the purposes of the 2001 Regulations.[8]

6.124 If the President considers that the notice of appeal does not include, and is not accompanied by, sufficient reasons to enable the LEA to respond to the appeal, then he must direct the parent to send particulars of the reasons to the Secretary within

[1]   Regulation 7(1) and (2). The *President's Statement* regarding the lodging of a notice of appeal, reported at [1998] ELR 234, indicates the approach which will be taken by the Tribunal in relation to what appears to the Tribunal to be a defective notice of appeal as a result of a failure to comply with reg 7(1) and (2). Its former practice was apparently to reject such a notice. The new one is that 'when an incomplete appeal is registered, I expect immediately to direct that what is missing be provided within a short period. This will be a formal direction under reg 18; failure to comply with it may result in the appeal being dismissed under reg 23': ibid, at 234E.

[2]   Regulation 7(3). The President's Statement entitled *Notification of Right of Appeal: Appeal Time Limits* [2002] ELR 341 includes, in para (3), the following statement: 'I take the view that, since the amendment of the notice requirements by [the SENDA 2001], that regulation must be read as referring to 2 months from the date when a notice fully complying with the expanded requirements was given'. Those requirements are set out in that Statement as: '(a) the fact that the parents have a right to appeal; (b) the time-limit within which they must appeal; (c) the availability of alternative dispute resolution arrangements; (d) the fact that those arrangements do not prejudice the right to appeal'.

[3]   See reg 51, which applies to all of the time-limits in the 2001 Regulations.

[4]   *R v Special Educational Needs Tribunal, ex parte J* [1997] ELR 237.

[5]   Regulation 17(1).

[6]   Regulation 17(2).

[7]   Regulation 17(3)(a).

[8]   Regulation 17(3)(b).

10 working days of the direction.[1] Particulars given pursuant to the direction are treated as part of the notice of appeal.[2]

6.125 Both parties are given 30 working days from the date of a notice served under reg 18(1) (which is sent by the Secretary on receipt of the appeal[3]), to send a statement of their respective cases and written evidence to the Secretary. This period cannot start until any further particulars ordered by the President under reg 8(1) to be provided are in fact provided.[4] If no such particulars are ordered to be provided, or if such particulars are ordered to be, and are, provided, then the Secretary must send the LEA a copy of the notice of appeal and any accompanying papers, and send to both parties a notice under reg 18(1), which (as indicated above) commences the 30-day 'case statement period'.[5]

6.126 The Secretary must send a copy of any amendment to the notice of appeal received during the case statement period, and at the end of that period send a copy of each party's statement of case and written evidence to the other party.[6] If any amendments or supplementary statements, written representations, written evidence (except for late evidence, regarding which see below) or other documents are sent by a party to the Tribunal after the end of the case statement period, then the Secretary must send a copy of it or them to the other party.[7]

Statements of case

6.127 The appellant parent 'may', and the LEA 'shall' during the case statement period deliver to the Secretary a written statement of his or its case.[8] If the LEA (1) fails to deliver a statement of its case within that period, (2) states in writing that it does not resist the appeal, or (3) withdraws its opposition to the appeal, then the Tribunal must (subject to s 326A of the EA 1996, which obliges the Tribunal in certain circumstances to treat the appeal as having been determined in favour of the parent) either (a) determine the appeal on the basis of the notice of appeal without a hearing, or (b) hold a hearing of which the authority is not notified and at which the authority is not represented.[9]

The parent's statement of case

6.128 The parent's statement of case may include the views of the child and must be accompanied by all written evidence which the parent wishes to submit to the

---

[1] Regulation 8(1). Regulations 21 and 25 (regarding which see paras **6.133–6.138**) apply to the direction: reg 8(2).
[2] Regulation 8(3).
[3] Regulation 17(1)(b)(iv).
[4] Regulation 18(2).
[5] Regulation 17(2)(b)(iv) and (c). Regulation 2(1) defines the case statement period as the 30-day period specified in the notice under reg 18(1), including any extension ordered by the President under reg 51(1).
[6] Regulation 19(1)(a) and (b).
[7] Regulation 19(1)(c).
[8] Regulations 9(1) and 13(1).
[9] Regulation 15(1), as amended by SI 2002/2787.

Tribunal and which he has not already submitted.[1] In exceptional circumstances, the parent may amend the notice of appeal, deliver a supplementary statement of reasons for appealing or statement of case, or amend either such document, but only if the President gives permission to do so or the Tribunal gives such permission at a hearing.[2] In such circumstances the LEA regains any lost entitlement to be represented at the hearing.[3]

The LEA's statement of case

6.129 The LEA's statement of case must be accompanied by all the written evidence on which it intends to rely.[4] The statement of case must be signed by an officer of the authority who is authorised to sign such documents, and must state whether or not the authority intends to oppose the appeal. If the LEA does intend to oppose the appeal, then the statement of case must state (a) the grounds on which the LEA relies, (b) the name and profession of the representative of the authority and the authority's address for service for the purposes of the appeal, (c) a summary of the facts relating to the disputed decision, (d) the reasons for the decision if they are not already stated in the document setting out the decision, and (e) the views of the child concerning the issues raised by the appeal, or the reasons why the LEA has not ascertained those views.[5] If the LEA does not intend to resist the appeal and the appeal relates to the contents of the child's statement of SEN, no statement that the LEA does not intend to resist the appeal or that it withdraws its opposition to the appeal may take effect until the LEA sends the Tribunal a written statement of the amendments (if any) to the statement which it agrees to make.[6]

6.130 In exceptional circumstances, the LEA may amend its statement of case or deliver a supplementary statement of case or amend a supplementary statement of case if permission to do so is given by the President, or by the Tribunal at a hearing.[7] If the President gives such permission, however, then he may extend the case statement period.[8] Where permission to amend is given, the parent regains his entitlement to amend or be represented at the hearing.[9]

6.131 If an appeal relates to a child for whom a statement of SEN exists and the notice of appeal is amended in accordance with reg 9(2) so that the parent seeks an order that a maintained school, or a different maintained school (different, that is, from that which is already named in the statement) be named in the statement, then the Secretary must give the head teacher of that school notice of the appeal, stating

---

[1]   Regulation 9(1), as amended by SI 2002/2787.
[2]   Regulation 9(2), as amended by SI 2002/2787. It was held that the wording of reg 9(2) in its original form could not properly be regarded as overridden by any statement in any guidance issued by the Tribunal: see *L v Royal Borough of Kensington and Chelsea* [1997] ELR 155, at 160E.
[3]   See reg 9(5), as inserted by SI 2002/2787.
[4]   Regulation 13(1), as amended by SI 2002/2787.
[5]   Regulation 13(2). The LEA can change its representative at any time by notifying the Secretary of the Tribunal of the name and profession of its new representative: reg 14(1).
[6]   Regulation 15(2).
[7]   Regulation 13(3), as amended by SI 2002/2787.
[8]   Regulation 13(5), as amended by SI 2002/2787.
[9]   See reg 13(6), as inserted by SI 2002/2787.

the name and date of birth of the child and, where the school is maintained by a different LEA, the name of the LEA which is the respondent to the appeal.[1]

Enquiries; representation

6.132 The Secretary of the Tribunal is obliged to make certain enquiries of the parties 'at any time after he has received the notice of appeal'.[2] The parties must reply to those enquiries.[3] The questions asked by the Secretary include whether the party intends to attend the hearing, and whether the party wishes to be represented at the hearing. Both parties may be represented by one person, whether or not legally qualified, and the President or the Tribunal at a hearing may allow a party to be represented by more than one person.[4] A parent who attends may either present the case alone or with assistance from one person as of right, or more than one person with permission granted by the President before the hearing or the Tribunal at the hearing.[5] If either party does not intend to attend or be represented at the hearing then they may, no later than 5 days before the hearing, send to the Secretary additional written representations in support of their appeal or reply.[6]

Interlocutory matters

6.133 Directions 'to enable the parties to prepare for the hearing or to assist the tribunal to determine the issues' may be given by the President in advance of the hearing.[7] Such directions may require the provision of 'such particulars or supplementary statements as may reasonably be required for the determination of the appeal',[8] and may require the delivery by a party of 'any document or other material which the tribunal may require and which it is in the power of that party to deliver'.[9] Disclosure or the inspection of documents (including the taking of copies) may in addition be granted in the same way that these may be granted under the Civil Procedure Rules 1998.[10] The directions described in this paragraph may be given either on the President's own initiative or on the application of a party.[11]

6.134 The President may issue witness summonses,[12] but must before doing so 'take into account the need to protect any matter that relates to intimate personal or financial circumstances or consists of information communicated or obtained in

---

[1] Regulation 19(3). If the school is maintained by a different LEA, then notice must also be given to that LEA: see reg 19(4) as inserted by SI 2002/2787

[2] See reg 20, which sets out the matters in relation to which enquiry must be made.

[3] See regs 11(1) and 16(2).

[4] Regulations 12(6) and 16(1) as amended by SI 2002/2787. Note the *President's Statement* of 1 December 1995 regarding representation by counsel and solicitor, reported at [1996] ELR 280.

[5] Ibid.

[6] Regulations 11(2) and 16(3).

[7] Regulation 21(1). A hearing to determine a preliminary issue may be ordered under reg 21(6).

[8] Regulation 23.

[9] Regulation 24(1), under which the President must 'impose a condition on the supply of a copy of any document or other material delivered in compliance with a direction given under this paragraph that the party receiving it shall use such document only for the purposes of the appeal', and may require a written undertaking to observe that condition before supplying a copy.

[10] Regulation 24(2).

[11] Regulation 21(1).

[12] Regulation 26(1).

confidence'.[1] The witness can be required to answer any questions or produce any documents or other material in his custody or under his control which relate to any matter in question in the appeal,[2] but only so far as he could be compelled to do so in a court of law.[3]

6.135 If an application for a direction (including a witness summons) is made then the Secretary of the Tribunal must serve a copy of the application on the other party, unless it is accompanied by the written consent of the other party.[4] If objection is made to an application for either such direction by the other party, then the President must, if he considers it necessary for the determination of the application, give the parties the opportunity of an oral hearing before him.[5]

6.136 The President may not make a direction for which an application is made if in his opinion there would not be a reasonable time before a hearing of which notice has been given under reg 28(1) to comply with the direction.[6]

6.137 A person to whom a direction or witness summons is addressed who had no opportunity to object to the issue of the direction or summons, may apply by notice to the Secretary of the Tribunal to vary or set it aside.[7] The President must then give the party who applied for the direction the opportunity to make relevant representations, and must consider the representations.[8]

6.138 If a party fails to comply with a direction within the time specified in the direction, then the Tribunal may dismiss or determine the appeal without a hearing.[9] Alternatively, the Tribunal may hold a hearing (without notifying the party in default) at which the party in default is not represented, or, if the parties have been duly notified of the hearing, direct that neither the party in default nor any representative or witness of his be entitled to attend the hearing.[10] These possible consequences must be stated in any relevant direction.[11] Where relevant, so must the possibility of a summary conviction and fine for a failure without reasonable excuse to comply with a direction to allow the disclosure or inspection of documents.[12]

---

[1] Regulation 26(1)(b). Note reg 26(1)(e) in relation to persons under the age of 12.

[2] Regulation 26(1).

[3] Regulation 26(1)(a). Witnesses must also (unless they agree otherwise) be given at least 5 working days' notice of the hearing, and must have their expenses paid or tendered to them: reg 26(1)(c) and (d).

[4] Regulation 21(2).

[5] Ibid.

[6] Regulation 21(3). See para **6.139** regarding reg 28(1).

[7] Regulations 22 and 26(4).

[8] Ibid.

[9] Regulation 25(1)(a) and (b).

[10] Regulation 25(1)(c).

[11] Regulation 21(4)(a).

[12] Regulation 21(4)(b). The possibility of applying to the President under reg 22 to set aside the direction or witness summons must also be stated unless the person to whom the direction is addressed had an opportunity to object to the direction, or gave his written consent to the application for it: reg 21(4)(c).

Notification of hearing

6.139 Determination and notification of the date and venue of the hearing must normally be preceded by consultation with the parties.[1] Notification of the date of the hearing must normally be sent (not received) not less than 5 working days before the date fixed for a hearing[2] concerning the possible striking out of an appeal, reply, response or statement, for a hearing[3] where the LEA either has failed to send a statement of its case to the Tribunal within the case statement period or has stated in writing that it does not resist the appeal or withdraws its opposition to the appeal, or for a hearing[4] of a review.[5] In any other case, the notification must be sent not less than 10 working days before the date fixed for the hearing.[6] In either case, however, the parties may agree to a shorter period.[7] When sending a notice of a hearing, the Secretary of the Tribunal must at the same time send (among other things[8]) 'information and guidance, in a form approved by the President, as to attendance at the hearing of the parties and witnesses, the bringing of documents, and the right of representation or assistance'.[9] The Tribunal may alter the time and place of any hearing, on no less than 5 working days' notice from the Secretary of the Tribunal (unless the parties agree to a shorter period), to a date no sooner than the date originally notified (unless the parties agree otherwise).[10]

Determining appeals

6.140 Appeals may be determined without a hearing (1) where the parties agree, (2) where the authority does not resist the appeal, or (3) where a party has failed to comply with a direction.[11] The Tribunal may, if it thinks fit, make a decision in terms agreed in writing by the parties.[12] Where it does so, it may be necessary to cross-refer to, or annexe, a note or copy of the relevant part or parts of the statement of SEN with the amendments which have been agreed by the parties, signed by the parties and the tribunal.[13]

6.141 Hearings are normally in private, but they will be in public if both the parent and the authority so request or the President, or the Tribunal at a hearing so orders.[14] Disruptive persons may in any event be excluded from the hearing.[15] By analogy with *Peach Grey & Co v Sommers*,[16] it is likely that such persons could be in contempt of

---

[1]　Regulation 28(1).

[2]　Under reg 44.

[3]　Under reg 15.

[4]　Under reg 37.

[5]　Regulation 28(2)(a).

[6]　Regulation 28(2)(b).

[7]　Regulation 28(2)(c).

[8]　As to which see reg 28(3) generally.

[9]　Regulation 28(3)(a).

[10]　Regulation 28(4).

[11]　Regulation 29(1).

[12]　Regulation 42(2).

[13]　*Crean v Somerset County Council* [2002] ELR 152, at 161, para 40.

[14]　Regulation 30(1), as amended by SI 2002/2787, but see reg 30(2) and (3).

[15]　Regulation 30(4).

[16]　[1995] ICR 549.

court. A parent of a child who is not a party to the appeal (and, as indicated above,[1] there may be more than two 'parents' for this purpose) may be permitted to address the Tribunal on the subject matter of the appeal.[2] The Tribunal may also permit the child to whose education the appeal relates to both give evidence and address the Tribunal on the subject matter of the appeal.[3] No more than two persons other than a representative or any witness may normally attend a hearing at the desire of the parent.[4]

6.142 If a party fails to attend or be represented at a hearing of which he has been duly notified, then the Tribunal may, unless it is satisfied that there is sufficient reason for such absence, hear and determine the hearing in his absence.[5] Alternatively, the Tribunal may adjourn the hearing.[6]

6.143 Where a decision of the Tribunal relating to a case has been quashed, it will be unlawful to put the papers relating to that quashed decision before a differently constituted Tribunal which considers the remitted matter.[7]

6.144 The Tribunal must conduct the hearing:

> 'in such manner as it considers the most suitable to the clarification of the issues and generally to the just handling of the proceedings; it shall, as far as appears to it appropriate, seek to avoid formality in its proceedings.'[8]

6.145 The Tribunal may hear evidence of any fact which appears to it to be relevant,[9] which means that it can hear evidence which would be inadmissible in a court of law. It will not be irrelevant that the child in question has been excluded from school.[10]

6.146 However, the Tribunal, being a creature of statute, has no power to rule on questions outside its jurisdiction, such as whether an LEA has any funding obligation.[11] Similarly, as Laws J said in *G v Wakefield Metropolitan District Council*:[12]

> 'Economic problems faced by the child's parents, where for example different and perhaps more spacious accommodation would in an ideal world be suitable for the family because of the child's disabilities, are not ordinarily within the remit of the SENT. Nor are difficulties associated with the parent's disabilities, where the effect is that the child is, in physical terms, more difficult to look after.'

---

[1] Paragraph **5.6**.
[2] Regulation 30(8).
[3] Regulation 30(7).
[4] Regulation 30(2) and (9).
[5] Regulation 31(1)(a).
[6] Regulation 31(1)(b).
[7] *R v Special Educational Needs Tribunal, ex parte Fisher* [1999] ELR 417.
[8] Regulation 32(2).
[9] Regulation 34(3), but see reg 34(1) in relation to the number of witnesses.
[10] *AE and PE v Special Educational Needs Tribunal and Surrey County Council* [1999] ELR 341.
[11] *White v London Borough of Ealing* [1998] ELR 203, at 220E–F, applied in *G v London Borough of Barnet* [1998] ELR 480, at 486G–H.
[12] (1998) 96 LGR 69, at 80h–81a.

However, Laws J accepted[1] that it was 'clearly possible to envisage [circumstances] where some kinds of day-to-day domestic problems may directly relate to the child's learning difficulties. Such a direct relation must in my judgment be shown in order to involve such problems in the tribunal's jurisdiction under section 326'. In addition, what Laws J said in the case must now be read in the light of the enactment of the SENDA 2001.

6.147 The usual rule that the appellant goes first may be ruled by the Tribunal not to apply, and the Tribunal determines the order in which the issues are to be determined.[2] The Tribunal may, if it is satisfied that it is 'just and reasonable to do so', permit a party to adduce evidence not put before the LEA before or at the time when it took its disputed decision, or to rely on grounds not stated in the statement of its case.[3] In addition, reg 33 provides for the admission by the Tribunal of 'late written evidence', which may be submitted at the beginning of the hearing, subject to conditions set out in reg 33(2), but which the Tribunal may in any event refuse to admit if it is of the opinion, having considered any representations from the other party, that it would be 'contrary to the interests of justice' to admit it.[4] The conditions are that (1) the evidence was not, and could not reasonably have been, available to the party before the end of the case statement period, (2) a copy of the evidence was 'sent to or delivered to the Tribunal and to the other party to arrive at least 5 working days before the hearing' (which presumably means that it must actually have arrived at least 5 working days before the hearing), and 'the extent and form of the evidence is such that, in the opinion of the Tribunal, it is not likely to impede the efficient conduct of the hearing'. Even if these conditions are not satisfied, the Tribunal may admit further written evidence at the hearing if it is of the opinion that the case is 'wholly exceptional' and that, unless the evidence is admitted, there is 'a serious risk of prejudice to the interests of the child'.[5]

6.148 These provisions confirm that the Tribunal is not limited to reviewing the decision of the LEA, but is, rather, both entitled and bound to consider the needs of the child at the time of the appeal.[6] Moreover, where a child is approaching the end of his time at, for example, primary school, the Tribunal is bound to consider what sort

---

[1]   (1998) 96 LGR 69, at 81b–c.

[2]   Regulation 32(3).

[3]   Regulation 32(4). In *L v Salford City Council* [1998] ELR 28, the LEA took the point at the hearing of an appeal against a refusal to amend a statement, that the statement no longer needed to be maintained. The Tribunal allowed the authority to take that point, and its decision to do so was upheld on appeal to the High Court: see ibid, at 34E–F. See further, para **6.105** regarding that case.

[4]   Regulation 33(1).

[5]   Regulation 33(3). Note also reg 33(4). It is doubtful whether these provisions apply to the admission of evidence by the Tribunal when considering whether to grant an application for costs under reg 40. This is in part because reg 33 is clearly directed at evidence relating to the child in question. In any event, reg 32(2) (which is set out in para **6.144**) should be borne in mind when considering whether it would fair (and therefore just) to allow evidence to be adduced otherwise than in accordance with the strict provisions of reg 33 during the hearing of an application for costs. Naturally, it would be unfair to take a party by surprise at such a hearing, but protection in that regard is capable of being granted by the Tribunal under reg 32(2).

[6]   In the *Special Educational Needs Tribunal – President's Direction* [1995] ELR 335, the President confirmed that, despite views to the contrary expressed by half the members of the Tribunal, the Tribunal should consider what was appropriate at the hearing, and should not merely adjudicate on the correctness of the LEA's decision when it was taken.

of secondary education he should receive, although there is no need for the Tribunal in doing so to name any particular school.[1] This implies that the Tribunal may look to the future, and this was explicitly stated by Collins J in *S v London Borough of Hackney*,[2] with the caveat that the Tribunal may not speculate.

6.149 Evidence is adduced in the usual way, except that unless the President before the hearing or the Tribunal at the hearing otherwise permits, neither party may call more than two witnesses in addition to the makers of any written statement whose personal attendance is ordered by the Tribunal.[3] An LEA's representative may give evidence to the Tribunal in addition to evidence being given by witnesses on behalf of the LEA.[4] No written statement may in any event be relied upon by a party unless it was submitted (in the case of a parent) with the notice of appeal or with the statement of the party's case, or under reg 33 (ie as late written evidence).[5] However, the 2001 Regulations do not prevent a party from adducing oral evidence of which no written notice has been given.[6] Witnesses may be required to give evidence on oath or affirmation, and evidence given by written statement may be required to be given by a written statement containing a statement of truth.[7]

6.150 As with other tribunals, the rules of natural justice apply to proceedings before the Tribunal. However, it was held in *Richardson v Solihull Metropolitan Borough Council*[8] that those rules did not require an expert member of the Tribunal to advise a party to a hearing that the expert intended to apply his knowledge and experience in a particular way. There, the Tribunal decided that neither the appellant parent's choice of school, nor the only school chosen by the respondent LEA where a place was available, was suitable. However, the Tribunal decided that the needs of the children in question could be met at other, unspecified, schools. It did so on the apparent basis of the expert knowledge of the lay members, and it did not indicate its likely conclusion in that regard to the appellant. Although Beldam LJ (with whom Schiemann LJ agreed) determined that:

> 'the specialist member of a tribunal who had in mind a specific school which neither party had considered would regard it as fair and indeed in the child's interest to raise with the parties the possibility of the provision of such a school to meet the child's educational needs',[9]

the court also held that the use of specialist knowledge could reasonably be expected by the parties and did not render the procedure of the decision invalid for unfairness.

---

[1]   *Wilkin v Goldthorpe and Coventry City Council* [1998] ELR 345.

[2]   [2002] ELR 45, at 55, at para 41.

[3]   Regulation 34(1). In the case of a parent, this means two witnesses other than the parent. Reg 34(2) provides that if a written statement is relied upon by a party, then the Tribunal may require the personal attendance of the maker of the statement.

[4]   *H v Gloucestershire County Council* [2000] ELR 357.

[5]   Regulation 34(2). See para **6.147** regarding reg 33. The predecessor of this provision, reg 29(2) of SI 1995/3113, was held to be *intra vires* by Dyson J in *Duncan v Bedfordshire County Council* [1997] ELR 299, at 306D–E.

[6]   As noted by Dyson J, ibid, at 306E in relation to the 1995 predecessor regulations, SI 1995/3113.

[7]   Regulation 34(4).

[8]   [1998] ELR 319; [1998] EdCR 308.

[9]   Ibid, at 332A–B.

This seems wrong. Indeed, Beatson J, without having been referred to *Richardson*, in *R(L) v London Borough of Waltham Forest*[1] accepted that if the Tribual is proposing to rely on its own expertise in rejecting evidence before it, then 'the expert member of the tribunal should put, either directly or through the chair, the point to those representing the parties at the hearing'. Similiarly, in *B v Gloucestershire County Council*,[2] Sullivan J stated:

> 'I do not rule out the possibility that fairness might well require a tribunal in particular circumstances to advise an appellant that they felt that evidence was lacking in some particular area.'

6.151 However, as Sedley LJ said in *London Borough of Bromley v Special Educational Needs Tribunal*:[3]

> 'While proceedings before SENTs are not expected to mimic litigation, a SENT is in the ordinary way entitled to expect each side to bring its full case forward, at least to the extent of putting down the necessary markers.'

6.152 Similarly, Collins J in *S v London Borough of Hackney*[4] said that the Tribunal 'has no duty ... to assume parental preferences on any grounds other than those specifically put forward by the parents and those which are live before the tribunal'. Furthermore, where the Tribunal decides that the school named by the LEA in part 4 of the statement of SEN to which the appeal relates is inappropriate, it is not necessary for the Tribunal to give the LEA an opportunity to suggest alternatives which might be less expensive than an independent school preferred by the parent.[5] Similarly, if the LEA names a school in the statement and the parent does not want the child to attend that school, the Tribunal is not obliged to order the LEA to name only the type of school rather than the school which is actually named in the statement unless there is 'some evidence that a school or schools of that type [are] or might become available to meet the special educational needs of that particular child'.[6]

6.153 Where the LEA is making a proposal as to a specific establishment to be named in part 4 of the statement without giving the parent a chance to research it at all, there is a particular obligation on the LEA to be 'punctilious in presenting to the tribunal, as well as to the parents, all the arguably relevant material'.[7]

Adjournments

6.154 There is a general power to adjourn a hearing.[8] Directions (which may require a party to provide 'such particulars, evidence or statements as may reasonably be

---

1   [2003] EWHC 2907 (Admin), [2004] ELR 161, at paras 25 and 26.
2   [1998] ELR 539, at 550B–C.
3   [1999] ELR 260, at 296G–H
4   [2002] ELR 45, at para 43.
5   *Rhondda Cynon Taff County Borough Council v Special Educational Needs Tribunal* [2002] ELR 290, at 294, para 14.
6   *CB v Merton London Borough Council* [2002] ELR 441, at 451, para 26.
7   *T v London Borough of Islington* [2002] ELR 426, at 438, para 42, per Wilson J.
8   Regulation 35(1).

required for the determination of the appeal'[1]) may be given when a hearing is adjourned,[2] and they must be complied with before the resumed hearing.[3] Any failure to comply with such a direction must be taken into account by the Tribunal when determining the appeal or deciding whether to make an order for costs.[4] Where the Tribunal adjourns a hearing, the chairman may announce 'provisional conclusions reached by the tribunal', which are not a decision of the Tribunal.[5]

6.155 If the Tribunal refuses a request for an adjournment, the test to be applied on appeal will probably not be whether the decision to refuse an adjournment was *Wednesbury* unreasonable. Rather, according to *L v Royal Borough of Kensington and Chelsea*,[6] the court will have to decide 'whether fairness required an adjournment, due regard being had to the views of the tribunal on that question'. Words to the same effect were said in *R v Cheshire County Council and the Special Educational Needs Tribunal, ex parte C*[7] and *West Glamorgan County Council v Confrey*.[8] However, in the latter case, having indicated his agreement with the proposition just stated, Popplewell J seemed to indicate a slightly different test, namely: 'whether an adjournment should be granted is a matter for the discretion of the judge or the tribunal and he should be guided in the exercise of that discretion by his assessment of where justice lies'.[9] Furthermore, Sedley J in *ex parte C* went on to determine the case in the alternative on the basis that he was wrong to apply the test of fairness, and that the test was instead that of *Wednesbury* reasonableness. McManus, in *Education and the Courts*,[10] suggests a synthesis of the two different approaches: that a 'refusal to grant an adjournment may not lead to an unfair hearing but still be perverse'. It is suggested here that, as McManus says there, the balance of authority leads to the view that the proper test is the one of fairness, and not that of *Wednesbury* unreasonableness. In *S v London Borough of Hounslow and Vassie*,[11] Tomlinson J, having been referred to this conflict of authority, declined to decide what was the proper approach. This was because both tests were satisfied in the circumstances.[12] The circumstances were that the mother of a high functioning autistic child who was aged 7 but was not attending school, was unable as a result of unforeseen circumstances to be present at the hearing. These were that she found out on the morning of the hearing that her childcare arrangements for the day had fallen through. She spoke on the telephone to the duty member of the staff of the social services department of the local authority, a Miss Beard. The latter telephoned the Tribunal's staff, and a member of staff apparently told Miss Beard that the hearing would be adjourned. She then told the child's mother

---

1 Regulation 35(3).
2 Regulation 35(2)(a).
3 Ibid.
4 Regulation 35(4).
5 Regulation 35(2)(b).
6 [1997] ELR 155, at 159C–D.
7 [1998] ELR 66, at 73F–H.
8 [1998] ELR 121, at 123D–G.
9 Ibid, at 123G.
10 Sweet & Maxwell, 1998, at para 3.87. The case referred to by him as *R v Cheshire, ex parte Cherrih* (1997) 95 LGR 299 has now been reported also as *R v Cheshire County Council and the Special Educational Needs Tribunal, ex parte C* [1998] ELR 66.
11 [2001] ELR 88, at para 66.
12 See para 68 of the report.

that that was so. The hearing was not in fact adjourned, and the facts stated in the preceding sentences above were not put before the Tribunal.

6.156 In any event, assuming that the test is one of fairness, some guidance can be found in several of the reported cases. In R *v Cheshire County Council and the Special Educational Needs Tribunal, ex parte C*,[1] Sedley J said: 'It is only where ... the tribunal could properly be satisfied that advantage was being taken of the absence of a wholly unnecessary witness or representative that it would be right to refuse an adjournment'. However, in *L v Royal Borough of Kensington and Chelsea*,[2] Dyson J held that Sedley J 'somewhat overstate[d] the position' in that regard. Dyson J there overruled the refusal by the Tribunal of an adjournment which had been requested to allow an expert witness to attend. The need for the adjournment was not of the appellant's own making. It came about because at very short notice the hearing was brought forward. The evidence of the expert was 'plainly of great importance, since it went to a central issue in the case'.[3]

6.157 In R *v Cheshire County Council and the Special Educational Needs Tribunal, ex parte C*[4] Sedley J said something else which is helpful. He said:

> 'To conclude that because she was articulate there was no reason why the appellant should not present the appeal herself was to take the very decision about representation which it was the appellant's right alone to take and which she had taken in favour of being represented.'[5]

The Tribunal's decision

6.158 The decision of the Tribunal may be taken by a majority, and where two members hear the appeal under reg 32(5),[6] the chairman has a second or casting vote,[7] but the fact that the decision was made by a majority must not be revealed.[8] The decision may be given orally at the end of the hearing or may be reserved, but in any event must be in writing.[9] The reasons in summary form must be given, unless the decision is by consent.[10] The reasons must be sufficient to allow the parties to see why the decision was reached.[11] The parties are entitled to 'know why they have either won or lost, as the case may be, and what the tribunal's conclusion has been in relation to

---

[1]   [1998] ELR 66.

[2]   [1997] ELR 155, at 159D–E.

[3]   [1997] ELR 155, at 160B.

[4]   [1998] ELR 66.

[5]   Ibid, at 75C–D:

[6]   As to which, see para **6.118**.

[7]   Regulation 36(1).

[8]   Regulation 36(3).

[9]   Regulation 36(2). Where there is no hearing there must also be a decision in writing: ibid.

[10]   Regulation 36(2).

[11]   *S (A Minor) v Special Educational Needs Tribunal* [1995] 1 WLR 1627, at 1636C–D, [1996] ELR 102, at 112B–C (this aspect of the decision of Latham J was not discussed by the Court of Appeal in the same case, reported at [1996] 1 WLR 382; [1996] ELR 228). See also *H v Kent County Council* [2000] ELR 660, at para 42: 'the statement of reasons should deal in short form with the substantial issues raised in order that the parties can understand why the decision has been reached; in other words, what evidence is rejected and what evidence is accepted'.

the major issues that have been put before it'.[1] However, 'when a decision, which is rationally explicable, has been reached by an expert tribunal, charged with assessing these difficult matters ... the court should be slow to quash that decision for failing to set out every aspect of its reasoning in arriving at it'.[2] However, 'recitation of the evidence is no substitute for reasons which are essential in order to understand the logic which [led] the tribunal to reject an expert opinion as to appropriate provision'.[3] It has been said that if the Tribunal's reasons are insufficient, then an application for a review of the Tribunal's decision (as to which, see the following section) rather than an appeal to the High Court against it (as to which, see below[4]), may be the best course of action to take.[5] Nevertheless, it has also been said that although it is wrong to 'go through reasons, or go through a decision of a tribunal, with a fine tooth comb and seek to tease out discrepancies and to try and show that there have been errors and omissions ... a deficiency in reasons may indicate that there is an error of law which has been made by the tribunal'.[6] This is what occurred in *Crean v Somerset County Council*,[7] where the Tribunal failed to state its conclusions on several material matters, including how long the Tribunal thought it would take the school named in the statement, which did not have the necessary expertise at the time of the Tribunal hearing, to obtain such expertise.

6.159 A decision is treated as having been made on the day when a copy of the document recording it is sent to the parent (whether or not the decision was announced orally at the end of the hearing).[8] There are various time-limits for compliance by an LEA with an order of the Tribunal.[9]

6.160 It is not open to the Tribunal to order the amendment of a statement of SEN so as to name a school where it would otherwise be unlawful for the school to admit the child (for example because the child is older than the maximum age for pupils at the school).[10] Furthermore, the Tribunal is not empowered to order an LEA to provide more than is required to meet the SEN of a child.[11] In addition, the Tribunal may not order, as part of its decision on the content of a statement, that an assessment of (for example) whether the child in question is to have access to the National Curriculum be carried out.[12] However, the Tribunal is not bound to accept

---

[1] *Staffordshire County Council v J and J* [1996] ELR 418, at 424F.

[2] *S v Special Educational Needs Tribunal* [2002] EWHC 1047 (Admin); [2003] ELR 85, at 94, para 52, per Goldring J. To a similar effect is the judgment of Lawrence Collins J in *M v Worcestershire County Council* [2002] EWHC 1292 (Admin); [2003] ELR 31, especially at paras 55 and 60.

[3] *R(M) v Brighton City Council and SENDIST* [2003] EWHC 1722 (Admin); [2003] ELR 752, para 3, per Leveson J. See also *R(L) v London Borough of Waltham Forest* [2003] EWHC 2907 (Admin), [2004] ELR 161, at paras 13 and 14.

[4] Paragraphs **6.172** et seq.

[5] *South Glamorgan County Council v L and M* [1996] ELR 400, at 414B–D.

[6] *L v Kent County Council and the Special Educational Needs Tribunal* [1998] ELR 140, at 147D–E.

[7] [2002] ELR 152.

[8] Regulation 36(7).

[9] See reg 25 of the Special Educational Needs Regulations 2001, SI 2001/3455 and reg 3 of the Special Educational Needs Tribunal (Time Limits) (Wales) Regulations 2001, SI 2001/3982.

[10] *Council of the City of Sunderland v P and C* [1996] ELR 283.

[11] *Richardson v Solihull Metropolitan Borough Council* [1998] ELR 319; *Hackney London Borough Council v Silaydin* [1998] ELR 571; [1999] EdCR 479.

[12] *C v Special Educational Needs Tribunal* [1999] ELR 5; [1999] EdCR 625.

the evidence of an expert, however eminent, even in the absence of any expert evidence to the contrary effect.[1]

Reviews

6.161 A party may apply for a review of a decision of the Tribunal and the Tribunal may on its own initiative review its decision, on the grounds that (a) its decision was 'wrongly made as a result of an error on the part of the tribunal staff ', (b) a party who was entitled to be heard at a hearing but failed to appear or to be represented, had 'good and sufficient reason for failing to appear', (c) there was an 'obvious error in the decision of the tribunal which decided the case', or (d) 'the interests of justice require'.[2] In *South Glamorgan County Council v L and M*,[3] it was held by Carnwath J that where one party is of the view that the decision of the Tribunal has been reached 'on a radically flawed basis of fact', then the party should seek a review, instead of appealing to the High Court on a point of law.[4] As noted above,[5] it was also held in that case that an inadequacy in the reasons given by the Tribunal could be sufficient justification to apply for a review. However, a more restrictive approach was apparently taken by Latham J in *C v the Special Educational Needs Tribunal*.[6] It is of note that in *Richardson v Solihull Metropolitan Borough Council*,[7] Beldam LJ (with whom Schiemann LJ agreed) said that 'It would not be appropriate to seek a review merely to reargue the case', and that 'Generally [a review] will be appropriate only if it is apparent from the statement of reasons that the tribunal has either overlooked some significant matter or has made an obvious error on which it has based its conclusions'. Although Elias J subsequently stated in *E v Oxfordshire County Council*[8] that he agreed with the statement from the judgment of Carnwath J in *South Glamorgan County Council v L and M* set out above in this paragraph, he was not referred to what Beldam LJ said in *Richardson*.

6.162 An application for a review must be in writing, must be made not later than 10 working days after the date when the decision was sent to the parties, and must contain the grounds 'in full'.[9] Unless the President or the chairman of the tribunal which decided the case is of the opinion that the application has no reasonable prospect of success, the parties must have an opportunity to 'be heard' on the application for review, and that application for a review must, subject to reg 46,[10] be

---

1   *Manchester City Council v (1) Special Educational Needs Tribunal (2) S* [2000] EdCR 80.
2   Regulation 37(1) and (4). Some of these grounds are similar to those which apply to the review of a decision of an employment tribunal, and the relevant case-law may therefore be applied by analogy. This is certainly the approach expressed in the *President's Guidance* on applications to review decisions, reported at [1996] ELR 278.
3   [1996] ELR 400, at 414D–F.
4   See paras **6.172** et seq regarding appeals to the High Court.
5   Paragraph **6.161**.
6   Unreported, but referred to in Friel and Hay, *Special Educational Needs and the Law* (Sweet & Maxwell, 1996), at p 83.
7   [1998] ELR 319; [1998] EdCR 308, at 335D and 327E respectively.
8   [2002] ELR 156, at 163, para 31.
9   Regulation 37(2). The time-limit is accordingly almost the same as that in an employment tribunal, where the limit is expressed slightly differently as '14 days': para 13(4) of Sch 1 to the Employment Tribunals (Constitution and Rules of Procedure) Regulations 2001, SI 2001/1171.
10   Regarding which, see para **6.119**.

determined by the Tribunal which decided the case or, where it is not practicable for that to occur, by a Tribunal appointed by the President.[1] There is no duty to give reasons for a refusal to review a decision of the Tribunal.[2]

6.163 Where the Tribunal proposes to review its decision on its own initiative, it must serve notice on the parents[3] no later than 10 working days after the date on which the decision was sent to the parties, and the parties must have an opportunity to be heard on the proposal for a review.[4] Where the Tribunal is satisfied that any of the grounds set out in reg 37(1) may be made out and that the application for a review should proceed, it must order that the whole or a specified part of the decision be reviewed and it may give directions to be complied with before or at the hearing of the review.[5] Such a direction may require a party to provide 'such particulars, evidence or statements as may reasonably be required for the determination of the review'.[6] If a party fails to comply with a direction made under reg 37(6), the Tribunal must take that failure into account when determining the review or deciding whether to make an order for costs.[7] Having reviewed a decision, the Tribunal may set aside or vary the decision, or it may order a rehearing before the same or a differently constituted tribunal.[8]

6.164 The President may review and set aside or vary any of his own decisions, either on his own initiative or on the application of a party to the Secretary of the Tribunal,[9] if he is satisfied that any one of the grounds (read as appropriate) set out in para 6.161 (except for the one relating to the failure by a party to appear or be represented at the hearing) applies.[10] The parties must have an opportunity to be heard on any application or proposal for such a review, and the review must be determined by the President.[11] A decision by the President not to extend the parent's time for delivering a notice of appeal under reg 7(3) may be reviewed in this manner on the application of a parent as if the parent were a party, and in such a case the LEA may not be either heard or notified.[12]

Costs and expenses

6.165 As with employment tribunals, an order for costs and expenses is not normally to be made by the Tribunal.[13] Such an order may nevertheless be made against a party

---

[1] Regulation 37(3) and (4).

[2] *C v Special Educational Needs Tribunal* [1997] ELR 390, at 402G–403A.

[3] Not the parties, but the parents.

[4] Regulation 37(5).

[5] Regulation 37(6), the wording of which is capable of confusing: it applies where 'the tribunal is satisfied as to any of the grounds referred to in paragraph 1', but it seems clear that the effect of reg 37(6) is as stated in the text to this note.

[6] Regulation 37(7).

[7] Regulation 37(8).

[8] Regulation 38.

[9] The application must be in writing, must be made within 10 working days of the date when the party was notified of the decision, and must state the grounds in full: reg 39(2). The same time-limit applies for the service by the President of notice of a proposal to review: reg 39(3).

[10] Regulation 39(1).

[11] Regulation 39(4).

[12] Regulation 39(6).

[13] Regulation 40(1).

(including a party who has withdrawn his appeal or reply) if the Tribunal is of the opinion that the party has acted 'frivolously or vexatiously or that his conduct in making, pursuing or resisting an appeal was wholly unreasonable'.[1] Such an order may also be made against a party who has failed to attend or be represented at a hearing of which he has been duly notified,[2] against the LEA where it has not delivered a statement of its case under reg 13,[3] or against the authority where the Tribunal considers that the disputed decision was 'wholly unreasonable'.[4] However, no such order may be made unless the Tribunal gives the party against whom it is proposed to be made an opportunity to make representations against the making of the order.[5] An order under reg 40(1) may be for a specified sum to be paid by one party in respect of the costs and expenses incurred by the other party, or for the whole or part of the costs (as assessed if not otherwise agreed) incurred by the party in whose favour the order is made in connection with the proceedings.[6] Such an order may also be made in respect of any allowance (other than allowances paid to members of tribunals) paid by the Secretary of State under s 336(3) of the EA 1996 for the purpose of or in connection with the attendance of persons at the Tribunal.[7] If an order is made under reg 40 for costs to be assessed, then the order must allow the county court to make a detailed assessment of fast-track trial costs either on the standard or (if the order so specifies) the indemnity basis in accordance with the Civil Procedure Rules 1998.[8]

Power to strike out

6.166   An appeal may be struck out at any stage of the proceedings (1) for want of prosecution, (2) on the ground that it is not, or is no longer, within the jurisdiction of the Tribunal, or (3) on the ground that the notice of appeal or the appeal is or has become 'scandalous, frivolous or vexatious'.[9] The doctrine of issue estoppel does not apply as such to proceedings before the Tribunal, but this power to strike out the appeal may be applied to a similar effect.[10] However, the striking out by the President of the appeal in *G v (1) London Borough of Barnet and (2) Aldridge*[11] was overturned by Collins J on appeal in part because there was new material on the basis of which a further tribunal *could* have come to a different view from the first tribunal.[12] The argument that *Ladd v Marshall*[13] was applicable in the sense that if the evidence could

---

[1]   Regulation 40(1)(a). *C v London Borough of Lambeth* [1999] ELR 350 indicates that the carrying out of an assessment under s 323 of the EA 1996 shortly before the hearing of an appeal to the Tribunal against a refusal to make such an assessment, will not necessarily justify an order for costs. Indeed, Keene J's approach at 354–355 suggests that he fully approved of the refusal of the Tribunal to order the LEA to pay the appellant's costs.

[2]   Regulation 40(1)(b).

[3]   Regulation 40(1)(c).

[4]   Regulation 40(1)(d).

[5]   Regulation 40(3).

[6]   Regulation 40(4).

[7]   Regulation 40(2)(b). It is clear that the use of the word 'or' in reg 40(2)(a) does not mean that an order cannot be made under both reg 40(2)(a) and reg 40(2)(b).

[8]   Regulation 40(5).

[9]   Regulation 44(1) and (2). According to Simon Brown LJ in *O v London Borough of Harrow* [2002] ELR 195, at 201, para 22, these words apply to 'appeals which plainly should never have been brought'.

[10]   *White v (1) Aldridge and (2) London Borough of Ealing* [1999] ELR 150; [1999] EdCR 612.

[11]   [1999] ELR 161.

[12]   See ibid, at 172E–F.

[13]   [1954] 1 WLR 1489.

have been produced before, it ought not to be allowed to be produced later, was rejected by Collins J.[1] In *R(A) v London Borough of Lambeth*,[2] Ouseley J said this about the application of the power to strike out on the basis that an appeal 'seeks to relitigate the issues already considered':

> 'In my judgment the underlying principle, where an appeal seeks to relitigate the issues already considered, is that it will normally be an abuse of process and the appeal should be struck out. However, that power is not automatically to be used. Its exercise depends on the circumstances of each case and the decision is one that must be made with care, discretion and flexibility. That is because it is important to bear in mind the inquisitorial and informal nature of proceedings before the Special Educational Needs Tribunal and the issue which is at stake; that issue is the educational well-being of a child with special educational needs.'[3]

6.167 The parent must be given notice that the appeal may be struck out on the basis that the appeal is or has become 'scandalous, frivolous or vexatious' if the LEA applies for it to be so struck out or if the President directs that such a notice is to be given.[4] The notice must invite the parent to make representations[5] and must inform the recipient that he may, within a period which is no less than 5 working days and which is specified in the notice, either make written representations or request an opportunity to make oral representations.[6] Only the Tribunal has the power to strike out an appeal (the President having a power merely to order that a statement of a party's case be struck out or amended on the grounds that it is 'scandalous, frivolous or vexatious'),[7] and before doing so it must take into account any representations duly made.[8] The Tribunal need not hold a hearing before striking out the appeal, unless the parent requests the opportunity to make oral representations.[9]

6.168 The President may, 'if he thinks fit, at any stage of the proceedings order that a statement of a party's case should be struck out or amended on the grounds that it is scandalous, frivolous or vexatious'.[10] However, before doing so, the President must give the party against whom he proposes to make the order a notice inviting (written or oral) representations, and must consider any representations duly made.[11]

---

1   See [1999] ELR 161, at 173E
2   [2002] ELR 231, at 239, para 24.
3   See also paras 25–27 inclusive of Ouseley J's judgment, where, among other things, he said that he did not derive any assistance from any of the employment cases cited to him in relation to review.
4   Regulation 44(1). See *Special Educational Needs Tribunal – President's Statement – Applications to Strike Out Appeals (22 September 1998)* [1998] ELR 641 regarding applications by LEAs to strike out appeals.
5   Regulation 44(3).
6   Regulation 44(8), the wording of subpara (b)(ii) of which is a little odd, and depends on reg 44(4) and (5) for its sense.
7   Regulation 44(4)–(6). See further the following paragraph regarding the President's strike-out powers.
8   Regulation 44(4).
9   Regulation 44(5). Where the Tribunal holds a hearing, it may be held at the beginning of the hearing of the substantive appeal: ibid.
10 Regulation 44(6).
11 Regulation 44(7) and (8).

Irregularities

6.169 An irregularity resulting from a failure to comply with any provision of the 2001 Regulations or of any direction of the Tribunal before the Tribunal has reached its decision, 'shall not of itself render the proceedings void'.[1] Where any such irregularity comes to the Tribunal's attention, the Tribunal in any event may (and shall, if the Tribunal considers that any person may have been prejudiced by the irregularity) give directions before reaching its decision to cure or waive the irregularity.[2] There is also a slip rule.[3]

Change of Local Education Authority

6.170 If, after a date when a disputed decision of an LEA was taken in relation to a child with SEN, the child becomes the responsibility within the meaning of s 321(3) of the EA 1996[4] of an LEA other than the one which made the disputed decision, the President may order that the name of the new LEA is substituted for that of the original LEA.[5] Both LEAs and the parent must be given an opportunity to be heard before such an order is made.[6]

Transfer of proceedings

6.171 The President may, where it appears to him that an appeal which is pending before a tribunal could be determined more conveniently in another tribunal, direct that the proceedings are transferred to be determined by that other tribunal.[7] Such a direction may be made either on the President's own initiative or on the application of a party, but must be preceded by the sending of notice to both parties giving them an opportunity to make representations against the giving of the direction.[8]

APPEALING FROM THE SPECIAL EDUCATIONAL NEEDS AND DISABILITY TRIBUNAL

6.172 An appeal from the Tribunal lies to the High Court on a point of law, under s 11 of the Tribunals and Inquiries Act 1992 (as amended by s 181 of the Education Act 1993).[9] In determining whether a point of law is involved, the following statements of principle may be of assistance.[10] In *G v London Borough of Barnet*,[11] Ognall J stated that it is not open to the court 'to reopen the matter and investigate questions

---

[1]   Regulation 49(1).
[2]   Regulation 49(2).
[3]   Regulation 49(3).
[4]   Regarding which, see para **6.12**.
[5]   Regulation 43(1) and (2).
[6]   Regulation 43(3).
[7]   Regulation 41.
[8]   Ibid.
[9]   See now EA 1996, Sch 37, para 118.
[10]   *C v Special Educational Needs Tribunal* [1997] ELR 390 is helpful in regard to the question whether there has been an error of law regarding the classification of needs as educational or non-educational.
[11]   [1998] ELR 480, at 485G.

of fact de novo'. In *B v Gloucestershire County Council*,[1] Sullivan J said: 'Whether there is a sufficiency or a lack of evidence on a particular point is pre-eminently a question of judgment for the tribunal that hears all the evidence, and, in particular, sees the witnesses.' The approach of Sedley LJ in *London Borough of Bromley v Special Educational Needs Tribunal*[2] is also significant: he said that the existence of the Tribunal and the regulations governing its procedure has 'jurisprudential implications', which include that 'Where [the relevant] law is expressed in words which, while not terms of legal art, have a purpose dictated by – and therefore a meaning coloured by – their context, it is clearly Parliament's intention that particular respect should be paid to the tribunal's conclusions'. Although this aspect of that case was not specifically referred to by Goldring J in *S v Special Educational Needs Tribunal*,[3] Goldring J 'very much endorse[d]' the view of McCullough J that:

> 'On a question of educational judgment ... a judge should be suitably cautious before castigating an opinion of the tribunal as irrational.'

It is of note also that in *R v West Sussex County Council, ex parte S*,[4] it was said that a decision of the Tribunal 'should be interpreted (so far as possible) consistently with the powers of the tribunal'.

6.173 Section 11(3) of the Tribunals and Inquiries Act 1992 provides that rules of court are to determine the procedure to be adopted. These are now the Rules of the Supreme Court (RSC), Ord 94, rr 8 and 9, which provide for a straightforward appeal (r 8) or an appeal by way of case stated (r 9). It is open to the Tribunal of its own motion or on a request by a party to proceedings before it, to state a case on any question of law arising in the proceedings under r 9.[5] However, the case stated procedure is not appropriate for appealing against a final decision.[6] Furthermore, an application for judicial review of a decision of the Tribunal is not appropriate where a party could appeal against that decision under (now) Ord 94, r 8.[7]

6.174 In *B v London Borough of Harrow*,[8] it was held by the Court of Appeal that a parent should not be restricted, in an appeal to the High Court, to arguing only points which were raised in the Tribunal.[9] The Court of Appeal's conclusion in that regard may well have been made more easy by the fact that a point of general principle, which it was in the public interest to decide, was at stake in that case.[10] Indeed, in *T v Special Educational Needs Tribunal*,[11] Richards J distinguished *B v London Borough of Harrow*, and decided that a parent could not argue on appeal in the High Court that the Tribunal had failed to comply with Art 2 of Protocol 1 to the European

---

[1]   [1998] ELR 539, at 549F.
[2]   [1999] ELR 260, at 293G–H.
[3]   [2003] ELR 85.
[4]   [1999] ELR 40, at 43E; [1999] EdCR 509, at 513D.
[5]   See also *S (A Minor) v Special Educational Needs Tribunal* [1995] 1 WLR 1627, at 1631F.
[6]   *Altan-Evans v Leicester LEA* [1998] ELR 237, at 241B; *Brophy v Special Educational Needs Tribunal* [1997] ELR 291, at 297F.
[7]   *R v Special Educational Needs Tribunal, ex parte South Glamorgan County Council* [1996] ELR 326, CA.
[8]   [1998] ELR 351.
[9]   Ibid, 356B–C.
[10] See para **6.64** for the principle.
[11] [2002] ELR 704, at para 39(i).

Convention on Human Rights where that point had not been raised in the proceedings before the Tribunal.

6.175 An appeal to the High Court under either r 8 or r 9 of Ord 94 is governed by Part 52 of the Civil Procedure Rules 1998[1] (CPR). The time-limit for appealing under Part 52 is significantly shorter than the normal maximum period within which an application may be made for permission to apply for judicial review: in the case of a statutory appeal governed by Part 52 it is 28 days after the date of the decision against which the appeal is brought,[2] whereas an application for judicial review may normally be made within 3 months from the decision in question (although it must be made promptly in any event[3]). In both cases, the court may grant leave to extend the time-limit. It was held in *Ligouri v City of Salford*[4] that a failure by the Legal Aid Board (now the Legal Services Commission) to determine an application for legal aid (now public funding) might in appropriate circumstances be a good reason for extending time to appeal under Ord 55 (the extension of time would now have to be granted under CPR, r 3.1(2)(a)). According to Sedley J in *Phillips v Derbyshire County Council*,[5] forgetfulness may also be such a reason, although on the facts the application to extend time for appealing was refused, and it would not be wise to rely upon the possibility of such an extension for that reason.[6]

6.176 Only a parent may appeal against a decision of the Tribunal, a child may not.[7] It was stated by Latham J in *S (A Minor) v Special Educational Needs Tribunal*[8] that the Tribunal has no right to appear and be heard on such an appeal, but may be permitted by the court to do so. However, in *S and C v Special Educational Needs Tribunal*,[9] Latham J, having been referred to s 151 of the Supreme Court Act 1981, held that the correct respondent would be the chairman of the Tribunal, and not the tribunal. Yet he indicated that he would expect that, in practical terms, the argument would be

---

[1]   SI 1998/3132.

[2]   See para 17.3 of the Practice Direction to Part 52.

[3]   CPR, r 54.5(1); the continuing validity of this requirement to act promptly – rather than within 3 months – has been called into question by what was said by the House of Lords in paras 53 and 59–60 of *R (Burkett) v Hammersmith London Borough Council* [2002] 1 WLR 1593 and what was said by Sedley LJ in paras 7–8 of the transcript of *R (Boulton) v Leeds School Organisation Committee* [2002] EWCA Civ 884.

[4]   [1997] ELR 455, at 459A.

[5]   [1997] ELR 461, at 466A–B.

[6]   However, it is of interest that in both *Re F* [1999] ELR 251 and *Sage v South Gloucestershire County Council* [1998] ELR 525; [1999] EdCR 420, extensions of time were granted. In the former, *Phillips v Derbyshire County Council* was applied in circumstances which were similar to those in issue in *Phillips*. In *Sage*, the circumstances were somewhat unusual, but not so unusual that they are unlikely to recur. However, the delays in *S v Special Educational Needs Tribunal* [2003] ELR 85 (where the court was referred to *Phillips*), which were caused by a 'catologue of errors' (para 23), were such that permission to appeal out of time was refused, despite Goldring J's 'very considerable sympathy in this case for' both the pupil in question and his parent.

[7]   *S (A Minor) v Special Educational Needs Tribunal* [1996] 1 WLR 382, CA. In *Council of the City of Sunderland v P and C* [1996] ELR 283, at 297–298, the approach of Carnwath J in *South Glamorgan County Council v L and M* [1996] ELR 400, 416A, regarding the joining of a child as a party to an appeal brought by the LEA, was disapproved.

[8]   [1995] 1 WLR 1627, at 1631F–1632A. The Court of Appeal in that case made no reference to this question (see [1996] 1 WLR 382).

[9]   [1997] ELR 242, at 245B.

between those who are parties to the proceedings to the Tribunal, and that the chairman would only seek to appear and be heard where there were particular matters he wished to put before the court.[1] He also said that the chairman cannot be required to submit evidence to the court if he does not wish to do so, whether he is a party or not.[2]

6.177 However, where the chairman does submit evidence, it cannot be unlimited in scope. In *A v Kirklees Metropolitan Council*,[3] Sedley LJ stated that where contentious evidence is admitted, it is not appropriate for the chairman to 'express ... his own view as to what the outcome would have been had the contentious evidence not been omitted'. He went on to say this:

> 'What the chairman's evidence has unfortunately done is make it impossible, should we conclude that there has been a material exclusion of evidence, simply to send the case back to the same tribunal so that it may reopen its findings and review its conclusions in the light of the further evidence. Were this now to be done, there would be a legitimate concern that the chairman, at least, was already committed to a particular course.'

However, although Schiemann LJ agreed with this in the circumstances of that case, he had some reservations.[4] He also stated that the chairman 'quite correctly and sensibly' responded to assertions in the various documents served on him 'about what the tribunal considered and what was before the tribunal'.[5]

6.178 It has been stated that an appeal should not be made where the party simply thinks that the decision in question was arrived at 'on a radically flawed basis of fact': rather, a review should be sought.[6] However, this seems mistaken, given that this might be a good ground for appealing on the basis that the decision was erroneous in law on the basis of the test in *Edwards v Bairstow*.[7] Furthermore, if a third party inadvertently misleads the Tribunal on a material matter of fact, then an appeal is the proper route for the seeking of redress.[8] It has been held that a mere defect in the

---

[1]   [1997] ELR 242, at 245D.

[2]   Ibid, at 245E–F.

[3]   [2001] ELR 657, at para 17.

[4]   Ibid, at para 33.

[5]   Ibid.

[6]   *South Glamorgan County Council v L and M* [1996] ELR 400, at 414D–F. The case contains (at 410B–411E) a helpful analysis of when it will, and when it will not, be possible or necessary to examine in detail the evidence or the chairman's notes of the proceedings, or to admit evidence, when a case is appealed on a point of law to the High Court. In relation to the question whether such a note should be provided, see also *Staffordshire County Council v J and J* [1996] ELR 418, at 427H–429B. See also *Oxfordshire County Council v GB* [2001] EWCA Civ 1358, [2002] ELR 8, at para 9. In *Joyce v Dorset County Council* [1997] ELR 26, at 34B, Latham J said that it would only be in very rare cases that a transcript would be necessary and the court would be unlikely to be impressed by any arguments based upon the transcript which have not been raised by the appeal. In *Fisher v Hughes* [1998] ELR 475; [1999] EdCR 409, Keene J 'concur[red] wholly' with that statement, but nevertheless in the unusual circumstances of that case ordered the provision of the transcript. All of these cases must now be read in the light of paras 5.15–5.18 of the Practice Direction supplementing CPR Part 52. Normally, only para 5.16 will apply. The Practice Direction will require the production of a chairman's notes only when the evidence to which the notes relate is 'relevant to the appeal'.

[7]   [1956] AC 14.

[8]   *R v Special Educational Needs Tribunal, ex parte South Cambridgeshire County Council* [1996] CLY 2493. It is clear from, among other cases, that of *R v Bolton Justices, ex parte Scally* [1991] 1 QB 537, that an error of

reasons would not be sufficient to empower the High Court to remit a matter for rehearing.[1] However, this is contrary to the approach taken in relation to the failure by an employment tribunal to give proper reasons.[2] Nevertheless, the decision of the Tribunal must be read 'as a whole and in the common sense way'.[3] Thus, 'One would normally assume that a factor which was specifically mentioned at an earlier descriptive stage in a decision would not be lost sight of when the tribunal was reaching its conclusions'.[4] In any event, it is implicit in CPR, r 52.11(3)(b) that the court will not allow an appeal if there was only a minor procedural or other irregularity in the proceedings. This is because as a result of that provision the Appeal Court must allow the appeal if the decision of the lower court was 'unjust because of a serious procedural or other irregularity in the proceedings of the lower court'.[5]

6.179 A stay of the decision of the Tribunal may be sought.[6] A stay is by no means automatic, and should not generally be granted unless there is good reason to do so.[7] The mere fact that not granting a stay might pre-empt the decision of the fresh tribunal should the appeal be successful will not be conclusive: it must be weighed in the balance along with any other relevant factors.[8]

SPECIAL SCHOOLS

6.180 A special school is a school which is 'specially organised to make special educational provision for pupils with special educational needs'.[9] There are only three kinds of special school within the meaning of that term as used in the EA 1996. These are community special schools, foundation special schools, and schools which are

---

law could occur as a result of an inadvertent misleading of the Tribunal by a third party. See further *de Smith, Woolf and Jowell, Judicial Review of Administrative Action* (Sweet & Maxwell, 5th edn, 1995), at paras 10.37–10.38.

[1] *South Glamorgan County Council v L and M* [1996] ELR 400, at 413G–H; *Staffordshire County Council v J and J* [1996] ELR 418, at 426C–E.

[2] See most recently the majority decision of the Court of Appeal in *Tran v Greenwich Vietnam Community* [2002] ICR 1101, [2002] IRLR 735.

[3] *B v Gloucestershire County Council* [1998] ELR 539, at 547A–B.

[4] Ibid.

[5] In *Catchpole v Buckinghamshire County Council* [1998] ELR 463, at 473D–E; [1999] EdCR 430, at 442F, Laws J said that he conceived the predecessor of this provision, RSC Ord 55, r 7(7), 'to be in broad terms, conferring at least an analogue of the discretion that arises in the judicial review jurisdiction, where the court has power to refuse relief even though an error of law is made out'. In *B v Gloucestershire County Council* [1998] ELR 539 (reported also under the name of *Beddis v Gloucestershire County Council* [1999] EdCR 446), Sullivan J (at 548E and 456F respectively) agreed with that proposition. However, in *C v Buckinghamshire County Council* [1999] ELR 179, at 186D–E; [1999] 690, 698D, Sedley LJ accepted that Ord 55, r 7(7) 'bears an analogy ... with the discretionary power to refuse leave in judicial review proceedings notwithstanding the existence of an error of law', but said that 'it is no more than an analogy: the subrule has to be interpreted and applied as it stands'.

[6] An example of a case where a stay was sought is *The Mayor and Burgesses of the London Borough of Camden v Hodin and White* [1996] ELR 430. The application could be made either under Part 25 of the CPR or under CPR, r 54.10.

[7] [1996] ELR 430, at 433E.

[8] This is clearly to be inferred from the case of *Hodin and White*: see [1996] ELR 433E–H

[9] EA 1996, s 337(1).

approved by the Secretary of State under s 342(1) of the EA 1996 (as substituted by the SSFA 1998).

Approval of special schools under section 342

6.181 As a result of s 342(4) of the EA 1996, any school in Wales which is approved under s 342(1) of that Act must comply with the Education (Special Schools) Regulations 1994,[1] and any school in England which is so approved must comply with the Education (Non-Maintained Special Schools) (England) Regulations 1999.[2] Any school which was a special school immediately before 1 April 1994 (the date when s 184 of the EA 1993 came into force) is treated (subject to s 342(4)) as approved under s 342.[3] All special schools must also comply with regulations made under s 537A of the 1996 Act.[4] If the Secretary of State is considering whether to withdraw approval for a school under s 342, he must consult the governing body of the school, unless the interests of health, safety or welfare of the children at the school preclude such consultation.[5] Despite this scheme of statutory regulation, a school which is approved under s 342(1) is not susceptible to a judicial review.[6]

Non-maintained special schools – obligation to keep educational records

6.182 A non-maintained special school will (naturally) need to be governed in the manner provided for by its constitution. Such a school is, however, obliged to comply in addition with the duty to keep, and in appropriate circumstances disclose, educational records imposed by the Education (Pupil Information) (England) Regulations 2000[7] and the Education (Pupil Records) (Wales) Regulations 2001.[8]

APPROVAL OF INDEPENDENT SCHOOLS AS SUITABLE FOR THE ADMISSION OF CHILDREN FOR WHOM STATEMENTS ARE MAINTAINED UNDER SECTION 324

6.183 If a child is to be given education at an independent school[9] under a statement maintained under s 324 of the EA 1996, the school must either be approved under s 347 as suitable for the admission of children for whom such statements are

---

[1] SI 1994/652.

[2] SI 1999/2257, as amended by SI 2002/1982.

[3] Section 342(3).

[4] See para **7.182** regarding s 537A of the EA 1996.

[5] See reg 5 of the Education (Non-Maintained Special Schools) (England) Regulations 1999, SI 1999/2257 in relation to England. In relation to Wales, consent is now given by the National Assembly (see SI 1999/672) and the relevant regulation is reg 7 of the Education (Special Schools) Regulations 1994, SI 1994/652, which must, as a result of s 17(2)(a) of the Interpretation Act 1978, be read in the light of s 342 of the EA 1996 as it currently stands.

[6] See *R v Muntham House School, ex parte R* [2000] ELR 287.

[7] SI 2000/297 as amended by SI 2001/1212. See in particular regs 4 and 5 of SI 2000/297.

[8] SI 2001/832. See in particular reg 5 of those regulations.

[9] For the definition of an independent school, see para **13.1**.

maintained,[1] or the Secretary of State must consent to the child being educated there.[2]

RELEVANT FURTHER EDUCATION FUNCTIONS OF LOCAL EDUCATION AUTHORITIES

6.184   An LEA's powers in relation to further education under ss 15A and 15B of the EA 1996 are noted elsewhere.[3] In exercising those powers, an LEA 'shall in particular have regard to the needs of persons with learning difficulties (within the meaning of section 13(5) and (6) of the Learning and Skills Act 2000)'.[4] Furthermore, the LEA must conscientiously take into account non-statutory guidance in the form of the relevant circular issued by the Department for Education.[5] However, the duty and power contained in the predecessor of s 15A (s 15 of the EA 1996, which was repealed by the LSA 2000) were held to be only in the nature of 'target' functions,[6] and there is no good reason to think that it is otherwise with the powers in ss 15A and 15B.

RELEVANT FUNCTIONS OF THE LEARNING AND SKILLS COUNCIL AND THE NATIONAL COUNCIL FOR EDUCATION AND TRAINING FOR WALES

6.185   The LSC and the CETW have responsibility for special education in the further education sector as a result of a number of provisions in the LSA 2000. These include ss 2, 3, 13, 31, 32 and 41. Sections 13 and 41 require the LSC and the CETW respectively to 'have regard – (a) to the needs of persons with learning difficulties, and (b) in particular, to any report of an assessment conducted under section 140' when exercising their functions under ss 2, 3, 31 and 32 and several related provisions.

---

[1]   Such a school must comply with the requirements contained in the Education (Special Educational Needs) (Approval of Independent Schools) Regulations 1994, SI 1994/651 (as amended by SI 1998/417, SI 2001/3710, and SI 2002/2072), which are now, as a result of s 17(2)(b) of the Interpretation Act 1978, treated as made under s 347(2). The Secretary of State must consult the proprietor of the school before withdrawing his approval under such regulations unless the interests of health, safety or welfare of the children at the school preclude such consultation: reg 5 and *R v Secretary of State for Education and Employment, ex parte McCarthy* (1996) *The Times*, July 24.

[2]   Section 347(5).

[3]   See paras **2.81–2.82**, **16.53** and **16.54**.

[4]   Section 15A(3).

[5]   *R v Islington London Borough Council, ex parte Rixon* [1997] ELR 66. The relevant circular at the time was, and remains, number 1/93. See also para **6.196** regarding further guidance, concerning relevant social services functions, which an LEA may have to take into account in relation to young persons with special educational needs. See paras **2.34–2.36** for the impact on a public body of a duty to 'have regard' to something.

[6]   *R v Further Education Funding Council, ex parte Parkinson* [1997] ELR 204, at 220D–G.

SECTION 140 OF THE LEARNING AND SKILLS ACT 2000

6.186 Section 140 of the LSA 2000 requires the Secretary of State (or, in Wales, the National Assembly[1]) in certain circumstances to arrange for an assessment of the educational and training needs and the provision required to meet those needs of a person for whom an LEA maintains a statement of SEN under s 324 of the EA 1996. The circumstances are that the Secretary of State believes that the person will leave school at the end of his last year of compulsory schooling to receive post-16 education or training (within the meaning of Part I of the LSA 2000) or higher education (within the meaning of the ERA 1988). The assessment must result in a written report of the relevant needs and provision.[2]

6.187 Section 140 empowers the Secretary of State at any time to:

'arrange for an assessment to be conducted of a person -

(a)   who is in his last year of compulsory schooling or who is over compulsory school age but has not attained the age of 25,

(b)   who appears to the Secretary of State to have a learning difficulty (within the meaning of section 13), and

(c)   who is receiving, or in the Secretary of State's opinion is likely to receive, post-16 education or training (within the meaning of Part I of this Act) or higher education (within the meaning of the Education Reform Act 1988).'

6.188 Another statutory provision needs to be borne in mind in this context. Paragraph 11(5) of Sch 27 to the EA 1996 (which is referred to in para **6.104** and was inserted by s 6 of the SENDA 2001) provides:

'A local education authority may not, under this paragraph, cease to maintain a statement if -

(a)   the parent of the child has appealed under this paragraph against the authority's determination to cease to maintain the statement, and

(b)   the appeal has not been determined by the Tribunal or withdrawn.'

Relationship between special education functions of the Learning and Skills Council (or the National Council for Education and Training for Wales) and of a Local Education Authority

6.189 Among other things, the statutory provisions described in the paragraphs above appear to be designed to avoid difficulties of the kind which occurred in *R v Dorset County Council and Further Education Funding Council, ex parte Goddard*,[3] *R v Oxfordshire County Council, ex parte B*[4] and *Wakefield Metropolitan District Council v E*[5] in

---

[1]   See LSA 2000, ss 140(6) and 150. References below to the Secretary of State's functions under s 140 are to be read as applying also to the National Assembly.

[2]   See s 140(4).

[3]   [1995] ELR 109.

[4]   [1997] ELR 90.

[5]   [2002] ELR 203.

relation to young persons for whom statements of SEN were maintained under what is now s 324 of the EA 1996 but whose statements named a school for pupils no older than 16 where the young persons were approaching the end of compulsory school age. These difficulties continue to arise from the fact that an LEA is obliged to maintain a statement of SEN under s 324 only while the person to whom the statement relates is at a school and because as a result of s 321 of the EA 1996, an LEA is responsible only for children who are either at school or not above compulsory school age. Although the statutory provisions introduced by the LSA 2000 and the SENDA 2001 do appear to avoid some of the difficulties which occurred in *ex parte Goddard* and *ex parte B*, they may not do so completely. In any event, those cases continue to be relevant for at least some purposes. Their continuing effects (taking into account subsequent developments) can be stated as follows.

6.190 If a pupil with SEN continues after the age of 16 to need to be educated at a school (including a special school), then the duty to fund that education is primarily that of the LEA, and not that of the LSC or the CETW.[1] In that situation, only if the LEA lawfully decides to cease to maintain a pupil's statement of SEN will it be lawful for the LEA not to pay for the pupil's schooling after the age of 16. An LEA cannot escape its liability to a pupil with SEN merely by ceasing to send him to a school and arguing that as a result he is no longer its responsibility.[2] As Auld J put it:

> 'In summary, a local education authority cannot divest itself of responsibility for a pupil's schooling when he reaches the age of 16 by wrongfully failing to specify it, either by silence or express exclusion, in his statement and by refusing to provide it when he reaches 16 so that he cannot then satisfy the condition of the authority's continuing responsibility under s 4(2)(a) of the 1981 Act, namely by being a registered pupil at a school appropriate to his needs.'[3]

6.191 However, according to the Court of Appeal in *R v Oxfordshire County Council, ex parte B*, where an LEA has a genuine policy of educating its special needs children in school to the age of 16 and after that at a college of further education, the LEA could lawfully cease to maintain a relevant statement of SEN made (now) under s 324 of the EA 1996.[4]

6.192 By analogy with the decision of Jowitt J in *R v Further Education Funding Council, ex parte Parkinson*,[5] the best view is probably that any duty to make educational provision for a person who is over compulsory school age (and by implication for whom no statement of SEN is maintained) which the LSC or the CETW believes, in the light of a report made under s 140 of the LSA 2000, to be required, rests upon the LSC or the CETW and not the LEA. Similarly, the best view is probably that the

---

[1]   *Ex parte Goddard*, at 132C–E.
[2]   Ibid, at 129B–C.
[3]   *Ex parte Goddard*, at 129G. This statement is unaffected by the replacement by the relevant provisions of the EA 1993 (and now the EA 1996) of those in the EA 1981 to which Auld J was referring.
[4]   *Ex parte B*, at 96–97. See paras **6.104–6.105** regarding ceasing to maintain a statement. For cogent criticism of the case, see S Hocking, 'Further education, learning difficulties and the law' (1997) 9 *Education and the Law* 13.
[5]   [1997] ELR 204, at 220E–F.

discretionary power of an LEA in what is now s 15B(1) of the EA 1996 is not a power to make provision which is tailor-made for the needs peculiar to a specific case.[1]

RELEVANT NON-EDUCATION FUNCTIONS OF A LOCAL AUTHORITY

6.193 An LEA has a number of further (non-education) functions in relation to young persons with SEN.[2] These functions arise under the Chronically Sick and Disabled Persons Act 1970, the Employment and Training Act 1973 (as amended by the Trade Union Reform and Employment Rights Act 1993), the Disabled Persons (Services, Consultation and Representation) Act 1986, the Children Act 1989, the National Health Service and Community Care Act 1990 and the Children (Leaving Care) Act 2001.

6.194 The duty in s 3 of the Disabled Persons (Services, Consultation and Representation) Act 1986 regarding assessments,[3] was considered in R *v Mayor and Burgesses of the London Borough of Merton, ex parte Wiggins*.[4] It was there held that s 3 involves:

> 'not only an assessment, but an involvement of the person who may have need of services or his parents in the process at a stage at which they are to be consulted and that all leading to what can for convenience be described as an "action plan".'[5]

6.195 In R *v Further Education Funding Council, ex parte Parkinson*,[6] Jowitt J decided that s 2(1)(c) of the Chronically Sick and Disabled Persons Act 1970 (which refers to the provision of 'lectures, games, outings or other recreational facilities outside [a person's] home or assistance to that person in taking advantage of educational facilities available to him') could not embrace the funding of a purely educational facility.[7] He decided the same in relation to s 29(4)(b) of the National Assistance Act 1948 (which refers to giving certain disabled persons 'instruction in their own homes or elsewhere in methods of overcoming the effects of their disabilities').[8]

FURTHER GUIDANCE TO BE TAKEN INTO ACCOUNT

6.196 In R *v Islington London Borough Council, ex parte Rixon*,[9] it was held by Sedley J that an LEA must take into account ministerial guidance in relation to the application

---

[1]   *Ex parte Parkinson*, at 220F. See para **16.53** regarding s 15B(1).
[2]   Paragraphs 9:58–9:60 and 9:68 of the SEN Code refer to most of these other functions. See also chapter 10 of the SEN Code.
[3]   In that case the assessment, carried out under s 47 of the National Health Service and Community Care Act 1990, concerned community care services.
[4]   [1996] ELR 332, CA.
[5]   Ibid, at 337C; see also at 338A–B.
[6]   [1997] ELR 204.
[7]   Ibid, at 218E.
[8]   Ibid, at 218G.
[9]   [1997] ELR 66, as to which see further, para **2.34**.

of s 2(1) of the Chronically Sick and Disabled Persons Act 1970.[1] In addition, Sedley J held that an LEA must also take into account practice guidance issued by the Department of Health in relation to the same provision.[2]

---

[1]   At the time, the guidance was contained in *Caring for People: Community Care in the Next Decade and Beyond: Policy Guidance* (HMSO 1990).

[2]   At the time it was *Care Management and Assessment* (HMSO, 5th impression, 1994).

Chapter 7

THE ESTABLISHMENT, FUNDING AND CONDUCT OF SCHOOLS MAINTAINED BY LOCAL EDUCATION AUTHORITIES

INTRODUCTION

7.1   This chapter concerns the establishment, alteration and funding of maintained schools. The main differences in practical terms between the various types of maintained school currently in existence consist of the differing responsibilities of the governing bodies of the various kinds of school for the provision and maintenance of property. These differences are most evident in relation to the establishment and alteration of those schools, and those responsibilities are accordingly described in that context. However, before these matters can be described, it is necessary to consider what is meant by the word 'school'.

DEFINITION OF 'SCHOOL'

7.2   The word 'school' in this context is defined in s 4 of the EA 1996. According to s 4(1), a school is an educational institution which is outside the further education sector and the higher education sector and which provides (a) primary education, (b) secondary education, or (c) both primary and secondary education, whether or not it also provides part-time education suitable to the requirements of junior pupils or further education. Clearly, this definition itself relies on a number of other definitions.[1] In any event, s 4(2) provides that nothing in s 4(1) is to be taken to preclude the making of arrangements under s 19(1) of the EA 1996, under which part-time education is provided at a school, and that for the purposes of the EA 1996, an educational institution that would fall within s 4(1) but for the fact that it provides part-time rather than full-time education is nevertheless to be treated as a school if that part-time education is provided under arrangements made under s 19(1).

7.3   Primary education is defined in s 2(1) of the 1996 Act. As amended by s 156 of the EA 2002, that subsection provides that primary education means (a) full-time or part-time education suitable to the requirements of children who have attained the age of 2 but are under compulsory school age, (b) full-time education suitable to the requirements of junior pupils of compulsory school age who have not attained the age of 10 years and 6 months, and (c) full-time education suitable to the requirements of junior pupils who have attained the age of 10 years and 6 months and whom it is expedient to educate together with junior pupils who have not attained that age but

---

[1]   See paras **16.2** and **17.14** respectively regarding institutions within the further education sector and the higher education sector. Otherwise, see the following passages below.

are above compulsory school age. Section 156 is in force only in England, so in Wales the former definition in s 2(1) applies. That differs from the new s 2(1) in that it does not include full-time or part-time education suitable to the requirements of children who have attained the age of 2 but are under compulsory school age. The word 'pupil' is defined by s 3 of the EA 1996 to mean a person who is provided with education at a school other than a person who is aged 19 or over for whom further education is being provided or a person who is over compulsory school age for whom part-time education is being provided.[1]

7.4   Secondary education is neither further education nor higher education.[2] Secondary education is defined by ss 2(2)(a) and 3 of the EA 1996 to include full-time education suitable to the requirements of pupils of compulsory school age who are aged 12 or over but less than 19 ('senior pupils') or of pupils who are below the age of 12 but who are aged at least 10 years and 6 months and whom it is expedient to educate together with senior pupils of compulsory school age.[3] Secondary education is also full-time education suitable to the requirements of persons who are over compulsory school age but under the age of 19, where it is provided at a school at which education of the sort referred to in the previous sentence is provided.[4] Education which is provided at an institution which is maintained by an LEA or at an Academy[5] and which is principally concerned with the provision of full-time education suitable to the requirements of persons of compulsory school age but under the age of 19, is also secondary education.[6] Where a person is in full-time education which is provided (a) partly at a school, and (b) partly at another institution under arrangements made by the school, that is also secondary education as long as the education provided at the school would be secondary education if it were provided full time at the school.[7] In addition, where a person has begun a particular course of secondary education before attaining the age of 18 and continues to attend that course, the education remains secondary education despite his reaching the age of 19.[8]

7.5   Further education means for the purposes of the EA 1996 full-time and part-time education suitable to the requirements of persons who are over compulsory school age, including vocational, social, physical and recreational training, and organised leisure-time occupation[9] provided in connection with the provision of such

---

[1]   EA 2002, Sch 21, para 34 has been brought into force only in England. Thus the new EA 1996, s 3(1A), which provides that 'A person is not for the purposes of this Act to be treated as a pupil at a school merely because any education is provided for him at the school in the exercise of the powers conferred by section 27 of the Education Act 2002', does not yet apply in Wales.

[2]   EA 1996, s 2(3) and (7).

[3]   For the definition of 'compulsory school age', see s 8 of the EA 1996, as to which, see paras **2.40** and **2.41**.

[4]   EA 1996, s 2(2)(b).

[5]   Within the meaning of EA 1996, s 482, regarding which see paras **3.68** et seq.

[6]   EA 1996, s 2(2A).

[7]   Ibid, s 2(2B).

[8]   Ibid, s 2(2)(b), (2A), (2B) and (5).

[9]   'Organised leisure-time occupation' means 'leisure-time occupation, in such organised cultural training and recreative activities as are suited to their requirements, for any persons over compulsory school age who are able and willing to profit by facilities provided for that purpose': EA 1996, s 2(6).

education.[1] Thus, unless it is secondary education as defined in para **7.4**, full-time education which is suitable to the requirements of persons who are over compulsory school age but below the age of 19 is further education and not secondary education for the purposes of the EA 1996.[2]

7.6 Section 20(6) of the SSFA 1998 provides that for the purposes of s 20, 'school' means 'a primary, secondary or special school including a nursery school which is a special school, but excluding – (a) a nursery school which is not a special school, and (b) a pupil referral unit'. Otherwise, the word 'school' means for the purposes of the SSFA 1998 the same as it means for the purposes of the EA 1996.[3]

THE VARIOUS TYPES OF MAINTAINED SCHOOL

7.7 There are now six kinds of maintained school (other than nursery schools), which now means schools maintained by LEAs.[4] These are (1) community schools, (2) voluntary controlled schools, (3) voluntary aided schools, (4) foundation schools, (5) community special schools, and (6) foundation special schools.[5]

Community schools

7.8 A community school is the modern equivalent of what used (before the SSFA 1998 was enacted) to be called county schools, and which were (before the EA 1994 was enacted) known as provided schools. The LEA's duty to maintain the school includes: '(a) the duty of defraying all the expenses of maintaining it, and (b) the duty of making premises available to be used for the purposes of the school'.[6] The LEA is the contractual employer of the staff in a community school.[7] The governing body of a community school is not a charity.[8]

Foundation schools

7.9 Foundation schools were introduced by the SSFA 1998. An LEA's duty to maintain a foundation school is the same as for a voluntary controlled school. This includes 'the duty of defraying all the expenses of maintaining it' (including the payment of rates[9]),[10] and the duty in certain circumstances of providing a site for it.[11]

---

[1] EA 1996, s 2(3) and (6A). This is subject to s 2(5), concerning the effect of which see the final sentence of para **7.4**.

[2] See EA 1996, s 2(4).

[3] See SSFA 1998, s 142(8) and (9).

[4] See ibid, s 20(1).

[5] According to ibid, s 20(7): 'In this Act – ... "maintained school" means (unless the context otherwise requires) a community, foundation or voluntary school or a community or foundation special school'.

[6] Ibid, s 22(3).

[7] See s 53 of, and Sch 16 to, the SSFA 1998 and s 35(2) of the EA 2002 (which was is in force only in England).

[8] SSFA 1998, s 23(1). See further, para **7.208** concerning the impact which this provision may have.

[9] SSFA 1998, s 22(6).

[10] Ibid, s 22(4)(a).

[11] Ibid, s 22(4)(b).

Those circumstances are referred to below.[1] However, the position relating to the staff of a foundation school is the same as that relating to voluntary aided schools.[2] This is a major difference between a foundation school and a community or community special school. The governing body of a foundation school is an exempt charity for the purposes of the Charities Act 1993.[3]

7.10   Section 21(1) of the SSFA 1998 provides that there may be three kinds of foundation school:

> '(a)   those having a foundation established otherwise than under this Act;
> (b)   those belonging to a group of schools for which a foundation body acts under this section; and
> (c)   those not falling within either of paragraphs (a) and (b) but having been either of the following immediately before the appointed day,[4] namely –
>> (i)   a voluntary school, or
>> (ii)   a grant-maintained school that was a voluntary school immediately before becoming grant-maintained,
>> within the meaning of the Education Act 1996.'

7.11   Somewhat confusingly, there may be a foundation not only for a foundation school but also for a voluntary school. Accordingly, the nature of a 'foundation' for the purposes of both kinds of school is considered below, after reference has been made to all the other kinds of maintained school.

Voluntary controlled schools

7.12   Voluntary controlled schools were introduced by the SSFA 1998, and replaced what were previously the kind of voluntary schools which were called controlled schools. The duty of the LEA to maintain a voluntary controlled school is the same as its duty to maintain a foundation school: it 'includes ... the duty of defraying all the expenses of maintaining it [including the payment of rates[5]],[6] and the duty of providing new premises for the school in certain circumstances.[7] The position relating to the staff of voluntary controlled schools is the same as that relating to community schools.[8] The governing body of a voluntary controlled school is an exempt charity for the purposes of the Charities Act 1993.[9]

7.13   Section 21(2) of the SSFA 1998 provides that there may be three kinds of voluntary controlled (or, indeed, voluntary aided) schools:

---

[1]   Paragraph **7.114**, read with paras **7.8** and **7.112**.
[2]   See (1) SSFA 1998, s 55, Sch 10, para 3(6), and (2) EA 2002, s 36(2). See further, paras **15.74** and **15.75**.
[3]   SSFA 1998, s 23(1).
[4]   The 'appointed day' was 1 September 1999: see SSFA 1998, s 20(7) and the School Standards and Framework Act 1998 (Appointed Day) Order 1998, SI 1998/2093.
[5]   SSFA 1998, s 22(6).
[6]   Ibid, s 22(4)(a).
[7]   Ibid, s 22(4)(b). See paras **7.108** and **7.112**.
[8]   See SSFA 1998, s 54 and EA 2002, s 35(2).
[9]   SSFA 1998, s 23(1).

'(a)   those having a foundation established otherwise than under this Act;[1]

(b)   those belonging to a group of schools for which a foundation body[2] acts under this section; and

(c)   those not falling within either of paragraphs (a) and (b) but having been either of the following immediately before the appointed day,[3] namely –

    (i)   a voluntary school, or

    (ii)   a grant-maintained school that was a voluntary school immediately before becoming grant-maintained,

within the meaning of the Education Act 1996.'

Voluntary aided schools

7.14   Voluntary aided schools were introduced by the SSFA 1998, and replaced what were previously the kind of voluntary schools which were called aided schools. The duty of the LEA to maintain the school includes: '(a) the duty of defraying all the expenses of maintaining it,[4] except any expenses that by virtue of paragraph 3 of Schedule 3 are payable by the governing body, and (b) the duty, under paragraph 4 of Schedule 3 or paragraph 14 of Schedule 6, of providing new premises for the school under and in accordance with that paragraph'.[5] The governing body of a voluntary aided school are the employers of the school's staff.[6] As stated above, there are three kinds of voluntary aided school, of the sorts referred to in s 21(2) of the SSFA 1998.[7] The governing body of a voluntary aided school is an exempt charity for the purposes of the Charities Act 1993.[8]

Maintained special schools: community special schools and foundation special schools

7.15   There are two kinds of maintained special school (1) community special schools, which are very much like what were, before the SSFA 1998 came into force, called maintained special schools, and (2) foundation special schools, the provisions governing which are very much like those governing foundation schools. For example, the provisions relating to the staff of community and foundation special schools are those which apply also to community and foundation schools respectively.[9]

7.16   The duty of an LEA to maintain a community special school is the same as that relating to a community school.[10] The duty of an LEA to maintain a foundation

---

1   The nature of a 'foundation' for this purpose is considered below, in paras **7.17–7.20**.

2   See paras **7.17–7.20** in relation to a foundation body.

3   The 'appointed day' was 1 September 1999: see SSFA 1998, s 20(7) and the School Standards and Framework Act 1998 (Appointed Day) Order 1998, SI 1998/2093.

4   Including the payment of rates: SSFA 1998, s 22(6).

5   SSFA 1998, s 22(5). See further below regarding the expenses for which the governing body is responsible.

6   Ibid, s 55 and Sch 10, para 3(6); EA 2002, s 36(2).

7   See para **7.13**, where s 21(2) is set out.

8   SSFA 1998, s 23(1).

9   See (1) SSFA 1998, ss 54 and 55, and (2) EA 2002, ss 35 and 36 respectively.

10   See SSFA 1998, s 22(3).

special school is in substance the same as its duty in relation to a foundation or voluntary controlled school.[1]

FOUNDATIONS

7.17   The provisions in the SSFA 1998 relating to foundations for the purposes of that Act, are complex. A foundation for those purposes 'in relation to a foundation or voluntary school, means – (i) any body of persons (whether incorporated or not but excluding the governing body) which holds land on trust for the purposes of the school, or (ii) a foundation body'.[2] Further, 'a school "has" a foundation if – (i) such a body of persons exists for holding land on trust for the purposes of the school, or (ii) the school belongs to a group of schools for which a foundation body acts under this section'.[3] A 'foundation body' for the purposes of the SSFA 1998 'means a body corporate established under this section to perform, in relation to three or more schools each of which is either a foundation or a voluntary school, the following functions, namely – (i) to hold property of those schools for the purposes of the schools, and (ii) to appoint foundation governors for those schools'.[4] Furthermore, 'the group' means, in relation to a foundation body, 'the group of three or more schools for which the body performs those functions'.[5]

7.18   The establishment, membership, functions, and winding up of a foundation body are the subject of regulations made by the Secretary of State[6] under s 21(5) of the SSFA 1998. So are 'the steps to be taken in connection with schools joining or leaving the group' for which the foundation body performs functions. Those regulations may make provision (a) with respect to the transfer of property, rights and liabilities to and from a foundation body when schools join or leave the group but do not change category in accordance with Sch 8 to the SSFA 1998,[7] (b) authorising a foundation body to appoint foundation governors to every school in the group, (c) prescribing a model instrument of government for adoption by a foundation body subject to variations approved by the Secretary of State, (d) for conferring functions, on a person or body specified in the regulations, with respect to the resolution of disputes between (i) schools in the group or (ii) one or more schools in the group and a foundation body, (e) requiring a governing body which is proposing that its school should leave the group, to publish proposals under para 2 of Sch 8 to the SSFA 1998[8] as if they were proposing to make a prescribed alteration to the school, (f) for the dissolution of a foundation body by order of the Secretary of State, and (g) for

---

[1]   See ibid, ss 22(4) and (6).
[2]   SSFA 1998, s 21(3)(a).
[3]   Ibid, s 21(3)(b).
[4]   Ibid, s 21(4)(a).
[5]   Ibid, s 21(4)(b).
[6]   In this chapter, as elsewhere in this book, references to the Secretary of State are, unless otherwise stated, to be read as references also to the National Assembly for Wales. On occasion, because of the express differences in the legislation relating to England and Wales as a result of amendments made (mostly) by or under the EA 2002, for the sake of clarity express reference is made to the National Assembly as well as to the Secretary of State.
[7]   See para **7.45** in regard to a change of category under Sch 8.
[8]   As to which, see para **7.45**.

enabling the Secretary of State, in the case of any land held by a foundation body immediately before its dissolution which by virtue of the SSFA 1998 could not be disposed of without his consent, to determine how that land is to be dealt with on its dissolution.[1] Regulations made under s 21(5) may also provide for the revision or replacement of instruments of government of schools joining or leaving the group and the reconstitution of their governing bodies.[2] Such regulations may also confer functions on school organisation committees (SOCs) and adjudicators, including functions which might otherwise be conferred on the Secretary of State.[3] The current regulations are the Education (Foundation Body) (England) Regulations 2000,[4] and the Education (Foundation Body) Wales Regulations 2001.[5]

7.19　The Secretary of State may by order modify the instrument of government adopted by a foundation body, after consulting that body.[6]

7.20　A foundation body is an exempt charity for the purposes of the Charities Act 1993,[7] as is 'any institution which – (a) is administered by or on behalf of [a foundation body established under s 21 of the SSFA], and (b) is established for the general purposes of, or for any special purpose of or in connection with, that ... body', but only so far as it is a charity.[8] Any foundation established otherwise than under the SSFA 1998 which has no property other than the premises (including a teacher's dwelling-house) of any foundation, voluntary or foundation special school or schools is a charity which (subject to s 3(5B) of the Charities Act 1993[9]) is not required to be registered for the purposes of that Act.[10] It is nevertheless subject to the jurisdiction of the Charity Commissioners under that Act, since it is not an exempt charity.[11]

ESTABLISHMENT, ALTERATION, CHANGE OF SITE AND DISCONTINUANCE OF MAINTAINED SCHOOLS

Introduction and overview

7.21　After the enactment of the SSFA 1998, there was a self-contained set of statutory provisions governing the establishment, alteration and discontinuance of maintained schools. There were also ss 482 and 483 of the EA 1996 concerning city

---

[1]　SSFA 1998, s 21(6). Land which could not be disposed of without the consent of the Secretary of State includes that to which para 2 of Sch 22 to the SSFA 1998 applies. (See para **7.42** regarding Sch 22.) It also includes playing fields to which s 77 of the SSFA 1998 applies (as to which, see para **8.58**).

[2]　Ibid, s 21(6)(b); see also s 21(7).

[3]　Ibid, s 21(6)(i).

[4]　SI 2000/2872.

[5]　SI 2001/2709,

[6]　SSFA 1998, s 21(8).

[7]　Ibid, s 23(1)(b).

[8]　Ibid, s 21(10).

[9]　As inserted into the Charities Act 1993 by SSFA 1998, Sch 30, para 48. Section 3(5B) permits the Charity Commissioners by order, or regulations made by the Secretary of State, to provide that s 23(3) is not to apply to a particular foundation or to foundations of a description specified in the order or regulations.

[10]　SSFA 1998, s 23(3).

[11]　Ibid.

technology colleges and city colleges for the technology of the arts, but they were clearly part of a separate regime. In addition, new statutory provisions were introduced by the LSA 2000 and the EA 2002. The latter sets of provisions add to, rather than amend, those in the SSFA 1998.

7.22   The establishment, alteration or discontinuance of a community, foundation or voluntary school are primarily governed by ss 28–30 of, and Sch 6 to, the SSFA 1998. Section 28 concerns the establishment or alteration of a community, foundation or voluntary school (other than a special school). Section 29 concerns the discontinuance of such a school, or of a maintained nursery school. The governing body of a voluntary school or a foundation school may discontinue the school on the giving of 2 years' notice of their intention to do so in accordance with s 30. Schedule 6 is a slightly complicated schedule, which applies to the procedures required by ss 28 and 29 (but not s 30).

7.23   Sections 31 and 32 of the SSFA 1998 govern the establishment, alteration and discontinuance of community and foundation special schools. Section 31 (together with Sch 6) governs the establishment, alteration and discontinuance of a community or foundation special school, and s 32 confers a power on the Secretary of State to direct the discontinuance of such a school on health, safety or welfare grounds. These are where the Secretary of State:

> 'considers it expedient to do so in the interests of the health, safety or welfare of pupils at a community or foundation special school.'[1]

7.24   Under s 34 of, and Sch 7 to, the SSFA 1998, the Secretary of State may direct an LEA to exercise its powers to make proposals for the establishment or discontinuance of schools, and may direct the governing body of a foundation, voluntary or foundation special school to exercise their powers to make proposals for the alteration of their school. In England, the Secretary of State has an additional power, conferred by s 71 of the EA 2002, which supplements the power in s 34 of the SSFA 1998.

7.25   There are three other sets of provisions under which changes may be made to maintained schools. The first is s 113 of, and Sch 7 to, the LSA 2000, the second is s 113A of, and Sch 7A to, the LSA 2000, as inserted by s 72 of the EA 2002, and the third is s 70 of, and Sch 8 to, the EA 2002. Section 70 of, and Sch 8 to, the EA 2002 concern only (1) maintained schools which are not special schools, and (2) Academies. The other two sets of provisions concern (only) community, foundation and voluntary schools and community and foundation special schools. All three of these sets of provisions supplement ss 28–33 and Sch 6. Indeed, s 34 of, and Sch 7 to, the SSFA 1998 can also be said to supplement ss 28–33 of, and Sch 6 to, that Act. Accordingly, the statutory scheme in ss 28–33 and Sch 6 is described below first.

---

1   See para **7.34** for the procedure which the Secretary of State must follow before serving a notice under s 32.

Procedure for the establishment or alteration of a community, foundation or voluntary school

7.26 Where an LEA proposes (a) to establish a new community or foundation school, (b) to make any prescribed alteration to a community school,[1] or (c) to make any prescribed alteration to a foundation school consisting of an enlargement of the premises of the school,[2] then it must publish its proposals under s 28.[3] An alteration for this purpose includes the transfer of the school to a new site, but does not include any change in the religious character of the school, or any change as a result of which the school will acquire or lose a religious character.[4] If the transfer is to a site in a different LEA's area or the proposals relate to a school which is not, or it is proposed will not be, situated in the maintaining LEA's area, then s 28(6) and Sch 6 have effect subject to modifications.[5]

7.27 Where any persons (referred to in Part II of the SSFA 1998 as 'promoters') propose to establish a new foundation or voluntary school, or the governing body of a foundation or voluntary school propose to make any prescribed alteration to the school, those persons or (as the case may be) the governing body must publish proposals under s 28.[6] Such proposals must contain the information and be published in the manner prescribed by regulations made under s 28(3).[7] Middle schools may be proposed.[8] Consultation is required before the publication of the

---

[1]   The alterations prescribed for this purpose are set out in Sch 2 to the Education (School Organisation Proposals) (Wales) Regulations 1999, SI 1999/1671 (as amended by SI 2004/908), and Sch 1 to the Education (School Organisation Proposals) (England) Regulations 1999, SI 1999/2213 (as amended, including by SI 2003/1229). They include alterations to admission arrangements of certain sorts, but it should be noted that the Education (Proposals for Grammar Schools to cease to have Selective Admission Arrangements) Regulations 1999, SI 1999/2103 make the governing body of a community school responsible for the publication of such proposals. The latter regulations apply only in England.

[2]   To which SI 1999/1671 and SI 1999/2213 also apply.

[3]   SSFA 1998, s 28(1).

[4]   Ibid, s 28(11). A foundation or voluntary school has a religious character for the purposes of Part II of the SSFA 1998 if it is designated as a school having such a character by an order made by the Secretary of State: SSFA 1998, s 69(3). The orders so made up to the time of writing included the Designation of Schools Having a Religious Character (Wales) Order 1999, SI 1999/1814 (as amended by SI 2004/1734), the Designation of Schools Having a Religious Character (England) Order 1999, SI 1999/2432, the Designation of Schools Having a Religious Character (England) Order 2000, SI 2000/3080, the Designation of Schools Having a Religious Character (England) Order 2003, SI 2003/800, SI 2003/2552, SI 2003/2749, SI 2004/1513 (all of which have similar names), SI 2004/1734 (relating to Wales) and several orders relating to individual schools: SI 2003/3259 and SI 2003/3262.

[5]   See SSFA 1998, s 28(9) and reg 15(2) and Part 1 of, Sch 5 to, the Education (School Organisation Proposals) (England) Regulations 1999, SI 1999/2213, as amended by SI 2003/1229.

[6]   SSFA 1998, s 28(2). The alterations are prescribed by reg 3 of, and Sch 2 to, SI 1999/1671 and reg 3 of, and Sch 1 to, SI 1999/2213. If the school is a Church of England school, then the governing body and the trustees of any church educational endowment held wholly or partly for or in connection with the school must obtain the advice of the relevant Diocesan Board of Education and have regard to that advice before publishing proposals under s 28(2)(b): Diocesan Boards of Education Measure 1991 (No 2), s 3(1), as amended by SSFA 1998, Sch 30, paras 30 and 32.

[7]   In relation to Wales, see the Education (School Organisation Proposals) (Wales) Regulations 1999, SI 1999/1671, reg 4 and Sch 3 for the information and reg 5 for the manner of publication. In relation to England, see the Education (School Organisation Proposals) (England) Regulations 1999, SI 1999/2213 (as amended, including by SI 2003/1229), reg 4 and Sch 2 for the information and reg 5 for the manner of publication.

[8]   See SSFA 1998, s 28(4).

proposals.[1] The consultation period need only be adequate; in one case, *R v Leeds City Council, ex parte N*,[2] the Court of Appeal was of the view that 3 weeks was sufficient in the circumstances.

7.28   Where the proposals relate to a school or proposed school in England, the relevant body or promoters (that is, the LEA, the governing body or the promoters, as the case may be[3]) must send a copy of the published proposals to the SOC for the area of the LEA which maintains, or it is proposed should maintain, the school, together with information prescribed by regulations.[4] The SOC must within 2 weeks of their receipt send a copy of any such proposals relating to mainstream schools to the Secretary of State and the LSC if such proposals relate to sixth-form education.[5] In Wales, the proposals (and any information which is prescribed by regulations) must be sent to the National Assembly for Wales.[6] The procedure to be followed in relation to schools in both England and Wales is set out in Sch 6 to the SSFA 1998, the effect of which is described below,[7] as supplemented by the Education (School Organisation Proposals) (Wales) Regulations 1999[8] and the Education (School Organisation Proposals) (England) Regulations 1999.[9]

Discontinuance of mainstream maintained schools

7.29   The procedure for the discontinuance of a community, foundation or voluntary school or of a maintained nursery school is contained in s 29 of, and Sch 6 to, the SSFA 1998, except where the governing body of a foundation or voluntary school gives notice under s 30.

7.30   The procedure in s 29 is not materially different from that in s 28, which is described above. The procedure in Sch 6 is described in paras **7.33** et seq.

7.31   Section 30(1) of the SSFA 1998 empowers the governing body of a foundation or voluntary school to discontinue the school by serving on the Secretary of State and the LEA at least 2 years' notice of its intention to do so.[10] However, if expenditure has been incurred on the school's premises otherwise than in connection with repairs by (a) the Secretary of State, (b) the Funding Agency for Schools, (c) any LEA, or (d) any authority which was an LEA within the meaning of any enactment repealed by the EA 1944 or an earlier Act, then no such notice may be served without the consent of the Secretary of State.[11] If discontinuing the school would affect the facilities for full-

---

[1]   See SSFA 1998, s 28(5).

[2]   [1999] ELR 324; [1999] EdCR 949.

[3]   SSFA 1998, s 28(10).

[4]   Ibid, s 28(6). See paras **2.52** and **2.53** regarding school organisation committees. See reg 6 of SI 1999/2213 for the prescribed information.

[5]   See reg 12 of SI 1999/2213, as amended by reg 11 of SI 2003/1229.

[6]   SSFA 1998, s 28(7), read with SI 1999/672.

[7]   See paras **7.35** et seq.

[8]   SI 1999/1671.

[9]   SI 1999/2213.

[10]   Nothing in s 29 or s 33 applies to such a notice: s 30(9).

[11]   SSFA 1998, s 30(2). Where such consent is given, the Secretary of State may impose requirements relating to, for example, the repayment of some or all of the expenditure incurred by the Secretary of State: see SSFA 1998, Sch 22, para 8.

time education suitable to the requirements of persons over compulsory school age who have not attained the age of 19, then the governing body must before serving a notice under s 30 consult the LSC or (as the case may be) the CETW.[1] If the school is a Church of England school,[2] then the governing body and the trustees of any church educational endowment held wholly or partly for or in connection with the school must obtain the advice of the Diocesan Board of Education and have regard to that advice before serving notice of an intention to discontinue the school under s 30.[3] Once a notice has been served under s 30(1), it can be withdrawn only with the consent of the LEA.[4] If, while the notice is in force, the governing body of the school inform the LEA that it is unable or unwilling to carry on the school until the notice expires, then the LEA may conduct the school for the rest of the notice period as if it were a community school, and may use the school premises free of charge for that purpose.[5]

7.32   If land which is occupied by a voluntary or foundation school is held by trustees for the purposes of the school, and the termination of the school's occupation of that land would have the result that it was not reasonably practicable for the school to continue to be conducted at its existing site, then any notice given by the trustees to the school's governing body which purports to terminate the school's occupation of the land will not be effective unless it is of at least 2 years' duration.[6] If there is a dispute as to whether that result would occur, then it is to be determined by the Secretary of State.[7]

Procedure for the establishment, alteration or discontinuance of a community or foundation special school

7.33   The procedure for the establishment, alteration or discontinuance of a community or foundation special school is governed primarily by s 31 of, and Sch 6 to, the SSFA 1998. Those provisions are similar to those which relate to mainstream maintained schools. The regulations which apply to the procedure in s 31 are the Education (Maintained Special Schools) (Wales) Regulations 1999[8] and the Education (Maintained Special Schools) (England) Regulations 1999.[9] One major difference between foundation and foundation special schools is that only an LEA may propose the establishment of a foundation special school: there is no provision by which promoters may do so. Furthermore, the Secretary of State has power to direct the

---

1   SSFA 1998, s 30(3).

2   As defined by ibid, s 142(1).

3   Diocesan Boards of Education Measure 1991 (No 2), s 3(1), as amended by SSFA 1998, Sch 30, paras 30 and 32.

4   SSFA 1998, s 30(7).

5   Ibid, s 30(5). The governing body may nevertheless use the premises, or any part of them, when they are not required for the purposes of the school, as if the governing body had continued to carry on the school during the unexpired period of the notice: s 30(6).

6   Ibid, s 30(10) and (11). See also s 30(12) for the position where the trustees hold two or more pieces of land for the purposes of the school and give notices at the same, or substantially the same, time purporting to terminate the school's occupation of the land.

7   Ibid, s 30(13).

8   SI 1999/1780.

9   SI 1999/2212.

discontinuance of a community or foundation special school under s 32 of the SSFA 1998.[1]

Procedure for the issuing of a direction by the Secretary of State under section 32 of the SSFA 1998

7.34   Before issuing a direction under s 32, the Secretary of State must consult (a) the LEA, (b) any other LEA who in the opinion of the Secretary of State would be affected by the discontinuance of the school, (c) in the case of a foundation special school which has a foundation, the person who appoints the foundation governors, and (d) such other persons as the Secretary of State considers appropriate.[2] It is provided (presumably for the avoidance of doubt) that the procedure in s 31 does not apply where a direction is made by the Secretary of State under s 32.[3]

The procedure in Schedule 6 to the SSFA 1998: establishment, alteration and discontinuance of maintained schools

7.35   Any person may make objections to, or comments on, any proposals published under ss 28, 29 or 31 of the SSFA 1998.[4] The objections or comments must be sent within 6 weeks in England (2 months in Wales) or (where s 15 of the SSFA 1998 applies to the school in question) one month of the date of the publication of the proposals.[5] Objections to or comments on proposals published by the LEA must be sent to the LEA.[6] Objections to or comments on proposals published by the governing body of a school or promoters in England must be sent to the SOC for the relevant area.[7] In Wales, such objections or comments must be sent to the National Assembly for Wales.[8] Objections or comments sent to the LEA must be sent on to the SOC or (as the case may be) the National Assembly for Wales within one month or (where s 15 of the SSFA 1998 applies to the school) 2 weeks.[9] The procedure to be followed in relation to the proposals in England and Wales differs slightly.

7.36   In England, where the proposals under ss 28, 29 or 31 were published by a governing body or promoters, then they must be determined under para 3 of Sch 6 to the SSFA 1998, unless they are withdrawn by notice in writing to the SOC before they are so determined.[10] That paragraph applies also (subject to the same qualification) if (1) proposals are published by the LEA under s 28, 29 or 31, (2) objections are made to the proposals, and (3) those objections have not all been withdrawn in writing within the period prescribed by regulations for the making of objections ('the

---

[1]   See para **7.23** for the operative words of s 32(1).
[2]   SSFA 1998, s 32(3). On giving a direction under s 32(1), the Secretary of State must give notice in writing of the direction to the governing body of the school and its head teacher: s 32(4).
[3]   Ibid, s 32(5).
[4]   Ibid, Sch 6, para 2(1), as amended by EA 2002, Sch 10, para 2.
[5]   See SI 1999/1671, reg 7, SI 1999/1780, reg 8, SI 1999/2212, reg 8 and SI 1999/2213, reg 7 as amended by reg 7 of SI 2003/1229.
[6]   SSFA 1998, Sch 6, paras 2(2)(a) and 7(2)(a).
[7]   Ibid, Sch 6, para 2(3). See paras **2.52** and **2.53** in regard to school organisation committees.
[8]   Ibid, Sch 6, para 7(3), read with SI 1999/672.
[9]   SI 1999/1671, reg 7(3), SI 1999/1780, reg 8(3), SI 1999/2212, reg 8(3) and SI 1999/2213, reg 7(3) as amended by reg 7 of SI 2003/1229.
[10]   SSFA 1998, Sch 6, para 3(1) and (8).

representation period'[1]).[2] Under para 3(2) of Sch 6, the proposals must be considered in the first instance by the SOC. When deciding whether to approve the proposals, the committee must have regard to the school organisation plan for the area as well as to any guidance given from time to time by the Secretary of State.[3] The committee may not approve the proposals 'unless they are satisfied that adequate financial resources will be available to enable the proposals to be implemented'.[4] The committee may approve the proposals with or without modifications, but if modifications are made then the committee must first carry out consultation with persons or bodies prescribed by regulations.[5] A conditional approval is possible.[6] Although an objector has no general right to be heard orally by an SOC, such a committee:

> 'are entitled to hear any objector orally if they consider that to do so will help them. Failure to invite or accept particular oral submissions may, depending on the circumstances, amount to an error of law.'[7]

7.37   If the proposals are rejected by the SOC, then that is the final decision concerning those proposals (subject of course to an application for judicial review), unless the committee exercises its discretion to refer the proposals to the adjudicator under Sch 6, para 3(2)(d) as inserted by EA 2002, Sch 10.[8] The same is true if the proposals are approved by the committee. If, however, the SOC has not voted on the question whether to give any approval under para 3 of Sch 6 by the end of the period of 2 months from certain events (depending on the circumstances),[9] and the body or promoters by whom the proposals were published request the committee to refer the proposals to the adjudicator, then the committee must refer the proposals to the adjudicator within 2 weeks of the request.[10] If the SOC has voted on any matter

---

1   SSFA 1998, Sch 6, para 2(2)(a), as amended by EA 2002, Sch 10, para 4(2).

2   SSFA 1998, Sch 6, para 3(1)(a)(i). Paragraph 4(5) of Sch 6 (as amended by EA 2002, Sch 10, para 4) sets out the other situations in which proposals have to be dealt with under para 3 of Sch 6: see Sch 6, para 3(1)(a)(ii). These are (1) where no objections or comments are made, or any such objections or comments which have been made are withdrawn, and the LEA does not make a determination within 4 months of the date of publication of the proposals, (2) the proposals are related to other relevant proposals (of the sorts set out in para 4(3)) which have not been determined or to a direction made by the Secretary of State under Sch 7, para 2(2) or 3(2), and (3) where the LEA refer the proposals to the SOC under para 4(4A) of Sch 6 (which was inserted by EA 2002, Sch 10, para 4(3)).

3   SSFA 1998, Sch 6, para 3(4). See paras **2.54–2.56** concerning the school organisation plan. See paras **2.34–2.36** for the impact of a duty to 'have regard' to something.

4   SSFA 1998, Sch 6, para 3(4).

5   See ibid, Sch 6, para 3(2)(c) and, for the persons or bodies, SI 1999/2213, reg 8.

6   Ibid, Sch 6, para 3(3), under which regulations may prescribe events on which proposals may be conditional; for the events, see reg 9 of SI 1999/2213, as amended by reg 8 of SI 2003/1229. If the relevant event does not occur, then a fresh approval is required: Sch 6, para 5(10) and (11), as inserted by EA 2002, Sch 10, para 5(5).

7   *R (WB and KA) v Leeds School Organisation Committee* [2002] EWHC 1927 (Admin), [2003] ELR 67, at para 38 (Scott Baker J).

8· A referral under Sch 6, para 3(2)(d) may only occur where the committee '(a) ... have voted on the proposals or matter, but (b) at least two groups of members (within the meaning of regulation 13(1)) did not vote because members of each group had declared an interest in the proposals or matter in question': SI 1999/2213, reg 10A, as inserted by SI 2003/1229, reg 10.

9   See SI 1999/2213, reg 10(2).

10 SSFA 1998, Sch 6, para 3(5), read with SI 1999/2213, reg 14. See paras **2.18** and **2.19** regarding the adjudicator.

arising under para 3 of Sch 6 to the SSFA 1998 which it is required by regulations made under para 4 of Sch 5 to that Act to determine by a unanimous decision, but it has failed to reach such decision on that matter, then, again, it must refer the proposals to the adjudicator.[1] Where the committee rejects proposals published by promoters for the establishment of a new foundation or voluntary school, the committee must, if the promoters so request, refer the proposals to the adjudicator, unless the promoters are the Diocesan Board of Education for a diocese of the Church of England or the Bishop and Trustees of a diocese of the Roman Catholic Church.[2] Where the committee rejects proposals to enlarge a school which were published by the governing body of the school under s 28 and the school is a popular school within the meaning of reg 10C of the Education (School Organisation Proposals) (England) Regulations 1999,[3] but not a grammar school, the committee must refer the proposals to the adjudicator if the governing body so requests within 28 days of the formal notification of the rejection.[4] In all these cases, the adjudicator must 'consider proposals afresh'.[5]

7.38   If para 3 of Sch 6 to the SSFA 1998 does not apply to proposals made by an LEA, then the LEA are under an obligation to determine under para 4 of Sch 6 whether to implement the proposals, unless it decides to refer the proposals to the SOC under para 4(4A) of Sch 6 as inserted by EA 2002, Sch 10.[6] Such determination must be made within the period of 4 months beginning with the date of publication of the proposals.[7]

7.39   Once approved in the above manner, proposals published under ss 28, 29 or 31 must be implemented in the form in which they were approved under para 3 of Sch 6 or determined under para 4 of Sch 6, unless the SOC subsequently determines under para 5 of Sch 6 that they do not need to be so implemented.[8] For example, that may occur if the SOC is satisfied that implementation of the proposals would be unreasonably difficult, or that circumstances have so altered since approval was given under para 3 that implementation of the proposals would be inappropriate.[9] However, that will be possible only once further proposals have been published, proposing that the original proposals be not implemented.[10] Proposals may also be modified by the SOC at the request of the persons or body who published the proposals.[11] If the SOC

---

[1]   SSFA 1998, Sch 6, para 3(6).
[2]   Ibid, Sch 6, para 3(6A) and (6B), as inserted by EA 2002, Sch 10, para 3(4).
[3]   Regulation 10C was inserted by reg 10 of SI 2003/1229.
[4]   SSFA 1998, Sch 6, para 3(6C)(a) and (b), as inserted by EA 2002, Sch 10, para 3(4), and reg 10C of SI 1999/2213.
[5]   SSFA 1998, Sch 6, para 3(7), as amended by EA 2002, Sch 10, para 3(5).
[6]   Such a referral may occur only where it appears to the LEA that 'it may be appropriate, if the proposals are approved, for the approval to be expressed (in accordance with paragraph 3(3) of Schedule 6) to take effect only if an event specified in the approval occurs by the date so specified': SI 1999/2213, reg 10B, as inserted by SI 2003/1229, reg 10.
[7]   See SSFA 1998, Sch 6, para 4(2), which must be read with SI 1999/2213, reg 5.
[8]   Ibid, Sch 6, para 5(1).
[9]   Ibid, Sch 6, para 5(3).
[10]   Ibid, Sch 6, para 5(4), which empowers regulations applying any part of ss 28, 29 and 31 and Sch 6, with or without modification, to the proposals. Regulations have been made under para 5(4): reg 15(1) of, and Sch 4 to, SI 1999/2213, as amended, including by SI 2003/1229.
[11]   See ibid, Sch 6, para 5(2) and SI 1999/2213, reg 11.

has not voted on any matter falling to be decided by them under para 5 of Sch 6 by the end of such period as may be specified in or determined in accordance with regulations, and the body or promoters who published the relevant proposals request the committee to refer that matter to the adjudicator, then the committee must refer the matter to the adjudicator.[1] If the SOC has voted on any matter which it is required by regulations made under para 5 of Sch 4 to the SSFA 1998 to decide by a unanimous decision but have failed to reach such a decision on that matter, then they must refer the matter to the adjudicator.[2] The committee 'may, if they think it appropriate to do so and subject to regulations, refer to the adjudicator any matter which would otherwise fall to be determined by the committee under [para 5 of Sch 6]'.[3] In all three cases, the adjudicator must 'consider the proposals afresh'.[4]

Adjudicator's inquiry

7.40   The adjudicator may hold an inquiry into any matter arising from his consideration of proposals published under ss 28, 29 or 31 of, or para 5(4) of Sch 6, or para 5(1) of Sch 23 to, the SSFA 1998, which is duly referred to him.[5] The procedure to be followed in the inquiry is governed by the Education (Adjudicators Inquiry Procedure etc) Regulations 1999.[6]

The procedure for determining school organisation proposals in Wales

7.41   The procedure for the determination of proposals relating to schools in Wales differs, since there are no school organisation committees in Wales and since there is accordingly no provision for the determination of school organisation proposals by an adjudicator. Rather, the determination in the event of a dispute is made by the National Assembly for Wales.[7] In other respects, the procedure is similar, but simpler.[8] One difference is that the National Assembly for Wales may, by giving notice to the body or promoters by whom relevant proposals were published under s 28 or s 31 of the SSFA 1998 within 2 months of their publication, require the proposals to be approved by the Assembly.[9]

---

1   SSFA 1998, Sch 6, para 5(5). The relevant period is set out in SI 1999/2213, reg 10(3), and is either one month or two months, depending on the circumstances.
2   Ibid, Sch 6, para 5(6).
3   Ibid, Sch 6, para 5(6A), as inserted by EA 2002, Sch 10, para 5(2).
4   Ibid, Sch 6, para 5(7).
5   Education (Adjudicators Inquiry Procedure etc) Regulations 1999, SI 1999/1286, reg 3(1)(a).
6   SI 1999/1286.
7   See SSFA 1998, Sch 6, paras 6–10. Regulations made under s 27 of the SSFA 1998 may apply the new procedure, involving school organisation committees and adjudicators, to Wales, but none have so far been made.
8   The regulations which prescribe the various matters referred to in paras 7–10 of Sch 6 are the Education (School Organisation Proposals) (Wales) Regulations 1999, SI 1999/1671 and the Education (Maintained Special Schools) (Wales) Regulations 1999, SI 1999/1780.
9   SSFA 1998, Sch 6, para 8(1)(a).

Disposals of land, other property and liabilities of a maintained school, including on its discontinuance

7.42   Schedule 22 to the SSFA 1998 makes detailed provision in relation to (1) the disposal of land held for the purposes of a foundation, voluntary or foundation special school, (2) the disposal of land, other property and liabilities on the discontinuance of such a school, and (3) the destination of the property held by the governing body of a maintained school on its dissolution. One useful provision in Sch 22 is para 10(1), which defines 'the trustees' in relation to a school as 'any person (other than the governing body) holding property on trust for the purposes of the school'.

7.43   Somewhat obscured by the title to Sch 22 and the headings within that Schedule are the provisions of para 7 concerning the disposal of a relevant governing body's liabilities on its dissolution. Paragraph 7(2) is to the effect that subject to the exceptions in para 7(3), where the governing body of a maintained school is dissolved by virtue of para 5 of Sch 1 to the EA 2002 or para 4 of Sch 10 to the SSFA 1998: (1) all land or other property which is used or held for the purposes of the school; and (2) all rights and liabilities (including rights and liabilities in relation to staff) subsisting immediately before the date of dissolution which were acquired or incurred for the purposes of the school, are transferred to, and by virtue of the SSFA 1998, vested in either (a) the LEA, or (b) the governing body of a maintained school[1] and/or the temporary governing body of a new school within the meaning of s 72(3) of the SSFA 1998,[2] if the Secretary of State so directs before the date of the dissolution. The exceptions in para 7(3) are that para 7(2) does not apply to (a) any land or other property for which provision has been made for transfer or payment under para 5(4) or para 6(2) of Sch 22,[3] (b) any property of any nature which is held by the governing body on trust for the purposes of the school, or (c) unless the Secretary of State directs otherwise by an order made before the dissolution, any liabilities of the governing body in respect of any loan made to the governing body.

7.44   Provision needed to be made for property which is held on trust by the governing body of a maintained school for the purposes of the school where the school is discontinued or the governing body is dissolved. Paragraph 7(4) of Sch 22 provides that the governing body may before its dissolution transfer any land or other property which it holds on trust for the purposes of the school to 'any person to hold such land or other property on trust for purposes connected with the provision of education in maintained schools', unless the school is a foundation, voluntary or foundation special school and any other persons also hold any property on trust for the purposes of the school. In the latter situation, the property held by the governing body on trust for the purposes of the school is transferred to those other persons.[4]

---

[1]   Within the meaning of SSFA 1998, s 20(7): see SSFA 1998, s 142(1).

[2]   See ibid, Sch 22, para 10(1)(d).

[3]   Such provision is made by the Secretary of State: see ibid, Sch 22, paras 5(4) and 6(2).

[4]   Ibid, Sch 22, para 7(5). Any dispute about the persons to whom the transfer should take place is to be determined by the Secretary of State: ibid, para 7(6).

Change of category of school

7.45 A maintained school may change its category in accordance with (and only in accordance with) the provisions of Sch 8 to the SSFA 1998.[1] Paragraph 2 of Sch 8 requires the publication of proposals for any permitted change of category, and regulations made under that paragraph may apply any of the provisions of ss 28 and 30 and Part I or II of Sch 6 (with modifications if necessary) to the procedure.[2] If the governing body of an aided school is unable or unwilling to carry out its obligations under Sch 3, then it must publish proposals for the school to become a voluntary controlled school or a foundation school.[3] On the other hand, a school may not change its category to become a voluntary aided school unless the governing body satisfies the SOC established for the area of the LEA which maintains the school, that the governing body (as the governing body of a voluntary aided school) will be able to carry out its obligations under Sch 3 to the SSFA 1998 'for a period of at least five years following the implementation date'.[4]

Additional secondary schools

7.46 Section 70 of the EA 2002 empowers an LEA in England to publish a notice inviting proposals for the establishment of additional secondary schools for its area,[5] and obliges the LEA to publish any proposals submitted pursuant to the notice. Schedule 8 to the EA 2002 provides that the Secretary of State, and not the adjudicator (within the meaning of s 25 of the SSFA 1998), makes the final decision as to whether the additional secondary school so proposed is to be established. Where s 70 may be utilised, s 28(1) of the SSFA 1998 may not be utilised by the LEA.[6]

7.47 Regulations are required to give effect to s 70, and they are the Education (Additional Secondary School Proposals) Regulations 2003.[7]

SECRETARY OF STATE'S POWER TO COMPEL A RATIONALISATION OF PLACES IN MAINTAINED SCHOOLS

7.48 Under Sch 7 to the SSFA 1998, the Secretary of State and the National Assembly for Wales[8] may direct what is called (only) in the title to that Schedule a 'rationalisation of school places'. This is a power by order to direct an LEA to

---

[1]   See SSFA 1998, s 35(1).
[2]   See the Education (Change of Category of Maintained Schools) (England) Regulations 2000, SI 2000/2195, as amended by SI 2003/2136, and the Change of Category of Maintained Schools (Wales) Regulations 2001, SI 2001/2678 for the provisions and modifications.
[3]   SSFA 1998, Sch 8, para 3.
[4]   SI 2000/2195, reg 5. The position is the same in Wales, except that the governing body must so satisfy the National Assembly for Wales: see SI 2001/2678, reg 5(1). Note also the restrictions in reg 7 of SI 2000/2195 and reg 5(2) of SI 2001/2678.
[5]   The word 'additional' is defined by s 70(8).
[6]   See SSFA 1998, s 28(1A), inserted by EA 2002, Sch 21, para 97.
[7]   SI 2003/1200, as amended by SI 2003/1421.
[8]   In what follows in this section, a reference to the Secretary of State is not to be read as including a reference to the National Assembly for Wales.

'exercise their powers to make proposals for the establishment, alteration or discontinuance of schools', or to direct the governing body of a foundation, voluntary, or foundation special school to 'exercise their powers to make proposals for the alteration of their school'.[1] The order must be for the purpose of remedying what the Secretary of State or the National Assembly perceives to be excessive or (in certain circumstances) insufficient provision for primary or secondary education in maintained schools in the area of the LEA.[2] Where the direction is given to an LEA, the order may not require the proposals to relate to any named school.[3] Where any proposals are published in accordance with such a direction which relates to an area in England, the body concerned must send a copy of the proposals and certain information to the Secretary of State.[4]

7.49   The Secretary of State must send a copy of any order made by him under paras 2(2) or 3(2) of Sch 7 to the SOC for the LEA's area and to 'any adjudicator who appears to him to be likely to be considering proposals in relation to that area'.[5] The SOC must then in turn send to the Secretary of State a copy of all relevant proposals which it has already received for the area but which have not yet been determined, and a copy of all relevant proposals made subsequently otherwise than by the Secretary of State under para 5.[6] Neither of them may, once the Secretary of State has sent them an order under para 2(2) or 3(2), make a determination or (in the case of an SOC) reference to the adjudicator without the Secretary of State's consent.[7]

7.50   If an LEA publishes proposals in pursuance of an order directing it to do so under para 2(2) or para 3(2), then those proposals must be approved under para 3 of Sch 6 to the SSFA 1998.[8] The proposals may not be withdrawn without the consent of the Secretary of State or (in Wales) the National Assembly, and such consent may be given subject to conditions.[9] Where the governing body of a foundation, voluntary or foundation special school publish proposals pursuant to an order under para 2(2) or 3(2), the LEA must reimburse any expenditure reasonably incurred by the governing body in making the proposals.[10] Where such proposals are determined to be implemented, or approved or adopted, under Sch 7, the LEA is obliged to defray the cost of implementing the proposals.[11]

7.51   The Secretary of State may publish his own proposals under Sch 7, para 5, but only once he has made a direction under para 2(2) or 3(3) of Sch 7 and either such proposals have been published or the time allowed for their publication under the order has elapsed. He may then make 'any such proposals as might have been made in

1   SSFA 1998, Sch 7, paras 2(2) and 3(2).
2   Ibid. For the definition of 'maintained schools', see ss 142(1) and 20(7) of the SSFA 1998.
3   Ibid, Sch 7, paras 2(4) and 3(4).
4   Ibid, Sch 7, paras 2(5) and 3(5). For the requisite information, see reg 6 of the Education (School Organisation Proposals) (England) Regulations 1999, SI 1999/2213.
5   Ibid, Sch 7, para 4(1).
6   Ibid, Sch 7, para 4(2).
7   Ibid, Sch 7, para 4(3).
8   Ibid, Sch 7, para 4(6). See paras **7.36** et seq in regard to para 3 of Sch 6.
9   Ibid, Sch 7, para 4(7).
10   Ibid, Sch 7, para 4(8).
11   Ibid, Sch 7, para 4(9).

accordance with the order relating to that area or that part of the area by the body to whom the directions were given'.[1]

7.52   The other provisions of Sch 7 are similar to those in Sch 6. So, for example, any person may object to, or comment on, the proposals.[2] However, unlike Sch 6, Sch 7 requires the adjudicator in England where the proposals are referred to him, and the National Assembly in Wales where objections to the proposals have been made within the requisite period[3] and not withdrawn, to hold a local inquiry into the proposals.[4] Part IV of Sch 7 caters for the situation where proposals are published that a single-sex establishment should cease to admit pupils of one sex only.

Additional power in England to direct that proposals are published

7.53   Section 71 of the EA 2002 empowers the Secretary of State to give a direction to an LEA in England where he is of the opinion that the provision for primary or secondary education in the area, or any part of the area, of the LEA is, or is likely to become, insufficient. The direction may include that the LEA exercises the power in s 70(1) of the EA 2002.[5] Section 71 can thus be seen to supplement the existing provision in Sch 7 to the SSFA 1998, incorporating s 70 into the scheme for the remedying of an insufficiency of school places in an LEA's area.

Inadequate sixth-forms

7.54   The LSC and the CETW have power to publish, under Sch 7 to the LSA 2000, proposals for a school to cease to have a sixth-form, or to close a sixth-form college which is maintained by an LEA. The provisions of Sch 7 are similar to those in Sch 6,[6] and accordingly they are not described in detail here. In general, Sch 7 applies where a school provides (a) full-time education suitable to the requirements of pupils over compulsory school age, and (b) full-time education suitable to the requirements of pupils who are of compulsory school age.[7] Paragraph 2 of Sch 7 provides that where a person inspecting the school under the SIA 1996 states in his report in accordance with ss 13(8), 14(2) or 14(4) of that Act[8] an opinion that the school no longer requires special measures (and by implication therefore it did so before that report was written), but is of the opinion that the school has an 'inadequate sixth-form', he must

---

[1]   SSFA 1998, Sch 7, para 5(1). Note the other provisions of para 5 concerning the information which must be published, the manner of publication of the proposals, and the sending of a copy of the proposals to the school organisation committee or (in Wales) the LEA and the governing body of every school to which the proposals relate.

[2]   Ibid, Sch 7, paras 7(1) and 12(1).

[3]   This period is 2 months or one month, depending on the circumstances: see SI 1999/1671, reg 7, and SI 1999/1780, reg 8.

[4]   See ibid, Sch 7, paras 9 and 13 respectively.

[5]   See ibid, Sch 7, paras 7.46 and 7.47 concerning s 70.

[6]   See ibid, Sch 7, paras 15–18, 23–26, 31, 32–38, 45, and the School Organisation Proposals by the Learning and Skills Council for England Regulations 2003, SI 2003/507, in relation to England and paras 19–22 and 27–30, 39–45 and the School Organisation Proposals by the National Council for Education and Training for Wales Regulations 2004, SI 2004/1576 in relation to Wales.

[7]   LSA 2000, Sch 7, para 1.

[8]   See paras **12.23**–**12.26** concerning such inspection reports generally.

state the latter opinion in his report. Paragraph 3 of Sch 7 provides that where the Chief Inspector in the course of an area inspection under s 65 of the LSA 2000[1] forms the opinion that a particular school has an inadequate sixth-form, he must make a report about the school stating that opinion, and the report is to be treated as if it were made under s 10 of the SIA 1996.[2]

7.55   An 'inadequate sixth-form' is defined for these purposes by para 1(2) of Sch 7. A school has an inadequate sixth-form if either '(a) the school is failing or likely to fail to give pupils over compulsory school-age an acceptable standard of education, or (b) the school has significant weaknesses in one or more areas of its activities for pupils over compulsory school age'.

7.56   Paragraphs 9–14 of Sch 7 apply to maintained sixth-form colleges where an inspection report made under ss 13(8), 14(2) or 14(4) contains an opinion that the college has 'significant weaknesses in one or more areas of its activities' (but does not require special measures),[3] or where the Chief Inspector in the course of an area inspection forms the opinion either that special measures are required to be taken in relation to the college or that the college has such weaknesses.[4]

7.57   The remaining paragraphs of Sch 7 contain a scheme, which draws on both Sch 6 to the SSFA 1998 and the SIA 1996, for the closure of either the relevant sixth-form or the relevant sixth-form college. Regulations are required by those paragraphs, and they are currently the School Organisation Proposals by the Learning and Skills Council for England Regulations 2003[5] and the School Organisation Proposals by the National Council for Education and Training for Wales Regulations 2004.[6]

Restructuring of sixth-form education

7.58   Closely related to s 113 of, and Sch 7 to, the LSA 2000 are s 113A of, and Sch 7A to, that Act. The latter provisions were inserted by s 72 of the EA 2002. Section 113A gave the LSC and the CETW a significant new role in relation to the making of proposals for the alteration of the provision made by an LEA of maintained schools and sixth-form colleges in the LEA's area. The proposals must be made for the purpose of meeting recommendations made in the report of an area inspection under s 65 of the LSA 2000,[7] or with a view to meeting 'one or more of the relevant objectives'.[8] These are[9] '(a) an improvement in the educational or training achievements of persons who are above compulsory school age but below the age of 19, (b) an increase in the number of such persons who participate in education or training suitable to the requirements of such persons, [or] (c) an expansion of the

---

[1]   Concerning which, see para **16.40**.
[2]   Concerning which, see paras **12.13** and **12.14**.
[3]   See SSFA 1998, Sch 7, para 9.
[4]   See ibid, Sch 7, para 10.
[5]   SI 2003/507.
[6]   SI 2004/1576.
[7]   Concerning which, see para **16.40**.
[8]   See s 113A(2).
[9]   See s 113A(3).

range of educational or training opportunities suitable to the requirements of such persons'.

7.59 Proposals made under s 113A may be for (1) the establishment by an LEA of one or more new maintained schools to provide secondary education which would, if it were provided by a further education college, be further education (and only such secondary education), (2) an alteration of one or more maintained schools which relates to the provision of such education, and/or (3) the discontinuance of one or more maintained secondary schools which provide such education (and only such education).[1] Such proposals may be made either alone or in addition to proposals relating to further education corporations made under s 51 of the FHEA 1992.[2]

7.60 Schedule 7A relates to the implementation of proposals for restructuring sixth-form education made and approved under s 113A of the LSA 2000. Regulations are required to give effect to s 113A and Sch 7A, and they are currently in relation to England the School Organisation Proposals by the Learning and Skills Council for England Regulations 2003.[3]

FEDERATIONS OF SCHOOLS

7.61 The grouping of schools under a single governing body was, from 1944 until 1998, permissible. Under the SSFA 1998, however, such grouping ceased to be possible. What amounts to grouping has been reintroduced by the EA 2002, under the name of a federation. Sections 24 and 25 of the EA 2002 empower the making of regulations concerning federations of schools and supplementary matters. Section 24(1) allows for two or more maintained schools, 'after complying with prescribed conditions and in accordance with prescribed procedure, [to] provide for their respective schools to be federated for the purposes of this Chapter'. Section 24(1) also allows for two or more existing federations to become one.

7.62 Regulations have been made for England only (ss 24 and 25 having come into force in relation only to England[4]). The first set of regulations was the Federation of Schools (Community Schools, Community Special Schools, Voluntary Controlled Schools and Maintained Nursery Schools) (England) Regulations 2003[5]. They allowed only the kinds of schools referred to in their title to join in a federation. They have been replaced by the School Governance (Federations) (England) Regulations 2004 (the Federation Regulations).[6]

7.63 Apart from the provisions which one would expect to be made in regulations made under ss 24 and 25 (such as that the governing bodies of federated schools are dissolved on the formation of the federation, at which time the governing body of the

---

[1]   See LSA 2000, s 113A(4).
[2]   Ibid, s 113A(8).
[3]   SI 2003/507.
[4]   See SI 2003/124 and SI 2003/1667.
[5]   SI 2003/1965.
[6]   SI 2004/2042, which came into force on 30 August 2004.

federation is incorporated[1]), there are several features of the Federation Regulations which are of note. The maximum number of schools which may become a federation under the Federation Regulations is five.[2] Where the intended members of a federation are maintained by different LEAs, the governing bodies of the schools which are intending to become a federation may choose which LEA is to make the instrument of government for the federation.[3] The regulations envisage the appointment of a head teacher for a federation and the co-existence of head teachers for schools in the federation.[4] The governing body of a school which is to become a federated school must 'prepare, for the purpose of assisting the governing body of the federation, a written report on the action which they have taken in the discharge of their functions relating to the school'.[5] Once a school is part of a federation, it may not leave it if the Secretary of State (who is the ultimate arbiter in this connection) decides that it cannot do so.[6] Regulation 39 provides for the 'de-federation date'. The Federation Regulations also apply s 198 of, and Sch 10 to, the ERA 1988: (1) where a school leaves the federation, to property which is held by the governing body of the federation 'for the purposes of the de-federated school';[7] and (2) where a federation is dissolved.[8]

CONSTITUTION OF THE GOVERNING BODY OF A MAINTAINED SCHOOL

7.64   Each maintained school has a governing body which is a corporate body. Under the SSFA 1998, it is constituted in accordance with s 36 of, and Sch 9 to, that Act,[9] and its powers, membership, proceedings and instrument of government are provided for by s 37 of, and Schs 10–12 to, that Act. Under the EA 2002,[10] the governing body is constituted in accordance with regulations made under ss 19 and 20 and Sch 1 (which are currently in force in England only). The only regulations made under the latter sections are currently the School Governance (Constitution) (England) Regulations 2003,[11] which came into effect on 1 September 2003. Those regulations allow the governing body of a maintained school in England to retain its existing instrument of government until 1 September 2006, by which time it must have a new instrument of government, made by the LEA.[12] The regulations are relatively straightforward. One development from their predecessors (the Education (School Government) (England) Regulations 1999[13]) is that they make provision for

---

[1]   See reg 12(1).
[2]   See reg 4.
[3]   See para 5 of Sch 7 to the Federation Regulations, which substitutes in relation to federations a new para 30 into the School Governance (Constitution) (England) Regulations 2003, SI 2003/348.
[4]   See, for example, regs 14(1) and 21(7).
[5]   Regulation 32(1).
[6]   See regs 35–37.
[7]   Regulation 40.
[8]   Regulation 45.
[9]   SSFA 1998, s 36(1).
[10]   Sections 19 and 20 of, and Sch 1 to, EA 2002 replace ss 36 and 37 of, and Schs 9–12 to, SSFA 1998.
[11]   SI 2003/348, as amended by SI 2003/1916 and SI 2004/450.
[12]   See ibid, reg 33.
[13]   SI 1999/2163.

associate members of committees.[1] These are persons who are not members of the governing body but who are appointed by the governing body to be members of committees of the governing body. However, this is in reality a development in name only, since the 1999 Regulations allowed for the same thing.[2] Another development of interest, which is of more substance, is that the 2003 Regulations provide that one-third or more of the members of the governing body must be parent governors.[3] A further change worthy of note is that there is rather more scope for the removal of governors by the governing body than formerly.[4] However, this greater power of removal is subject to (1) the safeguard (which it can confidently be said would otherwise have been implied by the courts) of a right to be heard before the decision to remove the governor is made, and (2) the requirement that the resolution be confirmed by a second resolution at a second meeting of the governing body held not less than 14 days after the first meeting.[5]

7.65   The constitution of a new school in England is provided for in the New Schools (General) (England) Regulations 2003,[6] made under s 34 of the EA 2002. The Education (New Schools) (Wales) Regulations 1999,[7] made under s 44 of the SSFA 1998, provide for the constitution of a new school in Wales. As one would expect, they reflect the position in existing schools.

SCHOOL GOVERNANCE

7.66   The topic of school governance is closely allied to, but different from, that of the constitution of the governing body. This has been expressly recognised by Parliament since the Education Act 1944 was enacted, because since then there has been provision for both an instrument of government and either articles of government or (since the enactment of the SSFA 1998) regulations governing the procedure to be followed by the governing body. Rather more consideration is given here to the governance of a maintained school than to its constitution, but that is merely because of the greater likelihood of problems occurring in practice in relation to the governance of a school than in relation to the constitution of its governing body.

7.67   As with many other aspects of the law of education, the current statutory provisions for Wales currently differ from those for England. This is mainly because the National Assembly for Wales has yet to bring into force and then to make regulations under many relevant provisions in the EA 2002. In Wales, regulations made under s 38(3) of the SSFA 1998 apply to the governance of maintained schools. Those regulations are the Education (School Government) (Wales) Regulations 1999[8] ('the School Government Regulations 1999', or, where appropriate, 'the 1999

---

1   See SI 2003/348, reg 11.
2   See reg 46(2)(c).
3   Regulations 13(1)(a), 14(1)(a), 15(1)(a) and 16(1)(e).
4   Contrast regs 23–26 of SI 2003/348 with regs 18–20 of SI 1999/2163.
5   See SI 2003/348, reg 26(2). This could be thought of as a 'cooling off' period.
6   SI 2003/1558.
7   SI 1999/2243.
8   SI 1999/2242.

Regulations'). In England, the School Governance (Procedures) (England) Regulations 2003,[1] ('the School Governance Procedure Regulations 2003', or, where appropriate, 'the 2003 Regulations') made under s 21(3) of the EA 2002, apply to the governance of maintained schools. The Education (School Government) (England) Regulations 1999,[2] which were in similar terms to their Welsh equivalent, were revoked and replaced by a combination of the Governance Regulations 2003, the School Governance (Constitution) (England) Regulations 2003,[3] and the New Schools (General) (England) Regulations 2003.[4] If nothing else, this serves to emphasise that the School Government Regulations 1999 covered more than merely that which is referred to here as school governance. The new regulations in England make changes other than merely of nomenclature, however, and accordingly the salient aspects of the situations in Wales and England are described below in tandem rather than in sequence.

Clerk to the governing body

7.68   Every governing body must have a clerk. Under the School Government Regulations 1999, the clerk to the governing body of a community, voluntary controlled or community special school must be appointed by the LEA.[5] The clerk to a foundation, voluntary aided or foundation special school must under those regulations be appointed by the governing body.[6] In contrast, under the School Governance Procedure Regulations 2003, the clerk must be appointed by the governing body, irrespective of the kind of maintained school in question.[7] Under the 1999 Regulations, the clerk may be neither a governor nor the head teacher,[8] unless the clerk fails to attend a meeting of the governing body, in which case it may appoint any one of its members to act as clerk for the purposes of that meeting.[9] Under the 2003 Regulations, the clerk may not be a governor, the head teacher, or an associate member, unless the clerk fails to attend a meeting of the governing body, in which case it may appoint any one of its number who is not the head teacher to act as clerk for the purposes of that meeting.[10]

7.69   The functions of the clerk are not specified in the School Government Regulations 1999, except in so far as they are specified in particular contexts. In contrast, reg 9 of the School Governance Procedure Regulations 2003 states those functions explicitly. It is of note that it is not there specified that the clerk must inform the governing body of his view that a proposed procedure or decision would be invalid, although in reg 9(g) it is said that the clerk shall 'perform such other functions as shall be determined by the governing body from time to time'.

---

[1]   SI 2003/1377, as amended by SI 2003/1916 and SI 2004/450.
[2]   SI 1999/2163.
[3]   SI 2003/348, as amended by SI 2003/1916.
[4]   SI 2003/1558, as amended by SI 2004/450.
[5]   See reg 23(2).
[6]   See reg 23(3).
[7]   See reg 8(2).
[8]   See reg 22(1).
[9]   See reg 22(2).
[10]   See reg 8(4).

7.70   Regulations 24 and 25 of the School Government Regulations 1999 provide for the removal of the clerk, but refer to his removal as a dismissal and provide for (1) the governing body of a community, voluntary controlled or community special school to notify the LEA of a decision to dismiss the clerk and the reasons for it, and (2) the dismissal by the LEA of the clerk on receipt of such notification. Regulation 25 makes detailed provision for the dismissal of the clerk where the school does not have a delegated budget, the procedure differing according to whether the school is (1) a community, voluntary controlled or community special school, or (2) a foundation, voluntary aided or foundation special school. The process for the removal of the clerk is more simple under the 2003 Regulations: the governing body may remove the clerk under reg 8(5), unless[1] the school does not have a delegated budget, in which case the LEA may remove the clerk and appoint a substitute, as long as the LEA consults the governing body before doing so.

Convening of meetings

7.71   The governing body of a maintained school in Wales must hold a meeting at least once in every school term.[2] The governing body of a maintained school in England must meet at least three times in every school year.[3] The clerk must convene the meeting, but must comply with any direction given in that regard by the governing body or the chair (or, in his absence, the vice-chair) as long as the latter's direction is consistent with that of the governing body.[4]

7.72   Any three members of the governing body may 'requisition' a meeting of the governing body by means of a notice in writing to the clerk, and the clerk must then convene such a meeting as soon as is reasonably practicable.[5] However, under the School Governance Procedure Regulations 2003, the members must in doing so include 'a summary of the business to be transacted'.

7.73   Written notice of at least 7 clear days must be given of a meeting of the governing body to each governor and the head teacher,[6] unless the chair (or, in certain circumstances, the vice-chair) decides that 'there are matters demanding urgent consideration', in which case such shorter notice as he directs may be given.[7] Under the 1999 Regulations, notice must also be given to the LEA of a meeting of the governing body, while under the 2003 Regulations, there is no need to give such notice, although notice must be given to an associate member.[8] The power of shortening the period of notice does not apply in relation to certain decisions.[9]

---

[1]   See reg 8(6).
[2]   School Government Regulations 1999, reg 34(1).
[3]   Regulation 11(1) of the 2003 Regulations.
[4]   See reg 34(3) of the 1999 Regulations and reg 11(2) of the 2003 Regulations.
[5]   Regulation 34(4) of the 1999 Regulations and reg 11(3) of the 2003 Regulations.
[6]   See reg 34(5) of the 1999 Regulations and reg 11(4) of the 2003 Regulations.
[7]   Ibid.
[8]   Ibid.
[9]   See regs 34(6) and 11(5) respectively.

Chair(man) and vice-chair(man)

7.74   The School Government Regulations 1999 refer (in regs 29–31) to the 'chairman' and 'vice-chairman' of the governing body. Regulations 5–7 of the School Governance Procedure Regulations 2003 refer to the 'chair' and 'vice-chair' (and this terminology is applied here to both sets of regulations). The 1999 Regulations provide for an annual election of a chair and vice-chair (subject to s 18 of the SSFA 1998 applying[1]),[2] but in the case of the 2003 Regulations, it is instead provided that before the election, the governing body must determine 'the date on which the term of office of the chair or vice-chair shall end', which must be either the first meeting of the governing body after the anniversary of his election as chair or vice-chair, or 'not less than one year or more than four years from the date of his election'.[3]

7.75   Although reg 31(6) of the School Government Regulations 1999 provides for the election of a chair for a meeting of the governing body at which there is neither a chair nor a vice-chair of the governing body, the School Governance Procedure Regulations 2003 make no such provision. Instead, it is merely provided in reg 7 that:

> 'Where the chair is absent from any meeting or there is at the time a vacancy in the office of chair, the vice-chair shall act as chair for all purposes.'

7.76   Both sets of regulations make provision for the removal of the chair.[4] However, the School Governance Procedure Regulations 2003 in addition provide for the removal of the vice-chair.[5] In both circumstances, the chair or vice-chair has the right to make a statement in response to the reasons for his proposed removal.

Quorum

7.77   The failure by the School Governance Procedure Regulations 2003 to cater for the situation in which neither the chair nor the vice-chair is present may stem from the fact that under reg 12(1) of those regulations, the quorum for a meeting of the governing body is 'one half (rounded up to a whole number) of the membership of the governing body when complete'. Thus one can expect either the chair or the vice-chair to be present. In contrast, reg 37 of the School Government Regulations 1999 provides that, except where reg 37(2) or (3) applies, the quorum for a meeting of the governing body is either 'any three members of that body or, where greater, any one third (rounded up to a whole number) of the membership when complete'. In relation to the matters set out in reg 37(2), the quorum is 'two-thirds (rounded up to a whole number) of the persons who are at the time members of the governing body entitled to vote on those respective matters'. In relation to the removal of the chair, the formula for the quorum is the same as under reg 37(2), with 'one-half' substituted for 'two-thirds'.[6]

---

1   This confers a power on the Secretary of State to appoint additional governors where s 15(4) or (6) of the SSFA 1998 applies to the school; see para **12.39**.
2   Regulation 29(1).
3   Regulation 5(2).
4   Regulation 30 of the 1999 Regulations and reg 7(1), (3) and (4) of the 2003 Regulations.
5   Regulation 7(2)–(4).
6   Regulation 37(3).

Proceedings of the governing body

7.78   However, reg 12(3) of the School Governance Procedure Regulations 2003 refers to the chair or a 'person who is acting as chair for the purposes of the meeting (provided that such a person is a governor)' as having a second, or casting, vote, where there is an equal division of votes. Provision to the same effect is contained in reg 38(2) of the School Government Regulations 1999, but that is consistent with the possibility, catered for in reg 31(6), of a chair being elected for the purposes of a meeting at which neither the chair nor the vice-chair is present.

7.79   Under both sets of regulations, 'every question to be decided at a meeting of the governing body shall be determined by a majority of the votes of the members present and voting on the question'.[1] Also, under both sets of regulations, a decision to serve notice of the discontinuance of the school under s 30 of the SSFA 1998[2] may not validly be made unless certain conditions are met. Under the School Government Regulations 1999, the decision must be confirmed by a meeting of the governing body held not less than 28 days later.[3] In the case of the School Governance Procedure Regulations 2003 (1) the matter must be specified as an item of business on the agenda for both that meeting and the meeting at which the initial decision was taken, and (2) notice under reg 11(4) must have been given of the second meeting.[4]

7.80   It is clear from these provisions that if there is to be a valid meeting of the governing body, the relevant members of the governing body must either be in the same room together, or, perhaps, must hold a telephone conference. The latter is, however, recommended only if it is the only practicable manner in which a meeting could properly be regarded as taking place. Wherever possible, the power of the chair or (if there is no chair or the chair would be unable to exercise the function in question before the detriment in question were suffered) the vice-chair to discharge any function of the governing body in cases of urgency should be relied upon instead. That power arises under reg 43 of the School Government Regulations 1999 and reg 6 of the School Governance Procedure Regulations 2003. In both cases it misleadingly referred to a delegation of power in cases of urgency: there is simply a power to act in the circumstances referred to in each regulation. Those are that in the opinion of the chair (or, as the case may be, the vice-chair):

> 'a delay in exercising the function would be likely to be seriously detrimental to the interests of –
> (a) the school;
> (b) any pupil at the school, or his parent; or
> (c) a person who works at the school.'[5]

7.81   For this purpose,

---

1   Regulation 38(1), read in the light of reg 38(2), of the School Government Regulations 1999; reg 12(2), read with reg 12(3), of the School Governance Procedure Regulations 2003.
2   Regarding which, see para **7.31**.
3   Regulation 38(2A).
4   Regulation 12(4).
5   These are the words of reg 6(2) of the 2003 Regulations. Slightly different words, which are to the same effect, are used in reg 43(2) of the 1999 Regulations.

'"delay" means delay for a period extending beyond the earliest date on which it would be reasonably practicable for a meeting of the governing body, or of a committee to which the function in question has been delegated, to be held.'[1]

7.82   When the power has been exercised, the chair or vice-chair who has exercised it must report any action or decision taken in the exercise of the power to the next meeting of the governing body.[2]

Defects in procedure

7.83   Both the School Government Regulations 1999 and the School Governance Procedure Regulations 2003 provide that the proceedings of the governing body shall not be invalidated by (1) any vacancy among their number, (2) any defect in the election, appointment or nomination of any governor, (3) any defect in the appointment of the chair or vice-chair, or (4) the school having more governors of a particular category than are provided for in the instrument of government.[3]

7.84   It is of note that the Secretary of State nevertheless has power under s 498 of the EA 1996 to 'make such appointments and give such directions as he thinks desirable for the purpose of securing that there is a properly constituted governing body' of a school in relation to which there is no such governing body by reason of the default of any person. It was held in *Harries v Crawfurd*[4] that a defect in the appointment of a governor includes a fundamental defect in such appointment so that it can properly be said that the appointment was illegal or that there was a vacancy. Accordingly, the Secretary of State's power in s 498 need not be exercised to remedy a relevant defect or vacancy.[5] A defect in the appointment of a member of a committee established under reg 41 of the School Government Regulations 1999 or reg 20 of the School Governance Procedure Regulations 2003 would not, however, be saved by reg 38(3) or reg 12(5) respectively if it were objected to at the outset of the meeting of the committee in question.[6]

7.85   Regulation 34(8) of the 1999 Regulations provides:

'The convening of a meeting and the proceedings conducted thereat shall not be invalidated by reason of an individual not having received written notice of the meeting or a copy of the agenda therefor.'

However, there is no equivalent provision in the 2003 Regulations.

---

1   These are the words used in reg 6(3) of the 2003 Regulations. Words to the same effect are used in reg 43(3) of the 1999 Regulations.
2   See reg 44 of the 1999 Regulations and reg 18 of the 2003 Regulations.
3   See reg 38(3) of the School Government Regulations 1999 and reg 12(5) of the School Governance Procedure Regulations 2003.
4   [1919] AC 717.
5   This was apparently the view of the court in *R v Secretary of State for Education and Science, ex parte Gray* (unreported) (1988) 20 July, referred to in J Rabinowicz, A Widdrington and K Nicholas, *Education: Law and Practice* (FT Law & Tax, London, 1996) at p 88.
6   Cf *R v Secretary of State for Education, ex parte Prior* [1994] ICR 877, at 885B–E.

Suspension of governors

7.86   There is no power to suspend governors in the School Government Regulations 1999. In contrast, reg 15 of the School Governance Procedure Regulations 2003 provides for such suspension in four circumstances. These are:

'(a)   that the governor, being a person paid to work at the school, is the subject of disciplinary proceedings in relation to his employment;

(b)   that the governor is the subject of proceedings in any court or tribunal, the outcome of which may be that he is disqualified from continuing to hold office as a governor under Schedule 6 to the Constitution Regulations;

(c)   that the governor has acted in a way that is inconsistent with the ethos or with the religious character of the school and has brought or is likely to bring the school or the governing body or his office into disrepute; or

(d)   that the governor is in breach of his duty of confidentiality to the school or to any member of staff or to any pupil at the school.'

Right of head teacher to attend

7.87   A head teacher of a maintained school who is not a governor has the right to attend any meeting of the governing body unless he is prevented from attending by the provisions in the relevant regulations concerning conflicts of interest.[1] (The head teacher has a right to be a member of the governing body unless he chooses not to be so.[2])

Withdrawal from proceedings

7.88   In certain circumstances, a person must withdraw from a meeting of the governing body, and, if a member, not vote in relation to the matter in issue. The circumstances are set out in reg 57 of, and Sch 7 to, the School Government Regulations 1999, and reg 14 of, and the Schedule to, the School Governance Procedure Regulations 2003.[3] The 2003 Regulations make simpler provision, but it is to the same effect as that made in the 1999 Regulations. Accordingly, for the sake of clarity and simplicity, reference is made below only to the wording of the School Governance Procedure Regulations 2003 (although references are given to the corresponding provisions in the School Government Regulations 1999). The circumstances in which a person must withdraw from and not vote on a matter arise where there is, or may be, a conflict of interest.

7.89   Although a person may, notwithstanding anything in reg 14 of, or the Schedule to, the 2003 Regulations be allowed to attend any hearing conducted by the governing body or a committee of the governing body 'conducted by them into any matter and to present his evidence', or to make representations when acting in a capacity other

---

[1]   See regs 32(1) and 57 of, and Sch 7 to, the School Government Regulations 1999, and regs 10(1)(b), 14 and the Schedule to, the School Governance Procedure Regulations 2003.

[2]   See, in relation to Wales, SSFA 1998, Sch 9, paras 9(1)(a), 10(1)(a), 11(1)(a), 12(1)(a), 13(1)(a) and 14(1)(a), EA 1996, and, in relation to England, reg 5(1)(a) of the School Governance (Constitution) (England) Regulations 2003, SI 2003/348.

[3]   A new para 14 and Schedule were substituted into SI 2003/1377 by SI 2003/1916.

than in his own capacity,[1] a governor, associate member, the head teacher, or a person appointed as clerk to the governing body or a committee (referred to in both sets of regulations, and below, as 'a relevant person') must in three circumstances withdraw from a meeting and not vote on the matter in question. Those are where (a) 'there may be a conflict between the interests of a relevant person and the interests of the governing body', (b) 'a fair hearing is required and there is any reasonable doubt about a relevant person's ability to act impartially in relation to any matter', or (c) 'a relevant person has a pecuniary interest in any matter'.[2]

7.90   One might have thought that this would for the most part be sufficient, but a number of specific circumstances are dealt with in the Schedule.[3] The one which is dealt with last, but which is most needed, relates to the 'pay or appraisal of persons working at the school'. Paragraph 3 of the Schedule[4] precludes a teacher from taking part in the consideration and determination of the pay or performance appraisal of any other person at the school. Paragraph 3 (unnecessarily, in the light of the para 1 of the Schedule, regarding which see para **7.91**) also precludes a head teacher from participating in a consideration of his own pay or performance appraisal.

7.91   Regulation 14(2) and para 1 of the Schedule[5] concern the situation in which a relevant person has a direct or indirect pecuniary interest in a contract, or proposed contract, or other matter, and is present at a meeting of the governing body or a committee of the governing body at which that contract, proposed contract, or other matter, is the subject of consideration. He must then at the meeting, and as soon as practicable after its commencement (1) disclose the fact that he has such an interest, and (2) withdraw from the meeting during the consideration or discussion of the contract or matter. Furthermore, he may not vote on any question with respect to the contract or matter. Paragraph 1 of the Schedule specifies when a pecuniary interest is, and in several cases is not, to be taken to have arisen for this purpose. One is that a relevant person is not to be taken to have a pecuniary interest in any matter:

> 'provided his interest in the matter is no greater than the interest of the generality of those paid to work at the school.'[6]

7.92   Furthermore, members of the governing body are not precluded by the relevant provisions from:

> 'considering and voting upon proposals for the governing body to take out insurance protecting its members against liabilities incurred by them arising out of their office and

---

[1]   Regulation 14(3); reg 57(3).

[2]   Regulation 14(2); reg 57(2).

[3]   The following discussion is not exhaustive, and reference should accordingly be made to the Schedule (as substituted), or to Sch 7 to the 1999 Regulations, in cases of doubt.

[4]   Replicating the effect of para 4 of Sch 7 to the 1999 Regulations.

[5]   Paragraph 2 of Sch 7 to the 1999 Regulations.

[6]   Paragraph 1(2) of the Sch to the 2003 Regulations, as substituted by SI 2003/1916; para 2(5) of Sch 7 to the 1999 Regulations makes more elaborate provision to the same effect. It is to be noted that the wording of the latter is also a little more extensive than that of the former, in that it refers to two specific situations – where the school's curriculum is to be discussed and where the matter under consideration or discussion involves expenditure by the governing body – but that the effect of the new provision is not lessened by its failure to be so specific.

the governing body shall not, by reason of the pecuniary interest of its members, be prevented from obtaining such insurance and paying the premiums.'[1]

7.93   In *Bostock v Kay*,[2] it was held on the facts that a teacher governor had a pecuniary interest in the question whether the school at which he taught should be converted into a city technology college. The circumstances were that there was 'a very real chance that the proposal would be adopted' with the result that 'any teacher invited to vote on the proposal would understandably be tempted at the very least to ask how it would affect him financially'. The teachers in question were in a position either to receive redundancy payments or a higher salary if the proposal was adopted.

7.94   The effect of the participation of a governor who has a pecuniary interest on a decision can be seen in *Noble v ILEA*,[3] where the participation of the governor concerned made the decision void.

Delegation of functions of a governing body

7.95   Many functions of a governing body may be delegated to either a committee, a governor, or the head teacher. The School Governance Procedure Regulations 2003 make rather simpler provision than do the School Government Regulations 1999. This is partly because aspects of the latter regulations are dealt with in regulations now made concerning staffing matters in England.[4] There is in reg 42(1) of the 1999 Regulations a long list of the functions which may *not* be delegated. This provision is far from replicated in the 2003 Regulations. Regulation 16 of those regulations empowers the delegation of functions to (a) a committee, (b) any governor, or (c) the head teacher (whether or not he is a governor). Regulation 17 then lists a (rather smaller) number of functions which may not be delegated *to an individual,* and imposes an outright prohibition on the delegation of functions relating to powers conferred, and the duties imposed, on governing bodies by or under the School Governance (Constitution) (England) Regulations 2003,[5] except as permitted by those regulations.

7.96   Sub-delegation (for example a determination by a committee that a member of the governing body should instead exercise a function of the governing body) is not possible. It is specifically prohibited by reg 42(1)(v) of the School Government Regulations 1999. Although specific provision is not made in the School Governance Procedure Regulations 2003 in relation to sub-delegation, sub-delegation is generally not permitted at common law, and it seems clear that that general rule applies here. Similarly, if a function has been delegated to a committee, then that committee (and not only its chairman) must exercise it.[6]

---

[1]   2003 Regulations, Sch, para 1(3); Sch 7, para 2(7).
[2]   (1989) 87 LGR 583; (1989) 1 Admin LR 73.
[3]   (1984) 82 LGR 291.
[4]   The School Staffing (England) Regulations 2003, SI 2003/1963, made under ss 19, 26, 34, 35 and 36 of the EA 2002. See para **15.75** concerning those regulations.
[5]   SI 2003/348.
[6]   *R v (1) Wakefield Diocesan Board of Education (Schools Appeal Tribunal) (2) Holy Trinity School, Wakefield* [1999] EdCR 566, concerning which, see further, para **10.71**.

7.97   A committee (which in general must have at least two members[1] and in the case of the School Governance Procedure Regulations 2003 must have at least three members[2]) may include persons who are not members of the governing body,[3] and except in relation to some issues,[4] such persons may vote in proceedings of the committee if the governing body so decides.[5] However, under the 2003 Regulations, an associate member may be excluded from any part of a committee meeting when the business under consideration concerns an individual member of staff or pupil.[6] In the case of the 1999 Regulations, the majority of the members of the committee must nevertheless be members of the governing body,[7] and in the case of both the 1999 Regulations and the 2003 Regulations, no vote may be taken at a committee meeting unless the majority of the members of the committee present are members of the governing body.[8]

7.98   Under the School Government Regulations 1999, some functions may be delegated only to a committee. These functions are those concerning staff dismissal, school discipline, and admissions.[9] Under the 1999 Regulations, the head teacher may not be a member of a committee determining whether an excluded pupil should be reinstated,[10] but the fact that there is no equivalent provision in the 2003 Regulations does not mean that the head teacher can be such a member: reg 14(2)(b) (and the rules of natural justice) preclude that.

7.99   The constitution, membership and proceedings of the committee are (subject to what is said above in the preceding two paragraphs and in the rest of this paragraph) determined by the governing body.[11] However, the quorum of a committee may not, under the 2003 Regulations, be less than three governors who are members of the committee.[12] Under the 1999 Regulations, the chair at a committee meeting must be taken by the chairman of the committee unless he is absent, in which case a chairman must be elected from among the members of the committee who are present and who are members of the governing body but are neither (1) employed at the school, nor (2) a registered pupil at the school, to take the chair at the meeting during such absence.[13] Many provisions of both sets of regulations apply to the proceedings of a committee of the governing body in the same way that they apply to the proceedings of the governing body. Thus, for example, there must be a clerk to

---

1   See *R v Secretary of State for the Environment, ex parte Hillingdon LBC* [1986] 1 WLR 192, 199D–E, approved by the Court of Appeal at [1986] 1 WLR 807 (Note).
2   See reg 20(2).
3   See reg 46(2)(c) of the 1999 Regulations and reg 22(1) of the 2003 Regulations.
4   See regs 47(5) and 48(1) of the 1999 Regulations and reg 22(3) of the 2003 Regulations.
5   Regulations 46(2)(c) and 22(2) respectively.
6   Regulation 23(2).
7   Regulation 46(2)(c).
8   Regulation 46(2)(f) and reg 24(4) respectively.
9   See regs 47–49. The membership of such committees differs, and reference should accordingly be made to those regulations if necessary.
10   Regulation 48(1).
11   Regulation 46(2)(a) of the 1999 Regulations and reg 20(1) of the 2003 Regulations.
12   Regulation 20(2).
13   Regulation 46(2)(g) and (h).

each committee,[1] proper notice of a meeting of the committee must be given,[2] and minutes of the meetings must be made and made available to interested persons.[3]

7.100 There are in addition several functions which may be delegated under specific provisions other than the 1999 Regulations or the 2003 Regulations. These include (1) the power (applicable now only in Wales) under the SSFA 1998 to appoint permanent teaching staff other than the head teacher or the deputy head teacher of a maintained school where there is a delegated budget,[4] and the corresponding power in England in the School Staffing (England) Regulations 2003,[5] and (2) the delegation by a head teacher of responsibility for his SEN functions under reg 3 of the Education (Special Educational Needs) (England) (Consolidation) Regulations 2001[6] or (as the case may be) reg 3 of the Education (Special Educational Needs) (Wales) Regulations 2002.[7]

Rescission or variation of resolutions

7.101 Resolutions may be rescinded or varied under reg 35 of the School Government Regulations 1999, but only if the consideration of the rescission or variation of the previous resolution is a specific item of business on the agenda for the meeting at which the rescission or variation takes place. Although there is no similar provision in the School Governance Procedure Regulations 2003, it is clear that a resolution of the governing body (or a committee or member with delegated power) may be rescinded or varied, but that the same restriction would not apply if the power to make the decision had been delegated to an individual.

Public access

7.102 A governing body may under reg 33 of the School Government Regulations 1999 allow a member of the public to attend a governing body meeting. A committee may also do so, under reg 56(2) of those regulations. Regulations 10(1) and 23(1) of the School Governance Procedure Regulations 2003 make similar provision.

Minutes of proceedings and papers

7.103 Minutes of proceedings of meetings of the governing body of a maintained school or of a committee of the governing body must be drawn up and signed (subject to the approval of the governing body) by the chair at the next meeting.[8] The governing body (or, as the case may be, committee) must, subject to exceptions, make those minutes, together with an agenda for the meeting and any report or other paper

---

[1]   Regulation 51 of the 1999 Regulations and reg 21 of the 2003 Regulations.
[2]   Regulation 52 and reg 24(1) and (2) respectively.
[3]   Regulations 54 and 55 and reg 24(7)–(9) respectively.
[4]   See SSFA 1998, Sch 16, para 17 and Sch 17, para 17.
[5]   SI 2003/1963, reg 4.
[6]   SI 2001/3455.
[7]   SI 2002/152.
[8]   See regs 13(1) and 24(7) of the 2003 Regulations and regs 39(1) and 54(1) of the 1999 Regulations. The latter provisions provide for signature at the same meeting, and the omission of this provision from the 2003 Regulations is probably a consequence of its lack of practical effect. Regs 39 and 54 of the 1999 Regulations are more specific than regs 13 and 24 of the 2003 Regulations in several other respects, but regs 13 and 24 provide no less protection of the public interest.

considered at the meeting, available for inspection as soon as reasonably practicable to any interested person.[1] The exceptions are that the governing body may exclude from any item which is required to be made available any material relating to:

'(a)   a named person who works, or who it is proposed should work, at the school; or
(b)   a named pupil at, or candidate for admission to, the school; or
(c)   any other matter that, by reason of its nature, the governing body is satisfied should remain confidential.'[2]

7.104 An LEA in Wales may require the governing body of a school which is maintained to give it a copy of the minutes of the proceedings of the governing body.[3] There is no equivalent of this power in the School Governance Procedure Regulations 2003, although the LEA will clearly be entitled to see the minutes, but with confidential information withheld.[4]

THE FUNDING OF MAINTAINED SCHOOLS

7.105 As stated in para **7.8**, the LEA is under a duty to meet all the expenses of maintaining a community school or a community special school, and to provide all the necessary premises for it. The duty to maintain the school and make available premises to be used for the purposes of the school is placed on the LEA by s 22(3) of, and para 12 of Sch 6 to, the SSFA 1998. No more needs to be said here about the duty to meet the expenses of community or community special schools, apart from in relation to the delegation of budgets to the governing bodies of such schools.[5]

7.106 The situation concerning maintained schools other than community schools is intricate. This is a product of legislation requiring persons or bodies who wish to influence the manner in which children in England and Wales are educated in state schools to contribute something financially towards the establishment and (in some cases) upkeep of those schools. Foundation schools are something of an anomaly in this regard, but it seems that it was thought necessary to allow the governing bodies of schools which before 1 September 1999 were grant-maintained to retain greater independence (without significant financial responsibility for the establishment or upkeep of the school) than they would have had if the schools had been community schools. The position of voluntary controlled schools is considered below first, after which the positions of (1) foundation and foundation special schools, and (2) voluntary aided schools are considered.

Voluntary controlled schools

7.107 The governing body of a voluntary controlled school is not responsible for any of the expenses of maintaining the school, except that it is responsible for the

---

1   Regulations 13(2) and 24(8) and regs 40(1) and 55(1) respectively.
2   Regulations 13(3) and 24(9) and regs 40(2) and 55(2) respectively.
3   See regs 39(4) and 54(4) of the 1999 Regulations.
4   See reg 13 and reg 24(7)–(9) respectively.
5   See paras **7.132** et seq.

repayment of the principal of, or interest on, a loan made to the governing body.[1] The obligations of the governing body in relation to the premises are set out in para 2 of Sch 3 to the SSFA 1998. The obligations of the LEA in that regard are set out in part also in para 2 of Sch 3, and otherwise in paras 13 and 16 of Sch 6 to the SSFA 1998.

The LEA's obligations regarding the funding of voluntary controlled schools

7.108 Subject to two exceptions, para 2 of Sch 3 to the SSFA 1998 obliges the LEA to provide any new site which is to be provided in addition to, or instead of, the existing site (or part of the site) of a voluntary controlled school. A 'site' for this purpose (and all other purposes of para 2 of Sch 3) 'does not include playing fields but otherwise includes any site which is to form part of the premises in the school in question'.[2] The LEA is also obliged by para 2 of Sch 3 to provide (subject to the same exceptions) any buildings which are to form part of the school's premises. The two exceptions are set out in para 2(2) of Sch 3. The first occurs where statutory proposals are made under s 28 of the SSFA 1998, in which case paras 13 and 16 of Sch 6 to the SSFA 1998 apply instead. The second exception is that if a site is, or buildings are, to be provided for the school otherwise than by the LEA, then the LEA is under no obligation to finance that acquisition.

7.109 Where a site is provided for a voluntary controlled school by the LEA under para 2 of Sch 3 to the SSFA 1998, the LEA is obliged to transfer its interest in the site, and in any buildings on the site which are to form part of the school premises (in other words, any rights of ownership which the LEA has in respect of the site and, where relevant, the buildings) to:

> 'the trustees of the school, to be held by them on trust for the purposes of the school, or ... if the school has no trustees, to the school's foundation body or (in the absence of such a body) to the governing body, to be held by that body for the relevant purposes.'[3]

The LEA must pay to the persons to whom the transfer is made their reasonable costs in connection with the transfer.[4]

7.110 Just who or what may be the 'trustees of the school' is an interesting question, since a trust is a relationship to property, and a state school at least is an institution rather than a kind of property. This question is returned to in para **7.201**. If any doubt or dispute arises as to the persons to whom an LEA is required to make the transfer, then the transfer is to be made to 'such persons as the Secretary of State thinks proper'.[5]

7.111 Where a transfer is made under para 2 of Sch 3 to the SSFA 1998 to persons who possess, or are or may become entitled to, any sum representing the proceeds of the sale of other premises which have been used for the purposes of the school, those

---

1   SSFA 1998, s 22(4) and Sch 3, para 1.
2   Ibid, Sch 3, para 2(11).
3   Ibid, Sch 3, para 2(3). The relevant purposes means, in relation to a transfer to a school's foundation body, the purposes of the schools in the group for which the body acts: see Sch 3, para 2(11).
4   Ibid, Sch 3, para 2(5).
5   Ibid, Sch 3, para 2(4).

persons must notify the LEA of that fact, and they or their successors (in other words any persons who subsequently become entitled in law to the proceeds of sale in question) must pay the LEA 'so much of that sum as, having regard to the value of the interest transferred, may be determined to be just, either by agreement between them and the authority or, in default of agreement, by the Secretary of State'.[1]

Obligations regarding the funding of a voluntary controlled school where statutory proposals are made under s 28 of the SSFA 1998

7.112 Where proposals which are published by an LEA under s 28(1) of the SSFA 1998 for the establishment or alteration of a voluntary controlled school fall to be implemented, then the LEA must implement them.[2] Where proposals for the establishment of such a school which are published by the promoters under s 28(2) fall to be implemented, then they must be implemented by the LEA and by the promoters to such extent (if any) as the proposals state.[3] Similarly, where proposals for the alteration of a voluntary controlled school are published by the governing body of the school under s 28(2), then the proposals must be implemented by the LEA and by the governing body to such extent (if any) as the proposals state.[4]

7.113 If, in any of the situations mentioned in para **7.112**, the LEA is under an obligation to provide a site for a voluntary controlled school, the LEA must transfer its interest in the site and in any buildings in the site which are to form part of the school premises to 'the school's trustees, to be held by them on trust for the purposes of the school'. If the school has no trustees, then the LEA must transfer such interest either (1) to the school's foundation body to be held by that body on trust for the purposes of the schools in the group for which the body acts, or (in the absence of such a body) (2) to the governing body to be held by that body on trust for the purposes of the school.[5] As with transfers under para 2 of Sch 3 to the SSFA 1998, the LEA must pay to the persons to whom the transfer is made their reasonable expenses in connection with the transfer.[6]

Foundation and foundation special schools

7.114 The position relating to the funding of foundation and foundation special schools is almost identical to that of voluntary controlled schools under the SSFA 1998.[7] There is, however, one major difference in that only the LEA may propose the

---

[1]   SSFA 1998, Sch 3, para 2(6); see further, para 2(7) of Sch 3 with regard to what is included in the term 'the proceeds of sale'. Schedule 3 contains further provisions concerning the School Sites Act 1841 and the Reverter of Sites Act 1987. Those Acts are referred to further in paras **8.25** et seq.

[2]   Ibid, Sch 6, para 13(2).

[3]   Ibid, Sch 6, para 13(3).

[4]   Ibid.

[5]   Ibid, Sch 6, para 16(2) and (10). As with transfers under para 2 of Sch 3, if there is any doubt about the appropriate persons to whom the transfer should be made, then the Secretary of State must decide to whom the transfer should be made: Sch 6, para 2(3). Similarly, the effect of para 2(6)–(10) of Sch 3 to the SSFA 1998 – concerning which see para **7.111** – is repeated in para 16(5)–(9) of Sch 6.

[6]   Ibid, Sch 16, para 2(4).

[7]   This is because (1) para 2 of Sch 3 to the SSFA 1998 applies not only to a voluntary controlled school but also to a foundation or foundation special school, and (2) para 13 of Sch 6 to the SSFA 1998 applies to foundation schools as well as to voluntary controlled schools.

establishment of a foundation special school,[1] and if it does so then it must pay the costs of implementing the proposal.[2]

Voluntary aided schools

7.115   The provisions relating to the funding of voluntary aided schools in the SSFA 1998 are a little complex. The responsibilities of the governing body of a voluntary aided school are discussed here first. The relevant responsibilities of the LEA are then discussed. Mention is then made of the responsibilities of the promoters of a new voluntary aided school. Finally, the routes by which assistance may be given to the governing body or the promoters of a voluntary aided school by the LEA or the Secretary of State are discussed.

Responsibilities of the governing body of a voluntary aided school in relation to the provision of premises for, and the maintenance of, the school

7.116   As with voluntary controlled schools, the LEA is obliged to meet all the expenses of maintaining a voluntary aided school except where the SSFA 1998 specifically provides otherwise.[3] Unlike the governing body of a voluntary controlled school, however, the governing body of a voluntary aided school are obliged to meet some of the expenses of maintaining the school. Those expenses are as follows.

7.117   The governing body of a voluntary aided school in England must meet all 'capital expenditure in relation to the school premises' (including in relation to boundary walls and fences[4]) except in relation to (1) 'playing fields or any building or other structure erected thereon in connection with the use of playing fields',[5] (2) capital expenditure which is necessary in consequence of the use of the school premises in pursuance of a direction or requirement of the LEA for purposes other than those of the school, or (3) capital expenditure on the provision of a new site which the LEA is to provide by virtue of para 4 of Sch 3 to the SSFA 1998.[6]

7.118   The governing body of a voluntary aided school in Wales must discharge any liability incurred by or on behalf of (a) the governing body of the school, (b) any former governors of the school, or (c) any trustees of the school (a difficult term, the meaning of which is considered below[7]) 'in connection with the provision of premises or specified equipment for the purposes of the school'.[8] 'Specified equipment' for these purposes means equipment of any description specified by the National Assembly for Wales for such purposes.[9] The governing body of a voluntary aided

---

[1]   See SSFA 1998, s 31(1).

[2]   See ibid, Sch 6, para 15(2).

[3]   See ibid, s 22(5).

[4]   Ibid, Sch 3, para 3(2)(a), as substituted in relation to England by the Regulatory Reform (Voluntary Aided Schools Liabilities and Funding) (England) Order 2002, SI 2002/906.

[5]   Ibid. 'Capital expenditure' is defined for this purpose by Art 13 of the Regulatory Reform (Voluntary Aided Schools Liabilities and Funding) (England) Order 2002, SI 2002/906: SSFA 1998, Sch 3, para 3(3), as substituted by that Order.

[6]   SSFA 1998, Sch 3, para 3(2), as substituted by SI 2002/906.

[7]   Paragraphs **7.201–7.204**.

[8]   SSFA 1998, Sch 3, para 3(1), as originally enacted.

[9]   Ibid.

school is also responsible for the expenses of certain repairs to the school buildings. Those repairs do not include repairs to the interior of the school buildings, or repairs to school buildings which are necessary in consequence of the use of the school premises, in pursuance of a direction or requirement of the LEA, for purposes other than those of the school.[1] The expenses concerning repairs for which the governing body of a voluntary aided school is responsible are any expenses incurred in making any alterations to the school buildings in order to secure that the school's premises conform to the standards prescribed under s 542 of the EA 1996,[2] and any expenses incurred in effecting repairs other than the ones mentioned in the preceding sentence.[3] If a voluntary aided school in Wales has not always been a voluntary aided school, then its governing body is not obliged to meet any liability of the sorts described in this paragraph if the liability was incurred at any time before the school became a voluntary aided school and at that time no liability was imposed under either the SSFA 1998 or the EA 1996 on the governing body of the school as it then was.[4]

7.119 Where the governing body of a voluntary aided school in England has published proposals under s 28(2) of the SSFA 1998 for the alteration of the school, the governing body is obliged to implement the proposals except in so far as they involve the provision of playing fields.[5] In relation to Wales, the governing body is obliged to implement the proposals except in so far as they involve the provision of playing fields and/or buildings which are to form part of the school premises but are not to be school buildings.[6]

Obligations of the LEA in regard to the provision of premises for a voluntary aided school

7.120 The LEA must provide any new site (other than playing fields or buildings which are to form part of the school premises but are not to be school buildings) which is to be provided in addition to, or instead of, the existing site of a voluntary aided school (or part of such site), unless the governing body or any other person is under a duty to provide the site under (in England) any enactment, or under (in Wales) Part III of Sch 6 to the SSFA 1998.[7] However, this does not mean that the LEA is under an obligation to finance the acquisition by the governing body of any site or buildings provided otherwise than by the LEA.[8] The exclusion of playing fields from this obligation of an LEA is probably a result of the obligations of an LEA

---

[1]   SSFA 1998, Sch 3, para 3(3) as originally enacted.
[2]   Regarding which, see paras **8.4** and **8.5**.
[3]   SSFA 1998, Sch 3, para 3(2).
[4]   Ibid, Sch 3, para 3(4).
[5]   Ibid, Sch 6, para 14(2) as substituted by SI 2002/906, Art 11.
[6]   Ibid, Sch 6, para 14(2) and (4) as originally enacted.
[7]   Ibid, Sch 3, para 4(1), (2) and (9), in relation to England as amended by para 114 of Sch 21 to the EA 2002. The provisions in Sch 3 for agreement between the governing body and the LEA in relation to the clearing of a site or making it suitable for building purposes, or for the making of payments or adjustments of the respective rights and liabilities of the LEA and the governing body where a site to be provided by the LEA for the school has on it buildings which are of value for the purposes of the school, should be noted. Those provisions are para 4(6) and (7) of Sch 3. Paragraph 4(8) of Sch 3 empowers the Secretary of State to give directions for the making of relevant payments or other adjustments where he thinks that appropriate.
[8]   Ibid, para 4(2).

where a voluntary aided school is established or altered pursuant to proposals published under s 28 of the SSFA 1998. Those obligations are set out in para 14 of Sch 6 to the SSFA 1998, and are as follows.

7.121   Where proposals for the establishment of a voluntary aided school have been published by promoters under s 28(2) of the SSFA 1998, the LEA is under a duty to implement the proposals in so far as they relate to the provision of premises which are to be playing fields (or, Wales, buildings which are to form part of the school premises but are not to be school buildings), unless the new school is to be established in place of one or more existing independent, foundation or voluntary schools which will be discontinued on or before the date of implementation of the proposals.[1] In the latter case, if any part of the premises of any such discontinued school is to be used for the purposes of the new school, and (in relation to a voluntary or foundation school) the premises were not provided by the LEA, then the LEA need not provide the premises in question.[2]

7.122   Where proposals for the alteration of a voluntary aided school have been published by the governing body of the school under s 28(2) of the SSFA 1998, the LEA must implement the proposals in so far as they relate to the provision of playing fields (or, in Wales, buildings which are to form part of the school premises but are not to be school buildings).[3]

Obligations of promoters of new voluntary aided schools

7.123   Where a new voluntary aided school is established following the publication of proposals for its establishment under s 28(2) of the SSFA 1998, the obligation to implement the proposals falls on the promoters of the school, except in so far as the proposals relate to the provision of premises which are to be provided by the LEA in the manner described in the preceding paragraphs.[4]

Assistance which may be given by the LEA to the promoters or governing body of a voluntary aided school

7.124   The LEA may provide assistance to the governing body of a voluntary aided school in regard to the governing body's duties described in the preceding paragraphs.[5] If that assistance takes the form of the provision of premises, the LEA must transfer its interest in the premises to (a) the trustees of the school (the meaning of which is considered below[6]) to be held by them on trust for the purposes of the school, or (b) if there are no such trustees, to the school's foundation body to be held by that body for the purposes of the schools for which the body acts.[7] If any doubt or dispute arises as to the persons to whom the LEA should make the transfer, then it is

---

[1]   In relation to Wales, SSFA 1998, Sch 6, para 14(3) and (4) as originally enacted, and in relation to England, Sch 6, para 14(3) as amended by SI 2002/906, Art 11.

[2]   SSFA 1998, Sch 14, para 14(5).

[3]   In relation to England, SSFA 1998, Sch 6, para 14(2) as amended by SI 2002/906, Art 11, and in relation to Wales, SSFA 1998, Sch 6, para 14(2) and (4) as originally enacted.

[4]   SSFA 1998, Sch 6, para 14(3)(b).

[5]   Ibid, Sch 3, para 8.

[6]   Paragraphs **7.201–7.204.**

[7]   SSFA 1998, Sch 3, para 9(1) and (4).

to be made to such persons as the Secretary of State 'thinks proper'.[1] The LEA is obliged to pay to the persons to whom the transfer is made 'their reasonable costs in connection with the transfer'.[2]

7.125   The LEA may in addition provide assistance to the governing body of a voluntary aided school in connection with the provision of premises for the school which are to be provided by the governing body where proposals have been published by the governing body under s 28(2) of the SSFA 1998.[3] Similarly, the LEA may provide assistance to the promoters of a new voluntary aided school in connection with the obligations of the promoters in respect of the establishment of the school.[4] Where it provides assistance in either situation, the LEA must convey its interest in any premises which it provides to (a) the trustees of the school to be held by them on trust for the purposes of the school, or (b) if there are no such trustees, to the school's foundation body to be held by that body for the purposes of the schools for which the body acts, in the same manner as described in the preceding paragraph.[5]

Assistance which may be given by the Secretary of State or the National Assembly for Wales to the promoters or governing body of a voluntary aided school

7.126   The Secretary of State (or, in Wales, the National Assembly for Wales) may provide assistance to the governing body of a voluntary aided school in relation to expenditure incurred by the governing body in respect of (in England) any capital expenditure[6] or (in Wales) the provision, alteration or repair of premises or equipment for the school.[7] The Secretary of State or the National Assembly may also provide assistance of the same sort to 'the appropriate diocesan authority or the school's trustees' where that body or those trustees has or (as the case may be) have incurred the relevant expenditure on behalf of the governing body.[8] The amount of any grant made by the Secretary of State for this purpose may not exceed 90 per cent of the expenditure (unless he considers that the circumstances are exceptional, in which case the grant may not exceed 100 per cent of the expenditure), and in relation to any kinds of expenditure specified in regulations, must be of such amount as may be decided upon in accordance with regulations.[9] In relation to Wales, the amount of any grant made by the National Assembly for this purpose may not exceed 85 per cent of

---

1   SSFA 1998, Sch 3, para 9(2).
2   Ibid, Sch 3, para 9(3).
3   Ibid, Sch 6, para 18. See para **7.119** concerning the duty of the governing body in this regard.
4   Ibid, Sch 6, para 19.
5   See ibid, Sch 6, para 20.
6   This means (see Art 13 of the Regulatory Reform (Voluntary Aided Schools Liabilities and Funding) (England) Order 2002, SI 2002/906): (a) the acquisition, reclamation, enhancement or laying out of any land; (b) the acquisition, construction, preparation, enhancement, replacement or demolition of any building or part of a building (including any fixtures and fittings affixed to a building), wall, fence or other structure, or any playground or other hard-standing; or (c) the acquisition, installation or replacement of any movable or immovable plant, machinery, apparatus or furniture (in all cases) used or intended to be used for the purposes of the school.
7   SSFA 1998, Sch 3, para 5(1) as amended by SI 2002/906, Art 7, and, in relation to Wales, para 5(1) and (2) as originally enacted.
8   Ibid, Sch 3, para 5(1), (2) and (12). See paras **7.201–7.204** regarding who or what may be the school's trustees.
9   Ibid, Sch 3, para 5(3), as amended by Art 7 of SI 2002/906.

the expenditure.[1] In making grants under para 5 of Sch 3 to the SSFA 1998, the Secretary of State must give priority to paying grants in respect of expenditure which is necessary to make such alterations as may be required by the LEA for the purpose of securing that the school premises conform to the standards prescribed under s 542 of the EA 1996 or as may be required for the purpose of securing that the school premises conform to standards specified by or under any other enactment relating to health and safety.[2] The amount of such grants must be at least 90 per cent of the expenditure.[3] In making grants in connection with expenditure on the repair of the school buildings of a voluntary aided school or in connection with alterations to the school buildings in order to secure that the school's premises conform to the standards prescribed under EA 1996, s 542, the National Assembly for Wales must 'give priority to paying grants in respect of expenditure which is necessary for the performance by [the governing body of its duties]'.[4] The amount so paid by the National Assembly must be 85 per cent of the expenditure.[5] Conditions may be attached to the assistance given by the Secretary of State or the National Assembly for Wales in the circumstances described in this paragraph.[6]

7.127 The Secretary of State or the National Assembly for Wales may also give assistance to the governing body of a voluntary aided school in the manner just described, in connection with the governing body's obligation under para 14(2) of Sch 6 to the SSFA 1998 to provide premises for the school where proposals have been published by the governing body under s 28(2) of the SSFA 1998.[7] Similarly, the Secretary of State or the National Assembly may give assistance to the promoters of a new voluntary aided school in connection with the promoters' obligations concerning the establishment of that school.[8]

7.128 The Secretary of State or (in Wales) the National Assembly for Wales may also give financial assistance by way of grants in respect of what is called 'preliminary expenditure' in connection with any scheme for (a) the transfer of a voluntary aided school to a new site, or (b) the enlargement or alteration of the school premises. Such assistance may be given to the governing body of the school or to the appropriate diocesan authority or the school's trustees where that authority has or those persons have incurred (or, in England, intend to incur) such preliminary expenditure on behalf of the governing body.[9] Similarly, the Secretary of State (or the National Assembly) may give financial assistance to any persons who propose or are considering whether to propose the establishment of a voluntary aided school. The assistance must take the form of grants in respect of preliminary expenditure incurred (or, in England, to be incurred) by those persons for the purposes of a scheme for the provision of (a) a site for the school, or (b) any buildings which would be school buildings (or, in

---

[1]   SSFA 1998, Sch 3, para 5(1) and (2) as originally enacted.
[2]   Ibid, Sch 3, para 5(5) as substituted by Art 7 of SI 2002/906.
[3]   Ibid.
[4]   Ibid, Sch 3, para 5(5) as originally enacted.
[5]   Ibid.
[6]   See ibid, Sch 3, para 5(6)–(10).
[7]   See ibid, Sch 6, para 17(1). See para **7.119** for the governing body's obligations in this regard.
[8]   Ibid, Sch 6, para 17(2). See para **7.123** for the promoters' obligations in that regard.
[9]   Ibid, Sch 3, para 6(1) and (7); in relation to England, para 6(1) was amended by Art 8 of SI 2002/906. See paras **7.201–7.204** regarding who or what may be a school's trustees.

England, any buildings which would be used for the purposes of the school).[1] Grants payable in the manner described in this paragraph are payable (among other things) even if the scheme to which they relate is not implemented.[2] The grants may not, however, be paid in respect of sums expended in carrying out the relevant works.[3] A grant payable by the National Assembly for Wales as described in this paragraph may not exceed 85 per cent of the expenditure to which it relates.[4] A grant payable by the Secretary of State as described in this paragraph may not exceed 90 per cent of the expenditure to which it relates, unless the Secretary of State considers that the circumstances are exceptional, in which case the grant may not exceed 100 per cent of the expenditure in respect of which it is paid.[5]

7.129 The Secretary of State may also give loans to the governing body of any voluntary aided school in England where he is 'satisfied that the governing body's share of any initial expenditure required in connection with the school premises will involve capital expenditure'.[6] Such initial expenses are ones in respect of which the Secretary of State could give assistance to the governing body under para 5 of Sch 3 to the SSFA 1998,[7] and do not include any expenses which are to be met by such assistance.[8] The Secretary of State may also give loans to the appropriate diocesan authority or the school's trustees where that authority or those persons have incurred the same kind of expenses on behalf of the governing body.[9] The Secretary of State may in addition give loans to the promoters of a new voluntary aided school in England in relation to the same kind of expenses.[10] The National Assembly has the same powers in relation to Wales, but in relation to initial 'expenses' rather than initial 'expenditure'.[11]

Common provisions relating to the funding of all foundation, voluntary and foundation special schools

7.130 There are two statutory provisions relating to the funding of foundation, voluntary and foundation special schools which are common to all of them. First, all foundation, voluntary and foundation special schools are entitled to the benefit of the default powers of the Secretary of State (or, in the case of a relevant school in Wales, the National Assembly for Wales[12]) under para 10 of Sch 3 to the SSFA 1998. That power arises where it appears to the Secretary of State or the National Assembly (as the case may be) that an LEA has defaulted in the discharge of its duties relating to the maintenance of a foundation, voluntary or foundation special school. In that situation, he (or it) may:

---

1   SSFA 1998, Sch 3, para 6(2), amended in relation to England by Art 8 of SI 2002/906.
2   Ibid, Sch 3, para 6(3).
3   Ibid, Sch 3, para 6(4).
4   Ibid, Sch 3, para 6(5) as originally enacted.
5   Ibid, Sch 3, para 6(5) as substituted by Art 8 of SI 2002/906.
6   Ibid, Sch 3, para 7(1), as amended by Art 10 of SI 2002/906.
7   See ibid, Sch 3, para 7(3). See para **7.126** regarding the funding powers conferred by para 5 of Sch 3.
8   Ibid, Sch 3, para 7(4).
9   Ibid, Sch 3, para 7(5). See paras **7.201–7.204** regarding the meaning of the phrase 'the school's trustees'.
10 Ibid.
11 See ibid, Sch 3, para 7 as originally enacted.
12 See SI 1999/672.

(a)   direct that any act done by or on behalf of the school's governing body for the purpose of securing the proper maintenance of the school shall be taken to have been done by or on behalf of the authority;

(b)   reimburse to the governing body any sums which in his [or its] opinion [the governing body] has expended for that purpose; and

(c)   recover the sum so spent by him or it as a debt due from the LEA to him or it.[1]

7.131 The second common provision applies where any sums accruing in respect of the income of an endowment are required by virtue of the provisions of a trust deed to be applied towards the maintenance of a foundation, voluntary or foundation special school. In that situation, those sums are not payable to the LEA but must be applied by the governing body of the school in accordance with any scheme for the administration of the endowment made after 1 April 1945.[2] If there is no such scheme, then, if the school is a voluntary aided school, the income of the endowment must be applied by the governing body towards the discharge of its obligations under para 3 of Sch 3 to the SSFA 1998.[3]

DELEGATED BUDGETS

Introduction

7.132 The Education Reform Act 1988 (ERA 1988) introduced the delegation of budgets to the governing bodies of maintained schools. The system introduced by that Act has come to be known as 'local management', and involves an unusual kind of delegation of power. That system is now governed by Chapter IV of Part II of the SSFA 1998, as amended by the EA 2002.

7.133 Section 45 of the SSFA 1998 requires that:

'For the purposes of the financing of maintained schools by local education authorities, every such school shall have, for each financial year, a budget share which is allocated to it by the authority which maintains it.'[4]

7.134 Sections 45A–45C of the SSFA 1998 apply to the determination of a maintained school's budget share.[5]

The determination of budget shares

England

7.135 Section 45A of the SSFA 1998[6] provides for the determination of specified budgets of LEAs in accordance with regulations made under s 45 relating to (1) the

---

[1]   SSFA 1998, Sch 3, para 10.
[2]   Ibid, Sch 3, para 11.
[3]   Ibid.
[4]   Section 45 applies also to new schools: see s 45(3)(b).
[5]   These were inserted by ss 41 and 42 of the EA 2002, and s 46 of the SSFA 1998 was repealed by Part 3 of Sch 22 to the EA 2002.
[6]   As amended by para 66 of Sch 7 to the Local Government Act 2003.

'LEA budget', (2) an LEA's 'schools budget', and (3) an LEA's 'individual schools budget'. The current regulations in relation to England are the LEA Budget, Schools Budget and Individual Schools Budget (England) Regulations 2002,[1] and, for the school year 1 April 2004 onwards, the LEA Budget, Schools Budget and Individual Schools Budget (England) Regulations 2003.[2] In relation to Wales the regulations are the LEA Budget, Schools Budget and Individual Schools Budget (Wales) Regulations 2003.[3]

7.136 Sections 45B and 45C empower the Secretary of State (and, in relation to Wales, the National Assembly for Wales[4]), by means of a notice given under s 45B(4), to set a 'minimum schools budget' for an LEA where he is satisfied that the LEA's schools budget for a financial year is 'inadequate',[5] or where the LEA has not set a schools budget for the following financial year by the schools budget deadline in any financial year.[6] The Secretary of State must give reasons for the giving of such a notice.[7] No minimum budget may be so set where the LEA (or LEAs) to which the notice relates object under s 45C(1). In that case, the Secretary of State must set the minimum budget by means of a statutory instrument,[8] approved by a resolution of the House of Commons.[9] Such minimum budget may not be greater than that which was specified in the notice given under s 45B(4).[10]

7.137 Section 47 of the SSFA 1998 provides for the determination of a school's budget share, but leaves the mechanics to regulations made under that section. Section 48 of the SSFA 1998 provides for the preparation of schemes for the delegation of budgets, and again leaves much to regulations made under that section. The current regulations made under those sections in relation to England are the Financing of Maintained Schools (England) Regulations 2003[11] and the Financing of Maintained Schools (England) (No 2) Regulations 2003.[12] These make extensive provision, including in connection with the amounts to be deducted from the budget share of a school which has permanently excluded a pupil and the amounts to be added to the budget share of any school which that pupil now attends.[13] It is of note that an LEA's formula for determining (or redetermining) budget shares for primary and secondary schools must provide that at least 75 per cent of the amount which is their individual schools budget, less certain amounts, is allocated in certain ways.[14] There are several important differences between these two sets of regulations. Unlike the first set of

---

[1]   SI 2002/3199.
[2]   SI 2003/3170, as amended by SI 2004/659.
[3]   SI 2003/3118.
[4]   References to the Secretary of State in what follows are to be read as including references to the National Assembly for Wales.
[5]   SSFA 1998, s 45B(1).
[6]   Ibid, s 45B(2), as amended by para 66 of Sch 7 to the Local Government Act 2003.
[7]   Ibid, s 45B(6).
[8]   See ibid, ss 45C(2), 138(1) and 142(1).
[9]   See ibid, s 45C(5).
[10] Ibid, s 45C(3).
[11] SI 2003/453.
[12] SI 2003/3247, as amended by SI 2004/659.
[13] See reg 22 of both sets of regulations.
[14] See reg 26(1) of both sets of regulations.

regulations, the later regulations apply to maintained nursery schools.[1] They also provide for a (new) minimum funding guarantee.[2]

Schools forums

7.138 Section 43 of the EA 2002 inserted a new s 47A into the SSFA 1998, requiring every LEA to establish schools forums for their area in accordance with regulations to be made under the new section. One main purpose of a schools forum is 'to advise the relevant authority on such matters relating to the authority's schools budget as may be prescribed by regulations'. Another main purpose is to be consulted as to matters prescribed by regulations concerning the schools budget. The current regulations for all of these purposes are the School Forums (England) Regulations 2002[3] and the Schools Forums (Wales) Regulations 2003.[4]

The making, revision and publication of schemes of local management

7.139 Schedule 14 to the SSFA 1998 governs the making, revision and publication of schemes of local management. In England, schemes must be approved by the Secretary of State. In Wales, schemes must be approved by the National Assembly for Wales.[5]

The effect of local management

7.140 Section 49 of the SSFA 1998 requires every maintained school to have a delegated budget. Section 50 of that Act states the effect of having a delegated budget. Those sections make clear several matters which had to be deduced under the 1996 Act. Two of those matters are set out in s 49(5) as follows:

> 'Any amount made available by a local education authority to the governing body of a maintained school (whether under section 50 or otherwise) –
> (a)   shall remain the property of the authority until spent by the governing body or the head teacher; and
> (b)   when spent by the governing body or the head teacher, shall be taken to be spent by them or him as the authority's agent.'[6]

7.141 Section 51A(1) of the SSFA 1998 makes some related, but rather different, provision concerning expenditure incurred by a governing body in the exercise of the power conferred by s 27 of the EA 2002 to provide community facilities. This is that as against third parties, such expenditure is to be treated as part of the expenses of

---

[1]   See SI 2003/3247, reg 1(3)(p).
[2]   See reg 15 and Sch 2.
[3]   SI 2002/2114, as amended by SI 2004/447.
[4]   SI 2003/2909.
[5]   See SI 1999/672.
[6]   This is subject to the exceptions that amounts spent (a) by way of repayment of the principal of, or interest on, a loan, or (b) to meet expenses payable by the governing body of a voluntary aided school in respect of the maintenance of the school under (in England) para 3(1) of Sch 3 to the SSFA 1998, or (in Wales) para 3(1) or (2) of Sch 3, or (in both England and Wales) para 14(2) of Sch 6, are not spent as the agent of the authority: s 49(6), as amended in relation to England by SI 2002/906, Art 4.

maintaining the school under s 22 of the SSFA 1998, but if it is met by the LEA then it may be recovered by them from the governing body.

7.142   Section 50 of the SSFA 1998 sets out the effect of financial delegation:

> '(1)   Where a maintained school has a delegated budget in respect of the whole or part of a financial year the local education authority shall secure that in respect of that year there is available to be spent by the governing body –
>
> (a)   where the school has a delegated budget in respect of the whole of that year, a sum equal to the school's budget share for the year, or
>
> (b)   where the school has a delegated budget in respect of only part of that year, a sum equal to that portion of the school's budget share for the year which has not been spent.'

7.143   The governing body may then 'Subject to any provision made by or under the scheme, ... spend any such amounts as they think fit – (a) for any purposes of the school, or (b) (subject also to any prescribed conditions) for such purposes as may be prescribed'.[1] Section 50 of the SSFA 1998 does not, however authorise the governing body of a maintained school to pay governors allowances otherwise than in accordance with regulations.[2] Moreover, the 'purposes of the school' do not include purposes wholly referable to the provision of (a) facilities and services under s 27 of the EA 2002,[3] (b) part-time education suitable to the requirements of persons of any age over compulsory school age, or (c) full-time education suitable to the requirements of persons who have attained the age of 19.[4] Furthermore, s 51A(2) of the SSFA 1998 provides that except as provided by regulations made under s 50(3)(b), no expenditure incurred by the governing body in the exercise of the power conferred by s 27 of the EA 2002 to provide community facilities may be met from the school's budget share for any financial year. This is so both when the school has a delegated budget and when its right to such a budget has been suspended under s 17 of, or Sch 15 to, the SSFA 1998.[5]

Suspension of the right to a delegated budget

7.144   A governing body's right to a delegated budget may be suspended where it appears to the LEA that the governing body:

> '(a)   have been guilty of a substantial or persistent failure to comply with any delegation requirement or restriction,[6]
>
> (b)   are not managing in a satisfactory manner the expenditure or appropriation of the [school's budget share],[7] or

---

[1]   SSFA 1998, s 50(3). Purposes have been prescribed for England, in the School Budget Shares (Prescribed Purposes) (England) Regulations 2002, SI 2002/378, as amended by SI 2004/444.

[2]   Ibid, s 50(5). The current regulations are the Education (Governors' Allowances) Regulations 1999, SI 1999/703 and the Education (Governors' Allowances) (England) Regulations 2003, SI 2003/523.

[3]   Regarding which, see paras **7.166** et seq.

[4]   SSFA 1998, s 50(4).

[5]   Ibid, s 51A(3). See para **12.37** regarding s 17. See paras **7.144** et seq concerning Sch 15.

[6]   A 'delegation requirement or restriction' is 'any requirement or restriction applicable, under or by virtue of the scheme or s 50(3), to the management by the governing body of the school's budget share': SSFA 1998, Sch 15, para 1(7).

[7]   Ibid, para 1(1).

(c)   are not managing in a satisfactory manner any expenditure, or sums received, in the exercise of the power conferred by section 27 of the Education Act 2002.'[1]

7.145 The LEA must give the governing body not less than one month's notice in writing of the suspension unless 'by reason of any gross incompetence or mismanagement on the part of the governing body or other emergency it appears to the authority to be necessary' to give the governing body a shorter period of notice or to give the governing body a notice suspending its right to a delegated budget with immediate effect.[2] A copy of the notice must at the same time be given to the head teacher of the school,[3] and the LEA must send a copy of the notice to the Secretary of State.[4]

7.146 The notice must specify the grounds for the suspension, giving particulars of any alleged failure on the part of the governing body to comply with any delegation requirement or restriction, of any alleged mismanagement on the part of the governing body and, if applicable, the basis on which notice of less than one month was given.[5] The notice must also inform the governing body of its right to appeal against the suspension to the Secretary of State and of the time within which the appeal may be brought.[6] That period is 2 months from the date when the notice was received by the governing body, unless the notice did not inform the governing body of the right of appeal, in which case the period is 2 months from the time when the LEA informed the governing body in writing of its right of appeal.[7]

7.147 The LEA must review the suspension before the beginning of every financial year unless the suspension took effect less than 2 months before then.[8] The LEA may review the suspension at any other time if it considers it appropriate to do so. The LEA must give the governing body and the head teacher an opportunity of making representations with respect to the suspension when carrying out a review in either circumstance.[9] The governing body may appeal to the Secretary of State against a refusal to revoke the suspension in the same manner as it may appeal against the imposition of the suspension.[10]

7.148 The effect of the suspension of a maintained school's right to a delegated budget is that the duty imposed on the LEA by s 50(1) of the SSFA 1998 does not apply in relation to the school, but the LEA may permit the governing body to take decisions as to the spending of sums to be met from the school's budget share.[11] If the governing body decides in that situation that a particular sum should be spent,

---

[1]   SSFA 1998, as amended by EA 2002, Sch 3, para 5.
[2]   Ibid, Sch 15, para 1(2).
[3]   Ibid, Sch 15, para 1(5).
[4]   Ibid, Sch 15, para 1(6).
[5]   Ibid, Sch 15, para 1(3).
[6]   Ibid, Sch 15, para 1(4). The right of appeal arises under para 3 of Sch 15.
[7]   Ibid, Sch 15, para 3(2) and (3).
[8]   Ibid, Sch 15, para 2(1).
[9]   Ibid, Sch 15, para 2(2).
[10]   Ibid, Sch 15, para 3(1)(b). The exercise by LEAs of their functions under paras 1 and 2 of Sch 15 to the SSFA 1998 may be the subject of guidance in the code of practice issued by the Secretary of State under s 127 of the SSFA 1998.
[11]   Ibid, Sch 15, para 4(1).

then it must in spending the sum comply with 'such reasonable conditions as the authority think fit to impose'.[1] The governing body may delegate its powers in relation to that sum to the head teacher.[2]

Financial statements concerning LEAs' education expenditure

7.149 Financial statements are required under regulations made under s 52 of the SSFA 1998. The current regulations are the Education (Budget Statements) (Wales) Regulations 2002,[3] the Education (Budget Statements) (England) Regulations 2004,[4] the Education (Outturn Statements) (Wales) Regulations 2003[5] and the Education (Outturn Statements) (England) Regulations 2004.[6] An LEA may be directed by the Secretary of State to require the Audit Commission for Local Authorities and the National Health Service to make arrangements under s 28(1)(d) of the Audit Commission Act 1998 for certifying a statement or statements, or part or parts of a statement or statements, made under s 52.[7] Such a direction may be given in relation either to an individual LEA or LEAs generally, or to a class or description of LEAs.[8]

ACCOUNTS OF MAINTAINED SCHOOLS

7.150 Section 44 of the EA 2002 confers a power on the Secretary of State to make regulations requiring the governing body of a maintained school to keep accounts and records of sorts specified by the regulations and comply with conditions so specified with respect to audit in relation to (1) resources held by the governing body, and (2) 'other resources whose application is controlled by the governing body'.[9] Regulations have so far been made only in relation to England. They are the Consistent Financial Reporting (England) Regulations 2003.[10]

CONDUCT OF A MAINTAINED SCHOOL

7.151 There are several general duties imposed by statute on the governing body of a maintained school. One is a duty to conduct the school with a view to promoting high standards of educational achievement at the school.[11] Another is a duty to 'make arrangements for ensuring that their functions relating to the conduct of the school are exercised with a view to safeguarding and promoting the welfare of children who

---

1 SSFA 1998, Sch 15, para 4(2).
2 Ibid, Sch 15, para 4(3).
3 SI 2002/122.
4 SI 2004/417.
5 SI 2003/873.
6 SI 2004/1279.
7 SSFA 1998, s 53(1).
8 Ibid, s 53(3).
9 See ibid, s 44(1) and (2). Section 44 is currently in force in relation only to England: see SI 2003/124 and SI 2003/1667.
10 SI 2003/373, as amended by SI 2004/393.
11 SSFA 1998, s 38(2); EA 2002, s 21(1).

are pupils at the school'.[1] A third is to have regard to any guidance given by the Secretary of State about consultation with pupils in connection with the taking of decisions affecting them.[2]

7.152 As to the mechanics of the conduct of the school, s 21(1) of the EA 2002 states simply that:

'Subject to any other statutory provision, the conduct of a maintained school shall be under the direction of the school's governing body.'

7.153 However, s 21(3) is slightly different from its predecessor, s 38(3) of the SSFA 1998. Section 38(3) provided that regulations may:

'(a)　set out terms of reference for governing bodies of maintained schools;
(b)　define the respective roles and responsibilities of governing bodies and head teachers of such schools, whether generally or with respect to particular matters, including the curriculum for such schools;
(c)　confer functions on governing bodies and head teachers of such schools.'

7.154 The current regulations are the School Government (Terms of Reference) (Wales) Regulations 2000.[3] The provision in s 21(3)(a) and (c) is identical to that made in s 38(3)(a) and (c). However, s 21(3)(b) of the EA 2002 is more satisfactory than s 38(3)(b) because it includes the LEA in its scope, in that any regulations made under it may:

'define the respective roles and responsibilities in relation to the conduct of a maintained school (whether generally or with respect to particular matters) of –
(i)　the local education authority
(ii)　the governing body, and
(iii)　the head teacher.'

7.155 This therefore allows for a filling of the gap in the statutory scheme relating to the conduct of a maintained school which was exposed in cases such as *Ching v Surrey County Council*[4] and was acknowledged by Staughton LJ in *R v Secretary of State for Education and Science, ex parte E*,[5] where he said: 'The relationship between a local education authority and school governors is a thorny topic'. No regulations have so far been made under s 21(3), however, and therefore the (unamended) Education (School Government) (Terms of Reference) (England) Regulations 2000,[6] made under s 38(3) of the SSFA 1998, remain in force. Those regulations provide welcome clarity about the overall responsibilities of the governing body and the head teacher, but they of course make no provision for the respective functions of the LEA and the governing body of a maintained school. It may be that they were left unamended

---

[1]　EA 2002, s 175(2), which is currently in force in England only. There is a duty also to have regard to any guidance given to it by the Secretary of State or (as the case may be) the National Assembly: s 175(4). See further, para **2.63**.
[2]　See EA 2002, s 176.
[3]　SI 2000/3027, as amended by SI 2002/1396.
[4]　[1910] 1 KB 736.
[5]　[1992] 1 FLR 377, at 392D.
[6]　SI 2000/2122.

because of the reasonably comprehensive existing statutory regime. Reference is made in the following sections to the salient aspects of that regime which are not dealt with elsewhere in this book. Before turning to those aspects, however, it is noted that the particular difficulties which gave rise to *Ching v Surrey County Council* have been ameliorated by the enactment of s 29(5) of the EA 2002, which empowers the LEA to give a binding direction to the governing body and/or the head teacher of a community or voluntary controlled school, a community special school, or a maintained nursery school, 'concerning the health and safety of persons on the school's premises or taking part in any school activities elsewhere'.

School attendance targets

7.156 Section 63(1) of the SSFA 1998 empowers the making of regulations which may require, or enable the Secretary of State to require, 'governing bodies of maintained schools to secure that annual targets are set for reducing the level of unauthorised absences on the part of relevant day pupils at their schools'.[1] The circumstances in which such a requirement may be imposed are provided for in the regulations.[2] The current regulations are the Education (School Attendance Targets) (England) Regulations 1999[3] and the Education (School Performance and Unauthorised Absence Targets) (Wales) Regulations 1999.[4] When regulations made under s 53 of the EA 2002 are in force, s 63 of the SSFA 1998 will apply also to authorised absences.[5]

Determining school terms and times of school sessions

7.157 Section 41 of the SSFA 1998 used to provide and s 32 of the EA 2002 currently provides for the responsibilities of the governing body of a maintained school and of the LEA in relation to the fixing of dates of terms and holidays and the times of school sessions, and empower the making of regulations concerning related matters. The Changing of School Session Times (England) Regulations 1999[6] (which apply only to community, voluntary controlled and community special schools) and the Changing of School Session Times (Wales) Regulations 2000[7] (which also apply only to such schools) were made under s 41.

School meals

7.158 An LEA's duties under s 512 of the EA 1996 with regard to school meals are referred to above.[8] The governing body of any school maintained by an LEA is obliged by s 533(1) of the EA 1996 among other things to afford facilities to the LEA in connection with the LEA's functions under s 512. However, the governing body is

---

[1] A 'relevant day pupil' means a pupil who is registered at a maintained school, who is of compulsory school age, and who is not a boarder: s 63(4).

[2] See s 63(2)–(3).

[3] SI 1999/397, as amended by SI 2001/3785.

[4] SI 1999/1811.

[5] Section 53 is in force in England only (see SI 2004/1318) and no regulations have yet been made under it.

[6] SI 1999/2733.

[7] SI 2000/2030.

[8] See paras **4.30** et seq.

not obliged to incur expenditure in doing so.[1] If the school has a delegated budget and the governing body provides milk, meals or other refreshment to pupils or other persons who receive education at the school, then, as a result of s 533(3) of the EA 1996 (as amended by para 54 of Sch 21 to the EA 2002), it is obliged to charge for that provision and to charge every person the same price for the same quantity of the same item.[2]

7.159 As stated in para **4.36**, under s 512A(1) of the EA 1996, the governing body of a maintained school may be given the function of the provision of school lunches under s 512(1A) and (1B) of the EA 1996 and of providing free school lunches and milk in accordance with s 512(3)(a) and (b) of the EA 1996. Where such a governing body has the function of providing school lunches or milk free of charge under s 512(3)(a) or (b) as a result of such an order, s 533(3) of the EA 1996 does not apply to any school lunches or milk provided by the governing body in pursuance of the order.[3]

Power to form or invest in companies to provide services or facilities for schools

7.160 Under s 11(1) of the EA 2002 (which is currently in force in England only[4]), the governing body of a maintained school[5] which has a delegated budget[6] may 'form or participate in forming' companies to: (1) provide services or facilities for 'any schools';[7] (2) 'make, or facilitate the making of, arrangements under which facilities or services are provided for any schools by other persons';[8] or (3) 'exercise relevant local education authority functions'.[9] A 'relevant local authority function' for this purpose is one which is or may become 'exercisable by the company in accordance with an authorisation given or direction made by virtue of any enactment'.[10]

7.161 Furthermore, the governing body of a maintained school may:

'with a view to securing or facilitating –
(a)   the provision by a company of services or facilities for any schools,
(b)   the exercise by a company of relevant local education authority functions, or
(c)   the making by any person of arrangements of the kind referred to in subsection (1)(c),

---

[1]   EA 1996, s 533(2).
[2]   In Wales, s 533 applies in its original form, and in that form it allows for differential charging as between pupils and other persons, but (1) all pupils must be charged the same as each other, and (2) all other persons must be charged the same as each other, for the same quantity of the same item.
[3]   EA 1996, s 512A(4)(b).
[4]   See SI 2002/2952.
[5]   The term 'maintained school' for this purpose includes a maintained nursery school: see EA 2002, s 11(9).
[6]   See EA 2002, s 12(1)(b).
[7]   Ibid, s 11(1)(a).
[8]   Ibid, s 11(1)(c).
[9]   Ibid, s 11(1)(b).
[10]   Ibid, s 11(9).

invest in the company which is to provide the services or facilities or exercise the functions or by which the arrangements are to be made or facilitated.'[1]

7.162 Moreover, the governing body of a maintained school may form, or participate in forming, one or more companies to purchase services or facilities for that school and other schools which are members of the company or companies.[2] Similarly, the governing body may 'with a view to securing or facilitating the purchase by a company of services or facilities for that school and other participating schools, become a member of the company'.[3]

7.163 It is of considerable significance that s 11(5) provides that the governing body may provide staff to any company in relation to which they have exercised a power of the sorts described in paras **7.160–7.162**.[4] Clear lines of responsibility will be required in case difficulties in the form of poor performance or misconduct on the part of the staff arise. Similarly, the extent to which a person is required to work for the company rather than in connection with the school itself will need to be clear, although some flexibility is likely to be beneficial for both affected members of staff and the governing body.

7.164 In exercising its powers under s 11(5), a governing body will need to have regard to any guidance given by the Secretary of State.[5] Furthermore, the governing body may not exercise any of its powers under s 11(1)–(4) without the consent of the LEA,[6] although regulations may be made restricting the circumstances in which an LEA may refuse to give such consent.[7] In addition, any company in relation to which such powers are exercised must satisfy any requirements of regulations made under s 12(3) of the EA 2002.[8] Regulations may be made under s 12(4)–(6) concerning the supervision of a relevant company by an LEA. The School Companies Regulations 2002[9] were made for all of these purposes. They are for the most part uncontroversial. One interesting provision is reg 26, which states that a supervising LEA must (a) 'monitor the management and finances of the school company', and (b) 'notify members of the company and relevant local education authorities if it considers that the company is poorly managed or there is a risk of the company becoming insolvent'.

7.165 In addition, the School Companies (Private Finance Initiative Companies) Regulations 2002[10] were made under s 12. Of most interest is reg 6, which provides that the governing body of a maintained school which is a member of a school company may pay part of its delegated budget to that company (which, it is to be presumed, is a school PFI company within the meaning of reg 4 of those regulations)

---

[1]   EA 2002, s 11(2). The definition of 'invest' is in s 11(10).
[2]   Ibid, s 11(3) and (9).
[3]   Ibid, s 11(4). A 'participating school' in relation to a company is a school whose governing body is, or is to be, a member of the company: s 11(9).
[4]   Ibid, s 11(5).
[5]   Ibid, s 11(6). Such guidance was issued on 20 January 2003. It is available online at www.teachernet.gov.uk.
[6]   Ibid, s 12(1)(a).
[7]   Ibid, s 12(8).
[8]   Ibid, s 12(2).
[9]   SI 2002/2978, as amended by SI 2003/2049.
[10] SI 2002/3177.

only (a) as consideration for services or facilities that the company has supplied or procured for the school, or (b) where such payment is 'necessary or expedient to enable the company to pursue its objects'.

Provision of community services and facilities

7.166 Section 27(1) of the EA 2002[1] allows the governing body of a maintained school to:

> 'provide any facilities or services whose provision furthers any charitable purpose for the benefit of -
> (a)   pupils at the school or their families, or
> (b)   people who live or work in the locality in which the school is situated.'

7.167 This power includes a power to '(a) incur expenditure, (b) enter into arrangements or agreements with any person, (c) co-operate with, or facilitate or co-ordinate the activities of, any person, and (d) provide staff, goods, services and accommodation to any person'.[2]

7.168 A governing body may charge for such services, subject to the prohibitions in Chapter 3 of Part 6 of the EA 1996.[3] However, the powers in s 27 are limited by the restrictions in s 28, which include that s 27 is limited by existing restrictions in a school's instrument of government and in a scheme of local management under s 48 of the SSFA 1998.[4] Regulations may be made under s 28(2) imposing further restrictions, and as a result of s 28(3), a governing body may exercise the power in s 27(1) 'only if and to the extent that they are satisfied that anything which they propose to do will not to a significant extent interfere with the performance of any duty imposed on them by section 21(2) or by any other provision of the Education Acts'.[5] Furthermore, the governing body must have regard to any guidance given by the Secretary of State under s 28(5)(a),[6] and[7] to any advice given to them from time to time by the LEA.

7.169 The words 'to a significant extent' in s 28(3) may be difficult to apply in practice. According to Baroness Ashton of Upholland, the Parliamentary Under-Secretary of State, Department for Education and Skills, speaking in Committee of the House of Lords on 9 May 2002:[8]

> 'The inclusion of the wording "to a significant extent" ensures that insignificant incidental effects on a school's main educational role are not seen as obstacles that would prevent

---

1   Which is in force both in England and in Wales. In relation to Wales, see SI 2003/1718.
2   EA 2002, s 27(2).
3   Ibid, s 27(3); see paras **2.136** et seq concerning charges and the prohibitions on them in Chapter 3 of Part 6 of the EA 1996.
4   Ibid, s 28(1).
5   See ibid, s 28(3); the duty in s 21(2) is to 'conduct the school with a view to promoting high standards of educational achievement at the school'.
6   Such guidance has been issued under the title 'Extended schools – providing opportunities and services for all'. It is available online at www.teachernet.gov.uk.
7   See EA 2002, s 28(5)(b).
8   *Hansard*, vol 634, col 1372.

worthwhile services being established. For instance, it might be argued that adults using an [information and communications technology] suite on school premises during school hours could potentially impact on teachers' and pupils' flexibility to use that suite. But the other side of that example is, of course, that it should have no significant effect in practice on children's learning; and evidence shows that this type of activity can have a positive impact on the achievement of those pupils. Adults learning in schools provide good role models for all pupils, developing positive attitudes towards teaching and learning.'

7.170   In any event, before exercising the power in s 27(1), the governing body must consult (1) the LEA, (2) the staff of the school, (3) the parents of registered pupils at the school, (4) such of the pupils as the governing body consider appropriate in the light of their age and understanding, and (5) 'such other persons as the governing body consider appropriate'.[1]

Collaboration with other governing bodies

7.171   Section 26 of the EA 2002 empowers the making of regulations allowing the governing bodies of two or more maintained schools 'to arrange for any of their functions to be discharged jointly or by a joint committee of theirs' and for making consequential provisions. Regulations have been made under s 26 in relation to England only (since s 26 has come into force only in England[2]), and they are the School Governance (Collaboration) (England) Regulations 2003.[3] These allow two or more governing bodies to arrange for 'any of their functions to be discharged jointly'.[4]

Complaints procedures

7.172   Section 29(1) of the EA 2002 requires the governing bodies of maintained schools to establish procedures dealing with all complaints relating to the school or to the provision of facilities or services under s 27 of the EA 2002 which are not provided for in some other statutory provision. The governing body must publicise the procedures so established.

Governor training

7.173   Section 22 of the EA 2002 requires the LEA to 'secure that every governor is provided, free of charge, with such information as they consider appropriate in connection with the discharge of his functions as a governor' and to 'secure that there is made available to every governor, free of charge, such training as they consider necessary for the effective discharge of those functions'.

---

[1]   EA 2002, s 28(4).

[2]   See SI 2003/124.

[3]   SI 2003/1962.

[4]   Regulation 3(1); this is expressed to be subject to regs 16–18 of the School Governance (Procedures) Regulations (England) 2003, SI 2003/1377, which relate to delegation of functions internally: see paras **7.95** et seq. It is also subject to the rest of the School Governance (Collaboration) (England) Regulations 2003.

Provision of teaching services to day nurseries

7.174 Section 535(1) of the EA 1996 Act empowers the governing body of a community, foundation or voluntary primary school which has one or more nursery classes to make arrangements under which it makes available to a day nursery[1] the services of any teacher who is employed by it in the school and who has agreed to provide his services for the purposes of the arrangements. However, this power can be exercised only at the request of the LEA and only on terms approved by it.[2] A teacher so employed remains a member of the teaching staff of the school and remains subject to the general directions of the head teacher.[3]

Further education in maintained schools

7.175 The governing body of a community, foundation or voluntary school or a community or foundation special school is responsible for determining whether or not to provide part-time education suitable to the requirements of persons of any age over compulsory school age or full-time education suitable to the requirements of persons who have attained the age of 19.[4] However, the governing body of a maintained special school must obtain the consent of the LEA to a determination either to commence or to cease such provision.[5] The governing body must secure that such education is provided in a room separate from that in which pupils are taught, unless a teacher[6] is present at the time.[7] A teacher is deemed to be present despite no teacher being present if it would be impracticable to secure the presence of a teacher in the room at that time and the absence does not last more than 5 minutes.[8]

Prohibition of political indoctrination

7.176 Section 406(1)(b) of the EA 1996 requires the LEA, the governing body of a maintained school (including a community or foundation special school established in a hospital[9]) and the head teacher of such a school to forbid the promotion of partisan political views in the teaching of any subject in the school. Section 407 requires the same persons to take such steps as are reasonably practicable to secure that where political issues are brought to the attention of pupils in relevant circumstances, 'they are offered a balanced presentation of opposing views'. Section 406(1)(a) prohibits 'the pursuit of partisan political activities by any of those registered pupils at a maintained school who are junior pupils'. Activities which take place otherwise than on the school's premises are affected by this prohibition only where they have been arranged for junior pupils either (1) by a member of staff, acting in his capacity as

---

1   Meaning a day nursery provided under s 18 of the Children Act 1989: EA 1996, s 535(4).
2   EA 1996, s 535(2). As for the terms, see s 535(3); for example, equipment may be supplied for use in connection with the arrangements. Section 535 complements the power of an LEA under s 515 of the EA 1996, as to which see para **2.76**.
3   Ibid, s 535(5); see also s 535(3)(b).
4   SSFA 1998, s 80(1).
5   Ibid.
6   Defined for the purpose by reg 2(2) of the Education (Further Education in Schools) Regulations 1999, SI 1999/1867.
7   SSFA 1998, s 80(2).
8   SI 1999/1867, reg 2(3).
9   EA 1996, s 406(3).

such or (2) by a person acting on behalf of (a) that member of staff (acting in his capacity as a member of staff) or (b) the school.[1]

Home-school agreements

7.177 Section 110(1) of the 1998 Act obliges the governing body of a maintained school to adopt a 'home-school agreement for the school, together with a parental declaration to be used in connection with the agreement'. A 'home-school agreement' for this purpose is a statement specifying:

'(a)   the school's aims and values;
(b)   the school's responsibilities, namely the responsibilities which the school intends to discharge in connection with the education of pupils at the school who are of compulsory school age;
(c)   the parental responsibilities, namely the responsibilities which the parents of such pupils are expected to discharge in connection with the education of their children while they are registered pupils at the school; and
(d)   the school's expectations of its pupils, namely the expectations of the school as regards the conduct of such pupils while they are registered pupils there.'[2]

7.178 A 'parental declaration' for this purpose is 'a document to be used by qualifying parents for recording that they take note of the school's aims and values and its responsibilities and that they acknowledge and accept the parental responsibilities and the school's expectations of its pupils'.[3] The governing body is under an obligation to take reasonable steps to secure that the parental declaration is signed by every registered parent of a pupil at the school who is of compulsory school age, unless the governing body considers, having regard to any special circumstances which apply to the parent or the pupil in question, that it would be inappropriate to do so.[4] Where the governing body considers that a registered pupil at the school 'has a sufficient understanding of the home-school agreement as it relates to him, they may invite the pupil to sign the parental declaration as an indication that he acknowledges and accepts the school's expectations of its pupils'.[5] The home-school agreement must be reviewed by the governing body from time to time.[6] Before adopting the home-school agreement or parental declaration, or revising the agreement, the governing body must consult the registered parents referred to above and any other person prescribed by regulations.[7]

7.179 In discharging any function under s 110, the governing body must have regard to any guidance given from time to time by the Secretary of State.[8] The Secretary of

---

1   EA 1996, s 406(2).
2   SSFA 1998, s 110(2).
3   Ibid. A 'qualifying parent' is 'a registered parent of a pupil at the school who is of compulsory school age': s 110(10). A 'registered parent' is one who is registered in the register required to be kept under s 434 of the EA 1996 Act, as to which see para **9.24**.
4   SSFA 1998, s 110(3) and (4).
5   Ibid, s 110(5).
6   Ibid, s 110(7).
7   Ibid, s 110(9). No such regulations have so far been made.
8   Ibid, s 111(1). See paras **2.34–2.36** concerning the impact of a duty to have regard to something. The relevant guidance is available on the DfES website at http://www.dfes.gov.uk/hsa.

State may by regulations oblige the governing body of a maintained school to ensure that any form of words, or form of words having a particular effect, is not used in a home-school agreement or (as the case may be) in a parental declaration.[1] Most importantly, neither the governing body nor the LEA where it is the admission authority may penalise a child because of a failure by his parents to sign a parental declaration by refusing to admit, or excluding him from, the school.[2] Furthermore, these bodies may not invite any person to sign the parental declaration at a time when the child in question has not been admitted to the school.[3] Finally, a home-school agreement 'shall not be capable of creating any obligation in respect of whose breach any liability arises in contract or in tort'.[4]

Publication and provision of information

7.180 The statutory provisions and regulations referred to in paras **4.52**, **4.53** and **4.55** apply not only to LEAs but also to the governing bodies of maintained schools. In addition, the Education (Pupil Information) (England) Regulations 2000[5] (which replace the Education (School Records) Regulations 1989[6] but are wider in their scope than those regulations were) and the Education (Pupil Information) (Wales) Regulations 2004[7] require the head teacher of a maintained school, except a nursery school, to keep a 'curricular record, updated at least once a year, in respect of every registered pupil at the school'.[8] Both sets of regulations also require the making, where necessary the transfer, and the disclosure of an 'educational record' for each pupil.

7.181 In addition, as indicated elsewhere in this book, information has to be made available in a number of other contexts, for example to parents of registered pupils at maintained schools in relation to sex education,[9] and in relation to school inspections.[10]

Provision of information to the Secretary of State

7.182 The governing body (or temporary governing body) of a community, foundation or voluntary school or a community or foundation special school must make such reports and returns, and give such information, to the Secretary of State as he may require for the purpose of the exercise of his functions in relation to education.[11] In addition, the governing bodies of all maintained schools must comply

---

[1]   SSFA 1998, s 111(2).
[2]   See ibid, s 111(4)(b) and (c) and s 111(5).
[3]   Ibid, s 111(4)(a).
[4]   Ibid, s 111(6).
[5]   SI 2000/297, as amended by SI 2001/1212, SI 2002/1680, SI 2003/1006 and SI 2004/1076.
[6]   SI 1989/1261.
[7]   SI 2004/1026.
[8]   Regulation 4 of both sets of regulations.
[9]   See para **11.23**.
[10]   See para **12.22**.
[11]   EA 1996, s 538.

with regulations made under s 537A of the EA 1996, which relate to 'individual pupil information'.[1]

Distribution of information concerning secondary and further education

7.183 Section 540 of the EA 1996 applies where the governing body of any school[2] providing primary education receives a request made by the governing body of any school providing secondary education relating to the distribution (free of charge) by the school providing primary education to parents of pupils at that school of information about the school providing secondary education. The governing body of the school providing primary education must secure that the request is treated no less favourably than any such request made by the governing body of any other school providing secondary education.[3]

7.184 Regulations made under s 541 of the EA 1996 require the governing bodies of all schools providing secondary education[4] to which information published under s 50 of the FHEA 1992 is given in accordance with the regulations by institutions within the further education sector, to distribute the information to all pupils who are in the second year of the fourth key stage[5] (unless the number of copies of the relevant document is not sufficient, in which case the manner of distribution is to be determined by the governing body).[6]

Governors' annual report and annual parents' meeting

7.185 Under s 42(1) and (2) of the SSFA 1998, the governing body of a maintained school was obliged to prepare a governors' report dealing with such matters as were specified in regulations. Section 42 has been repealed and replaced by s 30 of the EA 2002, but the regulations made under s 42(1) and (2) when those subsections were still in force continue to have effect. They are the Education (Governors' Annual Reports)

---

[1] See the Education (Individual Pupil Information) (Prescribed Persons) Regulations 1999, SI 1999/903, as amended by SI 2004/1377, the Education (School Performance Information) (England) Regulations 2001, SI 2001/3446, as amended by SI 2002/2017, SI 2003/537, SI 2003/2135 and SI 2004/1076, the Education (Information About Individual Pupils) (England) Regulations 2001, SI 2001/4020, as amended by SI 2002/3112 and SI 2003/3277, the Education (Information About Post-16 Individual Pupils) (Wales) Regulations 2003, SI 2003/2453, the Education (Information About Individual Pupils) (Wales) Regulations 2003, SI 2003/3237, the Education (Individual Pupil Information) (Prescribed Persons) (Wales) Regulations 2004, SI 2004/549 and the Education (School Performance Information) (Wales) Regulations 2004, SI 2004/1025.

[2] A 'school' means for this purpose a community, foundation or voluntary school or a community or foundation special school which is not established in a hospital: s 540(2).

[3] EA 1996, s 540(1).

[4] A 'school' means for this purpose a community, foundation or voluntary school or a community or foundation special school which is not established in a hospital: s 541(4).

[5] See para **11.7** regarding the fourth stage.

[6] The current regulations are the Education (Distribution by Schools of Information about Further Education Institutions) (Wales) Regulations 1994, SI 1994/1321. They appear to go slightly further than s 541 in that they apply to all maintained special schools, and not merely those which are not established in a hospital. The Education (Further Education Institutions Information) (England) Regulations 1995, SI 1995/2065 were revoked by SI 2003/51.

(England) Regulations 1999[1] and the School Governors' Annual Reports (Wales) Regulations 2001.[2]

7.186 Section 43(1) of the SSFA 1998 requires the governing body of a maintained school in Wales to hold a parents' meeting every year. The purpose of the meeting must be to provide an opportunity for discussion of (1) the governors' annual report, (2) the discharge by the governing body, the head teacher and the LEA of their functions in relation to the school, (3) 'the aims and values of the school', (4) 'how the spiritual, moral, cultural, mental and physical development of pupils is to be promoted at the school', (5) 'how pupils are to be prepared for the opportunities, responsibilities and experiences of adult life and citizenship', (6) 'the standards of educational achievement of pupils', and (7) 'how the governing body are to promote the good behaviour discipline and well-being of pupils'.[3] Regulations made under s 43(4) may govern the proceedings of the meeting; the current regulations are the Education (Annual Parents' Meetings) (Wales) Regulations 1999.[4]

7.187 Section 43 was repealed and replaced in relation to England by s 33 of the EA 2002.[5] It is rather less detailed than s 43. The purpose of the annual parents' meeting is now merely:

> 'to provide an opportunity for discussion of the manner in which the school has been, and is to be, conducted, and of any other matters relating to the school raised by parents of registered pupils.'[6]

7.188 Furthermore, although regulations may be made under s 33(3), their purpose can merely be to 'make provision as to circumstances in which a governing body are to be exempt from the obligation imposed by subsection (1)'.[7]

Provision of information by governing body and head teacher to LEA

7.189 Section 42(3) and (4) of the SSFA 1998 require the governing body of a maintained school in Wales to provide the LEA with 'such reports in connection with the discharge of their functions as the authority may require (either on a regular basis or from time to time)', and the head teacher to provide the same kind of report in the same manner to either the governing body or the LEA. The governing body is entitled to be notified of a requirement given by the LEA to the head teacher of this sort, and to be given a copy of the resulting report.[8] Section 42 has now been repealed and replaced in relation to England by s 30 of the EA 2002, but s 30(3)–(5), which replace s 43(3)–(5), are in materially the same terms as those of the latter subsections.

---

[1] SI 1999/2157, as amended by SI 2002/1171, SI 2002/2214 and SI 2004/1076.
[2] SI 2001/1110, as amended by SI 2002/1401 and SI 2004/1735.
[3] SSFA 1998, s 43(2).
[4] SI 1999/1407.
[5] See SI 2003/1667.
[6] EA 2002, s 33(2).
[7] See the Annual Parents' Meetings (Exemptions) (England) Regulations 2003, SI 2003/1921.
[8] SSFA 1998, s 43(5).

School voluntary funds

7.190 A maintained school voluntary fund may be held by any one or more of a number of people or bodies. For example, it may be held by an individual member of staff or by the head teacher *ex officio*. Alternatively, the voluntary fund could have been given to the governing body of the school, or to the LEA. Furthermore, the fund may be held for one or more of a number of possible purposes. However, it seems unlikely that the parents (who would be the main or only contributors to the fund) would have given their voluntary contributions to be used for (say) gifts to staff, or for gifts to pupils. It also seems unlikely that the contributions will have been intended by those who made them to be given to the employer of the staff, for the purposes of the employer. Rather, it seems most likely that the contributions will have been given to be used for the purpose of supplementing the money spent by the party or (in the case of a voluntary or foundation school) parties responsible for maintaining the school. On this basis, the contributions will have been given to be used for charitable purposes. The money will therefore probably be held (by whoever does hold it) either under a charitable trust for the general purposes of the school[1] or (if the money is given to the governing body of the school) beneficially.[2] Alternatively, the money may have been given to be used for a particular purpose such as the purchase of books for the school. The money so held would then in any event be held under a separate charitable trust.[3] The same would be true if the money had been given for the specific purpose of buying equipment such as a computer or computers.[4] The implications of this include that teachers could not automatically be disciplined for a failure to administer the fund properly.[5] They also include that if the governing body of the school were the trustee of the fund, then they would not be absolved from liability for breach of trust merely because they had validly delegated (under the relevant regulations, such as the School Governance Procedure Regulations 2003[6]) decisions in relation to the use of the fund.[7] However, the impact of such liability on individual governors is not entirely clear.[8]

7.191 In the event of the dissolution of the governing body of a maintained school, 'any land or other property which is held by them on trust for the purposes of the school' may be transferred by the governing body before their dissolution to 'any person to hold such land or other property on trust for purposes connected with the

---

[1] See Warburton, *Tudor on Charities* (Sweet & Maxwell, 9th edn, 2003), at p 49: 'Following the preamble [to the Charitable Uses Act 1601], gifts for the establishment or support of schools of learning generally are charitable'.

[2] See SSFA 1998, Sch 10, para 3(2)(c); EA 2002, Sch 1, para 3(3)(c).

[3] *Att-Gen v Marchant* (1866) LR 3 Eq 424.

[4] Cf *Re Harrow School Governors and Murray's Contract* [1927] 1 Ch 556.

[5] See further, O Hyams, 'Misapplication of state school voluntary funds' (1994) 6 *Education and the Law* 133. The overturning by the House of Lords of the decision of the Court of Appeal in *Target Holdings v Redferns* (see [1996] AC 421) does not affect the analysis in that article.

[6] SI 2003/1377, reg 16, regarding which, see para **7.95**.

[7] The possibility of such delegation, and of delegation under trust law, is discussed in the article referred to in footnote 5 above. See further, D Morris, *Schools: an education in charity law* (1996, Dartmouth). However, Morris's description (ibid, p 29) of county schools as not being charities 'because usually no assets are held on charitable trusts or dedicated to charitable purposes' is probably misleading, given the powers referred to in footnote 2 above, and the existence of school voluntary funds.

[8] See paras **19.17** et seq.

provision of education in maintained schools'.[1] If no such transfer occurs, however, then (subject to exceptions) such property vests in the LEA.[2] If the governing body holds property beneficially (albeit for the purposes of the school in question), then, subject to the same exceptions, that property will also pass to the LEA.[3]

Insurance

7.192 Where the governing body of a maintained school has liabilities which are different from those of the LEA and in respect of which the LEA have no liability, insurance in respect of those liabilities will (as a matter of law) have to be obtained by the governing body rather than the LEA. It may be that the governing body could properly look to the LEA to meet the cost of obtaining such insurance, as part of the duty of the LEA to maintain the school,[4] but that is another matter. In addition, where the governing body of a maintained school holds property in its own right, the insurance policies of the LEA will as a matter of law be incapable of applying to that property unless the LEA are under some obligation to replace that property in the event of its loss. The basis for both of these propositions is that before an insurance policy can properly be relied upon by an insured party, the insured party must normally have suffered a loss in respect of which the policy was intended to provide an indemnity. This in turn is because if no loss will be suffered by an insured party if the insured event occurs, then, unless one of a few exceptions applies, that party has no insurable interest, and that party will be unable to enforce the contract of insurance.[5] (If there is no insurable interest at all under a policy, then the policy is a wagering contract, and therefore void.[6]) Accordingly, for example, an LEA's insurance policy could not properly be relied upon by the LEA in respect of a loss suffered only by the governing body of a school maintained by the LEA (and which the LEA will not be under a duty to make good).

7.193 A governing body may, however, despite this principle, obtain insurance in respect of property held by the governing body not only for their general purposes but also under a charitable trust. This is because property held by a trustee may be insured, despite the trustee having no beneficial interest in the property, the situation of a trustee being one of the exceptions to the general rule referred to above.[7]

School trips

7.194 A school trip may be purely educational, it may be part educational and part recreational, or it may be purely recreational. Where the trip is purely educational, then s 29(3) of the EA 2002 may be relevant. That provides:

---

[1]   SSFA 1998, Sch 22, para 7(4).
[2]   See ibid, Sch 22, para 7(2).
[3]   Ibid.
[4]   Under s 22 of the SSFA 1998.
[5]   See eg ER Hardy-Ivamy, *General Principles of Insurance Law* (6th edn, Butterworths, London, 1993) at pp 23–24; N Legh-Jones, *MacGillivray on Insurance Law* (10th edn, Sweet & Maxwell, 2003), at para 1.123. The case of *Cosford Union v Poor Law and Local Government Officers' Mutual Guarantee Association Ltd* (1910) 103 LT 463, at 465 per Phillimore J, is particularly apposite.
[6]   ER Hardy-Ivamy, *General Principles of Insurance Law*, ibid.
[7]   See *Lonsdale & Thompson Ltd v Black Arrow plc* [1993] Ch 360, at 369B–D.

'The governing body of a maintained school may require pupils in attendance at the school to attend at any place outside the school premises for the purpose of receiving any instruction or training included in the secular curriculum for the school.'[1]

7.195 Where a trip is recreational (albeit that there is an educational element to it, for example because the trip is to a foreign country), the school is likely either to request or to acquiesce in the attendance of staff or parents for the purpose of looking after the pupils while they are on the trip. Unless (for example) the governing body of the school engage those staff or parents as agents of the governing body, the governing body will not be able to insure against the liability of those staff or agents in respect of negligence. This is for the reason indicated above:[2] that the governing body will have no insurable interest in respect of such liability. It could, however, bear the cost to the staff or parents of obtaining insurance to cover their individual liabilities.

7.196 Furthermore, it will be necessary to be clear about the party which is organising the trip and purchasing, for example, tickets in connection with it: it could be, for example, the governing body acting in its own right or a teacher acting in his own right, or it could be either of these (or some other party) acting as agent for the parents of the children. If there is no such clarity, then obtaining damages in respect of a breach of contract by, for example, a tour operator will be more time-consuming and therefore potentially more costly.

A DISCUSSION CONCERNING THE RELATIONSHIPS BETWEEN THE VARIOUS BODIES CONCERNED IN THE RUNNING OF A VOLUNTARY SCHOOL

7.197 A number of bodies or persons may be involved in the establishment of a voluntary school. Furthermore, others may have rights and responsibilities in relation to the property used for the school. For these reasons, and in any event, it is helpful to consider the relationships between the various persons or bodies who may have rights or duties in relation to the conduct, or running, of a voluntary school.

7.198 In the first instance real property (that is, rights in relation to land) must be given or purchased for the use of a voluntary school. When such property is given, it is usually given on trust to be used for the purposes of a school of the sort required by a declaration of trust. (Such a trust is clearly a charitable one.) Where that occurs, the trustees have duties in relation to that part of the school property which was given to them on trust, under the instrument governing the trust. It appears that sometimes the trust deed[3] gives the property to the foundation governors as such, or to the governors by virtue of their office,[4] with the result that some members of the

---

[1]   The power of the LEA to give a binding direction concerning health and safety to certain governing bodies, under s 29(5) of the EA 2002, should be noted in this context. See para **7.155** concerning this power.

[2]   Paragraph **7.192**.

[3]   Or the scheme where the trust is administered under a scheme made by eg the Charity Commissioners.

[4]   See, for example, s 180 of the EA 1996, which has been repealed and replaced by s 83 of the SSFA 1998 but which provides a good illustration for present purposes.

governing body may have two roles. Nevertheless that does not mean that the distinction between the role and responsibilities of the trustees as compared with that of the governing body is blurred: a relevant governor would need simply to be clear about the role which he was fulfilling in relation to any relevant act.[1]

7.199 At times under now repealed statutes, the governing body of a voluntary school has had to provide real property to be used for the purposes of the school. Where that has occurred and the governing body owns the property, it either owns and holds the property 'beneficially' (retaining outright ownership) or holds it under a (charitable) trust for the purposes of the school. Where this occurs, the governing body have a dual role – first, as the owner or trustee of property held for the purposes of the school; and, secondly, as a governing body under the Education Acts.

7.200 The governing body of a voluntary aided school simply has the function of the management of part of the school's premises. The governing body is not as a result of the Education Acts the owner of the premises and does not manage them as a trustee under those Acts, although it is true that the governing body's functions under SSFA 1998 and its predecessors have meant that in practice the trustees need no longer be concerned with their corresponding responsibilities.[2]

7.201 What then, or who, are the trustees of a school? Guidance may be thought to be capable of being found in the definition of a charity for the purposes of the Charities Act 1993 (CA 1993), and hence for example for the purpose of registration with the Charity Commissioners. That definition is as follows:

> 'any institution, corporate or not, which is established for charitable purposes and is subject to the control of the High Court in the exercise of the court's jurisdiction with respect to charities.'[3]

7.202 According to s 97 of the CA 1993, ' "institution" includes any trust or undertaking', and ' "charitable purposes" means purposes which are exclusively charitable according to the law of England and Wales'.

7.203 However, in some respects, these definitions are not helpful, since the word 'institution' could be interpreted to mean a school, and the trustees of the school would then be the body responsible for managing the school. However, in the case of a state school, the body responsible for managing the school is the governing body of the school as established under (currently) the SSFA 1998 or the EA 2002, and that body is clearly not the school's trustees for present purposes.

7.204 A trust is a relationship to property, and a school is not normally thought of as a piece of property. Property is required for the purposes of the school, but that does not make that property the school. Accordingly, the phrase 'the school's trustees' in

---

[1]   Cf the speeches of Viscount Simon LC and Lord Porter in *Griffiths v Smith* [1941] AC 170, at 174–175 and 202–203 respectively.

[2]   Cf *Griffiths v Smith* [1941] AC 170, at 174–175 and 202–203.

[3]   CA 1993, s 96(1).

relation to a maintained school should be interpreted to mean 'any persons who hold property exclusively for the purposes of the school'.

The role of the governing body of a maintained school

7.205 This division – and occasional possible overlap – of functions between the various bodies involved in the running of a maintained school illustrates the unusual situation of the governing body of such a school. The fact that the governing bodies of voluntary aided schools are the employers of their staff (although the power of appointment is subject to restrictions except where there is a delegated budget[1]) can be seen to reflect the compromise reached in the Education Act 1944 in relation to denominational schools. It also emphasises the fact that the governing body in particular of a voluntary aided school is a hybrid.

7.206 The governing body of a maintained school constituted under SSFA 1998 is still something of an odd creature, although its peculiarities have been lessened as compared with the situation under EA 1996 and its predecessors. The same is true of the governing body of a maintained school constituted under the EA 2002. It is helpful that the SSFA 1998 recognises that the only institution (other than a simple trust or charitable company set up for purposes related to the school) which can properly be called a charity in relation to a maintained school, is the governing body. This is a product of s 23(1) of the SSFA 1998, which provides that the governing body of a foundation, voluntary, or foundation special school (and not the school itself) is an exempt charity for the purposes of CA 1993. Accordingly, it is possible to assert with some conviction that the word 'school' means the educational institution conducted by the body of persons (whether natural or legal, for example, in the case of a maintained school, the incorporated governing body) which is responsible for running the school.

7.207 Section 23(2) of the SSFA 1998 provides also that any 'institution' which is administered by or on behalf of the governing body of a foundation, voluntary or foundation special school or which is established for the general purposes of, or for any special purpose of or in connection with, that body or any school or schools of those types is, so far as it is a charity, also an exempt charity. However, the word 'institution' in s 23(2) should not be regarded as including the school itself. This is because (1) as mentioned above, the school as an institution is conducted by the governing body, (2) clearly the word 'school' is distinguished from the word 'institution' in s 23(2), (3) in order to have any practical purpose, a charity will need to have property, and (4) clearly a state school (as distinct from its governing body) does not hold or administer property.

7.208 The fact that the governing body of a community or community special school is, however, not an exempt charity, and indeed is not a charity for any purposes,[2] is puzzling, bearing in mind that (1) the incorporated governing body of any maintained school has power to 'acquire and dispose of land and other property',[3] and 'accept

---

1   See para **15.74**.
2   See the final words of SSFA 1998, s 23(1).
3   SSFA 1998, Sch 10, para 3(2)(b); EA 2002, Sch 1, para 3(3)(b).

gifts of money, land or other property and apply it, or hold and administer it on trust',[1] and (2) the purposes of a community or community special school are no less charitable than those of the other kinds of maintained school. It may be that Parliament has thought it necessary to emphasise the connection between a community or community special school and the LEA, and to do so by providing that community and community special schools are not to be charities. This may have been on the basis that although the purposes of an LEA are in many respects charitable, they are not exclusively so. In any event, it is clear that although (1) the purposes of the governing body of a community or community special school are no less charitable than those of the governing bodies of other maintained schools, and (2) the governing body may hold property for those (apparently charitable) purposes, in contrast to the position of the governing body of any other kind of maintained school, the governing body of a community or community special school is not a charity for any purpose.

ARE (A) THE GOVERNING BODY AND (B) THE HEAD TEACHER OF A MAINTAINED SCHOOL PUBLIC AUTHORITIES FOR THE PURPOSES OF THE HUMAN RIGHTS ACT 1998?

7.209 In *A v Head Teacher and Governors of the Lord Grey School*,[2] the Court of Appeal accepted that the governing body of a maintained school is a public authority for the purposes of the Human Rights Act 1998. The court also accepted that the head teacher of a maintained school is such a public authority, although Sedley LJ, with whom Lord Justice Clark and Dame Butler-Sloss P agreed, confessed to 'a visceral unease at the conclusion that the headteacher of a maintained school is a public authority for the purposes of the Human Rights Act'.[3]

---

[1]   SSFA 1998, Sch 10, para 3(2)(e); EA 2002, Sch 1, para 3(3)(e).
[2]   [2004] EWCA Civ 382, [2004] 2 WLR 1442, [2004] ELR 169, at paras 36–38.
[3]   Ibid, at para 38.

Chapter 8

SCHOOL PREMISES AND STATUTORY TRANSFERS OF PROPERTY

INTRODUCTION

8.1   In this chapter, the law of education relating to school premises is described. The sources of such law are diverse. This chapter concerns (1) the powers of LEAs to acquire such premises, (2) the control of those premises, including by means of regulations made under the EA 1996 and by governing bodies under Sch 13 to the SSFA 1998 or (in the future) regulations made under s 31 of the EA 2002, and (3) the first statutes made specifically in relation to education in what are now known as maintained schools – the School Sites Acts of 1841 onwards, as affected by the Reverter of Sites Act 1987. This chapter is also concerned with the statutory provisions relating to the transfer of property to or from the proprietors of educational institutions.

ACQUISITION BY LOCAL EDUCATION AUTHORITIES

8.2   An LEA may 'accept, hold and administer any property on trust for purposes connected with education'.[1] However, any intention by an LEA that a school other than a nursery school or a special school should be vested in them as trustees is treated as an intention to maintain the school as a community school.[2] As a result, s 28 of the SSFA 1998 needs to be complied with in relation to the intention.[3]

8.3   The Secretary of State may authorise an LEA to acquire compulsorily land which is required for (1) any of their functions under the Education Acts, (2) the purposes of any school or institution which is, or is to be, maintained by the LEA or which the LEA has a power to assist, or (3) the purposes of any Academy which has been or is to be established as a result of the implementation of proposals made pursuant to a notice published by the LEA under s 70 of the EA 2002 as long as the land forms the whole or part of the site identified in that notice in accordance with s 70(3)(a).[4] It is specifically provided for the avoidance of doubt that an LEA may also acquire land by agreement for the purposes of a school or institution which is, or is to be, maintained by the LEA or which the LEA has a power to assist, even though the land will not be held by the authority.[5]

---

[1]   EA 1996, s 529(1).
[2]   See ibid, s 529(2) and (3).
[3]   Ibid, s 529(2).
[4]   Ibid, s 530(1), as amended by the SSFA 1998 and para 9(2) of Sch 8 to the EA 2002. The provisions of s 530(2)–(4) are consequential.
[5]   Ibid, s 531(1); but see s 531(2).

APPROVAL OF SCHOOL AND RELATED PREMISES UNDER SECTIONS 542–545 OF THE EDUCATION ACT 1996

8.4   Section 542 of the EA 1996 enables the prescribing in regulations of standards for the premises of maintained schools. The LEA must secure that the premises of a school maintained by them conform to the prescribed standards.[1] The requirements in the regulations may, however, be relaxed by the Secretary of State in relation to a particular school by a direction made under s 543. That section applies where, for various reasons, the Secretary of State is satisfied that it would be unreasonable to require conformity with any relevant prescribed requirement, including in relation to playing fields.

8.5   The Education (School Premises) Regulations 1999 were made under s 542 of the EA 1996.[2] They concern the facilities which are to be provided in schools (including pupil referral units[3]). Such facilities include playing fields for pupils aged 8 or over (although that particular requirement does not apply to a pupil referral unit[4]), washrooms, changing facilities for pupils aged 11 or over, facilities for staff, and 'ancillary facilities'[5] such as for the passage of persons, storage, and food preparation. The regulations also concern load-bearing structures in a school building.[6]

8.6   Section 545 of the EA 1996 empowers the Secretary of State by order to direct that any provision in a local Act or a byelaw made under a local Act is not to apply, or is to apply only with modifications, in relation to a building required for the purposes of any school or other educational institution the plans for, or particulars in respect of which, the Secretary of State has approved. This power of exemption applies to, among other things, particulars submitted or approved under regulations made under s 544 or s 218(7) of the ERA 1988.[7]

8.7   Section 544 empowers the making of regulations requiring the Secretary of State's approval for the provision of new premises for, or the alteration of the premises of, any maintained school and any non-maintained special school. The regulations may also apply in the same way to any boarding hostel provided by an LEA for persons receiving education at any such school and may in addition make provision for the inspection of any such hostel.[8] The Education (Schools and Further and Higher Education) Regulations 1989[9] were made under the predecessor to s 544, but they now (as amended) make no reference to the Secretary of State's approval of premises or to the inspection of hostels.

---

1   EA 1996, s 542(2). The test whether the regulations have been breached is objective: *Reffell v Surrey County Council* [1964] 1 All ER 743, at 747D–E. As for enforcement, see *Bradbury v Enfield London Borough* [1967] 1 WLR 1311, the effect of which is discussed in para **3.35**.
2   SI 1999/2. DfEE Guidance 29/2000 is relevant.
3   This is the effect of the definition of a school in s 4 of the EA 1996.
4   Regulation 24(1).
5   See reg 7.
6   Regulation 15.
7   EA 1996, s 545(2)(a). See para **8.7** for the relevant regulations.
8   Ibid, s 544(1) and (2).
9   SI 1989/351.

OTHER STANDARDS WITH WHICH SCHOOL PREMISES MUST COMPLY

8.8 School premises must, in addition to being approved in the manner described above, comply with s 8 of the Chronically Sick and Disabled Persons Act 1970. This requires that appropriate provision be made regarding means of access to and within school buildings, parking facilities and sanitary conveniences.[1]

NUISANCE ON SCHOOL PREMISES

8.9 Section 547 of the EA 1996 applies where a person is, without lawful authority, present on the premises (including playgrounds, playing fields and other premises for outdoor recreation[2]) of (1) any school maintained by a LEA, (2) any non-maintained special school, (3) any independent school, or (4) any premises which are used by an LEA under s 508 of the EA 1996 wholly or mainly in connection with the provision of instruction or leadership in sporting, recreational or outdoor activities.[3] If that person 'causes or permits nuisance or disturbance to the annoyance of persons who lawfully use those premises (whether or not any such persons are present at the time)', he is guilty of an offence, punishable by a fine not exceeding level 2 on the standard scale.[4] He may also be removed from the premises in question under s 547(3) if (1) a police constable, (2) in relation to the premises of a school which is maintained by a LEA, a person whom the LEA has authorised for the purpose (but in the case of a foundation, voluntary aided or foundation special school, only with the consent of the governing body), (3) in the case of a foundation, voluntary aided or foundation special school, a person whom the governing body has authorised for the purpose, or (4) in the case of a non-maintained special school or an independent school, a person whom the proprietor has authorised for the purpose, has 'reasonable cause' to suspect that the person causing the nuisance or disturbance is committing or has committed an offence under s 547(1).[5] Proceedings for such offence may be brought only by (1) a police constable, (2) in relation to an offence committed on the premises of any maintained school, the LEA, or, in relation to the premises of a foundation, voluntary aided or foundation special school, a person whom the governing body have authorised to bring the proceedings, or (3) in relation to an offence committed on the premises of a non-maintained special school or an independent school, a person whom the proprietor has authorised to bring such proceedings.[6]

---

[1]   The provisions of the DDA 1995 concerning school premises are considered in paras **18.47** and (albeit obliquely) **18.50–18.55**.

[2]   EA 1996, s 547(2).

[3]   Ibid, s 547(1) and (2), as amended by para 1 of Sch 20 to the EA 2002.

[4]   Ibid, s 547(1). Level 2 is currenlty £500.

[5]   See Ibid, s 547(4).

[6]   Ibid, s 547(6) and (7), as amended.

USE OF MATERIALS OR APPARATUS WHICH COULD OR MIGHT INVOLVE A SERIOUS RISK TO HEALTH

8.10   There is a need to obtain the Secretary of State's approval for the use in maintained schools and non-maintained special schools of certain materials and apparatus which could or might involve a serious risk to health. The requirement arises under regulations made under s 546 of the EA 1996. The current provision is reg 7 of the Education (Schools and Further and Higher Education) Regulations 1989.[1] That regulation applies to radioactive substances with an activity in excess of 0.002 of a microcurie per gram, and to any apparatus in which electrons are accelerated by a potential difference of at least 5 kilovolts other than a television or (broadly) a visual display unit.

CONTROL OF THE PREMISES OF MAINTAINED SCHOOLS

Introduction

8.11   Section 31 of the EA 2002 has not yet come into force. That section provides:

> 'Regulations may make provision relating to the control by the governing body of a maintained school of the occupation and use of school premises.'

8.12   Those regulations will replace the detailed provisions of Sch 13 to the SSFA 1998. It is likely that the regulations will be similar in their effects to those of Sch 13, which are described below. It should be noted that the exercise by LEAs and governing bodies of their functions under Sch 13 may be (and in the case of Wales is) the subject of guidance in the code of practice issued under s 127 of the SSFA 1998.[2] Furthermore, para 8 of Sch 13 to the SSFA 1998 provides, presumably for the avoidance of doubt, that the power of the governing body of any maintained school to control the use of the premises of the school is subject to any arrangements made under or by virtue of (a) an agreement made under para 1 or 2 of Sch 10 to the ERA 1988, (b) a determination made in accordance with para 62 or 63 of Sch 8 to the FHEA 1992, (c) an agreement made under para 1 or 2 of Sch 5 to the FHEA 1992, or (d) a determination made in accordance with para 3 or 4 of that Schedule.[3]

Community and community special schools

8.13   The occupation and use of the premises of a community or community special school, both during and outside school hours, is under the control of the governing body subject to some significant limitations.[4] The most notable of these is the power of the LEA to give such directions as to the occupation and use of the premises 'as

---

[1]   SI 1989/351.
[2]   See paras 55–70 of the code for Wales; there is no such guidance in the current code for England.
[3]   As to all of which, see paras **8.48** et seq.
[4]   SSFA 1998, Sch 13, para 1(1) and (2).

they think fit'.[1] There are two other limitations, and they are that the use and control is subject: (1) if the governing body have entered into a transfer of control agreement under para 2 of Sch 13, to that agreement, and (2) to any requirement of any other enactment.[2] In exercising control of the occupation and use of the school's premises outside school hours, the governing body must 'have regard to the desirability of those premises being made available for community use'.[3]

8.14   The governing body may enter into a transfer of control agreement under para 2 of Sch 13 only if (1) its purpose, or one of its purposes, in doing so is to promote community use of the whole or any part of the premises,[4] and (2) if the agreement makes or includes provision for the use of the whole or any part of the school premises during school hours, only if it has first obtained the LEA's consent to the agreement in so far as it makes such provision. Where the governing body enter into such a transfer of control agreement, it must secure so far as reasonably practicable that the body which has control of the premises under the agreement (the 'controlling body'[5]) exercises control of the school premises in accordance with any directions given by the LEA under para 1(3).[6]

8.15   A transfer of control agreement is to be taken to include certain terms. These are as follows. The controlling body must have regard to the desirability of the premises being made available for community use.[7] Any directions given by the LEA to the governing body under para 1(3) must be notified by the governing body to the controlling body.[8] The controlling body must comply with any such directions so notified to it.[9] If reasonable notice in writing is given to the controlling body by the governing body that the premises (or a part of the premises specified in the notice) are reasonably required for use by or in connection with the school at times specified in the notice, the controlling body must allow the premises to be used by or in connection with the school for the purposes specified in the notice.[10] However, if a transfer of control agreement makes express provision for the use of the school premises to be occasionally under the control of the governing body instead of the controlling body, the express provision in the agreement is to prevail over the term just referred to if, at the time of entering into the agreement, the governing body was of the opinion that the express provision would be more favourable to the interests of the school than the term which would otherwise have been included by virtue of para 2(3)(c) of Sch 13.[11]

---

1   SSFA 1998, Sch 13, para 1(3).
2   Ibid, Sch 13, para 1(2). The definition of a 'transfer of control agreement' is in para 2(7).
3   Ibid, Sch 13, para 1(4). The definitions of 'community use' and 'school hours' are in Sch 13, para 9.
4   Ibid, Sch 13, para 2(1).
5   Ibid, Sch 13, para 2(7).
6   Ibid, Sch 13, para 2(6).
7   Ibid, Sch 13, para 2(3)(b)(ii).
8   Ibid, Sch 13, para 2(3)(a).
9   Ibid, Sch 13, para 2(3)(b)(i).
10   Ibid, Sch 13, para 2(3)(c).
11   Ibid, Sch 13, para 2(4) and (5).

Foundation and foundation special schools

8.16   The occupation and use of the premises of a foundation or foundation special school, both during and outside school hours, are, subject to two limitations, under the control of the governing body and/or if there is a trust deed for the school which provides for any person other than the governing body to be entitled to control the occupation and use of the school premises to any extent, that person (references to the governing body in this section are to be read as referring also to that person).[1] These limitations are that the use and control is subject (1) if the governing body has entered into a transfer of control agreement under para 4 of Sch 13, to that agreement, and (2) to any requirement of any other enactment.[2] In exercising control of the occupation and use of the school's premises outside school hours, the governing body must 'have regard to the desirability of those premises being made available for community use'.[3]

8.17   The governing body may enter into a transfer of control agreement under para 4 of Sch 13 only if (1) its purpose, or one of its purposes, in doing so is to promote community use of the whole or any part of the premises,[4] and (2) if the agreement makes or includes provision for the use of the whole or any part of the school premises during school hours, only if it has first obtained the Secretary of State's consent to the agreement in so far as it makes such provision.[5]

8.18   A transfer of control agreement is to be taken to include two terms. These are that the controlling body must have regard to the desirability of the premises being made available for community use,[6] and that if reasonable notice in writing is given to the controlling body by the governing body that the premises (or a part of the premises specified in the notice) are reasonably required for use by or in connection with the school at times specified in the notice, the controlling body must allow the premises to be used by or in connection with the school for the purposes specified in the notice.[7] However, if a transfer of control agreement makes express provision for the use of the school premises to be occasionally under the control of the governing body instead of the controlling body, the express provision in the agreement is to prevail over the term just referred to if, at the time of entering into the agreement, the governing body was of the opinion that the express provision would be more favourable to the interests of the school than the term which would otherwise have been included by para 4(3)(b) of Sch 13.[8]

---

[1]   SSFA 1998, Sch 13, para 3(1), (2) and (4).

[2]   Ibid, Sch 13, para 3(2). The definition of a 'transfer of control agreement' is in para 4(6).

[3]   Ibid, Sch 13, para 3(3). The definitions of 'community use' and 'school hours' are in para 9 of Sch 13.

[4]   Ibid, Sch 13, para 4(1).

[5]   Ibid, Sch 13, para 4(2).

[6]   Ibid, Sch 13, para 4(3)(a).

[7]   Ibid, Sch 13, para 4(3)(b).

[8]   Ibid, Sch 13, para 4(4) and (5).

Voluntary schools

Voluntary controlled schools

8.19   The occupation and use of the premises of a voluntary school, both during and outside school hours, is under the control of the governing body and/or if there is a trust deed for the school which provides for any person other than the governing body to be entitled to control the occupation and use of the school premises to any extent, that person (references to the governing body in this section are to be read as referring also to that person), subject to (1) any direction given by the LEA under para 5(3) of Sch 13, (2) any transfer of control agreement entered into by the governing body under para 6 of Sch 13, and (3) any requirements of an enactment other than the EA 1996 or regulations made under it.[1] The power of an LEA to give a direction under para 5(3) of Sch 13 is subject to para 7(1), and (2) of Sch 13, the effect of which is as follows. The governing body has the power to determine the use to which the school premises (or any part of them) are put on Saturdays when they are not required for (a) the purposes of the school, or (b) any purpose connected with education or the welfare of the young for which the LEA desires to provide accommodation on the premises (or the relevant part of the premises).[2] The foundation governors may determine the use to which the premises (or any part of them) are put on Sundays.[3] Transfer of control agreements for controlled schools reflect this power of the foundation governors (see further, below).

Voluntary aided schools

8.20   The regime in relation to the control of the premises of a voluntary aided school is similar to that for a voluntary controlled school. Most of the statutory provisions which apply to voluntary controlled schools also apply to voluntary aided schools. The difference between voluntary controlled and voluntary aided schools in this context is that the LEA's power to give directions is more limited. This is because the LEA may give directions in relation to the occupation and use of the school premises of an aided school only in relation to weekdays.[4] Even then, the directions may not concern more than 3 days in any week.[5] Furthermore, the directions may be given only if the premises (or relevant part of them) are not needed for the purposes of the school, and may only be given if both of two conditions are satisfied.[6] The first condition is that the LEA wishes to provide accommodation for any purpose connected with education or with the welfare of the young, and the second is that it is satisfied that there is no suitable alternative accommodation in its area for that purpose.[7]

---

[1]   See SSFA 1998, Sch 13, para 5(2), (3) and (4). For the definition of a transfer of control agreement, see para 6(7) of Sch 13.
[2]   Ibid, Sch 13, para 7(1).
[3]   Ibid, Sch 13, para 7(2).
[4]   Ibid, Sch 13, para 7(3).
[5]   Ibid, Sch 13, para 7(4).
[6]   Ibid, Sch 13, para 7(3).
[7]   Ibid.

Transfer of control agreements for voluntary schools

8.21   Transfer of control agreements for both kinds of voluntary schools are governed by para 6 of Sch 13. Paragraph 6(1) reflects the fact that there may be a trust deed for the school. That deed may be contravened by the transfer of control agreement, but only in so far as the transfer of control agreement, as empowered by para 6, is inconsistent with it. The governing body of a voluntary aided school may enter into a transfer of control agreement only if its purpose, or one of its purposes, in doing so is to promote community use of the whole or any part of the school premises.[1]

8.22   A transfer of control agreement for a voluntary school is to be taken to include the following terms. One is that the controlling body must have regard to the desirability of the premises being made available for community use.[2] In the case of a voluntary controlled school (1) any directions given by the LEA to the governing body under para 5(3), and (2) any determination made by the foundation governors under para 7(2), must be notified by the governing body to the controlling body.[3] In the case of a voluntary aided school, any directions given by the LEA to the governing body under para 7(3) must be notified by the governing body to the controlling body.[4] The controlling body must comply with any such directions so notified to it.[5] If reasonable notice in writing is given to the controlling body by the governing body that the premises (or a part of the premises specified in the notice) are reasonably required for use by or in connection with the school at times specified in the notice, the controlling body must allow the premises to be used by or in connection with the school for the purposes specified in the notice.[6] However, if a transfer of control agreement makes express provision for the use of the school premises to be occasionally under the control of the governing body instead of the controlling body, the express provision in the agreement is to prevail over the term just referred to if, at the time of entering into the agreement, the governing body was of the opinion that the express provision would be more favourable to the interests of the school than the term which would otherwise have been included by para 6(3)(c) of Sch 13.[7] The governing body must then 'so far as reasonably practicable secure that the controlling body exercises control in accordance with any such directions or determinations as are notified to that body' as mentioned.[8]

USE OF SCHOOL PREMISES IN CONNECTION WITH ELECTIONS AND FOR OTHER PUBLIC PURPOSES

8.23   If a parish council (or, in Wales, a community council) do not have a suitable public room vested in them, then a suitable room in the premises of a maintained

---

1   SSFA 1998, Sch 13, para 6(1). The definition of 'community use' is in para 9 of Sch 13.
2   Ibid, Sch 13, para 6(3)(b)(ii).
3   Ibid, Sch 13, para 6(3)(a)(i).
4   Ibid, Sch 13, para 6(3)(a)(ii).
5   Ibid, Sch 13, para 6(3)(b)(i).
6   Ibid, Sch 13, para 6(3)(c).
7   Ibid, Sch 13, para 6(4) and (5).
8   Ibid, Sch 13, para 6(6).

school may be used by them free of charge for specified meetings about parish affairs or for administrative purposes.[1] Reasonable notice must be given and the use by the council must not interfere with use of the premises for educational purposes.[2]

8.24 A candidate in a local, parliamentary or European Parliament election may, on giving reasonable notice, use a suitable room in a maintained school at reasonable times when it is not being used for educational purposes or in connection with a previously agreed letting, for holding public meetings.[3] Any expenses incurred and the cost of remedying any damage caused by such use must be borne by the candidate.[4] Such a room may also be used by the returning officer free of charge as a polling station for such elections.[5] Any expenses incurred or the cost of remedying any damage resulting from such use must be met by the returning officer.[6]

SCHOOL SITES ACTS 1841 ONWARDS

8.25 According to KP Poole,[7] the purposes of the School Sites Act 1841 (SSA 1841) were (1) to facilitate the acquisition of land for use in connection with the provision of elementary schools by voluntary bodies, and (2) to enable the conveyance of land where the grantor was not the absolute owner or was under some other legal disability. Section 2 contains the main operative provision. Its terms (as amended) among other things reflect the then somewhat convoluted drafting style of enactments, and are as follows.

'Any person, being seised in fee simple, fee tail, or for life, of and in any manor or lands of freehold, copyhold or customary tenure, and having the beneficial interest therein ... may grant, convey or enfranchise by way of gift, sale, or exchange, in fee simple or for a term of years, any quantity not exceeding one acre of such land, as a site for a school for the education of poor persons, or for the residence of the schoolmaster or schoolmistress, or otherwise for the purposes of the education of such poor persons in religious and useful knowledge; provided that no such grant made by any person seised only for life of and in any such manor or lands shall be valid, unless the person next entitled to the same in remainder, in fee simple or fee tail, (if legally competent) shall be a party to and join in such grant; Provided also, that where any portion of waste or commonable land shall be gratuitously conveyed by any lord or lady of a manor for any such purposes as aforesaid, the rights and interest of all persons in the said land shall be barred and divested by such conveyance; Provided also, that upon the said land so granted as aforesaid, or any part thereof, ceasing to be used for the purposes in this Act mentioned,[8] the same shall thereupon immediately revert to and become a portion of the

---

1   Local Government Act 1972, s 134. However, any expenses incurred in connection with the council's use of the premises must be paid for, and any damage made good, by the council: ibid.
2   Ibid.
3   Representation of the People Act 1983, ss 95 and 96, as amended, and Sch 5; applied to European Parliamentary Elections by Sch 1 to SI 1999/1214.
4   Ibid, ss 95(4) and 96(4).
5   Ibid, ss 23 and 36, and Sch 1, para 22.
6   Ibid, Sch 1, para 22(2).
7   *Education Law* (Sweet & Maxwell, London, 1988), at para 1.150.
8   The words 'the purposes in this Act mentioned' were determined in *A-G v Shadwell* [1910] 1 Ch 92, at 99 to mean 'such of those purposes as are applicable to the case in question, namely, the purposes to

said estate held in fee simple or otherwise, or of any manor or land as aforesaid, as fully to all intents and purposes as if this Act had not been passed, any thing herein contained to the contrary notwithstanding.'[1]

8.26	The final words of this section have been called the 'right of reverter' in the section. That right has now been superseded by the provisions of s 1 of the Reverter of Sites Act 1987 (RSA 1987), which are considered below. However, the right of reverter in s 2 is also in apparent conflict with s 14 of the SSA 1841, which provides for a right on the part of trustees holding school property conveyed under the other provisions of that Act or under the provisions of its predecessor,[2] to sell or exchange:

> '[the] land or building, or part thereof, for other land or building suitable to the purposes of their trust, and to receive on any exchange any sum of money by way of effecting an equality of exchange, and to apply the money arising from such sale or given on such exchange in the purchase of another site, or in the improvement of other premises used or to be used for the purposes of such trust.'

8.27	This power is exercisable only on the direction or with the consent of any 'managers and directors' of the school. There are two provisos to s 14. The first is that if the land was given by an ecclesiastical corporation sole, then the consent of the bishop of the diocese is necessary for the sale or exchange. The second proviso is that if a portion of any parliamentary grant has been or will be applied towards the erection of any school, then no sale or exchange may take place without the consent of (now) the Secretary of State. The obvious solution of the apparent conflict of s 14 with the right of reverter in s 2 was to interpret s 2 as being subject to s 14. Section 6(2) of the RSA 1987 now makes explicit provision for the situation, by declaring that the exercise of the power conferred by s 14 of the SSA 1841 prevents any trust from arising under s 1 of the RSA 1987 in relation to the land sold or any land representing the proceeds of its sale. Apparently, it has been assumed that if a site is sold under s 14, any right of reverter is not transferred to some other site or the proceeds of sale: rather, such right is destroyed.[3]

8.28	Section 6 of the SSA 1841 enables corporations and:

> 'any officers, justices of the peace, trustees, or commissioners, holding land for public, ecclesiastical, parochial, charitable or other purposes or objects, subject to the provisions next hereinafter mentioned, to grant, convey or enfranchise, for the purposes of this Act, such quantity of land as aforesaid in any manner vested in such corporation, officers, justices, trustees, or commissioners.'

---

which the land was devoted by the grantor'. The Court of Appeal approved this determination in *Fraser v Canterbury Diocesan Board of Finance* [2001] Ch 669, at 680–682, paras 28–34.

[1]	In *Fraser v Canterbury Diocesan Board of Finance*, the Court of Appeal said (at para 47): 'No doubt section 2 of the 1841 Act could have been drafted more simply and more clearly, but it does make good sense once the purpose and the context of the 1841 Act are fully appreciated. As already explained the purpose of the Act was to facilitate and encourage grants of school sites by removing legal obstacles present in the then unreformed law of real property. The context of section 2 involves a consideration of the complex, and now increasingly unfamiliar, state of real property law at the time of the 1841 Act'.

[2]	School Sites Act 1836. That Act contained no reverter proviso.

[3]	See *Property Law, Rights of Reverter* (Law Commission No 111), Cmnd 8410, para 42, at p 15. The assumption was approved by the Law Commission working party whose report is printed in that document: see ibid, at para 43.

8.29 The provisions 'next hereinafter mentioned' require the consent of the poor law commissioners to the grant of parochial property under the section.[1] In addition, the grant of relevant property by any ecclesiastical corporation sole 'being below the dignity of a bishop' requires the consent of the bishop of the diocese to whose jurisdiction that corporation is subject. The third proviso to s 6 enables decisions to be made otherwise than by an outright majority of the actual body of the relevant officers, trustees (other than parochial trustees) or commissioners. There is no reverter provision in s 6, and it seems to have been accepted by the Court of Appeal that no right of reverter arose under s 6.[2]

8.30 The provisions of the SSA 1841 were supplemented by those of the School Sites Acts of 1844, 1849, 1851 and 1852. That of 1852 extended the scope of the SSA 1841 to sites to be used for the purpose of 'schools or colleges for the religious or educational training of the sons of yeomen or tradesmen or others, or for the theological training of candidates for holy orders'. The other provisions of those subsequent Acts were enacted to explain and extend the machinery of the SSA 1841.

8.31 A number of difficulties have arisen in relation to the interpretation of the provisions of the SSA 1841. Some of those difficulties were solved by the enactment of the RSA 1987, but others remain. Those which remain are considered below, after the provisions of the RSA 1987 have been described.

REVERTER OF SITES ACT 1987

8.32 The RSA 1987 applies not only to sites granted under the SSA 1841 and the other School Sites Acts referred to above[3] but also to those granted under the Literary and Scientific Institutions Act 1854 and the Places of Worship Sites Act 1873.[4] Section 1 of the RSA 1987 (as amended by the Trusts of Land and Appointment of Trustees Act 1996) replaces the right of reverter in (so far as relevant) s 2 of the SSA 1841 with a trust. The trust is in favour of those in whom the right of reverter would otherwise have arisen under s 2. The trustees are those who had title to the land before the trust arose under s 1 of the RSA 1987. That section is retrospective in that it is deemed 'always' to have had effect.[5] However, as a result of s 1(4), s 1 does not confer any right on any person as a beneficiary in relation to (a) any property in respect of which that person's claim was statute-barred before the commencement of the RSA 1987 or any property derived from such property, or (b) any rents or profits received, or breach of trust committed, before the commencement of the RSA 1987. Similarly, as a further result of s 1(4), anything validly done before the commencement of the RSA 1987 in relation to relevant land is, if done by the beneficiaries, deemed so

---

1   That power to consent is now held by the Secretary of State (meaning one of Her Majesty's Principal Secretaries of State: Interpretation Act 1978, s 5, Sch 1): see Local Government Board Act 1871, s 2; Ministry of Health Act 1919, s 3(1)(a), (5), Sch 1; SI 1951/142, as amended by SI 1951/753 and SI 1951/1900 (see in particular Art 2(1) and First Sch to SI 1951/753); and SI 1970/1681.

2   See *Hornsey DC v Smith* [1897] 1 Ch 843, at 863.

3   The Act applies to 'the School Sites Acts': s 7(1)(a). That expression means the 1841, 1844, 1849, 1851 and 1852 Acts: Short Titles Act 1896, s 2, Sch 2.

4   RSA 1987, s 7(1).

5   Ibid, s 1(1).

far as necessary for preserving its validity, to have been done by the trustees. If a change of use of relevant land occurs with the result that the original purpose for which the land was given ceases, then there is a reversion of the ownership of the land at that point. There is no need for the change to be 'institutional', but there must be more than merely the incidental carrying out of activities which are not authorised by the trust.[1]

8.33   The question whether the limitation period has run may be affected by the question of how the right of reverter in s 2 of the SSA 1841 took effect before the RSA 1987 was enacted. In *Re Clayton's Deed Poll*,[2] Whitford J held that when a site reverted under s 2, an equitable interest arose in favour of the person entitled to the site under the reverter, and that those who held the site as trustees now did so on trust for that person.[3] The trustees were then under a duty, as a result of s 3(3) of the Law of Property Act 1925, to convey the legal estate in the site to that person. The limitation period therefore could not at any time commence in favour of the trustees.[4] However, in *Re Rowhook Mission Hall*,[5] Nourse J held that time began to run for the purpose of the limitation period once the reverter operated.[6] The RSA 1987 appears to have been drafted on the assumption that the decision in *Re Rowhook* is the correct one. Section 3(3) of the Law of Property Act 1925 was in any event repealed by the RSA 1987.[7]

8.34   Where, as a result of s 1(4) of the RSA 1987, there are no beneficiaries, the trustees may act in relation to the property in question only: (1) for the purposes for which they could have acted in relation to the property if the RSA 1987 had not been passed; or (2) for the purpose of securing (a) the establishment of a scheme under s 2 of the RSA 1987 or (b) the making of an order under s 554 of the EA 1996.[8]

8.35   Under s 2(1) of the RSA 1987, the Charity Commissioners may, on the application of the trustees of property which is subject to a trust which has arisen under s 1 of that Act, as long as the requirements referred to below are satisfied, by order establish a scheme which (a) extinguishes the rights of beneficiaries under the trust, and (b) requires the trustees to hold the property on trust for such charitable purposes as may be specified in the order. Those purposes 'shall be as similar in character as the Charity Commissioners think is practicable in all the circumstances to the purposes (whether charitable or not) for which the trustees held the relevant land before the cesser of use in consequence of which the trust arose'.[9] However, in determining the character of those purposes, the Commissioners may, 'if they think it appropriate to do so, ... give greater weight to the persons or locality benefited by the

---

[1]   See *Fraser v Canterbury Diocesan Board of Finance (No 2)* [2004] EWCA Civ 15, (2004) 148 SJLB 149, at paras 24–27.

[2]   [1980] Ch 99.

[3]   Ibid, at p 108D–E.

[4]   See s 21 of the Limitation Act 1980.

[5]   [1985] Ch 62.

[6]   Once the limitation period had expired, the trustees held the land for charitable purposes.

[7]   RSA 1987, s 8(2).

[8]   Ibid, s 1(5). As for s 554 of the EA 1996, see para **3.83**.

[9]   Ibid, s 2(3).

purposes than to the nature of the benefit'.[1] The order must, however, be so framed as to secure that if a person who (a) but for the making of the order would have been a beneficiary under the trust, and (b) has not consented to the establishment of a scheme under s 2, notifies a claim to the trustees within the period of 5 years after the date of the making of the order, then the person is paid an amount equal to the value of his rights at the time of their extinguishment.[2] Furthermore, the Charity Commissioners must have given public notice of the order in such manner as they think sufficient and appropriate,[3] and a copy of the order must have been available for public inspection at all reasonable times at the Commissioners' office and at some convenient place in the locality where the relevant land is situated, for not less than one month after the date of the giving of the notice.[4]

8.36 Unless certain conditions are satisfied, the Charity Commissioners cannot make an order under s 2 unles (1) the requirements of s 3 have been satisfied or by virtue of s 3(4) do not apply, (2) public notice of the Commissioners' proposals has been given inviting representations to be made to them within a period specified in the notice (which must be not less than one month after the date of the giving of the notice), and (3) that period has ended and the Commissioners have taken into consideration any representations which have been made during that period and not withdrawn.[5] The conditions which need to be satisfied are set out in s 2(6), and concern claims in relation to the property which are outstanding or which have been accepted as valid, for example, by the trustees. Section 3 requires the trustees (except in certain circumstances[6]) to publish a notice setting out the relevant circumstances, stating that an application is to be made for the establishment of a scheme with respect to the property subject to the trust, and containing a warning to every beneficiary that, if he wishes to oppose the extinguishment of his rights, he should notify his claim to the trustees in the manner, and within the period specified, in the notice.[7] That period must be not less than 3 months from the date when the last notice of the relevant sort was published.[8] Such a notice must be published in two national newspapers and a local newspaper circulating in the locality where the relevant land is situated.[9] In addition, a copy of the notice must have been 'affixed to some object on the relevant land in such a position and manner as, so far as practicable, to make the notice easy for members of the public to see and read without going on to the land' for a period of not less than 21 days during the first month of the period of 3 months during which the beneficiary was able to notify his claim to

---

[1]   RSA 1987.

[2]   Ibid, s 2(4).

[3]   Ibid, s 4(1)(a).

[4]   Ibid, s 4(1)(b).

[5]   Ibid, s 2(5). Where the proposals are modified by the Commissioners after the giving of public notice under s 2(5), there is no need for a further notice: s 2(8).

[6]   Those circumstances are where the right of reverter under s 2 of the SSA 1841 arose before the commencement of the RSA 1987, and more than 12 years have elapsed since that time: s 3(4).

[7]   Ibid, s 3(2). The trustees may pay or apply capital money for any of the purposes of ss 2–4 of the RSA 1987: s 4(5).

[8]   Ibid, s 3(1)(b).

[9]   Ibid, s 3(1)(a).

the trustees.[1] Furthermore, the trustees must have considered what other steps could be taken to trace the persons who are or may be beneficiaries and to inform those persons of the application to be made under s 2.[2] They must also have taken such of those steps as it was reasonably practicable for them to take.[3]

8.37   An appeal against an order made under s 2 may be made to the High Court by (1) the Attorney General, (2) the trustees of the trust established under the order, (3) a beneficiary of the trust in respect of which the application for an order was made, (4) the trustees of that trust,[4] (5) any person 'interested in the purposes for which [those] trustees or any of their predecessors held the relevant land before the cesser of use in consequence of which the trust arose under s 1 [of the RSA 1987]', or (6) any two or more inhabitants of the locality where the land is situated.[5] The time-limit for the making of an appeal is 3 months from the date on which public notice of the order was given, unless the appeal is brought by the Attorney-General.[6] In addition, unless the appeal is brought by the Attorney-General, either the High Court must grant leave to appeal or the Charity Commissioners must give a certificate that the case is a proper one for an appeal.[7]

8.38   In *Bath and Wells Diocesan Board of Finance v Jenkinson*,[8] the successor in title to the original grantor of land under s 2 of the SSA 1841 had sold all of the land to a company, which was subsequently dissolved. The land ceased to be used for the purposes of a school in 1984 and was sold in 1990. It was held that the person entitled to the reversion (and therefore under the RSA 1987 as it then stood to the proceeds of sale) was the company, but that since the company had been dissolved, the beneficial entitlement was now vested in the Crown as bona vacantia.

RELATIONSHIP BETWEEN THE REVERTER OF SITES ACT 1987 AND SECTION 554 OF THE EDUCATION ACT 1996

8.39   An order made by the Secretary of State under s 554 of the EA 1996[9] may extinguish any rights to which a person is or may become entitled as a beneficiary under a trust arising under s 1 of the RSA 1987 in relation to relevant land or other property.[10] However, the Secretary of State may not extinguish any such rights by an order under s 554 unless he is satisfied that all reasonably practicable steps to trace the

---

[1]   RSA 1987, s 3(1)(d). This duty does not apply where the land is not under the control of the trustees and it is not reasonably practicable for them to arrange that a copy of the notice is affixed in the relevant manner: s 3(3).

[2]   Ibid, s 3(1)(e).

[3]   Ibid.

[4]   The trustees of a trust which has arisen under s 1 may pay or apply capital money for the purpose: see footnote 7 at para **8.36**.

[5]   RSA 1987, s 4(2).

[6]   Ibid, s 4(3)(a).

[7]   Ibid, s 4(3)(b).

[8]   [2003] Ch 89.

[9]   As to which, see para **3.83**.

[10]   RSA 1987, s 5(1).

persons who are or may become entitled to any of those rights have been taken, and that one of two sets of circumstances prevail. These are that either (a) there is no relevant claim which (i) is outstanding, (ii) has been accepted as valid by the trustees or those whose acceptance binds or will bind the trustees, or (iii) has been held in concluded proceedings to be valid, or (b) consent to the making of an order under s 554 has been given by every person whose claim to be so entitled is outstanding or has been so accepted or upheld.[1] Where applications for the extinguishment of the rights of any beneficiaries are made with respect to the same trust property both to the Secretary of State under s 554 and to the Charity Commissioners under s 2 of the RSA 1987, the Commissioners may consider or further consider the application to them only in two circumstances. Those are that the Secretary of State either (a) consents to the application made to the Commissioners being considered before the application made to him, or (b) disposes of the application made to him without extinguishing the rights of one or more of the beneficiaries.[2]

OUTSTANDING ISSUES OF INTERPRETATION CONCERNING THE SCHOOL SITES ACT 1841

8.40 There are several issues of interpretation concerning the SSA 1841 which remain unresolved by the RSA 1987. One is when the use which gives rise (now) to a trust under s 1 of the RSA 1987 ceases. A second is whether the cessation of the use of only a part of a relevant site can give rise to a trust under s 1 in respect of only that part of that site. A third question of interpretation which remains unresolved by the RSA 1987 arises most acutely where a trust arises under s 1 in relation to a school site which was at the time of its conveyance under the SSA 1841 part of a larger estate, and the ownership of the land comprising the estate other than the school site has since that conveyance been split so that that other land is now in multiple ownership. The question is then whether the trust under s 1 of the RSA 1987 arises in favour of the successors in title to those who owned the site which was conveyed under the SSA 1841, or in favour of the current owners of the rest of the estate of which that site formed a part.[3]

When does the cessation of relevant use occur?

8.41 The case of *Re Chavasse*[4] concerned a former school site which had been bombed during the Second World War and was later purchased compulsorily for other purposes by Birmingham Corporation. The court held that the cessation of use of the site for the purposes for which it was conveyed under the SSA 1841 occurred

---

1   RSA 1987, s 5(2).
2   Ibid, s 5(3).
3   See also paras 44–48 of Cmnd 8410, at pp 16–17. The questions there raised are: (1) where land was granted by the tenant for life of an entailed estate, what is the effect of the breaking of the entail; (2) what is the effect of a change relating to manorial waste or commonable land out of which the school site was granted; and (3) what is the effect of reverter on the quasi-corporate status of ministers and churchwardens under s 7 of the SSA 1841.
4   (1954) unreported, but referred to so far as relevant in Poole, op cit (see p 297), at para 1.152 and *Property Law: Rights of Reverter* (Law Commission No 111), Cmnd 8410, in para 18 at pp 6–7 and in para 23 at p 9.

not when the site was bombed but, rather, when its intentional permanent discontinuance occurred.[1] In *Attorney-General v Shadwell*,[2] it was held that when land which had been granted for a day school started to be used for the purposes of a Sunday school, reverter occurred. The House of Lords in *Price v A-G*[3] appears to have assumed that the trustees of the school site whose future was in issue in that case could suspend rather than abandon the authorised use.

8.42   The Law Commission working party in their report on the matter suggested that there may be a cessation of use even where there is no intentional (or enforced) permanent discontinuance. The example given was of the situation where a teacher's house is not in fact used as such, but the trustees do not know whether they will need the house for a school teacher at some future date, and let the house as an interim measure. The Law Commission working party commented that it would be open to the court to find that the authorised use had ceased, and that the court might well so find if it appeared that resumption of the authorised use in the future was unlikely or if the letting was for a substantial period.[4]

8.43   The Law Commission working party also pointed out that where a school site has been transferred to the LEA under, for example, s 38 of the Education Act 1921,[5] and the use of the site is changed following the exercise by the LEA of its statutory powers in respect of what are now community schools, it could be said that the authorised use for the purposes of the SSA 1841 has changed. The Commission suggested, however, that it was 'unlikely that the legislation under which the powers were granted was intended to be self-defeating in relation to schools whose premises were subject to reverter.'[6]

Can a trust arise under section 1 of the Reverter of Sites Act 1987 when there is a cessation of use of only part of a site?

8.44   It seems clear that there can be a cessation of the use of part of a relevant site, so as to give rise to a trust under s 1 of the RSA 1987 in relation to that part only. That was the view of the Law Commission working party whose report gave rise to the RSA 1987.[7] However, as pointed out by that working party,[8] practical problems would occur if the cessation was only of, for example, the use of the top floor of a building, and the school continued to use the ground floor.

---

[1]   See Cmnd 8410, p 9 (para 23), and Poole, op cit, para 1.153.
[2]   [1910] 1 Ch 92.
[3]   [1914] AC 20.
[4]   Cmnd 8410, para 25, at p 10.
[5]   As to which, see paras **8.46** and **8.47**.
[6]   Cmnd 8410, para 26, at p 10.
[7]   Cmnd 8410, para 27, at p 10.
[8]   Ibid, para 28.

Do rights arise under section 1 of the Reverter of Sites Act 1987 in favour of the successors in title to neighbouring land where the school site was originally a part of the same site?

8.45 It appears that the original expectation on the part of those who drafted the SSA 1841 was that it would not matter whether a site granted under the provisions of that Act reverted, on ceasing to be used for the purposes for which it was granted, to the successor of the owner of the site itself or to the owner of the estate of which it formed part at the time of its conveyance.[1] This is because it was probably thought then that the Act would facilitate the granting of small parts of landowners' existing estates, which would revert to the estate or the owner of it, and that the result in either case would be the same. However, many of the large estates which existed then have been broken up. Accordingly, it would make most sense for the ownership to revert to the successor in title to the land itself, and not to the owner or owners of the relevant neighbouring land. However, that is not what was assumed in *Dennis v Malcolm*[2] and *Re Cawston's Conveyance*[3] and held in *Attorney-General v Shadwell*,[4] and *Marchant v Onslow*,[5] although in *Re Cawston's Conveyance* and in *Marchant v Onslow* it was nevertheless held on the facts that the site in each case reverted to the successors in title to the site which was originally granted. *Marchant v Onslow* was disapproved by the Court of Appeal in *Fraser v Canterbury Diocesan Board of Finance*,[6] where the court decided (in fact obiter) that the reversion under the section is to the holder of the estate, and not to the neighbouring land.[7]

Arrangements made under section 23 of the Elementary Education Act 1870 or section 38 of the Education Act 1921

8.46 A maintained school's site may be held by the LEA under an arrangement entered into under s 23 of the Elementary Education Act 1870 or s 38 of, and Part I of the Fourth Schedule to, the Education Act 1921 (EA 1921). Only the provisions of s 38 will be considered here, since they were largely a consolidation of s 23. Section 38 of the 1921 Act allowed the managers (that is what would today be called the governing body) of an elementary school to make an arrangement with the LEA for transferring the school to that authority. The school then was deemed to be a school which was 'provided' by the LEA while the LEA had any control over the school under the arrangement. Arrangements made under the relevant provisions could take many possible forms. However, their terms will have to be construed in the light of the legislation which was in force at the time the arrangements were entered into. Accordingly, it may be necessary to refer to that legislation in order to determine the meaning of a relevant arrangement.

---

[1] See Cmnd 8410, para 29.
[2] [1934] Ch 244, at 251.
[3] [1940] Ch 27, at 37–38.
[4] [1910] 1 Ch 92, at 99.
[5] [1995] Ch 1, at 7B–8C; [1994] ELR 451, at 456A–457B.
[6] [2001] Ch 669.
[7] Ibid, at 682–684, paras 40–48, especially at para 44: 'The reverter is of that estate held on that tenure to the original grantor of the site and not to the land out of which the site granted was carved and conveyed'.

8.47 If, for example, an arrangement entered into under s 38 of the EA 1921 provided that the site of the school could be used by the LEA only while it continued to be needed by the LEA for the purpose of a 'public elementary school', then the question might arise whether what would now be called a maintained special school was within the meaning of those words. It seems clear that the better view is that a maintained special school would indeed be within the meaning of those words. This is because of the references in the EA 1921 to 'ordinary public elementary schools',[1] the implication being that there were also 'special' public elementary schools, although the EA 1921 contained no specific reference to such schools. There are apparently contrary indications in the EA 1921, but they can all be seen on a close analysis to be inconclusive.

PROPERTY TRANSFER PROVISIONS IN THE EDUCATION REFORM ACT 1988 AND SUBSEQUENT EDUCATION ACTS

Introduction

8.48 The ERA 1988 introduced grant-maintained schools and higher education corporations. The FHEA 1992 introduced further education corporations. All of these educational institutions were formerly maintained by LEAs. Under those Acts, the new corporations were given the premises used solely by the institutions and took on liabilities which had been incurred solely for the purposes of the institutions. In many cases, however, the institutions shared premises with other institutions maintained by the LEA or which were used for other purposes of the local authority which was the LEA, or benefited from obligations incurred by the local authority (whether or not acting as the LEA) also for other purposes of that authority.

8.49 It was therefore necessary to provide a mechanism by means of which the property which was to be, or had been, transferred was identified and, where necessary, shared between the new corporation and the local authority. This was done primarily by means of ss 197 and 198 of, and Sch 10 to, the ERA 1988 and s 36 of, and Sch 5 to, the FHEA 1992. Those (and related) provisions have subsequently been amended significantly. Their precise effect at various times may on occasion need to be ascertained, and the effect of those provisions and the history of the changes made to them was described at some length in the first edition of this book.[2] Accordingly, only the current provisions are described here. Furthermore, only the most salient of those issues of interpretation which may arise in relation to those provisions are considered here.

The current situation

8.50 By way of introduction, it needs to be said that s 197 of the ERA 1988 has no continuing application, since the Education Transfer Council (as the Education Assets

---

[1]   See ss 18(5) and 36(4).

[2]   Paragraphs 17.22–17.57.

Board was renamed by s 136 of the SSFA 1998) no longer exists.[1] Thus the main relevant provisions in that Act are now only s 198 of, and Sch 10 to, the ERA 1988, and the main operative provisions in the FHEA 1992 are s 36 and Sch 5. Those have been modified by the Education (New Procedures for Property Transfers) Regulations 2000[2] (the Property Transfer Regulations) in different ways. Thus s 198 of, and Sch 10 to, the 1988 Act apply to transfers of land held by a foundation body, with modifications,[3] and transfers of property, rights and liabilities under the FHEA 1992 are governed by s 36 of, and Sch 5 to, that Act as modified by regs 8–14 of the Property Transfer Regulations. Transfers in relation to grant-maintained schools (which of course now no longer exist) are affected by the amendments made by regs 15–19 of those regulations to the applicable statutory provisions as they stood after the enactment of the SSFA 1998.

8.51 Disputes as to the application of the relevant property transfer provisions are now determined in relation to England by the Secretary of State, and in relation to Wales by the National Assembly for Wales.[4]

Several unresolved issues of interpretation

8.52 Some difficulties of interpretation remain, however. For example, para 4 of Sch 10 to the ERA 1988 as set out in Sch 1 to the Property Transfer Regulations continues to provide that any property:

'the nature of which does not permit its division or apportionment ... shall be transferred to the transferee (or to one or other of the transferees) or retained by the transferor authority or body according to –

(a)   in the case of an interest or estate in land, whether on the transfer date the transferor authority or body or the transferee (or one or other of the transferees) appears to be in greater need of the security afforded by that estate or interest, or, where none of them appears to be in greater need of that security, which of them appears on that date to be likely to make use of the land to the greater extent.'

8.53 It is a little difficult to ascertain what is meant by the words 'appears to be in greater need of the security afforded by that estate or interest'. This could be physical security, or it could be the security afforded by having all those rights which adhere to the ownership of land (including the right to control the use of or access to land and therefore the power to protect the physical security of that or other land). The latter appears to be the better interpretation.

8.54 Paragraph 2(1) of Sch 10 as set out in Sch 1 to the Property Transfer Regulations provides that it is the duty of the transferor and transferee:

'whether before or after the transfer date so far as practicable to arrive at such written agreements, and to execute such other instruments, as are necessary or expedient to

---

[1]   See the Education Transfer Council (Winding Up) Regulatons 2000, SI 2000/2729 and the Education (New Procedures for Property Transfers) Regulations 2000, SI 2000/3209.

[2]   SI 2000/3209.

[3]   See Property Transfer Regulations, reg 5.

[4]   Ibid, reg 4.

identify or define the property, rights and liabilities transferred to the transferee or retained by the transferor or for making any such arrangements as are mentioned in paragraph 1(4) above and as will –

(a)   afford to the transferor and the transferee as against one another such rights and safeguards as they may require for the proper discharge of their respective functions, and

(b)   make as from such date, not being earlier than the transfer date, ... such clarifications and modifications of the effect of the provisions of this Act or of the 1998 Act (or any regulations made under it) under which the transfer is required on the property, rights and liabilities of the transferor as will best serve the proper discharge of the respective functions of the transferor and the transferee.'

8.55   One question of interpretation which arises in relation to para 2 is what is meant by the words 'such clarifications and modifications of the effect of the provision of this Act or of the 1998 Act (or any regulations made under it) under which the transfer is required on the property, rights and liabilities of the transferor as will best serve the proper discharge of the respective functions of the transferor and the transferee'. On one view, such a modification could properly include transferring property to which Sch 10 did not apply. However, given (among other things[1]) that (1) as a result of 198(2)(d), the provisions in Sch 10 are 'supplementary [to] and consequential' on the provisions of s 198(2)(a)–(c), and (2) those provisions apply only to property which has been used or held for the purposes of more than one school or other educational institution, that view is probably not correct. It is noted that the relevant modifications are likely to be of the effect of, for example, s 74 of the ERA 1988, which required the transfer or, as the case may be, retention of all property held or used by the transferor authority for the purposes of the institution in question. The modifications could, for example, take the form of a lease being granted to the transferor in respect of property the fee simple in which is transferred in accordance with s 74.

8.56   Similarly, it may be asked whether the Secretary of State or the National Assembly for Wales could, under para 1(4) of Sch 10 to the ERA 1988, determine that property of a local authority which was never used or held in any way for the purposes of a potential transferee, is to transfer to such transferee. This would be on the basis that para 1(2) of Sch 10 applies to property, rights and liabilities of a transferor body, and does not contain the word 'such' before the first usage of the word 'property'. It is suggested here that that could not properly occur, for the following reasons. The first is that, as mentioned in para **8.55**, s 198(2) provides that Sch 10 applies (only) to property which has been used or held for the purposes of more than one school or other educational institution,[2] and that s 198(2)(d) provides that Sch 10 has effect for the purposes of 'making supplementary and consequential provisions in relation to transfers to which this section applies'. The second reason is that (a) Sch 5 to the FHEA 1992 contains no equivalent of para 1(2) of Sch 10, (b) para 1(3) of Sch 5, which contains the equivalent of para 1(4) of Sch 10, expressly

---

[1]   As to which, see para 17.038 of the first edition of this book.

[2]   ERA 1988, Sch 10 para 1(1) applies to property, rights and liabilities for a transferor authority held, used or subsisting for such purposes but also for 'other purposes of the transferor authority'. It is assumed that s 198(2)(a) should be read as applying in the same way, if only because as a matter of common sense s 198(2)(a) must have been intended so to apply.

refers back to para 1(1), which expressly refers only to property held at least partly for the purposes of the potential transferee, and (c) it would be odd if Sch 10 applied more widely than Sch 5.

8.57 Finally, it is noted that an agreement or instrument made under para 2 of Sch 10 must 'so far as it is expedient' provide for (among other things) the granting of leases and the creation of other liabilities and rights over land 'whether amounting in law to interests in land or not'.[1] Presumably, if a right is not attached to the land, then it will be capable of being regarded as contractual in the circumstances. If that were not so, then the right would be best regarded as a private law right arising out of a statutory framework, and therefore enforceable in a private action by analogy with the case of *Roy v Kensington and Chelsea and Westminster Family Practitioner Committee*.[2]

RESTRICTION ON THE DISPOSAL OR CHANGE OF USE OF PLAYING FIELDS

8.58 Section 77 of the SSFA 1998 restricts the freedom of (1) local authorities, (2) the governing bodies of maintained schools, and (3) foundation bodies in England,[3] to dispose of playing fields[4] (a) which are, immediately before the date of the disposal, used by a maintained school for the purposes of the school, or (b) which are not then so used but have been so used at any time within the period of 10 years ending with that date. Such disposal is permitted only with the consent of the Secretary of State.[5] A local authority must (with one exception) obtain the consent of the Secretary of State before taking any action (other than such disposal) which is intended or likely to result in a change of use of any playing fields (a) which are, immediately before the date when the action is taken, used by a maintained school for the purposes of the school, or (b) which are not then so used but have been so used at any time within the period of 10 years ending with that date, 'whereby the playing fields will be used for purposes which do not consist of or include their use as playing fields by such a school for the purposes of the school'.[6] The exception is that where the land in question will, on the relevant change of use, become used in connection with the provision by any local authority of educational facilities for a maintained school, or any recreational facilities.[7]

---

[1]   ERA 1988, Sch 10, para 2(2)(a).

[2]   [1992] 1 AC 624.

[3]   Section 77 does not apply to Wales: s 77(9).

[4]   By 'playing fields' is meant 'land in the open air which is provided for the purposes of physical education or recreation, other than any prescribed description of such land': s 77(7). No regulations prescribing any such description have so far been made.

[5]   SSFA 1988, s 77(1). A general consent has been given by the Secretary of State: see The Protection of School Playing Fields and Land for City Academies, DfES/0580/01, which also contains relevant guidance.

[6]   Ibid, s 77(3).

[7]   Ibid, s 77(4).

Chapter 9

ADMISSIONS TO MAINTAINED SCHOOLS

LIMITED DUTY TO GIVE EFFECT TO PARENTAL PREFERENCE[1]

9.1   The current law relating to admissions to maintained schools has its origins in the Education Act 1980. Although the current statutory provisions are markedly different in some respects from those which were originally enacted, a number of principles have survived. Accordingly, many of the cases reported since the 1980 Act came into force remain relevant. The current regime is contained in the SSFA 1998, as a result of s 86(1) of which, an LEA must:

> 'make arrangements for enabling the parent of a child[2] in the area of the authority –
> (a)   to express a preference as to the school at which he wishes education to be provided for his child in the exercise of the authority's functions, and
> (b)   to give reasons for his preference.'[3]

9.2   Subject to the exceptions described below, as a result of s 86(2), the governing body of a maintained school (which in this context means a community, foundation or voluntary school[4]) and the LEA must comply with such a preference so expressed. This duty applies also in relation to the parent of a child who is not in the area of the LEA where the parent seeks the admission of the child to a school maintained by the LEA.[5] It applies in addition to an application made under s 438(4) or s 440(2) of the EA 1996 by a parent for a particular school to be specified in a school attendance order.[6] However, s 86 and related provisions do not apply to (1) nursery schools,[7] (2) special schools[8] (although regulations 'may make provision in connection with the arrangements for the admission of pupils to community or foundation special schools, and for the allocation between the local education authority and the governing body of such a school of functions in connection with such arrangements'[9]), or (3) children

---

[1]   For the sake of simplicity, except where indicated otherwise (such as in relation to s 86(3)(b) of the SSFA 1998) this chapter is written on the assumption that all of the changes made by the EA 2002 to the law relating to admissions are in force in Wales as well as in England. However, those changes have been brought into force only in England.

[2]   A 'child' for this purpose must not have attained the age of 19: SSFA 1998, s 84(6).

[3]   It may be arranged by the LEA that applications for admission are to be made by a parent to the governing body of a maintained school or a person acting on behalf of the governing body: see SSFA 1998, s 86(7).

[4]   See ibid, s 84(6).

[5]   Ibid, s 86(8)(a).

[6]   Ibid, s 86(8)(b).

[7]   Ibid, s 98(3).

[8]   Ibid, s 98(6).

[9]   Ibid, s 98(5).

with statements of SEN.[1] Those provisions also do not apply to children who will be under compulsory school age at the time of their proposed admission to a school; however, those provisions apply 'in relation to the admission of such pupils to the school otherwise than for nursery education'.[2] When a child is admitted to a school for nursery education and is subsequently transferred to a reception class at the school, the child is to be regarded for the purposes of the rest of Chapter I of Part III of the SSFA 1998 (ie ss 84–89) as having been admitted to the school on being so transferred.[3]

9.3   The exceptions to the duty of an LEA and the governing body of a maintained school to comply with a parent's preference expressed under s 86(1) are as follows:

(1)   'if compliance with the preference would prejudice the efficient provision of education or the efficient use of resources'[4] (the oversubscription exception);

(2)   (in relation to Wales only) if the preferred school is a foundation or voluntary aided school and compliance with the preference would be incompatible with any special arrangements under s 91 of the SSFA 1998 (which allows for admission arrangements which are designed to preserve the religious character of such a school, but which was repealed by the EA 2002);[5]

(3)   if the arrangements for admission to the preferred school are wholly based on selection by reference to ability or aptitude and are so based with a view to admitting only pupils with high ability or with aptitude, and compliance with the preference would be incompatible with selection under those arrangements;[6]

(4)   if a parent has expressed a preference for more than one maintained school under a scheme made under s 89A of the SSFA 1998 (under which regulations may be made requiring an LEA to formulate a scheme for the co-ordinating of admissions to maintained schools in their area), and a place is being offered at one of the other schools for which a parent has expressed a preference under that scheme;[7]

(5)   if the child to whom the application relates has been permanently excluded from two or more maintained schools, the last such exclusion having occurred within the 2 preceding years;[8] or

(6)   in relation to the education at a secondary school of pupils who are over compulsory school age, if the admission arrangements are selective (being wholly based on selection by reference to ability or aptitude), and compliance

1   SSFA 1998, s 98(7).

2   Ibid, s 98(4).

3   Ibid, s 98(1).

4   Ibid, s 86(3)(a). It was held by Burton J in *R v Sheffield City Council, ex parte M* [2000] ELR 85 that the mere fact that a school could physically take a given number of pupils is not to be taken by itself to mean that there would be no prejudice to the provision of efficient education or the efficient use of resources by the admission of that number of pupils.

5   Ibid, s 86(3)(b).

6   Ibid, s 86(3)(c). See the School Admissions Code of Practice for England, DfES/0031/2003, paras 3.17, 3.20–3.25 and 3.31 concerning selection tests.

7   Ibid, s 86(2A).

8   See ibid, s 87.

with the preference would be incompatible with selection under those arrangements.[1]

9.4 By far the most common exception in practice is the first of these, if only because a successful school is likely to be oversubscribed. The word 'oversubscription' does not appear in the legislation, but it is commonly used in practice[2] to describe the legal effect of the number of admissions for places being above a certain number. In England that number used to be called the admission[3] or standard number (and is still so called in Wales[4]), but is now (unless the number concerns admissions to an infant class within the meaning of s 4 of the SSFA 1998, as to which, see para **9.6**) the number determined under s 89 of the SSFA 1998 (as substituted by the EA 2002) as the number of pupils in a relevant age group that it is intended to admit to the school during a school year.[5] If the number of applications for places does not exceed that number, then no prejudice may be taken to arise for the purposes of s 86(3)(a).[6] However, if the number of applications for places exceeds that number, then the admission authority for the school must decide which applications should be accepted and which should be rejected. In doing so, it is likely to apply certain criteria, such as the proximity of the home of the child to whom the application relates to the school, and whether or not that child has a sibling at the school. These are commonly known (understandably) as the proximity and sibling admission criteria, and are part of the admission policy of the school. There is a considerable body of case-law concerning the application of admission criteria such as these, and its effects are described below.

9.5 It is of note that in R *v Governors of the Hasmonean High School, ex parte N and E*,[7] the Court of Appeal accepted that the refusal to admit a pupil with SEN because of those needs was not a rejection on the ground of academic selection as used by grammar schools and therefore unlawful because the school in question was non-selective. Rather, the refusal to admit was (properly) based on what is now s 86(3)(a).[8] That decision has been overtaken by the new regime relating to a child with SEN where a statement of such needs is made and maintained for the child,[9] but where a child has SEN which are not sufficiently serious to require a statement of such needs to be made and maintained, the decision will still be relevant. Nevertheless, the

---

1   SSFA 1998, s 86(3A) and (3B), which are currently in force only in England.
2   For example, it is used throughout the current School Admissions Code of Practice for England, DfES/0031/2003, concerning which, see para **9.17**.
3   Determined under s 93 of the SSFA 1998.
4   See ibid, s 86(5) as originally enacted. Section 93 of the SSFA 1998 is repealed in relation to England and is prospectively repealed by the EA 2002 in relation to Wales: see EA 2002, Sch 22.
5   See ibid, s 86(5) as substituted by the EA 2002. The position of maintained boarding schools is dealt with in the substituted provisions, and may appear to be more complicated than it actually is. Essentially, in relation to a boarding school the admission authority – as defined by s 88 of the SSFA 1998, regarding which see below – may make a determination as to both the number of boarders and non-boarders whom it is intended to admit to the school. In that case, the test as to oversubscription is applied in relation to both numbers: see ss 86(5), (5A) and (5B), and 89A.
6   Ibid, s 86(5).
7   [1994] ELR 343.
8   See per Glidewell LJ at ibid, 352A–C.
9   See paras **6.57** et seq concerning statements of SEN, and para **9.2** concerning the impact of having such a statement in relation to admission to a maintained school.

position is affected by para 7.19 of the School Admissions Code of Practice for England,[1] which among other things reminds admission authorities that children with SEN but without statements of SEN 'must be treated as fairly as other applicants'.

ADMISSIONS TO INFANT CLASSES

9.6   Prejudice to the provision of efficient education or the efficient use of resources within the meaning of s 86(3)(a) of the SSFA 1998 is to be taken to occur 'by reason of measures required to be taken in order to ensure compliance with the duty imposed by section 1(6)' of the SSFA 1998.[2] That subsection requires the LEA and the governing body of a maintained school which has an infant class within the meaning of s 4 of that Act to 'exercise their functions with a view to securing that [any limit imposed under s 1 of the SSFA 1998] is complied with'.[3] This is the infant class size limit, which is currently 30.[4]

THE ADMISSION AUTHORITY FOR A MAINTAINED SCHOOL

9.7   The admission authority for a community or voluntary controlled school is the LEA, unless the LEA has, with the agreement of the school's governing body, delegated to the governing body responsibility for determining the admission arrangements for the school.[5] In relation to a foundation or voluntary aided school, the admission authority is the governing body.[6]

WHAT IS MEANT BY THE WORDS 'ADMISSION ARRANGEMENTS'?

9.8   According to s 88(2) of the SSFA 1998:

> 'In this Chapter, "admission arrangements", in relation to a maintained school, means the arrangements for the admission of pupils to the school, including the school's admission policy.'

Accordingly, the admission authority for a maintained school is the body which decides the admission arrangements for the school. Although it is not expressly stated in the SSFA 1998 (or elsewhere in the legislation), it is clear that the admission authority not only determines the admission arrangements for the school, but also which children should be admitted under those arrangements. In other words, the admission authority not only decides the admission arrangements, but it applies them

---

[1]   DfES/0031/2003.
[2]   SSFA 1998, s 86(4).
[3]   See para **2.12** in connection with s 1.
[4]   See SI 1998/1943 and SI 1998/1973.
[5]   SSFA 1998, s 88(1)(a).
[6]   Ibid, s 88(1)(b).

to applications made for places at the school, and it applies the admission policy and therefore the admission criteria in the event of oversubscription.

DETERMINING THE ADMISSION ARRANGEMENTS

9.9   There is now a detailed procedure for the determination of the arrangements for admissions to maintained schools. These must be determined before 15 April in the school year preceding that to which the arrangements relate.[1] Before they are determined, the admission authority must consult various bodies. These are (1) the LEA or the governing body of the school (whichever is not the admission authority for the school, (2) the admission authorities for all other maintained schools in the area or for such class of such schools as may be prescribed (ie specified in a statutory instrument), (3) the governing bodies of all community or foundation schools in the relevant area (so far as not already consulted), and (4) 'the admission authorities for maintained schools of any prescribed description'.[2] The regulations which specify these matters are the Education (Relevant Areas for Consultation on Admission Arrangements) Regulations 1999[3] and the Education (Determination of Admission Arrangements) Regulations 1999.[4] It is of note in relation to the former that if an LEA 'determine any relevant area which comprises part (or all) of the area of that education authority and part (or all) of the area of another education authority (or of the areas of other education authorities)', and one or more of the other education authorities object to that determination, then 'the objecting authority may refer that determination to the adjudicator'.[5] It is also of interest that under the Education (Determination of Admission Arrangements) Regulations 1999, there may be a suspension of the consultation requirements.[6]

9.10   An admission authority's determination of the admission arrangements for a school must be notified in writing to each of the bodies which the authority were required to consult (or would have been so required if the requirement to consult had not been suspended as described at the end of para **9.9**), within 14 days from the date of that determination.[7] This notification may be in electronic form (unless there are grounds for believing that the intended recipient is unable to make use of it in that form).[8]

---

[1]   See SSFA 1998, s 89(1) and reg 3(3) of the Education (Determination of Admission Arrangements) Regulations 1999, SI 1999/126. As a result of reg 3 of the Education (Determining School Admission Arrangements for the Initial Year) Regulations 1998, SI 1998/3165, admission authorities were prevented from determining admission arrangements earlier than 1 April 1999 for the school year 1999–2000 or any later year. Although those regulations would not expressly prevent an admission authority in the future from determining such arrangements for, say, the year after the next school year, it is clear that doing so would breach the statutory scheme.

[2]   SSFA 1998, s 89(2).

[3]   SI 1999/124.

[4]   SI 1999/126.

[5]   See SI 1999/124, reg 9.

[6]   See SI 1999/126, reg 5A, inserted by SI 2002/2896, which currently applies only in England.

[7]   Education (Determination of Admission Arrangements) Regulations 1999, SI 1999/126, reg 8(3).

[8]   Ibid, reg 8(4).

VARYING ADMISSION ARRANGEMENTS DURING A SCHOOL YEAR

9.11   An admission authority may decide 'in view of a major change in circumstances' to vary the admission arrangements which were to apply for a particular year.[1] In addition, the Education (Variation of Admission Arrangements) (England) Regulations 2002,[2] made under s 89(8)(e) of the SSFA 1998, permit the variation of admission arrangements where necessary to implement school organisation proposals made under s 28 of the SSFA 1998. In both cases (albeit subject to an exception in the case of a variation of an admission number which results from the implementation of proposals made under s 28 of the SSFA 1998[3]), the LEA must refer the proposed variations to the adjudicator. Before doing so, the LEA must first notify the appropriate bodies whom they consulted under s 89(2)[4] and, if the admission authority is the LEA and any school to which the variations relate is a community or voluntary school, consult the governing body of that school.[5]

REFERENCES TO THE ADJUDICATOR[6]

9.12   A body which an admission authority is required to consult (or which the admission authority would, if the consultation requirements had not been suspended as indicated in para **9.11**, have been required to consult) which objects to the proposed admission arrangements, may (subject to several exceptions[7]) refer that objection to the adjudicator.[8] A parent (1) who is an individual (that is, not a 'corporate' parent such as the local authority where a pupil is being looked after by such an authority), (2) whose child is a pupil of compulsory school age and receiving primary education, and (3) is resident in the area for which consultation under s 89(2)(b) is required in relation to the arrangements, may object to the adjudicator against admission arrangements which (a) make provision for the selection of pupils by ability or aptitude within the meaning of s 99(5) of the SSFA 1998 (regarding which, see below), (b) have continuously been in existence in relation to the school in question since the beginning of the 1997/98 school year, and (c) depend solely for their lawfulness on

---

[1]   SSFA 1998, s 89(5); s 89(8)(d) permits the making of regulations specifying matters which are, or are not, to constitute major changes in circumstances for the purposes of s 89(5)(b). No such regulations have so far been made.

[2]   SI 2002/2898.

[3]   See reg 4(2) of SI 2002/2898.

[4]   Ibid.

[5]   SSFA 1998, s 89(9).

[6]   By 'adjudicator' is meant a person appointed by the Secretary of State under s 25 of the SSFA 1998, regarding which, see para **2.18**.

[7]   See reg 2 of the Education (Objections to Adjudicator or Secretary of State) Regulations 1999, SI 1999/125 (in relation to England, that regulation was substituted by SI 2002/2901). These include that the substance of the objection is to seek an alteration to the admission arrangements which would constitute a prescribed alteration for the purposes of s 28 of the SSFA 1998. See *R v Downes, ex parte Wandsworth London Borough Council* [2000] ELR 425 in relation to that exception.

[8]   SSFA 1998, s 90(1).

s 100 of the SSFA 1998.[1] A parent in England of a child who has attained the age of 2 but has not attained the age of 5 or whose child is of compulsory school age and is receiving primary education, may refer to the adjudicator an objection to arrangements which adopt an admission number for any relevant age group which is lower than the 'indicated admission number' for the group.[2] However, the adjudicator is not obliged to determine an objection made by a parent as described in this paragraph unless at least 10 parents of the relevant type have referred objections under s 90(2) which are about the same admission arrangements and raise the same, or substantially the same, issue.[3]

9.13 All of the references to the adjudicator referred to in para **9.12** must be made within 6 weeks of the notification, or (in the case of objections to continuing selection arrangements of the sort referred to in para **9.12**) the publication, by the admission authority of its decision on the proposed admission arrangements, unless the adjudicator is satisfied that it was 'not reasonably practicable for the objection to have been received earlier than the time it was received'.[4] Such publication is provided for in reg 9 of the Education (Determination of Admission Arrangements) Regulations 1999.[5]

REFERENCES TO THE SECRETARY OF STATE

9.14 The adjudicator must refer to the Secretary of State an objection which has been made to the adjudicator where the objection is about 'any criterion for admission to a school relating to a person's religion, religious denomination or religious practice'.[6] Where that occurs, the adjudicator must, if the Secretary of State so requests, give his advice to the Secretary of State on the question so referred.[7]

ADJUDICATOR'S PROCEDURE IN OTHER CASES

9.15 In other cases, the adjudicator must simply decide whether to uphold the objection, and, if so, to what extent. In doing so, he will be bound to have regard to the provisions of the School Admissions Code of Practice published under s 84 of the

---

[1] See SSFA 1998, s 90(2) and the Education (Objections to Adjudicator or Secretary of State) Regulations 1999, SI 1999/125, regs 4 and 5. In relation to England, reg 5(1) was substituted by SI 2002/2901. Selective admission arrangements depend solely for their lawfulness on s 100 if they are not rendered lawful by virtue of s 99(1)(b) or (2)(b) (which relate to grammar schools and sixth forms respectively), s 101 (which relates to pupil banding) or s 102 (which concerns aptitude for particular subjects): ibid, reg 5(3).

[2] Education (Objections to Adjudicator or Secretary of State) Regulations 1999, SI 1999/125, reg 5(1). The definition of 'indicated admission number' is in ibid, reg 1(1), as substituted by SI 2002/2901.

[3] Ibid, reg 6.

[4] Ibid, reg 3. This is the wording used in relation to claims of unfair dismissal (see s 111 of the Employment Rights Act 1996) and a number of other statutory claims to employment tribunals. Accordingly, the case-law concerning such claims (the leading authority being *Palmer v Southend-on-Sea Borough Council* [1984] ICR 372) may be applied by analogy.

[5] SI 1999/126.

[6] Education (Objections to Admission Arrangements) Regulations 1999, SI 1999/125, reg 7.

[7] SSFA 1998, s 90(3)(b).

SSFA 1998 (concerning which, see para **9.17**). In this connection, the following passage from the judgment of Ouseley J in R *(ota Metropolitan Borough of Wirral) v The Chief Schools Adjudicator*[1] is both relevant and illuminative:

> 'The duty is as set out in the statutory language. It is to have regard to the code. It is not a duty to apply the code. Of course, if there is specific guidance in relation to a particular problem and that guidance is not followed, the duty to give reasons would necessarily entail that reasons be given for that exceptional approach being adopted. But, as I have said, it is inherent in the function of the code and in the breadth of its language that it requires considerable judgment on the part of a LEA or adjudicator as to its application and as to the balance to be struck between the competing considerations which it contains. The duty on the adjudicator to have regard to the code is not one which can possibly be taken as yielding any obligation on the court to assess for itself the weight to be given to the code or to say whether the adjudicator gave it adequate weight.'

9.16   Otherwise, the adjudicator is bound simply by the principles of public law – there being no statutory provisions applicable to the procedure which needs to be followed by the adjudicator in this context.[2]

CODE OF PRACTICE ON SCHOOL ADMISSIONS

9.17   Section 84 of the SSFA 1998 obliges the Secretary of State to issue (and from time to time to revise) a code of practice 'containing such practical guidance as he thinks appropriate' in respect of the discharge by LEAs, the governing bodies of maintained schools, appeal panels (regarding which see below) and adjudicators, of their respective functions under Chapter I of Part III of the SSFA 1998.[3] It is the duty of such bodies or persons when exercising such a function to have regard to any relevant provisions of that code.[4] There are four such codes in existence: two in relation to England and two in relation to Wales. They are the School Admissions Code of Practice,[5] the School Admission Appeals Code of Practice,[6] the Code of Practice on School Admission Arrangements (Wales) and the School Admission

---

[1]   [2001] ELR 574, at 592, para 75.

[2]   In addition to R *(ota Metropolitan Borough of Wirral) v The Chief Schools Adjudicator*, the relevant case-law includes R *v The Schools Adjudicator, ex parte Metropolitan Borough of Wirral* [2000] ELR 620, which confirmed that the adjudicator has an original jurisdiction and is not confined to a review of the admission authority's decision, R *v Downes, ex parte Wandsworth London Borough Council* [2000] ELR 425, concerning among other things the adjudicator's duty to give reasons for his decision, and R *(Watford Grammar Schools) v Adjudicator for Schools* [2003] EWHC 2480, [2004] ELR 40, in which (at paras 62–65) Collins J confirmed that admission arrangements within the meaning of s 103 are made annually and therefore may be challenged even if they have been in place for several years. In R *(Wandsworth LBC) v Schools Adjudicator* [2003] EWHC 2969 (Admin), [2004] ELR 274, Goldring J allowed an application for judicial review on the basis that the adjudicator's decision was irrational.

[3]   See s 85 of the SSFA 1998 concerning the making and approval of a code of practice under s 84. It must be laid before the Houses of Parliament for 40 days, but is subject only to the negative approval procedure: see s 85(5).

[4]   Ibid, s 84(2).

[5]   DfES/0031/2003, which was given effect by the Education (School Admissions Code of Practice and School Admission Appeals Code of Practice) (Appointed Day) (England) Order 2003, SI 2003/163.

[6]   DfES/0030/2003, given effect by the same Order.

Appeals: The National Assembly for Wales Code of Practice.[1] For the sake of simplicity, for the most part, reference is made below only to the codes which relate to England. However, it should be noted that both of the English codes were issued more recently than those for Wales, and that some aspects of the current English codes are not to be found in those which relate to Wales.

ADMISSION FORUMS

9.18 Section 85A of the SSFA 1998 requires every LEA, in accordance with regulations made under that section, to establish an admission forum within the meaning of the section. The functions of such a forum are clearly advisory only, and relate only to functions concerning admissions to maintained schools conferred by Chapter I of Part III of the SSFA 1998. The current regulations are the Education (Admission Forums) (England) Regulations 2002[2] and the Education (Admission Forums) (Wales) Regulations 2003.[3] Their salient features include that such a forum must meet at least three times in its first year of existence and at least twice a year in following years.[4]

CO-ORDINATED ADMISSIONS

9.19 Section 89B(1) of the SSFA 1998 empowers (currently in relation to England only[5]) the making of regulations requiring an LEA to formulate a scheme for co-ordinating the arrangements for the admission of pupils to maintained schools in its area, and to take 'prescribed action with a view to securing the adoption of the scheme by themselves and each governing body who are the admission authority for a maintained school in their area'. The Secretary of State is given power by s 89B(2) to make a scheme for co-ordinating, or assisting the co-ordination of, the arrangements for the admission of pupils to maintained schools in an LEA's area for an academic year,[6] but only if the LEA has not made such a scheme in accordance with s 89B(1) before a prescribed date in the previous academic year and given the Secretary of State a copy of it.

9.20 Regulations may require LEAs to give other LEAs information in connection with the exercise by those other LEAs of their functions in relation to admissions

---

[1] Given effect by the Education (School Admission Appeals: The National Assembly for Wales Code of Practice) (Appointed Day) Order 1999, SI 1999/2893. Both this code and the Code of Practice on School Admission Arrangements (Wales) are available on the National Assembly for Wales' website, http://www.wales.gov.uk.

[2] SI 2002/2900.

[3] SI 2003/2962.

[4] See reg 9 of both sets of regulations.

[5] See SI 2002/2439. None of the provisions whose effect is described in this section are yet in force in Wales.

[6] An academic year for this purpose is 1 August to 31 July: SSFA 1998, s 89B(6).

under Chapter I of Part III.[1] Regulations may also provide that each LEA must secure that, subject to exceptions:

> '(a)   ... no decision made by any admission authority for a maintained school in their area to offer or refuse a child admission to the school shall be communicated to the parent of the child except on a single day, designated by the local education authority, in each year, or
>
> (b)   that, subject to such exceptions as may be prescribed, a decision made by the admission authority for a maintained school to offer or refuse a child admission to the school shall not be communicated to the parent of the child except on a prescribed day.'[2]

9.21   Section 89C makes further provision about the regulations which may be made under s 89B. This includes that LEAs must consult before proposing a co-ordinated admissions scheme under s 89B, including 'with a view to securing that the arrangements for the admission of pupils to maintained schools in the areas of different local education authorities are, so far as is reasonably practicable, compatible with each other'. The regulations made under s 89C may also apply ss 496 and 497 of the EA 1996[3] to functions exercisable under a co-ordinated admission scheme. The Education (Co-ordination of Admission Arrangements) (Primary Schools) (England) Regulations 2002[4] and the Education (Co-ordination of Admission Arrangements) (Secondary Schools) (England) Regulations,[5] are currently in force.

NEW SCHOOLS

9.22   Mention needs to be made here of the position relating to new schools. Provision is made for these in the Education (New Schools) (Admissions) (Wales) Regulations 1999[6] and the New School (Admissions) (England) Regulations 2003.[7]

DIRECTED ADMISSIONS

9.23   The power to direct admissions under s 96 of the SSFA 1998 is considered in detail above.[8] It is mentioned here for the sake of completeness.

---

1   SSFA 1998, s 89B(4).
2   Ibid, s 89B(5).
3   Concerning which, see Chapter 3.
4   SI 2002/2903, as amended by SI 2003/2751 and 2004/1515.
5   SI 2002/2904, as amended by SI 2004/1516.
6   SI 1999/2800.
7   SI 2003/1041.
8   See paras **2.77–2.78**.

WITHDRAWAL OF PUPILS UNDER SECTION 435 OF THE EA 1996; REGISTRATION OF PUPILS UNDER SECTION 434

9.24   Under s 435 of the EA 1996, an LEA has power to make arrangements for the withdrawal of registered pupils below the age of 12 but above the age of 10 years and 6 months from a primary school which for the time being provides no secondary education. The withdrawal must be so that they can receive secondary education. A pupil is registered if he is registered as a pupil in a register kept under s 434 of the EA 1996, the effect of which is as follows. Once a pupil is admitted to a school (and, indeed, not just a maintained school), the proprietor of the school (as defined in s 579(1) of the EA 1996, which in the context of a maintained school means the governing body) is obliged by s 434 of the EA 1996 to put the requisite particulars of the child in the register kept by the proprietor under that section. The proprietor is obliged by s 434 to keep a register containing those particulars and the requisite particulars of all persons known to be parents of the pupil. The requisite particulars are as prescribed by regulations. The current regulations are the Education (Pupil Registration) Regulations 1995.[1]

PUBLICATION OF INFORMATION REGARDING ADMISSIONS

9.25   Local education authorities and the governing bodies of foundation and voluntary aided schools in England may be required by regulations made under s 92 of the SSFA 1998 as substituted by the EA 2002, to publish information about admissions (that is, to maintained schools). In Wales, the original s 92 continues in force, but it is to similar (albeit more extensive) effect. The relevant regulations are referred to in para **4.55**.[2] The information which is published must be accurate.[3] It was held in *R v Hackney London Borough Council, ex parte T*[4] that dates specified in such information are not to be construed as if they were statutory. Accordingly, the words 'parents should apply well before [certain] dates' could not properly be regarded as having the effect that applications for places made after the stated date could not be considered.[5]

---

[1]   SI 1995/2089, as amended by SI 1997/2624, and, in relation to England, by SI 2001/2802 and SI 2002/3178, and, in relation to Wales, by SI 2001/1109. Concerning deletion from the register under reg 9, see *R v Governing Body of Gateway Primary School, ex parte X* [2001] ELR 321 and *R (M-P) v London Borough of Barking and Dagenham and Barking Abbey Comprehensive School* [2002] EWHC 2483 (Admin); [2003] ELR 144.

[2]   These are currently SI 2002/2897 in relation to England and SI 1999/1812 in relation to Wales.

[3]   *R (ota South Gloucestershire Local Education Authority) v South Gloucestershire Schools Appeal Panel* [2002] ELR 309, at para 42. Parts of the decision in that case were overruled by the Court of Appeal in *School Admissions Appeals Panel for the London Borough of Hounslow v London Borough of Hounslow* [2002] EWCA Civ 900; [2002] 1 WLR 3147; [2002] ELR 602, at paras 60 and 61, but, understandably, not this part.

[4]   [1991] COD 454.

[5]   Ibid.

SELECTIVE ARRANGEMENTS FOR ADMISSION TO MAINTAINED SCHOOLS

9.26 Chapter II of Part III (ss 99–109) of the SSFA 1998 concerns selective admissions to community, foundation and voluntary schools. Section 99 provides that selection by ability[1] is lawful only in certain circumstances.[2] One is that the school is a grammar school (as defined by s 104(7); see further below). Another is that the admission arrangements make what is called a 'permitted form' of selection, and that means (1) pre-existing arrangements within the meaning of s 100, (2) any selection by ability authorised by s 101 (pupil banding), and (3) any selection by ability conducted in connection with the admission of pupils to the school for secondary education suitable to the requirements of pupils who are over compulsory school age.

9.27 Section 99 also provides that admission arrangements for a maintained school may make provision for selection by aptitude only if (1) they are pre-existing arrangements within the meaning of s 100, or (2) they are authorised by s 102 (which concerns aptitude for particular subjects).[3]

9.28 For these purposes (and those of the rest of Chapter II of Part III), 'a school's admission arrangements make provision for selection by ability or by aptitude if they make provision for all or any of the pupils who are to be admitted to the school in any relevant age group to be so admitted by reference to ability or to aptitude (as the case may be)'.[4]

9.29 Section 100 permits existing provision in admission arrangements for a maintained school (other than a grammar school within the meaning of s 104(2)[5]) for selection by ability or aptitude to continue, as long as there is (1) no increase in the 'proportion of admissions' (as defined in s 100(3) and the Education (Proportion of Selective Admissions) Regulations 1998[6]) in any relevant age group, and (2) no significant change in the basis of selection as compared with the beginning of the 1997–98 school year.

Selection by reference to ability

9.30 Section 101(1)[7] permits selection by reference to ability to the extent that the admission arrangements are designed to secure that (a) in any year the pupils admitted to the school in any relevant age group are representative of all levels of ability among applicants for admission to the school in that age group, and (b) no level of ability is substantially over-represented or substantially under-represented. The introduction of

---

[1] Which means either general ability or ability in any particular subject or subjects: s 99(5)(b).
[2] See s 99(1) and (2).
[3] See SSFA 1998, s 99(3) and (4).
[4] Ibid, s 99(5)(a).
[5] As to which, see para **9.33**.
[6] SI 1998/2229.
[7] SSFA 1998, s 101(1) does not apply if some further process is required or authorised to be carried out in relation to the applicant for the purpose of determining whether or not he is to be admitted to the school: s 101(2). However, that does not prevent selection by aptitude under s 101 of the SSFA 1998, as to which see para **9.31**.

such arrangements requires the public notice procedure in s 28 of the SSFA 1998 to be followed.[1] Furthermore such arrangements are not authorised by s 101 unless that procedure has been followed and the arrangements have fallen to be implemented.[2]

Selection by reference to aptitude

9.31 Section 102 (subject to an exception) permits the selection of pupils by reference to their aptitude for one or more subjects prescribed by regulations[3] where (a) the admission authority for the school[4] is satisfied that the school has a specialism in the subject or subjects in question, and (b) the proportion of selective admissions (as defined by s 102(4) and the Education (Proportion of Selective Admissions) Regulations 1998[5]) in any relevant age group does not exceed 10 per cent. The exception is where the admission arrangements make provision for any test to be carried out in relation to an applicant for admission which is either a test of ability, or one designed to elicit any aptitude of his for a subject which is not that (or one of those) in question.[6] 'Aptitude' in this context, as contrasted with 'ability', was described by Mr S Byers, MP, the Minister for School Standards, in the relevant House of Commons Standing Committee, on 24 February 1998:

> 'Ability is what a child has already achieved. Aptitude is the natural talent and interest that a child has in a specific subject: in other words, the potential to develop a skill or talent. That is the distinction in the Bill. I am pleased to put that on record. With ability, we are talking of where a child is already. With aptitude, we are talking of a child's scope for development in the future – an innate talent in a particular area.'

Introducing, varying, or abandoning selective admission arrangements

9.32 The introduction, variation or abandonment of selective admission arrangements by reference to ability or aptitude (other than by grammar schools, as to which see below) must be effected by following the procedure in ss 89 and 90 of the SSFA 1998 governing the determination of admission arrangements, unless the change is one which regulations require to be implemented by means of the public notice procedure in s 28 of that Act.[7]

---

[1] SSFA 1998, s 101(3). See paras **7.22** et seq concerning s 28 of the SSFA 1998.

[2] Ibid, s 101(4).

[3] See the Education (Aptitude for Particular Subjects) Regulations 1999, SI 1999/258. These are one or more of any modern foreign language, any performing art, any visual art, any sport, and physical education, design and technology and information technology: see reg 2.

[4] Although this is not expressly provided, it is clear that this means an admission authority within the meaning of s 88 of the SSFA 1998, concerning which, see para **9.8**.

[5] SI 1998/2229.

[6] SSFA 1998, s 102(2). This is itself subject to s 101(1): s 102(3).

[7] See ibid, s 103. See paras **9.9–9.15** concerning ss 89 and 90, and paras **7.22** et seq concerning s 28. Note also s 103(3) in relation to the variation of admission arrangements to which s 101(1) applies.

GRAMMAR SCHOOLS

9.33   Section 104 of the SSFA 1998 defines a grammar school for the purposes of Chapter II of Part III of that Act. A school is a grammar school for those purposes only if it is designated as such a school by the Secretary of State under s 104(1), and he was permitted by that subsection only if he 'is satisfied that [the school] had selective admission arrangements at the beginning of the 1997–98 school year'.[1] Selective admission arrangements for a school for this purpose are 'admission arrangements [which] make provision for all (or substantially all) of its pupils to be selected by reference to general ability, with a view to admitting only pupils with high ability'.[2]

9.34   Sections 104–109 of the SSFA 1998 have the effect that grammar schools may continue in existence only if a ballot of parents under s 105 (held at the request of not less than 20 per cent of certain of the parents[3]) is not in favour of the school ceasing to be a grammar school. The word 'parents' is defined for this purpose by s 106 as (1) 'registered parents of registered pupils'[4] at (i) maintained and (ii) independent schools within the area, or a prescribed part of the area of, the LEA (in the case of the parents of pupils at independent schools, as long as the parents are themselves resident within the relevant area), and (2) parents of children of a description prescribed by regulations who are resident in the relevant area and have registered with the relevant body in order to be eligible to request or vote in a ballot under s 105.[5] Much of the procedure for such ballots and much of the provision for determining who is eligible to vote in them must be determined by reference to regulations.[6] Furthermore, once a grammar school's admission arrangements have been altered so that the school no longer has selective admission arrangements within the meaning of s 104(2), it may not regain its former status as a grammar school.[7] Such an alteration must, however, be effected by means of the public notice procedure in s 28 of the SSFA 1998,[8] although any proposals for such an alteration to

---

1   See the final sentence of para **9.34** for the exception to this general rule. A designation order has been made under s 104(1): the Education (Grammar School Designation) Order 1998, SI 1998/2219, which was amended by SI 1999/2456.

2   SSFA 1998, s 104(2).

3   See ibid, s 106(3).

4   For the meaning of the words 'registered parents of registered pupils', see para **9.24**.

5   See the Education (Grammar School Ballots) Regulations 1998, SI 1998/2876, which are modified by the Education (Substituted Grammar Schools) Regulations 1999, SI 1999/2102 and the Education (Proposals for Grammar Schools to Cease to have Selective Admissions Arrangements) Regulations 1999, SI 1999/2103.

6   See, in particular (but by no means exclusively), SSFA 1998, s 105. There are, however, restrictions in section 107 on (among other things) the publication by LEAs and the governing bodies of maintained schools of material which is to any extent designed (broadly) to influence (1) the question whether a relevant ballot should be held, or (2) the outcome of such a ballot. The current regulations are the Education (Grammar School Ballots) Regulations 1998, SI 1998/2876 which are modified by the Education (Substituted Grammar Schools) Regulations 1999, SI 1999/2102 and the Education (Proposals for Grammar Schools to Cease to have Selective Admissions Arrangements) Regulations 1999, SI 1999/2103. A challenge to the validity of SI 1998/2876 was rejected in *R v Secretary of State for Education and Employment, ex parte RCO* [2000] ELR 307.

7   This is the combined effect of ss 104(1) and (7), 108(3) and 109(5).

8   As to which, see paras **7.22** et seq.

a community school must be made by the governing body and not the LEA.[1] Nevertheless, regulations made under s 104(5) may enable the Secretary of State to make an order designating as a grammar school for the purposes of Chapter II of Part III of the SSFA 1998, a maintained school established in substitution for one or more discontinued schools each of which either has been or could have been so designated.[2]

DETERMINING ADMISSIONS

Human Rights Act 1998

9.35   In *R ota O v St James Roman Catholic Primary School Appeal Panel*,[3] Newman J accepted:

> 'without deciding, that the right to respect for family life under Art 8 of the Convention can be engaged by an admissions decision to a religious school, where one sibling is already attending, and that equally the right to respect for parents' religious convictions under Art 2 of Protocol 1 can thereby be engaged.'

9.36   However, he said:

> 'It is of course plain that those rights do not confer any absolute right to admission and there will be circumstances where competing considerations, for example the provision of efficient education to others and the efficient use of resources, will justify a refusal for admission.
>
> Article 8 confers no absolute right to have a child admitted to a school already attended by a sibling. In my judgment a school will act compatibly with Art 8 by having in its admission policy a sibling criterion. In this instance priority is given in the ordinary admissions round, and where it is not the ordinary admissions round, priority is given on the waiting list.
>
> So far as Art 2 of Protocol 1 is concerned, it is material to point out that the United Kingdom did enter a reservation in respect of the second sentence of Art 2 when ratifying that protocol, affirming the principle with respect to parents' religious and philosophical conviction "only so far as it is compatible with the provision of additional instruction and training and the avoidance of unreasonable public expenditure".
>
> In my judgment, no question of incompatibility arises upon the content of these statutory provisions and the Convention.'[4]

9.37   This is consistent with the decision of the Court of Appeal in *School Admissions Appeals Panel for the London Borough of Hounslow v London Borough of Hounslow*,[5] where May LJ, with whom Tuckey and Kennedy LJJ agreed, said:

---

1   See SSFA 1998, s 109(2). The Education (Proposals for Grammar Schools to cease to have Selective Admission Arrangements) Regulations 1999, SI 1999/2103 apply to that situation.
2   See the Education (Substituted Grammar Schools) Regulations 1999, SI 1999/2102.
3   [2001] ELR 469, at para 36.
4   Ibid, at paras 36–37.
5   [2002] EWCA Civ 900; [2002] ELR 602, at para 62.

'Of course, Hounslow, the panel and this court are public authorities within s 6 of the Human Rights Act 1998 and the court is required by s 2 of the Act to take into account, among other things, decisions of the European Court of Human Rights. But in the present cases the relevant considerations are obvious and can be simply expressed. A local education authority's school admission arrangements must be fair and fairly operated. If a school is over-subscribed, there will necessarily be discrimination, because not every child whose parents apply for admission can be admitted. This may be particularly acute with admissions to infants classes, because of the statutory limit on their size. No one suggests that a limit of this kind is other than desirable. Discrimination needs to have reasonable objective justification. Some children will have stronger cases than others for admission. A child with an elder brother or sister in a school may well have a strong case wherever they live; but so may a child who lives close to the school.'[1]

9.38   In *R(K) v London Borough of Newham*,[2] Collins J said that as a result of the incorporation by the HRA 1998 of Art 2 of Protocol 1 to the European Convention on Human Rights, 'the religious conviction of a parent is something to which due weight must be given in considering admission to a particular school'. Thus the LEA and, on appeal, the appeal panel should, he said,[3] give 'due weight' to the fact that a parent's desire for the education of his or her child in a single-sex school stems from a real religious conviction. Although these comments must be read in the light of the comments of the Court of Appeal in *Hounslow* concerning the relevance of the Convention to admission appeals, it is suggested here that Collins J's reliance on the Convention in relation to religious convictions should not be regarded as overruled by *Hounslow*. However, the weight to be accorded to the motivation of the parent's desire is probably best regarded as diminished by *Hounslow*.

Preference based on racial grounds

9.39   If a parent expresses a preference for a school on racial grounds, then, as a result of s 86(2) of the SSFA 1998, the LEA and the governing body of the relevant school must nevertheless comply with the preference unless excused by one of the provisions referred to in para **9.3**: to do so would not contravene s 17 or s 18 of the Race Relations Act 1976, which make discrimination on the ground of race unlawful in relation to (among other things) admissions to schools.[4] This is one result of *R v Cleveland County Council, ex parte The Commission for Racial Equality*,[5] where the court ruled that s 41(1) of the Race Relations Act 1976 applied an LEA's compliance with what is now s 86(2) of the SSFA 1998.[6] Section 41(1) provides:

---

[1]   This passage was applied by Richards J in R *(Khundakji and Salahi) v (1) Admissions Appeal Panel of Cardiff County Council and (2) Cardiff County Council* [2003] EWHC 436 (Admin); [2003] ELR 495, at paras 52 and 53.

[2]   [2002] ELR 390, at para 29.

[3]   Ibid, at para 38.

[4]   As to which, see para **18.32**. There are equivalents of ss 17 and 18 of the Race Relations Act in the Sex Discrimination Act 1975: ss 22 and 23, as to which see paras **18.6** and **18.7**.

[5]   [1994] ELR 44, CA. Although both the judge at first instance and the Court of Appeal accepted that the parent in question had not in fact expressed her preference on racial grounds, both courts ruled on the question of principle involved. The Court of Appeal determined in any event that the Council did not act on racial grounds: see ibid, at 52G–53A.

[6]   See ibid, at 51H.

'Nothing in Parts II to IV [which include sections 17 and 18] shall render unlawful any act of discrimination done –

(a)   in pursuance of any enactment or Order in Council; or

(b)   in pursuance of any instrument made under any enactment by a Minister of the Crown.'

9.40   This ruling appears to be unaffected by the enactment of the HRA 1998.

When should parents be required to express a preference for a selective school?

9.41   The time when a parent should be required to express a preference for a selective school can be problematic. This is because if a parent is allowed first to express a preference for a selective school and then, if the preference is not met because either the child in question is adjudged to be of insufficiently high academic ability or not to have the relevant aptitude, to express a fresh preference for a non-selective school, the parent will have two opportunities to express a first preference. Furthermore, the first preference will in fact be for a selective school, and a parent who does not apply for a place at a selective school could be regarded as treated unfairly if the parent who applies for a place at a selective school is then treated as expressing a first preference for a non-selective school. Accordingly, adjudicators 'have consistently held that to delay the expression of preferences until parents interested in grammar schools know whether their children do or do not meet selective schools' entry standards is unfair to other parents who want a place only at a non-selective school or schools'.[1] Accordingly, 'In those areas where grammar schools exist, parents should be asked to express school preferences before they know the outcome of selective tests'.[2]

Policies which may or may not be applied in the event of oversubscription

9.42   As stated above, if the proposed number of pupils to be admitted to a school does not exceed the number determined under s 89 of the SSFA 1998 as the number of pupils in that age group that it is intended to admit to the school in that year and the school is not selective, then the LEA and the governing body of the school will have no power to refuse admission to a pupil whose parent expresses a preference under s 86(1) in respect of the school.[3] If, however, the school is oversubscribed – that is the number of applicants (or, as the case may be, qualified applicants) for places at the school is greater than the number determined under s 89 – then the

---

[1]   School Admissions Code of Practice, DfES/0031/2003, para 3.20.

[2]   Ibid.

[3]   In R *v Stockton-on-Tees Borough Council, ex parte W* [2000] ELR 93, the Court of Appeal decided that it is open to an LEA to decide that the admission of a further child to a school would prejudice the provision of efficient education and the efficient use of resources even though the LEA in practice planned subsequently to admit to the school pupils whose parents moved into the catchment area for the school when there had been no subsequent reduction in the number of pupils admitted to the school. This seems to be contrary to s 86(5) of the SSFA 1998. It is of note that the School Admissions Code of Practice for England (DfES/0031/2003) is of the same view: see para 7.9, where it is also said that 'admission authorities ... should not hold back or reserve places e.g. in the expectation that there may be later applications from families moving into the catchment area'.

admission authority may apply policies to determine which applications should be successful. This is implicitly recognised in para 3 of Sch 2 to the Education (School Information) (England) Regulations 2002,[1] which requires the 'composite prospectus' within the meaning of reg 8 of those regulations to include 'The particulars of the admissions policy determined for each school in relation to each relevant age group at the school ... including particulars of ... any oversubscription criteria which will be applied to allocate places if there are more applicants than places to a particular school'.

9.43   The School Admissions Code of Practice for England refers extensively to the policies which may be applied in the event of oversubscription. The position of children who are in public care is dealt with for the first time in that Code.[2] There, it is recommended that 'all admission authorities give these children top priority in their oversubscription criteria'.

9.44   The application of policies in the event of oversubscription was first endorsed by the Court of Appeal in *R v Greenwich London Borough Council, ex parte Governors of John Ball Primary School*[3] and by the House of Lords in *Choudhury v Governors of Bishop Challoner Roman Catholic Comprehensive School*.[4] In the former, Lloyd LJ said:

> 'I do not regard efficient education or the efficient use of resources as being the sole source of lawful policy ... In my judgment a local education authority can have any reasonable policy they think fit, provided it does not conflict with their duties under section [86 of the SSFA 1998], or any other enactment ... Sibling priority and the proximity rule are sound and lawful policies whether or not they promote efficient education.'[5]

9.45   The House of Lords in *Choudhury v Governors of Bishop Challoner Roman Catholic Comprehensive School* also approved the application of criteria such as sibling priority and geographical proximity.[6] However, it is clear that an admission authority cannot '[resolve] the sibling issue' by assuming that a child at a school to which application has been made on behalf of a sibling could be moved to a school at which the sibling has been offered a place.[7] Furthermore, where a child's parents are divorced and the child spends a considerable time with both of them separately, the admission authority must take both addresses into account in determining proximity.[8] Nevertheless, if the application of a geographical criterion before the sibling criterion results in parents being unable in practical terms to avoid one or other of their children being late to

---

1   SI 2002/2897.
2   At paras 3.14, 3.15 and 7.22. The position of such children is not mentioned in the current such code for Wales.
3   (1990) 88 LGR 589.
4   [1992] 2 AC 182.
5   88 LGR 589, at 599. Farquharson LJ said words to the same effect at pp 602–603.
6   [1992] 2 AC 182, at 192A–D.
7   See *R v Essex County Council, ex parte Jacobs* [1997] ELR 190, at 200H–201B.
8   Ibid, at 202F–203A. In that case, there was a rare quashing of the original decision. Often, relief is refused because of the administrative difficulties which would be caused by the granting of relief.

school, that does not of itself make the admission criteria unlawful (either in domestic law or as a result of the HRA 1998).[1]

9.46 In R *v Greenwich London Borough Council, ex parte Governors of John Ball Primary School*[2] the Court of Appeal ruled that an LEA's policy of favouring applicants living within its area at the expense of applicants living outside that area was unlawful. This was because to do so would contravene what is now s 86(8)(a) of the SSFA 1998. However, it has since been held that an LEA may apply a catchment area in the event of oversubscription, as long as it does not contravene that provision.[3] The mere fact, however, that the boundary of a catchment area coincides with that of the LEA does not make it unlawful.[4] Such a catchment area may alter from year to year[5] and may be justified by tradition.[6]

> 'One cannot simply place the point to a pair of compasses on the school and draw a circle of so many miles radius around it. If you did that with each school you would have a series of circles, some of which overlap, so some people might live in two or more catchment areas and some people might miss out altogether. Catchment areas have to be carefully considered so that they interlock with each other and have regard to areas of population and bus routes, safe walking distance and matters of that sort.'[7]

9.47 However, the automatic allocation of a place at a school in whose catchment area a pupil lives is unlawful, since a preference in favour of the school has to be expressed by a parent of the pupil under s 86(1) before a place at the school can be allocated, and an opportunity afforded to give reasons for that preference.[8]

9.48 The complexity of admission criteria may make it impossible in practice to challenge the manner in which the criteria were applied by the admission authority. That occurred in R *v South Gloucestershire Education Appeals Committee, ex parte Bryant.*[9] However, the School Admissions Code of Practice for England[10] is firmly in favour of the need for admission criteria to be capable of being assessed objectively. Thus, for example, in para 3.6, it is said that 'It is important that all oversubscription criteria are clearly defined and objectively assessable'.

---

[1] R *(Khundakji and Salahi) v (1) Admissions Appeal Panel of Cardiff County Council and (2) Cardiff County Council* [2003] EWHC 436 (Admin); [2003] ELR 495, at paras 50 and 51, per Richards J.

[2] (1990) 88 LGR 589, followed in R *v Bromley London Borough Council, ex parte C* [1992] 1 FLR 174 and R *v Royal Borough of Kingston upon Thames, ex parte Kingwell* [1992] 1 FLR 182. See para **9.49** regarding *ex parte Kingwell.*

[3] R *v Wiltshire County Council, ex parte Razazan* [1997] ELR 370, CA; R *v Rotherham Metropolitan Borough Council, ex parte LT* [2000] ELR 76, CA. The School Admissions Code of Practice for England states that catchment areas are acceptable in the event of oversubscription: para **3.5**. See also paras **3.8** and **4.17** concerning the application by admission authorities of catchment areas.

[4] R *v Rotherham Metropolitan Borough Council, ex parte LT*, ibid, at 82.

[5] R *v Bradford Metropolitan Borough Council, ex parte Sikander Ali* [1994] ELR 299. There is no need to consult parents on such alteration: R *v Stockton-on-Tees Borough Council, ex parte W* [2000] ELR 93.

[6] R *v Bradford Metropolitan Borough Council, ex parte Sikander Ali*, ibid.

[7] R *v Rotherham Metropolitan Borough Council, ex parte LT*, op cit, at 82.

[8] R *v Rotherham Metropolitan Borough Council, ex parte Clark* [1998] ELR 152, at 169 (where the report of the Court of Appeal's judgment begins).

[9] [2001] ELR 53, CA.

[10] DfES/0031/2003.

9.49   In *R v Kingston upon Thames Royal London Borough, ex parte Kingwell*,[1] the court upheld a revision of an admissions policy which had the effect that applicants resident both within and outside the LEA's area were treated equally, where as a result of that revision a resident of Kingston had less chance of securing a place at a single-sex school for his child than a resident outside the borough. This revision was made because of the *Greenwich* case. As Watkins LJ said:

> 'If primary duty there is in this sphere, it is, in our view, to ensure that there is no discrimination against out-borough residents. Thereafter, the duties to make available efficient education within the area of the local education authority will remain. Presumably this education will be available at schools in the area of another local education authority.'[2]

9.50   A subsequent revision of the same authority's admissions policy in relation to two selective schools in the borough was challenged in *R v Kingston upon Thames Royal London Borough, ex parte Emsden*.[3] Although the subsequent revision was geographically based, it was on its face neutral as far as those inside and outside the borough were concerned. However, it had the effect that those inside the borough were in practice favoured, and the challenge was in part that the purpose behind the revision was to obtain that effect. The judge did not rule on this ground, because the application was made too late in relation to it.

9.51   In *Choudhury v Governors of Bishop Challoner Roman Catholic Comprehensive School*,[4] the House of Lords held that even if no arrangements had been made under what is now s 91 of the SSFA 1998 for preserving the character of what would now be a foundation or voluntary aided school, the admission authority for the school was able to rely, in determining which applications to reject in the event of oversubscription, upon criteria which could have formed such arrangements. However, Sedley J in *R v Governors of La Sainte Union Convent School, ex parte T*[5] commented that:

> 'if a publicly funded school, with statutory permission, adopts an exclusionary rule which shuts out many children who may live nearby and want to go to the school upon religious grounds, then it must expect it to be strictly construed.'[6]

9.52   Although s 91 is prospectively repealed in relation to Wales, and has been repealed in England,[7] this case-law will continue to be of relevance. It is of interest that the School Admissions Code of Practice for England[8] specifically envisages the giving, by a school which is designated by the DfES (presumably under s 69(3) of the SSFA 1998) as having a religious character, of preference in its admission arrangements to members of a particular faith or denomination '(as may be required

1   [1992] 1 FLR 182.
2   [1992] 1 FLR 182, at 188B–C.
3   (1993) 91 LGR 96; [1993] 1 FLR 179.
4   [1992] AC 182.
5   [1996] ELR 98.
6   Ibid, at 101D. Cf *R v Governing Body of Dame Alice Owen's School, ex parte S* [1998] EdCR 101, where a selective admissions policy was construed strictly, albeit that it was construed purposively rather than literally.
7   See EA 2002, s 49 and Sch 22; in relation to England, see SI 2002/2439.
8   DfES/0031/2003, at para 3.9.

by their Trust Deed), providing this does not conflict with other legislation, such as race relations legislation'. This is consistent with the House of Lords' ruling in *Choudhury v Governors of Bishop Challoner Roman Catholic Comprehensive School.* However, although the previous version of the School Admissions Code of Practice for England allowed interviewing parents and/or prospective pupils for the purpose of assessing religious or denominational commitment where this was provided for in the admission arrangements or oversubscription criteria, the current Code prohibits, for the 'admission round leading to September 2005 intakes and subsequent admissions' the interviewing of parents or children as any part of the application or admission process, unless a school is a boarding school and the interview is 'necessary to assess the suitability of the child for a boarding place'.[1] However, this does not mean that auditions which are 'part of objective testing for aptitude conducted by a school with a specialism in a prescribed subject ... or discussion of subject choice with those applying for sixth forms' are prohibited.[2]

9.53   In *R v Kingston upon Thames Royal London Borough Council, ex parte Emsden,*[3] Schiemann J approved the application of a geographical criterion to be applied where there were more than enough applicants able to satisfy the selection criteria for a selective school, on the basis of what is now s 86(3)(c). However, it is suggested here that the proper basis was in fact what is now section 86(3)(a).

9.54   In *R v Lancashire County Council, ex parte F,*[4] it was held that in the circumstances of that case it was lawful for non-Roman Catholic schools maintained by the LEA to have an admission policy of rejecting applications from Roman Catholic pupils in favour of those who were non-Roman Catholic in the event of oversubscription. This was despite the fact that the policy was contrary to the then relevant DfE Circular.[5] The circumstances were that if such a policy were not applied then there would be a number of children who could not be given places in the areas in which they lived.[6]

Irrelevant considerations

9.55   It was held in *R v Secretary of State for Education and Employment and the Governors of Southlands Community Comprehensive School, ex parte W*[7] to have been contrary to the respondent grant-maintained school's articles of government and therefore unlawful to decline to accept an applicant for a place because of her parent's past behaviour. (The applicant's sister was already a pupil at the school, and the parent's behaviour was in response to the school staff's actions in relation to that sister.[8])

---

[1]   At para 3.16.
[2]   Ibid.
[3]   (1993) 91 LGR 96; [1993] 1 FLR 179.
[4]   [1995] ELR 33.
[5]   6/93. See [1995] ELR 33, at 37. That circular had been considered by the respondent LEA: ibid.
[6]   Ibid, at 41C.
[7]   [1998] ELR 413; [1998] EdCR 135.
[8]   It is of interest that the court nevertheless declined to order the governing body to admit the child: see further, para **3.40**.

9.56   The School Admissions Code of Practice for England[1] refers to the analogous situation of a pupil whose own behaviour causes the admission authority to wish to decline to offer him a place to which he is apparently entitled. In some circumstances, according to that Code, it will be possible to do so; this will normally be 'where a school has a particularly high concentration of pupils with challenging behaviour, or the child is particularly challenging' and the school is in one or more of five particular circumstances, including that the school 'is a Fresh Start School or Academy open for less than two years'.[2]

Late applications

9.57   Paragraph 7.14 of the School Admissions Code of Practice for England[3] states that LEAs and other admission authorities:

> 'should, as far as possible, be willing to accept applications which are received late for a good reason, for example, when a single parent has been ill for some time, or a family have just moved into the area, or a family are returning from abroad - if applications are received before offers of places are made.'

THE EFFECT OF A MISTAKEN OFFER OF A PLACE AT A MAINTAINED SCHOOL

9.58   A mistaken offer of a place at a maintained school will only rarely lead to an entitlement to a place at such school. The principle of irrevocability might be relied upon by a parent in arguing that the offer could not be withdrawn,[4] but that principle was not applied on the facts in *R v Birmingham City Council, ex parte L*.[5] An alternative submission that a legitimate expectation had arisen in favour of a parent who had received an erroneous decision letter, was also rejected. In *R v Beatrix Potter School, ex parte K*,[6] it was held that a legitimate expectation had arisen in favour of a parent that his child would be admitted to a particular school, but that it was not unlawful in the circumstances to withdraw the offer of a place at that school.[7]

---

[1]   DfES/0031/2003, paras 7.5– 7.7.

[2]   At para 7.7.

[3]   DfES/0031/2003.

[4]   On the principle of irrevocability, see paras 14.44 and 14.45 of the first edition of this book. *Rootkin v Kent County Council* [1981] 1 WLR 1186 contains a reasonably recent analysis of the principle.

[5]   [2000] ELR 543.

[6]   [1997] ELR 468.

[7]   See further, paras 7.26 and 7.27 of the School Admissions Code of Practice for England, DfES/0031/2003, concerning the withdrawal of offers.

APPEALS AGAINST REFUSALS OF ADMISSION[1]

Introduction: responsibility for making the appeal arrangements

LEA responsibility

9.59 An LEA must make arrangements for enabling the parent of a child to appeal against a decision as to the school at which education is to be provided for the child in the exercise of the authority's functions, other than a decision leading to or embodied in a direction under s 96 (concerning directed admissions[2]).[3] An LEA must also make arrangements for enabling the parent of a child to appeal against any decision made by or on behalf of the governing body of a community or voluntary controlled school maintained by the LEA, refusing the child admission to the school.[4]

9.60 Where a child has been permanently excluded from two or more schools[5] (no matter how long the gap between them[6]), during the period of 2 years from the last of those exclusions,[7] no obligation to make such appeal arrangements in favour of the parent of such a child arises.[8] However, if the LEA direct a community or voluntary controlled school to admit such a child and (currently only in England) the LEA is the admission authority for the school,[9] the LEA are under a duty to permit the governing body to appeal to an appeal panel constituted in accordance with such arrangements.[10] The obvious reason for the confinement of this right to the governing body of such schools is that any other school would be able to refer under s 97 of the SSFA 1998 to the Secretary of State a decision of the LEA made under s 96 of that Act to direct a child's admission to the school.[11]

9.61 The LEA must also make arrangements for enabling the parent of a child who has been admitted to a community or voluntary controlled school maintained by the LEA to appeal against any decision made by or on behalf of the governing body refusing permission for the child to enter the school's sixth form.[12] Entering the school's sixth form in this context means 'being transferred to a class at the school in which secondary education suitable to the requirements of pupils who are over

---

[1] Where unlawful discrimination contrary to the Disability Discrimination Act 1995 is claimed in relation to a refusal of admission to a maintained school, the claim must be made to an appeal panel of the type described below. See further, para **18.58**.

[2] See paras **2.77** and **2.78** concerning directed admissions.

[3] SSFA 1998, s 94(1)(a).

[4] SSFA 1998, s 94(1)(b).

[5] For the definition of 'permanent exclusion' in this context, see ibid, s 87(4).

[6] Ibid, s 87(3).

[7] Ibid, s 87(2). The permanent exclusion takes effect for this purpose when the head teacher of the school decided that the pupil should be permanently excluded: s 87(6).

[8] Ibid, s 95(1).

[9] EA 2002, Sch 4, para 10; see SI 2002/2439.

[10] SSFA 1998, s 95(2).

[11] See paras **2.77** and **2.78**.

[12] SSFA 1998, s 94(1A), as inserted by para 8 of Sch 4 to the EA 2002 in relation to England by SI 2002/2439 and in relation to Wales by SI 2002/3185.

compulsory school age is provided from a class in which such education is not provided'.[1]

Responsibility of governing body of a foundation or voluntary aided school

9.62   The governing body of a foundation or voluntary aided school must make arrangements for enabling the parent of a child to appeal against any decision made by or on behalf of the governing body refusing the child admission to the school.[2] The governing bodies of two or more such schools which are maintained by the same authority may make joint arrangements of this kind.[3] An LEA and the governing body or bodies of one or more foundation or voluntary aided schools maintained by the LEA may make joint arrangements under s 94.[4]

9.63   The governing body of a foundation or voluntary aided school must make arrangements for enabling the parent of a child who has been admitted to the school to appeal against any decision made by or on behalf of the governing body refusing permission for the child to enter the school's sixth form.[5]

Appeal panel: constitution and procedure

9.64   In Wales, the appeal is to an appeal panel constituted in accordance with Part I of Sch 24 to the SSFA 1998, and the procedure which must be followed by such a panel is provided for in Part II of that Schedule. In England, the constitution and procedure of the appeal panel is governed by regulations made under s 94(5), (5A), (5B) and (5C) of the SSFA 1998, as substituted by s 50 of the EA 2002 (which is not yet in force in relation to Wales). These are the Education (Admission Appeals Arrangements) (England) Regulations 2002.[6]

Constitution

9.65   The constitution of the appeal panel is provided for in Sch 1 to those regulations. The panel must consist of three or five members appointed in the case of a panel arranged by the LEA from (a) persons who are eligible to be lay members, and (b) persons who have experience in education, are acquainted with educational conditions in the area of the authority or are parents of registered pupils at a school.[7] For this purpose, 'a person is eligible to be a lay member if he is a person without personal experience in the management of any school or the provision of education in any school (disregarding any such experience as a governor or in any other voluntary capacity)'.[8] There must be at least one lay member and one person with experience of

---

[1]   SSFA 1998, s 94(7A).

[2]   Ibid, s 94(2).

[3]   Ibid, s 94(3).

[4]   Ibid, s 94(4).

[5]   SSFA 1998, s 94(2A), as inserted by para 8(2) of Sch 21 to the EA 2002. See para **9.61** concerning what it means to enter the sixth form.

[6]   SI 2002/2899.

[7]   Ibid, Sch 1, para 1(1).

[8]   Ibid, Sch 1, para 1(3).

education of the relevant sort.[1] Certain persons are disqualified from membership of an appeal panel. These are:[2]

> '(a) any member of the authority or governing body of the school in question;
>
> (b) any person employed by the authority or the governing body or governing bodies, other than a person employed as a teacher;[3]
>
> (c) any person who has, or at any time has had, any connection with the authority or the school, or with any person within paragraph (b), of a kind which might reasonably be taken to raise doubts about his ability to act impartially in relation to the authority or the school.'

9.66 However, a person who is employed as a teacher by the LEA is not, by reason only of that employment, to be taken to have such a connection.[4] Furthermore, a person who is a teacher at a school may not be a member of an appeal panel which is considering an appeal 'involving a question whether a child is to be admitted to that school'.[5] Moreover (presumably for the avoidance of doubt, although it is hard to see why this is the subject of specific provision), a person may not be a member of an appeal panel considering an appeal against a decision 'if he was among those who made the decision or took part in discussions as to whether the decision should be made'.[6]

9.67 If a member of a five-person panel dies after the commencement of the appeal or becomes unable through illness to continue as a member, the panel may nevertheless continue to consider the relevant appeal(s) as long as the number of members does not fall below three and there are two members of the sort required by para 1(2) of Sch 1.[7]

9.68 Appeal panels arranged pursuant to s 95(2) are constituted in accordance with para 1 of Sch 1 to the Education (Admission Appeals Arrangements) (England) Regulations 2002,[8] although in that case a person may not be a member of the appeal panel if he has 'to any extent been involved in any previous consideration of the question whether the child in question should or should not be reinstated at any school from which he has at any time been permanently excluded, or in any previous appeal relating to the child under section 95(2)'.[9]

Indemnity in respect of costs of legal proceedings

9.69 The members of an appeal panel have the benefit of an indemnity against 'any reasonable legal costs and expenses reasonably incurred by those members in

---

[1] SI 2002/2899, Sch 1, para 1(2).
[2] Ibid, Sch 1, para 1(6).
[3] This does not include a firm of solicitors retained from time to time: *R (L) v The Independent Appeal Panel of St Edward's College* [2001] EWHC Admin 108; [2001] ELR 542, at para 33.
[4] SI 2002/2899, Sch 1, para 1(7).
[5] SSFA 1998, Sch 1, para 1(9). This is hardly surprising.
[6] SI 2002/2899, Sch 1, para 1(8).
[7] Ibid, Sch 1, para 1(10).
[8] Ibid, Sch 1, para 5(1).
[9] Ibid, Sch 1, para 5(2).

connection with any decision or action taken by them in good faith in pursuance of their functions as members of that panel'.[1]

Allowances of members

9.70   The members of an appeal panel constituted under the Education (Admission Appeals Arrangements) (England) Regulations 2002 have the right to financial allowances in certain circumstances.[2]

Infant classes

9.71   In an appeal against a refusal of a place in an infant class:

> 'an appeal panel shall determine that a place is to be offered to the child only if they are satisfied -
>
> (a)   that the decision was not one which a reasonable admission authority would make in the circumstances of the case; or
>
> (b)   that the child would have been offered a place if the admission arrangements (as published in accordance with regulations made under section 92) had been properly implemented.'[3]

9.72   The procedure to be followed in relation to such an appeal was helpfully and clearly set out by May LJ in *School Admissions Appeals Panel for the London Borough of Hounslow v London Borough of Hounslow*:[4]

> 'parents need to make a particular case which is so compelling that the decision not to admit the child is shown to be perverse. A local education authority opposing an appeal will need to explain their admission arrangements, explain their particular problems in relation to the school in question, and show that, unfortunate though it may be, it was objectively fair not to admit the child in question. They may wish to show that they had to refuse admission to several children with good cases, but that admitting one or more of those children would have entailed refusing one or more of those who were admitted because of the class size limit. As to the panel, their task is not simply to rubber stamp the local education authority's decision, but they can only uphold the appeal if they conclude that it was perverse in the light of the admission arrangements to refuse to admit the particular child. Their task is not to take again the original decision.'

Matters to be taken into account

9.73   The matters to be taken into account by an appeal panel hearing an appeal under arrangements made under ss 94 and 95 are affected by reg 6 of the Education (Admission Appeals Arrangements) (England) Regulations 2002.[5] In relation to an 'ordinary' appeal (that is, not one concerning admission to an infant class), under s 94(1)–(4) inclusive, the matters 'to be taken into account' by a panel 'include' the

---

1   SI 2002/2899, reg 8(1).
2   See ibid, reg 7.
3   SI 2002/2899, Sch 1, reg 6(2).
4   [2002] EWCA Civ 900; [2002] ELR 602, at para 63.
5   SI 2002/2899.

parent's expressed preference and the published arrangements for the admission of pupils to the school.[1]

9.74 In *School Admissions Appeals Panel for the London Borough of Hounslow v London Borough of Hounslow*,[2] the Court of Appeal held that even where an appeal relates to an infant class, the panel must apply para 11 of Sch 24 (now reg 6(1) of the Education (Admission Appeals Arrangements) (England) Regulations 2002), so that parental preference 'remains relevant', although the scope for a successful appeal is 'limited'.[3] In *R v London Borough of Richmond, ex parte JC*,[4] the Court of Appeal held that in applying what is now reg 6(2)(a) of the Education (Admission Appeals Arrangements) (England) Regulations 2002, the appeal panel can have regard to fresh evidence in certain circumstances, although it cannot conduct a rehearing.[5] The court also held that what is now reg 6(2)(b) 'is really a slip clause empowering the appeal committee to put right any error made by the admissions authority ... on the information available to it'.[6]

9.75 In relation to an appeal under arrangements made under s 95(2) of the SSFA 1998, the appeal committee must 'have regard' to:

'(a)   the reasons for the local education authority's decision that the child in question should be admitted; and

(b)   any reasons put forward by the governing body as to why the child's admission would be inappropriate.'[7]

9.76 The relevant provisions of the admissions appeals code of practice need also to be taken into account.[8] These include guidance as to the effect of *R v London Borough of Richmond, ex parte JC*.[9]

9.77 One effect of *R v Sheffield City Council, ex parte H*[10] is that an appeal panel hearing an appeal against a refusal of admission to a maintained school where the child is not an infant (and to whose class the class size limit imposed by s 1 of the SSFA 1998 therefore does not apply) may take into account an unlawfulness in the detail of the admissions procedure.[11] However, this does not mean that a panel must

---

1   Regulation 6(1). See para **9.25** regarding the duty to publish the arrangements.
2   [2002] EWCA Civ 900; [2002] ELR 602.
3   [2002] EWCA Civ 900; [2002] ELR 602, at para 51.
4   [2001] ELR 21.
5   See paras 52 and 53.
6   [2001] ELR 21, para 41.
7   SI 2002/2899, reg 6(3).
8   SSFA 1998, s 84(1). See para **9.17** concerning the codes for England and Wales.
9   See para 4.57.
10   [1999] ELR 511.
11   This is the interpretation of the Court of Appeal in *School Admissions Appeals Panel for the London Borough of Hounslow v London Borough of Hounslow* [2002] EWCA Civ 900; [2002] ELR 602, at para 22.

adjourn its hearing while judicial review proceedings take place.[1] Rather, such a challenge should be made only in 'quite exceptional' circumstances.[2] Indeed:

> 'Appeal panels are obliged to take appropriate account of procedural or substantive errors, if they are relevant to the question they have to determine. This may readily apply to relevant errors which are established or self-evident. By contrast, although general admission arrangements are not, as I have said, immune from examination, it will scarcely ever be necessary to go further than to consider whether their application to the particular child was perverse.'[3]

9.78   However, *R v Sheffield City Council, ex parte H* 'should [not] be read as absolutely limited to established or self-evident unlawfulness'.[4] Nevertheless, appeal panels should not 'embark on wide-ranging inquiries which will normally be neither appropriate nor necessary, thus tending to divert them from their main task'.[5]

9.79   In any event, one clear effect of *R v Sheffield City Council, ex parte H*[6] is that an appeal panel other than one determining an appeal against a refusal of admission to an infant class must consider the circumstances of the case afresh, and are not limited to reviewing the decision of the admission authority.[7] According to Pill LJ, 'an appellant is intended to have the right to an independent and general scrutiny of his case'.[8]

Procedure

Generally

9.80   Parents must be informed of their rights of appeal under s 94 where a decision against which they may appeal under s 94 is notified to them.[9] An appeal must be made by notice in writing, setting out the grounds on which it is made.[10] The appellant must be given the opportunity to appear and make oral representations, whether himself or by a representative, and has the right to be accompanied if not represented.[11] Appeals must be held in private unless the body or bodies by whom the arrangements are made under s 94 'direct otherwise'.[12] In the event of disagreement,

---

[1]   *School Admissions Appeals Panel for the London Borough of Hounslow v London Borough of Hounslow* [2002] EWCA Civ 900; [2002] ELR 602, at para 60.

[2]   Ibid.

[3]   Ibid, at para 61.

[4]   Ibid.

[5]   Ibid. *R (M-P) v London Borough of Barking and Dagenham and Barking Abbey Comprehensive School* [2002] EWHC 2483 (Admin); [2003] ELR 144 involved an appeal against a refusal of admission to a maintained school where the application for admission followed the deletion of the relevant child's name from the school's register. Nevertheless, it is of interest that it was held there that since it was impossible to draw 'a sensible distinction between the factual circumstances of removal and legality, ... the panel should have considered the legality of the removal from the roll'.

[6]   [1999] ELR 511.

[7]   Ibid, at 522 per Pill LJ, and 526, per Peter Gibson LJ.

[8]   Ibid.

[9]   See the Education (Admission Appeals Arrangements) (England) Regulations 2002, SI 2002/2899, Sch 2, para 1(2).

[10]   Ibid, Sch 2, para 1(3).

[11]   Ibid, Sch 2, para 1(4).

[12]   Ibid, Sch 2, para 1(5). However, a panel constituted under para 1 of Sch 1 may allow one member of the LEA to attend as an observer the hearing of the appeal, and a panel constituted in accordance with

appeals are to be determined by a majority vote with the chairman having a second or casting vote in the case of an equality of votes.[1] Subject to these matters, the procedure relating to appeals, including the time-limit for appealing, is to be determined by the body which arranges the appeals.[2]

9.81   An appeal panel must comply with the rules of natural justice. A statement of some significance regarding the application of the rules of natural justice to the proceedings of an appeal committee was made by Scott Baker J in *R v Birmingham City Council Education Appeals Committee, ex parte B*:[3]

> 'Where an appeal committee of this nature is minded to disbelieve a case that is being advanced by an appellant, they should give that appellant an opportunity of dealing specifically with the points that are troubling them and are leading them towards making such a finding and give the appellant an opportunity of dealing with them.'

9.82   In any event, it has been held that a committee hearing an appeal against a refusal of admission on the ground that the admission of the child would prejudice the provision of efficient education or the efficient use of resources has to follow a certain procedure. That procedure is a two-stage one, as described in *R v Commissioner for Local Administration, ex parte Croydon London Borough Council*[4] (where Woolf LJ followed and approved *R v South Glamorgan Appeals Committee, ex parte Evans*[5]) and as approved by the Court of Appeal in *W (A Minor) v Education Appeal Committee of Lancashire County Council*.[6] The first stage is to determine whether or not the admission of the child would cause prejudice to the provision of efficient education or the efficient use of resources of the school in question. This is a matter which it is primarily for the body against whose decision the appeal is brought to show, although it is not right to say that that body has the burden of proof in that regard.[7] However, it is not enough for the school to show the appeal panel merely that the school has a reasonable case to the effect that such prejudice would be caused if the child were admitted.[8]

9.83   The second stage of the procedure will arise only if prejudice of the relevant sort is shown, and consists of determining whether that prejudice outweighs the parent's preference. If the application of the second stage of the test results in only one parent's appeal being successful, then that is the end of the matter. However, according to Sedley J in *R v Education Appeal Committee of Leicestershire County Council, ex*

---

para 1 or 2 of Sch 1 may allow one member of the governing body of the school in question to attend as an observer. Furthermore, one member of the Council on Tribunals may attend as an observer any panel considering an appeal: ibid.

[1]   Ibid, Sch 2, para 1(7). The case of *R v (1) Wakefield Diocesan Board of Education (Schools Appeal Tribunal) (2) Holy Trinity School, Wakefield* [1999] EdCR 566 (regarding which see para **10.71**) should be noted in this context.

[2]   SI 2002/2899, Sch 2, para 1(9).

[3]   [1999] ELR 305, at 312C–D; [1999] EdCR 573, at 581G–582A.

[4]   [1989] 1 All ER 1033.

[5]   (1984), unreported, QBD.

[6]   [1994] ELR 530; see per Hirst LJ (with whom Peter Gibson LJ agreed) at 538A–C.

[7]   [1989] 1 All ER 1033, at 1041a–c.

[8]   *R v Brighouse School Appeal Committee, ex parte G and B* [1997] ELR 39, at 44F–H.

parte Tarmohamed,[1] if more than one parent's preference outweighs the relevant prejudice but the admission of all of the relevant children would 'create such further stress upon the school's provision and resources that they cannot, in the committee's judgment, all be admitted', then there is 'no alternative but to rank the children in order of priority'.[2]

9.84   Sedley J made the following further helpful comment in *ex parte Tarmohamed*:

> 'If, I would add, in the present form of procedure one parent does gratuitously make an adverse comment upon another parent's case, whether that parent is present or absent at the time, then the committee's duty would in the ordinary way be to ignore the comment and to make it clear that it is doing so. If, however, the comment were something which the committee felt duty-bound to consider then it would of course be wrong to do so without giving the parent affected the opportunity to deal with it.'[3]

9.85   It was held in *R v Commissioner for Local Administration, ex parte Croydon London Borough Council*[4] that although there is a clear advantage in terms of fairness to parents in the determination of all the appeals of parents relating to a particular school at the same time by the same members of the appeal committee, if it is impractical to do so then that procedure need not be followed.[5] Nevertheless, in *R v Camden London Borough Council, ex parte S*,[6] it was held that if the appeals are not heard at the same time but are determined together (in other words if the appeal hearings occur over a period but the appeals are all determined at the same time), the members of the committee hearing and determining the appeals must be the same: substituting a member before all the appeals had been heard was therefore unlawful.

9.86   According to *R v Governors of Pates' Grant-maintained School, ex parte T*,[7] where there is a waiting list in operation at a school and a parent appeals against a refusal of admission to that school, the appeal panel may take into account the status of those on the waiting list. In contrast, the School Admission Appeals Code of Practice for England states, in para 4.76:

> 'There is no statutory requirement for admission authorities to maintain waiting lists, and appeal panels have no power to determine where a child should be placed on the waiting list for a school. Panels should take no account of where the admission authority has placed a child on the waiting list, or of the fact that the parents of other children on the waiting list may not be appealing.'

9.87   Presumably this is on the basis that the duty of the appeal panel is to consider the cases in accordance with their respective merits, as indicated in *Tarmohamed*, with

---

1   [1997] ELR 48, at 59B–E.
2   See also *R v Essex County Council, ex parte Jacobs* [1997] ELR 190, at 194F–H, per Collins J. The effect of these cases is stated in paras 4.69 and 4.71–4.72 of the School Admission Appeals Code of Practice, DfES/0030/2003. Direct reference to *Tarmohamed* is made in para 4.68 of the National Assembly for Wales School Admission Appeals Code of Practice.
3   [1997] ELR 48, at 60G–H.
4   [1989] 1 All ER 1033.
5   [1989] 1 All ER 1033, at 1041d–h.
6   (1990) 89 LGR 513.
7   [1994] COD 297.

the result that the placing by the admission authority of a child's name on the waiting list is irrelevant, as is the fact that other parents may not be appealing.[1] However, it is at least possible (if not arguably correct to say) that every time that it is decided by an admission authority (within the meaning of s 88 of the SSFA 1998) that a place at the school in question should be offered to a particular parent, there is necessarily a decision that the prospective pupils whose names are on the waiting list should not be given a place at that school. Accordingly, it could properly be said that every time that an admission authority makes such a decision, a right of appeal arises in favour of the parents of the children who are not offered a place at the school. This is because that is (it seems clear) a decision within the meaning of s 94(1) of the SSFA 1998. However, if admission authorities were obliged to inform parents of their right of appeal in these circumstances and make arrangements for the appeals, one can surmise that the system would become unworkable. This does not, however, mean, it is suggested here, that the place of a child on a waiting list is irrelevant. Rather, that place is allocated as a result of the application by the admission authority of its admission criteria, and an appeal panel is obliged by reg 6(1)(b) of the Education (Admission Appeals Arrangements) (England) Regulations 2002[2] to take into account those criteria. The correctness of para 4.76 of the School Admission Appeals Code of Practice for England must therefore be doubted.

9.88 It has been said that the hearing should not be regarded as an adversarial process in the usual sense. This is because parents 'do not normally have any sort of professional assistance and the details of the schools would be matters known to the school and to the local education authority rather than to them'.[3]

9.89 In *McKeown v Appeal Committee and Governors of Cardinal Heenan High School and Leeds City Council*,[4] an appeal committee rejected a parent's application for a place at a secondary school for her son in the circumstance that she reasonably believed that her son was better placed to be admitted (if the admission criteria were applied properly) than 14 or 15 other children who *were* admitted. She had not been present at the hearing as a result of a misunderstanding. She protested about the rejection of her appeal, and was granted a further appeal hearing. At that hearing, the committee rejected the appeal because the prospective pupil's case was now because of changed circumstances weaker (applying the admission criteria properly) than the cases of some 10 other children. The High Court held that the first appeal hearing was unfair, and although it held that there was nothing unlawful about the second appeal hearing as such, it was part of an unlawful process, since the first appeal hearing could not realistically be seen as standing on its own, and the decision taken at the second appeal hearing 'was part of a process which included the earlier decision'.[5] Accordingly, the decisions of both appeal committees were quashed. It is open to question why there was a second appeal hearing in any event, since it appears that the appeal committee

---

1 See further, concerning waiting lists, paras 7.29 and 7.30 of the School Admissions Code of Practice for England, DfES/0031/2003.
2 SI 2002/2899.
3 *R v Rotherham MBC, ex parte Clark* [1998] ELR 152, at 162D, per Collins J at first instance, no comment on this aspect of his judgment having been made by the Court of Appeal.
4 [1998] ELR 578.
5 Ibid, at 585D.

was *functus officio* (in other words, that the principle of irrevocability applied so that the second appeal committee had no jurisdiction).[1]

Appeals against refusals of admission to selective schools

9.90   The School Admission Appeals Code of Practice for England[2] makes extensive reference to the manner in which an appeal panel should approach an appeal against a refusal of admission to a selective school. Perhaps of most interest are paras 4.65 and 4.66. Paragraph 4.65 includes the following statement:

> 'Panels may take account of parents' arguments as to why their child did not perform their best on the day of the test, or of any evidence to support their contention that the child is suitable for admission to a grammar school or to a 6th form.'

9.91   However, it is then said (in the same paragraph) that the panel 'should not attempt to make its own assessment of a child's ability, but may need to decide whether the original decision that the child was not of the required standard was reasonable'. These statements are apparently inconsistent.

9.92   In para 4.66, after it is said that admission authorities for selective schools must consider applications which are made at any time during the school year, and, if such applications are refused, offer a right of appeal, it is said that:

> 'Many selective schools do not offer a facility for testing applicants for admission outside the normal admission round. In that situation, if the admission authority is not willing to accept that such a casual applicant is of the required academic ability for admission, it must make arrangements for an appropriate assessment of the child's ability to be made if their parent lodges an appeal. If this is not done, the panel must work on the assumption that the child is of the required academic standard.'

9.93   Paragraph 4.66 continues by stating that the panel must then adopt the usual procedure of first seeing whether prejudice of the relevant sort would be caused by the admission of the child to the school in question, and then determining whether the child should nevertheless be admitted in the circumstances.

Reasons for the decision

9.94   The decision of the appeal committee 'and the grounds on which it is made' must be communicated to the relevant parties in writing.[3] In *R v Hackney London Borough Council, ex parte T*,[4] it was held that all that was required by way of reasons was that the committee explained their conclusion in 'broad and simple terms, which indicated a correct appreciation of the task they had and a correct approach to its resolution'. Similarly, in *R v Lancashire County Council, ex parte M*,[5] Macpherson J said that he accepted the submission 'that broad grounds must be set out rather than what may be termed detailed reasons'. He also said that there was 'absolutely nothing

---

1   On the principle of irrevocability, see para **9.58**.
2   DfES/0030/2003.
3   SI 2002/2899, Sch 2, paras 1(8) and 2(10).
4   [1991] COD 454.
5   [1995] ELR 136, at 139E–F.

wrong with a local authority having a standard form letter which can be modified if required'.[1] However, In *R v Birmingham City Council Education Appeals Committee, ex parte B*,[2] Scott Baker J said this:

'If Macpherson J was there saying that a standard letter without more is sufficient, I respectfully disagree. But I do not think that that is what the judge was saying. He certainly referred to a standard form of letter but he added these important words, "which can be modified if required".'

9.95 Dyson J in *R v South Gloucestershire Appeals Committee, ex parte C*[3] agreed with what Macpherson J said in *R v Lancashire County Council, ex parte M*, and said that he did not 'believe that the decision in *R v Birmingham City Council Education Appeals Committee, ex parte B* lays down any general principle save perhaps to say that a minimum requirement of the grounds of a decision is that they explain broadly the basis of the decision.' He also stated, when dismissing the application for judicial review:

'What is required will depend on the issues that have been raised on the appeal. In a complex case the grounds may well have to be more elaborate than in a simple one. Where however there is no dispute as to the primary facts, I do not consider that the grounds are required to make findings about those facts.'[4]

9.96 Even if a decision letter is insufficient, a remedy may be refused by the High Court. This occurred in *R(L) v The Independent Appeal Panel of St Edward's College*,[5] where the failing was said to be one of form rather than one of substance. It also occurred in *R v Governors of the Buss Foundation Camden School for Girls, ex parte Lukasievicz*,[6] because the parents knew of the reasons for the rejection of their appeal. According to the summary of the case: 'Even though the reasons might have been expressed differently, the failure did not undermine the decision nor did it flaw the decision-making process nor was it of such materiality that the decision of the tribunal should be set aside'.

---

[1]   [1995] ELR 136, at 139D–E.
[2]   [1999] ELR 305, at 310H.
[3]   [2000] ELR 220, at 225.
[4]   Ibid. See also *W (A Minor) v Education Appeal Committee of Lancashire County Council* [1994] ELR 530, at 538; *R v Education Committee of Blackpool Borough Council, ex parte Taylor* [1999] ELR 237, at 240C–D; *R v Lancashire County Council, ex parte M* [1994] ELR 478, at 482G–H and 485C; and *R v Northamptonshire County Council, ex parte D* [1998] EdCR 14; [1998] ELR 291.
[5]   [2001] EWHC Admin 108; [2001] ELR 542, at para 37.
[6]   [1991] COD 98.

Chapter 10

DISCIPLINE IN, AND EXCLUSION FROM, MAINTAINED SCHOOLS

10.1   The main focus of this chapter is the law relating to discipline in maintained schools and the principles applicable to, and the procedural requirements governing, the exclusion of pupils from those schools. After those matters are considered, however, reference is made to two measures which were introduced by the Anti-Social Behaviour Act 2003, one of which (parenting contracts) applies also where a pupil has not attended regularly at the school at which he is a registered pupil.

DISCIPLINE IN A MAINTAINED SCHOOL

10.2   The legal basis for the discipline of a school pupil is to an extent unclear. It used traditionally to be thought that the power to discipline a pupil derived from a delegation of parental authority.[1] However, according to Neville Harris, writing in 1993:

> 'Today, the prevalent view is that the teacher's authority is probably independent of parental delegation.'[2]

10.3   In the following passage, Professor Harris says that:

> 'the independent nature of a teacher's authority to discipline a child, within the limits the law allows ... is reinforced by section 1(7) of the Children and Young Persons Act 1933. This states that "nothing in this section (prescribing offences of cruelty) shall be construed as affecting the right of any parent, teacher, or other person having lawful control or charge of a young person to administer punishment to him".'

10.4   That section must, however, be viewed in the light of developments since 1933. In particular, the decision of the House of Lords in *Gillick v West Norfolk and Wisbech Area Health Authority*[3] suggests that the punishment which a court would now approve as lawful would be considerably lighter than that which in 1933 a court would have been willing to countenance. This is because of the connection made in that case between the rights of a parent in relation to a child and the duties of the parent in relation to the child.

---

[1]   See, eg, *Fitzgerald v Northcote* (1865) 4 F&F 856; *Cleary v Booth* [1893] 1 QB 465, at 468; *Ryan v Fildes* [1938] 3 All ER 517, at 521C–E; and *R v Newport (Salop) JJ, ex parte Wright* [1929] 2 KB 416, at 428–429.
[2]   N Harris, *Law and Education* (Sweet & Maxwell, 1993), p 213.
[3]   [1986] AC 112; see para **14.3**.

10.5   In any event, the suggestion that a teacher's authority is today independent of parental delegation could be an over-simplification. In some respects, it may be that a parent's wishes are either determinative or at least of great importance. For example, in *Terrington v Lancashire County Council*,[1] the judge ruled that if the parent of a pupil clearly informed the pupil's school that detention of the pupil at the end of the school day was not to take place, then any subsequent such detention would amount to an unlawful imprisonment.[2] Furthermore, s 2(9) of the Children Act 1989 provides as follows:

> 'A person who has parental responsibility for a child may not surrender or transfer any part of that responsibility to another but may arrange for some or all of it to be met by one or more persons acting on his behalf.'

10.6   Moreover, s 3(5) of the same Act provides as follows:

> 'A person who –
> (a)   does not have parental responsibility for a particular child, but
> (b)   has care of the child,
> may (subject to the provisions of this Act) do what is reasonable in all the circumstances of the case for the purpose of safeguarding or promoting the child's welfare.'

10.7   These provisions suggest that a teacher's authority over a child is now in part the result of a delegation by the parent of his authority, and in part derived from statutes of general application. It was recommended by the committee of enquiry chaired by Lord Elton, in its report *Discipline in Schools*[3] that a teacher's disciplinary authority be enshrined in statute. However, that did not occur. It is suggested here that the current position is sufficiently catered for as a result of the provisions of the Children Act set out in the text, the common law in the form in particular of *Gillick*, and the provisions in the SSFA 1998 concerning discipline, to which reference will now be made.

Policies concerning good behaviour

10.8   Section 61 of the SSFA 1998 requires the governing body of a maintained school[4] to 'ensure that policies designed to promote good behaviour and discipline on the part of its pupils are pursued at the school'. Section 61(2)(a) requires the governing body to make, and from time to time to review, a written statement of general principles to which the head teacher is to have regard in determining any measures under s 61(4). Section 61(4) provides as follows:

---

[1]   (1986) Blackpool County Court; unreported, but see the note of the case in Butterworths' *Law of Education* at F[56].
[2]   This aspect of the situation is now affected by s 550B of the EA 1996, concerning which, see paras **10.22–10.23**.
[3]   HMSO, 1999.
[4]   Meaning a community, foundation or voluntary school, or a community or foundation special school and a maintained nursery school: SSFA 1998, s 20(7) and 61(8) as inserted by EA 2002, Sch 21, para 102, with effect from 1 September 2003 by SI 2003/1667.

'The head teacher[1] shall determine measures (which may include the making of rules and provision for enforcing them) to be taken with a view to –
(a)   promoting, among pupils, self-discipline and proper regard for authority,
(b)   encouraging good behaviour and respect for others on the part of pupils,
(c)   securing that the standard of behaviour of pupils is acceptable, and
(d)   otherwise regulating the conduct of pupils.'

10.9   Where the governing body:

'consider it desirable that any particular measures should be so determined by the head teacher or that he should have regard to any particular matters [they] –
(i)   shall notify him of those measures or matters, and
(ii)   may give him such guidance as they consider appropriate;
and in exercising their functions under this subsection the governing body shall have regard to any guidance given from time to time by the Secretary of State.'[2]

10.10   As one would expect, the head teacher is obliged, when determining measures under s 61(4), to act in accordance with the current statement made by the governing body under s 61(2)(a), and to 'have regard' to any notification or guidance given to him under s 61(2)(b).[3]

10.11   Before making or reviewing a statement under s 61(2)(a), the governing body must consult 'in such manner as appears to them to be appropriate' (a) the head teacher, and (b) parents of registered pupils at the school.[4]

10.12   Section 61(6) places residual power in the head teacher, by providing that:

'The standard of behaviour which is to be regarded as acceptable at the school shall be determined by the head teacher, so far as it is not determined by the governing body.'

10.13   The head teacher must publicise any measures determined by him under s 61(4) in the form of a written document by which he makes the measures 'generally known within the school and to parents of registered pupils at the school'.[5] The head teacher must also, at least once in every school year, take steps to bring those measures to the attention of all such pupils and parents and all persons employed, or otherwise engaged, at the school.[6]

Is a head teacher obliged to administer a caution to a teacher who may have assaulted a child?

10.14   Despite the predecessor to s 61 of the SSFA 1998, when investigating circumstances in which a teacher may have assaulted a pupil, a head teacher is not to

---

1   This includes an acting head teacher: EA 1996, s 579(1).
2   SSFA 1998, s 61(2)(b). See paras **2.34–2.36** concerning the impact of a duty imposed on a public body to 'have regard' to something. An example of relevant guidance is the DfES document entitled 'Drugs: Guidance for Schools', DfES/0092/2004.
3   Ibid, s 61(5).
4   Ibid, s 61(3).
5   Ibid, s 61(7)(a).
6   Ibid, s 61(7)(b).

be regarded as 'charged with investigating offences' under s 67(9) of the Police and Criminal Evidence Act 1984, and therefore does not normally need to administer a caution prior to questioning the teacher about the incident. This was expressly held by the Court of Appeal in *R v Headteacher and Independent Appeal Committee of Dunraven School, ex parte B*,[1] where Brooke LJ said this:

> 'In conducting his investigations Mr Townsend [the head teacher] was not a person charged with the duty of investigating offences within the meaning of s 67(9) of the Police and Criminal Evidence Act 1984 (PACE). He was none the less obliged to conduct his investigation fairly, and if he secured an admission from a pupil through conduct tantamount to oppression it would be as unfair to rely on it in exclusion proceedings as it is in court proceedings where the principles set out in s 76(2) of PACE must be strictly applied.'[2]

Is disciplinary action against a pupil at a maintained school in respect of conduct otherwise than at school lawful?

10.15 In *R v London Borough of Newham, ex parte X*,[3] disciplinary action in relation to the behaviour of pupils of a school towards each other off the school premises was said to be capable of being lawful.[4] However, that was said in the context of the facts of that case, and there must be a limit to the extent of a head teacher's disciplinary power in regard to actions outside school. Nevertheless, this aspect of the approach taken in *R v London Borough of Newham, ex parte X* was specifically endorsed by the Court of Appeal in *Bradford-Smart v West Sussex County Council*.[5]

10.16 The Secretary of State's guidance on exclusions issued in January 2003 states that pupils' behaviour outside school 'on school business – for example on school trips, away school sports fixtures, or work experience placements – is subject to the school's behaviour policy', so that bad behaviour in such circumstances 'should be dealt with as if it had taken place in school'.[6] The guidance goes on to say:

> 'For behaviour outside school, but not on school business, a head teacher may exclude a pupil if there is a clear link between that behaviour and maintaining good behaviour and discipline among the pupil body as a whole. This will be a matter of judgment for the head teacher. Pupils' behaviour in the immediate vicinity of the school or on a journey to or from school can, for example, be grounds for exclusion.'[7]

10.17 This guidance is likely to be influential in relation to the question whether an exclusion for conduct outside school was lawful.

---

1   [2000] ELR 156, at 201–202.
2   Sedley LJ said words to a similar effect at 194.
3   [1995] ELR 303.
4   Ibid, at 306H–307A. See also *Cleary v Booth* [1893] 1 QB 465 and *R v Newport (Salop) JJ, ex parte Wright* [1929] 2 KB 416.
5   [2002] EWCA Civ 07; [2002] ELR 139, at para 34 of the judgment of the court.
6   DfES/0087/2003, para 12.1 of Part 1.
7   Ibid.

Penalty must normally be proportionate to offence

10.18 In relation to any disciplinary action, it appears that the penalty should normally be proportionate to the offence,[1] although the principle of proportionality will not be determinative.[2] It is of interest that s 550B of the EA 1996[3] provides specifically that any detention must, if it is to be lawful, be 'a proportionate punishment in the circumstances of the case'. Otherwise, there is no reference to proportionality in the statutory framework concerning discipline in schools. It is also of interest that it was said by Stanley Burnton J in *A v The Head Teacher and Governors of the Lord Grey School*[4] that 'the operation of reasonable disciplinary sanctions will not give rise to a breach of [Art 2 of the First Protocol to the European Convention on Human Rights]'. Although the High Court's ruling was overturned on appeal,[5] that statement was not the subject of adverse comment.

Prohibition of corporal punishment in schools

10.19 Corporal punishment[6] is now unlawful in all schools. This is the product of s 548 of the EA 1996 as substituted by s 131 of the SSFA 1998. Section 548(1) does not expressly state that corporal punishment is unlawful. Instead, it provides that in any proceedings where it is shown that corporal punishment has been given by, or on the authority of, a member of staff[7] to a child[8] (a) for whom education is provided at any school, (b) for whom education is provided, otherwise than at school, under any arrangements made by a LEA, or (c) for whom specified nursery education[9] is provided otherwise than at school, the punishment cannot be justified on the ground that it was given in pursuance of a right exercisable by the member of staff 'by virtue of his position as such'.[10] This applies no matter where the punishment is given.[11] However, corporal punishment is not to be taken to be given to a child by virtue of anything done for reasons that include averting (a) an immediate danger of personal injury to, or (b) an immediate danger to the property of, any person (including the child himself).[12]

---

[1] *R v London Borough of Newham, ex parte X*, [1995] ELR 303, at 307A.

[2] Ibid.

[3] Regarding which see paras **10.22–10.23**.

[4] [2003] EWHC 1533, [2003] ELR 517, at paras 80–81.

[5] [2004] EWCA Civ 382.

[6] This means 'doing anything for the purpose of punishing [a] child (whether or not there are other reasons for doing it) which, apart from any justification, would constitute battery': EA 1996, s 548(4) as substituted by s 131 of the SSFA 1998.

[7] Defined in s 548(6).

[8] This means a person under the age of 18, although in relation to nursery education this definition is excluded: s 548(7).

[9] 'Specified nursery education' is defined in s 548(8), which is amended (prospectively as far as Wales is concerned) by Sch 22 to the EA 2002.

[10] A challenge to s 548 on the basis that it breaches various Convention rights of a parent (art 8 and/or 9 and/or 10 and/or Art 2 of Protocol 1), was rejected by the Court of Appeal in *R (Williamson) v Secretary of State* [2002] EWCA Civ 1926; [2003] ELR 176. An appeal to the House of Lords is currently pending.

[11] EA 1996, s 548(2).

[12] Ibid, s 548(5).

Physical restraint of pupils

10.20 Despite s 548 of the EA 1996, teachers are given statutory authority for the physical restraint of pupils in certain circumstances. This is the result of the insertion by the Education Act 1997 of s 550A into the EA 1996. This enacts for the purposes of the staff of a school some defences which would have applied in any event, such as the defence of reasonable force used in the prevention of crime,[1] and confers additional protection. For example, s 550A protects a member of the staff of a school[2] who uses:

> 'such force as is reasonable in the circumstances for the purpose of preventing the pupil from ... engaging in any behaviour prejudicial to the maintenance of good order and discipline at the school or among any of its pupils, whether that behaviour occurs during a teaching session or otherwise.'[3]

10.21 The definition of a member of the staff is particularly interesting in that it seems clearly to cover a voluntary helper who, with the head teacher's authority, accompanies pupils on a school trip. It is also helpful that the word 'offence' is defined[4] in accordance with the common law relating to the defence of the prevention of crime (and not that in s 3 of the Criminal Law Act 1967) in that it is not necessary for the defence to apply that a crime would otherwise in fact be committed.

Detention

10.22 The detention of a pupil outside school hours as a form of punishment is made lawful in certain circumstances by s 550B of the EA 1996. That applies to pupils at all maintained schools (ie community, foundation and voluntary schools and community and foundation special schools[5]) and at city technology colleges, city colleges for the technology of the arts and Academies.[6] Where such a pupil is required on disciplinary grounds to spend a period of time in detention at his school after the end of any school session, as long as certain conditions are satisfied, the detention will not be unlawful merely because the parent has not consented to it.[7] Those conditions include that the head teacher of the school must have (1) previously determined that the detention of pupils after the end of a school session is one of the measures that may be taken with a view to regulating the conduct of pupils, (2) made that generally known within the school, and (3) taken steps to bring it to the attention of the parent of every person who is for the time being a registered pupil there.[8] In addition, (1) the detention must be imposed by the head teacher or by another teacher at the school

---

[1]   See s 3(1) of the Criminal Law Act 1967.
[2]   A 'member of the staff' is defined by s 550A(4) as 'any teacher who works at the school and any other person who, with the authority of the head teacher, has lawful control or charge of pupils at the school'.
[3]   EA 1996, s 550A(1). The protection afforded by s 550A(1) is available wherever the reasonable force is used as long as the member of staff is acting as such and has lawful control or charge of the pupil concerned: s 550A(2).
[4]   By ibid, s 550A(4).
[5]   SSFA 1998, s 20(7), which must be read for this purpose with s 142(8) of that Act.
[6]   EA 1996, s 550B(2).
[7]   Ibid, s 550B(1).
[8]   Ibid, s 550B(3)(a).

specifically or generally authorised by the head teacher for the purpose, (2) the detention must be reasonable in all the circumstances, and (3) the pupil's parent must have been given at least 24 hours' notice in writing that the detention was due to take place.[1]

10.23 If a court were asked to determine whether or not a pupil's detention was reasonable in all the circumstances of the case, within the meaning of s 550B(3)(c), the court would have to take into account the matters set out in s 550B(4). These are (1) 'whether the detention constitutes a proportionate punishment in the circumstances of the case', and (2) any special circumstances relevant to its imposition on the pupil which are known to the person imposing it (or of which he ought reasonably to be aware). These special circumstances include (a) the pupil's age, (b) any SEN he may have, (3) any religious requirements affecting him, and (4) where arrangements have to be made for him to travel from the school to his home, whether suitable alternative arrangements can reasonably be made by his parent.

Other forms of punishment

10.24 The limitations on any other kind of action by a teacher will, however, remain only those of the law of tort generally. As a result, the case of *Gillick v West Norfolk and Wisbech Area Health Authority*[2] will be highly relevant. Although *Gillick* concerned a different area of the law (the legality of a statement in a circular letter from the Department of Health and Social Security relating to the giving of contraceptive advice to girls under the age of 16), the approach taken in that case to the times when a young person may give a valid consent to medical treatment is likely to be highly influential in any future court proceedings concerning the rights of young people and their parents to consent to actions which would otherwise be unlawful.[3]

10.25 A state school would be potentially liable to a public law challenge if any disciplinary sanction which did not involve a breach of private law rights were excessive.[4] However, since the ultimate sanction is exclusion from school, and since there is a specific procedure to follow in relation to such exclusion, it is highly unlikely that public law proceedings (or a complaint to the Secretary of State under s 496 of the EA 1996) would be initiated in respect of a response to a disciplinary matter other than exclusion.

Local education authority's reserve power to prevent a breakdown of discipline

10.26 Before turning to exclusions, however, mention needs to be made of the power of an LEA in certain circumstances to take, under s 62(1) of the SSFA 1998,

---

1   EA 1996, s 550B(3)(b)–(d). The notice need not be given in accordance with s 572 of the EA 1996: s 550B(5).
2   [1986] AC 112; see para **14.3**.
3   See further, paras **14.3–14.5**.
4   Guidance in regard to disciplinary sanctions is provided by DfEE Circular 10/99.

'such steps in relation to a maintained school[1] as they consider are required to prevent the breakdown or continued breakdown of discipline at the school'. Those circumstances are that (1) in the opinion of the LEA the behaviour of registered pupils at the school, or any action taken by those pupils or their parents, is such that the education of any registered pupils at the school is (or is in the immediate future likely to become) severely prejudiced, and (2) the governing body of the school have been informed in writing of the LEA's opinion.[2] The steps which the LEA may take include the giving of any direction to the governing body or the head teacher.[3] Such a direction may, where (1) a warning notice has been given under s 15(2) of the SSFA 1998[4] referring to the safety of pupils or staff at the school being threatened by a breakdown of discipline at the school, and (2) that warning has in the view of the LEA not been acted on sufficiently, be combined with a notice under s 15(1)(c) of the SSFA 1998.[5]

10.27   Guidance in relation to the exercise by an LEA of its power in s 62(1) of the SSFA 1998 is set out in para 8 of Annex 2 to the DfES Code of Practice on LEA School Relations, issued under s 127 of the SSFA 1998. According to that para, the 'initial criterion' for its exercise:

> 'is that there must be, either now or in immediate prospect, a breakdown of discipline at the school. "Breakdown" implies problems such that the school can no longer function in an orderly way, that staff cannot maintain discipline, that large numbers of pupils are truanting, or that the safety or welfare of pupils or staff is at risk.'

School attendance targets

10.28   Section 63(1) of the SSFA 1998 empowers the making of regulations which may require, or enable the Secretary of State to require, 'governing bodies of maintained schools to secure that annual targets are set for reducing the level of unauthorised absences on the part of relevant day pupils at their schools'. The circumstances in which such a requirement may be imposed must be specified in the regulations.[6] The current regulations are the Education (School Attendance Targets) (England) Regulations 1999,[7] and the Education (School Performance and Unauthorised Absence Targets) (Wales) Regulations 1999.[8]

---

1   This means a community, foundation or voluntary school, or a community or foundation special school and a maintained nursery school: SSFA 1998, s 20(7) and 62(5) as inserted by EA 2002, Sch 21, para 103, with effect from 1 September 2003 by SI 2003/1667.

2   SSFA 1998, s 62(2). It is of interest that the power exists where the breakdown in discipline is caused by action taken by a pupil's parent.

3   Ibid, s 62(4).

4   Regarding which, see para **12.33**.

5   SSFA 1998, s 62(3). See para **12.33** concerning s 15(1)(c).

6   See ibid, s 63(1)–(3). A 'relevant day pupil' means a pupil who is registered at a maintained school, who is of compulsory school age, and who is not a boarder: s 63(4). An 'unauthorised absence' is 'any occasion on which the pupil is recorded as absent without authority pursuant to regulations under [s 434 of the EA 1996]': s 63(4).

7   SI 1999/397, as amended by SI 2001/3785.

8   SI 1999/1811.

The exclusion of pupils from maintained schools

10.29 Exclusions from maintained schools are governed by s 52 of the EA 2002 and regulations made under that section.[1] Those are the Education (Pupil Exclusions and Appeals) (Maintained Schools) (England) Regulations 2002,[2] the Education (Pupil Exclusions and Appeals) (Pupil Referral Units) (England) Regulations 2002,[3] the Education (Pupil Exclusions and Appeals) (Maintained Schools) (Wales) Regulations 2003,[4] and the Education (Pupil Exclusions and Appeals) (Pupil Referral Units) (Wales) Regulations 2003.[5]

10.30 Section 52(1) permits the head teacher[6] of a maintained school[7] to exclude a pupil from the school on disciplinary grounds[8] either for a fixed period, or permanently. Section 52(2) permits the teacher in charge of a pupil referral unit to do the same. A pupil may not be excluded for fixed periods which, in total, exceed 45 school days in any one school year.[9] Any exclusion for a fixed period 'consisting of the period between the morning and afternoon school sessions' must for the purposes of both sets of regulations 'be taken as equivalent to half a school day'.[10]

Guidance on exclusions

10.31 The regulations require[11] the head teacher and governing body of a maintained school, the LEA and an appeal panel when exercising any function under s 52(1) or regulations made under s 52 (the salient effects of all of which are described below) to 'have regard to any guidance given from time to time by the Secretary of State'. The main current guidance was issued on 20 January 2003,[12] and where relevant it is referred to further below (as 'the Secretary of State's Guidance' or, as the case may be, 'the Secretary of State's current Guidance').[13] Other guidance may be relevant, for

---

1   This is the case in England only (since only s 52(1) to (6) are currently in force in Wales: see SI 2003/2961), but for the sake of simplicity, and because s 52 will in time be brought fully into force in relation to Wales, reference is made here only to the position as if s 52 were fully in force also in Wales.

2   SI 2002/3178.

3   SI 2002/3179.

4   SI 2003/3227, as amended by SI 2004/1805.

5   SI 2003/3246, as amended by SI 2004/1805.

6   This includes an acting head teacher: EA 1996, s 579(1).

7   Meaning a community, foundation or voluntary school, a community or foundation special school, or a maintained nursery school: EA 2002, ss 52(11) and 39(1). References in the rest of this chapter to a maintained school are to be read accordingly.

8   See EA 2002, s 52(10).

9   SI 2002/3178, reg 3; SI 2002/3179, reg 4.

10   Regulation 2(2) of both SI 2002/3178 and SI 2002/3179.

11   Regulation 7 of SI 2002/3178 and reg 8 of SI 2002/3179.

12   DfES/0087/2003.

13   The guidance refers to discrimination against a person contrary to the DDA 1995, as amended by SENDA 2001 (see para 14 of Part 1). In connection with a pupil who is disabled within the meaning of the DDA 1995, reference should also be made to the Disability Rights Commission's code of practice, as to which, see para **18.48**.

example the good practice guide issued by the Commission for Racial Equality,[1] and that which relates to drugs in schools.[2]

Role of the head teacher

10.32 The head teacher of a maintained school who excludes any pupil (for whatever reason and, if the exclusion is for a fixed period, for whatever period) is required by reg 4 of the Education (Pupil Exclusions and Appeals) (Maintained Schools) (England) Regulations 2002 'without delay' to take reasonable steps to give certain information to a parent of the pupil if the pupil is under the age of 18 or (if the pupil has attained that age) the pupil himself (defined in reg 2(1) and referred to below as 'the relevant person'). The information is (1) the period of the exclusion, or, if the exclusion is permanent, that fact, (2) the reasons for the exclusion, (3) that the recipient of the information may make representations about the exclusion to the governing body of the school, and (4) the means by which such representations may be made.[3] If the head teacher decides that an exclusion of a pupil for a fixed period should be made permanent, then he must without delay take reasonable steps to inform the relevant person of (1) the decision, (2) the reasons for it (3) that he may make representations about the decision to the governing body, and (4) the means by which such representations may be made.[4]

10.33 The head teacher is required without delay to inform the LEA and the governing body of the school of any permanent exclusion and the reasons for it.[5] If the head teacher decides that an exclusion of a pupil for a fixed period should be made permanent, then he must without delay inform the governing body of the school and the LEA of that decision and the reasons for it.[6] Where an exclusion would result in the pupil being excluded for a total of more than 5 school days in any one term, or in the pupil losing an opportunity to take any public examination, the head teacher must without delay inform the LEA and the governing body of the school of (1) the period of the exclusion (or, as the case may be, that the pupil is being excluded permanently), and (2) the reasons for it.[7]

10.34 If in any school term the head teacher excludes any pupil otherwise than in the manner described in paras **10.32–10.33**, then he must inform the LEA and the governing body of that exclusion and the reasons for it.[8]

10.35 Where the head teacher is directed by the governing body to reinstate a pupil who has been excluded from the school in the manner described in para **10.39**, he must comply with that direction.[9] Such a direction is not a direction to reintegrate the

---

[1]   This is available at www.cre.gov.uk/pdfs/excl12pp.pdf.
[2]   See 'Drugs: Guidance for Schools', DfES/0092/2004, where, in para 5.4, guidance is given in relation to exclusions from maintained schools.
[3]   Regulation 4(1).
[4]   Regulation 4(2).
[5]   Regulation 4(3)(b) and (4).
[6]   Regulation 4(3)(c) and (4).
[7]   Regulation 4(3)(a) and (4).
[8]   Regulation 4(5).
[9]   Regulation 5(5).

pupil.[1] Although the school-pupil relationship must be 'reinstated and the responsibilities and obligations of the school towards the pupil resumed',[2] whatever occurs after such reinstatement is a separate matter, 'unless the resumption can be shown to have been a sham or to be so nugatory as to evince an intention not in truth to resume them at all.'[3] In this respect 'The test is stringent and is directed to the realities not mere formalities.'[4] To require the school to treat the incident as if it had never happened and to treat the pupil as if he had never offended 'is not merely wholly impractical but gives the decision of the independent panel a content beyond that authorised by the statute'.[5] Thus, the fact that teachers have threatened to take industrial action having followed the appropriate relevant ballot procedure is a relevant factor which a head teacher cannot be required to ignore.[6]

10.36 It goes without saying that a head teacher is obliged to comply with the principles of public law in relation to a decision to exclude a pupil, although his decision and that of the governing body as described in the following paragraphs below should be regarded as one.[7] It was held in *R (K) v Governors of the W School*[8] that the head teacher should not have accepted the verbal opinion of the police on the reliability of the allegations made against the excluded pupil.

Relevance of investigation by the police of the situation as a result of which a pupil is excluded

10.37 If the (alleged) conduct for which a pupil has been excluded is the subject of an investigation by the police, it may be appropriate to exclude the pupil for one or more fixed periods while the investigation continues. That was certainly the view taken by Moses J in *R v Independent Appeal Panel of Sheffield City Council, ex parte N*,[9] a view which was endorsed by Scott Baker J in *A v Head Teacher and Governors of the Lord Grey School*.[10]

Role of the governing body

10.38 Where the governing body of a maintained school is informed of a fixed period or permanent exclusion in the circumstances described in the section above, or of the exclusion of any pupil where the pupil would as a result of the exclusion be excluded from the school for a total of more than 5 school days in any one term and the relevant person expresses a wish to make representations in pursuance of reg 4(1)(c), the governing body must consider the circumstances in which the pupil

---

1   *R (L (A Minor)) v Governors of J School* [2003] UKHL 9; [2003] 2 AC 633.
2   Ibid, per Lord Hobhouse, at para 36.
3   Ibid, per Lord Hobhouse, at para 36. See also at para 48.
4   Ibid.
5   Ibid, at para 46.
6   Ibid, at para 75, per Lord Walker.
7   *R (DR) v Head Teacher and Governing Body of S School and Independent Appeal Panel of W City Council* [2002] EWCA Civ 1822; [2003] ELR 104, para 37; see para **10.77**.
8   [2001] ELR 311, at para 31.
9   [2000] ELR 700.
10   [2003] EWHC 1533 (QB); [2003] ELR 517, at para 91. This view was not commented upon by the Court of Appeal when overturning the decision in that case: see [2004] EWCA Civ 382, [2004] ELR 169.

was excluded.[1] It must also consider any representations about the exclusion made to them by the relevant person or by the LEA.[2] The governing body must have a meeting in order to allow the relevant person and an officer of the LEA nominated by the LEA to make oral representations about the exclusion, or at least offer to do so.[3] The governing body must then consider any representations so made.[4] If as a result of the exclusion the pupil will lose an opportunity to take a public examination, these steps must, if it is practical to do so, be taken before the date when the pupil is due to take the examination.[5] Subject to this, these steps must be taken by the governing body at least 6 school days after the date on which they were informed of the exclusion pursuant to reg 4(4).[6] In the case of a permanent exclusion or an exclusion for a fixed period of more than 15 school days, the steps must be taken not later than 15 school days after that date.[7] In the case of an exclusion for a fixed period of 15 or fewer school days, the steps must be taken not later than 50 school days after that date.[8] A failure to comply with any of these time-limits does not relieve the governing body of the duty in question.[9]

10.39 The governing body must consider 'whether or not the pupil should be reinstated', and, if they decide that he should be reinstated, whether that should occur immediately or by a particular date.[10] If they decide that the pupil should be reinstated, then it must 'forthwith ... give the appropriate direction to the head teacher' and inform the relevant person and the LEA of their decision.[11] If the governing body decides that the pupil should not be reinstated, then it must 'forthwith ... inform the relevant person, the head teacher' and the LEA of its decision.[12] Where the pupil has been permanently excluded, the governing body must also give the relevant person notice in writing referring to that decision and stating the matters set out in reg 5(6)(b) relating to his right to appeal against the decision.[13] This notice may be delivered to the person's last known address or sent to it by first-class post.[14]

10.40 If reg 5(2)–(6) do not apply to an exclusion (that is, it is a fixed-period exclusion and the pupil will not as a result of it have been excluded for more than 5 days in a term once its period is completed), but the relevant person makes representations pursuant to reg 4(1)(c), the governing body must consider those representations.[15] The implication appears to be that there is no need for the

---

1 Regulation 5(1) and (2)(a).
2 Regulation 5(2)(b).
3 See reg 5(2)(c), the terms of which are potentially misleading. The obligation is to allow those persons to attend a meeting of the governing body and to make oral representations about the exclusion.
4 Regulation 5(2)(d).
5 Regulation 5(9).
6 Regulation 5(8)(a).
7 Regulation 5(8)(b).
8 Regulation 5(8)(c).
9 Regulation 5(10).
10 Regulation 5(3).
11 Regulation 5(4).
12 Regulation 5(6)(a).
13 Regulation 5(6)(b).
14 Regulation 5(11).
15 Regulation 5(7).

governing body in this case to give the relevant person an opportunity to make oral representations.

Right of appeal against permanent exclusion from a maintained school [1]

10.41   Regulation 6(1) of the Education (Pupil Exclusions and Appeals) (Maintained Schools) (England) Regulations 2002 obliges an LEA to make arrangements for enabling the relevant person to appeal against a decision by a governing body not to reinstate a pupil who has been permanently excluded. The right to appeal is conferred on the relevant person,[2] so if the pupil is over the age of 18, this right is conferred on him. Otherwise, the right is conferred on the parent of the pupil. The right must be exercised within 15 school days of the day on which the relevant person was given notice in writing under reg 5(6)(b).[3] If the relevant person notifies the LEA in writing that he does not intend to appeal against a decision not to reinstate the pupil, that notice is final.[4]

10.42   The constitution of the appeal panel is determined in accordance with para 2 of the Schedule to the Education (Pupil Exclusions and Appeals) (Maintained Schools) (England) Regulations 2002. The procedure to be followed by the panel in hearing the appeal is governed by paras 6–16 of that Schedule.

Appeal panel constitution

10.43   An appeal panel constituted in accordance with para 2 of the Schedule to the Education (Pupil Exclusions and Appeals) (Maintained Schools) (England) Regulations 2002 must have three or five members appointed by the LEA from (1) 'persons who are eligible to be lay members', which means persons 'without personal experience in the management of any school or the provision of education in any school (disregarding any such experience as a governor or in any other voluntary capacity)',[5] (2) persons who are, or who have been within the previous 5 years, head teachers of maintained schools who may[6] be employed by the LEA (this is new: there was in the superseded provisions in the SSFA 1998 no requirement to have a head teacher as a member of the appeal panel),[7] and (3) persons who are or have been governors of maintained schools, but have not been teachers or head teachers during the last 5 years, and who have served as a governor for at least 12 consecutive months within the last 6 years.[8] If the panel consists of three members, then there must be one of each of these categories as a member.[9] Certain persons are disqualified, by

---

[1]   Where unlawful discrimination contrary to the Disability Discrimination Act 1995 is claimed in relation to an exclusion from a maintained school, the claim must be made to an appeal panel of the type described below. See further, para **18.59**.

[2]   See reg 5(6)(b)(ii).

[3]   SI 2002/3178, Sch, para 1(1). See para 1(2) in relation to the date when notice is to be regarded as having been given.

[4]   Ibid, Sch, para 1(3).

[5]   Ibid, Sch, para 2(2)(a) and (4).

[6]   See ibid, Sch, para 2(8), which is subject to para 2(7)(d).

[7]   Ibid, Sch, para 2(2)(b).

[8]   Ibid, Sch, para 2(2)(c), as inserted by SI 2004/402.

[9]   Ibid, Sch, para 2(3)(a).

para 2(7) of the Schedule, for membership of an appeal panel. These include any person employed by the LEA other than as a head teacher.[1]

10.44   The impact of the inclusion of a person who was disqualified for membership of an appeal panel would probably be that the court would order that a new appeal panel be appointed to consider the matter afresh.[2]

10.45   When the panel consists of five members, one must be a lay member, two must be head teachers or former head teachers and two must be governors or former governors.[3] If at any time after an appeal panel consisting of five members has begun to consider an appeal, a member dies or becomes unable through illness to continue as a member, then the panel may continue with their consideration and determination of the appeal as long as the number of remaining members is not less than three and there continues to be at least one each of all three kinds of member.[4]

10.46   No matter how many members an appeal panel has, it must be chaired by the person appointed as a lay member.[5]

Appeal panel procedure

10.47   An appeal must be made by notice in writing, setting out the grounds on which it is made.[6] The hearing of the appeal must take place on a date determined by the LEA which is no later than the fifteenth school day after the day on which the appeal is lodged.[7] The LEA must take reasonable steps to ascertain when the relevant person or his proposed representative (who is entitled to attend) would not be able to attend such a hearing, and must fix the time of the hearing so far as it is reasonably practicable to do so to enable the relevant person and/or his representative to be present and make representations.[8] The appeal panel must then give the relevant person an opportunity to appear and make oral representations, and allow that person to be represented or accompanied by a friend.[9]

10.48   The panel must also allow (1) the head teacher to make written representations and to appear and make oral representations, (2) the LEA and the governing body to make written representations, and (3) the LEA and the governing body to be represented and make oral representations.[10]

10.49   Appeals must be heard in private, but one member of the LEA may attend, as an observer, any hearing of an appeal by an appeal panel, but only if the panel so

---

[1]   SI 2002/3178, Sch, para 2(7)(c).
[2]   Cf *R v The Board of Governors of Stoke Newington School, ex parte M* [1994] ELR 131.
[3]   SI 2002/3178, Sch, para 2(3)(b).
[4]   Ibid, Sch, para 2(9).
[5]   Ibid, Sch, para 2(10).
[6]   Ibid, Sch, para 7.
[7]   Ibid, Sch, paras 6 and 8.
[8]   Ibid, Sch, para 9.
[9]   Ibid, Sch, para 10(1).
[10]   Ibid, Sch, para 10(2).

direct.[1] One member of the Council on Tribunals may in any event attend such a meeting as an observer.[2]

10.50 Two or more appeals may be heard together if the panel consider it to be expedient to do so because the issues raised by the appeals are 'the same or connected'.[3]

10.51 In making any decision on the appeal, the appeal panel must 'have regard both to the interests of the excluded pupil and to the interests of other pupils and persons working at the school (including persons working at the school voluntarily)'.[4] Furthermore, the panel may not determine that a pupil is to be reinstated merely because of a failure to comply with any procedural requirement imposed by the Education (Pupil Exclusions and Appeals) (Maintained Schools) (England) Regulations 2002 in relation to either the decision against which the appeal is brought or the exclusion or decision by the head teacher to which that decision related.[5]

10.52 An appeal must be determined by a majority of the votes cast by those present, but if there is an equality of votes, the chairman of the panel has a second or casting vote.[6] The decision of the panel 'and the grounds on which it is made'[7] must be communicated in writing by the end of the second working day[8] after the conclusion of the appeal hearing to (1) the relevant person, (2) the LEA, (3) the governing body; and (4) the head teacher.[9] The decision is binding on 'the relevant person, the governing body, the head teacher and the [LEA]'.[10] The panel may either (1) uphold the exclusion, (2) direct that the pupil is to be reinstated (either immediately or by a date specified in the direction), or (3) 'decide that because of exceptional circumstances or for other reasons it is not practical to give a direction requiring his reinstatement, but that it would otherwise have been appropriate to give such a direction'.[11]

10.53 Except as described in the preceding paragraphs above, the procedure of the appeal panel is to be determined by the LEA, which must when setting time-limits have regard to the desirability of avoiding delay.[12] In addition, there is a growing body of case-law affecting the manner in which an appeal panel should proceed.

---

[1] SI 2002/3178, Sch, para 11(a).

[2] Ibid, Sch, para 11(b).

[3] Ibid, Sch, para 12.

[4] SI 2002/3178, reg 6(3). This gives statutory effect to the ruling in R *v Camden London Borough and the Governors of the Hampstead School, ex parte* H [1996] ELR 360.

[5] SI 2002/3178, reg 6(4).

[6] Ibid, Sch, para 13.

[7] See paras **9.94–9.96** concerning the impact of this duty, where the case-law concerning the duty which arises in relation to admission appeals (which is in the same terms), is discussed.

[8] A 'working day' is defined in para 16 of the Schedule.

[9] SI 2002/3178, Sch, para 14.

[10] Ibid, reg 6(5).

[11] Ibid, reg 6(6). See para 10.4 of Part 4 of the Secretary of State's guidance on exclusions for relevant considerations which should be taken into account in this context, and for guidance generally about the exercise of the power to decline to direct the reinstatement of a pupil whose appeal has been allowed.

[12] Ibid, Sch, para 15.

RELEVANT CASE LAW AFFECTING APPEAL PANELS

GENERAL PRINCIPLES

10.54 In *S v Brent LB*,[1] the predecessor to the Secretary of State's current Guidance, issued under s 68 of the SSFA 1998, was considered. That predecessor set out, in paras 17 and 18, certain views, including that an appeal panel 'should not normally direct reinstatement' where a head teacher has 'excluded a pupil in accordance with clearly stated provisions in the school's published discipline policy, for example zero tolerance of drug dealing' and that 'the Secretary of State would normally regard it as inappropriate to reinstate a pupil who has been permanently excluded in circumstances involving ... sexual abuse'. In para 16 of the guidance, it was said that if the panel were 'satisfied on the balance of probabilities that the pupil did what they are alleged to have done, then the panel should decide whether permanent exclusion is a reasonable response to that conduct'. These passages are in substance repeated in the Secretary of State's current Guidance.[2]

10.55 In *S v Brent LB*, the court said that 'great circumspection is required on the part of ministers in formulating guidance under s 68',[3] but that 'the promotion of consistency is a necessary purpose of [such] guidance',[4] although it is not a sufficient one.[5] Paragraphs 17 and 18 of the then current guidance were held to be lawful,[6] but the court commented that in saying the words quoted above from para 16, the guidance 'enters choppy waters'.[7] The panel must decide by asking itself: 'ought this child to be reinstated or not?'[8]

10.56 A number of other statements from the Court of Appeal's judgment in *S v Brent LB* are worthy of note. One is that it is 'no part of the function of the LEA to press for a particular conclusion in relation to a particular pupil'.[9] Equally, the appeal panel must avoid being, or appearing to be, unduly influenced by what the LEA's representative says about the exclusion.[10] A panel must 'entertain any credible material, written or oral, which is reasonably and fairly capable of affecting what they have to decide'.[11] Where there is a 'material conflict of evidence involving an adult witness, there is no legal reason why the witness cannot be invited to attend and be questioned',[12] although 'panels are perfectly entitled to refuse to allow confrontational cross-examination of witnesses and to require questions to be put by or through the chair'.[13] The use of anonymised statements would be unfair 'if they are damaging to

---

[1]   [2002] EWCA Civ 693; [2002] ELR 556.
[2]   See paras 1.4, 1.6, 8.1 and 8.3.
[3]   [2002] ELR 556, at para 17.
[4]   Ibid, at para 16.
[5]   Ibid.
[6]   Ibid, at para 32.
[7]   Ibid, at para 20.
[8]   Ibid.
[9]   Ibid, at para 24.
[10]   Ibid, at para 25.
[11]   Ibid, at para 27.
[12]   Ibid, at para 28.
[13]   Ibid.

the pupil in ways which the pupil cannot be expected to deal with without knowing who has made the statement'.[1]

10.57 It is of considerable interest that the court made the 'perfectly tenable assumption ... that domestic human rights law, and arguably the European Court of Human Right's jurisprudence too, will today regard at least the right not to be permanently excluded from school without good reason as a civil right for Art 6 purposes'.[2] However, there was no need to decide that question, as the common law was found to supply the necessary answers to the criticisms made by the appellants as to the independence and impartiality of exclusion appeal panels established under the SSFA 1998.[3]

10.58 In R *v Headteacher and Independent Appeal Committee of Dunraven School, ex parte B*,[4] the Court of Appeal ruled that since a pupil has the right to be heard in an exclusion appeal hearing, where what was being said against the pupil had taken at least two different and arguably inconsistent forms, fairness would ordinarily require enough disclosure to reveal the inconsistency.[5] Moreover, it was unfair for the decision-maker to have access to damaging material to which the person at risk, here the pupil through his parent, had no access.[6] Furthermore, an appellant was not obliged to ask for the disclosure of such damaging material:[7] the governing body's duty to ensure fairness was not conditional upon applications or demands more appropriate to adversarial litigation.[8]

10.59 In relation to anonymised statements, the Court of Appeal ruled in *Dunraven* that the governing body should have proceeded by taking an approach which was similar to that indicated in the case of *Linfood Cash and Carry Ltd v Thomson*[9] to the use of anonymised statements when dismissing employees. According to Sedley LJ, a governing body in such a situation should first ask whether they wish to take into account any such statement. If it does so wish, then it must consider whether the informant's identity can be concealed. If it cannot, then the governing body must consider whether to go ahead without relying on anything which the maker of the statement has said, or to drop the case and reinstate the excluded pupil.[10] However, in

---

[1]   [2002] ELR 556, at para 29.
[2]   Ibid, at para 30. This appears not to have been taken into account in *A v The Head Teacher and Governors of the Lord Grey School* [2003] EWCH 1533; [2003] ELR 517, at para 75, where it was accepted on behalf of the claimant that 'on the basis of the current jurisprudence of the European Court of Human Rights, the right to education under Art 1 of Protocol 1 [sic] to the Convention is not a civil right with the meaning of Art 6'.
[3]   *S v Brent LB* [2002] EWCA Civ 693; [2002] ELR 556, at para 30.
[4]   [2000] ELR 156.
[5]   Ibid, at 190, per Sedley LJ.
[6]   Ibid.
[7]   Ibid, at 193.
[8]   Ibid. It is of interest that on the facts of the case in R *(S) v The Governing Body of YP School* [2002] EWHC 2975 (Admin); [2003] ELR 578 (Maurice Kay J), the giving by the school's discipline committee to solicitors acting for the excluded pupil of only a synopsis of the evidence against the pupil, was, although unfair, not such as to cause an injustice. This was primarily because the excluded pupil did not attend the committee's hearing, and did not advance any kind of 'positive narrative about the events' which led to the pupil's exclusion (see para 24).
[9]   [1989] IRLR 235.
[10]   Ibid, at 192.

R (T) v Head Teacher of Elliott School,[1] Schiemann LJ commented in relation to the submission that anonymised statements were inadmissible that:

> 'These cases can involve difficult choices between fairness to those who face exclusion and fairness to others. They are very fact sensitive and the decision maker must, in each case, be conscious of any possible unfairness.'[2]

10.60 However, he also said this:

> 'It must, I think, be presumed in the absence of evidence to the contrary that the head teacher will not place before the panel statements from pupils known to him to be unreliable or to have some disconnected grudge. If a head teacher had a reason to suspect such a thing, then he should tell the appeal panel of his concerns.'[3]

10.61 That case also concerned the question whether it was unfair for a teacher who was (as Sedley LJ put it[4]) 'familiar with the pupil' sitting on the school's discipline committee. On the facts, the allegation of unfairness was rejected, but it is clear from the judgments of both Schiemann LJ[5] and Sedley LJ that (as Sedley LJ put it[6]): 'The right course is always to err on the side of caution, for it is not necessarily going to be an answer that the pupil or the parent failed to object.'

10.62 According to Brooke LJ in *Dunraven* (and only he referred to this aspect of the case, Morritt LJ merely agreeing with Sedley LJ), if a pupil has been excluded for what amounts to a criminal offence (in *Dunraven* it was an offence of dishonesty), although the case needs to be proved against the pupil only on the balance of probabilities, that balance must be struck on the basis that he should be found to have committed the act of which he is accused only if it is distinctly more probable than not that he committed it.[7] In *R (J) v Birmingham City Council Exclusion Appeals Committee*,[8] Davis J nevertheless said that it was 'important to stress that matters of this kind are not to be conducted as though they are some kind of formal criminal proceeding'. He ruled that it was not unfair in that case that the appeal panel heard no oral evidence from any person who saw the incident which led to the exclusion, nor any evidence (at all) from any person who carried out the investigation which followed it. The only oral evidence which the panel heard from the school was the head teacher's evidence, and she had neither witnessed the incident which led to the exclusion nor investigated it. She therefore relied purely on hearsay evidence.

---

[1]   [2002] EWCA Civ 1349; [2003] ELR 160, CA (Schiemann and Sedley LJJ).

[2]   Ibid, at para 36; and see para 52, per Sedley LJ. Sedley LJ also in effect reiterated (at para 50) in this respect the ruling in *Dunraven*.

[3]   [2002] EWCA Civ 1349, at para 37; see also at para 48, per Sedley LJ. At para 42, Schiemann LJ gave this indication as to the procedure which appeal panels would be well-advised to adopt: 'Clearly, if the panel can reach a firm decision one way or the other, quite apart from any such statements, then it will be well advised to say so. In such circumstances it will be relieved of the difficult task of deciding what weight to give to the statements'.

[4]   Ibid, at para 46.

[5]   Ibid, at paras 16 and 17.

[6]   Ibid, at para 46.

[7]   Ibid, at para 204.

[8]   [2003] EWHC 1747 (Admin); [2003] ELR 743, para 13.

10.63 With this may be contrasted the ruling of the Court of Appeal in R *(S) v The Governing Body of Y P School*.[1] There, it was conceded by the respondent that Maurice Kay J was wrong in law when, in giving judgment in the High Court, he said in relation to the standard of proof which is required in deciding whether (in the case of a head teacher) an exclusion from a maintained school should occur (or in the case of a governing body or an appeal panel) such an exclusion should have occurred:

> 'The appropriate standard, in the sense of the standard required by the law, is less than the criminal standard and is properly described as being "the balance of probabilities", albeit that a gloss is placed upon that language by the authorities in relation to an allegation of seriousness as this one was.'

10.64 The (3-judge) Court of Appeal accepted that this concession was correct, and held (without having heard any oral submissions) that:

> 'The right approach is as conceded: namely, that in dealing with a disciplinary matter where the accusation amounts to a crime under the general law, the head teacher and governors must be sure that the child has done what he has been accused of before so finding.'

10.65 It may be that the rigour which this statement implies should be adopted in exclusion appeals would in practice have been tempered by the statement of Schiemann LJ in R *(T) v Head Teacher of Elliott School*[2] set out in para **10.59**, namely that cases of this sort 'are very fact sensitive'. In any event, the Education (Pupil Exclusions) (Miscellaneous Amendments) (England) Regulations 2004[3] were enacted in swift response to the judgment of the Court of Appeal in R *(S) v The Governing Body of YP School*. They inserted a new regulation into each relevant set of regulations,[4] providing that 'any question as to whether [a relevant] fact is established shall be decided on a balance of probabilities'. This new regulation appears to be fully retrospective. It seems clear, however, that it does not mean that the case-law concerning the higher standard of proof where what is alleged is a criminal offence (albeit that the test is still regarded as being whether the matter in question is proved on the balance of probabilities rather than beyond reasonable doubt) is ousted; rather, that case-law (referred to in *Dunraven*) should, it seems, still apply.

10.66 If a new issue is to be considered by an appeal panel, then the panel must consider it properly. So, if the issue is one which was not considered by the head teacher to be important when making the challenged decision to exclude a pupil, then it must be investigated properly.[5] However, it will not always be necessary to 'carry out searching inquiries involving the calling of bodies of oral evidence'.[6] Nevertheless, the panel must decide what central issues of fact they should resolve and what enquiries could reasonably be made to resolve those issues.[7] They must also give

---

[1]   [2003] EWCA Civ 1306, [2003] All ER (D) 202.

[2]   Ibid, at para 36.

[3]   SI 2004/402.

[4]   SI 2002/3178, the new reg being reg 7A, and SI 2002/3179, the new reg being reg 8A.

[5]   R *v Camden London Borough and Governors of Hampstead School, ex parte H* [1996] ELR 360, at 376G–377G.

[6]   Ibid, at 377F.

[7]   R *v Solihull Borough Council, ex parte W* [1997] ELR 489, at 499F–G.

careful and even-handed consideration to all the available evidence in relation to those issues.[1] The overriding principle is that a pupil must have a fair opportunity to exculpate himself.[2] In determining what sanction to impose in respect of misconduct, the committee must take into account the school's disciplinary regime.[3]

RELEVANCE OF CONDUCT OF A PARENT

10.67   In *R v Neale, ex parte S*,[4] it was held that the actions of a parent may be relevant in determining whether an appeal against an exclusion should be upheld. Although at first sight this may seem odd, in practice the actions of a parent may be very disruptive. Furthermore, as mentioned above, s 62 of the SSFA 1998 confers on the LEA a reserve power to intervene in the event of indiscipline, and makes express reference to the action of parents as well as of pupils.[5] This accordingly provides some support for the ruling in *ex parte S*.[6] However, the Secretary of State's guidance refers to a number of matters for which exclusion 'should not be used', and one of these is 'punishing pupils for the behaviour of their parents'.[7] This must be right. Perhaps the discretion to decline to reinstate a pupil whose appeal against a permanent exclusion has been successful[8] should now be relied upon instead of dismissing the appeal where the conduct of a parent has made the reinstatement of the pupil unduly problematic.

IDENTIFICATION EVIDENCE

10.68   According to Moses J in *R v Roman Catholic Schools, ex parte S*:[9] 'There may be cases where it is unnecessary to have the identifying witness give oral evidence but I should have thought that such cases would be rare'. However, this was said against the background that the identification evidence was central. This should be borne in mind in relation to the court's statement that those conducting the inquiry 'should remind themselves of the dangers of identification evidence and the need for safeguards to avoid such dangers'[10]. However, if there is a 'clear opportunity' for the pupil or his representative to raise and the panel to consider the 'areas of caution and areas where

---

1   *R v Roman Catholic Schools, ex parte S* [1998] ELR 304, at 312.
2   *R v Roman Catholic Schools, ex parte S*, ibid, at 312A, applying *R v Board of Visitors of Hull Prison, ex parte St Germain* [1979] 1 WLR 1401. See also *R v Governors of Bacon's City Technology College, ex parte W* [1998] ELR 488, at 498F–499G; [1998] EdCR 236, at 247G–249A, concerning the need to be even-handed in portraying the excluded pupil's character.
3   This was said in *R v Governors of St Gregory's RC Aided High School and Appeals Committee, ex parte M* [1995] ELR 290, at 300B–301D, but it is in any event stated in the Secretary of State's Guidance at para 8.2(b) that an appeal panel should have regard to 'the school's published behaviour policy ... and, if appropriate, anti-bullying policy'.
4   [1995] ELR 198, at 211B–E.
5   See para **10.26**.
6   The case of *R v Secretary of State for Education and Southlands Comprehensive School, ex parte W* [1998] ELR 413; [1998] EdCR 135 also provides support for the ruling that the actions of a pupil's parent may be taken into account when deciding to exclude the pupil.
7   DfES/0087/2003, para 54.1(f) of Part 1.
8   See para **10.52**.
9   [1998] ELR 304, 315B; [1998] EdCR 277, at 289E.
10   [1998] ELR 313C.

particular attention [is] required' but those areas are not expressly raised by the pupil or his representative, a decision to uphold an exclusion is unlikely to be vitiated.[1]

FAIRNESS OF EXCLUSION – CONSISTENCY OF PENALTY

10.69 In R *v Governors of Bacon's City Technology College, ex parte W*,[2] Collins J said that 'one cannot look at punishment in isolation, one must look at it in the context of the others involved. Otherwise there may be unfairness if one is picked out and others are not.' The Secretary of State's Guidance now states that an appeal panel must have regard to 'the fairness of the exclusion in relation to the treatment of any other pupils involved in the same incident'.[3]

LIMITING THE TIME FOR THE HEARING

10.70 In R *v Governors of Bacon's City Technology College, ex parte W*,[4] it was said that if an appeal committee had a policy of allowing only a certain period of time for an appeal (in that case it was 30 minutes):

> 'then it is a dangerous policy because there may be cases where it is necessary to go into more detail than others where, for example, primary facts are disputed and there has been no chance before the hearing before the governors for the student or the parents to challenge those primary facts. In those circumstances, as it seems to me, it may be necessary for the governors to involve themselves in a fact-finding exercise because it would clearly be, on the face of it, wrong to rely upon evidence which has not been able to be challenged at all by the student in question.'

IMPERMISSIBLE DELEGATION

10.71 It was held in R *v (1) Wakefield Diocesan Board of Education (Schools Appeal Tribunal) (2) Holy Trinity School, Wakefield*[5] that a chairman of an appeal panel may not make decisions on the law without consulting his colleagues. This was decided on the basis that there was no provision in the relevant legislation (in that case it concerned a grant-maintained school, but there was no material difference from the legislation affecting other maintained schools) for the delegation of the power to make such decisions. This was despite the facts that (1) the principle that the power to exercise a discretion may not be delegated is by no means immutable or universally applicable,[6] and (2) a tribunal does not have a discretion as to whether it applies the law.

APPEAL PANEL'S INQUISITORIAL ROLE

10.72 In R *v Governors of Bacon's City Technology College, ex parte W*[7] it was held that a failure to indicate to a loquacious representative that the appeal panel wished to hear from the pupil himself 'led in itself to a degree of unfairness'. In the circumstances of

---

1   See R *(A) v Head Teacher and Governing Body of North Westminster Community School* [2002] EWHC 2351 (Admin); [2003] ELR 378, at paras 28–29.
2   [1998] ELR 488, 500C–D; [1998] EdCR 236, at 249F.
3   Ibid, at para 8.2(c).
4   [1998] ELR 488, at 493C–D; [1998] EdCR 236, at 241F–G.
5   [1999] EdCR 566.
6   See de Smith, Woolf and Jowell, *Judicial Review of Administrative Action* (Sweet & Maxwell, 5th edn, 1995), at para 6.104.
7   [1998] ELR 488, at 498E; [1998] EdCR 236, at 247D–E.

that case, the chairman 'ought to have firmly and clearly indicated why he wanted to hear from [the excluded pupil] and [that] it would not be in [the excluded pupil's] interest if he did not hear from him'.[1]

Can an excluded pupil who was excluded for violence against another pupil lawfully attend school to take public examinations?

10.73 The question whether an excluded pupil who was excluded for violence to another pupil could lawfully be allowed back to take public examinations arose in *R (MB) v Independent Appeal Panel of SMBC*.[2] The question arose because the appeal panel decided to reinstate the excluded pupil and he was accordingly allowed back to school, but it was subsequently accepted (in judicial review proceedings) that the decision that the pupil should be reinstated was made unlawfully. Moses J commented that in the circumstances he could see 'no legal reason why the headmaster should not continue the present arrangements of allowing him in as a visitor under the authority of the local education authority to continue to sit the exams at the school under the present arrangements'.[3]

Exclusions from pupil referral units

10.74 Exclusions from pupil referral units are, as stated above, governed by a different set of regulations. Those regulations, the Education (Pupil Exclusions and Appeals) (Pupil Referral Units) (England) Regulations 2002,[4] are in substance the same as the Education (Pupil Exclusions and Appeals) (Maintained Schools) (England) Regulations 2002, and in the main differ only as a result of the need to take account of the differences in the structures of pupil referral units as compared with maintained schools. Indeed, the regulations relating to pupil referral units incorporate the Schedule in those relating to maintained schools, but with modifications.[5]

10.75 Section 52(7) of the EA 2002 conferred a retrospective right to appeal against an exclusion from a pupil referral unit after they first came into existence, which was on 1 September 1994. That right was given effect by the Education (Pupil Referral Units) (Appeals against Permanent Exclusion) (England) Regulations 2002.[6] However, those regulations allowed a period of only 30 days from 4 November 2002 for the bringing of the appeal.[7] Those regulations were repealed by the Education (Pupil Exclusions and Appeals) (Pupil Referral Units) (England) Regulations 2002,[8] although their continuing application was provided for in the Education Act 2002 (Commencement No 3 and Savings and Transitional Provisions) Order 2002.[9]

---

[1]   [1998] ELR 488, at 498E; [1998] EdCR 236, at 247D–E.
[2]   [2002] ELR 677.
[3]   [2002] ELR 677, at para 9.
[4]   SI 2002/3179.
[5]   See reg 7(2) of SI 2002/3179.
[6]   SI 2002/2550.
[7]   See regs 1 and 5.
[8]   See reg 10.
[9]   SI 2002/2952.

CHALLENGING A DECISION OF A GOVERNING BODY NOT TO ORDER REINSTATEMENT IN PUBLIC LAW PROCEEDINGS

10.76 In R *v London Borough of Newham, ex parte X,*[1] both the governing body of a school and the LEA decided not to direct the reinstatement of a pupil, with the result that under the then current legislation there was a right of appeal to an appeal committee arranged by the LEA available to the excluded pupil's parent. Counsel for the LEA argued in the hearing of the application for judicial review that that appeal route should have been used, but the court rejected that argument, and even granted interim relief.

10.77 This was (understandably) said by the Court of Appeal (obiter) in R *(DR) v Head Teacher and Governing Body of S School and Independent Appeal Panel of W City Council*[2] to be one of the 'very few and far between' cases where judicial review may be appropriate, bearing in mind that there is a statutory appeal procedure which can be followed within a short period of time. In *DR*, it was held that the statutory scheme under the SSFA 1998 relating to exclusions from maintained schools (which currently still applies in Wales and is in all material respects the same as that which is described above) required an excluded pupil to seek a remedy before the appeal panel.[3] Only if a procedural unfairness at the first stage of the decision-making process (namely that of the head teacher and the governing body, which 'can sensibly be regarded as a single process given that any case of permanent exclusion is automatically referred to the governing body'[4]) 'can be shown in some way to have tainted the subsequent appeal process' will the appeal panel's decision itself be 'necessarily unsustainable'.[5] This would be so where the procedural defect was 'so gross, and the prejudice so extreme, that it would be appropriate to quash [the first-tier] decision on that ground'.[6] However, apart from in circumstances such as these, Simon Brown LJ found it 'difficult to think of any case in which a decision reached upon an otherwise fairly conducted appeal by an independent tribunal following a full merits hearing should be impugnable by reference to unfairness at an earlier stage'.[7]

10.78 However, since a right of appeal to an appeal panel arises only where a pupil has been excluded permanently, there may still be occasions when an application for judicial review may be appropriate (assuming that a complaint to the Secretary of State under s 496 or s 497 of the EA 1996 would not be the better option). In R *v Governors of McEntee School, ex parte Mbandaka,*[8] Collins J said that an application for permission to apply for a judicial review of a temporary exclusion should be made as quickly as

---

1   [1995] ELR 303.
2   [2002] EWCA Civ 1822; [2003] ELR 104, at para 45, per Simon Brown LJ, with whom Kay and Keene LJJ agreed.
3   See ibid, para 37.
4   Ibid, para 37.
5   Ibid, para 43.
6   Ibid.
7   Ibid.
8   [1999] EdCR 656.

possible – in days or at most two weeks from the exclusion. Furthermore, he said, an internal appeal against the exclusion should be made first.

Judicial review of a decision to order reinstatement

10.79 When the reinstatement of a pupil occurs as a result of a direction by the governing body of a maintained school, the decision to direct reinstatement will be the final decision in relation to the pupil's exclusion. There will be no right to appeal against such a decision, so a challenge to it could be made only by way of an application for judicial review or a complaint to the Secretary of State under s 496 or s 497 of the EA 1996. The question which route should be followed would then arise. It seems clear that if the challenge were purely to the reasonableness of the decision (in narrow *Wednesbury* terms), then, as long as the complaint was likely to be considered quickly, a challenge by way of an application for judicial review could be rejected by the court. This would be on the basis that there was an appropriate alternative route for complaining, and that an application for permission to apply for judicial review should accordingly as a matter of practice be refused. Nevertheless, it may be that a court would be sympathetic to an application for permission to apply for judicial review in such circumstances. This is apparent from several cases. One example is *R v London Borough of Newham, ex parte X*.[1] In contrast to that case, the point that there was an alternative to an application for judicial review (in the form of a complaint to the Secretary of State under s 496 or s 497 of the EA 1996) was not taken in *R v Camden London Borough and the Governors of the Hampstead School, ex parte H*,[2] where the governing body had directed the reinstatement of a pupil. It may be that the reason for not taking the point that there was an alternative remedy was that the applications for judicial review were made on the basis that the decisions in question were *ultra vires*. In *R v Governing Body of the Rectory School, ex parte WK*,[3] *R v London Borough of Newham, ex parte X* was referred to and cited in support of a decision to allow an application for permission to apply for judicial review despite the fact that an appeal to an independent appeal panel could have been made. The circumstances of *ex parte WK* were, however, different from those of the other cases referred to in this paragraph. This is because in *ex parte WK* an insistence by the court on the appeal route being followed would in practice have deprived the child's parent of a right to make representations about an earlier fixed-period exclusion, and that deprivation could have had a material effect on the outcome of the appeal.[4]

Challenging a decision of an appeal panel

10.80 Any challenge to a decision of an appeal panel would have to be made by way of an application for permission to apply for judicial review, since ss 496 and 497 of the EA 1996 do not apply to the decisions of such panels. The members of the panel would, however, be indemnified by the local education authority against any reasonable legal costs and expenses reasonably incurred by them in connection with

---

[1] [1995] ELR 303; see para **10.76**.
[2] [1996] ELR 360.
[3] [1997] ELR 484, at 488C–E.
[4] See ibid, at 486F–487B. See also 488C–E.

any decision or action taken by them in good faith in pursuance of their functions as members of that committee.[1]

Funding of education for permanently excluded pupils

10.81 Section 494 of the EA 1996 applies where a pupil is permanently excluded from a maintained school and in the financial year in which the exclusion first takes effect he is then provided with education in a school which is maintained by a different LEA (the new LEA) from that which maintained the school from which he was excluded (the old LEA).[2] In that situation, s 494(2) provides that the funding for his education must follow him from the old LEA to the new LEA in accordance with regulations made under the subsection. If there is a third LEA involved in any year, for example because the pupil is educated at a school maintained by one LEA, the pupil is then educated in a pupil referral unit for which another LEA is responsible, and then the pupil is admitted to a school which is maintained by neither of those two LEAs, then s 494(2) is applied in relation to each change.[3]

10.82 Any dispute as to whether any LEA is entitled to be paid any amount under s 494 by any other LEA must be determined by the Secretary of State.[4] Regulations may prescribe the time when the permanent exclusion of a pupil is to be regarded as taking effect for the purposes of the section.[5] The current regulations are the Education (Amount to Follow Permanently Excluded Pupil) Regulations 1999.[6]

Effect of removal of a permanently excluded pupil's name from the admission register for a maintained school

10.83 Regulation 9(1)(k) of the Education (Pupil Registration) Regulations 1995[7] requires the removal from the admission register for a maintained school of the name of a pupil who has been permanently excluded from the school. However, the permanent exclusion does not take effect for this purpose until the governing body of the school have discharged their duties in relation to the exclusion, and (a) the relevant person has stated in writing that he does not intend to appeal against the exclusion, or (b) the time-limit for bringing such an appeal has expired, or (c) an appeal brought within that time-limit has been determined or abandoned.[8] However:

> 'removal from the school roll is not an act with legal consequences. It is the administrative consequence of other acts, and if those acts are not lawfully done, neither is the removal from the school roll.'[9]

---

[1] SI 2002/3178, Sch, para 5.

[2] EA 1996, s 494(1).

[3] Ibid, s 494(3).

[4] Ibid, s 494(4); s 208(2) of the EA 2002 will, when it is in force, transfer this function of resolving disputes to the National Assembly for Wales. (Section 208 was brought into force 'except in relation to Wales' by SI 2003/124.)

[5] Ibid, s 494(5).

[6] SI 1999/495, amended in relation to England by SI 2001/870 and SI 2004/402, and in relation to Wales by SI 2002/408.

[7] SI 1995/2089.

[8] Ibid, reg 9(4)(d).

[9] *A v Head Teacher and Governors of the Lord Grey School* [2004] EWCA Civ 382, [2004] ELR 169, at para 62.

MEASURES INTRODUCED BY THE ANTI-SOCIAL BEHAVIOUR ACT 2003

10.84 The Anti-Social Behaviour Act 2003 introduced two new measures for LEAs to use in relation to pupils who have been excluded from school. These are (1) parenting contracts, empowered by s 19 (which apply also in relation to pupils who have not attended regularly at the schools at which they are registered pupils), and (2) parenting orders. Parenting contracts are described in paras **5.65** et seq. Parenting orders are described below.

Parenting orders

10.85 Where a pupil has been excluded, either (a) for a fixed period after the pupil has been excluded for a fixed period from any school within the previous 12 months, or (b) permanently, on disciplinary grounds from a relevant school (for the meaning of which see para **5.65**), an LEA may apply to a magistrates' court for a parenting order in respect of a parent of the pupil.[1] In the case of a fixed-period exclusion, the application must be made within either (a) 40 school days from the next school day after the day on which the exclusion was considered by the governing body (or in the case of a pupil referral unit, the LEA), or, if it was not so considered, the day on which it began, or (b) 6 months from the day on which a parent of the pupil entered into a parenting contract.[2] In the case of a permanent exclusion, the application must be made within either (1) the period of 40 school days beginning with the next school day after either (a) the day on which an appeal panel constituted under regulations made under s 52 of the EA 2002 decided to uphold the exclusion, or (b) if there was no such appeal, the last day on which an appeal could have been made, or (2) the period of 6 months beginning with the day on which a parent of the pupil entered into a parenting contract.[3]

10.86 A parenting order is an order which requires the parent (1) to comply, for a period of no more than 12 months, with any requirements specified in the order and, where no such order has previously been made in respect of the parent, (2) to attend, for a concurrent period of no more than 3 months, 'such counselling or guidance programme as may be specified in directions given by the responsible officer'.[4] A 'responsible officer' for this purpose is either an officer of the LEA or a head teacher or (with his consent) a person nominated by a head teacher.[5] If a parenting order has

---

[1] Anti-Social Behaviour Act 2003, s 20(1) and (2) and reg 3 of the Education (Parenting Orders) (England) Regulations 2004, SI 2004/182. Sections 19–24 of that Act are in force in England only: see SI 2003/3300, Art 4. For the purposes of s 20, the term 'pupil' is to be construed in accordance with s 3(1) and (1A) of the EA 1996, and the term 'parent' is to be construed in accordance with s 576 of the EA 1996, except that it does not include a person who is not an individual: Anti-Social Behaviour Act 2003, s 24.

[2] SI 2004/182, reg 4(1). If both are applicable, the period is whichever expires later: ibid. For the meaning of a parenting contract, see para **5.65**.

[3] SI 2004/182, reg 4(2). If both are applicable, the period is whichever expires later: ibid.

[4] Anti-Social Behaviour Act 2003, s 20(4).

[5] Ibid, s 24. The term 'head teacher' includes an acting head teacher, teaching in charge and acting teacher in charge: ibid.

previously been made in respect of the parent in question, then the order may include a requirement to attend such a counselling or guidance programme.[1]

10.87　Any counselling or guidance programme which is a requirement of a parenting order may be or include a residential course, but only if (1) the attendance of the parent at a residential course is likely to be more effective than his attendance at a non-residential course in improving the behaviour of the pupil, and (2) any interference with family life which is likely to result from the attendance of the parent at a residential course is 'proportionate in all the circumstances'.[2]

10.88　The costs associated with the requirements of parenting orders, including the costs of providing counselling or guidance programmes, must be met by the LEA.[3]

10.89　In deciding whether to make a parenting order under s 20 of the Anti-Social Behaviour Act 2003, a court must take into account (among other things) (a) any refusal by the parent to enter into a parenting contract under s 19 in respect of a pupil who has been excluded from a relevant school on disciplinary grounds, or (b) if the parent has entered into any such contract, any failure by the parent to comply with the requirements specified in it.[4] The magistrates' court may make such a parenting order only if it is satisfied that 'making the order would be desirable in the interests of improving the behaviour of the pupil'.[5] Where the order would relate to a pupil under the age of 16, the court must 'obtain and consider information about the pupil's family circumstances and the likely effect of the order on those circumstances'.[6]

10.90　An appeal lies to the Crown Court against the making of a parenting order under s 20.

---

[1]　Anti-Social Behaviour Act 2003, s 20(5).
[2]　Ibid, s 20(6)–(8).
[3]　Education (Parenting Orders) (England) Regulations 2004, SI 2004/182, reg 5.
[4]　Anti-Social Behaviour Act 2003, s 21(1).
[5]　Ibid, s 20(3).
[6]　Ibid, s 21(2).

Chapter 11

THE CURRICULUM FOR A
MAINTAINED SCHOOL

INTRODUCTION

11.1 The chapter is concerned with statutory obligations imposed on maintained schools in relation to (1) the secular curriculum, including the National Curriculum (which does not apply to independent schools, although of course they may choose to follow it), (2) external qualifications, (3) careers education, (4) sex education, (5) religious education, and (6) religious worship.

11.2 It is the duty of the governing body of a maintained school (which for this purpose does not include a special school established in a hospital[1]) and every maintained nursery school, the head teacher and the LEA to 'exercise their functions with a view to securing that the curriculum for the school satisfies the requirements of section 78 [or (in relation to Wales) 99 of the EA 2002]'.[2] The relevant functions include those concerning religious education and religious worship, and those conferred by the EA 2002 in relation to the National Curriculum.[3]

11.3 Sections 78 and 79 of the EA 2002 provide that it is the duty of the Secretary of State in relation to every maintained school,[4] every LEA as respects every maintained school which is maintained by them, and the governing body or the head teacher of every maintained school as respects that school, to exercise their functions with a view to securing that the curriculum for the school is a:

'balanced and broadly based curriculum which –

 (a)   promotes the spiritual, moral, cultural, mental and physical development of pupils at the school and of society; and
 (b)   prepares such pupils at the school for the opportunities, responsibilities and experiences of later life.'[5]

11.4 It is the duty of the Secretary of State, the LEA and the teacher in charge of a pupil referral unit[6] to do the same in relation to the curriculum for the unit.[7] In

---

1   EA 2002, ss 76(1) and 97(1).
2   Ibid, ss 79(3) and 100(3).
3   Ibid, ss 79(4) and 100(4).
4   Defined by ibid, ss 76(1) and 97(1) as any community, foundation or voluntary school which is maintained by an LEA, or, except where otherwise stated, any community or foundation special school which is maintained by an LEA and which is not established in a hospital.
5   See ibid, ss 99 and 100 in relation to Wales. By virtue of ss 79(4) and 100(4), the functions in question include those relating to religious education and religious worship.
6   As to which see s 19 of the EA 1996, concerning which see para **4.2**.
7   EA 1996, Sch 1, para 6(2).

exercising any function which may affect the provision of sex education in maintained schools, every LEA in England must have regard to the guidance issued by the Secretary of State under s 403(1A) of the EA 1996.[1] Except to this extent, nothing in s 79 imposes duties on an LEA with regard to sex education.[2]

11.5 A similar duty applies in relation to the curriculum for a maintained nursery school[3] or the curriculum for any nursery education which is: (a) funded by an LEA under s 118 of the SSFA 1998; and (b) provided otherwise than at a maintained school or maintained nursery school.[4] However, nursery education in England is only affected by the National Curriculum where the child is aged at least 3 years.[5]

11.6 Sections 80 and 101 of the EA 2002 provide for a 'basic curriculum' which every maintained school is required to follow. The basic curriculum includes (1) provision for religious education[6] for all registered pupils at the school except[7] in relation to a nursery class in a primary school, and (2) sex education for (a) all registered pupils at a secondary school, and (b) all registered pupils at a special school who receive secondary education.[8] Perhaps most significantly, the basic curriculum also includes 'a curriculum for all registered pupils at the school who have attained the age of 3 yeras but are not over compulsory school age (known [in England] as "the National Curriculum for England")'.[9] The Secretary of State may by order[10] (a) alter the age range of pupils to whose education the National Curriculum applies, or (b) add to the requirements of that curriculum.[11]

The National Curriculum

11.7 Sections 81–87 and 102–108 of the EA 2002 contain the substantive provisions concerning the content of the National Curriculum.[12] There is a foundation stage[13] and four key stages.[14] Broadly, these are for pupils who are aged

---

[1]   EA 2002, s 79(6).
[2]   Ibid, s 79(7).
[3]   Defined by ibid, ss 76(1) and 97(1) as a nursery school which is maintained by an LEA and is not a special school.
[4]   See ibid, ss 77, 78, 79, 98, 99 and 100.
[5]   See ibid s 81(2); s 102 is not yet in force.
[6]   In accordance with such of the provisions of Sch 19 to the SSFA 1998 as apply in relation to the school, as to which, see further, paras **11.34** et seq. In the case of a maintained special school, however, provision is made under regulations made under s 71(7) of the SSFA 1998: EA 2002 ss 80(2)(b) and 101(2)(b) (although the latter is not yet in force).
[7]   See EA 2002, ss 80(2)(a) and 101(2)(a).
[8]   Ibid, s 80(1). 'Sex education' is defined by EA 1996, s 579(1) as amended by the EA 2002, to include 'education about – (a) Acquired Immune Deficiency Syndrome and Human Immunodeficiency Virus, and (b) any other sexually transmitted disease'. As for the right of a parent to withdraw his child from sex education outside the National Curriculum, see para **11.24**.
[9]   Ibid, ss 80(1)(b). See ibid s 101(1)(b) in relation to Wales, although that provision is not yet in force. See paras **2.40** and **2.41** for the definition of compulsory school age.
[10] Made by statutory instrument approved, in England, by a positive resolution of both Houses of Parliament: EA 2002, ss 210(1) and (3).
[11] See ibid, ss 80(3) and 101(3).
[12] Of the provisions relating to Wales only, ibid, ss 103, 105–107, and part of s 108 are currently in force. They were brought into force by SI 2002/3185.
[13] See EA 2002, ss 81, 83, 102 and 104.
[14] See ibid, ss 82, 84–86, 103 and 105–107.

5–7, 8–11, 12–14 and 15–16.[1] There are foundation subjects and core subjects. The core subjects (which are also foundation subjects) in England are mathematics, English and science.[2] In relation to Welsh-speaking schools in Wales they are the same subjects plus Welsh.[3] The rest of the foundation subjects differ according to the key stage in question.[4] The core and foundation subjects may be altered by an order made by the Secretary of State or the National Assembly for Wales.[5] Such an order must take the form of a statutory instrument, which, in relation to England, must be approved by a positive resolution of each House of Parliament.[6]

11.8   The Secretary of State is under a duty so to exercise his powers in s 87(2) and (3) as to establish a complete National Curriculum for England for the foundation stage as soon as is reasonably practicable and to revise the National Curriculum for England for the foundation stage and the key stages 'whenever he considers it necessary or expedient to do so'.[7] The Secretary of State has the power by order to specify attainment targets, programmes of study and 'such assessment arrangements ... as he considers appropriate' in relation to each of the foundation subjects.[8] In respect of the foundation stage, the Secretary of State has the power by order to specify in relation to the 'areas of learning' referred to in s 83(1) 'early learning goals', 'educational programmes' and 'assessment arrangements'.[9] The manner in which the order may be made is unusual, in that the order may 'instead of containing the provisions to be made, refer to provisions in a document published as specified in the order and direct that those provisions are to have effect'.[10] Section 87(4) does, however, contain some limits on the power of the Secretary of State to specify attainment targets, programmes of study and assessment arrangements. These are that an order made under s 87(2) or (3) may not require:

---

[1]   In each case, the period actually begins with the beginning of the school year in which the majority of pupils in the class attain the age of the minimum plus one year (ie 6, 8, 12 and 15 respectively) and ends with the end of the school year in which the majority of pupils attain the relevant upper age: see ss 82(1) and 103(1). The Secretary of State and the National Assembly for Wales have the power by order to amend these provisions: ss 82(4) and 103(4), and note that (1) s 96 applies to the making of the order, and (2) if the order amends the provisions otherwise than merely by changing the ages in relation to which key stage 1 ends and key stage 2 begins, the order must be approved by a resolution of each House of Parliament: s 210(3)(b). Where there is difficulty in the application of s 82(1) or s 103(1), the provisions of s 82(3) or s 103(3) may assist.

[2]   EA 2002, ss 84(2) and 85(2).

[3]   Ibid, ss 105(2) and 106(2).

[4]   See ibid, ss 84(3), 85(3), 105(3) and 106(3).

[5]   Ibid, ss 84(6), 86, 105(6) and 107.

[6]   Ibid, s 210(3)(d) and (e). See s 96 of the EA 2002 concerning the procedure which needs to be followed in the making of an order under s 84(6).

[7]   Ibid, s 87(1). See s 108(1)–(3) for the equivalent provision relating to Wales.

[8]   Ibid, s 87(3), subject to s 87(4). See s 210(4) and (5)(b) concerning the making of such an order. See s 108(3) and (4) in relation to Wales. The effect of ss 87(4) and 108(4) is described at the end of this paragraph.

[9]   Ibid, s 87(2) and, in relation to the making of such an order, s 210(4) and (5)(b). See 108(2) in relation to Wales, where there are 'desirable outcomes' rather than 'early learning goals'. The Education (National Curriculum) (Foundation Stage Early Learning Goals) (England) Order 2003, SI 2003/391 was made under s 87.

[10]   Ibid, s 87(5). In relation to Wales, see s 108(5). A similar provision exists in the relation to the employment of school teachers: see EA 2002, s 124(3)

'the allocation of any particular period or periods of time during the foundation stage or any key stage to the teaching of any educational programme or programme of study or any matter, skill or process forming part of it or ... the making in school timetables (or the timetables of any person providing funded nursery education) of provision of any particular kind for the periods to be allocated to such teaching during any such stage.'[1]

11.9   The LEA and the governing body of a maintained school 'shall exercise their functions with a view to securing', and the head teacher 'shall secure' that the National Curriculum subsisting for that year is implemented in relation to the school.[2] The EA 2002 is silent about the duties of teachers in maintained schools in relation to the implementation of the National Curriculum. At first instance in *NAS/UWT v Wandsworth London Borough Council*,[3] Mantell J held in relation to the statutory predecessors to the current provisions (which do not differ materially) that teachers were not under a statutory duty to implement the National Curriculum and as part of that duty to carry out standard assessment tasks (sometimes known as 'SATs'). In the Court of Appeal in that case, the argument that teachers are under a statutory duty to implement the National Curriculum was abandoned.[4]

Exemptions from the National Curriculum

11.10   There is provision in the EA 2002 for the National Curriculum not to apply in certain circumstances. Section 90[5] provides that the Secretary of State may '[f]or the purpose of enabling development work or experiments to be carried out' direct in respect of a particular maintained school or maintained nursery school that the National Curriculum is for a specified period not to apply to the school, or is to apply only with modifications.[6] Section 91[7] provides that regulations may provide that the National Curriculum for England or any part of it either is not to apply in cases or circumstances specified in the regulations, or is to apply only as modified in cases or circumstances so specified.[8] Section 92[9] provides that a statement of SEN may exclude the application of the National Curriculum or apply it only with such modifications as may be specified in the statement.

Temporary exceptions for individual pupils

11.11   Section 93[10] of the EA 2002 provides that regulations may enable the head teacher of a maintained school[11] or maintained nursery school[12] in certain circumstances to direct that the National Curriculum is not to apply (or is to apply

---

1   EA 2002, s 87(4). See s 108(4) in relation to Wales.
2   Ibid, ss 88 and 109. See ss 89 and 110 in relation to nursery education.
3   (1993) *The Times*, 7 April.
4   [1994] ICR 81, 94A.
5   EA 2002, s 111 in relation to Wales.
6   For the manner in which the power must be exercised, see s 90(2)–(5).
7   EA 2002, s 112 in relation to Wales.
8   See the Education (National Curriculum) (Exceptions at Key Stage 4) (England) Regulations 2003, SI 2003/252 in relation to England, and, in relation to Wales, SIs 1990/2187, 1991/1657, 1994/1270, 1995/1574 and 1996/2083.
9   EA 2002, s 113 in relation to Wales.
10   See EA 2002, s 114 in relation to Wales.
11   As to which, see footnote 8 at para **11.10**.
12   As to which, see footnote 4 at para **11.5**.

with modifications specified in the direction) to a registered pupil at the school for a period, which is to be subject to a maximum of 6 months in the first instance.[1] The head teacher may also revoke or vary the direction, but not so as to extend its operative period.[2] However, there is nothing in s 93 (or s 114) which would preclude the making of a series of consecutive directions under the regulations (and the regulations allow for that: see below). Presumably, the restriction of the life of a direction under the section to 6 months was imposed to avoid exceptions being made and never reviewed.

11.12 The current regulations made under the predecessor to s 93 are the Education (National Curriculum) (Temporary Exceptions for Individual Pupils) (Wales) Regulations 1999[3] and the Education (National Curriculum) (Temporary Exceptions for Individual Pupils) (England) Regulations 2000.[4] Section 94[5] requires the giving of certain information concerning the direction, in a manner prescribed by regulations. Section 95[6] gives a parent of a pupil in relation to whom a direction under regulations made under s 93 has been given, revoked or varied (or whose request made under the regulations for a direction, or for a revocation or variation of a direction, has been refused or not acted on within a period specified by the regulations) a right of appeal to the governing body (see further, para **11.3**). The governing body's determination of that appeal is binding on the head teacher.[7] The parent has the right to appeal further to the LEA by way of a complaint made under s 409 of the EA 1996,[8] and only after that to the Secretary of State under s 496 or s 497 of that Act.

11.13 A direction under the regulations made under s 93 may be general or special.[9] A general direction may be given where the head teacher of the school is of the opinion that it is not appropriate for the time being to offer a registered pupil at the school the National Curriculum as it would otherwise apply to him, and the circumstances that gave rise to that opinion are likely to change significantly so that, within 6 months from the date when the direction comes into force, the pupil will be able to follow the National Curriculum as it would otherwise apply to him.[10] A special direction may be given where the head teacher has the same opinion in relation to a registered pupil but the circumstances are instead indicative of a need for the pupil to be assessed under s 323 of the EA 1996 with a view to the making or amendment of a statement of SEN in respect of him.[11] A direction may not normally come into force sooner than one month from the time when it was given.[12] The maximum period

---

1   See EA 2002, ss 93(3) and 114(3).
2   See ibid, ss 93(5) and 114(5).
3   SI 1999/1815.
4   SI 2000/2121.
5   EA 2002, s 115 in Wales
6   Ibid, s 116 in Wales.
7   Ibid, ss 95(3) and 116(3).
8   As to which, see paras **4.8–4.11**.
9   Regulations 3 and 4 of both SI 1999/1815 and SI 2000/2121 (which are so far as relevant in the same terms). See reg 5 concerning the form and content of the direction. Regulation 6 requires the sending of the direction to certain parties.
10   Regulations 1(3) and 3(1)(b)(i).
11   Regulations 1(3) and 3(1)(b)(ii). As noted above, a statement of SEN may exclude the application of the National Curriculum or apply it with modifications: EA 2002, ss 92 and 113.
12   Regulation 4(2).

during which the National Curriculum may not apply (or apply in full) as a result of a single direction is 6 months.[1] However, further directions may be given to run from the expiry of the initial 6-month period.[2] A parent may request the head teacher at any time to give a direction or a further direction, or to revoke or vary a direction currently in force.[3] The request may be made orally or in writing, and must include the reasons for which it is made.[4] However, the head teacher need not entertain a request to vary or revoke a direction more than once during the operative period of the direction or more than once during the operative period of any further direction or directions given under regs 9 and 10.[5] As indicated in para **11.12**, under ss 95 and 116 of the EA 2002, the parent has a right of appeal to the governing body against the refusal of the request.[6] The right arises in any event if the head teacher has not within 2 weeks given the parent notice of his decision.[7]

EXTERNAL QUALIFICATIONS

External qualifications for pupils below the age of 19

11.14   As a result of ss 96 and 98–103 of the LSA 2000, the approval of either the Secretary of State under s 98 or the National Assembly for Wales under s 99, or of a body designated either by the Secretary of State under s 98 or the National Assembly under s 99, is required for certain purposes for a course of education or training (a) which is provided (or proposed to be provided) by or on behalf of 'a school or institution or employer', (b) which leads to an external qualification as defined by s 96(5)–(7), and (c) which is provided (or proposed to be provided) for pupils who are of compulsory school age or for 'pupils who are above that age but have not attained the age of 19'. If such approval is not so given, then the course may not lawfully be funded by an 'authorised body' within the meaning of s 100. Such a body is defined by s 100 as (a) the LSC or the CETW, (b) an LEA, and (c) a body specified in an order (in the form of a statutory instrument[8]) made by the Secretary of State under s 100(1)(c) or the National Assembly for Wales under s 100(2)(c).[9] Nor may such a course be provided by or on behalf of a maintained school,[10] and the LEA and governing body of such a school must carry out their functions with a view to securing that this does not occur.[11]

---

[1]   Regulation 4(4).
[2]   See regs 9 (concerning general directions) and 10 (concerning special directions). See also reg 11.
[3]   Regulation 12(1).
[4]   Regulation 12(2).
[5]   Regulation 12(3).
[6]   The relevant provisions in the regulations are regs 13 and 14.
[7]   Regulation 14(a).
[8]   See LSA 2000, s 152.
[9]   LSA 2000, s 96(2)(a). As to enforcement see ss 101 and 102.
[10] Ibid, s 96(2)(b); maintained schools are for this purpose community, foundation and voluntary schools and community and foundation special schools: s 96(8).
[11] Ibid, s 96(3).

External qualifications for persons over the age of 19

11.15   As a result of ss 97–102 of the LSA 2000, an authorised body within the meaning of s 100 must carry out its functions with a view to securing that any funding which it gives to an institution or employer in respect of a course of education or training which is provided by that institution or employer and which leads to an external qualification within the meaning of s 97(4)–(6), is not used by the institution or employer in respect of the qualification unless the qualification is approved by either the Secretary of State under s 98 or the National Assembly for Wales under s 99, or by a body designated by the former under s 98 or the latter under s 99.[1]

THE SECRETARY OF STATE'S POWERS IN RELATION TO THE QUALIFICATIONS AND CURRICULUM AUTHORITY

11.16   Section 26(1)(a) of the EA 1997 requires the Qualifications and Curriculum Authority to 'comply with any directions given by the Secretary of State'.[2] This Authority is a body corporate,[3] whose members are appointed by the Secretary of State.[4]

BASELINE ASSESSMENTS

11.17   Sections 15–18 of the EA 1997 require maintained primary schools (other than special schools established in hospitals) in Wales[5] to conduct 'baseline assessments' as provided for in those sections and regulations made under ss 17 and 18.[6] They are mentioned here because they appear to be intended to supplement the assessment provisions of the National Curriculum.

SCHOOL PERFORMANCE TARGETS

11.18   Section 19 of the EA 1997 empowers the Secretary of State to make regulations requiring the governing body of a maintained school other than a special school established in a hospital to set 'annual targets ... in respect of the performance of pupils' in public examinations or other external examinations or (in the case of pupils of compulsory school age) in assessments for the purposes of the National Curriculum.[7]

---

[1]   See ibid, s 97(7) for how a payment may be made in respect of a qualification.

[2]   In relation to Wales, see EA 1997, s 32(1).

[3]   See ibid, s 21(1). In relation to Wales, see s 27(1).

[4]   Ibid, s 21(2). In relation to Wales, see s 27(1). See further, para **2.105** in relation to the Qualifications and Curriculum Authority and its Welsh equivalent, the Qualifications, Curriculum and Assessment Authority for Wales.

[5]   Sections 15–18 of the EA 1997 were repealed in relation to England by EA 2002, Sch 22 and SI 2002/2002 on 2 September 2002.

[6]   See the Education (Baseline Assessment) (Wales) Regulations 1999, SI 1999/1188.

[7]   See the Education (School Performance Targets) (England) Regulations 1998, SI 1998/1532 as amended by SI 1999/2267, SI 2001/827, SI 2001/2944, SI 2002/840, SI 2002/2105 and SI 2003/1970

OBLIGATIONS CONCERNING PUBLIC EXAMINATIONS

11.19 As a result of s 402(1) of the EA 1996, the governing body of a maintained school (including a maintained special school established in a hospital[1]) is under a duty to secure that each registered pupil at the school is entered, at such times as the governing body considers appropriate, for each prescribed public examination[2] for which he is being prepared at the school in each syllabus for that examination for which he is being so prepared.[3] Section 402(2), however, gives the governing body the power to determine whether a pupil is to be entered for any examination (other than one which is part of the assessment arrangements for the fourth key stage[4]) or for an examination in any syllabus for such an examination in two circumstances. The first is where there are 'educational reasons' for the duty in s 402(1) not to apply, and the second is where 'the parent' of the pupil has requested in writing that the pupil should not be entered for the relevant examination or (as the case may be) for that examination in that syllabus. A parent's request that a child is not entered for a relevant public examination is accordingly not determinative. The governing body must inform the parent of a relevant pupil as soon as practicable after any determination whether or not to secure the entry of any pupil for a relevant prescribed public examination.[5]

SEX EDUCATION

11.20 Sex education is part of the basic curriculum for every maintained secondary school and for pupils in a maintained special school who are provided with secondary education.[6] The governing body of a maintained school (including a maintained special school established in a hospital[7] and a pupil referral unit[8]) and the head teacher are obliged by s 403(1) of the EA 1996 to:

> 'take such steps as are reasonably practicable to secure that where sex education is given to any registered pupils at [the school] it is given in such a manner as to encourage those pupils to have due regard to moral considerations and the value of family life.'

11.21 Under s 403(1A) of the EA 1996,[9] the Secretary of State must:

> 'issue guidance designed to secure that when sex education is given to registered pupils at maintained schools –

---

and the (School Performance and Unauthorised Absence Targets) (Wales) Regulations 1999, SI 1999/1811.

[1] EA 1996, s 402(6).

[2] As to which, see ss 402(6)(b) and 462 of the EA 1996 and the Education (Prescribed Public Examinations) Regulations 1989, SI 1989/377.

[3] EA 1996, s 402(1) and (6).

[4] As to key stages, see para **11.7**.

[5] EA 1996, s 402(5).

[6] EA 2002, ss 80(1)(c) and (d) and 101(1)(c) and (d).

[7] EA 1996, s 403(2).

[8] Ibid, Sch 1, para 8.

[9] Subsection (1A) was inserted by s 148 of the LSA 2000, which was brought into force in relation to England by SI 2000/2559 and in relation to Wales by SI 2001/1274.

(a)   they learn the nature of marriage and its importance for family life and the bringing up of children, and

(b)   they are protected from teaching and materials which are inappropriate having regard to the age and the religious and cultural background of the pupils concerned.'[1]

11.22   In exercising their functions under s 403(1), governing bodies and head teachers must have regard to such guidance.[2] In exercising any function which may affect the provision of sex education in maintained schools, every LEA must also have regard to the guidance.[3]

11.23   The governing body of a maintained school (including a special school established in a hospital, but only in relation to pupils who are provided with secondary education there[4]) and the LEA in relation to a pupil referral unit[5] must also 'make, and keep up to date, a separate written statement of their policy with regard to the provision of sex education' and of the effect of s 405 of the EA 1996,[6] and must make copies of such statement available at all reasonable times for inspection by parents of registered pupils at the school.[7]

Right of withdrawal of pupil from sex education

11.24   Section 405 of the EA 1996 provides that if a parent of a pupil at a maintained school requests that he be wholly or partly excused from receiving sex education at the school, the pupil must be so excused from all such education which is not comprised in the National Curriculum, unless and until the request is withdrawn.

CAREERS EDUCATION AND GUIDANCE[8]

11.25   Section 43 of the EA 1997 requires the governing bodies and head teachers of community, foundation and voluntary schools and of community and foundation special schools (other than those established in hospitals), 'to secure' that all registered pupils are provided 'during the relevant phase of their education, with a programme of careers education'. That phase is from the beginning of the school year when the majority of pupils in the relevant class[9] attain the age (in England) of 12[10] or (in

---

[1]   The guidance must 'include guidance about any material which may be produced by NHS bodies for use for the purposes of sex education in schools': EA 1996, s 403(1C).

[2]   EA 1996, s 403(1B).

[3]   EA 2002, ss 79(6) and 100(6).

[4]   EA 1996, s 404(2).

[5]   SI 1994/2103, reg 4.

[6]   Concerning which, see para **11.24**.

[7]   EA 1996, s 404(1), (1A) and (2). If a copy is sought by a parent, then it must be supplied free of charge: s 404(1)(b).

[8]   In this section, in order to avoid repetition in other chapters, reference is made to all the various bodies and persons to which or to whom the relevant obligations apply. Thus, reference is made to students at institutions within the further education sector, and to students at city technology colleges, city colleges for the technology of the arts and Academies.

[9]   'Class' is defined for the purposes of EA 1997, s 43 in s 43(6).

[10]   See the Education (Extension of Careers Education) (England) Regulations 2003, SI 2003/2645. These came into force on 1 September 2004.

Wales) of 14, to the end of the school year in which the majority of pupils in that class attain the age of (in England) 16 or (in Wales[1]) 19 'a programme of careers education'.[2] LEAs and the teachers in charge of pupil referral units are under the same duty,[3] as are the proprietors and head teachers of city technology colleges, city colleges for the technology of the arts and Academies.[4]

11.26 Section 44(1) of the EA 1997 provides that where a careers adviser 'has responsibilities in relation to persons attending an educational institution to which this section applies',[5] then he must (subject to a significant exception), on request, be provided with certain information by the institution. That information is the name and address of every relevant pupil or student at the institution, and any information in the institution's possession about any such pupil or student which the careers adviser needs in order to be able to provide him with advice and guidance on decisions about his career or with other information relevant to such decisions.[6] If the registered address of a parent of any such pupil is different from the pupil's registered address, then the address of the parent must be provided as well.[7] The significant exception is that s 44(1)(a) or (b) does not apply to any pupil or student to the extent that (where he is under the age of 16) a parent of his, or (where he has attained that age) he himself, has indicated that any information falling within either or both of s 44(1)(a) or (b) should not be provided to the careers adviser.[8] It seems that a relevant parent or pupil would have to be informed that such information was to be provided under s 44(1) before it was so provided, because otherwise that right to object would be rendered nugatory.

11.27 Where a careers adviser 'has responsibilities in relation to persons attending an educational institution to which [s 44] applies',[9] he must also, on request, be permitted to have access to any relevant pupil or student specified by him '(a) on the institution's premises, and (b) at a reasonable time agreed by or on behalf of the head teacher, principal or other head of the institution, for the purpose of enabling him to provide that person with advice and guidance on decisions about his career and with any other information relevant to such decisions'.[10] Such access must include 'an opportunity

---

1   See the Education (Extension of Careers Education) (Wales) Regulations 2001, SI 2001/1987.
2   The definitions of 'career' and 'careers education' for this purpose are set out in EA 1997, s 43(6).
3   EA 1997, s 43(3)(c).
4   The duty in s 43(3) is enforceable against the proprietors of such a college under ss 496 and 497 of the EA 1996 (as to which see Chapter 3): see EA 1997, s 43(4).
5   A careers adviser is defined for the purposes of s 44 as 'a person who is employed by a body providing services in pursuance of arrangements made or directions given under section 10 of the Employment and Training Act 1973 and who is acting, in the course of his employment by that body, for the purposes of the provision of any such services': s 44(11)(a). (The Secretary of State may by regulations amend this definition: EA 1997, s 46(4).) Such an adviser 'has responsibilities for any persons' for the purposes of s 44 'if his employment by that body includes the provision of any such services to them': s 44(11)(b). The institutions to which s 44 applies are those to which s 43 applies apart from pupil referral units, and institutions within the further education sector: see s 44(8).
6   EA 1997, s 44(1). A relevant pupil or student is defined for the purposes of s 44 in s 44(10), and the word 'career' has the same meaning as in s 43: s 44(12).
7   Ibid, s 44(2).
8   Ibid, s 44(3), as amended.
9   As to which, see para **11.26**.
10   EA 1997, s 44(4).

for the careers adviser to interview that person about his career, if he agrees to being so interviewed'.[1] The careers adviser must also be permitted to have access on request to any group of relevant pupils or students specified by him, in the manner specified in s 44(4)(a) and (b) and 'to such of the institution's facilities as can conveniently be made available for his use', for the purpose of enabling him to provide those persons with 'group sessions on any matters relating to careers or to advice or guidance about careers'.[2] Any request made by a careers adviser for the purposes of s 44 must be made in writing to the head teacher, principal or other head of the institution in question.[3]

11.28 The governing body of each relevant institution (or, in the case of a city technology college, a city college for the technology of the arts, or an Academy, its proprietors) and its head teacher, principal 'or other head' are placed under a duty 'to secure' that the duties in s 44(1), (4) and (6) are complied with.[4]

11.29 Section 45 of the EA 1997 applies to the same institutions as those to which s 44 of that Act applies, except that it is specifically provided that s 45 does not apply to a primary school.[5] The effect of the provisions regarding the age range of relevant pupils for the purposes of ss 43 and 44 is that the duties in those sections in any event do not at present apply to primary school pupils. It should be noted that the Secretary of State was given power by s 46(1) of the EA 1997 to extend by regulations the scope of operation of s 43 or s 44 'by substituting for the period specified in section 43(5) or section 44(10)(a)(i) such other period as is specified'. Such orders have been made, as indicated in para **11.25**. Furthermore, the Secretary of State was given power by s 46(2) to make provision by regulations for extending the scope of s 43, s 44 or s 45 to primary schools or to 'any specified description of such schools'.

11.30 Persons attending any institution to which s 45 applies must be provided with access to both guidance materials and 'a wide range of up-to-date reference materials' relating to 'careers education and career opportunities'.[6] The bodies and persons upon whom this duty is imposed are the same as those on whom the duties in s 44(1), (4) and (6) are imposed.[7] Those bodies and persons must seek assistance with discharging that duty from a body providing services in pursuance of arrangements made or directions given under s 10 of the Employment and Training Act 1973.[8]

---

1 EA 1997, s 44(5).
2 Ibid, s 44(6).
3 Ibid, s 44(7).
4 Ibid, s 44(9). Sections 496 and 497 of the EA 1996 apply in relation to that duty on the part of the proprietors of a city technology college, a city college for the technology of the arts, or an Academy: ibid.
5 See ibid, ss 44(8), 45(2) and 45(6).
6 Ibid, s 45(1). The terms 'career' and 'careers education' have the same meaning as in s 43: s 45(5).
7 See ibid, ss 44(9) and 45(3). See paras **11.26** and **11.27** for the bodies and persons on whom the duties in s 44(1), (4) and (6) are imposed. Sections 496 and 497 of the EA 1996 apply to the duty imposed by s 45(3) on the proprietors of city technology colleges, city colleges for the technology of the arts and Academies in the same way as those sections apply to the duty imposed by s 44(9): s 45(3).
8 Ibid, s 45(4).

RELIGIOUS EDUCATION AND WORSHIP

11.31   Subject to a parent's right under s 71 of the SSFA 1998 to excuse a pupil from receiving religious education,[1] as a result of s 69 of the SSFA 1998, it is the duty of the LEA and the governing body of any community, foundation or voluntary school to exercise their functions with a view to securing, and the head teacher to secure, that religious education is given in accordance with the provision for such education included in the school's basic curriculum by virtue of s 80(1)(a) or s 101(1)(a) of the EA 2002.[2]

The 'agreed syllabus'

11.32   Although the requirements relating to religious education differ as between (1) community schools and foundation and voluntary schools which do not have a religious character, (2) foundation and voluntary controlled schools which have a religious character, and (3) voluntary aided schools which have a religious character (see further below), the situation of each such type of school is affected by what is referred to in the EA 1996 and the SSFA 1998 as the 'agreed syllabus' of religious education. That agreed syllabus has effect under the provisions of s 375 of and Sch 31 to the EA 1996. The agreed syllabus may be adopted for use in all the schools maintained by the LEA or for use in particular such schools, or in relation to any particular class or description of pupils in such schools.[3] However, s 375(3) provides:

> 'Every agreed syllabus shall reflect the fact that the religious traditions in Great Britain are in the main Christian whilst taking account of the teaching and practices of the other principal religions represented in Great Britain.'

11.33   Schedule 31 provides for the convening by an LEA of conferences for the purpose of reconsidering any agreed syllabus for the time being adopted by them.[4] Such a conference must be convened no later than 5 years from the date when (a) the syllabus was adopted, or (b) the authority gave effect to a unanimous recommendation by a previous such conference under para 10(2) of Sch 31 (or its predecessor, para 13 of Sch 5 to the Education Act 1944) that the syllabus should continue to be the agreed syllabus.[5] Meetings must normally be open to the public.[6] If a syllabus cannot be agreed unanimously, or if it appears to the LEA that the syllabus which has been the subject of a recommendation under para 10(2) (which may be either that the existing syllabus should continue to be the agreed syllabus, or a recommendation of a new syllabus to be adopted) does not reflect 'the fact that the religious traditions in

---

[1]   As to which see paras **11.43** and **11.44**.

[2]   See paras **11.34** et seq regarding such religious education. See footnote 4 at para **11.43** in relation to maintained special schools.

[3]   EA 1996, s 375(2).

[4]   Ibid, Sch 31, paras 1(1) and 2(1). The constitution of the conference is dealt with in paras 4–9. It is recognised in para 8(b) that a person may cease to be representative of the religion, denomination or associations which he was appointed to represent.

[5]   Ibid, Sch 31, paras 1(2) and 2(2). A conference convened under the 1944 Act remains subject to the provisions of that Act: EA 1996, Sch 39, para 39.

[6]   See Religious Education (Meetings of Local Conferences and Councils) Regulations 1994, SI 1994/1304, reg 3. See the other provisions of those regulations with regard to the procedure to be followed generally.

Great Britain are in the main Christian while taking account of the teaching and practices of the other principal religions represented in Great Britain', or if it appears to the Secretary of State that the LEA has failed to give effect to a recommendation under para 10(2), then the Secretary of State must 'appoint a body of persons having experience in religious education to prepare a syllabus of religious education'.[1] The resulting syllabus is then deemed to be the agreed syllabus.[2]

Religious education in community, foundation and voluntary schools without a religious character

11.34 Subject to what is said in para **11.35**, the religious education which a community school, or a foundation or voluntary school which does not have a religious character, is required by s 69(1) of the SSFA 1998 to give is religious education in accordance with an agreed syllabus adopted for the school or for pupils at the school.[3] Schedule 19, para 2(5) ensures that such a school's religious education does not favour any particular denomination. It provides as follows:

'No agreed syllabus shall provide for religious education to be given to pupils at a school to which this paragraph applies by means of any catechism or formulary which is distinctive of a particular religious denomination (but this is not to be taken as prohibiting provision in such a syllabus for the study of such catechisms or formularies).'

11.35 Section 71 of the SSFA 1998 empowers a parent of a pupil at a maintained school to request that the pupil be excused from receiving religious education given in the school in accordance with the school's basic curriculum, and in certain circumstances for the withdrawal of the pupil from the school for the purpose of enabling him to receive religious education of a kind desired by the parent.[4] In the case of a relevant secondary school which is so situated that arrangements cannot conveniently be made for the withdrawal of pupils from it in accordance with s 71 to receive religious education elsewhere, the LEA may be under an obligation to provide facilities for the carrying out of arrangements for the provision to pupils of religious education in the school in accordance with the tenets of a particular religion or religious denomination. The LEA will be under such an obligation where they are satisfied that (1) the parents of any pupils at the school desire them to receive such education, and (2) satisfactory arrangements have been made for the provision of such education and for securing that the cost of its provision to those pupils will not fall to be met from the school's budget share or otherwise by the LEA, but they will not be under such an obligation if they are satisfied that because of any special circumstances it would be unreasonable to provide the relevant facilities.[5]

11.36 However, if on 31 August 1999 the school was a grant-maintained school within the meaning of the EA 1996, and in relation to the school or any pupils at the

---

[1] EA 1996 Sch 31, paras 10(3) and 12(1). The body must be representative in the same manner so far as practicable as that required by para 4 (para 12(2)), and must follow the procedure required by para 13.

[2] Ibid, Sch 31, para 14. Presumably the 5-year period referred to in para 2(2) runs from the date when the Secretary of State directs under para 14(a) that the new syllabus is deemed to be the agreed syllabus.

[3] SSFA 1998, Sch 19, para 2(2). See the paragraphs above regarding the agreed syllabus.

[4] See paras **11.43** and **11.44** concerning s 71.

[5] SSFA 1998, Sch 19, para 2(3).

school the appropriate agreed syllabus as defined by s 382 of that Act was a syllabus falling with s 382(1)(c), then that syllabus is treated as an agreed syllabus adopted for the school or (as the case may be) those pupils until either 31 August 2004 or such earlier date as the governing body may determine.[1]

Religious education in foundation and voluntary controlled schools with a religious character

11.37 Subject to what is said in the following paragraph, the religious education which is required by s 69(1) of the SSFA 1998 to be given to the pupils at a foundation or voluntary controlled school which has a religious character must be in accordance with an agreed syllabus adopted for the school or for those pupils,[2] unless the parents of any pupils at the school have requested that the pupils may receive religious education either (1) in accordance with any provisions of the trust deed relating to the school, or (2) where provision for that purpose is not made by such a deed, in accordance with the tenets of the religion or religious denomination specified in relation to the school under s 69(4) of the SSFA 1998.[3] If any such parents have made such a request, then, unless the foundation governors are satisfied that because of any special circumstances it would be unreasonable to do so, those governors must make arrangements for securing that such religious education is given to those pupils during not more than two periods each week.[4]

11.38 However, if on 31 August 1999 the school was a grant-maintained school within the meaning of the EA 1996 and in relation to the school or any pupils at the school the appropriate agreed syllabus as defined by s 382 of that Act was a syllabus falling within s 382(1)(c), then that syllabus is treated as an agreed syllabus adopted for the school or (as the case may be) those pupils until either 31 August 2004 or such earlier date as the governing body may determine.[5]

Religious education in voluntary aided schools with a religious character

11.39 The religious education which is required by s 69(1) of the SSFA 1998 to be given at a voluntary aided school must be made (1) in accordance with any provisions of the trust deed relating to the school, or, where provision for that purpose is not made by such a deed, in accordance with the tenets of the religion or religious denomination specified in relation to the school under s 69(4) of the SSFA 1998, or (2) in certain circumstances in accordance with any agreed syllabus adopted by the LEA.[6] Those circumstances are that (1) the parents of any pupils at the school want the pupils to receive religious education in accordance with such an agreed syllabus, (2) the parents cannot with reasonable convenience cause the pupils to attend a school

---

[1] SSFA 1998, Sch 19, para 3(4) and the Agreed Syllabus for Religious Education (Prescribed Period) Order 1999, SI 1999/1728.

[2] Concerning the agreed syllabus, see paras **11.32** and **11.33**.

[3] SSFA 1998, Sch 19, para 3(2) and (3).

[4] Ibid, Sch 19, para 3(3).

[5] Ibid, Sch 19, para 3(4) and the Agreed Syllabus for Religious Education (Prescribed Period) Order 1999, SI 1999/1728.

[6] Ibid, Sch 19, para 4(2). See paras **11.32** and **11.33** with regard to the agreed syllabus.

at which that syllabus is in use, and (3) the governing body of the school is not satisfied that it would be unreasonable to do so 'because of any special circumstances'.[1] In those circumstances, the governing body must make arrangements for religious education in accordance with the agreed syllabus to be given to those pupils at the school,[2] and that education must be given during the times set apart for the giving of religious education in the school in accordance with the provision for that purpose included in the school's basic curriculum.[3] Such arrangements must be made by the governing body of the school unless the LEA is satisfied that the governing body is unwilling to make them, in which case the LEA must make them.[4] Except where such arrangements are made, the religious education given to pupils at a foundation or voluntary controlled school with a religious character is under the control of the governing body of the school.[5]

Religious worship

11.40 All pupils in attendance at a maintained school other than a maintained special school must on each school day take part in an act of collective worship unless in the case of any pupil his parent requests that he be wholly or partly excused from such worship under s 71 of the SSFA 1998.[6] If the governing body of the school is of the opinion that it is 'desirable that any act of collective worship in the school required by section 70 should, on a special occasion, take place elsewhere than on the school premises, they may, after consultation with the head teacher, make such arrangements for the purpose as they think appropriate'.[7] Subject to this, the arrangements for such worship must be made in the case of a community or foundation school which does not have a religious character by the head teacher after consulting the governing body.[8] In the case of a foundation school which has a religious character or a voluntary school, such arrangements must be made by the governing body after consulting the head teacher.[9] Except when the governing body is of the opinion that it is desirable that any act of collective worship should on a special occasion take place elsewhere than on the school premises, collective worship of the sort required by s 70 must take place on the school premises.[10]

11.41 The collective worship in a community school or a foundation school without a religious character must normally be 'wholly or mainly of a broadly Christian character' unless a standing advisory council on religious education has determined under s 394 of the EA 1996 that it is not appropriate for that to be so in the case of

---

[1]   SSFA 1998, Sch 19, para 4(3).
[2]   Ibid.
[3]   Ibid, Sch 19, para 4(4). See para **11.6** concerning the school's basic curriculum.
[4]   Ibid, Sch 19, para 4(5).
[5]   Ibid, Sch 19, para 4(6).
[6]   Ibid, s 70(1). For the manner in which the act of collective worship may take place, see SSFA 1998, Sch 20, para 2. See paras **11.43** and **11.44** concerning s 71.
[7]   Ibid, Sch 20, para 2(6).
[8]   Ibid, Sch 20, para 2(4)(a).
[9]   Ibid, Sch 20, para 2(4)(b).
[10]   Ibid, Sch 20, para 2(5), which is reinforced by Sch 20, para 2(7).

the school or in the case of any class or description of pupils at the school.[1] Collective worship in this context is wholly or mainly of a broadly Christian character if it 'reflects the broad traditions of Christian belief without being distinctive of any particular Christian denomination'.[2] Not every act of collective worship in the school which is required by s 70 need be wholly or mainly of a broadly Christian character provided that, taking any school term as a whole, most such acts which take place in the school are of that character.[3] Subject to the requirements described above in this paragraph (1) the extent to which (if at all) any acts of collective worship required by s 70 which are not wholly or mainly of a broadly Christian character take place in the school, (2) the extent to which any act of collective worship in the school which is of such a character reflects the broad traditions of Christian belief, and (3) the ways in which those traditions are reflected in any such act of collective worship, must be 'such as may be appropriate having regard to' certain considerations relating to the pupils concerned.[4] Those considerations are (a) any circumstances relating to the family backgrounds of the pupils which are relevant for determining the character of the collective worship which is appropriate to their case, and (b) their ages and aptitudes.[5]

11.42 As a result of s 395 of the EA 1996, a standing advisory council must review a determination made under s 394 in relation to a school or a class or description of pupils at a school if the head teacher of the school requests it to do so, and in any event such council must review such a determination within 5 years from the date when the determination either took effect or was last reviewed.[6] The public normally have a right of access to meetings of an advisory council.[7] The Secretary of State has a default power in relation to the exercise of functions under ss 394 and 395 by a standing advisory council on religious education, and a power to intervene under a provision analogous to s 496 of the EA 1996.[8]

Exceptions and special arrangements concerning religious education and worship

11.43 Section 71 of the SSFA 1998 provides for exceptions from the requirements described above concerning religious education and worship. It allows the parent of a pupil at a community, foundation or voluntary school (that is, a maintained school

---

[1]   SSFA 1998, Sch 20, paras 3(2) and 4. See EA 1996, ss 390 to 393 in relation to the constitution and functions of an advisory council on religious education. See further, para **11.42** concerning determinations under s 394.

[2]   Ibid, Sch 20, para 3(3). On what constitutes worship which is wholly or mainly of a broadly Christian character, see further *R v Secretary of State for Education, ex parte R and D* [1994] ELR 495.

[3]   Ibid, Sch 20, para 3(4).

[4]   Ibid, Sch 20, para 3(5).

[5]   Ibid, Sch 20, para 3(6).

[6]   EA 1996, s 395(1).

[7]   See the Religious Education (Meetings of Local Conferences and Councils) Regulations 1994, SI 1994/1304, reg 3. See the other provisions of those regulations and s 395 concerning the procedure to be followed generally.

[8]   EA 1996, s 396. These powers are to be exercised in the same manner as those in ss 496 and 497, as to which see Chapter 3.

other than a special school[1]) to request that the pupil be wholly or partly excused from receiving religious education given in the school in accordance with the school's basic curriculum, or from attendance at religious worship in the school, or from both. In *R v Secretary of State for Education, ex parte R and D*,[2] it was alleged that the school at which the pupils in question had been registered pupils had integrated religious education into the secular curriculum to such an extent that it was not possible to withdraw the pupils from religious education without also withdrawing them from the secular education provided with it. Although the argument was rejected on the facts (because there was no evidence that withdrawal from the religious education provided as part of the basic curriculum would result in any interference with the pupils' secular education), it would remain open to a complainant in appropriate circumstances to repeat the argument.

11.44 In the circumstances referred to in s 71(3), a pupil may be withdrawn from a community, foundation or voluntary school for the purpose of enabling him to receive religious education elsewhere than at the school, but not unless the LEA is satisfied that the resulting arrangements will not interfere with the pupil's attendance at school on any school day except at the beginning or end of a school session on that day.[3] A pupil who is a boarder at such a school must be given reasonable opportunities by the governing body of the school for receiving religious education in accordance with the tenets of a particular religion or religious denomination outside school hours, or for attending worship in accordance with such tenets on Sundays or other days exclusively set apart for religious observance by the religious body to which his parent belongs, where his parent requests that he be permitted to do so.[4] The governing body may make facilities available on the school premises for such education or worship as long as no expenditure entailed by the arrangements is met from the governing body's delegated budget or otherwise by the LEA.[5]

No requirement to attend Sunday school permissible

11.45 No pupil may be required as a condition of attending a maintained school[6] to attend or abstain from attending a Sunday school or place of religious worship.[7] The same is true of a person attending a maintained school to receive further education or teacher training.[8]

---

[1]   To which regulations made under s 71(7) apply. The current regulations are the Education (Maintained Special Schools) (England) Regulations 1999, SI 1999/2212, reg 18, and the Education (Maintained Special Schools) (Wales) Regulations 1999, SI 1999/1780, reg 12.
[2]   [1994] ELR 495.
[3]   SSFA 1998, s 71(4).
[4]   Ibid, s 71(5).
[5]   Ibid, s 71(6).
[6]   This means a community, foundation or voluntary school or a community or foundation special school: see SSFA 1998, ss 142(8) and 20(7).
[7]   EA 1996, s 398.
[8]   Ibid.

Chapter 12

INSPECTION OF MAINTAINED SCHOOLS, RELATED INSTITUTIONS AND LOCAL EDUCATION AUTHORITIES

INSPECTION OF SCHOOLS AND RELATED INSTITUTIONS

Introduction

12.1   The inspection of schools and certain related institutions is an area of the law which had at the time of the first edition of this book been subjected to a considerable number of changes over recent years. The first major change came with the Education (Schools) Act 1992 (ESA 1992). That Act replaced the previous regime, which was contained mainly in s 77 of the EA 1944. The EA 1993 introduced further changes, providing for schools which were regarded as failing among other things to be taken over and conducted by a new body, called an education association. That regime was hardly relied upon at all.[1] It was then repealed by the SSFA 1998. The replacement provisions consisted in the main of ss 14–19 of the SSFA 1998. Those provisions survived largely intact up to the time of writing (although they were added to and amended by the EA 2002), and are considered below.[2] First, however, the current statutory provisions concerning inspections are considered. Those originate in the ESA 1992, although they have been amended to a certain degree. They are now contained in the School Inspections Act 1996 (SIA 1996), which was a consolidation Act.

School inspections

12.2   A maintained school may be inspected under ss 1–25 of the SIA 1996. Section 1 provides for the office and appointment by Order in Council of Her Majesty's Chief Inspector of Schools in England ('the Chief Inspector for England'), and for the office and appointment, also by Order in Council, of individuals as Her Majesty's Inspectors of Schools in England.[3] The latter serve, in accordance with the terms and conditions on which they are appointed, as members of the staff of the former.[4] The Chief Inspector holds office under the terms of his appointment, but (a) may not be appointed for a term of more than 5 years, (b) may resign at any time, and (c) may be removed from office by Her Majesty on the ground of incapacity or misconduct.[5]

---

[1]   There is only one reported case concerning an education association: *R v Secretary of State for Education and Employment and the North East London Education Association, ex parte M* [1996] ELR 162.
[2]   See paras **12.33–12.42**.
[3]   SIA 1996, s 1(1) and (2).
[4]   Ibid, s 1(3).
[5]   Ibid, s 1(4).

However, the Chief Inspector may be re-appointed.[1] Section 4 of the SIA 1996 makes equivalent provision in relation to a person called in s 4 the Chief Inspector of Schools in Wales, but who was renamed by s 73 of the LSA 2000 'Her Majesty's Chief Inspector of Schools in Wales'. He is referred to below as 'the Chief Inspector for Wales'.

Functions of the Chief Inspector for England

Duties

12.3 The primary functions of the Chief Inspector for England in relation to schools are set out in s 2 of the SIA 1996.[2] As a result of s 2(1), the Chief Inspector has the 'general duty of keeping the Secretary of State informed about' four things. Those are (a) the quality of education provided by schools in England, (b) the educational standards achieved in those schools, (c) the quality of the leadership in and management of those schools, including whether the financial resources made available to those schools are managed efficiently, and (d) the spiritual, moral, social and cultural development of pupils at those schools. When asked to do so by the Secretary of State, the Chief Inspector must also give advice on any matter specified by the Secretary of State in the request,[3] or inspect and report on a particular school or a class of schools specified in the request.[4] In addition, the Chief Inspector is obliged to establish and maintain a register of persons whom he considers are 'fit and proper person[s] for discharging the functions of a registered inspector' and 'will be capable of conducting inspections under [Part I of the SIA 1996] competently and effectively'.[5] Furthermore, the Chief Inspector is obliged to give guidance to inspectors registered in that register, and 'such other persons as he considers appropriate', in connection with inspections of schools in England under s 10 of the SIA 1996 and the making of reports of such inspections.[6] The Chief Inspector is obliged to keep under review the system of inspecting schools under that section so far as it relates to schools in England, in particular the standard of the inspections and of the reports made by registered inspectors.[7] The Chief Inspector is also required to keep under review the extent to which any requirement in relation to inspections of schools in England imposed by or under any enactment on any (a) registered inspector, (b) LEA, (c) proprietor of a school, or (d) governing body, is complied with.[8] The Chief Inspector is also required to '[promote] efficiency in the conduct and reporting of inspections of schools in England by encouraging competition in the provision of services by registered inspectors'.[9]

---

1   SSFA 1998, s 1(5).
2   The Chief Inspector's functions in relation to the inspection of further education are described in Chapter 16.
3   SIA 1996, s 2(2)(a).
4   Ibid, s 2(2)(b).
5   Ibid, ss 2(3)(a) and 7(3). A reference below to a 'registered inspector' should be read as a reference to an inspector registered in that register. See paras **12.43–12.45** concerning such registration.
6   Ibid, s 2(3)(b). See paras **12.13** et seq concerning inspections under s 10.
7   Ibid, s 2(3)(c).
8   Ibid, s 2(3)(d).
9   Ibid, s 2(3)(e).

12.4 In exercising his functions, the Chief Inspector must 'have regard to such aspects of government policy as the Secretary of State may direct'.[1] The Chief Inspector must also make an annual report to the Secretary of State, who must lay a copy of it before each House of Parliament.[2]

12.5 One duty of the Chief Inspector which is perhaps the most important in practice is not mentioned in s 2. That is the duty imposed by s 10 of the SIA 1996 to 'secure' that schools are inspected under s 10. That duty is considered below.[3]

Powers

12.6 The Chief Inspector (a) may at any time give advice to the Secretary of State on any matter connected with schools, or a particular school, in England,[4] (b) may make such reports to the Secretary of State on matters which fall within the scope of his functions 'as he considers appropriate',[5] and (c) may arrange for any such report or any annual report made by him to the Secretary of State under s 2(7)(a), to be published.[6]

12.7 The Chief Inspector may cause any school in England to be inspected by one or more of Her Majesty's Inspectors of Schools in England.[7] Where an inspection of a school in England is being conducted by a registered inspector under s 10, the Chief Inspector may arrange for that inspection to be monitored by one or more such Inspectors.[8]

12.8 The Chief Inspector has at all reasonable times a right of entry to the premises of any school for the purposes of the exercise of any function conferred by or under s 2, and a right to inspect and take copies of (a) any records kept by the school, and (b) any other documents containing information relating to the school, which he requires for the purposes of the inspection.[9] The Chief Inspector has the same right of entry to any premises (other than school premises) on which, by virtue of any arrangements made by a school in England, any pupils who (a) are registered at the school, and (b) have attained the age of 15 (or will do so during the current school year) but have not ceased to be of compulsory school age, are provided with part of their education by 'any person'.[10] The Chief Inspector also has a similar right in respect of records and other documents kept on computer.[11] Any of Her Majesty's Inspectors of Schools in England inspecting, or monitoring the inspection of, a school under s 3 has rights of the same sort.[12]

---

[1]   SIA 1996, s 2(6).
[2]   Ibid, s 2(7)(a).
[3]   See paras **12.13–12.32**.
[4]   SIA 1996, s 2(4).
[5]   Ibid, s 2(7)(b).
[6]   Ibid, s 2(7)(c).
[7]   Ibid, s 3(1).
[8]   Ibid, s 3(2).
[9]   Ibid, s 2(8).
[10]   Ibid, s 2(8A).
[11]   Ibid, s 42.
[12]   Ibid, ss 3(3) and 42.

Assignment of further functions

12.9   The Secretary of State may assign to the Chief Inspector other functions in connection with schools in England, including functions with respect to the training of teachers for such schools.[1]

Offences relating to obstruction of inspections

12.10   It is an offence wilfully to obstruct the Chief Inspector for England in the exercise of his functions in relation to the inspection of a school under s 2(2)(b) or in the exercise of any right under s 2(8) or 2(8A) for the purpose of the exercise of any other function.[2] It is also an offence wilfully to obstruct any of Her Majesty's Inspectors of Schools in England in the exercise of any of his functions under s 3.[3] Both offences are summary,[4] the maximum penalty for which is a fine at level 4 on the standard scale.[5]

Functions of the Chief Inspector for Wales

12.11   The Chief Inspector for Wales has equivalent functions to those of the Chief Inspector for England in relation to schools. Those functions are conferred by ss 5 and 6 of the SIA 1996, which, in contrast to ss 2 and 3 of that Act, are stated specifically not to extend to 'any education of a kind brought within the remit of Her Majesty's Chief Inspector of Education and Training in Wales by [Part IV of the LSA 2000] that [in the case of s 6] is provided by a school'.[6]

Staffing of the inspectorates of England and Wales

12.12   Schedule 1 to the SIA 1996[7] provides for the staffing of the Inspectorates of England and Wales and the appointment of 'additional inspectors', who may or may not be members of the Chief Inspector's staff.[8] The Chief Inspector may delegate his functions to any Inspector, 'any other member of his staff', or any additional inspector.[9]

Inspections under section 10 of the SIA 1996

12.13   The most significant obligation of the Chief Inspector is to 'secure' that every school in England to which s 10 of the SIA 1996 applies is inspected at prescribed intervals by an inspector registered under s 7, or, in certain circumstances, by one of Her Majesty's Inspectors (referred to below as a member of the Inspectorate).[10] The

---

[1]   SIA 1996, s 2(5).
[2]   Ibid, s 2(9). See the text to footnote 5 at para **12.3** concerning s 2(2)(b). See para **12.8** concerning s 2(8) and (8A).
[3]   Ibid, s 3(4).
[4]   That is, triable in a magistrates' court only.
[5]   See SIA 1996, ss 2(10) and 3(5). Level 4 is currently £2,500.
[6]   Ibid, ss 5(11) and 6(6).
[7]   Schedule 1 is empowered by ss 1(6) and 4(6).
[8]   See Sch 1, para 2, subpara (3) of which makes it clear that additional inspectors need not be members of the Chief Inspector's staff.
[9]   See Sch 1, para 5.
[10]   See s 10(1) and (2), which are subject to s 12, where the circumstances where the inspection may be by a member of the Inspectorate are set out. Under s 12(3), the Chief Inspector may elect to treat an

interval is currently as set out in reg 4 of the Education (School Inspection) Regulations 1997[1] and reg 4 of the Education (School Inspection) (Wales) Regulations 1998.[2] Once the school has first been inspected (and there are different time-limits for different types of school) a subsequent inspection must take place within 6 years. The schools to which s 10 applies are (1) community, foundation and voluntary schools, (2) community and foundation special schools, (3) special schools which are neither community nor foundation special schools but which are for the time being approved by the Secretary of State under s 342 of the EA 1996 as suitable for admitting children with statements of SEN, (4) city technology colleges, (5) city colleges for the technology of the arts, (6) Academies, and (7) maintained nursery schools.[3] There is no obligation imposed on the Chief Inspector to secure the inspection under s 10 of a 'closing school' (as defined by s 10(4B)) in respect of which the Chief Inspector has decided that, because of the date on which the closure is to take effect, no useful purpose would be served by the school being inspected under s 10.[4]

Content of report under section 10

12.14 Any registered inspector who conducts an inspection of a school under s 10 must report on:

'(a)   the quality of the education provided by the school;
(b)   the educational standards achieved in the school;
(c)   the quality of the leadership in and management of the school, including whether the financial resources made available to the school are managed efficiently; and
(d)   the spiritual, moral, social and cultural development of pupils at the school.'[5]

However, an inspection under s 10 does not extend to (a) denominational education,[6] or (b) the content of collective worship which falls to be inspected under s 23 of the SIA 1996.[7]

Procedure for an inspection under section 10

12.15 The procedure to be followed in relation to an inspection under s 10 is set out in ss 11–16 of, and Sch 3 to, the SIA 1996, and regulations made under those provisions. The Chief Inspector has to:

'invite tenders from at least two persons who can reasonably be expected to tender for the proposed inspection and to do so at arm's length from each other, and each of whom is either –

---

inspection of a school by a member of the Inspectorate under s 2(2)(b), 3(1), 5(2)(b) or 6(1) as if it were an inspection under s 10, and in the case of ss 10(1) and (2) and 13(1) as if the member of the Inspectorate were a registered inspector. See the text to footnote 5 at para **12.3** and para **12.7** concerning ss 2(2)(b) and 3(1), which apply in England; ss 5(2)(b) and 6(1) are the equivalent provisions for Wales.

1   SI 1997/1966.
2   SI 1998/1866.
3   SIA 1996, s 10(3).
4   Ibid, s 10(3) and (4A).
5   Ibid, s 10(5).
6   As defined in ibid, s 23(4): s 46(1). See para **12.46** concerning s 23(4).
7   Ibid, s 10(8). See paras **12.46** and **12.47** regarding s 23.

(a)   a registered inspector, or

(b)   a person who the Chief Inspector is satisfied would, if his tender were successful, arrange with a registered inspector for the inspection to be carried out.'[1]

12.16   Before inviting such tenders, the Chief Inspector must consult the LEA where the school is maintained by the authority but does not have a delegated budget.[2] Otherwise, the Chief Inspector must consult the governing body or the proprietor of the school (as appropriate).[3]

12.17   Every inspection team must be conducted by a registered inspector with the assistance of an inspection team of the sort described in para 3 of Sch 3 (as amended by the EA 2002).[4] Certain persons may be prevented by regulations from being a member of such a team.[5] The inspector and all the members of the team must normally, in the opinion of the Chief Inspector, have satisfactorily completed a course of training provided by, or complying with arrangements approved by, the Chief Inspector.[6] The exception is that the Chief Inspector may specify otherwise in any particular case or class of case.[7]

12.18   Where an inspection is arranged, the same body as that which the Chief Inspector must consult before inviting tenders[8] must take such steps as are reasonably practicable to notify the parents of registered pupils at the school and certain other persons of the time when the inspection is to take place.[9] That body must also arrange a meeting between the inspector conducting the inspection and those parents of registered pupils at the school who wish to attend.[10]

12.19   A registered inspector conducting an inspection under s 10, and the members of the inspection team, have a right at all reasonable times to enter onto the premises of the school concerned and, where the inspector is satisfied that it is necessary, of any other school at which pupils of the first school are by agreement receiving part of their education.[11] A registered inspector and the members of his team also have the right when conducting an inspection of a school at all reasonable times to go onto premises which are not school premises but at which, by virtue of arrangements made by the school, any registered pupils of the school who are in the last 2 years of their

---

[1]   SIA 1996, Sch 3, para 2(1).

[2]   Ibid, Sch 3, paras 1 and 2(2).

[3]   Ibid.

[4]   The EA 2002 among other things inserted a new para 3A requiring the Chief Inspector to keep a list of persons who may act as members of an inspection team by virtue of para 3(1)(a).

[5]   See SIA 1996, Sch 3 para 3(2)(b). No regulations have so far been made for this purpose. The provision is rendered largely otiose in practical terms by the new para 3A.

[6]   Ibid, Sch 3, paras 4 and 5. The Chief Inspector may charge reasonable fees for the purpose of recovering the whole or part of the cost of providing the training: paras 4(2) and 5(2).

[7]   Ibid, Sch 3, paras 4(3) and 5(3).

[8]   That body is defined as the 'appropriate authority' for the purposes of Sch 3: see ibid, Sch 3 para 1. See para **12.16** for the relevant bodies.

[9]   Ibid, Sch 3, para 6(a). The other persons are those set out in the amended versions of SI 1997/1966, reg 5 and SI 1998/1866, reg 5.

[10]   SIA 1996, Sch 3, para 6(b). The amended versions of SI 1997/1996, reg 6 and SI 1998/1866, reg 6 apply to such meetings.

[11]   Ibid, Sch 3, para 7(1) and (2).

compulsory schooling are receiving part of their education from any person.[1] The inspector and the members of his team may also inspect relevant documents[2] and computer records.[3] It is an offence wilfully to obstruct a registered inspector or a member of an inspection team in the exercise of his functions in relation to an inspection of a school.[4]

12.20 An inspection under s 10 which is carried out by a registered inspector must take no longer than 2 weeks, unless the Chief Inspector considers it necessary to extend that period.[5] A registered inspector or (where relevant) a member of the Inspectorate must make a report of a s 10 inspection and a summary of the report.[6] Where the inspector is a registered inspector, that report and summary must be produced within 6 weeks (or, in Wales, 35 working days), again, unless the Chief Inspector considers it necessary to extend that period.[7] The inspection and the making of a s 10 report by a registered inspector must be completed within a maximum period of 3 months.[8] Certain persons must be notified of any extension of these time periods.[9]

Schools to which section 11(2) of the SIA 1996 applies (maintained schools)

21.21 Once a report relating to a school named in s 11(2) (that is, a community, foundation, or a voluntary school or a community or foundation special school, or, in England, a maintained nursery school[10]) has been made, the person who has made it must 'without delay' send it and a summary of it to the 'appropriate authority' within the meaning of s 11(4).[11] The 'appropriate authority' within the meaning of that subsection in the case of all schools maintained by an LEA is the governing body if the school has a delegated budget, and the LEA if it does not have such a budget.

12.22 The report and summary must also be sent to the persons referred to in s 16(3), who include the head teacher of the school. The appropriate authority must (a) make a copy of the report and summary available for inspection by members of the public at such times and at such place as may be reasonable, (b) provide such a copy free of charge (or in certain cases on payment of such fee as they think fit, not exceeding the cost of supply[12]) to any person who asks for one, and (c) take 'such steps as are reasonably practicable to secure that every registered parent of a registered

---

1   SIA 1996, Sch 3, para 7(3).
2   Ibid, Sch 3, para 7(1) and (3).
3   See ibid, s 42 regarding the inspection of computer records.
4   Ibid, Sch 3, para 8(1). The maximum penalty is the same as that for an offence under ss 2(9) and 5(9) of the SIA 1996 (as to which see para **12.10**), that is a fine at level 4 on the standard scale (currently £2,500): Sch 3, para 8(2).
5   Ibid, s 15(1), (2) and (5), SI 1997/1966, reg 7(1) and SI 1998/1866, reg 7(1).
6   Ibid, ss 12(2) and 13(1).
7   Ibid, s 15(1), (2) and (5), and SI 1997/1966, reg 7(2) (as amended by SI 1999/601) and SI 1998/1866, reg 7(2), as amended by SI 2004/784.
8   Ibid, s 15(2) and (5).
9   See ibid, s 15(3) and (4), read in the light of s 11(4) and (5).
10 See EA 2002, Sch 21, para 60, for the inclusion of a maintained nursery school within the subsection; that para is currently in force only in England: see SI 2003/1667.
11 SIA 1996, s 16(1)(a).
12 See SI 1997/1966, reg 10 and SI 1998/1866, reg 10 for the cases where a fee may be charged.

pupil at the school receives a copy of the summary' within 10 working days from the date of the receipt of the report by the appropriate authority.[1]

ACTION PLANS; SPECIAL MEASURES IN RELATION TO A SCHOOL

INTRODUCTION

12.23 The obligations placed on the person or body responsible for the conduct of a school and (where relevant) the LEA where an inspection of the school has been made, are difficult to state clearly. This is because the obligations depend in part on whether the person inspecting the school was a registered inspector or a member of the Inspectorate. Furthermore, the obligations are greater where the person who made the report states in it that special measures are required to be taken in relation to the school, *and* either that person is a member of the Inspectorate or the person is a registered inspector and the report states that the Chief Inspector agrees with his opinion. 'Special measures' are defined for this purpose and all other purposes of the SIA 1996 as measures which are 'required to be taken in relation to a school [because an inspection under s 10 has resulted in the view that] the school is failing or likely to fail to give its pupils an acceptable standard of education'.[2]

REPORT WHERE INSPECTOR IS OF THE OPINION THAT SPECIAL MEASURES ARE NECESSARY

12.24 If a registered inspector or a member of the Inspectorate who (in each case) has carried out a s 10 inspection is of the opinion that special measures are required to be taken in relation to the school, then he must state that opinion in the requisite report of his inspection.[3] If a member of the Inspectorate carries out an inspection under s 2(2)(b), 3(1), 5(2)(b) or 6(1) (which are inspections at the request of the Secretary of State[4] or which the Chief Inspector himself initiates without being under any obligation to do so), and the member of the Inspectorate in question is of the opinion that special measures are required to be taken in relation to the school, then he must (1) prepare in writing a report of the inspection and a summary of the report,[5] and (2) state his opinion in the report.[6]

12.25 There is an elaborate set of procedures to be followed where in the opinion of a relevant inspector special measures are required to be taken in relation to a school. The procedure concerning the writing and completion of the necessary written report is more involved where the inspector is a registered inspector than where he is a member of the Inspectorate.[7] The inspection report and a summary of it must in all cases be sent to the appropriate authority and the persons referred to in s 16(3).[8] If the report of a registered inspector concerning a community, foundation or voluntary school, or a community or foundation special school, states that the Chief Inspector

---

[1]   SIA 1996, s 16(4) and SI 1997/1966, reg 7(3) and SI 1998/1866 reg 7(3).
[2]   Ibid, s 13(9).
[3]   Ibid, ss 12(2)(b), 13(1), 13(7)(a) and 14(3).
[4]   In relation to Wales, references here and below in this chapter to the Secretary of State should be read as references to the National Assembly for Wales: see SI 1999/672.
[5]   SIA 1996, s 14(1)(a).
[6]   Ibid, s 14(1)(b).
[7]   See ibid, ss 13 and 14.
[8]   See ibid, s 16(1) and (3).

agrees with the opinion of the inspector that special measures are required to be taken in relation to the school, then the report and a summary of it must be sent to the appropriate authority and the Secretary of State.[1] Similarly, if the inspection of such a school was carried out by a member of the Inspectorate and he is of the opinion that special measures are required to be taken in relation to the school, then the inspector must send the report and a summary of it to the appropriate authority for the school and the Secretary of State.[2]

REPORT WHERE INSPECTION SHOWS A SCHOOL IS CAUSING CONCERN

12.26 If a member of the Inspectorate who carries out under an inspection s 10 of the SIA 1996 informs the Secretary of State of his opinion that the school has serious weaknesses or that special measures are required to be taken in relation to the school, the Chief Inspector must without delay give the Secretary of State a notice in writing stating that that is so.[3] For this purpose, a school has serious weaknesses if 'although giving its pupils in general an acceptable standard of education, it has significant weaknesses in one or more areas of its activities'.[4] On receipt of such a notice, the Secretary of State must without delay give the LEA notice in writing that he has been informed by the Chief Inspector of this opinion of the member of the Inspectorate.[5] Similarly, if (a) a registered inspector carries out such an inspection and notifies the Chief Inspector in writing that the school has serious weaknesses, or (b) the Chief Inspector agrees with the opinion of a registered inspector, expressed in a draft report submitted to the Chief Inspector under s 13(2), that special measures are required to be taken in relation to the school, the Chief Inspector must without delay inform the Secretary of State in writing that that is so, who must then inform the LEA accordingly.[6]

STATEMENTS UNDER SECTIONS 17 AND 18 OF THE SIA 1996

12.27 The appropriate authority for a relevant school[7] must (unless the Secretary of State directs otherwise in the circumstances referred to in the following sentence) within 40 working days (45 working days in Wales) from the date on which it receives a report of an inspection under s 10 or of an inspection by a member of the Inspectorate in which that member is required by s 14(1)(b) to state that he is of the opinion that special measures are required to be taken in relation to the school, 'prepare a written statement of the action which they propose to take in the light of the report and the period within which they propose to take it'.[8] If (a) the report states that the person making it is of the opinion that special measures are required to be taken in relation to the school, and either that person is a member of the Inspectorate

---

1   SIA 1996, s 16(1)(b).
2   Ibid, s 16(2).
3   Ibid, s 16A(1)(a) and (2).
4   Ibid, s 16A(4).
5   Ibid, s 16A(3).
6   Ibid, s 16A(1)(b) and (c), (2) and (3).
7   The 'appropriate authority' for this purpose is defined by s 11(4) of the SIA 1996.
8   SIA 1996, s 17(1) and (2), SI 1997/1966, reg 8(1) and SI 1998/1866 reg 8(1), as amended by SI 2004/784. A failure to comply with the requirement to prepare the statement within the requisite period will not absolve the appropriate authority from making such a statement: s 17(2). What is now a s 17 statement used to be called an 'action plan' (see ESA 1992, Sch 2, para 10), but that phrase now appears in the context of s 10 inspections only in the above regulations.

or the report states that the Chief Inspector agrees with his opinion, and (b) the Secretary of State is of the opinion that the urgency of the case requires a shorter period, the period by which such statement must be prepared is such shorter period as the Secretary of State directs.[1] The appropriate authority must next send a copy of the statement to the persons referred to in s 17(3)–(5), and make it available in accordance with s 17(6) and (6A).[2] If the report does not state that the registered inspector is of the opinion that special measures are required to be taken in relation to the school, or it does so but it also states that the Chief Inspector disagrees with that opinion, then the s 17(2) statement (the 'action plan') must be sent to the persons referred to in s 17(3) and (4) within 5 working days of the date on which the appropriate authority complete the preparation of the action plan.[3] If the report states that the person making the report is of the opinion that special measures are required to be taken in relation to the school and either that person is a member of the Inspectorate or the report states that the Chief Inspector agrees with his opinion, then the action plan must be sent to the persons referred to in s 17(3) and (4) within 2 days (excluding Saturdays, Sundays, Good Friday, Christmas Day and bank holidays) from the date on which the appropriate authority completes the preparation of the action plan, or 2 days from the expiry of the 40-day period referred to at the beginning of this paragraph, whichever is the earlier.[4]

12.28   If the appropriate authority is the governing body of the school, then it must state in its annual report made under s 30 of the EA 2002 (or, currently, in Wales, s 42 of the SSFA 1998) 'the extent to which the proposals set out in the [s 17] statement (or if there is more than one, the most recent statement) have been carried into effect'.[5]

12.29   Where (1) a report of an inspection is of a community, foundation or voluntary school, or a community or foundation special school, which (in all cases) has a delegated budget, (2) the person who made the report stated that in his opinion special measures were required to be taken in relation to the school, (3) either that person was a member of the Inspectorate or the report stated that the Chief Inspector agreed with his opinion, and (4) either the LEA has received a copy of a s 17 statement or the time-limit for complying with s 17(3) has expired,[6] the LEA must prepare a statement under s 18(2) of the SIA 1996. That statement must either be of any action which it proposes to take in the light of the report and the period within which it proposes to take it, or, if it does not propose to take any such action, of its reasons for not doing so.[7] It must prepare that statement within 10 days from the date on which it receives a copy of the action plan in respect of the school in question, or 12 days from the expiry of the 40-day period referred to at the beginning of

[1]   SIA 1996, s 17(2).
[2]   Ibid, s 17(3)(d) requires that copies be sent to 'such other persons ... as may be prescribed'. Those persons are prescribed in SI 1997/1966, reg 8(3) and SI 1998/1866 reg 8(3).
[3]   SI 1997/1966, reg 8(2)(a); SI 1998/1866, reg 8(2)(a). In contrast, no time-limit applies to the duty to comply with s 17(5).
[4]   See reg 8(2)(b) and (4) of both sets of regulations.
[5]   SIA 1996, s 17(7).
[6]   See para **12.27** for the relevant period, as prescribed by reg 8 of both sets of regulations.
[7]   SIA 1996, s 18(2)(a).

para **12.27**, whichever occurs first,[1] unless the Secretary of State is of the opinion that the urgency of the case requires a shorter period. In the latter case, the statement must be prepared within 'such shorter period as the Secretary of State may direct'.[2] The LEA must also send a copy of its statement made under s 18(2) and its comments on any 'statement prepared under section 17' (in other words, an action plan) of which it has received a copy, to the Secretary of State, the Chief Inspector, and, in the case of a voluntary aided school, the person who appoints the foundation governors and (if different) the 'appropriate appointing authority' within the meaning of s 11(4) of the SIA 1996.[3]

MONITORING SPECIAL MEASURES

12.30 Section 19 of the SIA 1996 provides that regulations may make provision with a view to securing that measures taken by the appropriate authority and, in the case of a school with a delegated budget, the LEA, for improving the standard of education at the school are, in certain circumstances, monitored 'in accordance with the regulations by such persons as may be prescribed'.[4]

SCHOOLS TO WHICH SECTION 11(3) REFERS

12.31 Schools other than those to which s 11(2) refers[5] which are inspected under s 10 are subject to a slightly different regime from that described in the preceding paragraphs. (The schools in question are special schools approved by the Secretary of State under s 342 of the EA 1996, city technology colleges, city colleges for the technology of the arts, Academies, and maintained nursery schools. These are referred to below as the schools to which s 11(3) refers.) However, the differences are minor, and result from the different circumstances of the schools: ss 13–15 of the SIA 1996 apply also to the schools to which s 11(3) refers, but instead of ss 16–19, ss 20–22 of that Act apply to them. The 'appropriate authority' for the purposes of the schools to which s 11(3) refers is defined by s 11(5). In the case of special schools approved under s 342, city technology colleges, city colleges for the technology of the arts, and Academies, the appropriate authority is the proprietor of the school. In the case of a maintained nursery school, it is the LEA unless the school has a delegated budget, in which case it is the governing body. Otherwise, the provision made in ss 20–22 is equivalent to that made in ss 16–19 and described above (with equivalent time-limits), albeit suitably adapted.

Publication of reports of inspections carried out under the SIA 1996

12.32 If the Chief Inspector considers it appropriate, a report of an inspection carried out by a member of the Inspectorate under any provision of the SIA 1996

---

[1] SIA 1996, s 18(3)(a) and SI 1997/1966, reg 9(1) or (as the case may be) SI 1998/1866, reg 9(1). Saturdays, Sundays, Good Friday, Christmas Day and bank holidays are not counted for the purposes of those provisions: see reg 9(2) of both sets of regulations.

[2] Ibid, s 18(3)(b).

[3] Ibid, s 18(2)(b). There is no time-limit for complying with s 18(2)(b).

[4] Ibid, s 19(2). The circumstances in question are set out in s 19(1). The other provisions of s 19 empower the regulations to set out the mechanics of the monitoring. No regulations have so far been made under s 19.

[5] See para **12.21** for the schools to which s 11(2) refers.

(whether the report is required by any such provision or is otherwise made in pursuance of his functions under that provision), or of an inspection under s 10 by a person who is not a member of the Inspectorate, may be published.[1] Such publication may be made by electronic means.[2] Such publication is protected for the purposes of the law of defamation by being privileged unless it is shown that it was made with malice.[3]

Powers of intervention in schools in relation to which an inspection report is critical

12.33 As a result of s 14 of the SSFA 1998, an LEA may intervene in the conduct of a maintained school[4] (including a maintained nursery school[5]) under s 16, s 16A or s 17 of the SSFA 1998 (concerning which, see paras **12.36–12.38**) in three situations.[6] The first is where s 15(1) of the 1998 Act applies, which is where (a) the school is subject to a formal warning notice given by the LEA to its governing body under s 15(2), (b) the governing body have failed to comply, or secure compliance, with the notice to the LEA's satisfaction within the compliance period (defined as indicated below), and (c) the LEA have given reasonable notice to the governing body that they propose to exercise their powers under either or both of s 16 or s 17 of the SSFA 1998.[7] Section 15(2) empowers the LEA to give a warning notice where three conditions are satisfied. The first is that the LEA is satisfied that (a) the standards of performance of pupils at the school are unacceptably low and are likely to remain so unless the LEA exercise their powers under either or both of ss 16 and 17, (b) there has been a serious breakdown in the way the school is managed or governed which is prejudicing, or likely to prejudice, such standards of performance, or (c) the safety of pupils or staff of the school is threatened (whether by a breakdown of discipline or otherwise).[8] The second condition is that the LEA have previously informed the governing body and the head teacher of the matters on which that conclusion is based.[9] The third condition is that those matters have not been remedied to the LEA's satisfaction within a reasonable period.[10] The warning notice must set out (a) the matters on which the conclusion is based, (b) the action which the LEA require the governing body to take in order to remedy those matters, and (c) the period within which that action is to be taken by the governing body ('the compliance period').[11] The exercise by an LEA of its functions under s 15(2) is the subject of guidance given

---

1   SIA 1996, s 42A(1).
2   Ibid, s 42A(2).
3   See ibid, s 42A(3), which does not affect any privilege which would otherwise attach: s 42A(4).
4   A maintained school for this purpose is a community, foundation or voluntary school, or a community or foundation special school: SSFA 1998, s 20(7).
5   See ibid, s 14(1A), as inserted by EA 2002, Sch 21, para 92, which is currently in force in England (see SI 2003/1667) but not in Wales. For the sake of simplicity, and because it is highly likely that all relevant provisions will shortly come into force in Wales, it is assumed that all of ss 14–19 inclusive of the SSFA 1998 which apply both to England and Wales will at the time of publication be in force in Wales as well as in England.
6   See ibid, s 14(1).
7   Although ibid, s 14(2) was amended by the EA 2002 to reflect the enactment of s 16A, s 15(1) and (2) were not so amended.
8   Ibid, s 15(2)(a).
9   Ibid, s 15(2)(b).
10   Ibid, s 15(2)(c).
11   Ibid, s 15(3).

in the code of practice issued by the Secretary of State under s 127 of the SSFA 1998.[1]

12.34 The second situation in which the LEA may intervene under s 16, s 16A or s 17 of the SSFA 1998 is where s 15(4) applies, which is where (a) a report of an inspection has been made under Part I of the SIA 1996 and the Chief Inspector has given the Secretary of State a notice under s 16A(1)(a) or (b) and s 16(2) of the SIA 1996,[2] and (b) no subsequent such report has been made in which the person making it has stated that in his opinion either (i) the school no longer has serious weaknesses, or (ii) special measures are required to be taken in relation to the school. A school has 'serious weaknesses' for this purpose if, although giving its pupils in general an acceptable standard of education, it has significant weaknesses in one or more of its activities.[3]

12.35 The third situation in which the LEA may intervene under s 16, s 16A or s 17 is where s 15(6) applies. That is where (1) following an inspection of the school under Part I of the SIA 1996, the Chief Inspector has given the Secretary of State a notice under s 16A(1)(c) and (2) of that Act,[4] and (2) if a subsequent such report has been made, the person making it did not state that, in his opinion, special measures were not required to be taken in relation to the school. However, s 15(6) does not permit the LEA to intervene under s 16, s 16A or s 17 of the SSFA 1998 if in connection with the same inspection falling within s 15(6)(a), (a) the Secretary of State has exercised his power under s 18 of that Act to appoint additional governors and any additional governors appointed in the exercise of that power remain in office, or (b) he has exercised his power under s 19 of that Act to direct the closure of the school.[5]

Local education authority's power to appoint additional governors

12.36 Section 16(1) of the SSFA 1998 empowers the LEA to appoint 'such number of additional governors as they think fit'. However, this power may be exercised in relation to a school to which s 15(1) applies[6] only within the period of 2 months following the end of the compliance period (within the meaning of s 15(3)).[7] The power in s 16(1) applies to a school falling within s 15(6) (that is, a school requiring special measures) only if the Secretary of State has given the LEA a notice under s 16A(3) of the SIA 1996, and a period of not less than 10 days (or a shorter period determined by the Secretary of State) has elapsed since the date of the notice.[8] In the case of a voluntary aided school other than one falling within s 15(4) or (6) of the SSFA 1998 (in other words, such a school to which s 15(1) applies), the 'appropriate appointing authority' (within the meaning of s 16(11) of the SSFA 1998) may appoint 'such number of additional foundation governors as is equal to the number of additional governors appointed by the [LEA]'.[9] Those additional governors cease to

---

1   SSFA 1998, s 127(6); the code for England gives guidance in paras 1–3 of Annex 2, and that for Wales does so in paras 99–104 of Part 2. See paras **2.31–2.32** concerning s 127.
2   Concerning which, see para **12.26**.
3   SSFA 1998, s 15(5).
4   Concerning which, see para **12.26**.
5   SSFA 1998, s 14(3).
6   See para **12.33** for the circumstances in which s 15(1) applies.
7   SSFA 1998, s 16(2). See para **12.33** as to the compliance period.
8   Ibid, s 16(3) and (12A). As to s 16A(3), see para **12.26**.
9   SSFA 1998, s 16(6).

hold office at the time when the additional governors appointed by the LEA cease to do so and are not eligible to be re-appointed except where, and to the extent that, those governors are re-appointed.[1] In the case of a voluntary aided school to which s 15(4) or (6) applies and in regard to which the Secretary of State has not exercised his powers under s 18 or 19 of the SSFA 1998, the appropriate appointing authority 'may appoint such number of additional governors as they think fit'.[2] The exercise by an LEA of its functions under s 16(1) is subject to the code of practice issued by the Secretary of State under s 127 of the SSFA 1998.[3]

Local education authority's power under section 17 of the SSFA 1998 to suspend right to delegated budget

12.37 An LEA has power under s 17 of the SSFA 1998 to suspend the right of a maintained school to a delegated budget.[4] This power applies in the same circumstances so far as relevant, and subject to the same conditions so far as relevant, as the power in s 16 to appoint additional governors. The LEA must give notice in writing of the suspension to the governing body and the head teacher of the school,[5] and the suspension comes into effect on receipt by the governing body of that notice.[6] The exercise by an LEA of its functions under s 17(1) is the subject of guidance in the code of practice issued by the Secretary of State under s 127 of the SSFA 1998.[7]

Local education authority's power to appoint interim executive members of the governing body

12.38 Under s 16A of the SSFA 1998, in the same circumstances so far as relevant, and subject to the same conditions so far as relevant (but with one additional condition), as the power in s 16 to appoint additional governors of a maintained school, an LEA may cause the governing body of the school to be constituted in accordance with Sch 1A to the SSFA 1998. That Schedule was inserted by the EA 2002. It provides for a governing body to be replaced by an 'interim executive board'. The additional condition is that before exercising the power, the LEA must consult (a) the governing body of the school, and (b) in the case of a foundation or voluntary school which is a Church of England school, a Church in Wales school or a Roman Catholic school, the appropriate diocesan authority, and in the case of any other foundation or voluntary school, the person or persons by whom the foundation governors are appointed.[8] The interim executive board cannot publish proposals to close the school under s 29(2) of the SSFA 1998 or serve notice of its discontinuance

1   Ibid, s 16(7)(a).
2   Ibid, s 16(8), which is subject to s 16(9). See below regarding the Secretary of State's powers under ss 18 and 19. See paras **12.34** and **12.35** for the circumstances in which s 15(4) and (6) apply. See s 16(11) and (12) concerning the appointment of governors under s 16(8).
3   See ibid, s 127(6); the code for England gives guidance in paras 4–6 of Annex 2, and that for Wales does so in paras 105–113 of Part 2. See paras **2.31– 2.32** concerning s 127.
4   See paras **7.132** et seq in relation to delegated budgets.
5   SSFA 1998, s 17(1) and (5).
6   SSFA 1998, s 17(1).
7   Ibid, s 127(6); the code for England gives guidance in para 7 of Annex 2, and that for Wales does so in paras 117–120 of Part 2. See paras **2.31–2.32** concerning s 127.
8   Ibid, s 16A(4). The definition of 'appropriate diocesan authority' is in SSFA 1998, s 142(1).

under s 30(2) of that Act,[1] but may recommend to the LEA and the Secretary of State that the school be discontinued.[2] The 'appropriate authority' (in this case the LEA[3]) may give notice under para 17 of Sch 1A to the SSFA 1998, specifying a date on which the governing body 'are to become a normally constituted governing body', and by virtue of paras 18 and 19 of Sch 1A and the School Governance (Transition from an Interim Executive Board) (England) Regulations 2004,[4] a shadow governing body must be formed, which then takes over as the normally constituted governing body at the end of the interim period.

Power of the Secretary of State to appoint additional governors

12.39 The Secretary of State may under s 18(1) of the SSFA 1998 appoint additional governors to a maintained school governing body where s 15(4) or (6) applies.[5] He may also in that situation nominate such an additional governor as chairman of the governing body to be the chairman instead of the person who has been elected to be the chairman of the body.[6] A governor so appointed holds office for such term, and, if so nominated as the chairman, is chairman of that body for such period, as the Secretary of State determines.[7] The Secretary of State may pay any additional governor appointed by him under s 18 'such remuneration and such allowances as the Secretary of State may determine'.[8]

12.40 Where the Secretary of State has exercised his power under s 18 in relation to a school, the LEA may not exercise its power under para 1 of Sch 15 to the SSFA 1998[9] to suspend the governing body's right to a delegated budget, and if it has already exercised that power of suspension, or its power under s 17(1) of the SSFA 1998,[10] the Secretary of State must revoke that suspension if requested to do so by the governing body.[11]

Secretary of State's power to appoint interim executive members of the governing body

12.41 The Secretary of State may under s 18A of the SSFA 1998 cause the governing body of a maintained school to be constituted in accordance with Sch 1A to the SSFA 1998 in the same circumstances as those which empower the appointment of additional governors under s 18 (concerning which, see para **12.40**), although the Secretary of State must with two exceptions also consult the LEA and the governing body of the school before exercising the power under s 18A. One exception is that

---

[1]   See paras **7.29–7.31** concerning ss 29 and 30 of the SSFA 1998.

[2]   SSFA 1998, Sch 1A, para 15.

[3]   See ibid, Sch 1A, para 1(1).

[4]   SI 2004/530.

[5]   See paras **12.34** and **12.35** for the circumstances in which s 15(4) and (6) apply. Before making such an appointment in relation to a voluntary aided school, the Secretary of State must consult the appropriate diocesan authority in relation to a Church of England school, a Church in Wales school or a Roman Catholic School, and, in any other case, the person who appoints the foundation governors: s 18(2)(b).

[6]   SSFA 1998, s 18(1).

[7]   Ibid, s 18(3).

[8]   Ibid, s 18(4).

[9]   As to which, see para **7.144**.

[10] See para **12.37** concerning the power in s 17(1).

[11] SSFA 1998, s 18(6)(a). The revocation must be notified to the LEA in writing, and takes effect from the date specified in the notification: s 18(7).

the LEA has previously consulted the governing body under s 16A(4) in relation to a proposed notice under s 16A(1), in which case there is no need to consult the governing body.[1] The other exception is that in the same circumstances, that is, when the LEA has consulted the appropriate diocesan authority or the person or persons by whom the foundation governors are appointed under s 16A(4) in relation to a proposed notice under s 16A(1), the Secretary of State does not need to consult such person(s) or body.[2]

Secretary of State's power of closure

12.42 Where s 15(4) or (6) of the SSFA 1998 applies to a maintained school,[3] the Secretary of State may give a direction to the LEA under s 19(1) of the SSFA 1998, requiring the school to be discontinued on a date specified in the direction. Before giving such a direction, the Secretary of State must consult (a) the LEA and the governing body of the school, (b) the appropriate diocesan authority in the case of a foundation or voluntary school which is a Church of England school, a Church in Wales school, or a Roman Catholic school, (c) in the case of any other foundation or voluntary school, the person who appoints the foundation governors, (d) in the case of a school which provides education suitable to the requirements of persons over compulsory school age, the LSC or (if the school is in Wales, which case as stated above, 'the Secretary of State' means 'the National Assembly') the CETW, and (e) such other persons as the Secretary of State considers appropriate.[4] When giving a direction under s 19(1), the Secretary of State must give notice in writing to the governing body of the school and its head teacher.[5] The LEA must cease to maintain the school from the date specified in the direction, and none of the 'public notice' provisions in ss 29–33 of the SSFA 1998 apply to the discontinuance.[6]

Registration of inspectors

12.43 As stated above, an inspection of a school under s 10(1) of the SIA 1996 may be carried out only by a registered inspector or a member of the Inspectorate. Inspectors are registered for this purpose in a register kept by the Chief Inspector under s 7 of that Act. A person may not be registered in that register unless it appears to the Chief Inspector that the person is 'a fit and proper person for discharging the functions of a registered inspector' and that the person 'will be capable of conducting inspections under this Part competently and effectively'.[7] No person who falls within a category of persons prescribed for the purposes of s 7(3) may be registered.[8] An application to be registered under s 7 must be made in such manner as the Chief

---

[1]   SSFA 1998, s 18A(3).
[2]   Ibid. See para **12.38** for the manner in which the interim executive board ceases to exist; where the Secretary of State has caused a school to be governed by such a board, the Secretary of State is the 'appropriate authority' for the purposes of Sch 1A.
[3]   See paras **12.34** and **12.35** for the circumstances in which s 15(4) or (6) applies.
[4]   SSFA 1998, s 19(2). The appropriate diocesan authority is defined by SSFA 1998, s 142(1).
[5]   Ibid, s 19(3).
[6]   Ibid, s 18(4) and (5).
[7]   Ibid, s 7(3).
[8]   Ibid.

Inspector may direct and must be accompanied by the appropriate fee.[1] The Chief Inspector may refuse to register the applicant, or may register him only subject to conditions.[2] The registration may be for a period only.[3]

12.44 Inspectors may be removed from the register under s 8(1) in the circumstances set out in s 8(2), which include that an inspector has 'without reasonable explanation, produced a report of an inspection which is, in whole or in part, seriously misleading'. In addition, if the Chief Inspector is 'satisfied ... (a) that he is authorised by subsection (2) to remove the name of an inspector from his register, or (b) that it would otherwise be in the public interest to act under this subsection', then he may vary any condition subject to which the inspector's registration has effect, or impose a condition subject to which it will have effect.[4] In determining whether to take any action under s 8, each Chief Inspector may have regard to any action taken by the other Chief Inspector with respect to the registered inspector in question.[5]

12.45 There is a right of appeal by any person who is aggrieved by (a) the refusal of the Chief Inspector to renew his registration under s 7, (b) the imposition or variation of any condition subject to which he is registered under that section, or (c) the removal of his name from the relevant register under s 8. That right of appeal is conferred by s 9 of the SIA 1996. The appeal is made to a tribunal constituted in accordance with Sch 2 to that Act. The tribunal is chaired by a lawyer with a 7-year general qualification within the meaning of s 71 of the Courts and Legal Services Act 1990, and two other members appointed by the Secretary of State.[6] There are detailed rules which apply to the appeal, and they are in the Education (Registered Inspectors of Schools Appeal Tribunal and Registered Nursery Education Inspectors Appeal Tribunal) (Procedure) Regulations 1999.[7]

Inspections of religious education and collective worship

12.46 Section 23 of the SIA 1996 applies to religious education given in a voluntary or foundation school which has been designated by the Secretary of State under s 69(3) of the SSFA 1998 as having a religious character.[8] It is the duty of the governing body of such a school to ensure that denominational education given to any pupils and the content of the school's collective worship (required by s 70 of the SSFA 1998) is inspected under s 23.[9] Denominational education for this purpose is defined by s 23(4), and is that which is required by s 80(1)(a) or 101(1)(a) of the

---

[1] SSFA 1998, s 7(4). The appropriate fee is currently £150: see Education (Registered Inspectors) (Fees) Regulations 1992, SI 1992/2025.

[2] Ibid, s 7(5).

[3] Ibid, s 7(8).

[4] Ibid, s 8(3).

[5] Ibid, s 8(4).

[6] SIA 1996, Sch 2, para 1.

[7] SI 1999/265.

[8] See para **7.26** as to how a school acquires such a designation.

[9] SIA 1996, s 23(1). See paras **11.40** et seq concerning s 70.

EA 2002 to be included in the school's basic curriculum[1] but which is not required by any enactment to be given in accordance with any agreed syllabus.[2]

12.47 Inspections under s 23 need not be carried out by a registered inspector.[3] The person carrying out the inspection must be chosen by the foundation governors in the case of a controlled school and by the governing body in any other case.[4] If the inspection is of the denominational education under s 23(1) then the inspector must report on the quality of the denominational education provided by the school.[5] If the inspection is of the school's collective worship under s 23(2), then the inspector must report on the content of that worship.[6] The inspector may in addition report on the spiritual, moral, social and cultural development of pupils at the school.[7] Inspections under s 23 are to be carried out at intervals prescribed under s 23(7). Under the current regulations, after the initial such inspection, inspections under s 23 must be repeated at intervals of 6 years.[8]

Inspections by local education authorities

12.48 An LEA may provide a school inspection service for schools in its area under s 24 of the SIA 1996 and regulations made under that section. Inspections under that section may, however, be made of schools which are not maintained by the authority, as well as those which are so maintained.[9] The inspection service provided by the LEA under s 24 must be operated by the authority in such a way that they 'can reasonably be expected to secure that the full cost of providing the service is recovered by way of charges made by the authority to those using the service'.[10] Regulations made by the Secretary of State under s 24(5) may (among other things) require the keeping of accounts in relation to such inspections.[11]

12.49 An LEA may also in certain circumstances cause an inspection of a school which is maintained by it to be made by one or more of its officers, under s 25. The circumstances are that (a) the LEA requires, for the purpose of enabling it to exercise any of its functions, information about any matter in connection with a school maintained by it, and (b) it is not reasonably practicable for them to obtain the information in any other manner. The officer who inspects the school has at all reasonable times a right of entry to the premises of the school. The exercise by an

---

1   See para **11.6** regarding the basic curriculum.
2   The agreed syllabus is considered at paras **11.32** and **11.33**.
3   SIA 1996, s 23(6).
4   Ibid, s 23(5). The inspector may be assisted by persons chosen by him under s 23(9).
5   Ibid, s 23(8)(a).
6   Ibid, s 23(8)(b). Schedule 4 to the SIA 1996 applies to reports under s 23(8). Among other things, Sch 4 requires the governing body of the school to prepare what is referred to specifically as an 'action plan', as well as providing for the manner in which the report is to be produced. Regulations 11–14 of SI 1997/1966 and regs 11–14 of SI 1998/1866 apply also to the inspection.
7   Ibid, s 23(8).
8   See SI 1997/1966, reg 12 and SI 1998/1866, reg 12.
9   SIA 1996, s 24(3).
10   Ibid, s 24(4).
11   See SI 1997/1966, reg 15 and SI 1998/1866, reg 15 concerning the keeping of accounts. There are currently no other regulations which apply to inspections under ibid, s 24.

LEA of its functions under s 25 is the subject of guidance in the code of practice issued by the Secretary of State under s 127 of the SSFA 1998.[1]

Inspection of nursery education provided elsewhere than in maintained nursery schools

12.50 There is a separate set of provisions (in Sch 26 to the SSFA 1998) for the inspection of nursery education which is provided (a) by an LEA (as opposed to by a maintained nursery school), and (b) by persons who are in receipt of financial assistance given by a LEA and whose provision of nursery education is taken into account by the LEA in formulating proposals for the purposes of s 120(2)(a) of the SSFA 1998.[2] The provisions of Sch 26 are in large part equivalent to those contained in the SIA 1996 relating to primary and secondary schools, adapted as necessary to take account of the different circumstances concerning nursery education. For example, Sch 26 requires the Chief Inspector to keep a register of nursery education inspectors, under a regime which is in essence the same as that in ss 7–9 of the SIA 1996.[3] Indeed, Sch 26 was amended by the EA 2002 so that an inspection of nursery education may be made in addition by a member of the Inspectorate.[4] However, the right of appeal against a relevant decision concerning a person's registration is to the Care Standards Tribunal.[5]

12.51 A report of an inspection under Sch 26 to the SSFA 1998 may be published under s 42A(2)–(4) of the SIA 1996.[6]

Inspections of local education authorities

12.52 Under s 38(1) of the EA 1997, the Chief Inspector[7] may, and if requested by the Secretary of State, must, inspect any LEA under s 38. The inspection must consist of:

> 'a review of the way in which the authority are performing any function of theirs (of whatever nature) which relates to the provision of education –
> (a)   for persons of compulsory school age (whether at school or otherwise), or
> (b)   for persons of any age above or below that age who are registered as pupils at schools maintained by the authority.'[8]

12.53 Section 39(1) of the EA 1997 provides for the making of a written report 'on the matters reviewed in the course of the inspection' by the inspector. The inspector

---

1   SSFA 1998, s 127(6); the code for England does not appear to give guidance as to the exercise by a LEA of their functions under s 25, but the code for Wales does so in paras 105–113 of Part 2. See paras **2.31–2.32** concerning s 127.
2   See SSFA 1998, Sch 26, paras 1, 6(1)(a) and 6(2). See para **2.72** concerning s 120(2)(a) of the SSFA 1998.
3   As to which, see paras **12.43–12.45**.
4   EA 2002, Sch 14, para 1.
5   See SSFA 1998, Sch 26, para 10(1A), as inserted by EA 2002, Sch 14, para 5.
6   Ibid, Sch 26, para 13. See para **12.32** concerning s 42A.
7   The Chief Inspector is defined by s 38(7) for this purpose, and it is in relation to an LEA in England, Her Majesty's Chief Inspector of Schools in England, and in relation to an LEA in Wales, Her Majesty's Chief Inspector of Education and Training in Wales.
8   EA 1997, s 38(2). There are mechanical and consequential provisions in s 38(3)–(6).

must send copies of the report to the Secretary of State and any LEA to which the inspection relates.[1] The LEA must then prepare 'a written statement of the action which they propose to take in the light of the report and the period within which they propose to take it'.[2] The LEA are required by s 39(3) and regulations made under that subsection to publish that report and statement within the period and in the manner provided for by those regulations. The current regulations are the Education (Publication of Local Education Authority Inspection Reports) Regulations 1998.[3] The Chief Inspector is empowered to publish the report made under s 39(1), and may do so by electronic means under s 42A of the SIA 1996.[4] Section 42A protects the report from an action in defamation unless it is published with malice.[5]

12.54 Section 40(1) of the EA 1997 (as substituted by s 180 of the EA 2002) confers rights of (a) entry to the premises of the LEA to which the inspection relates, and (b) inspection, of the same sort as those which apply in relation to school inspections. Section 40 also applies s 42 of the SIA 1996 to the inspection.[6] Without prejudice to this, an LEA which is being inspected under s 38 must give the inspector carrying out the inspection, and any person assisting him, 'all assistance in connection with the exercise of his functions which they are reasonably able to give'.[7] These provisions are applied also to the governing bodies of schools maintained by the LEA which is being inspected, and both the LEA and the governing body are obliged to 'secure that all such assistance is also given by persons who work at the school'.[8] However, ss 38–41 of the EA 1997 provide for no offence equivalent to that in (for example) s 2(9) of the SIA 1996.[9]

12.55 The Chief Inspector may call upon the Audit Commission to assist with any inspection under s 38 of the EA 1997, but if he does so then he must pay the full cost to the Commission of providing such assistance.[10]

INSPECTIONS OF TEACHER TRAINING INSTITUTIONS

12.56 Under s 18A of the EA 1994, as inserted by s 20 of the THEA 1998, the Chief Inspector (or any person authorised to act on his behalf under para 5(1) or (2) of Sch 1 to the SIA 1996[11]) may inspect and report upon (a) any initial training of teachers, or of specialist teaching assistants, for schools, and (b) any in-service training[12] of such teachers or assistants, where, in both cases, such training is provided

---

[1]   EA 1997, s 39(1).
[2]   Ibid, s 39(2).
[3]   SI 1998/880.
[4]   EA 1997, s 39(4); see para **12.32** concerning s 42A.
[5]   SIA 1996, s 42A(3).
[6]   See para **12.8** regarding the equivalent provisions relating to school inspections and s 42 of the SIA 1996.
[7]   EA 1997, s 40(5)(a).
[8]   Ibid, s 40(5)(b).
[9]   As to which, see para **12.10**.
[10] EA 1997, s 41(1) and (6). The other provisions of s 41 are consequential.
[11] EA 1994, s 18A(11). See para **12.12** concerning para 5 of Sch 1 to the SIA 1996.
[12] 'In-service training' includes any training provided to a teacher serving an induction period within the meaning of s 19 of the THEA 1998 (as to which, see paras **15.19** et seq): EA 1994, s 18A(10)(c).

by any eligible institution within the meaning of the EA 1994 or any other institution, body or person designated by the Secretary of State as being in receipt of public funding in respect of the provision of either of these sorts of training.[1] However, such an inspection may not be made in relation to any course which consists of instruction given wholly or mainly for purposes other than training of the sorts referred to in the first sentence of this paragraph.[2]

12.57 Section 42A(2)–(4) of the SIA 1996[3] apply to inspections under s 18A of the 1994 Act,[4] as does s 42 of that Act (which concerns the inspection of computer records).[5] The Chief Inspector must normally give at least 8 weeks' notice of his intention to carry out an inspection under s 18A(1).[6]

---

[1]   EA 1994, s 18A(1) and (10)(b). See para **15.6** as to what is an eligible institution for the purposes of the EA 1994.
[2]   Ibid, s 18A(9).
[3]   See para **12.32** regarding s 42A.
[4]   EA 1994, s 18A(4).
[5]   Ibid, s 18A(5).
[6]   See ibid, s 18A(7) and (8).

Chapter 13

INDEPENDENT SCHOOLS

WHAT IS AN INDEPENDENT SCHOOL?

13.1   An independent school is defined by s 463 of the EA 1996 as substituted by s 172 of the EA 2002. It is a school at which full-time education is provided for either (a) five or more pupils of compulsory school age, or (b) at least one pupil of that age for whom a statement is maintained under s 324 of the EA 1996 or who is looked after by a local authority (within the meaning of s 22 of the Children Act 1989) but which is neither (1) maintained by an LEA, nor (2) a non-maintained special school.[1] It is immaterial if full-time education is also provided at the school for pupils under or over compulsory school age.[2]

13.2   Independent schools can be conducted in a number of different ways. For example, an independent school may be conducted by a company established under the Companies Acts, or by one or more natural persons. Where the purposes of the body which conducts the school are exclusively charitable, there will be a charity in existence. The precise nature of the charity may be slightly difficult to discern, bearing in mind that the institution may have to be regarded at least for some purposes as distinct from the body which conducts it,[3] but that is not a matter which needs to be considered here. Those matters which need to be considered here are the statutory provisions which apply to independent schools and the relationships (1) between (a) a pupil at an independent school, and (b) the body which conducts it (except in so far as that relationship is considered in Chapter 14), and (2) between (a) the pupil's parent and (b) such body. Those matters are accordingly the subject of this chapter. In what follows, the body responsible for conducting an independent school is described as the 'proprietor' of the school, consistently with the definition of the word 'proprietor' in s 579(1) of the EA 1996, where the word is defined (so far as relevant) to mean in relation to a school:

> 'the person or body of persons responsible for the management of the school.'

STATUTORY REGULATION OF INDEPENDENT SCHOOLS

13.3   The main statutory provisions concerning independent schools as such are those in the EA 2002 which relate to the requirement for such a school to be registered in the register kept, under s 158 of that Act, in relation to England by the

---

[1]   EA 1996, s 463(1).
[2]   Ibid, s 463(2).
[3]   See, for example, paras **2.163–2.165**.

Secretary of State or in relation to Wales by the National Assembly for Wales (referred to below as 'the relevant register').

13.4   There are also certain provisions in the Children Act 1989 (CA 1989) which apply where the school provides accommodation for pupils. Furthermore, some provisions of the EA 1996 other than those relating to registration in the relevant register apply not only to maintained schools but also to independent schools.

The requirement to register an independent school; offence of conducting an unregistered school

13.5   A person who conducts an independent school which is not registered in the relevant register commits an offence, contrary to s 159(1) of the EA 2002. The maximum penalty for the offence is a fine at level 5 on the standard scale and a prison sentence of 6 months.[1] A prosecution for the offence may be instituted only by the registration authority,[2] which is the Secretary of State in relation to England and the National Assembly for Wales in relation to Wales.[3]

13.6   Where the Chief Inspector (in relation to a school in England this is Her Majesty's Chief Inspector of Schools in England, and in relation to a school in Wales it is Her Majesty's Chief Inspector of Education and Training in Wales[4]) has reasonable cause to believe that the offence in s 159(1) is being committed on any premises, he may at any reasonable time (a) enter and inspect the premises, and (b) inspect and take copies of any records or other documents which he has reasonable cause to believe may be required for the purposes of proceedings in relation to the offence.[5] It is an offence wilfully to obstruct the Chief Inspector when he is exercising this power,[6] the maximum penalty for which is a fine not exceeding level 4 on the standard scale.[7]

Applications for registration

13.7   An application for registration in the English register must be in the form, and contain the information, required by reg 5 of, and Part 2 of the Schedule to, the Education (Provision of Information by Independent Schools) (England) Regulations 2003.[8] In relation to a school in Wales, the form and information are as required by reg 3 of, and Part 2 of the Schedule to, the Education (Provision of Information by Independent Schools) (Wales) Regulations 2003.[9]

---

[1]   EA 2002, s 159(2). Level 5 is currently £5,000.

[2]   Ibid, s 159(3).

[3]   See ibid, s 171.

[4]   Ibid.

[5]   Ibid, s 159(4). Section 42 of the SIA 1996, relating to computer records, applies in relation to the inspection of such records or other documents: EA 2002, s 159(5).

[6]   Ibid, s 159(6).

[7]   Ibid, s 159(7). Level 4 is currently £2,500.

[8]   SI 2003/1934.

[9]   SI 2003/3230.

13.8   The registration authority (in England this is the Secretary of State, and in Wales this is the National Assembly[1]) must notify the Chief Inspector of any such application,[2] and the Chief Inspector must then inspect the school and report to the Secretary of State on the extent to which the independent school standards (within the meaning of s 157 of the EA 2002, concerning which, see para **13.9**) are, and are likely to continue to be met, in relation to the school.[3] The Secretary of State must then determine in the light of (a) that report 'and (b) any other evidence relating to the independent school standards, ... whether those standards are met, and are likely to continue to be met, in relation to the school'.[4] If the Secretary of State decides that those standards are met, and are likely to continue to be met, then he must enter the name and address of the school in the register,[5] together with the name of the proprietor and the information supplied pursuant to s 160(2)(a)–(e).[6] Any determination under s 161(1) must be notified to the proprietor of the school.[7]

Independent school standards

13.9   Section 157 of the EA 2002 empowers the making of regulations prescribing standards about a number of matters relating to independent schools. As indicated in para **13.8**, these standards are relevant to an application for the registration of an independent school in the relevant register. They are also applied when an independent school is inspected under s 163 of the EA 2002 (concerning which, see para **13.12**). The standards ('the independent school standards') relate to (1) the quality of the education provided to the pupils at the school, (2) the spiritual, moral, social and cultural development of such pupils, (3) the welfare, health and safety of such pupils, (4) the suitability of the proprietor and staff of the school, (5) the premises of, and accommodation at, the school, (6) the provision of information by the school; and (7) the manner in which the school handles complaints. The regulations which currently prescribe these standards are the Education (Independent School Standards) (England) Regulations 2003[8] and the Independent School Standards (Wales) Regulations 2003.[9] The standards are set out in the Schedule to both of those regulations. There is a considerable amount of detail in the standards.

Conditions for remaining in the register

13.10   If the information contained in the register in relation to an independent school changes, that change must be approved either by the registration authority under s 162 or, on appeal, under s 167 of the EA 2002.[10] If it is not so approved, the registration authority may remove the school from the register.[11] An application for approval under s 162 must be made in writing and, in the case of approval of a change

---

1   EA 2002, s 171.
2   Ibid, s 160(3).
3   Ibid, s 160(4).
4   Ibid, s 161(1).
5   Ibid, s 161(3).
6   Ibid, s 161(4). That information is prescribed by the regulations referred to in the preceding paragraph.
7   Ibid, s 161(2).
8   SI 2003/1910.
9   SI 2003/3234.
10   See para **13.19** concerning appeals under EA 2002, s 167.
11   EA 2002, s 162(1).

of proprietor of the school, must be made by the 'proposed new proprietor'.[1] The registration authority may then require the Chief Inspector to inspect the school and report to the authority 'on the extent to which, if the change is made, any [of the independent school standards] is likely to continue to be met in relation to the school'.[2] If the registration authority is satisfied, taking into account this report and 'any other evidence relating to the independent school standards', that those standards 'will continue to be met in relation to the school', then it must approve the change.[3] If, however, it is not so satisfied, then it must refuse to approve it.[4]

Removal from the register where a person who is barred from working with children carries out in relation to the school work to which section 142 of the Education Act 2002 applies

13.11   If the registration authority is satisfied that any person who is the subject of a barring direction under s 142 of the EA 2002[5] or is subject to an order, made under s 28 or s 29 of the Criminal Justice and Court Services Act 2000, disqualifying him from working with children, 'carries out [in relation to the school] any work to which section 142 applies', the authority may remove the school from the register.[6] There is no right of appeal against such a removal, but it will of course be subject to the principles of public law (including the requirement of fairness), and will therefore potentially be subject to a judicial review.

Power of registration authority at any time to require an inspection of an independent school

13.12   The registration authority may at any time require the Chief Inspector to inspect any registered independent school, or to secure its inspection by one or more registered inspectors.[7] Alternatively, the registration authority may arrange for the inspection of the school by a body approved by the registration authority for the purpose.[8] The inspection and report must relate to the independent school standards so far as relevant.[9] The report is privileged for the purposes of the law of defamation unless the publication is shown to be made with malice.[10] The person conducting the inspection, any person assisting him, and any person monitoring the inspection[11] has at all reasonable times a right of entry to the premises of the school and a right to inspect and take copies of any records or other documents (including records or other documents kept on computer[12]) containing information relating to the school which

---

1   EA 2002, s 162(3).
2   Ibid, s 162(4) and (5).
3   Ibid, s 162(6) and (7).
4   Ibid.
5   See paras **15.36** et seq concerning such a direction.
6   EA 2002, s 169.
7   Ibid, s 163(1)(a).
8   Ibid, s 163(1)(b).
9   See ibid, s 163(2) and (3). See in relation to England, SI 2003/1926 and in relation to Wales SI 2003/3232 for the manner in which an inspection report must be published.
10   Ibid, s 163(4). This is without prejudice to any privilege which would in any event have subsisted: ibid.
11   For the manner in which a person may come to assist or monitor the inspection, see ibid, s 164(2)–(4).
12   See EA 2002, s 164(6), applying s 42 of the SIA 1996.

are required for the purposes of the inspection.[1] It is an offence wilfully to obstruct a person 'in the exercise of his functions in relation to the inspection'.[2]

13.13 The proprietor of an independent school must pay the Chief Inspector a fee for an inspection carried out under s 163(1)(a).[3] The fee is currently £40 per pupil if the number of pupils is less than 50, and increases up to a maximum of £10,000.[4] If the proprietor fails to pay the fee then the registration authority can remove the school from the register.[5] The fee is paid into the Consolidated Fund.[6]

Effect of a failure to meet the independent school standards

13.14 If the registration authority is, taking into account (a) a report made under s 163, or (b) any other evidence in respect of a registered school, satisfied that any one or more of the independent school standards is not or are not being met in relation to the school, then it must take action of two possible sorts. If it considers that there is a risk of serious harm to the welfare of pupils at the school, the authority may determine that the school is to be removed from the register 'on such date after the appeal period as the authority may determine'.[7] The appeal period for this and other purposes of ss 157–171 of the EA 2002 is the period within which an appeal can be made under s 166 (concerning which, see para **13.19**).[8] If an appeal is made under s 166(1)(b) against this determination, the appellate tribunal may, if it considers that there is a risk of serious harm occurring to the welfare of pupils before the determination of the appeal, by order provide that the school is to be regarded as not registered for the purposes of s 159 until the tribunal either determines the appeal under s 167 or revokes the order before so determining the appeal.[9]

13.15 If the registration authority does not determine that the school is to be regarded as not registered for the purposes of s 159 for such period, then it must serve notice on the school's proprietor identifying the standard or standards in question and requiring the proprietor to submit an action plan to the authority by a time specified by the authority (either in the notice or after the service of the notice).[10] If no such plan is served, or such a plan is served but the registration authority rejects it, the authority may determine that the school is to be removed from the register on a date (after the end of the appeal period) determined by the authority, or make an order under s 165(8) requiring the proprietor to (1) cease using any part of the school premises for all purposes specified in the order, and/or (2) close any part of the school's operation; and/or (3) cease to admit new pupils, or new pupils of a

---

[1]   EA 2002, s 164(5).

[2]   Ibid, s 164(7); the maximum penalty for the offence is a fine at level 4 on the standard scale (which is currently £2,500): s 164(8).

[3]   Ibid, s 164(9) and the Education (Independent School Inspection Fees and Publication) (England) Regulations 2003, SI 2003/1926.

[4]   See the Schedule to SI 2003/1926.

[5]   EA 2002, s 164(10).

[6]   Ibid, s 164(11).

[7]   Ibid, s 165(1) and (2).

[8]   Ibid, s 165(13).

[9]   Ibid, s 166(5).

[10]   Ibid, s 165(3). An action plan must specify the steps which will be taken to meet the standard or standards, and the time by which each step will be taken: s 165(4).

description specified in the order.[1] A failure to comply with such an order constitutes an offence the maximum penalty for which is a term of imprisonment of 6 months and a fine at level 5 on the standard scale.[2] Furthermore, if the order is not complied with, the registration authority may decide that the school is to be removed from the register on such date after the ending of the appeal period as the authority determines.[3] However, the proprietor may appeal against the order under s 166(1)(c), and if that occurs then the order has no effect until the appeal is either determined under s 167 or withdrawn or otherwise disposed of.[4]

13.16   If an action plan submitted in accordance with s 165(3) is not rejected, then it must be approved, with or without modifications.[5] If any step which is set out in the plan is not taken by the date specified in the plan, the registration authority may substitute a later date for the taking of the step.[6] Alternatively, the authority can either make an order under s 165(8) as described in para **13.15**, or determine that the school is to be removed from the register on such date after the ending of the appeal period as the authority determines.[7]

13.17   If the proprietor of a registered school appeals under s 166 against any decision under s 165 to remove the school from the register, the registration authority may not remove the school from the register until the appeal has been withdrawn or otherwise disposed of before it is determined under s 167 (in which case the authority may remove the school from the register on such date as it may determine after the end of the appeal period), or in accordance with s 167 (which relates to the determination of appeals under s 166: see para **13.20**).[8]

13.18   If the proprietor of an independent school requests the revocation or variation by the registration authority of an order under s 165(8), the authority must comply with the request 'if it is satisfied that it is appropriate to do so because of any change of circumstance', but otherwise it must refuse to grant the request.[9] Such revocation or variation takes effect as from the date of its notification to the proprietor.[10]

Appeals against adverse determinations by the registration authority

13.19   The proprietor of a registered school may appeal to the 'tribunal established under section 9 of the Protection of Children Act 1999' (known, and referred to below, as the Care Standards Tribunal) against (1) a refusal to approve a material change, (2) a determination under s 165 to remove the school from the register, (3) an

---

[1]   EA 2002, s 165(6) and (8). An order made under s 165(8) is not made by statutory instrument: s 210(2).
[2]   Ibid, s 165(9)(a). Level 5 is currently £5,000.
[3]   Ibid, s 165(9)(b).
[4]   Ibid, s 166(4).
[5]   Ibid, s 165(5). The word 'may' is used, but it is clear that there are only two options open to the registration authority.
[6]   Ibid, s 165(7)(a). This may occur more than once: see the opening words of s 165(7).
[7]   Ibid, s 165(7)(b) and (c).
[8]   Ibid, s 166(3).
[9]   Ibid, s 165(10).
[10] Ibid, s 165(11).

order under s 165(8) requiring the taking of action specified in the order, or (4) a refusal under s 165(10) to vary or revoke such an order.[1] Such an appeal must be made within 28 days of the day on which notice of the relevant decision was served on the proprietor.[2]

13.20 The powers of the Care Standards Tribunal are set out in s 167, and they are largely consequential. However, if the tribunal revokes (under s 167(3)(b)) a determination made by the registration authority under s 165 that a school should be removed from the register, the tribunal may nevertheless order the proprietor to take one or more of the kinds of action set out in s 167(5) (which are the same as those in s 165(8), as to which see para **13.15**). A failure to comply with such an order constitutes an offence, the maximum penalty for which is a term of imprisonment of 6 months and a fine at level 5 on the standard scale.[3] In addition, if a proprietor fails to comply with such an order, the Care Standards Tribunal may, on the application of the registration authority, authorise the authority to remove the school from the register on a date determined by the tribunal.[4]

Requirement to supply information to the registration authority

13.21 Section 168(1) of the EA 2002 empowers the making of regulations requiring the proprietor of a registered school to provide the registration authority 'when the authority so requests' with 'such particulars relating to the school as may be prescribed'. The regulations prescribing this information are the Education (Provision of Information by Independent Schools) (England) Regulations 2003[5] and the Education (Provision of Information by Independent Schools) (Wales) Regulations 2003.[6] The former regulations require, by reg 8(1),[7] the supply of the facts of a case where the proprietor of the school has ceased to use a person's services on 'a ground – (i) that the person is unsuitable to work with children; (ii) relating to the person's misconduct; or (iii) relating to the person's health where a relevant issue is raised'.[8] In addition, reg 8(2) requires the proprietor to provide 'such further information as may be requested by the Secretary of State which he considers relevant to the exercise of his functions under section 142 of the 2002 Act'. The regulations relating to Wales are both more simple and (given the terms of s 168) appropriate in this respect, requiring merely that the proprietor, within 15 days of a request, provides the National Assembly with 'such information as may be requested by it which it

---

[1]   EA 2002, s 166(1).

[2]   Ibid, s 166(2). For the procedure which must be followed in relation to such an appeal, see the Protection of Children and Vulnerable Adults and Care Standards Tribunal Regulations 2002, SI 2001/816, as amended by SI 2003/626, SI 2003/1060 and SI 2003/2043.

[3]   Ibid, s 167(9)(a). Level 5 is currently £5,000.

[4]   Ibid, s 167(9)(b).

[5]   SI 2003/1934, regs 6, 7 and 8, although none of those regulations refer to a request made by the Secretary of State.

[6]   SI 2003/3230.

[7]   The same requirement is contained reg 4 of the Education (Prohibition from Teaching or Working with Children) Regulations 2003, SI 2003/1184 (see para **12.48**), which is empowered by s 142 of the EA 2002.

[8]   A 'relevant issue' for this purpose is 'one which arises where the circumstances of the case, including occasions of conduct other than that in question, are such as to raise an issue concerning the safety and welfare of children': reg 8(3).

considers is relevant to the exercise of its functions or the Secretary of State's functions under section 142 of the 2002 Act, and which has not already been provided under the Education (Supply of Information) (Wales) Regulations 2003[1]'.[2]

13.22 A failure to comply with any of the requirements imposed by reg 6, 7 or 8 of the Education (Provision of Information by Independent Schools) (England) Regulations 2003 in relation to the provision of information by the Secretary of State is an offence.[3] Such a failure also empowers the Secretary of State to remove from the register the school in respect of which the requirement was not complied with.[4] The Education (Provision of Information by Independent Schools) (Wales) Regulations 2003 make equivalent provision for Wales.[5]

The Children Act 1989

13.23 There are three sets of provisions of the CA 1989 which affect independent schools. These are s 63 and its related provisions, s 80, and s 87 and its related provisions. Section 87 is of general application, whereas ss 63 and 80 are of more limited application. Section 87 is accordingly considered first.

Duty to safeguard and promote welfare of child provided with accommodation

13.24 It is the duty of the proprietor of an independent school (and, in fact, the governing body of an institution in the further education sector[6] and the governing body of any other school) which provides accommodation for any child and any person who is not the proprietor but is responsible for conducting it to 'safeguard and promote the child's welfare'.[7] The duty to see so far as is reasonably practicable that this duty is complied with is placed by s 87(3) of the CA 1989 on the Care Standards Commission in relation to England and the National Assembly for Wales in relation to Wales. The Commission or (as the case may be) the Assembly may authorise any person to go onto the premises of a relevant school or college at any reasonable time, for the purpose of enabling the Commission or (as the case may be) the Assembly to see whether the welfare of a child who is accommodated by the school or college is adequately safeguarded and promoted while he is so accommodated.[8] The person so entering may inspect the premises, children and records in the manner authorised by s 87(6) and (8) of the CA 1989 and the National Care Standards Commission (Inspection of Schools and Colleges) Regulations 2002[9] or (as the case may be) the

---

[1]   SI 2003/542.

[2]   SI 2003/3230, reg 4.

[3]   SI 2003/1934, reg 10, made under EA 2002, s 168(2)(c). The maximum penalty is a fine at level 5 of the standard scale, which is currently £5,000: ibid.

[4]   SI 2003/1934, reg 9, made under EA 2002, s 168(2)(b).

[5]   See SI 2003/3230, regs 7 and 8.

[6]   This means a further education institution which is conducted by a further education corporation or an institution designated under s 28 of the FHEA 1992: see CA 1989, s 87(10) and FHEA 1992, s 91(3).

[7]   CA 1989, s 87(1), (10), (11) and (12), as amended by the Care Standards Act 2000.

[8]   CA 1989, s 87(5), as substituted by the Care Standards Act 2000.

[9]   SI 2002/552. One salient effect of those regulations is that a physical inspection of a relevant child may be carried out only by a registered medical practitioner or registered nurse who is authorised by the National Care Standards Commission for the purpose, and only if: (1) that person has reasonable cause

Inspection of Boarding Schools and Colleges (Powers and Fees) (Wales) Regulations 2002.[1] Any person exercising this power must, if asked to do so, produce some duly authenticated document showing his authority to do so.[2] Any person who intentionally obstructs another in the exercise of any power conferred by s 87 or the relevant regulations is guilty of an offence the maximum penalty for which is a fine at level 3 on the standard scale.[3] If the Commission 'are of the opinion that there has been a failure to comply with subsection (1) in relation to a child provided with accommodation by a school or college', they must (a) in the case of an independent school or a college, notify the Secretary of State, (b) in the case of a maintained special school, notify the LEA by which it is maintained, and (c) in the case of a school other than an independent school or a special school, notify the LEA for the area in which the school is situated.[4] If the National Assembly for Wales is of such opinion, in the case of a special school it must notify the LEA by which the school is maintained, and in the case of a school other than an independent school or a special school, it must notify the LEA for the area in which the school is situated.[5]

13.25 The Secretary of State may, however, appoint a person to be an inspector in place of the National Care Standards Commission or the National Assembly for Wales in the circumstances provided for in s 87A of the CA 1989, which was substituted by the Care Standards Act 2000. The circumstances are that (1) that person ('the inspector') already acts as an inspector for other purposes in relation to schools or colleges to which s 87(1) applies,[6] (2) the Secretary of State is satisfied that the inspector is an appropriate person to determine whether the welfare of children provided with accommodation by such schools or colleges is adequately safeguarded and promoted while they are accommodated by them,[7] (3) the inspector enters into an agreement with the proprietor of the school (or, as the case may be, the governing body of the college) that the inspector is to have in relation to the school (or college) the function in s 87(1),[8] and (4) the inspector notifies the National Care Standards Commission or (as the case may be) the National Assembly for Wales in writing that the agreement has come into effect.[9] The Secretary of State may, under s 87B of the CA 1989, impose duties on an inspector appointed under s 87A.

13.26 The Secretary of State may, under s 87C(1) of the CA 1989, make and publish statements of national minimum standards for safeguarding and promoting the welfare of children for whom accommodation is provided in a school or college.

---

to believe that the child's welfare is not being adequately safeguarded or promoted by the relevant person, and (2) either the child consents to the examination or the child is incapable of giving his consent: see regs 2(1) and 5(2). The examination must take place in private: reg 5(3).
[1] SI 2002/3161.
[2] CA 1989, s 87(7).
[3] Ibid, s 87(9). Level 3 is currently £1,000.
[4] Ibid, s 87(4) as substituted.
[5] Ibid, s 87(4A).
[6] Ibid, s 87A(1)(a).
[7] Ibid, s 87A(1)(b) and (4)(b).
[8] Ibid, s 87A(2)(a) and (b).
[9] Ibid, s 87A(2)(c).

13.27 Regulations made under s 87D of the CA 1989 may require the proprietor of an independent school, or the governing body of a further education college, to pay an annual fee in respect of inspections under s 87(3). The current regulations are the Inspection of Boarding Schools and Colleges (Powers and Fees) (Wales) Regulations 2002,[1] and the National Care Standards Commission (Fees and Frequency of Inspections) Regulations 2003.[2]

Inspection, by persons authorised by the Secretary of State, of schools and colleges providing accommodation for children

13.28 Section 80 of the CA 1989 enables the Secretary of State to cause a number of places to be inspected from time to time. Included in these is a 'school or college providing accommodation for any child'.[3] Certain individuals or bodies may also be required by the Secretary of State to furnish information and to allow the inspection of records, under s 80(4). The proprietor of an independent school is one such individual or body.[4] The inspection may involve (among other things) the inspection of the children at the school.[5] Access must be permitted in certain circumstances by the proprietor of the school,[6] and any person who intentionally obstructs another in the exercise of that power of entry is guilty of an offence.[7]

Section 537A of the Education Act 1996

13.29 Section 537A of the EA 1996 enables the Secretary of State by regulations to require independent schools as well as maintained schools to provide information regarding pupils' performance.[8]

RELATIONSHIPS BETWEEN (1) A PUPIL AT AN INDEPENDENT SCHOOL AND THE BODY WHICH CONDUCTS IT AND (2) THE PUPIL'S PARENT AND THAT BODY

Relationship between pupil and independent school

13.30 A pupil at an independent school is in some respects in no different a position so far as relevant from a pupil at a maintained (or state) school. This is because a pupil at an independent school, just as much as a pupil at a state school, is owed a duty in the law of negligence (both in relation to physical safety and in relation to the provision of education), and has rights in the law of trespass to the person in relation

---

[1]   SI 2002/3161, in part amending the Registration of Social Care and Independent Healthcare (Fees) (Wales) Regulations 2002, SI 2002/921.
[2]   SI 2003/753, reg 5.
[3]   CA 1989, s 80(1)(l), as amended by s 109 of the Care Standards Act 2000.
[4]   Ibid, s 80(5)(d).
[5]   See ibid, s 80(6).
[6]   See ibid, s 80(8).
[7]   Ibid, s 80(10). The maximum penalty is a fine on level 3 of the standard scale (ibid), which is currently £1,000.
[8]   See further, para **7.182**.

to physical contact (including in relation to corporal punishment).[1] The pupil will not, however, have rights in public law as against the school, merely because the school is subject to the registration regime under the EA 2002 described above.[2] It is of note that it was, however, held by Dyson J in *R v Cobham Hall School, ex parte S*[3] that where a pupil is attending an independent school only because of the assisted places scheme empowered by ss 479–481 of the EA 1996 (which have now been repealed, although at present some pupils continue to receive assistance under those sections), the pupil may in appropriate circumstances judicially review a decision to exclude him. This was on the basis that the exclusion in that case was not an exclusion of the sort which normally occurs in an independent school; rather, the head teacher had withdrawn and reallocated the assisted place. Dyson J so ruled despite the fact that it was only the independent school in question which had what one might refer to as direct public law rights. Such rights were exercisable primarily by the school against the Secretary of State, since the latter assisted the pupil by reimbursing the school in respect of the relevant fees.[4] Dyson J followed his own earlier decision in *R v Governors of Haberdashers' Aske's Hatcham College Trust, ex parte T*,[5] where he held that a decision of a city technology college was potentially judicially reviewable. That case concerned a quite different situation, because the city technology college owed its existence to the statutory provisions governing such colleges, whereas the independent school in *ex parte S* came into existence independently of any statutory provision concerning education. The school may have owed its continuing existence to the receipt of fees under the assisted places scheme, but that is irrelevant. Nevertheless, the reasoning of Dyson J in *ex parte S* was persuasive on the facts. It was, however, not applied in relation to a special school approved under s 342 of the EA 1996.[6]

13.31 In any event, although a pupil will usually be at a school only because of a contract between his parents and the school, the pupil will normally have rights in the law of contract as against the school only if the Contracts (Rights of Third Parties) Act 1999 can be relied upon by the pupil.[7] The provision of that Act which is most likely to be relied upon by an independent school is s 1(2), which has the effect that a third party such as a pupil at an independent school could not rely upon the contract between his parent(s) and the proprietor of the school 'if on a proper construction of the contract it appears that the parties did not intend the term to be enforceable by the third party'. However, if a pupil is benefiting from a means-tested scholarship or is in any other way being treated as a beneficiary of any charitable obligation on the part of the school, then he will be likely to be in a position to challenge acts of the body

---

1   See para **10.19**. An appeal to the House of Lords against the decision of the Court of Appeal in *R (Williamson) v Secretary of State* [2002] EWCA Civ 1926, [2003] QB 1300 is currently pending. In that case, there was a challenge to the ban on corporal punishment in independent schools imposed by s 548 of the EA 1996 on the basis that it was incompatible with the European Convention on Human Rights.
2   *R v Fernhill Manor School, ex parte A* [1993] 1 FLR 620, [1994] ELR 67.
3   [1998] ELR 389; [1998] EdCR 79.
4   See EA 1996, s 480(1)(c) as it then stood and the Education (Assisted Places) Regulations 1997, SI 1997/1968.
5   [1995] ELR 350.
6   See *R v Muntham House School, ex parte R* [2000] ELR 287. See para **6.181** concerning s 342.
7   See *Chitty on Contracts* (Sweet & Maxwell, 28th edn, 1999) ('*Chitty*') at paras 19.41 et seq and *R v Fernhill Manor School, ex parte A* [1994] ELR 67 at 77G–78C and 80A–B.

responsible for conducting the school if they contravene the terms of the instrument under which the charitable obligation is owed.[1]

Relationship between parent and independent school

13.32 The relationship between a parent of a pupil at an independent school and the body responsible for conducting the school will usually be subject primarily to the law of contract. In addition, however, the parent will in many situations have the right to consent to conduct which would in the absence of consent be unlawful in the law of trespass (whether to the person or chattels) or false imprisonment. In the latter regard, the position of the parent will be no different from that of a parent of a minor at a state school, and since that position is described in Chapter 14, no more will be said about it here.

Rights in the law of contract

13.33 The rights of a parent in the law of contract as against an independent school are typical of those of a party who contracts for the benefit of a person who is not a party to the contract. In outline, the parent will be able only to (a) seek a declaration of legal rights, and (b) claim damages in respect of alternative provision which he reasonably arranges.[2] Specific performance will probably not be available, because of the need to supervise the performance constantly,[3] and, possibly, because the contract will involve personal service.[4] However, given that a maintained school can be ordered to take a wrongly excluded pupil back, it seems that the latter objection should not necessarily prevail.[5]

13.34 As far as the terms of the contract are concerned, the case of *Hutt v The Governors of Haileybury College*[6] is instructive. There, the jury determined that expulsion could take place if the college acted upon reasonable grounds and honestly – for 'reasonable cause'. The case of *R v Fernhill Manor School, ex parte A*[7] is also instructive. There, it was stated that the:

> 'relevant principles of fair play ... apply ... just as much to the relationship between a schoolgirl of 16 and her school as they do to an undergraduate and his university or a trade unionist and his trade union.'[8]

1 See, for example, *Tudor on Charities* (Sweet & Maxwell, 9th edn, 2003), at paras 10.30–10.32. See further, para **13.36**.
2 See, for example, *Chitty*, at paras 19.42, 19.45 and 19.50.
3 See *Chitty*, at para 28.23.
4 See *Chitty*, at para 27.18. That was the reason for the refusal of an application for an injunction in *R v Incorporated Froebel Institute, ex parte L* [1999] ELR 488, and it formed part of the reasoning in *Ross v Stanbridge Earls School* [2002] EWHC 2255 (QB), [2003] ELR 400.
5 Cf *Chitty*, at para 28.20.
6 (1888) 4 TLR 623.
7 [1993] 1 FLR 620, [1994] ELR 67.
8 [1994] ELR 79H–80A. This statement of principle was approved and adopted by Tucker J in *R v Incorporated Froebel Institute, ex parte L* [1999] ELR 488 at 490D. As for the principles of fair play as they apply for example to a university student, see the cases cited in paras **12.76** et seq.

13.35 In *Price v Dennis*,[1] which was decided in 1988 but reported only in 1999, the Court of Appeal considered the terms of the contract between a parent and an independent school. The court there held that there is a duty on the proprietor of an independent school to take reasonable steps to retain the confidence of parents who themselves act reasonably.[2] The court also held that the broad terms of the prospectus, but not each detail in it, were incorporated into the contract between the parents and the proprietor. Accordingly, the prospectus contained the terms of the contract as to (a) the type of school, (b) the nature of the education, (c) the nature of the facilities, and (d) broadly the standard of education which the proprietor was obliged to provide.[3] Furthermore, it was held that it was an implied term of the contract that the proprietor would conduct the school in a fit, proper and responsible manner.[4]

Challenging decisions of an independent school which is a charity

13.36 In addition to claiming against a school in the law of contract, the parent of a child who is a pupil at an independent school which is a charity will (where appropriate) be able to challenge decisions of the trustees of the charity (that is the body of persons responsible for conducting the charity) in relation to the administration of the charity. This will be so even if the parents merely pay fees to the school for the education of their child, and do not benefit directly in any way from the fact that the school is a charity.[5] However, where the charity is subject to the jurisdiction of a visitor, then the challenge will have to be made by way of a complaint to the visitor, and not to the court.[6]

DESIGNATION OF INDEPENDENT SCHOOLS AS HAVING A RELIGIOUS CHARACTER

13.37 The Employment Equality (Religion or Belief) Regulations 2003[7] prohibit discrimination against persons on the ground of their religion or belief. In order to permit independent schools which have a religious character nevertheless so to discriminate, the Independent Schools (Employment of Teachers in Schools with a Religious Character) Regulations 2003[8] inserted new ss 124A and 124B into the SSFA 1998. Section 124A permits the giving of preference in connection with the appointment, promotion or remuneration of teachers at an independent school with a religious character, to persons (a) whose religious opinions are in accordance with the tenets of the religion or religious denomination specified in relation to the school

---

[1]   [1999] EdCR 747.

[2]   Ibid, at 761F–G.

[3]   Ibid, at 759C.

[4]   Ibid, at 759E–G.

[5]   *Gunning v Buckfast Abbey Trustees*, (1994) *The Times*, June 9. The consent of the Charity Commissioners would normally be required under s 33 of the Charities Act 1993 to an action for breach of trust of the sort envisaged.

[6]   *Thomas v University of Bradford* [1987] AC 795. See further, paras **17.49** et seq concerning the visitatorial jurisdiction in relation to higher education institutions, albeit that the abolition of that jurisdiction in relation to student complaints is currently proposed in the Higher Education Bill.

[7]   SI 2003/1660.

[8]   SI 2003/2037.

under s 124B(2), (b) who attend religious worship in accordance with those tenets, or (c) who give, or are willing to give, religious education at the school in accordance with those tenets. Section 124B applies s 69(3) and (5) of the SSFA 1998 to independent schools, so that such schools can be designated as having a religious character under s 69. Nine orders have so far been made under s 69 as amended by s 124B.[1]

---

[1]   These were the Religious Character of Schools (Designation Procedure) (Independent Schools) (England) Regulations 2003, SI 2003/2314 as amended by SI 2004/2262, the Designation of Schools Having a Religious Character (Independent Schools) (England) Order 2003, SI 2003/3108, the Independent Schools (Religious Character of Schools) (Designation Procedure) (Wales) Regulations 2003, SI 2003/3233 and the following orders of the same sort as the latter order: SIs 2003/3284 and 2003/3328 and SIs 2004/72, 2004/354, 2004/577, 2004/1378 and 2004/2089.

Chapter 14

ISSUES ARISING IN THE LAW OF TORT WHERE A MINOR IS PROVIDED WITH EDUCATION

INTRODUCTION

14.1   This chapter is mainly concerned with the law of tort[1] so far as it applies to the relationships between on the one hand school authorities (by which is meant those responsible for running or maintaining a school), teachers and other employees or agents of such authorities, and on the other hand pupils or their parents.[2] Many minors are educated at institutions within the further education sector, however, and the issues considered in this chapter which arise in relation to school pupils who are over the age of 16 but below the age of 18 will arise also in relation to those further education students. Occasionally, minors are educated at institutions within the higher education sector. The issues considered in this chapter will arise therefore also in relation to them. The legal issues arising in relation to students receiving further education or higher education which are unique to the context of further and higher education respectively, are considered in detail only in the chapters concerned with further and higher education.

14.2   Brief mention is made in this chapter of the possibility of claims for breach of statutory duty in relation to breaches of the Occupiers' Liability Acts 1957 and 1984. Brief mention is also made of the possibility of criminal liability for a breach of s 3 or s 4 of the Health and Safety at Work etc Act 1974, partly in order to set in context the possibility of civil liability for breaches of health and safety regulations made under that Act. Those matters are of course of general application, and do not apply only in the context of the education of minors. In what follows, the relationship in the law of tort between an education provider and the parent of a minor is considered first. The relationship in the law of tort between the minor recipient and the education provider is then considered.

---

[1]   For the definition of a tort (essentially a legal wrong which not based on, for example, a contract), see *Clerk and Lindsell on Torts* (Sweet & Maxwell, London, 18th edn, 2000), at para 1.1. For the validity of referring to the law of tort rather than the law of torts, see in addition to that paragraph, para 1.2 of *Clerk and Lindsell on Torts*.

[2]   The relationship between an education provider and a parent of a recipient of the education where the parent is purchasing the recipient's education gives rise to additional considerations. That relationship is considered in Chapter 13, where independent schools are considered. The impact of the criminal law is touched on briefly in paras **14.12–14.13**.

RELATIONSHIP IN THE LAW OF TORT BETWEEN AN EDUCATION PROVIDER AND THE PARENT OF A MINOR

Gillick

14.3   The main legal issue in the law of tort which is likely to arise in the context of the relationship between an education provider and the parent of a minor recipient of education is when the education provider will need to obtain the consent of the parent to actions which would in the absence of the parent's consent be unlawful.[1] The consent will then provide a defence to a claim of trespass brought on behalf of the minor (or by the minor within the time-limit for doing so from the time when he obtains the age of majority): the party who would be wronged if no relevant consent were given would be the child, and not the parent.[2] The need to obtain a parent's consent will occur where a child is unable validly to give the requisite consent. That is a question which must be considered in the light of the case of *Gillick v West Norfolk and Wisbech Area Health Authority.*[3] There, Lord Scarman made it clear that the rights of a parent in relation to a child exist primarily – or indeed as a matter of principle *only* – because of the parent's duties towards the child.[4] As the child grows older, so the duties – and hence the rights – of the parent towards the child diminish.[5] Lord Fraser's speech was so far as relevant to the same effect.[6] Lord Bridge agreed with the reasoning in both these parts of the speeches of Lord Scarman and Lord Fraser.[7] Although *Gillick* concerned the right of a minor to consent to medical treatment, with the result that the pivotal age of 16 in that case will not be relevant to questions concerning pure educational matters, the approach which the House of Lords said must be applied when determining when a minor can consent to medical treatment was drawn from statements of general principle. Accordingly, the general position is that where a certain course of action requires the consent of a participant in order to be lawful in relation to that participant, a child who has sufficient intelligence and understanding to appreciate what that course of action involves may give a valid consent to that course of action.

Re W

14.4   It was determined by the Court of Appeal in *In re W (A Minor) (Medical Treatment: Court's Jurisdiction)*[8] (*Re W*) that where a minor who has the power in law to consent to medical treatment refuses to consent to such treatment which in the absence of consent would amount to a battery, then a parent of the minor may

---

[1]   What constitutes a valid consent is a different matter from the occasions when such a consent will be necessary. The application of what has been called the doctrine of informed consent is considered in passing in paras **14.12** and **14.13**, but the issues of what that doctrine means and how far it applies, are outside the scope of this book. A fuller discussion of those issues can be found for example in *Clerk and Lindsell on Torts* (Sweet & Maxwell, 18th edn, 2000), at paras 8.25–8.34.

[2]   There is no tort of interference with a parent's right to determine how a child of his should be treated: *F v Wirral Metropolitan Borough Council* [1991] Fam 69, CA.

[3]   [1986] AC 112.

[4]   See ibid, at 184A–B.

[5]   See ibid, at 184A–185F.

[6]   See ibid, at 170D–G and 172G.

[7]   See ibid, at 194H–195B.

[8]   [1993] Fam 64.

nevertheless give a valid consent to the treatment. The case concerned a minor over the age of 16, but the principle just referred to was said to apply generally and was clearly applied by Lord Donaldson MR also to a minor who is under the age of 16 but has sufficient understanding and intelligence within the meaning of *Gillick* (and who is therefore '*Gillick* competent').[1] Lord Donaldson had earlier, in *In re R (A Minor) (Wardship: Consent to Treatment)*[2] (*Re R*), compared the power to consent to a key to a locked door: each person who had the power to consent to treatment had a key to unlock the door. In *Re W* he confirmed this approach (although he referred instead to a 'flak jacket', because a key can lock as well as unlock a door[3]), and this time (unlike in *Re R*) one of the other two members of the Court of Appeal agreed with him (Balcombe LJ: see further below).

14.5 As a matter of general principle, it seems partly right that the consent of any person who has the power to give a valid consent will suffice. This is because if there are a number of people who could give a valid consent to treatment, then the consent of any one of them other than the proposed recipient of the treatment should, where that proposed recipient cannot give that consent, be sufficient. However, the court's approach in *Re W* can be seen to have been reached on a mistaken understanding of what the House of Lords determined in *Gillick*. This is for the following reasons. Lord Donaldson was correct in concluding in *Re W*[4] that 'the central issue [in *Gillick*] was *not* whether a child patient under the age of 16 could refuse medical treatment if the parents or the court consented, but whether the parents could effectively impose a veto on treatment by failing or refusing to consent to treatment to which the child might consent'. Yet, as acknowledged by Lord Donaldson in *Re W*,[5] his judgment in *Re W* (with which so far as relevant Balcombe LJ concurred[6]) can be seen to be contrary to the clear words of Lord Scarman in *Gillick*.[7] However, as was *not* recognised by Lord Donaldson or Balcombe LJ in *Re W*,[8] the approach of Lord Fraser in *Gillick* was (so far as relevant) to the same effect as that of Lord Scarman.[9] Since, as indicated in para **14.3**, Lord Bridge agreed with the reasoning in the speeches of both Lord Scarman and Lord Fraser in this regard, *Re W* can be seen to have been (so far as relevant) mistaken. (The support which Lord Donaldson and Balcombe LJ derived from s 8(3) of the Family Law Reform Act 1969 can in any event be seen to have been misplaced, since that subsection 'can be explained as doing no more than ensuring that if a 16-year-old is unable to consent, or chooses to leave the decision to the parents, doctors can proceed on the basis of parental consent'.[10]) In any event, the

---

1   See [1993] Fam 64, at 83G–84A.

2   [1992] Fam 11.

3   See *Re W*, at 78D.

4   Ibid, at 75D–E.

5   Ibid, at 75H–76D.

6   See ibid, at 87. Nolan LJ merely referred to the proposition that the *court's* consent (given under its inherent jurisdiction) could override minor's refusal of treatment: see ibid, at 90C.

7   At [1986] AC 188H–189A.

8   See [1993] Fam 75H–76A and 87C–F respectively.

9   See [1986] AC 171A–E.

10   J Eekelaar, *White Coats or Flak Jackets? Doctors, Children and the Courts – Again* (1993) 109 LQR 182, at 183. The following passages in that case-note indicate further sustainable arguments why the reliance in *Re W* on s 8(3) was misplaced. See further, MM Davies, *Medical Law* (Oxford University Press, 1998), at pp 145–150.

statements of principle regarding the power of a parent to give a valid consent where a *Gillick* competent minor refused were *obiter*.[1]

In loco parentis

14.6   The phrase '*in loco parentis*' has often been used to justify action which could only be authorised by a parent. Whether that is now a correct approach is open to question.

14.7   It is true that it was held in *Fitzgerald v Northcote*[2] that:

> 'the authority of the schoolmaster is, while it exists, the same as that of the parent. A parent, when he places his child with a schoolmaster, delegates to him all his own authority, so far as it is necessary for the welfare of the child.'

14.8   However, ss 2(9) and 3(5) of the Children Act 1989[3] now regulate that aspect of the relationship between an education provider and the parent of a recipient minor. It is suggested here that it would be mistaken to refer to ss 2(9) and 3(5) as enacting whatever is meant by the *in loco parentis* principle, and that the matter should be regarded instead as governed both by those provisions and the principles to be drawn from *Gillick*.[4] Shorn as a result of meaning by those provisions, the phrase *in loco parentis* can only properly be applied in this context – if it is to be applied at all – to action in relation to a minor which a parent has actually authorised. It seems axiomatic (and it is consistent with the statement of principle set out above from *Fitzgerald v Northcote*) that a parent cannot be taken to have authorised anything which a teacher may wish to do in the course of the school day – or otherwise – merely by placing the child in the custody of the teacher. Accordingly, the phrase *in loco parentis* cannot be understood to denote that a parent, by placing his child in a teacher's care, gives the teacher authority to do whatever the teacher wishes in respect of the child. Accordingly, it seems clear that the phrase *in loco parentis* could now usefully be jettisoned, at least in this context.[5]

When is it necessary to obtain consent to conduct occurring in the course of the provision of education?

14.9   The need to obtain a relevant consent to conduct occurring in the course of the provision of education may arise in a number of contexts. These include the provision of physical education in certain situations (which are considered in the

---

[1]   See [1993] Fam 64, at 76D.

[2]   (1865) 4 F & F 856.

[3]   As to which, see paras **10.5** and **10.6**.

[4]   The same approach is suggested in para **10.7** in relation to discipline in a maintained school, but further statutory provisions apply in that context.

[5]   There is a slightly fuller discussion of this issue at (1997) 9 *Education and the Law* 187 (O Hyams). See further, paras **14.26–14.27** regarding the question whether the phrase *in loco parentis* has any meaning in relation to the law of negligence.

following paragraph), the teaching of, for example, dance, and detention after school hours as a form of punishment.[1]

14.10 In the case of physical education provided as part of the curriculum, a parent who makes no relevant protest can be taken to have consented to physical education which would otherwise be a trespass to the person, if only because by sending a child to a school at which the curriculum includes physical education, the parent must be taken to have consented to the physical education. (The fact that the National Curriculum includes physical education is not significant: all that matters in this context is that the curriculum at the school in question includes physical education.[2]) If games or sports are played or participated in outside school hours, however, then the consent of a parent will in theory be required if the game or sport involves the possibility of physical contact between participants. However, since games or sport outside school hours are very common, a parent's consent could again readily be inferred to have been given as necessary.

Medical treatment

14.11 For the reasons indicated above, there may be occasions when it will be necessary to obtain the consent of a parent to the procuring of medical treatment for a minor. Special considerations may then arise, because the religious or other beliefs of the parent may cause the parent to reject certain kinds of treatment. For example, a Jehovah's Witness may refuse to consent to the giving of a blood transfusion to his child. At common law, necessity arising out of an emergency may be a defence to a claim of trespass in respect of the giving of medical treatment.[3] It remains to be seen whether necessity would provide a defence to such a claim brought by a parent who is a Jehovah's Witness in respect of the giving to his child of a blood transfusion against the parent's previously expressed wishes, there being no clear authority on that question. However, as a matter of principle, it seems clear that the defence of necessity should be available in that situation.[4] If the circumstances were not an emergency, then (among other things) the local authority could apply to the court under s 100(3) of the CA 1989 for the court to exercise its inherent jurisdiction in relation to the child and give the necessary consent.

Overlap between criminal and civil law in this context

14.12 Although this chapter is concerned in the main with the law of tort in so far as it applies to the relationship between, among others, education providers and pupils or their parents, it is necessary to be aware of the overlap between civil and criminal law so far as relevant. For example, an assault or a battery is usually both a crime and

---

[1] See para **10.5**, and note that in the case of schools maintained by LEAs, city technology colleges, city colleges for the technology of the arts and Academies, s 550B of the EA 1996 makes the absence of a parent's consent irrelevant in certain circumstances (see paras **10.22** and **10.23**).

[2] As noted in para **11.1**, the National Curriculum in any event does not apply in independent schools.

[3] See, for example, *Gillick v West Norfolk and Wisbech Area Health Authority* [1986] AC 112, at 181G, per Lord Scarman, 194D per Lord Bridge, and 204G–205C, per Lord Templeman. See also *In re F (Mental Patient: Sterilisation)* [1990] 2 AC 1, at 52C–E, 55B–F per Lord Bridge, and 73H–74F, 76H–77A, per Lord Goff.

[4] M Davies is of the view that the defence of necessity should be available in such circumstances: see op cit, p 150, para 6.4.

a tort – although there is not usually criminal liability for an act or omission which could give rise to liability in the civil law of negligence.[1] However, the law of tort and criminal law are not co-extensive, as was made clear by the Court of Appeal in *R v Richardson*.[2] That case concerned the validity of a defence of consent to a criminal charge against a dentist of assault occasioning actual bodily harm. The 'victims' were regular patients of the dentist, and her defence was that they had consented to being treated by her. She had continued to treat them despite having been suspended from practice by the General Dental Council, and had done so without informing them of that suspension. It was apparent that the patients might not have given their consent to being treated by the defendant if she had informed them that she had been so suspended. The Crown Court had ruled that the patients had not given a valid consent to being treated by the defendant in those circumstances. Accordingly, the defendant had pleaded guilty in the Crown Court. She then appealed to the Court of Appeal, contending that her patients had indeed given a valid consent. The prosecution argued that if a consent was given, then it had to be fully informed before it could be valid. The prosecution therefore sought to import what is known as the law of informed consent into the criminal law. (That concept is to the effect that a consent which is obtained in circumstances in which the person giving consent knows less than the full material facts, is not sufficient to found a defence to an action in the law of trespass to the person.[3]) The Court of Appeal said this:

> 'It was suggested in argument that we might be assisted by the civil law of consent, where such expressions as "real" or "informed" consent prevail. In this regard the criminal and the civil law do not run along the same track. The concept of informed consent has no place in the criminal law ... The gravamen of the defendant's conduct in the instant case was that the complainants consented to treatment from her although their consent had been procured by her failure to inform them that she was no longer qualified to practise. This was clearly reprehensible and may well found the basis of a civil claim for damages. But we are quite satisfied that it is not a basis for finding criminal liability in the field of offences against the person.'[4]

14.13 As a result, the law of informed consent may have a place in the relationship between an education provider and a student in the law of trespass to the person, but it has no such place as far as the criminal law is concerned.

Alternative routes of redress

14.14 The possibility of a parent of a minor who is in receipt of education complaining to the Secretary of State under s 496 or s 497 of the EA 1996 is considered elsewhere,[5] and is mentioned here only for the sake of completeness. Also for the sake of completeness, mention should be made here of the possibility of applying for judicial review. Similarly, in the following section, consideration is given

---

[1]   See, for example, JC Smith and B Hogan *Criminal Law* (Butterworths, 10th edn, 2002), at pp 109–110. If a parent refused to consent to medical treatment and as a consequence his child died, then the parent might be liable for manslaughter (see *R v Senior* [1899] 1 QB 283), but that is not relevant to the matters considered in this chapter.

[2]   [1999] QB 444.

[3]   See further, *Clerk and Lindsell on Torts* (Sweet & Maxwell, 18th edn, 2000), at para 8.29.

[4]   [1999] QB 444, at 450.

[5]   See Chapter 3.

only to the principles of private law which apply to the relationship between an education provider and a minor recipient of education provided by it.

RELATIONSHIP BETWEEN AN EDUCATION PROVIDER AND THE MINOR RECIPIENTS OF EDUCATION PROVIDED BY IT

Introduction

14.15 The main principles of private law which apply to the relationship between an education provider[1] and a minor recipient of education provided by it are those concerning trespass to the person and negligence. In addition, there may be the possibility of a claim for damages in respect of a breach of statutory duty, although in some respects the scope for arguing such a claim has diminished dramatically as a result of the cases of *X v Bedfordshire County Council*[2] and *Phelps v Hillingdon London Borough Council.*[3]

14.16 The principles applicable to the law of trespass to the person are considered above.[4] No more needs to be said here except to reiterate that the effect of a trespass to the person will be that only the minor who is the subject of the trespass will be entitled to sue, either while a minor through his next friend or on achieving the age of majority.[5] In what follows, the potential for liability for negligence in relation to physical injury is considered first, after which the possibility of liability for negligence in relation to the provision of education itself is examined. Brief mention is then made of the possibility of liability for breach of statutory duty.

Liability for negligence in respect of physical injury

Introduction

14.17 Before liability in negligence can properly be found to have arisen in any case, there must have been a duty to take care owed by the defendant, that duty of care must have been breached (in other words there must have been a failure to take reasonable care) by the defendant, and damage (which was not too remote) must have been caused to the plaintiff by that failure to take reasonable care.[6]

14.18 It is clear that in some circumstances the person or body responsible for running a school owes a duty of care towards a pupil at the school. In others, however, it is by no means clear whether a duty of care is owed. Where a duty of care *is* owed, however, then determining what standard of care needs to be applied is often

---

[1] In most cases this will be a school, and for the sake of simplicity, where appropriate reference is made below only to schools.

[2] [1995] 2 AC 633.

[3] [2001] 2 AC 619; see para **14.64**.

[4] See paras **14.3** et seq.

[5] The general principles relating to trespass to the person and the time-limits for making claims in relation to such are outside the scope of this book. Reference should be made for example to *Clerk and Lindsell on Torts* (Sweet & Maxwell, 18th edn, 2000) in connection with those matters.

[6] See further, for example, *Charlesworth and Percy on Negligence* (Sweet and Maxwell, 10th edn, 2001).

not easy. The fact that there is a body of case-law relating to the specific situation of a school pupil does not in fact help as much as might have been thought, since the outcomes of many of the relevant cases look decidedly odd today. In any event, the question of the standard of care which it would have been reasonable to expect in any circumstances, and whether or not such care was forthcoming, is largely a question of fact (as opposed to one of law).[1] Accordingly, some of the decided cases can at best be only guides to the proper approach to apply in any situation. Having said that, there are a number of situations involving school pupils which are likely to recur, and there are some general principles which can usefully be deduced from the case-law. The salient features of the relevant case-law will therefore now be considered. Principles which are applicable in the law of negligence generally are not considered here, unless there is some factor which makes it helpful to refer to them in the school context.[2]

When is a duty of care owed to a school pupil?

14.19   It is clear that a duty of care is owed by an education provider such as a school to a pupil in respect of physical injury occurring as a result of the manner in which that education is provided or the manner in which pupils have been supervised; the standard of care required to satisfy that duty is considered below. In contrast, it is by no means clear whether an education provider owes a duty of care in respect of the acts of an outsider as far as the institution at which the education is provided is concerned. The reason for this is that a court in the United Kingdom will only rarely impose liability for the acts of a third party. The leading case on this issue is *Smith v Littlewoods Organisation Ltd*.[3] There, Lord Mackay said this:

> 'Unless the needle that measures the probability of a particular result flowing from the conduct of a human agent is near the top of the scale it may be hard to conclude that it has risen sufficiently from the bottom to create the duty reasonably to foresee it.'[4]

14.20   The speech of Lord Goff in that case was to a different effect with regard to the principles to be applied in determining whether a duty of care is owed in respect of the acts of a stranger, and it seems clear that the approach of Lord Mackay cannot

---

1   That there may be differences of opinion in relation to the same facts is amply illustrated by the case of *Moore v Hampshire County Council* (1981) 80 LGR 481, where at first instance the judge rejected the claim, but at the successful appeal although two judges thought that the case involved a 'fine point', Watkins LJ (at p 486) came to the conclusion 'without hesitation that this was a claim to which there was no defence'.

2   The relevant following paragraphs are not intended to be an exhaustive description of the existing case-law. A more comprehensive description is to be found in *Charlesworth and Percy on Negligence* op cit, at paras 8.158–8.185.

3   [1987] AC 241.

4   [1987] AC 241, at 261E–F. The United States case of *Tarasoff v Regents University of California* (1976) 55 P 2d 334 can be distinguished, and in any event might well not be followed in this country. There, a student medical centre was found liable for not warning the victim of a psychotic patient that the patient intended to commit violence against the victim and that the patient had a gun. The patient was the victim's rejected lover. The medical centre told the police, who decided to do nothing. The patient then murdered the victim.

be regarded as determinative.[1] Nevertheless, Lord Goff recognised that the law 'does not recognise a general duty of care to prevent others from suffering loss or damage caused by the deliberate wrongdoing of third parties',[2] and stated that 'any affirmative duty to prevent deliberate wrongdoing by third parties, if recognised in English law, is likely to be strictly limited'.[3]

Would a school be liable if a third party entered onto school premises and attacked pupils or staff?

14.21 The question whether a duty of care towards pupils has arisen in relation to the acts of a third party is most likely to arise where a third party has entered onto school premises and attacked pupils. It is suggested here that because of the case of *Smith v Littlewoods Organisation Ltd*,[4] a school authority (that is those who are responsible for maintaining the school to any extent) should not be regarded as being under a duty of care in relation to the acts of a third party who attacks pupils randomly. Alternatively, if a duty of care is owed in that regard, then the standard of care should be regarded as relatively low, bearing in mind the scarcity of resources in the case of at least maintained schools,[5] and bearing in mind the possible undesirability of turning schools into fortresses.

The standard of care generally

14.22 Where a duty of care is owed, however, then the question will be what standard of care needs to be applied. That standard has been thought to be one of a careful parent, a reasonably prudent parent, or one of a reasonably careful parent. For example, in the case of *Williams v Eady*,[6] it was said by Cave J with the approval of Lord Esher, MR, that a schoolmaster had to take 'such care of his boys as a careful father would take of his boys ... he was bound to take notice of the ordinary nature of young boys, their tendency to do mischievous acts, and their propensity to meddle with anything that came in their way'.[7] In *Lyes v Middlesex County Council*,[8] it was said that:

> 'the standard is that of a reasonably prudent parent judged not in the context of his own home but in that of a school, in other words, a person exhibiting the responsible mental qualities of a prudent parent in the circumstances of school life. School life happily differs from home life. The more the merrier. A lot of pupils are apt to make much more noise even than a few children in a small home and there is, to use an expression of one of the

---

1   See, for example, the discussion in *Clerk and Lindsell on Torts* (Sweet & Maxwell, 17th edn 1995), at para 7.36. That discussion was not repeated in the current, 18th edition, but no reference is made there in the relevant place (para 7.45) to the speech of Lord Mackay.
2   [1987] AC 241, at 271B.
3   Ibid, at 271G–H.
4   See above.
5   See para **14.37**.
6   (1893) 10 TLR 41.
7   Ibid, at 42.
8   (1963) 61 LGR 443.

witnesses, more skylarking, and a bit of rough play, but the reasonable parent in school premises would be mindful of such considerations as that.'[1]

14.23 In *Nicholson v Westmorland County Council,*[2] the Master of the Rolls applied the test by referring to 'a reasonably careful parent looking after a family as large as 20'. In *Beaumont v Surrey County Council,*[3] Geoffrey Lane J described the duty of the headmaster as one to take such care 'as a reasonably careful and prudent father would take of his own children'.[4] However, he also said that the situation there in issue was best approached in the light not of that standard but, rather, by using 'the ordinary language of the law of negligence'. In other words, it was the headmaster's duty:

> 'bearing in mind the known propensities of boys and indeed girls between the ages of 11 and 17 or 18,[5] to take all reasonable and proper steps to prevent any of the pupils under his care from suffering injury from inanimate objects, from the actions of their fellow pupils, or from a combination of the two. That is a high standard.'[6]

14.24 Indeed, it seems clear that in at least some circumstances it will be most helpful to use only the ordinary language of the law of negligence, albeit bearing in mind that it has to be applied on the basis that the alleged tortfeasor is to be treated as if he were a parent. This is because the 'reasonably careful (or prudent) parent' test seems to assume something which then has to be disregarded – the home or family environment. Furthermore, claims against parents as such in the law of negligence are rare, and give rise to different considerations from those which apply in schools. This can be seen from the following extract from the judgment of Sir Nicholas Browne-Wilkinson V-C in *Surtees v Kingston-upon-Thames Borough Council:*[7]

> 'There are very real public policy considerations to be taken into account if the conflicts inherent in legal proceedings are to be brought into family relationships. Moreover, the responsibilities of a parent (which in contemporary society normally means the mother) looking after one or more children, in addition to the myriad other duties which fall on the parent at home, far exceed those of other members of society. The studied calm of the Royal Courts of Justice, concentrating on one point at a time, is light years away from the circumstances prevailing in the average home. The mother is looking after a fast-moving toddler at the same time as cooking the meal, doing the housework, answering the telephone, looking after the other children and doing all the other things that the average mother has to cope with simultaneously, or in quick succession, in the normal household. We should be slow to characterise as negligent the care which ordinary loving and careful mothers are able to give to individual children, given the rough-and-tumble of home life.'[8]

---

[1] (1963) 61 LGR 443, at 446.

[2] (1962) *The Times*, October 25.

[3] (1968) 66 LGR 580.

[4] Ibid, at 585.

[5] In this connection the statement of Lord Hoffman in *Jolley v Sutton London Borough Council* [2000] 1 WLR 1082, at 1093, that children's 'ingenuity in finding unexpected ways of doing mischief to themselves and others should never be underestimated', should be borne in mind.

[6] Ibid.

[7] [1991] 2 FLR 559, at 583–584.

[8] In the case, the Court of Appeal dismissed (by a majority) a claim in respect of a scalding injury which occurred to a 2-year-old while in the care of a foster parent.

14.25   Furthermore, in *Barrett v Enfield London Borough Council*,[1] Lord Hutton (who must be taken to have spoken as part of the majority of the House of Lords on this point[2]), having agreed with the thrust of the above extract from Browne-Wilkinson LJ's judgment in *Surtees*,[3] said:

> 'I consider that the comparison between a parent and a local authority is not an apt one in the present case because the local authority has to make decisions of a nature which a parent with whom a child is living in a normal family relationship does not have to make, viz whether the child should be placed for adoption or placed with foster parents, or whether a child should remain with foster parents or be placed in a residential home.'[4]

14.26   The situation is not helped by the use of the phrase *in loco parentis* to describe the situation. The potentially misleading use of specific phrases in the law of negligence to describe standards of care required in typical situations is well-described in *Clerk and Lindsell on Torts*:[5]

> 'The standard of care required in particular circumstances is sometimes formulated in terms of a particular duty: e.g. the motorist is under a duty to give a turn signal. Such formulations may be regarded as helpful in a descriptive way. But this use of "duty" terminology is misleading. The standard of care required is what would be reasonable in the circumstances. ... To express the standard in terms of a duty is to confuse two distinct questions. The duty question is concerned with the general nature of the relationship between the parties and asks whether there should be a duty of care in that kind of relationship. The scope of any duty may be described by reference to the circumstances of the relationship. Thus the relationship between the parties may justify a duty of care to prevent the harm being caused by third parties and the restricted nature of that duty of care will tend to suggest that what is reasonably required should not place an onerous burden on the defendant. However, the specific level of care required, e.g. whether a warning should have been given, will depend on [the] particular circumstances of the case.'

14.27   Thus the phrase *in loco parentis* could usefully be regarded as indicating that a duty of care is owed in certain relevant situations, but not the standard of care in any particular situation. However, since it is clear that a duty of care is so owed, it is at least doubtful whether there is any purpose to be served by the continuing use of the phrase *in loco parentis* in this context. It is suggested here that since that phrase serves no real purpose, either in this context or that of the law of trespass to the person,[6] it may be misleading, and therefore that it would be best to let it fall into desuetude.

14.28   Some of the factors which may be relevant to a claim in negligence in respect of physical injury brought by a minor recipient of education against the provider of that education will now be considered. Afterwards, reference is made to some particular situations.

---

[1]   [2001] 2 AC 550.
[2]   Lord Nolan and Lord Steyn agreed with the speeches not only of Lord Hutton but also of Lord Slynn and Lord Browne-Wilkinson. However, only Lord Hutton referred to *Surtees*.
[3]   See [2001] 2 AC 550, at 587.
[4]   Ibid, at 588.
[5]   (Sweet & Maxwell, 18th edn, 2000, at para 7.160.
[6]   See paras **14.6–14.8**.

Factors which may be relevant to a claim of negligence[1]

The system

14.29 Even though an individual teacher may not have been negligent, the system of supervision applied at a school[2] may have been insufficient to comply with the standard of care which the law of negligence requires. So, for example, in *Martin v Middlesbrough Corporation*,[3] a child cut her hand on broken glass in the school playground, the glass having probably come from a milk bottle provided by the school. It was decided by the Court of Appeal that the defendant LEA should have made better arrangements for the disposal of empty milk bottles,[4] and that they had therefore been negligent. More recently, in *J v North Lincolnshire County Council*,[5] the Court of Appeal held that the judge was right to decide that the system for ensuring so far as was practicable that all five exits from a primary school playground were kept closed and fastened during school hours, was negligent. The system of supervision in the playground was not at fault, however. Thus the system which was negligent was that which related to the security of the perimeter. It was 'not so much a system but a "policy" (the headmaster's word) of staff closing gates which they found open', which, the judge found, was 'somewhat haphazard'.[6] The school in question could not say how the pupil (who was hit by a passing car and who, it was accepted, could not safely be out of school on his own) had left the school's premises. Thus 'the basic res ipsa loquitur principle applie[d]'.[7]

14.30 Even if the system is in itself sufficient, it may not have been applied properly, and negligence may have occurred as a result. For example, in *Beaumont v Surrey County Council*,[8] a piece of discarded trampette elastic was left in a waste bin within reach of pupils. An injury to the eye of a pupil which resulted from playing with the elastic was held to have been caused by negligence, the normal system of supervision having broken down at the time when the injury occurred.[9]

14.31 When a system is sufficient to satisfy the requisite standard of care and that system is applied properly, if an injury nevertheless occurs then there will be no liability in negligence.[10]

---

1   The eight factors referred to below are not set out in order of importance.
2   As indicated above, references are made in this section of this chapter below only to schools for the sake of simplicity. Where relevant, the word 'school' should be read as meaning also a provider of any other sort of education to a minor.
3   (1965) 63 LGR 385.
4   See ibid, at 389, per Willmer LJ, with whom Davies and Salmon LJJ both agreed and concurred.
5   [2000] ELR 245.
6   See ibid, at para 28, per Henry LJ.
7   Ibid, at para 31.
8   (1968) 66 LGR 580.
9   (1968) 66 LGR 580, at 587. See also *Barnes v Hampshire County Council* [1969] 1 WLR 1563.
10   See, for example, *Nwabudike v Southwark London Borough Council* [1997] ELR 35; *Jeffery v London County Council* (1954) 52 LGR 521 (the outcome of which might well have been different today); *Rich v London County Council* [1953] 2 All ER 376; and *Wilson v Governors of Sacred Heart Roman Catholic Primary School* [1998] ELR 637 (as to which, see para **14.44**).

Special knowledge

14.32 A school may have special knowledge which a parent does not have, for example of the safest manner in which to carry out scientific experiments. If so, then that would be relevant to a claim in negligence brought by a minor.[1]

Age of pupil

14.33 As one would expect, the age of a pupil will be relevant in determining the standard of care owed to him. This was a factor in *Black v Kent County Council*.[2] The age of a pupil will also be relevant in determining whether the pupil was contributorily negligent,[3] or whether the pupil had consented to the risk of negligence under the principle connoted by the maxim *volenti non fit injuria*.[4]

Need to encourage independence

14.34 In *Suckling v Essex County Council*,[5] it was said that it was 'better that a boy should break his neck than allow other people to break his spirit'. It may be that not everyone would agree with that proposition today, but the need to encourage the independence of children is clearly a factor which will be relevant in determining what was the standard of care in any case.[6] More recently, it was made clear that the mere fact that playing on a piece of dedicated playing field equipment such as a swing on a school's premises can be dangerous does not mean that an injury caused as a result of playing on that equipment will have been caused by negligence for which those responsible for the conduct of the school are liable.[7]

Warnings may protect against liability

14.35 A proper warning may protect an education provider from liability.[8] However, the greater the danger, the more clear the warning must be.[9] If injury occurs where the provision of a warning would be likely to have avoided it, the failure to warn may well be found to have been negligent.[10]

---

[1] *Van Oppen v Clerk to the Bedford Charity Trustees* (at first instance) [1989] 1 All ER 273, at 287b–d per Boreham J.

[2] (1983) 82 LGR 39.

[3] See, for example, *Gough v Thorne* [1966] 1 WLR 1387.

[4] See further, para **14.3** regarding the effect of *Gillick v West Norfolk and Wisbech Area Health Authority* [1986] AC 112 on the question whether a pupil could properly be said to have consented to the risk of negligence.

[5] (1955) *The Times*, January 27, [1955] CLY 1844.

[6] See, for example, *Jeffery v London County Council* (1954) 52 LGR 521.

[7] See *Simonds v Isle of Wight Council* [2003] EWHC 2303 (QB), [2004] ELR 59.

[8] See, for example, *Crouch v Essex County Council* (1966) 64 LGR 240.

[9] See, for example, *Noonan v Inner London Education Authority*, (1974) *The Times*, news item (at p 3), 14 December; the case is described in more detail by GR Barrell and JA Partington in *Teachers and the Law* (Methuen, 6th edn, 1985), at p 395.

[10] See, for example, *Foster v London County Council*, (1928) *The Times*, March 2 and the report of the case at first instance in (1927) *The Times*, December 7. The only reference to a warning is in the earlier report.

The existence of a statutory framework

14.36 There may on occasion be a statutory framework which may be thought to be relevant in determining the standard of care which a defendant was obliged to apply. For example, there used to be no requirement that seat belts were fitted to buses used in the provision of school transport.[1] That lack of a requirement could have been thought to be relevant in determining whether there was any obligation on the part of the LEA to ensure that seat belts were fitted on all seats used by pupils in vehicles used for the provision of school transport. However, the existence of a statutory framework will be relevant only as indicating what is acceptable to the community, and that framework cannot be determinative.[2] Accordingly, the absence of a requirement that vehicles used for the purpose of providing school transport had seat belts fitted could not have been determinative. In addition, it could be argued that the fact that it was not characterised by the court in *R v Gwent County Council, ex parte Harris*[3] as unlawful (in public law terms) to fail to ensure that seat belts were fitted in school transport at that time indicates clearly that there would be no obligation in the law of negligence in regard to such failure. But, it is suggested here, that would again be mistaken. That could merely be one factor to weigh in the balance, or it could be completely irrelevant.[4] On the other hand, the mere fact that an LEA (or an employee or agent of theirs) would now be criminally liable for causing the use of a minibus or coach without appropriate seat belts on a journey carrying pupils to or from their school's premises, would not determine the question whether there was any liability on the part of the authority for injuries caused as a result: the relevant obligation is a strict one, with the result that a breach of it cannot be regarded as determinative.[5]

The availability of resources

14.37 The scarcity of resources is a factor which is relevant (although clearly not conclusive) in determining the standard of care which should be imposed on a public body. As Pill J put it in *Knight v Home Office:*[6]

'In making the decision as to the standard to be demanded the court must, however, bear in mind as one factor that resources available for the public service are limited and that the allocation of resources is a matter for Parliament. ... [However, it would not be a

---

1   A change in that regard was introduced with effect from 10 February 1997 by SI 1996/163.
2   Cf *Bux v Slough Metals Ltd* [1973] 1 WLR 1358.
3   [1995] ELR 27.
4   In *X v Bedfordshire County Council* [1995] 2 AC 633, at 736–737, the House of Lords indicated that public law principles generally are irrelevant to a claim in the law of negligence. However, in *Storin v Wise and Norfolk County Council* [1996] AC 923, Lord Hoffman, with whose speech Lord Goff and Lord Jauncey agreed, stated that the 'minimum preconditions for basing a duty of care upon the existence of a statutory power, if it can be done at all, are, first, that it would in the circumstances have been irrational not to have exercised the power, so that there was in effect a public law duty to act'. This, however, was said in a rather different context, and need not be regarded as affecting the indication in *X v Bedfordshire County Council* that public law principles generally are irrelevant to a claim in the law of negligence.
5   Cf *Clerk and Lindsell on Torts* (Sweet & Maxwell, 18th edn, 2000), at para 7.188.
6   [1990] 3 All ER 237, at 243c.

complete defence for a government department] to say that no funds are available for additional safety measures.'[1]

General and approved practice

14.38 If injury occurs as a result of following a general and approved practice, then the fact that that practice was followed may well be determinative of a claim in negligence in respect of the injury. For example, in *Chilvers v London County Council*,[2] a child lost the sight of an eye when he fell on the lance of a toy soldier which a fellow pupil had, with the permission of the teacher, brought to school. The court held that there was no negligence because children were commonly allowed to play with toy soldiers of a similar sort.[3] It has to be said, however, that if the same situation as that in *Chilvers* occurred today, then the outcome might be to the opposite effect. That points towards the caveat which must be expressed here, which is that the mere fact that a practice is commonplace will not inevitably save a defendant from liability, even in this context.[4]

Physical education

14.39 The following of (or failure to follow) a general and approved practice will be particularly relevant where an injury occurs as a result of the provision of physical education.[5] This is one of the contexts in which some of the decisions in the old authorities might look odd to modern eyes, with the result that they should be treated with caution as indicators of the likely approach of courts today.[6] In any event, the general and approved practice must be that relating to a pupil of the age of the injured participant.[7]

14.40 A pupil's expressed wish to be allowed to participate in games or sports may be contrary to the expressed wish of his parent. (The parent's wish where the child is of compulsory school age will no doubt have to be soundly based, for example because the pupil has an injury or condition which makes it inappropriate to allow the

---

[1]   See further, *Clerk and Lindsell on Torts* (Sweet & Maxwell, 18th edn, 2000), at paras 7.181–7.182.

[2]   (1916) 80 JP 246.

[3]   See also *Wilson v Governors of Sacred Heart Catholic Primary School* [1998] ELR 637, as to which see para **14.44**.

[4]   See, for example, *Lyes v Middlesex County Council* (1963) 61 LGR 443, at 446. See also *Perry v Butlins Holiday World (Butlins Ltd T/A)*, [1998] EdCR 39, where the court considered the differing current practices prevailing in various circumstances in 1862, 1970 and 1994, and concluded that the circumstances in 1994 required more than did those of 1970, albeit that the circumstances of the situations in 1970 and 1994 were only loosely analogous. See also *Kearn-Price v Kent County Council* [2002] EWCA Civ 1539, [2003] ELR 17, concerning which see paras **14.45** and **14.46**.

[5]   See, for example, *Van Oppen v Clerk to the Bedford Charity Trustees* [1990] 1 WLR 235, where there was no liability in respect of an injury which occurred in the course of a rugby match; *Smolden v Whitworth* [1997] ELR 249, where the plaintiff's claim in negligence was successful against the referee of a rugby football match; and *Fowles v Bedfordshire County Council* [1996] ELR 51, where the plaintiff was successful in his claim against the defendant LEA for negligence in relation to a gymnastic activity, although he was held to have been contributorily negligent.

[6]   See, for example, *Wright v Cheshire County Council* [1952] 2 All ER 789, and *Webb v Essex County Council*, (1954) *The Times Educational Supplement*, 12 November (at p 1061), as to which see also Barrell and Partington, 'Teachers and the Law' (Methuen, 6th edn, 1985), at p 400.

[7]   See *Affutu-Nartoy v Clarke* (1984) *The Times*, February 9.

pupil to participate in games or sports.[1]) If a teacher nevertheless gave in to the pupil's request and allowed the pupil to participate in games or sports, and the pupil suffered injury, then the teacher and (vicariously) the teacher's employer could be held to have been negligent.[2] Whether they would be so liable would depend to an extent on the age of the pupil and his '*Gillick* competence'.[3]

No duty to insure against injury to pupil or to advise parent to do so

14.41 Despite the fact that an education provider owes a duty in negligence towards minor recipients of the education which it provides, the education provider is not under a duty to have regard to such a minor recipient's economic welfare, and accordingly is not obliged to insure such a recipient against accidental injury, or to advise a parent to do so.[4]

The administration of medicines; seeking medical help

14.42 A school may be under an obligation in the law of negligence to take positive steps to seek medical help for a pupil.[5] As one might expect, that will be so not only when a pupil is under the age of 16.[6] However, a school is likely to be under an obligation to administer medicines only in exceptional circumstances, which will almost certainly constitute an emergency.[7] School staff cannot be obliged to administer medicines unless it is an express term of their contracts of employment that they may be required to do so, and in any event, the inexpert administration of medicines could itself give rise to liability for negligence.

Duty of care arises only when child is in school's custody

14.43 A parent cannot impose liability in negligence on a school *merely* by depositing his child there before the commencement of the normal period during which pupils are supervised by the school.[8] Similarly, in *Good v Inner London Education Authority*,[9] one basis of the decision by the Court of Appeal that the defendant LEA was not

---

[1]   There does not seem to be any specific statutory provision concerning a physical condition preventing a pupil from participating in the physical education element of the National Curriculum. Accordingly, the case of *Osborne v Martin* (1927) 91 JP 197, could be relevant to the question whether the parent had ensured the regular attendance of his child at school: see footnote 8 in para **5.16** concerning *Osborne v Martin*, and cf *Bunt v Kent* [1914] 1 KB 207, regarding which, see para **5.35**.

[2]   See *Moore v Hampshire County Council* (1981) 80 LGR 481.

[3]   See text to footnote 1 in para **14.4** for what constitutes '*Gillick* competence'.

[4]   *Van Oppen v Clerk to the Trustees of the Bedford Charity* [1990] 1 WLR 235.

[5]   *Hippolyte v London Borough of Bexley* [1995] PIQR P309, at P314–315. The case concerned a failure to call an ambulance for a pupil who was suffering an asthma attack, and the decision of the Court of Appeal in part turned on the state of knowledge at the time of the incident in question. The outcome on the facts (the claim was rejected) should not therefore be regarded as in any way determinative of any later case.

[6]   *Hippolyte v London Borough of Bexley*, ibid.

[7]   This is also the view of the DfEE, expressed in Circular 14/96, at para 14.

[8]   See *Mays v Essex County Council* (1975) *The Times*, October 11. See also *Ward v Hertfordshire County Council* [1970] 1 WLR 356, at 359E, per Lord Denning MR, but see ibid, at 361E–F, per Salmon LJ. See further below, especially in relation to *Kearn-Price v Kent County Council*, concerning which, see paras **14.45** and **14.46**.

[9]   (1980) 10 Fam Law 213.

negligent was that the 'jurisdiction' of the teachers at the pupil claimant's school regarding the pupils at the school ended when the pupils left the school either to be collected by their parents or to go to an adjacent play centre at the end of the school day. The injury in question had been caused by another pupil's throwing of sand and a sharp object which he had obtained from a pile of sand or a pile of sand and stones which were to be used in the building of a swimming pool and which had been deposited in the playground only temporarily. Pupils had been warned during school assembly not to go near the piles, but the pupil who threw the object had obtained it from one of the piles while the play centre staff were getting things ready in the play centre. It was held in addition that the authority had not been negligent in not supervising the whole of the journey from the school to the play centre.[1]

14.44 *Wilson v Governors of Sacred Heart Catholic Primary School*[2] is to a similar effect. There, the situation during the lunch hour and that at the end of the school day was contrasted. The Court of Appeal overturned (on the facts) the first instance judge's finding of liability on the part of the governors in relation to an eye injury caused to a pupil while he was walking from the school door to the school yard gate, by another pupil's waving his coat like a lasso. There was, said Hirst LJ, an obvious need for supervision during the lunch hour.[3] However, he said:

> 'In my judgment, the very short period in which pupils moved from the exit from the school building to the gate at the other end of the playground is quite different, even allowing for the fact that ... departing pupils are likely to be high-spirited at that particular moment of the day. Moreover, and to my mind most importantly, there was no evidence that supervision at that juncture, as contrasted with the lunch-break, is standard practice, as it surely would be if it was an equally reasonable requirement.'[4]

14.45 In contrast, however, in *Kearn-Price v Kent County Council*,[5] the Court of Appeal upheld the first instance judge's finding of liability on the part of an LEA towards a pupil who had been standing in the playground and had been hit in the eye by a full-size leather football at 8.40 am, 3 minutes before pupils were let into the school and 5 minutes before the start of the school day. In so deciding, Dyson LJ, with whom Arden and Schiemann LJJ agreed, said that he would:

> 'unhesitatingly reject the proposition that, as a matter of law, no duty to supervise can be owed by a school to its pupils who are on school premises before or after school hours. As I have explained, *Ward v Hertfordshire County Council* [1970] 1 WLR 356 is not authority for such a proposition. ... The real issue is what is the *scope* of the duty of care owed to pupils who are on school premises before and after school hours. It may be that it is not

---

1   See also *Barnes v Hampshire County Council* [1969] 1 WLR 1563, [1969] 3 All ER 746, where, at 1572C, Lord Pearson (with whom Lords Reid and Donovan agreed) said this: 'The mothers might fairly be held responsible for the safety of the children after 3.30 p.m. [the end of the school day], when the school's responsibility would for most purposes, subject to emergencies and special arrangements, come to an end'.

2   [1998] ELR 637.

3   Ibid, at 639–640.

4   Ibid, at 640B–C.

5   [2002] EWCA Civ 1539, [2003] ELR 17.

reasonable to expect a school to do as much to protect its pupils from injury outside school hours as during school hours. All will depend on the circumstances.'[1]

14.46   He also said:

'I accept that evidence of what is standard procedure at schools generally is highly material to a determination of what is reasonably required of a school. But it is no more than that. Sometimes, although probably rarely, a court may conclude that the standard generally required is not sufficient to discharge the duty of care.'[2]

Duty of care applies to journey to school on transport provided by the local education authority

14.47   There may, however, be liability in relation to injury suffered in connection with the provision of transport to or from school. In *Shrimpton v Hertfordshire County Council*,[3] a pupil was injured when alighting from a school bus. If a supervisor had been present, then the accident might not have occurred. The LEA did not need to provide the transport free of charge. However, the House of Lords held that since the LEA had provided the transport, they had to take reasonable steps to ensure that its use was safe.[4]

School authorities will not normally be vicariously liable for pupils

14.48   It was held in *Watkins v Birmingham City Council*[5] that a pupil who does an errand for a teacher during the course of the school day should not be regarded as being in the same category as an employee of the party which is responsible for maintaining the school. Accordingly, the party responsible for maintaining the school will not be vicariously liable for the torts of the pupil when doing such an errand.[6] Although the case of *Pearce v Governing Body of Mayfield School*[7] concerned a claim of vicarious liability for unlawful discrimination, the relevant ruling of the House of Lords can be taken to confirm the rulings in *Watkins*.[8]

An education provider may nevertheless be liable in respect of the acts of pupils

14.49   As a result of the decision of the House of Lords in *Carmarthenshire County Council v Lewis*,[9] if a young pupil[10] is allowed to wander alone outside a school's gates

---

1   [2002] EWCA Civ 1539, [2003] ELR 17, at para 18.
2   Ibid, at para 30.
3   (1911) 104 LT 145.
4   See also *Ellis v Sayers Confectioners Ltd* (1963) 61 LGR 299, where the supervision which was provided was negligent, and *Jacques v Oxfordshire County Council* (1967) 66 LGR 440, where supervision by school prefects was held to have been sufficient. The question whether an LEA could be liable for the provision of school transport without seat belts is considered in para **14.36**.
5   (1975) *The Times*, August 1.
6   Ibid.
7   [2003] UKHL 34, [2003] ICR 937.
8   See ibid, per Lord Hope, at para 96 and per Lord Scott at para 120. Lord Nicholls' speech was to the same effect in this respect, but less clearly so: see para 37.
9   [1955] AC 549.
10   That is, one of 'such tender years that [he] may be presumed to be unable to take any care for [his] own safety and whom a prudent parent would not allow to go into a street unaccompanied': per Lord

and an accident occurs as a result, then any person who suffers injury by reason of the accident could succeed in a claim in negligence against the school's staff and those who employ them. Furthermore, a school may be liable if it fails to take reasonable precautions to prevent pupils from gaining access to a pile of building materials, and a pupil is injured as a result of one pupil gaining such access and throwing some of the material at the victim.[1] However, an education provider will not be liable in the law of negligence for the bullying by one pupil of another unless there was negligence in relation to the supervision of the bully.[2] In this context the reference in *Beaumont v Surrey County Council*[3] to the 'known propensities' of girls and boys aged between 11 and 18 is likely to be particularly relevant.[4] Indeed, the Court of Appeal has stated that a failure to exercise disciplinary powers against a pupil who has attacked another pupil outside school could be negligent.[5] Further, HHJ Wilkie QC held in *Faulkner v Enfield London Borough Council*[6] that the duty of care owed by the school in question was a duty:

> 'to take reasonable care to protect pupils from bullying and other mistreatment by other pupils when at school and, where parents were reasonably concerned about the continued safety of their children when at school, to act reasonably so as to provide information to enable them to take properly informed decisions about whether to permit the children to continue to attend the school or to withdraw them.'

Employment of an independent contractor

14.50 The rule that a person will not normally be liable for the acts of an independent contractor unless one of a number of exceptions can be relied upon (for example where the contractor was negligently selected) applies in the school context.[7] One situation where liability might nevertheless arise is where pupils go to an outdoor activity centre. It is possible that a failure to follow the detailed recommendations in relation to the choosing of such a centre contained in DfE Circular 22/94 would be regarded as negligent. Furthermore, the fact that certain outdoor activity centres must now be licensed under the Adventure Activities Licensing Regulations 1996[8] means

---

Goddard at ibid, at 560; or 'a child so young that it cannot safely be allowed on a busy street by itself': per Lord Keith at 570.

[1]   See *Jackson v London County Council and Chappell* (1912) 28 TLR 359; but note *Good v Inner London Education Authority* (1980) 10 Fam Law 213, as to which see para **14.43**.

[2]   See *Walker v Derbyshire County Council* (1994). The course of the hearing is reported as a news item in *The Times* of 7 June 1994, at p 10; the outcome of the hearing is indicated by NS Harris in *The Law Relating to Schools* (Tolley, 2nd edn, 1995), at 339. See also, for example, *Ricketts v Erith Borough Council* (1943) 42 LGR 71 and *Clark v Monmouthshire County Council* (1954) 52 LGR 246, CA.

[3]   (1968) 66 LGR 580. See para **14.23**.

[4]   Contrast, however, *Etheridge v Kitson and East Sussex County Council* [1999] EdCR 550, where the first defendant was a pupil.

[5]   *Bradford-Smart v West Sussex County Council* [2002] EWCA Civ 7, [2002] ELR 139, at para 34.

[6]   [2003] ELR 426, at para 63.

[7]   See, for example, *Myton v Woods* (1980) 79 LGR 440, and see further, for example, *Clerk and Lindsell on Torts* (Sweet & Maxwell, 18th edn, 2000) at paras 5.48 et seq.

[8]   SI 1996/772; those regulations apply to a local authority which provides relevant facilities to an educational establishment in respect of the pupils of such an establishment as well as to a person who provides relevant facilities in return for payment: reg 3(1). However, the exceptions in reg 3(2) should be noted; one occurs where in certain circumstances the facilities are provided by a voluntary association, and another occurs where the facilities are provided 'by an educational establishment to pupils of that establishment'.

that if the education provider chose a centre which was required to be but was not so licensed and an injury occurred to a relevant pupil, then the education provider might be held to have been negligent in choosing that centre.

School trips

14.51 Where pupils are taken on a school trip then a duty of care will clearly apply. The nature of that duty, and the standard of care, were stated by Auld LJ (with whom Carnwath LJ and Sir Swinton Thomas agreed) in *Woodbridge School v Chittock*[1] so helpfully but succinctly that the relevant paragraph bears repeating in full here:

'(i)   Mr Jackson and his fellow teachers on the skiing trip owed a duty to Simon [the claimant] to show the same care in relation to him as would have been exercised by a reasonably careful parent credited with experience of skiing and its hazards and of running school ski trips, but also taking into account Simon's known level of skiing competence and experience, the nature and conditions of the particular resort and the teachers' responsibilities for the school group as a whole.

(ii)   This could, in appropriate circumstances, include a duty to take positive steps by way of supervision or otherwise to protect Simon from doing himself harm. See eg *Van Oppen v Clerk to the Bedford Charity Trustees* [1990] 1 WLR 235, per Croom Johnson LJ, at 266D-F; *Hippolyte v Bexley London Borough Council* [1995] PIQR P309, per Steyn LJ, at 314; and *Gower v London Borough of Bromley* [1999] ELR 356, per Auld LJ, at 359G-H.

(iii)   It was not a duty to ensure his safety against injury from skiing mishaps such as those that might result from his own misjudgement or inadvertence when skiing unsupervised on-piste. It was a duty to take such steps as in all the circumstances were reasonable to see that he skied safely and otherwise behaved in a responsible manner. See, for example, *O'Shea v Royal Borough of Kingston-upon-Thames* [1995] PIQR P208, per Neill LJ, at 213.

(iv)   Where there are a number of options for the teacher as to the manner in which he might discharge that duty, he is not negligent if he chooses one which, exercising the Bolam test (*Bolam v Friern Hospital Management Committee* [1957] 1 WLR 582), would be within a reasonable range of options for a reasonable teacher exercising that duty of care in the circumstances. See eg *X (Minors) v Bedfordshire County Council* ... [1995] 2 AC 633, ... [1995] ELR 404, per Lord Browne Wilkinson, at 766E-G and 451E respectively; and *Gower v London Borough of Bromley* [1999] ELR 356, at 360H-361A.

(v)   The duty of care of organisers of school skiing trips should, as Mr Wilby submitted, be considered in the context of any available appropriate guidance for such activity. See, for example *Smoldon v Whitworth and Another* [1997] PIQR P133, [1997] ELR 249; and *O'Shea v Royal Borough of Kingston-upon-Thames* [1995] PIQR P208. Mr Wilby has taken us through the documents of guidance available here, including the Skiers' Code, but they do not seem to me to add materially to the other evidence and reasoning of the judge, namely that teachers in loco parentis should provide a level of supervision appropriate to the age, skiing experience, ability, and behaviour of the pupils in their charge.

(vi)   The standard of care should reflect the particular circumstances in which Simon went on the trip. These included the understanding with his parents that he should

---

[1]   [2002] EWCA Civ 915, [2002] ELR 735, para 18.

be allowed to ski unsupervised, but also an implicit assumption by the school of responsibility for general oversight of his skiing and other activities at the resort, backed, where necessary, by appropriate discipline to safeguard him and others from reasonably foreseeable harm. See *Smoldon v Whitworth and Another* [1997] PIQR P133, [1997] ELR 249, per Lord Bingham of Cornhill CJ, at 139 and 254 respectively.'

14.52   One issue which was not clarified by this passage is whether there would be a duty so to supervise pupils that they did not become intoxicated. Bearing in mind that a parent can often not prevent a young person nearing the age of 18 from drinking, it would seem wrong to make a teacher liable if a pupil of a similar age became intoxicated on a school trip unless there was something extra in the circumstances pointing towards liability. If, however, the teacher assumed responsibility for the pupil after the pupil became intoxicated and the pupil suffered injury as a result, liability in negligence for that injury might well arise.[1]

Work experience

14.53   One situation in which the ordinary principles in the law of negligence must apply is where a pupil is sent by a school or LEA to undertake work experience under s 560 of the EA 1996.[2] In particular, the body which sends the pupil on work experience must be under a duty to exercise reasonable care (but no more) as judged in the light of the relevant circumstances. This would mean reasonable care in the selection of the place to which a pupil was sent on work experience.

Indecent acts of teachers

14.54   In *Lister v Hesley Hall Ltd*,[3] the House of Lords held (overruling earlier decisions including that of the Court of Appeal in *Trotman v North Yorkshire County Council*[4]) that the employer of a teacher who had sexually abused a mentally disabled schoolboy entrusted to his care, was vicariously liable for the torts which were committed as a result of that abuse.

Contributory negligence

14.55   It was stated (*obiter*) in *Gough v Upshire Primary School*[5] by HHJ Grenfell that he would, if he had found the defendant liable in negligence, have found the claimant, a child aged 8 years old, contributorily negligent. As HHJ Grenfell put it:

'an 8-year-old has difficulty in comprehending the likely extent of an injury that he might suffer if he [climbed onto a smooth bannister]. For this reason, any contribution to the responsibility for his accident would be less than for an adult. Nevertheless, if I had found the defendant school to have been in breach of duty, I would have found a substantial percentage of contributory negligence, even against an 8-year-old, simply because clearly he knew there was serious danger involved in doing what he did. This

---

[1]   Cf *Barrett v Ministry of Defence* [1995] 1 WLR 1217, as to which, see para **17.105**.
[2]   See para **4.71** concerning s 560.
[3]   [2002] 1 AC 215.
[4]   [1998] ELR 625.
[5]   [2002] ELR 169, at para 25.

makes sufficient allowance for his age, because an adult who did the same thing would undoubtedly have been the sole cause of his injury.'

LIABILITY FOR NEGLIGENCE IN RELATION TO THE PROVISION OF EDUCATION WHERE NO PHYSICAL INJURY OCCURS

Duty of care

14.56 In *Phelps v Hillingdon London Borough Council*,[1] the House of Lords confirmed a number of matters of general principle relating to claims of negligence in connection with the provision of education. The main rulings are as follows.

(1)   If a duty of care would exist where advice was given other than pursuant to the exercise of statutory powers, such duty is not excluded because the advice was given pursuant to statutory powers.[2]

(2)   There may be cases where the recognition of vicarious liability on the part of an LEA may so interfere with the performance by the LEA of its duties that it would be wrong to recognise such liability on the part of the LEA. However, it is for an LEA to establish such interference: it cannot be presumed, and the circumstances in which such interference could be established are likely to be exceptional.[3]

(3)   Not only could a teacher or an educational psychologist be liable in the law of negligence towards people who, it could be foreseen, would be injured if due skill and care were not exercised in the performance by the teacher or (as the case may be) educational psychologist of his or her duties, but so could an education officer performing the functions of an LEA in regard to children with SEN.[4]

(4)   The fact that, for example, an educational psychologist was employed as part of a LEA's team to provide necessary services in connection with the exercise of the LEA's statutory functions and therefore owed a duty to the LEA to exercise skill and care in the performance of his or her contract of employment, does not mean that no duty of care could be, or was, owed to the child. Nor does the fact that the educational psychologist was called in in pursuance of the performance of the LEA's statutory duties mean that no duty of care was owed by him or her if, in exercising his or her profession, he or she would otherwise have a duty of care.[5]

(5)   Nevertheless, that will only be the beginning of the enquiry: it will still be necessary to show that the educational psychologist was acting in relation to a child in a situation where the law recognises a duty of care. So, for example, a casual remark, an isolated act, may occur in a situation where there was no

---

[1]   [2001] 2 AC 619.

[2]   See per Lord Slynn, with whose speech the majority of their Lordships agreed (although they also agreed with the speech of Lord Clyde), ibid, at 653.

[3]   Ibid.

[4]   Ibid. In *Carty v London Borough of Croydon* [2004] ELR 226, Gibbs J applied this ruling.

[5]   Ibid, at 654.

sufficient nexus between the two persons for a duty of care to exist. But where an educational psychologist was specifically called in to advise in relation to the assessment and future provision for a specific child, and it was clear that the parents acting for the child and the teachers would follow that advice, at first sight a duty of care arose. There was no need for the educational psychologist knowingly and deliberately to accept responsibility. Rather, responsibility is recognised or imposed by the law.[1]

(6)   If foreseeability of psychological injury (as opposed to a recognisable psychiatric condition) and causation is established, such injury can constitute damage (in the form of personal injury) for the purposes of the common law.[2]

(7)   Equally, where (1) a failure to diagnose a congenital condition and to take appropriate action occurred, (2) that failure led to a child's level of achievement being reduced, and (3) that in turn led to loss of employment and wages, a claim for damages for negligence can in appropriate circumstances be made. Questions in those circumstances of causation and the quantum of damage might be very difficult, especially if the claim was made long after the event, but there is no reason in principle to rule out such a claim.[3]

(8)   There is no reason of public policy why the courts should not recognise that an LEA should be vicariously liable for such negligence. Nevertheless, the difficulties of the tasks involved and the circumstances under which people have to work in the area in question must be borne fully in mind. The professionalism, dedication and standards of those engaged in the provision of educational services are such that cases of liability for negligence will be exceptional.[4]

(9)   A claim in negligence in relation to the provision of education to a pupil against an LEA directly cannot be ruled out: an LEA could in some circumstances owe a duty of care and be negligent in the performance of it. The facts that (a) the parents of a child of compulsory school age have their own duties under what is now s 7 of the EA 1996, and (b) consultation and appeal procedures exist (such as in relation to children for whom statements are prepared under s 324 of that Act), do not preclude the existence of such a duty of care. However, it may rarely be necessary to invoke a claim of direct liability in relevant circumstances, given that an LEA can act only through its employees or agents and given the existence in those circumstances of vicarious liability.[5]

---

[1]   [2001] 2 AC 619, at 654.
[2]   Ibid, at 654 and 664.
[3]   Ibid, at 654, 670, and 672–673.
[4]   Ibid, at 655.
[5]   [2001] 2 AC 619, at 658. In *Carty v London Borough of Croydon* [2004] ELR 226, at para 75, Gibbs J commented that 'the need for a separate "direct" duty is by no means clear'. However, that comment was made against the background of the facts of that case. In other circumstances the possibility of direct liability may be important.

Standard of care

14.57   The House of Lords confirmed in *Phelps* that the standard of care in education negligence claims is determined by applying the test in *Bolam v Friern Hospital Management Committee.*[1]

14.58   In *X v Bedfordshire County Council*,[2] it was pointed out by Lord Browne-Wilkinson (with whom the other members of the Judicial Committee of the House of Lords agreed) that the *Bolam* test applied, for example, to an educational psychologist requires only that the psychologist exercised the ordinary skill of a competent psychologist and that he acted in accordance with the accepted views of some reputable psychologist at the relevant time, even if other psychologists would have adopted a different view. The House of Lords also held in *X v Bedfordshire County Council* that a head teacher need not exercise the skill of an educational psychologist.[3]

14.59   In *Smith v London Borough of Havering*,[4] David Foskett QC, sitting as a Deputy High Court Judge, said that it was 'no part of [his] task to review discretionary decisions made by the education authority in relation to the allocation of resources', and in so doing relied on a statement in *X v Bedfordshire County Council*.[5] This, surely, cannot be right, for the following reasons. If an LEA deliberately decided to limit the funds devoted to the meeting of SEN, so that for example the making of a statement of SEN would not lead to the devotion to a child's SEN of any more by way of financial resources than would otherwise have been the case, that surely could be negligent. The fact that it was held by Collins J in *R v London Borough of Hillingdon, ex parte Governing Body of Queensmead School*[6] that if an LEA delegates to a school's governing body the funds for meeting the SEN of a pupil at the school for whom a statement is made under s 324 of the EA 1996, the amount so delegated must be sufficient to meet those needs, provides strong support for this proposition. The passage of the speech of Lord Browne-Wilkinson in *X v Bedfordshire County Council* on which David Foskett QC relied in *Smith* can, furthermore, be seen as inconsistent with the approach taken by the House of Lords in *Phelps*.[7]

Limitation period

14.60   Where a claim of negligence in relation to the education of a child includes a claim of a negligent failure to ameliorate dyslexia, that aspect of the claim at least will be a claim for damages for personal injury.[8] Thus the primary limitation period for such a claim is 3 years,[9] although that period will start to run only from the date of the child's attaining the age of 18 or (if later) the date of knowledge that the injury was significant and that it was attributable in whole or in part to the act or omission which

1   [1957] 1 WLR 582. See per Lord Slynn at [2001] 2 AC 619, 655, and per Lord Clyde at 672.
2   [1995] 2 AC 633, at 763F–G.
3   Ibid, at 766F–G.
4   [2004] EWHC 599, at para 90.
5   [1995] 2 AC 633, at 737.
6   [1997] ELR 331, at 347D.
7   See [2001] 2 AC 691 at 658, per Lord Slynn, and at 668, per Lord Nicholls.
8   *Adams v Bracknell Forest Borough Council* [2004] UKHL 29, [2004] 3 WLR 89.
9   Limitation Act 1980, s 11.

it is alleged constituted negligence.[1] Further, a claim may be permitted to be made after the primary limitation period has expired, under s 33 of the Limitation Act 1980.

14.61 That s 33 will only rarely assist a claimant is clear from the Court of Appeal's decisions in *Robinson v St Helens Metropolitan Borough Council*[2] and *Rowe v Kingston Upon Hull City Council*,[3] and that of the House of Lords in *Adams v Bracknell Forest Borough Council*.[4]

Amount of damages which may be awarded as a result of the negligent provision of education

14.62 The only reported case in which damages for loss arising out of the negligence of an educational psychologist were awarded, is *Phelps v Hillingdon London Borough Council*.[5] However, in several cases where the court decided against the claimant on liability, the court gave an indication of the amount of damages which it would have awarded had the claim succeeded on the facts.

14.63 In *Phelps*,[6] the court awarded the claimant £12,500 by way of general damages, £25,000 'for the loss of the opportunity to earn at a higher rate than that which the plaintiff is now able to command (if fit and willing) or may be able to command after 2 or 3 years' further tuition and education', and some special damages. In *Liennard v Slough Borough Council*,[7] although Henriques J rejected the claim on the facts, he indicated what he would have awarded by way of damages if the claim had succeeded. This was £15,000 by way of general damages, and £20,000 to represent 'the loss of the opportunity to gain employment at the end of a successful period of education'.[8] In *Smith v London Borough of Havering*,[9] the court would have awarded £7,500 as general damages for the claimant's not having 'a better two years or so after he left school' and '[s]omething in the region of £10,000' by way of compensation for 'a slower start on the earnings ladder'. However, in that case the claimant had apparently been able to overcome his difficulties rather well.

---

[1]   Limitation Act 1980, s 14. See further, *Adams v Bracknell Forest Borough Council* [2004] UKHL 29, [2004] 3 WLR 89.

[2]   [2002] EWCA Civ 1099, [2002] ELR 681.

[3]   [2003] EWCA Civ 1281, [2003] ELR 771. See also *Meherali v Hampshire County Council* [2002] EWHC 2655 (QB), [2003] ELR 338 (HC).

[4]   [2004] UKHL 29, [2004] 3 WLR 89.

[5]   [1998] ELR 38, [1998] EdCR 47. The claim in *Christmas v Hampshire County Council* [1998] ELR 1, which was one of the cases which were joined for the purpose of the appeal to the House of Lords in *X v Bedfordshire County Council*, was eventually unsuccessful on the facts. The same is true of *Keating v London Borough of Bromley* [2003] EWHC 1070 (QB), [2003] ELR 590, which was one of the other cases which had been joined for the purposes of the appeal in *X v Bedfordshire County Council*.

[6]   [1998] ELR 38, at 64–65.

[7]   [2002] EWHC 398 (QB), [2002] ELR 527.

[8]   See para 72.

[9]   [2004] EWHC 599, at paras 98–100.

BREACH OF STATUTORY DUTY

14.64   A claim for damages for breach of statutory duty in relation to the provision of education may not be made against a maintained school governing body or an LEA.[1]

EDUCATION (SCHOOL PREMISES) REGULATIONS 1989

14.65   There appears at present to be only one statutory duty arising in the education context alone and in relation to which it has been held that a breach could give rise to a claim for breach of statutory duty. That statutory duty is the one relating to the provision of premises, contained (now) in the Education (School Premises) Regulations 1999,[2] made under s 542 of the EA 1996 Act. The case where it was held that a breach of one of the predecessors to those regulations could give rise to a claim for breach of statutory duty is *Reffell v Surrey County Council*.[3] It was there held that the regulations were to be applied objectively rather than subjectively. There was also in the circumstances a breach of the Occupiers' Liability Act 1957, to which a brief reference will now be made.

Occupiers' Liability Acts

14.66   There are two Acts imposing liability in tort on the occupier of premises in certain circumstances. These are the Occupiers' Liability Act 1957 and the Occupiers' Liability Act 1984. The former concerns lawful visitors, and the latter concerns trespassers. The content of the duty imposed by those Acts on an occupier of premises is outside the scope of this book,[4] but the terms of s 2(3) of the former bear repeating here. According to that subsection, the circumstances which an occupier of land must take into account in determining what needs to be done to see that the visitor will be reasonably safe in using the premises for the purposes for which he is invited or permitted by the occupier to be there:

> 'include the degree of care, and of want of care, which would ordinarily be looked for in a visitor so that (for example) in proper cases –
>
> (a)   an occupier must be prepared for children to be less careful than adults.'

14.67   Despite the latter words, which were not referred to by the Court of Appeal in *Barrie v Cardiff City Council*,[5] Pill LJ (with whom Chadwick LJ agreed) there held that 'a playground is ... not to be criticised by the standards of a bowling green'.[6]

---

[1]   See *Phelps v Hillingdon London Borough Council* [2001] 2 AC 619, per Lord Slynn, at 652, with whose speech the majority of their Lordships agreed, although they also agreed with the speech of Lord Clyde. Lord Clyde did not refer specifically to this issue.

[2]   SI 1999/2.

[3]   [1964] 1 WLR 358.

[4]   Although the case of *Ratcliff v Governors of Harper Adams Agricultural College* [1999] EdCR 523 is of interest to all education institutions which have swimming pools in their grounds.

[5]   [2001] EWCA Civ 703, [2002] ELR 1.

[6]   Ibid, at para 23.

Health and Safety at Work etc Act 1974

14.68 The duties of an employer under the health and safety legislation (principally the Health and Safety at Work etc Act 1974 (HASAWA 1974) and the regulations made under that Act) concern in the main the duties of an employer to its employees. Accordingly, the majority of those duties are outside the scope of this book. However, several provisions of that Act need to be mentioned here. For example, it was held by the Divisional Court in *Moualem v Carlisle City Council*[1] that the children who were present at a children's play centre were within the scope of the duty of s 4 of the HASAWA 1974. That section:

'has effect for imposing on persons duties in relation to those who
(a)   are not their employees; but
(b)   use non-domestic premises made available to them ... as a place where they may use plant or substances provided for their use there,
and applies to premises so made available and other non-domestic premises used in connection with them.'[2]

14.69 Furthermore, s 3(1) of the HASAWA 1974 will almost certainly apply in favour of pupils at school. That subsection provides:

'It shall be the duty of every employer to conduct his undertaking in such a way as to ensure, so far as is reasonably practicable, that persons not in his employment who may be affected thereby are not thereby exposed to risks to their health or safety.'

14.70 It was assumed by the Court of Appeal (Criminal Division) in *R v Board of Trustees of the Science Museum*[3] that that subsection extended to danger to members of the public in the street from legionnaires' disease caused by contaminated water in cooling towers. If that assumption was correct then there can be no doubt that s 3(1) applies in favour of pupils.[4]

14.71 Neither s 3 nor s 4 of the HASAWA 1974 imposes civil liability; both give rise to possible criminal liability only.[5] However, liability may arise for breach of many of the numerous regulations which have been made under the HASAWA 1974.[6] The detail of those regulations and the numerous other health and safety regulations which apply in the school context are outside the scope of this book. However, it is noted that in *Purvis v Buckinghamshire County Council*,[7] it was held that reg 4 of the Manual Handling Operations Regulations 1992,[8] applied to the physical handling of a disruptive pupil.

---

[1]   [1995] ELR 22.
[2]   The plant in question consisted of the equipment provided at the play centre.
[3]   [1993] 1 WLR 1171.
[4]   This is the view of the DfEE expressed in Circular 14/96.
[5]   HASAWA 1974, s 47(1).
[6]   Ibid, s 47(2).
[7]   [1999] ELR 231, 235C–G; [1999] EdCR 542, at 547D–548A.
[8]   SI 1992/2793.

LEGAL ISSUES ARISING IN THE LAW OF TORT IN THE RELATIONSHIP BETWEEN A MINOR STUDENT OR HIS PARENT AND A FURTHER OR HIGHER EDUCATION PROVIDER

14.72 As indicated above, the legal issues in the law of tort which arise in regard to the relationship between a further education provider or a higher education provider and a minor student or his parent will be the same as those occurring in relation to a school pupil who is under the age of 18. Nothing more therefore needs to be said about them here.

Chapter 15

THE STAFFING OF SCHOOLS AND FURTHER EDUCATION INSTITUTIONS

INTRODUCTION

15.1   The regulation of the staffing in particular of a maintained school has in some respects increased considerably in recent years. This is in the main a result of the increase in legislation concerning checks into the past of applicants for posts in which the post-holder will come into contact with children. In contrast, however, once the provisions concerning dismissal procedures in the Employment Act 2002 are fully in force, the regulation of the procedure to be followed in dismissing members of the staff of a maintained school (as such) will be diminished.

15.2   In this chapter, the effects of the current legislation concerning the training, qualification, conduct and fitness to teach of teachers are first described. Reference is then made to the current statutory provisions affecting employment in maintained schools.

TEACHER TRAINING

The Teacher Training Agency

15.3   The Teacher Training Agency (TTA) was established by s 1 of the Education Act 1994 (EA 1994). The TTA must have between eight and 12 members, all appointed by the Secretary of State.[1] The primary functions of the TTA are to distribute government funding for the training of teachers and to provide information and advice on teaching as a career.[2] A little unusually, s 1(2) sets out the objectives of the Agency. These are (a) to contribute to raising the standards of teaching; (b) to promote teaching as a career; (c) to improve the quality and efficiency of all routes into the teaching profession; (d) to secure the involvement of schools in all courses and programmes for the initial training of school teachers; and (e):

> 'generally to secure that teachers are well fitted and trained to promote the spiritual, moral, social, cultural, mental and physical development of pupils and to prepare pupils for the opportunities, responsibilities and experiences of adult life.'

---

[1]   EA 1994, s 2(1). See the other provisions of s 2 concerning the membership, and Sch 1 to the EA 1994 in relation to the constitution, of the TTA.

[2]   Ibid, s 1(1).

15.4   The TTA must in exercising its functions 'have regard to the requirements of persons who are disabled persons for the purposes of the Disability Discrimination Act 1995'.[1]

15.5   There is no separate TTA for Wales: the TTA has functions in relation to Wales unless the EA 1994 provides otherwise in respect of particular functions, although the TTA may not do anything in relation to Wales, or institutions or students in Wales, except at the request of the National Assembly for Wales.[2] The TTA's main function is 'administering funds made available to them by the Secretary of State and others for the purpose of providing financial support for the carrying on by eligible institutions of qualifying activities', but that function is exercisable only in relation to England.[3] The Higher Education Funding Council for Wales (HEFCW) has the same function in relation to Wales.[4] Both bodies may, however, exercise that function in relation to the Open University.[5] Any dispute as to the funding body by which any functions are exercisable is to be determined by the Secretary of State.[6]

15.6   Activities for which funding may be provided include (1) the provision of teacher training and related facilities, (2) the carrying on of related activities by eligible institutions, and (3) the provision by any person of services for the purposes of, or in connection with, such training and/or activities.[7] Eligible institutions for this purpose are (1) any institution within the higher or further education sector, (2) any school, (3) any other institution or body designated by an order of the Secretary of State (which must be made by statutory instrument[8]), and (4) 'any partnership or association of eligible institutions, or body established by one or more such institutions, for the purpose of carrying on qualifying activities'.[9]

15.7   The terms and conditions on which the TTA or (in Wales) the HEFCW may give funding under the EA 1994 are very similar to those on which the higher education councils are empowered to give funding.[10] However, the provisions in the EA 1994 are tailored to fit the circumstances of teacher training. The provisions concerning the funding by the TTA and the HEFCW of teacher training are contained in ss 5 and 6. Those bodies receive their funding from the Secretary of State

---

[1]   EA 1994, s 1(4) as inserted by the DDA 1995 and (again, seemingly in error) by the SENDA 2001. See paras **2.34–2.36** concerning the impact of a requirement to 'have regard' to something. See s 1 of, and Sch 1 to, the DDA 1995 for the definition of a person who is disabled for the purposes of the DDA 1995.

[2]   EA 1994, s 1(3), read with the National Assembly for Wales (Transfer of Functions) Order 1999, SI 1999/672: see Sch 1 to that Order.

[3]   See ibid, s 3. See the following paragraphs regarding the institutions to which, and the activities for which, funds may be given under s 3.

[4]   Ibid.

[5]   Ibid, s 3(2).

[6]   Ibid.

[7]   Ibid, s 4(1).

[8]   See ibid, s 23(1). Many orders have been made under s 4.

[9]   Ibid, s 4(2).

[10] See paras **17.13** et seq for the provisions relating to the provision of higher education. It should be noted that the same conditions as may be required in respect of the levying of fees by higher education institutions as a result of s 26 of the THEA 1998 apply also to the TTA.

(or, as the case may be, the National Assembly for Wales;[1] in what follows, a reference to the Secretary of State should, unless otherwise stated, include a reference to the National Assembly, and, for the sake of simplicity, wherever possible reference is made only to the TTA) under s 7, the terms of which are similar to those which apply to the provision by the Secretary of State of funding to the higher education funding councils.[2]

15.8   The TTA must comply with any directions given by the Secretary of State under s 8 of the EA 1994, the provisions of which are, so far as relevant, the same as those of s 81 of the FHEA 1992.[3] The TTA and/or the HEFCW and any of (1) the Higher Education Funding Council for England, (2) the LSC, and (3) the CETW, may exercise any of their functions jointly, where it appears to them that to do so will be more efficient or will enable them more effectively to discharge any of their functions.[4]

15.9   The TTA may, under s 10 of the EA 1994, arrange efficiency studies relating to the management or operations of an institution which is receiving funding under Part I of the EA 1994. Any person promoting or carrying out such a study at the request of the TTA may require the institution to provide such information and make available for inspection their accounts and such other documents as he may reasonably require for the purpose.[5] In addition, the TTA may, under s 11 of the EA 1994, carry out or commission research with a view to improving (a) the training of teachers, or (b) the standards of teaching.

15.10   The Secretary of State may, under s 16(1) or (2) of the EA 1994, by order (made by statutory instrument[6]) confer or impose additional or supplementary functions on the TTA, under s 16(1) or (2) of the 1994 Act.[7] One such order was the Teacher Training Agency (Additional Functions) Order 2000,[8] under which the TTA now has 'the additional function of arranging the assessment of candidates undertaking national tests for teacher training candidates in numeracy and information and communications technology'. The Secretary of State may also, under s 16(4), direct either the TTA or the HEFCW to carry out activities which are ancillary to their functions under Part I of the EA 1994.

15.11   The TTA may also be given power under s 145 of the EA 2002 to approve or accredit a qualification, course, programme or institution for the purposes of ss 132–140 of that Act.[9]

---

[1]   See SI 1999/672.

[2]   See paras **17.10–17.12** for the provisions relating to the higher education funding councils.

[3]   The provisions of s 81 of the FHEA 1992 are described in para **17.27**, and because of the equivalence of those provisions, no further reference to the provisions of s 8 is made here.

[4]   EA 1994, s 9(1) and (2). The reference in s 9(2) to 'a funding authority for schools' is now redundant.

[5]   Ibid, s 10(2).

[6]   Ibid, s 23(1).

[7]   The power in relation to the HEFCW relates to existing functions of the Secretary of State of any sort: see ibid, s 16(2).

[8]   SI 2000/1000.

[9]   See further below in this chapter concerning ss 132–140.

Provision of initial teacher training by maintained schools

15.12 Under s 12(1)(a) of the EA 1994, the governing body of any community, foundation or voluntary or community or foundation special school may provide 'courses of initial training for school teachers'. They may also join in a partnership or association with other eligible institutions (within the meaning of s 4 of the EA 1994[1]) for the purpose of doing the same.[2] These initial teacher training courses must be open only to persons holding a degree or an equivalent qualification.[3] The governing body's delegated budget must not be spent on any such course.[4]

The provision of information

15.13 The TTA must provide information to the Secretary of State under s 15(1)(a) of the EA 1994, and may under s 15(1)(b) provide him with such information and advice as it thinks fit. Section 69 of the FHEA 1992 places the HEFCW under a parallel (albeit slightly differently worded) obligation.[5] Those two funding bodies must give each other any information which they may require for the purposes of the exercise of their functions under Part I of the EA 1994.[6] The governing body of any institution which is receiving, has received, or has applied for, funding under that Part, and any LEA, must give the TTA or the HEFCW any information which it may require for the purpose of the exercise of their functions under that Part.[7]

Inspection of teacher training institutions

15.14 Under s 18A(1) of the EA 1994, the Chief Inspector[8] may inspect and report on '(a) any initial training of teachers, or of specialist teaching assistants, for schools, or (b) any in-service training of such teachers or assistants, which is provided by a relevant institution'.[9]

15.15 The Chief Inspector has a right of entry and a right to inspect, and take copies of, documents and records for the purposes of an inspection under s 18A,[10] and s 42 of the SIA 1996 (concerning the inspection of computer records[11]) applies.[12] These rights of inspection are restricted by s 18A(9), in that nothing in s 18A applies 'in

---

1   As to which, see para **15.6**.

2   EA 1994, s 12(1)(b).

3   Ibid, s 12(2).

4   See ibid, s 12(6).

5   See paras **17.20** and **17.21** regarding s 69.

6   EA 1994, s 15(2).

7   Ibid, s 15(3).

8   The Chief Inspector for this purpose in relation to England means Her Majesty's Chief Inspector of Schools in England, and in relation to Wales, means Her Majesty's Chief Inspector of Schools in Wales: EA 1994, s 18A(10)(a). It also means any person authorised by either such Inspector under para 5(1) or (2) of Sch 1 to the School Inspections Act 1996: see EA 1994, s 18A(11).

9   A 'relevant institution' for this purpose is defined by s 18A(10)(b) as an eligible institution for the purposes of Part I of the EA 1994 (as to which, see para **15.6**), and 'any other institution, body, or person designated by the Secretary of State as being in receipt of public funding in respect of the provision of training falling within subsection (1)(a) or (b) [of s 18A]'.

10   EA 1994, s 18A(5).

11   See para **12.8** as to s 42.

12   EA 1994, s 18A(5).

relation to any course which consists of instruction given wholly or mainly for purposes other than training falling within subsection (1)(a) or (b)'.

THE QUALIFICATION REQUIREMENTS FOR TEACHING IN MAINTAINED SCHOOLS AND NON-MAINTAINED SPECIAL SCHOOLS

15.16 Regulations may prohibit the carrying out in a school which is maintained by an LEA[1] or a non-maintained special school of what is called in s 133 of the EA 2002 'specified work', except by a person who (a) is a 'qualified teacher' or (b) satisfies 'specified requirements'.[2] The nature of such specified work was left to be determined by regulations: it was not defined by the EA 2002. The Education (Specified Work and Registration) (England) Regulations 2003[3] define specified work for this purpose in England.[4] It is essentially the core work of a teacher (1) planning and preparing lessons and courses for pupils, (2) delivering lessons to pupils, (3) assessing the development, progress and attainment of pupils, and (4) reporting on such development, progress and attainment.[5] Those regulations also contain the relevant prohibition[6] and specify the relevant requirements.[7] A person who is neither a qualified teacher nor able to satisfy the requirements specified for the purpose by paras 2–9 of Sch 2 to those regulations may nevertheless carry out such specified work 'in order to assist the work of a qualified teacher or a nominated teacher in the school', but only if the head teacher is satisfied that the person has the skills, expertise and experience required to carry out such work.[8] Furthermore, the person must be subject to the direction of a qualified or nominated teacher in accordance with arrangements made by the head teacher of the school.[9] In determining whether a person has such skills, expertise and experience, the head teacher may (not must) have regard to 'such standards for higher-level teaching assistants, or guidance concerning school support staff as may be published from time to time by the Secretary of State', and to 'such guidance as to contractual matters relating to school support staff as may be published from time to time by any local education authority or other employer'.[10]

15.17 In order to be a 'qualified teacher' for this purpose (and any other purpose of the Education Acts), a person must satisfy the requirements of regulations made under s 132 of the EA 2002. The current regulations are the Education (School

---

[1]   Defined for this purpose by SSFA 1998, s 20(6) and (7): see EA 2002, s 212(2)–(4) and SSFA 1998, s 142(8). Thus, it includes a nursery school which is a special school, but not a nursery school which is not a special school. It also does not include a pupil referral unit.

[2]   EA 2002, s 133(1) and (6).

[3]   SI 2003/1663.

[4]   In relation to Wales, see the Education (Specified Work and Registration) (Wales) Regulations 2004, SI 2004/1744.

[5]   See SI 2003/1663, reg 6.

[6]   Ibid, reg 5.

[7]   See ibid, Sch 2.

[8]   Ibid, Sch 2, para 10(2)(a) and (c).

[9]   See ibid, Sch 2, para 10(2)(b); see Sch 2, para 10(3) for the definition of a 'nominated teacher' for this purpose.

[10]   Ibid, Sch 2, para 10(4).

Teachers' Qualifications (England) Regulations 2003[1] and the Education (School Teachers' Qualifications) (Wales) Regulations 2004.[2] It is of interest that qualified teacher status under those regulations is awarded by the General Teaching Council for England (GTC), although that appears simply to be a formality as long as the teacher satisfies the requirements in one of paras 2–13 of Sch 2 to those regulations.[3] The GTC does so by 'written notification'.[4] The regulations apply not only to what one might call 'ordinary' teachers, but also to mandatory additional qualifications for teachers of (1) hearing impaired pupils,[5] (2) visually impaired pupils,[6] and (3) pupils who are both hearing and visually impaired.[7] There are also provisions in the regulations relating to teachers of art, handicraft, music, needlework and domestic subjects, speech and drama, and to certain 'other qualifications'.[8]

REQUIREMENT TO BE REGISTERED

15.18 Regulations may provide that specified work is carried out in a school which is maintained by an LEA or non-maintained special school by a qualified teacher only if he is registered with full registration under s 3 of the THEA 1998.[9] Similarly, regulations may provide that specified work may be carried out by a person other than a qualified teacher only if that person is registered with provisional such registration.[10] Regulations may also provide that a person may undertake a specified course of training with a view to becoming a qualified teacher only if he is registered with such provisional registration.[11] Specified work for these purposes is defined by the Education (Specified Work and Registration) (England) Regulations 2003,[12] which also contain the relevant prohibition, subject to exceptions[13] and transitional provisions.[14]

---

[1] SI 2003/1662.

[2] SI 2004/1729.

[3] See reg 10. See below in this chapter concerning the GTC. The TTA has a number of functions in connection with the means by which persons may acquire qualified teacher status: see reg 11 and Sch 2, paras 7, 9 and 10.

[4] Regulation 10(1).

[5] Regulation 6.

[6] Regulation 7.

[7] Regulation 8.

[8] See Part 2 of Sch 2 to the regulations.

[9] EA 2002, s 134(1) and (5). See para **15.53** in relation to s 3 of the THEA 1998. For the definition of a maintained school for this purpose, see footnote 1 at para **15.16**.

[10] Ibid, s 134(2). This subsection is currently not in force in England or Wales.

[11] Ibid, s 134(3). This subsection is currently not in force in England or Wales.

[12] SI 2003/1663. See reg 6, as to which, see para **15.16**.

[13] See reg 7 and Sch 3.

[14] See reg 4 and Part 2 of Sch 1. For the current prohibition in relation to Wales, see the Teachers (Compulsory Registration) (Wales) Regulations 2000, SI 2000/3122, reg 2(1).

INDUCTION PERIOD TO BE SERVED SATISFACTORILY BY A SCHOOL TEACHER

15.19   As a result of s 19 of the THEA 1998, regulations may prohibit a person from working in a school which is maintained by an LEA or a non-maintained special school[1] unless he has served an induction period of not less than three school terms in (a) such a school, (b) an independent school, or (c) in circumstances prescribed by the regulations, a further education institution. The Education (Induction Arrangements for School Teachers) (Consolidation) (England) Regulations[2] and the Education (Induction Arrangements for School Teachers) (Wales) Regulations 2003[3] make provision for the purposes of s 19. For the sake of simplicity, reference is made below only to the regulations relating to England (and they are referred to as 'the English induction regulations').

15.20   Subject to the exceptions in Sch 2 to the English induction regulations (which include that the person in question has served an induction period in Wales[4]), reg 7 prohibits a person from being employed as a teacher at a school maintained by an LEA or a non-maintained special school unless he has satisfactorily completed an induction period of not less than three school terms in (a) such a school, (b) an independent school which (by and large) follows the National Curriculum in relation to the pupils taught by the person in question, or (c) a sixth-form college (that is, a further education institution principally concerned with the provision of full-time education suitable to the requirements of persons who have not attained the age of 19 years[5]).[6]

15.21   An induction period may not be served in a pupil referral unit.[7] Nor (subject to two exceptions) may such a period be served in a school which has been inspected under the SIA 1996 in relation to which the inspector has stated in his report on the inspection that in his opinion the school has serious weaknesses or that it requires special measures and either the inspector is a member of Her Majesty's Inspectorate, or the report states that the Chief Inspector agrees with the opinion, unless (in either case) a later such report states the contrary.[8] The exceptions to this prohibition are that (a) the person in question 'began his induction period at the school, or was employed as a graduate teacher, a registered teacher or a teacher on the employment-based teacher training scheme at the school' at a time when the school was not subject to such a report, or (b) one of Her Majesty's Inspectors of Schools in England has

---

[1]   See s 19(10)(b), as substituted by para 85 of Sch 21 to the EA 2002. See footnote 1 at para **15.16** for the meaning of the phrase 'a school which is maintained by a LEA'.

[2]   SI 2001/2897, as amended a number of times, most recently at the time of writing by SI 2003/2148.

[3]   SI 2003/543, as amended by SI 2004/872 and SI 2004/1745.

[4]   See SI 2001/2897, Sch 2, para 6. It is of note that a person who is employed as a supply teacher 'for a period of less than one term ... during the period of a school year and one term commencing on the date that he is first employed as a supply teacher (by that or any other employer)', need not have served an induction period under the regulations: ibid, para 4.

[5]   See ibid, reg 3(1).

[6]   Ibid, regs 7 and 8.

[7]   Ibid, reg 8(2)(b).

[8]   Ibid, reg 8(2)(a).

certified in writing that he is satisfied that the school is fit for the purpose of providing induction supervision and training.[1]

Length of induction period

15.22 A person's employment during an induction period of the sort required by s 19 of the THEA 1998 must be as a qualified teacher.[2] Where a person is employed full-time, the induction period must be of an academic year.[3] However, where the year is divided into terms, the year must consist of the relevant number of full terms.[4] No period as a supply teacher counts for this purpose unless the head teacher of the school or sixth form college agrees before the start of the period that it is to do so.[5] Where the person works part time, or in two or more relevant schools, the period must be 'the period of time it would take in accordance with his contract of employment or the terms of his engagement for him to complete 378 school sessions'.[6] Where the person works either wholly or partly in a sixth-form college, the period is that which 'it would take in accordance with his contract of employment or the terms of his engagement for him to complete 189 working days falling in term time'.[7]

15.23 If the person undergoing an induction period is absent from work for an aggregate period of more than 30 working days falling in term time, then the induction period must be extended by that aggregate period,[8] unless the absence is 'by reason of the maternity leave period specified in regulation 7(1) of the Maternity and Parental Leave etc Regulations 1999',[9] in which case the employee may choose whether it should be so extended.[10] There is provision for the extension (subject to limits) of the induction period before its end by agreement between the relevant person and the appropriate body within the meaning of the English induction regulations.[11] Otherwise, it may be extended only in certain circumstances.[12] Subject to the possibility of such an extension, only one induction period may be served.[13]

1   SI 2001/2897, reg 8(2)(a).
2   See ibid, reg 10.
3   Ibid, reg 9(1).
4   Ibid, reg 10.
5   Ibid, reg 10(3).
6   Ibid, reg 9(2).
7   Ibid, reg 9(3).
8   Ibid, reg 11(1).
9   SI 1999/3312.
10 SI 2001/2897, reg 11(2).
11 See ibid reg 11(3), and see reg 5 for the definition of 'the appropriate body'; it is usually an LEA. Where 5 years or more have passed since a teacher in full-time service started his induction period but he has not completed that period, he may with the agreement of the appropriate body choose to extend the induction period by a maximum of one school year. A teacher in part-time service whose induction period started 5 or more years ago and has not been completed may with the agreement of the appropriate body extend the period by a maximum of 378 school sessions or (in relation to an induction period spent in a sixth-form college) 189 working days falling within term time.
12 See ibid, regs 16, 16A, 17 and 19.
13 Ibid, reg 12.

Supervision and training during the induction period

15.24   A person who is undergoing an induction period under the induction period regulations is not explicitly entitled by the English induction regulations to supervision and training during that period. However, it is apparent from reg 13 that supervision and training is to be given to that person during that period. Regulation 13(2) provides that the 'duties assigned to a person serving an induction period, his supervision and the conditions under which he works shall be such as to facilitate a fair and effective assessment of his conduct and efficiency as a teacher'. Regulation 13(1) is to the effect that the head teacher of the school or sixth-form college at which a person is undergoing his induction period *and* the appropriate body in relation to the school or college[1] are responsible for the supervision and training of that person during that period. However, a teacher who is serving an induction period under the relevant regulations is not required to be appraised under regulations made under s 131 of the EA 2002.[2]

Completion of an induction period

15.25   Regulation 15 of the English induction regulations gives the Secretary of State power to decide what are the standards against which a person who has completed an induction period is to be assessed for the purpose of deciding whether he has satisfactorily completed an induction period.[3] Where a person's induction period has been completed, the head teacher of the school or sixth form college at which he is employed (or, if there is more than one such institution, the lead head teacher[4]) must make a written recommendation to the appropriate body as to whether the person has achieved those standards. That recommendation must be made within the period of 10 working days from the date when the period was completed, and the head teacher must at the same time send a copy of the recommendation to the person in question.[5]

Effect of failure satisfactorily to complete induction period

15.26   If a person who is employed at a maintained school or a non-maintained special school has failed satisfactorily to complete an induction period within the meaning of s 19 of the THEA 1998, his employer must secure the termination of his employment as a teacher unless the person appeals to the GTC under reg 19 of the English induction regulations against the decision of the appropriate body and the appeal is allowed.[6] The procedure to be followed in relation to the appeal is governed by Sch 3 to those regulations. Salient features of the procedure include that if an appeal is withdrawn then no further appeal may be instigated in relation to the

---

1   Defined by 2001/2897, reg 5.
2   THEA 1998, s 19(7). The current regulations are the Education (School Teacher Appraisal) (England) Regulations 2001, SI 2001/2855 and the Education (School Teacher Appraisal) (Wales) Regulations 2002, SI 2002/1394.
3   Such standards are published on the TTA's website, at http://www.tta.gov.uk/training/qtsstandards.
4   See reg 16(1); see reg 14 concerning employment in two or more institutions simultaneously.
5   See reg 16 generally regarding the completion of an induction period; its provisions are straightforward. The relevant person has a right to make written representations to the appropriate body within 10 days of that body's receipt of the head teacher's recommendation: reg 16(4).
6   SI 2001/2897, reg 18(2).

decision in question.[1] Furthermore, (1) an appeal may be decided without an oral hearing if neither party wants such a hearing and the GTC agrees,[2] and (2) an appeal hearing must be in public unless the appeal body determines that it is 'fair and reasonable for the hearing or any part of it to be in private'.[3]

15.27 If the person appeals under reg 19, his employer may allow his employment to continue pending the outcome of that appeal, but only if the employer secures that the person only undertakes such limited teaching duties as the Secretary of State may decide.[4] In any event, the employer must take whatever steps are necessary to secure the termination of the person's employment by no later than 10 working days from (a) the date when the employer received written notification from the person that he did not intend to appeal against the relevant decision of the appropriate body, (b) the expiry of the time-limit for so appealing (which is 20 working days from the date of receipt by the person of notification of the decision[5]), or (c) the date when the employer received notice that the person's appeal was unsuccessful.[6]

Charges for independent schools and sixth form colleges

15.28 The appropriate body in relation to an independent school or sixth form college may charge the governing body of the school or college a reasonable sum (not exceeding the cost of the provision) for the service provided to the governing body under the English induction regulations.[7] This is a little obscure. It appears that it was intended that the appropriate body would be able to impose such a charge on the proprietor of an independent school (which may[8] be the governing body of the school, but may be a private individual or a company). However, the wording is not apt to do this.

Secretary of State's guidance

15.29 Any person or body exercising a function under the English induction regulations must 'have regard' to any guidance given by the Secretary of State from time to time as to the exercise of that function.[9]

QUALIFICATION TO BE A HEAD TEACHER

15.30 In order to become a head teacher (for the first time) of a school which is maintained by an LEA or a non-maintained special school in England, after 1 April 2004, a person must (subject to an exception) have acquired the 'National

---

1   SI 2001/2897, Sch 3, para 4(3).
2   Ibid, Sch 3, para 11(1).
3   Ibid, Sch 3, para 16(2).
4   Ibid, reg 18(5).
5   See ibid, Sch 3, para 2(1).
6   Ibid, reg 18(3) and (4).
7   See ibid, reg 21.
8   See EA 1996, s 579(1).
9   Ibid, reg 22. Such guidance is published on the DfES website at http://www.teachernet.gov.uk/ professionaldevelopment/opportunities/nqt/induction/guidance. As to the impact on a public body of a duty to have regard to something, see paras **2.34–2.36**.

Professional Qualification for Headship' which is awarded by the Secretary of State to a person if he is satisfied that the person has successfully completed a course of training for that qualification which is approved by the National College for School Leadership Limited.[1] The exception to this requirement is that if (a) the person is appointed to such a post before 1 April 2009 and at the time of his appointment he has successfully applied for a training course for the purpose of gaining that qualification, and (b) the period of 4 years from the date of appointment has not expired, he may serve as such a head teacher without that qualification.[2] Acting head teachers are not affected by this requirement.[3]

FURTHER EDUCATION TEACHERS' AND PRINCIPALS' QUALIFICATIONS

15.31　Section 136 of the EA 2002 empowers the making of regulations prohibiting the provision of education at a further education institution which is either maintained by an LEA or within the further education sector[4] by a person who does not have a particular qualification, specified in the regulations. That section also empowers the making of regulations (1) prohibiting such provision by a person unless he has served, or is serving, a probationary period, and (2) specifying conditions to be complied with in respect of persons providing education at such an institution. Currently, s 136 is in force only in Wales,[5] and no regulations have yet been made under it. However, regulations had been made under the provisions which it replaced, and they were the Further Education Teachers' Qualifications (Wales) Regulations 2002[6] and the Further Education Teachers' Qualifications (England) Regulations 2001.[7]

15.32　Similarly, regulations may be made under s 137 of the EA 2002 prohibiting a person from serving as the principal of such a further education institution unless he has a qualification specified in the regulations, or is studying to attain such a qualification.

15.33　The Secretary of State will, when s 138(2) of the EA 2002 is in force, be able to make regulations prohibiting the provision without his consent in England by such a further education institution or an institution which is within the higher education sector and which receives financial support under s 65 of the FHEA 1992, of a course

---

[1]　See reg 3 of the Education (Head Teachers' Qualifications) (England) Regulations 2003, SI 2003/3111, which were made under s 135 of the EA 2002. Those regulations do not apply to a person who before then had been appointed as the head teacher of (1) a school maintained by an LEA (for the meaning of which, see EA 2002, s 212(2)–(4), SSFA 1998, ss 20 and 142(8), and EA 1996, s 4), (2) an independent school, or (3) a 'similar educational institution outside England and Wales': see reg 2(2).

[2]　Ibid, reg 5(1). The 4-year period is extended by the amount of any maternity, parental, paternity or adoption leave which the employee has taken (in the case of the last three only if the leave is taken pursuant to the right to do so granted by the Employment Rights Act 1996): see reg 5(2).

[3]　Ibid, reg 6.

[4]　See EA 2002, s 140; for the definition of an institution which is in the further education sector, see para **16.2**.

[5]　See SI 2003/1718. The same is true of ibid, ss 137–140.

[6]　SI 2002/1663. These have continued in force by virtue of s 17(2) of the Interpretation Act 1978. They were amended by SI 2003/1717 and SI 2004/1745.

[7]　SI 2001/1209, as amended by SI 2003/2039.

which is designed to lead to the award of a qualification which is specified under s 136 or s 137. He will also be able to make regulations under s 138(2) which limit the number of persons who may undertake such a course at such an institution. The National Assembly for Wales may do these things in relation to Wales, under s 138(3).

HEALTH AND FITNESS TO TEACH IN SCHOOLS AND FURTHER EDUCATION INSTITUTIONS

15.34 Section 141 of the EA 2002 is to the effect that regulations may be made prohibiting persons from carrying out certain kinds of work in a school or further education institution unless they satisfy conditions specified in the regulations as to health or physical capacity. Such regulations are the Education (Health Standards) (England) Regulations 2003.[1] The work in question is (1) planning and preparing lessons and courses for children,[2] (2) delivering lessons to children, (3) assessing the development, progress and attainment of children, and (4) reporting on such development, progress and attainment,[3] (5) an activity which assists or supports teaching, (6) supervising, assisting and supporting a child, (7) an administrative or organisational activity which supports the provision of education, and (8) an activity which is ancillary to the provision of education.[4] A person may only carry out any such work if he has the health and physical capacity to carry out that work, although whether he is to be regarded as having such health and physical capacity is to be determined in the light of his employer's duty to him under the DDA 1995.[5] A person who is in receipt of an early retirement pension granted on the ground of ill health is not to be regarded as fit to teach unless his entitlement to such a pension took effect before 1 April 1997, in which case he may teach, or carry out any other relevant activity, but only on a part-time basis.[6]

15.35 If it 'appears' to a person's employer that the employee may not have the health or physical capacity to carry out a relevant activity, the employer must afford

---

[1] SI 2003/3139. The regulations currently in force in Wales are the Education (Teachers' Qualifications and Health Standards) (Wales) Regulations 1999, SI 1999/2817, as amended most recently by SI 2003/2458; they were made under the predecessor provision, s 218(5) of the ERA 1988 and continue in effect by virtue of s 17(2) of the Interpretation Act 1978.

[2] For this purpose a child is a person below the age of 18: see EA 2002, s 141(5) and Interpretation Act 1978, s 11.

[3] These four kinds of work constitute specified work for the purposes of ss 123 and 133 of the EA 2002, as provided by the Education (Specified Work and Registration) (England) Regulations 2003, SI 2003/1663. They also constitute 'teaching' for the purposes of the Education (Health Standards) (England) Regulations 2003, SI 2003/3139: see reg 3 of those regulations.

[4] See SI 2003/3139, reg 5. Each one of these eight kinds of work is referred to in the rest of this section as a 'relevant activity'.

[5] See ibid, reg 6(1). The DDA 1995 imposes by ss 4–6 a duty to make reasonable adjustments to allow a disabled person within the meaning of that Act to continue to work. However, a failure to make such reasonable adjustments is not unlawful if it is justified. Whether it is justified is ultimately to be determined by an employment tribunal, but such a tribunal may not approach the matter by asking itself whether the failure to make the reasonable adjustment was justified. It must instead ask whether it was within the range of reasonable responses of a reasonable employer to fail to make the adjustment: see *Jones v Post Office* [2001] ICR 805.

[6] See SI 2003/3139, reg 6(2) and (3).

the employee an opportunity to submit medical evidence and make representations to the employer.[1] The employer must consider that evidence and those representations as well as any other medical evidence available to the employer, including medical evidence which has been furnished in confidence on the ground that it would not be in the best interests of the person concerned to see it.[2] The employer may require the employee, and at his request must arrange for him, to submit himself to a medical examination by a qualified medical practitioner appointed by the employer.[3] If the employee refuses or fails without good cause to submit to the examination or to make available medical evidence or information sought by the medical practitioner, the employer may reach a conclusion in the matter on the evidence and information which is available to the employer 'notwithstanding that further medical evidence may be desirable'.[4] The employee may arrange for the attendance at the examination of any duly qualified medical practitioner appointed by the employee.[5] It is of note that although the Education (Health Standards) (England) Regulations 2003 must, bearing in mind s 141(3)(b) and (4)(a) of the EA 2002, be read as applying to persons who work otherwise than under a contract of employment, the safeguards described above in this paragraph must (bearing in mind the express reference in reg 7 of those regulations only to a person's 'employer' and the absence of a definition of that word in the regulations) be read as applying in favour only of employees.

THE BARRING OF PERSONS FROM TEACHING OR OTHERWISE WORKING WITH CHILDREN IN RELATION TO THE PROVISION OF EDUCATION[6]

15.36 Section 142(1) of the EA 2002 empowers the Secretary of State in relation to England, and the Secretary of State acting concurrently with the National Assembly for Wales in relation to Wales,[7] to direct that a person may not carry out work to which s 142 applies, or may do so only in certain circumstances or subject to specific conditions. The section applies to (1) providing education at (a) a school[8] or (b) an institution within the further education sector or an institution which is maintained by a LEA and provides further education, (2) providing education as an employee or under a contract for services where the other party to the contract is an LEA or a person exercising a function relating to the provision of education on behalf of the

---

1   SI 2003/3139, reg 7(1)(a).
2   Ibid, reg 7(1)(b).
3   Ibid, reg 7(1)(c).
4   Ibid.
5   Ibid, reg 7(2).
6   The Secretary of State has issued guidance in relation to barring unsuitable people from working with children and young persons. The current guidance was issued in July 2003, and is available on the internet at http://www.teachernet.gov.uk. He has also issued guidance in relation to preventing unsuitable people from working with children and young persons in the education service. It is available on the same website, and has the number DfES/0278/2002.
7   References below in this section to the Secretary of State should be read as including the National Assembly for Wales on this basis.
8   The term 'school' for these purposes is defined by EA 2002, ss 142(9) and 212(2) and (3)(f), and EA 1996, s 4.

LEA, and (3) taking part in the management of an independent school.[1] It also applies[2] to work of a kind which brings a person regularly into contact with children[3] and which is carried out at the request or with the consent of a 'relevant employer', namely (1) an LEA, (2) a person exercising a function relating to the provision of education on behalf of an LEA, (3) the proprietor of a school,[4] which means the governing body in relation to a community, foundation or voluntary or community or foundation special school,[5] or (4) the governing body of a further education institution.[6]

15.37 A direction may be given under s 142(1) only on the grounds set out in s 142(4). These are (1) that the person to whom the direction relates is included (otherwise than provisionally) in the list kept under s 1 of the Protection of Children Act 1999 (POCA 1999), (2) that the person is 'unsuitable to work with children', (3) grounds relating to the person's misconduct, (4) grounds relating to the person's health, or (5) only in relation to the management of an independent school, grounds relating to the person's professional incompetence.

15.38 Regulations may be made relating to the procedure to be followed in the giving of a direction under s 142(1),[7] and the current regulations are the Education (Prohibition from Teaching or Working with Children) Regulations 2003.[8] They afford a person in relation to whom the Secretary of State is considering making a direction an opportunity to make representations to him and, where appropriate, to submit medical evidence or other evidence to him within 2 months of the date of notification of the opportunity to do so (unless the Secretary of State does not know the whereabouts of the person).[9] They require the Secretary of State to consult the employer of the person to whom the direction would relate, unless the Secretary of State is obliged by reg 8 to give a direction under s 142(1).[10] If the person is employed under arrangements made by an agent, then the Secretary of State must consult that agent.[11] Regulation 8 requires the Secretary of State to give a direction under s 142(1) in certain circumstances, such as that the person concerned pleads guilty to, or is convicted of, committing certain offences against children.[12]

---

[1]   EA 2002, s 142(2) and (9) and s 140.

[2]   See ibid, s 142(3).

[3]   That is, persons below the age of 18: ibid, s 142(9).

[4]   Including an independent school: ibid, s 142(9).

[5]   See EA 2002 s 212(2)–(4) and EA 1996, s 579(1).

[6]   See EA 2002, s 142(9), which also defines (by reference to s 140) the meaning of the term 'further education institution'.

[7]   Ibid, s 142(5).

[8]   SI 2003/1184, as amended by SI 2004/1493.

[9]   See ibid, reg 6(1) and (3); the time-limit may be extended by the Secretary of State if he considers that the person had good reason for not complying with the time-limit: reg 6(1). A notice is deemed to be served 48 hours after the date on which it was sent: reg 6(2).

[10] Ibid, reg 5.

[11] Ibid.

[12] See ibid, reg 8(1) and Sch 2; and see the rest of reg 8 for the other situations in which a person must be barred by a direction given under s 142(1). A person who was not over the age of 18 at the time of committing the offence is, perhaps surprisingly, not automatically to be barred. However, there remains a discretion under s 142(1) to bar him.

15.39 A person in respect of whom a direction has been given under s 142 may appeal 'to the Tribunal established under section 9 of the Protection of Children Act 1999' (known as, and referred to below as, the Care Standards Tribunal) against the decision to give the direction or against a decision not to vary or revoke the direction.[1] As a result of ss 142(6), 144(2) and 144(3), only that tribunal (referred to below as 'the Care Standards Tribunal', although it is also known as the Care Standards Tribunal) has the power to revoke a direction that a person is unsuitable to work with children. Such a revocation may occur only if the person in question makes an application to review the direction, and the application to review must be made in accordance with regs 10 and 11 of the Education (Prohibition from Teaching or Working with Children) Regulations 2003.[2] The Care Standards Tribunal's permission is required for the making of such an application.[3] No such application may be made in the case of an adult until 10 years have elapsed since the direction was made.[4]

15.40 The Secretary of State may revoke or vary a direction given under s 142 which he is entitled to revoke if he is 'in possession of information relevant to the decision to give the earlier direction which he did not have at the time that the decision was made' *and* he 'is in possession of evidence of a material change of circumstances of the person concerned occurring since the earlier direction was given'.[5]

15.41 Appeals to the Care Standards Tribunal other than applications to review are governed by reg 12 of the Education (Prohibition from Teaching or Working with Children) Regulations 2003. No such appeal may be made against a direction imposed pursuant to reg 8 of those regulations,[6] nor may such an appeal be made on the ground of information of the sort referred to in the preceding paragraph 'unless that information or evidence has first been brought to the attention of the Secretary of State under regulation 9'.[7] Furthermore, a finding of fact on which a conviction 'of

---

[1] EA 2002, s 144(1). The procedure of the tribunal is governed by the Protection of Children and Vulnerable Adults and Care Standards Tribunal Regulations 2002, SI 2002/816, as amended by SI 2003/626, SI 2003/1060, SI 2003/2043 and SI 2004/2073. It was held in R *v Secretary of State for Education, ex parte Standish* (1993) *The Times*, November 15, that the Secretary of State must, when barring a teacher, make express findings of fact and give reasons for his decision. However, the subsequently-conferred right of appeal to the Care Standards Tribunal has probably superseded this ruling, since a finding on the facts as to the suitability of the person concerned to teach or otherwise come into contact with children will have to be made by that tribunal, under the Education (Prohibition from Teaching or Working with Children) Regulations 2003, SI 2003/1184. This is because under reg 13(1) of those regulations, if the tribunal considers that the direction 'is not appropriate', then it may (not must) order the Secretary of State to revoke or vary the direction. It is difficult to envisage circumstances where, having arrived at such a conclusion, it would be lawful not to make such an order.

[2] SI 2003/1184.

[3] Ibid, reg 11(1).

[4] See ibid, reg 11(4). In the case of a person who was a child when the barring order was made, the period is 5 years: reg 11(3).

[5] Ibid, reg 9.

[6] Ibid, reg 12(1).

[7] SI 2003/1184, reg 12(2).

any offence involving misconduct' must be taken to have been based may not be challenged on an appeal under the regulations.[1]

15.42 The Care Standards Tribunal may order the Secretary of State to revoke or vary a direction given under s 142 (other than, of course, an automatic prohibition imposed under reg 8 of the Education (Prohibition from Teaching or Working with Children) Regulations 2003) if it 'considers that the direction is not appropriate'.[2] However, it is precluded by reg 13(2) from considering 'any information relevant to the decision to give a direction or not to revoke or vary a direction which the Secretary of State did not have at the time the decision was made' or 'any evidence of a material change of circumstances of the person concerned occurring since the decision to give a direction or not to revoke or vary a direction was given'. The apparent purpose of this prohibition is to ensure that such information must first be put to the Secretary of State under reg 12(2).

Effect of a barring direction under section 142

15.43 One effect of a direction given under s 142(1) in relation to a person is that a relevant employer may not lawfully use that person to carry out work in contravention of the direction.[3] Another – perhaps more stark – consequence of a direction given under s 142(1) in relation to a person is that it is a criminal offence to employ such a person in a position known as a 'regulated position' within the meaning of s 36(1) of the Criminal Justice and Court Services Act 2000 (CJCSA 2000) knowing that such a direction has been made in relation to him. This is the effect of s 35(2) of that Act, which makes it an offence for an individual – not a person, so the offence applies only to a natural person – knowingly to offer work in a regulated position to an individual who is disqualified from working with children, or to fail to remove an individual from such work. Such disqualification occurs (1) after an order has been made by a court under s 28 or s 29 of that Act in relation to a person, (2) if the person in question is included (otherwise than provisionally) in a list kept under s 1 of the POCA 1999, (3) he is included, 'on the grounds that he is unsuitable to work with children' in any list kept by the Secretary of State or the National Assembly for Wales under s 470 or s 471 of the EA 1996,[4] or (4) he is 'subject to a direction under' s 142 of the EA 2002 'given on the grounds that he is unsuitable to work with children'.[5]

15.44 A 'regulated position' for these purposes (so far as relevant) is:

(1)   'a position whose normal duties include work in an establishment mentioned in subsection (2)', which include 'an educational institution';[6]

(2)   'a position whose normal duties include caring for, training, supervising or being in charge of children';[7] and

---

1   SI 2003/1184, reg 12(3).
2   Ibid, reg 13(1).
3   EA 2002, s 142(8). See para **15.36** for the meaning of the term 'relevant employer'.
4   These have now been superseded: see generally paras **13.3** et seq.
5   CJCSA 2000, s 35(4).
6   Ibid, s 36(1)(a).
7   Ibid, s 36(1)(c).

(3)   'a position whose normal duties involve unsupervised contact with children under arrangements made by a responsible person'.[1]

15.45 A 'responsible person' for this purpose means so far as relevant a 'member of the governing body of an educational institution', the 'chief education officer of a local education authority', or 'the person in charge of any establishment mentioned in subsection (2) in which the child is accommodated ... or receives education, and any person acting on behalf of such a person'.[2] An 'educational institution' is defined for these purposes by s 42(1) of the CJCSA 2000, and it is 'an institution which is exclusively or mainly for the provision of full-time education to' persons under the age of 18.

15.46 Accordingly, a person who is employed by a higher education institution, or a further education institution which provides services as much to adults as to children, which (in both cases) provides secondary education,[3] will not commit the offence in s 35(2) of the CJCSA 2000 by employing a person who is subject to (for example) a direction under s 142 of the EA 2002, unless that person's post can properly be said to involve the training or supervision of the child. In this connection, it is of note that there is a clear distinction in s 2 of the LSA 2000 between education and training. Given the general rule that criminal statutes are to be construed strictly, this might mean that a prosecution could not properly be brought under s 35(2) of the CJCSA 2000 against a person employed by the governing body of a relevant higher or further education institution.

15.47 What is clear, however, is that a person who is disqualified from working with children for the purposes of the CJCSA 2000 and who knowingly applies for, or offers to do, or accepts or does any work in a regulated position, is guilty of an offence, contrary to s 35(1) of that Act.[4]

Information to be given to the Secretary of State where a person leaves a relevant employer's employment and is, or might have been, dismissed for misconduct

15.48 Regulation 11 of the Education (Restriction of Employment) Regulations 2000[5] (which were replaced by the Education (Prohibition from Teaching or Working with Children) Regulations 2003) required a person's employer where the person was dismissed from relevant employment on grounds of his misconduct, or where the person resigned in circumstances where his employer would have dismissed him or

---

[1]   CJCSA 2000, s 36(1)(d).

[2]   See ibid, s 36(13)(b) and (d) read together with s 36(6) of that Act.

[3]   The governing body of a higher education corporation was given power to do this by the amendment by para 15 of Sch 9 to the LSA 2000 of s 124 of the ERA 1988, which was subsequently further amended by para 8 of Sch 21 to the EA 2002, so that under s 124(1)(ba) the governing body may now provide 'secondary education suitable to the requirements of persons who have attained the age of fourteen years'. The same amendments were made to s 18 of the FHEA 1992 so that a further education corporation may do the same: see LSA 2000, s 142(1), and EA 2002, Sch 21, para 11.

[4]   The offence is triable either way, and the maximum penalty is imprisonment for 5 years and a fine: s 35(6).

[5]   SI 2000/2419.

considered dismissing him on those grounds if he had not resigned, to report 'the facts of the case and provide such further information in his possession or control as relates to the circumstances giving rise to the dismissal or resignation' to the Secretary of State. Regulation 4 of the Education (Prohibition from Teaching or Working with Children) Regulations 2003 is worded differently. It requires the giving of specific information (set out in Part 1 of Sch 1 to the regulations) where a relevant employer[1] has ceased to use a person's services on a ground (not *the* ground):

'(i)   that the person is unsuitable to work with children;

(ii)   relating to the person's misconduct; or

(iii)   relating to the person's health where a relevant issue is raised',

or where the employer 'might have ceased to use a person's services on such a ground had the person not ceased to provide those services'. Agents are also required by reg 4 to report information (set out in Part 2 of Sch 1 to the regulations) to the Secretary of State in analogous circumstances.[2]

15.49   A 'relevant issue' for these purposes is defined by reg 2 to be:

'an issue which arises where the circumstances of the case, including occasions of conduct other than that in question, are such as to raise an issue concerning the safety and welfare of children.'

15.50   The GTC now has disciplinary functions in relation to teachers,[3] but it is precluded from considering cases where such an issue arises and the Secretary of State wishes to consider the case with a view to exercising his powers under s 142.[4]

THE GENERAL TEACHING COUNCILS

15.51   The General Teaching Council for England (the GTC) and the General Teaching Council for Wales (the Welsh GTC) were first established only after the THEA 1998 was enacted. Their constitutions are provided for in Sch 1 to that Act, the provisions of which are uncontroversial. For the sake of simplicity, with exceptions, only the position of the GTC is described below.[5]

---

1   See para **15.36** for the meaning of the term 'relevant employer'.

2   For the equivalent obligation in relation to Wales, see regs 4 and 6 of the Education (Supply of Information) (Wales) Regulations 2003, SI 2003/542.

3   See the following section.

4   See reg 9 of the General Teaching Council for England (Disciplinary Functions) Regulations 2001, SI 2001/1268, as amended by SI 2003/1186.

5   The provisions of the THEA 1998 relating to the GTC are ss 1–7; those provisions are applied to the Welsh GTC by the order creating the latter, the General Teaching Council for Wales Order 1998, SI 1998/2911. In addition, s 9(2) of the THEA 1998 should be borne in mind in relation to the Welsh GTC; it empowers the National Assembly for Wales to require the Welsh GTC to undertake (or join with any other person or body in undertaking) activities designed to promote (a) recruitment to the teaching profession, or (b) the continuing professional development of teachers.

Functions of the GTC

Advice

15.52 The functions of the GTC are in part advisory, in that they must, when they think fit, advise the Secretary of State and such other bodies as he may designate on a number of matters.[1] Those matters are (1) standards of teaching, (2) standards of conduct for teachers, (3) the role of the teaching profession, (4) the training, career development and performance management of teachers, (5) recruitment to the teaching profession, (6) the supply of teachers, (7) the retention of teachers within the teaching profession, and (8) medical fitness to teach.[2] If the Secretary of State asks it to do so, the GTC must advise him (1) (in a general way[3]) on any of these matters, (2) on any other matter which he requires relating to teaching, or (3) as to whether any power of his under s 142 of the EA 2002 to prohibit or restrict the employment of a teacher should or should not be exercised in any particular case.[4]

Register of teachers

15.53 The GTC must establish and maintain a register of teachers under s 3 of the THEA 1998 containing the name of every person who is eligible for registration and who applies to be registered in the register in accordance with regulations made under s 4 of that Act.[5] A person is so eligible if he is a qualified teacher within the meaning of s 132 of the EA 2002 and he is not (1) barred by the Secretary of State under s 142 from teaching, (2) subject to a disciplinary order made by the GTC such that he may not be registered, (3) disqualified from being employed as a teacher in any school by virtue of an order made by an Independent Schools Tribunal under s 470 of the EA 1996 or by the Secretary of State under s 471 of that Act, or (4) ineligible for registration as a teacher, or disqualified from being a teacher in any school, by virtue of any prescribed provision of the Law of Scotland or Northern Ireland.[6] A person is not normally[7] eligible for registration if, having served an induction period in accordance with regulations made under s 19 of the THEA 1998,[8] he has failed to complete it satisfactorily for the purposes of those regulations.[9]

---

[1] See THEA 1998, s 2.

[2] Ibid, s 2(2), as amended by EA 2002, Sch 12, para 2.

[3] See ibid, s 2(6).

[4] Ibid, s 2(3) and (4).

[5] The current regulations are the General Teaching Council for England (Registration of Teachers) Regulations 2000, SI 2000/2176, as amended by SI 2001/23 and SI 2001/1267. In order to be eligible to teach in a maintained school or a non-maintained special school, it is necessary to be registered in the register: see the regulations made under s 134 of the EA 2002, as to which, see para **15.18**.

[6] THEA 1998, s 3(3). The prescribed provisions are set out in reg 3 of the General Teaching Council for England (Registration of Teachers) Regulations 2000, SI 2000/2176.

[7] That is, except in circumstances prescribed by regulations; in relation to England the exceptions are set out in Sch 3 to the Education (Specified Work and Registration) (England) Regulations 2003, SI 2003/1663.

[8] See paras **15.19** et seq regarding induction periods.

[9] THEA 1998, s 3(4).

15.54 Fees may be charged by the GTC for applications for registration or for the registration, restoration, or retention of entries on the register.[1] The deduction of such fees from teachers' salaries and their remission to the GTC is required by the General Teaching Council for England (Deduction of Fees) Regulations 2001,[2] which were made under s 12 of the THEA 1998.[3] The amount of the fees must be approved by the Secretary of State.[4]

15.55 When para 5 of Sch 12 to the EA 2002 is in force, a person will have a right of appeal to the High Court under regulations made under a new s 4A of the THEA 1998 against a decision by the GTC to refuse an application made by him for registration under s 3 where that decision is made on the ground that at the relevant time the GTC was 'not satisfied of the applicant's suitability to be a teacher'. This is not stated to be a right of appeal on a point of law. This, taken with the fact that on the appeal, the High Court may make 'any order which appears appropriate', suggests that the appeal will be on the facts.

The GTC's disciplinary powers in relation to teachers

15.56 The GTC has disciplinary powers as a result of Sch 2 to the THEA 1998, which empowers the making of regulations concerning disciplinary matters. The orders which can be made are set out in Sch 2. They are (a) a reprimand, (b) a conditional registration order, (c) a suspension order (suspending a person's registration as a teacher), and (d) a probation order.[5] However, a suspension order may not last for more than 2 years,[6] although conditions may be placed by the GTC on the ability of the person concerned again to become registered.[7]

15.57 The regulations concerning the disciplinary functions of the GTC are the General Teaching Council for England (Disciplinary Functions) Regulations 2001.[8] In relation to Wales the current regulations are the General Teaching Council for Wales (Disciplinary Functions) Regulations 2001.[9] Salient features of those regulations include that a disciplinary committee (which will be either an Investigating Committee, a Professional Conduct Committee, or a Professional Competence Committee[10]) may require the attendance of witnesses,[11] who may be required to give evidence on oath or affirmation.[12] Furthermore, the hearing of either of the latter two

---

[1] See ibid 1998, s 4(2)(g) and (4), and, in relation to England, reg 9 of the General Teaching Council for England (Registration of Teachers) Regulations 2000, SI 2000/2176.

[2] SI 2001/3993.

[3] See in relation to Wales the General Teaching Council for Wales (Fees) Regulations 2002, SI 2002/326, as amended by SI 2004/1745.

[4] THEA 1998, s 4(4).

[5] Ibid, Sch 2, paras 2(3) and 4.

[6] Ibid, Sch 2, para 4(1).

[7] See ibid, s 4(2), as inserted by EA 2002, Sch 12, para 12(1) and (2), in relation to both England (see SI 2002/2439) and Wales (see SI 2002/3185).

[8] SI 2001/1268, as amended by SI 2003/1186.

[9] SI 2001/1424, as amended by SI 2003/503. There are few material differences between the two sets of regulations so, for the sake of simplicity, except where necessary, reference is made below only to those concerning England.

[10] See reg 2(4) of SI 2001/1268.

[11] See ibid, reg 13.

[12] See ibid, reg 15.

kinds of committee must normally be in public.[1] There is a right of appeal to the High Court within 28 days against a disciplinary order made under the regulations.[2]

15.58 The GTC is empowered to issue, and from time to time to revise, a code 'laying down standards of professional conduct and practice expected of registered teachers'.[3] It must make this code available free of charge to each registered teacher at least once.[4] A failure by a teacher to comply with the code may be taken into account by a disciplinary committee of the GTC in any disciplinary proceedings against the teacher.[5]

Supply of information relating to teachers

15.59 The Education (Restriction of Employment) (Amendment) Regulations 2001[6] inserted a reg 5A into the Education (Restriction of Employment) Regulations 2000,[7] requiring the Secretary of State to refer an allegation of (1) 'unacceptable professional conduct' on the part of a registered teacher, or (2) that the teacher had been convicted of a 'relevant offence', to the relevant GTC unless the Secretary of State was of the view that a 'relevant issue' arose. There is no such requirement in the Education (Prohibition from Teaching or Working with Children) Regulations 2003 (although one may imagine that the Secretary of State would not hesitate to refer such an allegation to the GTC). In contrast, there is a duty imposed on a relevant employer by reg 29 of the General Teaching Council for England (Disciplinary Functions) Regulations 2001[8] and reg 5 of the Education (Supply of Information) (Wales) Regulations 2003[9] to inform the relevant GTC only of the ending by the employer of a teacher's employment on a ground relating to the teacher's professional incompetence or because the teacher left the employment in circumstances where the employer might have so ended that employment.[10]

15.60 This may be because s 14 of the THEA 1998 requires the provision by the Secretary of State to the two GTCs of such information relating to individual teachers as he considers it to be necessary or desirable for them to have for the purpose of carrying out any of the functions conferred on them by or under Chapter I of Part I of that Act. That section also requires each GTC to supply certain information to the Secretary of State, any information prescribed in regulations to any other person or body so prescribed, and to supply the other GTC with information which it is either necessary or desirable for that council to have for the purpose of carrying out any of the functions conferred on them by or under Chapter I of Part I of the THEA 1998.

---

1 See SI 2001/1268, reg 14.
2 See ibid, reg 24.
3 THEA 1998, s 5(1) and reg 13 of the General Teaching Council for England (Registration of Teachers) Regulations 2000, SI 2000/2176.
4 See SI 2000/2176, reg 14(1).
5 General Teaching Council for England (Disciplinary Functions) Regulations 2001, SI 2001/1268, reg 7.
6 SI 2001/1269.
7 SI 2000/2419.
8 SI 2001/1268, as amended by SI 2003/1186. The definition of an employer for this purpose is in reg 2 of SI 2001/1268. It is similar to, but not the same as, the meaning of the term 'relevant employer' for the purposes of s 142, as to which see para **15.36**.
9 SI 2003/542.
10 Agents are also so obliged: see reg 29(2) of SI 2001/1268 and reg 7 of SI 2003/542.

SCHOOL TEACHERS' PAY AND CONDITIONS

15.61 Under the Teachers' Pay and Conditions Act 1987, the Secretary of State was given power to determine the pay and conditions of teachers in state schools. Since pay and conditions of employment are in the vast majority of situations determined contractually (and at the time of the enactment of that Act were so determined in relation to teachers), this represented a considerable inroad into the freedom of the employers of teachers in state schools to negotiate the terms and conditions of staff. The 1987 Act was replaced by the School Teachers' Pay and Conditions Act 1991, which has now been replaced by ss 119–129 of the EA 2002.

15.62 Those sections apply to the employment of school teachers as defined by s 122(3) to (5) of the EA 2002 (unless they are in an Education Action Zone and the Secretary of State has ordered under s 128(2) that s 122(2) does not apply to the school[1]). This means (1) qualified teachers providing primary or secondary education under a contract of employment or for services where the other party to the contract is an LEA or the governing body of a foundation, voluntary aided or foundation special school, and the contract requires the teacher to carry out work specified in regulations made under s 133(1) of the EA 2002,[2] (2) head teachers of schools maintained by LEAs,[3] and (3) persons who fall within one of five categories (including that they are undertaking training), all of which require regulations to be given effect.[4]

15.63 The Secretary of State's power in s 122(1) 'by order [to] make provision for the determination of (a) the remuneration of teachers [and] (b) other conditions of employment of school teachers which relate to their professional duties or working time' is a re-enactment of similar provisions in the 1987 and 1991 Acts mentioned above. There has been a series of such orders. The most recent one is the Education (School Teachers' Pay and Conditions) (No 2) Order 2004.[5] Before making any order under s 122, the Secretary of State (and only the Secretary of State: the National Assembly for Wales has no powers in this respect) must normally refer the matter to which the proposed order relates to the School Teachers' Review Body whose continuing existence was given effect to by s 119 of the EA 2002.[6] He must also consult in accordance with s 126 of that Act.

15.64 The effect of an order under s 122(1) is that the remuneration of a school teacher to whom the order applies must be 'determined and paid in accordance with any provision of the order which applies to him'.[7] As regards any provision of the order which applies to him but does not concern remuneration, the provision takes

---

[1]   Such an order needs to be made by statutory instrument: see EA 2002, s 210. See para **15.73** concerning the making of such an order.

[2]   See EA 2002, s 122(3); see para **15.16** concerning regs made under s 133(1).

[3]   Ibid, s 122(4).

[4]   See ibid, s 122(5). The current regulations are the Education (School Teachers' Prescribed Qualifications, etc) Order 2003, SI 2003/1709.

[5]   SI 2004/2142.

[6]   See EA 2002, s 125, which sets out the circumstances when such a referral is not necessary.

[7]   EA 2002, s 122(2)(a).

effect as a term of his contract of employment.[1] Furthermore, 'a term of that contract shall have no effect in so far as it makes provision which is prohibited by the order or which is otherwise inconsistent with a provision of the order'.[2] Thus the nationally agreed terms of employment of teachers are ousted in so far as they are inconsistent with the order. This does not normally give rise to difficulty in practice, since pay and conditions documents made under the relevant Acts have not contained all the terms and conditions which one would expect in a contract of employment. So, for example, there is no provision in those documents concerning the rights and obligations of the parties in relation to notice periods and therefore pay in relation to such periods. Accordingly, in the event of a need to give notice, it would be necessary to consider the terms of the booklet known as the Burgundy Book (because of its colour) containing the terms agreed collectively at a national level. Those terms are in some respects not entirely straightforward, however, and several issues of interpretation of those terms, and related matters, have recently been the subject of judicial consideration. Similarly, the part of the School Teachers' Pay and Conditions Documents issued since 2001 relating to threshold payments has given rise to some difficulty in practice, and some of the issues which have arisen in both of these contexts are considered in the following section below.

15.65 Before turning to those issues, however, reference can usefully be made here to the Secretary of State's power to give guidance under s 127 'about the procedure to be followed in applying provision of an order under section 122' [sic]. The governing body of a school and the LEA must have regard to such guidance, and a failure to 'follow' the guidance may be taken into account in any proceedings in a court or tribunal.[3]

Issues concerning the application of the school teachers' pay and conditions documents

Reviews of determinations concerning threshold payments

15.66 One matter which may give rise to difficulty concerns the manner in which so-called threshold payments are assessed under the School Teachers' Pay and Conditions Document. Paragraph 19.1 of the 2003 Document requires the Secretary of State to appoint 'persons to act as assessors of applications to become threshold teachers'. Those persons are not employees of the teacher's employer. The assessor must 'exercise his functions without unlawful discrimination'.[4] The teacher can ask under para 22.1 for a review of the assessment on the (essentially public law) grounds in para 22.2. There is provision in para 22.3.3 for the request to be determined by a review officer (who is appointed by the Secretary of State under para 19.2), and in paras 22.8–22.15 for a complaint to be made by a teacher who has not been assessed to have crossed the threshold. The complaint is made to the teacher's employer, but can be made only on the basis that 'the review officer who carried out the view unlawfully discriminated against' the teacher. Only if the teacher's employers are

---

[1]   EA 2002, s 122(2)(b).

[2]   Ibid, s 122(2)(c).

[3]   Ibid, s 127(2) and (3). Such guidance has been issued. It is available at http://www.teachernet.gov.uk/management/payand performance/pay/strb2003.

[4]   Paragraph 19.3 of the 2003 Document.

satisfied that the complaint 'is justified' and that 'the unlawful discrimination may have affected the review officer's decision that the threshold assessment stood', must they 'refer the case to a replacement review officer for a further review and inform him of their conclusions and the reasons for their decision'. This involves requiring the employers to decide whether the (independent) review officer (appointed on behalf of the Secretary of State) has committed discrimination. This is a very unusual requirement, even if (as seems sensible) it is read as a request to refer the case to a replacement review officer merely where such discrimination may have occurred.

Is temporary safeguarding of pay lawful?

15.67   Another issue which has given rise to difficulty is whether it is open to an employer to award an employee only temporary safeguarding under what is now para 43.1.2 of the School Teachers' Pay and Conditions Document 2003. The employing LEA where that paragraph applies may pay a teacher who would otherwise have suffered a diminution in pay that which he would have been paid before the proposed diminution. There is no mention there of a power to do so only temporarily. In *Governing Body of the Plume School v Langshaw*,[1] the Employment Appeal Tribunal (EAT) decided that it is not open to an employer to grant a temporal limitation on the effect of such a determination.

Issues relating to the Burgundy Book

Dorling v Sheffield City Council

15.68   Under para 6.1 of s 4 of the Burgundy Book:

> 'In the event of a teacher exhausting in part or full his/her entitlements under paragraph 2.1 above [which confer a right to sick pay] and being given notice of the termination of his/her contract without returning to work on the ground of permanent incapacity or for some other reason related to the sickness absence, he/she shall be paid full salary for the notice period with normal deductions only.'

15.69   In R *(Dorling) v Sheffield City Council*,[2] the High Court held that reg 7 of the Education (Teachers' Qualifications and Health Standards) (England) Regulations 1999,[3] imposed an obligation not to employ a person who did not have the requisite capacity (in terms of health) to teach, with the result that such person's employer was obliged to dismiss him. This then meant, bearing in mind para 6.1 of section 4 of the Burgundy Book, that the employer was obliged to pay a teacher employed under the terms of that book his full pay for his notice period, even though the teacher was sick and even though the teacher might now be in receipt of an early retirement pension, granted on the basis that he was permanently incapacitated. The Court of Appeal

---

[1]   [2003] ELR 97.

[2]   [2003] ICR 424.

[3]   SI 1999/2166. There is no equivalent provision in the Education (Health Standards) (England) Regulations 2003, SI 2003/3139, possibly because of the difficulties caused by the *Dorling* case. Regulation 6 of the latter regulations (which are considerably more simple than the regulations which they replace) merely provides that 'A relevant activity may only be carried out by a person if, having regard to [the employer's duty to the employee under the DDA 1995], he has the health and physical capacity to carry out that activity'.

reached a different conclusion in the subsequent case of *Healey v Bridgend County Borough Council*,[1] but the case was not argued as fully as it might have been. The matter was then considered fully by Lindsay J in *R (Verner) v Derby City Council*.[2] His determination was that the teacher is not entitled to notice pay in the circumstances.

Is an employee entitled to the full amount of sick pay under the Burgundy Book before he is dismissed because of the incapacity?

15.70 In *Jones v Governing Body of Barton Court Grammar School*,[3] the EAT ruled that the fact that para 6.1 of section 4 of the Burgundy Book (set out in para **15.68**) refers to the termination of a teacher's contract of employment in the event that the teacher's entitlement to sick pay is only partly exhausted, means that an employer can lawfully terminate the contract of employment before the teacher's full sick pay entitlement has expired. This was despite the line of cases including *Aspden v Webbs Poultry & Meat Group (Holdings) Ltd*,[4] according to which in certain circumstances where an employee has the right to sickness benefits (in all the relevant cases, they were payable by insurers), an employer's express power to terminate the contract of employment will be restricted.

The required notice period

15.71 However, in the same case, the EAT concluded that a failure to give sufficient notice to ensure that a relevant teacher's contract of employment is terminated on or before the end of the period of notice to which he is entitled by reason of s 86 of the Employment Rights Act 1996 means that the teacher will be entitled to notice to the end of the following, and not just the current, term. This is a situation which can occur only in relation to the autumn or spring terms, since under the Burgundy Book an employer must give at least 3 months' notice before 31 August if the teacher's employment is terminated during the summer term. The Burgundy Book, however, requires the giving of only 2 months' notice to terminate on 31 December or 30 April (as the case may be).[5] The problem in issue arises if a teacher has 9 or more years of continuous employment by the time that notice needs to be given: this is because he will then be entitled to more than 2 calendar months' notice.

15.72 Arguably, the EAT erred in its finding on this issue: why, after all, should not the parties be taken to have agreed that if the employer gives at least 2 months' notice, but less than (say) 11 weeks' notice, the teacher then would receive pay for the part of the notice period which exceeds 2 months?

Where pay and conditions orders do not apply

15.73 As stated above, pay and conditions orders made under s 122 of the EA 2002 will not apply where an order is made under s 128 that Act. Such an order may be

---

1   [2002] EWCA Civ 1996, [2004] ICR 561.
2   [2003] EWHC 2708 (Admin), [2004] ICR 535.
3   EAT/0920/02.
4   [1996] IRLR 521.
5   See para 4 of section 3.

made only in respect of a school which is a member of an EAZ. The order is made under s 128(2) on the application of the governing body of such a school to the Secretary of State. The governing body must have consulted the school teachers at the school about the proposed application,[1] and the application must not state a date for its commencement earlier than 3 months after the date of the application.[2] Once an order made under s 128(2) is in force in relation to a school, the terms and conditions of the teachers at the school relating to remuneration and other conditions of employment at the school will be either as they have been determined by the governing body or, where the governing body have made no such determination, those terms which had effect under the latest School Teachers' Pay and Conditions Order before the order made under s 128(2) came into effect.[3] The Secretary of State may under s 128(6) make regulations about the application of s 122(2) where an order made under s 128(2) either (a) is revoked, or (b) lapses (in whole or in part) because one or more schools to which the order relates ceases to form part of an EAZ. No such regulations have yet been made.

APPOINTMENT AND DISMISSAL OF STAFF OF A MAINTAINED SCHOOL[4]

15.74   The primary legislation relating to the appointment and dismissal of staff in a maintained school is now much simpler, given the enactment of ss 35 and 36 of, and Sch 2 to, the EA 2002 and the replacement by those (short) provisions of the detailed provisions of Schs 16 and 17 to the SSFA 1998 with regulatory powers. Section 35 applies to community, voluntary controlled, community special and maintained nursery schools. A teacher in such a school is employed by the LEA.[5] If the school does not have a delegated budget, then the LEA has all of the relevant employment powers, fettered only by s 58 of the SSFA 1998 in relation to a voluntary controlled school.[6] Section 36 applies to foundation, voluntary aided and foundation special schools. A teacher or other employee appointed to work under a contract of employment at such a school must (unless regulations made under s 36(4) otherwise provide) be employed under a contract of employment the other party to which is the governing body of the school.[7] If the school does not have a delegated budget, the

---

[1]   EA 2002, s 128(4).

[2]   Ibid, s 128(5)(a).

[3]   Ibid, s 128(3).

[4]   Regulation 4(1) of the Education (Teachers' Qualifications and Health Standards) (Wales) Regulations 1999, SI 1999/2817, as amended, requires there to be employed at any maintained school or non-maintained special school (or, in fact, a further education institution as defined by reg 3), 'a staff of teachers suitable and sufficient in numbers for the purposes of securing the provision of education appropriate to the ages, abilities, aptitudes and needs of the pupils or students having regard to any arrangements for the utilisation of the services of teachers employed otherwise than at the school'. This staff must (see reg 4(2)) include a head teacher. The equivalent requirement in SI 1999/2166 in relation to England was repealed and not replaced by SI 2003/1662.

[5]   EA 2002, s 35(2).

[6]   See ibid, s 35(7) and Sch 2, paras 1–4. See paras **15.83** et seq concerning s 58 of the SSFA 1998.

[7]   Ibid, s 36(2).

LEA has extensive (but not unfettered) powers in relation to the staffing of the school.[1]

15.75 Currently, ss 35 and 36 are in force in England only. However, for the sake of simplicity, reference is made here only to those sections and the regulations made under them, the School Staffing (England) Regulations 2003.[2] Those regulations (the School Staffing Regulations) apply to all schools, including new schools. They also apply to situations in which the governing bodies of two or more schools act jointly.[3] The School Staffing Regulations make similar provision to that which was contained in Schs 16 and 17 to the SSFA 1998 (for example, in that the regulations give to the governing body the power to control the staff[4]), although the regulations make rather simpler provision than Schs 16 and 17.[5] For the most part, the School Staffing Regulations are uncontroversial. Provisions of note include reg 4, which permits the delegation to a single person by the governing body of its powers of appointment of staff other than the head teacher or deputy head teacher, and its power to dismiss staff. There is no provision in the regulations for an appeal against a decision to dismiss a member of staff, but that is subject to the transitional provisions in the Schedule to the regulations, which confer rights which are similar to (but not the same as) rights of the sort which formerly were contained in Schs 16 and 17 to the SSFA 1998, pending the commencement of s 29(1) of the EA 2002. The commencement date (assuming that this means the date when the regulations made under it come into force) is 1 October 2004.[6]

15.76 One matter which is likely to be problematic is who is the proper respondent to a claim of unfair dismissal where governing bodies which have delegated budgets have acted jointly. Presumably, they would all have to be respondents to such a claim unless they designated one governing body as the employer.[7]

---

[1]   See EA 2002, s 36(7) and Sch 2, paras 5–10.

[2]   SI 2003/1963.

[3]   See regs 28–32. Concerning acting jointly, see para **7.171**.

[4]   See regs 6, 16, 17 in relation to community, voluntary, controlled, community special, and maintained nursery schools.

[5]   For example, there is no provision relating to foundation, voluntary aided and foundation special schools which is equivalent to regs 6, 16 and 17 (concerning which, see the preceding footnote). This is in contrast to Sch 17, which included, in paras 21, 23 and 24, similar provision to that in regs 6, 16 and 17.

[6]   See the Employment Act 2002 (Commencement No 6 and Transitional Provision) Order 2004, SI 2004/1717 and the Employment Act 2002 (Dispute Resolution) Regulations 2004, SI 2004/752.

[7]   See the Education (Modification of Enactments Relating to Employment) (England) Order 2003, SI 2003/1964, as amended by SI 2004/2325.

PAYMENTS IN RESPECT OF THE DISMISSAL OR PREMATURE RETIREMENT, OR FOR THE PURPOSE OF SECURING THE RESIGNATION OF, ANY MEMBER OF THE STAFF OF A MAINTAINED SCHOOL WITH A DELEGATED BUDGET

15.77 Where a maintained school has a delegated budget, that budget will include the costs of employing the staff of the school. However, s 37(5) of the EA 2002 has the effect that, subject to exceptions, the cost of dismissing or securing the resignation of a member of staff of the school will not normally have to be met from the school's delegated budget.[1] Section 37(1) provides that it is nevertheless for the governing body of the school to decide 'whether any payment should be made by the local education authority in respect of the dismissal, or for the purpose of securing the resignation, of any member of the staff of the school', and the amount of such payment. The LEA must give effect to such a decision and may not make, or agree to make, a payment of that sort except in accordance with the governing body's decision.[2] As a result of s 37(2), the exceptions are that the LEA may nevertheless make a payment which is required to be made 'by virtue of any contract other than one made in contemplation of the impending dismissal or resignation of the member of staff concerned' or one which is required to be made 'under any statutory provision'.

15.78 Read literally, the words of s 37(2) appear to allow an LEA to enter into an agreement to compromise a claim made by a person who has been employed at a maintained school with a delegated budget and who has been dismissed from that employment. However, s 37(1) indicates that Parliament intended the conduct of any claim made by such an employee to a court or an employment tribunal in respect of the termination of his contract of employment to be under the control of the governing body. This is consistent with the fact that as a result of the Education (Modification of Enactments Relating to Employment) (England) Order 2003,[3] the governing body of a school with a delegated budget will be the primary respondent to such a claim brought by a person employed to work at the school.[4] Yet s 37(1) makes

---

1   See para **15.79**.

2   EA 2002, s 37(3).

3   SI 2003/1964. It is noted that Art 3(1)(d) of that Order must be read as referring to reg 18(3) of the School Staffing Regulations rather than reg 18(1) of those regulations, since that is an obvious typographical error, Art 3(1)(d) otherwise having no meaning.

4   In *Kent County Council v Green* [2004] EWCA Civ 11, [2004] ELR 75, the Court of Appeal overturned the decision of the EAT that the proper primary respondent to a claim of unfair constructive dismissal (that is, a dismissal within the meaning of s 95(1)(c) of the Employment Rights Act 1996) brought by an employee in a maintained school whose contractual employer is the LEA, and not the governing body of the school. In so deciding, the EAT had relied (see para 6 of its decision, reported at [2003] ELR 455) on the fact that the powers in paras 25 and 29 of Sch 16 to the SSFA 1998 of dismissal 'should more accurately be defined as powers to determine that a teacher who is employed to work at the school managed by the governing body must cease to work there'. The Court of Appeal's overturning of this ruling was welcome. In any event, the decision of the EAT in *Green* can properly be regarded as inconsistent with reg 3(1) of the School Staffing (England) Regulations 2003, which, unlike Sch 16, defines the word 'dismissal', and does so in the following terms: "'dismissal" is to be interpreted in accordance with sections 95 and 136 of the Employment Rights Act 1996'. Thus *Green* can properly be regarded as superseded by reg 3(1).

no reference to the making of a payment to settle a claim of, for example, sex discrimination where the applicant has not resigned or been dismissed. Furthermore, s 37(2) would on any view not prevent the making (against the governing body's wishes) by the LEA of a payment in respect of a resignation (which had already occurred) of a member of staff who could not claim 'constructive unfair dismissal' because he could not show a fundamental breach or repudiation of his contract of employment.[1] One might wonder why the LEA might wish to do so, and strictly speaking it would have to act lawfully in doing so, but that is irrelevant here.

15.79 Section 37(5) of the EA 2002 affords the delegated budget of a maintained school protection concerning costs arising in connection with the dismissal or resignation of a member of staff. Its terms shed light on the question of interpretation referred to in the preceding paragraph. According to s 37(5):

> 'Subject to subsection (7),[2] costs incurred by the local education authority in respect of the dismissal, or for the purpose of securing the resignation, of any member of the staff of a maintained school shall not be met from the school's budget share for any financial year except in so far as the authority have good reason for deducting those costs, or any part of those costs, from that share.'[3]

15.80 There is no reference in s 37(5) to costs incurred otherwise than in securing the resignation, or in respect of the dismissal, of a member of staff. Accordingly, Parliament can be inferred to have intended claims concerning the dismissal of staff (including for redundancy) to be under the control of the governing body of a school with a delegated budget (which would risk having to pay the costs arising out of such dismissal from that budget), and to have intended that other claims alleging breaches by the governing body of employment law could be compromised by the LEA without the consent of the governing body. This is presumably on the basis that the governing body would not be liable to meet the costs of any other kind of employment law claim from its delegated budget. However, that question is not specifically addressed in s 37.

15.81 Nevertheless, costs incurred by the LEA in respect of any premature retirement of a member of the staff of a maintained school with a delegated budget must be met from the school's budget share for one or more financial years 'except in so far as the authority agree with the governing body in writing (whether before or after the retirement occurs) that they shall not be so met'.[4]

Costs incurred in relation to the dismissal of staff employed for community purposes

15.82 The effect of s 37(7) of the EA 2002 is that where any costs are incurred by an LEA in respect of the dismissal or premature retirement of an employee who was

---

[1] By 'constructive dismissal' is meant a dismissal within the meaning of s 95(1)(c) of the Employment Rights Act 1996.

[2] As to which, see para **15.82**.

[3] Section 37(6) provides that the fact that the LEA have a policy precluding dismissals by reason of redundancy is not to be regarded as a good reason for the purposes of EA 2002, s 37(5).

[4] EA 2002, s 37(4).

employed for community purposes within the meaning of s 27 of the EA 2002, or for the purpose of securing the resignation of such a member of staff, those costs must be recovered from the governing body of the school unless the LEA agree otherwise in writing. The amount of those costs may not be met from the governing body's delegated budget.[1]

TEACHERS, RELIGIOUS EDUCATION AND RELIGIOUS OPINIONS

15.83 Section 58(2) of the SSFA 1998[2] provides that where the number of teachers at a foundation or voluntary controlled school which has a religious character (and such a school 'has a religious character' if it is designated as a school having such a character by an order made by the Secretary of State under s 69(4) of the SSFA 1998[3]) is more than two, the teachers must include persons who are selected for their fitness and competence to give religious education in accordance with arrangements made under para 3(3) of Sch 19 to the SSFA 1998 and are specifically appointed to do so. That subparagraph requires the governing body of such a school in some circumstances to arrange for religious education to be given in accordance with the trust deed for the school or, if none, in accordance with the tenets of the religion or religious denomination specified in relation to the school under s 69(4).[4] Such staff are called 'reserved teachers'.[5] They must not number more than one-fifth of the total number of teachers (including the head teacher) at the school.[6] For this purpose, where the total number of teachers is not a multiple of five, then it is to be treated as if it were the next higher multiple of five. The head teacher of a foundation or voluntary controlled school with a religious character may not be a reserved teacher while holding the post of head teacher.[7]

15.84 The LEA must consult the foundation governors[8] before appointing a person to be a reserved teacher in a voluntary controlled school with a religious character,

---

1   EA 2002, s 37(8).

2   This section, and the related ss 59–60 of the SSFA 1998, are amended by paras 6–8 of Sch 3 to the EA 2002. Those paras are currently in force only in England (see SI 2003/1667), but in what follows, it is assumed that ss 58–60 will by the time of publication have been amended also in relation to Wales. The amendments merely reflect the possibility of the engagement of staff otherwise than as employees. It should be noted that it is expressly provided by reg 39 of the Employment Equality (Religion or Belief) Regulations 2003, SI 2003/1660, that those regulations do not affect ss 58–60 of the SSFA 1998.

3   See SSFA 1998, s 58(1).

4   See para **11.37**.

5   See SSFA 1998, s 58(9).

6   Ibid, s 58(3).

7   Ibid, s 58(4).

8   A 'foundation governor' is a person appointed as such a governor under regulations made under s 19 of the EA 2002: see SSFA 1998, s 142(1) as amended by para 112 of Sch 21 to the EA 2002. Regulation 8 of the School Governance (Constitution) (England) Regulations 2003, SI 2003/348 currently applies. As far as a school with a religious character is concerned, a foundation governor is a governor appointed otherwise than by the LEA for the purpose of securing that that character is preserved and developed: reg 8(1)(a). If there is a trust relating to a school, a foundation governor may be a governor appointed otherwise than by the LEA for the purpose of securing that the school is conducted in accordance with the trust: ibid.

and may not appoint the person to be such a teacher unless the foundation governors are satisfied as to his fitness and competence to give religious education in accordance with arrangements made under para 3(3) of Sch 19 to the SSFA 1998.[1] The governing body of a foundation school with a religious character is bound in the same way: it must consult the foundation governors before appointing a person to be a reserved teacher in the school, and may not appoint the person to be such a teacher unless the foundation governors are satisfied as to his fitness and competence to give religious education in accordance with arrangements made under para 3(3) of Sch 19.[2] If the foundation governors of a relevant voluntary controlled school consider that a reserved teacher has failed to give religious education in accordance with arrangements made under para 3(3) of Sch 19 efficiently and suitably, then they may require the LEA to dismiss him from employment as a reserved teacher in the school or, in the case of a teacher who is engaged otherwise than under a contract of employment, require the governing body to terminate his engagement.[3] If the foundation governors of a relevant foundation school consider the same thing, then they may require the governing body of the school to dismiss the reserved teacher in question from employment as a reserved teacher at the school, or, in the case of a teacher who is engaged otherwise than under a contract of employment, require the governing body to terminate his engagement.[4]

15.85 Section 58(7) of the SSFA 1998 applies to a voluntary aided school which has a religious character[5] and is to the following effect. If a teacher appointed to give religious education in such a school (except in accordance with an agreed syllabus as defined by s 375(2) of the EA 1996[6]) fails to give such education 'efficiently and suitably', then he may be dismissed on that ground by the governing body without the consent of the LEA. It is provided by s 58(8) (presumably for the avoidance of doubt) that where such a school has a delegated budget, s 58(7) does not apply.

PROTECTION OF STAFF IN CERTAIN MAINTAINED SCHOOLS REGARDING RELIGIOUS OPINIONS, AND PERMITTED POSITIVE DISCRIMINATION IN VOLUNTARY AIDED AND FOUNDATION SCHOOLS WITH A RELIGIOUS CHARACTER

15.86 Sections 59 and 60 of the SSFA 1998 protect staff against discrimination on the ground of their religious opinions and related matters and permit some positive discrimination in those respects. Section 59 applies to schools which do not have a religious character: (1) community schools, community and foundation special schools, and (2) foundation and voluntary schools which do not have a religious character. Section 59(2) has the effect that no person may be disqualified from being a teacher at such a school or from being employed or engaged for the purposes of the

---

[1] SSFA 1998, s 58(5) and (9).
[2] Ibid.
[3] Ibid, s 58(6) and (9).
[4] Ibid.
[5] See ibid, s 58(1)(b).
[6] As to which, see para **11.32**.

school otherwise than as a teacher 'by reason of his religious opinions, or of his attending or omitting to attend religious worship'. According to s 59(3), no teacher at such a school may be required to give religious education. Section 59(4) has the effect that no teacher at such a school may be paid less or be deprived of, or disqualified for, any promotion or 'other advantage' (a) because he does or does not give religious education, (b) because of his religious opinions, or (c) because he attends or omits to attend religious worship. These provisions would, however, not entitle a teacher to take time off in breach of contract to attend a religious service.[1]

15.87 Section 60 of the SSFA 1998 applies to foundation and voluntary schools which have a religious character (and such a school 'has a religious character' if it is designated as a school having such a character by an order made by the Secretary of State under s 69(4) of the SSFA 1998[2]). The members of the staff of a foundation or voluntary controlled school which has a religious character are, unless they are reserved teachers or the head teacher, protected in the same way as are all the staff of a maintained school which does not have a religious character, since s 59(2)–(4) are specifically applied to them.[3] Section 60(4) and (5) permit some positive dis-crimination. In connection with the appointment of a person to be the head teacher of a foundation or voluntary school which has a religious character, s 60(4) allows regard to be had to that person's 'ability and fitness to preserve and develop the religious character of the school'. Section 60(5) permits preference to be given, in connection with the appointment, remuneration or promotion of teachers at a voluntary aided school which has a religious character or reserved teachers in a foundation or voluntary controlled school which has a religious character,[4] to persons of three sorts. These are (a) persons whose religious opinions are in accordance with the tenets of the religion or religious denomination specified in relation to the school under s 69(4) of the SSFA 1998, (b) persons who attend religious worship in accordance with those tenets, or (c) persons who give, or are willing to give, religious education at the school in accordance with those tenets.[5]

15.88 Section 60(5) also permits regard to be had, in connection with the termination of the employment or engagement of any teacher at a voluntary aided school which has a religious character or the termination of the employment or engagement of a reserved teacher at a foundation or voluntary controlled school which has a religious character, to 'any conduct on his part which is incompatible with the precepts, or with the upholding of the tenets, of the religion or religious denomination' specified in relation to the school under s 69(4) of the SSFA 1998. However, no person may be disqualified because of his religious opinions, or because he attends or omits to attend

---

[1] *Ahmad v Inner London Education Authority* [1978] QB 36, CA. The European Commission of Human Rights dismissed the employee's complaint under the European Convention on Human Rights: see (1982) 4 EHRR 126.

[2] See SSFA 1998, s 58(1).

[3] Ibid, s 60(2).

[4] Ibid, s 60(5) is applied to reserved teachers at a foundation or voluntary controlled school with a religious character by s 60(3).

[5] Since no distinction is drawn in SSFA 1998, s 60(5) between head teachers, deputy head teachers and other teachers, s 60(5) applies to all such teachers.

religious worship, from being employed or engaged otherwise than as a teacher for the purposes of a voluntary aided school which has a religious character.[1]

15.89 Finally, it is worth noting that s 60(7) of the SSFA 1998 has the effect that where immediately before 1 September 1999 a teacher at a school which on that day became a foundation or voluntary school which has a religious character enjoyed, by virtue of s 304 or s 305 of the EA 1996, any rights which are not conferred on him by s 60 of the SSFA 1998 as a teacher at a school to which s 60 applies, the teacher will continue to enjoy these rights (in addition to those conferred by s 60) until he ceases to be employed as a teacher at the school.

---

[1] SSFA 1998, s 60(6).

Chapter 16

FURTHER EDUCATION

INTRODUCTION

16.1   Until the FHEA 1992, there were relatively few statutory provisions concerning further education. However, even in the period since then, the law relating to the provision of further education has changed in a number of important ways. The law of further education is now to be found primarily in the FHEA 1992, the EA 1996 and the LSA 2000. Those Acts contain the main statutory powers and duties concerning the funding of further education and related matters. As is now the case with many other areas of the law of education, in some respects there are separate statutory provisions affecting Wales and England, although, as is common, the effect of the provisions does not differ markedly.

16.2   In this chapter, the funding of further education is considered first. The functions of the Learning and Skills Council for England (LSC) and the National Council for Education and Training for Wales (CETW) are described first,[1] after which reference is made to the funding powers of LEAs. A new regime for the inspection of further education was introduced by the LSA 2000, and that regime is then described. The law relating to further education colleges – which are, in the main, institutions within the further education sector[2] – is then considered, including statutory provisions concerning further education corporations (in so far as it differs from the law relating to corporations in general[3]) and institutions designated under s 28(4) of the FHEA 1992. Reference is then made to a number of miscellaneous matters, including the relationship between a student at a further education institution and the governing body of the institution, in so far as that relationship is not considered in Chapter 16 (concerning higher education). First, however, it is necessary to state what is meant by the term 'further education' in this context.

THE STATUTORY DEFINITION OF FURTHER EDUCATION

16.3   Further education is defined for the purposes of the EA 1996 (and any other enactments which are to be read as one with that Act) and the FHEA 1992[4] by

---

[1]   The LSC and the CETW replaced the further education funding councils, which were established under the FHEA 1992. Those funding councils were dissolved under ss 89 and 91 of the LSA 2000. See ss 90 and 92–95 of the LSA 2000 in relation to their property and staff.

[2]   This term is defined by s 91(3) of the FHEA 1992, to mean (a) institutions conducted by further education corporations, and (b) institutions designated under s 28(4) of that Act.

[3]   The law relating to corporations generally is considered in paras **2.157** et seq.

[4]   See s 90(1) of the FHEA 1992.

s 2(3)–(5) of the EA 1996 as certain specific kinds of education which is for persons who are over compulsory school age but which is neither secondary education nor higher education. This is the product of the following statutory framework.

16.4 Section 2(3) provides:

'Subject to subsection (5), in this Act "further education" means –
(a) full-time and part-time education suitable to the requirements of persons who are over compulsory school age (including vocational, social, physical and recreational training), and
(b) organised leisure-time occupation provided in connection with the provision of such education,
except that it does not include secondary education or ... higher education.'

16.5 According to s 2(5) of the EA 1996, education provided for persons who have attained the age of 19 is further education not secondary education, unless a person has begun a particular course of secondary education before attaining the age of 18 and continues to attend that course. In the latter case, the education does not cease to be secondary education by reason of the person's having attained the age of 19. Subject to this qualification, secondary education includes:

'full-time education suitable to the requirements of pupils who are over compulsory school age but under the age of 19 which is provided at a school at which education within paragraph (a) is also provided.'[1]

16.6 Secondary education also includes education which is provided by an institution which is (a) maintained by an LEA or an Academy, and (b) principally concerned with the provision of full-time education suitable to the requirements of pupils who are over compulsory school age but under the age of 19.[2] In addition, if (1) a person is in full-time education and receives his education partly at a school, and, by virtue of arrangements made by the school, partly at another institution or any other 'establishment' (a term which is not defined for this purpose), and (2) the education which he receives at the school would be secondary education if it were full-time education at the school, then (subject to s 2(5) of the EA 1996) the whole of that education is secondary education for the purposes of the EA 1996.[3]

16.7 Accordingly, unless it is secondary education of these sorts, full-time education suitable to the requirements of persons over compulsory school age who have not attained the age of 19 is further education and not secondary education.[4]

---

[1] EA 1996, s 2(2)(b). Section 2(2)(a) refers (so far as relevant) to education suitable to the requirements of pupils of compulsory school age. See paras **2.40** and **2.41** as to what is compulsory school age.
[2] Ibid, s 2(2A).
[3] Ibid, s 2(2B).
[4] Ibid, s 2(4).

THE FUNCTIONS OF THE LSC AND THE CETW

Introduction

16.8 In most respects, the LSA 2000 provides for the LSC and the CETW in the same way. The one major difference between the positions of the LSC and the CETW is that the LSC was obliged to establish local learning and skills councils for areas in England specified by the Secretary of State, which must carry out in relation to their areas the duties and powers of the LSC which the LSC specifies. The common provisions are considered first in what follows. Where there are material differences between the situations in England and Wales, attention is drawn to those differences.

Duty to secure the provision of proper facilities for education suitable to the requirements of persons aged 16–19

16.9 The LSC and the CETW must 'secure the provision of proper facilities for' both full-time and part-time education (other than higher education[1]) which is 'suitable to the requirements of persons who are above compulsory school age but have not attained the age of 19'.[2] They must also secure the provision of proper facilities for full-time and part-time training[3] suitable to the requirements of such persons,[4] organised leisure-time occupation connected with such education,[5] and organised leisure-time occupation connected with such training.[6] For these purposes, facilities are 'proper' if they are (a) 'of a quantity sufficient to meet the reasonable needs of individuals, and (b) of a quality adequate to meet those needs'.[7]

16.10 In performing the duties described in the preceding paragraph, the LSC and the CETW must take account of (a) the places where facilities are provided, the character of facilities and the way they are equipped, (b) the different abilities and aptitudes of different persons, (c) the education and training required in different sectors of employment for employees and potential employees, and (d) facilities whose provision they think might reasonably be secured by other persons.[8] The LSC and the CETW must also make the best use of their resources 'and in particular avoid provision which might give rise to disproportionate expenditure',[9] although provision is not to be considered as giving rise to disproportionate expenditure only because that provision is more expensive than comparable provision.[10]

---

[1] That is, 'education provided by means of a course of any description mentioned in Schedule 6 to the Education Reform Act 1988': LSA 2000, ss 2(5)(d) and 31(5)(d).

[2] LSA 2000, ss 2(1)(a) and (5)(a) and 31(1)(a) and (5)(a).

[3] Which for this purpose 'includes vocational, social, physical and recreational training': LSA 2000, ss 2(5)(c) and 31(5)(c).

[4] Ibid, ss 2(1)(b) and (5)(b) and 31(1)(b) and (5)(b).

[5] Ibid, ss 2(1)(c) and 31(1)(c).

[6] Ibid, ss 2(1)(d) and 31(1)(d).

[7] Ibid, ss 2(2) and 31(2).

[8] Ibid, ss 2(3)(a)–(d) and 31(3)(a)–(d).

[9] Ibid, ss 2(3)(e) and 31(3)(e).

[10] Ibid, ss 2(4) and 31(4).

Duty to secure the provision of reasonable facilities for education suitable to the requirements of persons aged 19 and above

16.11   The LSC and the CETW owe duties in relation to the provision of 'reasonable facilities for ... education (other than higher education) suitable to the requirements of persons who have attained the age of 19'.[1] Facilities for these purposes 'are reasonable if (taking account of the Council's resources) the facilities are of such a quantity and quality that the Council can reasonably be expected to secure their provision'.[2]

16.12   The wording of ss 3 and 32 of the LSA 2000 is otherwise the same as that of ss 2 and 31. Thus, for example, the LSC and the CETW are both required to 'make the best use of the Council's resources and in particular avoid provision which might give rise to disproportionate expenditure', but provision 'is not to be considered as giving rise to disproportionate expenditure only because that provision is more expensive than comparable provision'.[3]

16.13   The effect of the use of the word 'reasonable' in ss 3 and 32, as contrasted with the use of the word 'proper' in ss 2 and 31, was described by Lord Bach (speaking on behalf of the Government) in Committee in the House of Lords. He said:

> 'I prefer to say that there is an "entitlement" for those between 16 and 19 and to say that the LSC will do all that it can in relation to those who are over the age of 19. However, it cannot give them the entitlement which applies to those between the ages of 16 and 19.'[4]

16.14   It would seem, therefore, that the duty imposed by ss 3 and 32 is a duty of the sort imposed on an LEA by s 14 of the EA 1996, which was described by Woolf LJ in *R v Inner London Education Authority, ex parte Ali*[5] as a 'target' duty.

Duty to comply with directions given by the Secretary of State or (in Wales) the National Assembly for Wales

16.15   The LSC may be given binding directions by the Secretary of State under s 25 of the LSA 2000, and the CETW may be given binding directions by the National Assembly under s 47 of that Act. Such directions 'may contain – (a) objectives which the Council should achieve in seeking to carry out its functions; (b) time limits within which the Council should achieve the objectives; (c) provision relating to the management of the Council'. However, such directions 'may not concern the provision of financial resources in respect of activities carried on by a particular person or persons'.[6]

---

[1]   See LSA 2000, ss 3 and 32 respectively.
[2]   Ibid, ss 3(2) and 31(2).
[3]   Ibid, ss 3(3)(e) and (4) and 32(3)(e) and (4).
[4]   *Hansard*, HL vol 609, col 603.
[5]   (1990) 2 Admin LR 822. See para **3.33**.
[6]   LSA 2000, ss 25(6) and 47(6).

16.16 Where the Secretary of State or (as the case may be) the National Assembly is 'satisfied' that the LSC (or the CETW) 'has acted or is proposing to act unreasonably with respect to the exercise of a power conferred or the performance of a duty imposed by or under any Act', he (or it) may give a direction 'as to the exercise of the Council's powers and performance of its duties'.[1]

Funding powers

16.17 The LSC may 'secure the provision of financial resources' (meaning, presumably, 'ensure that money is given') to one or more of a number of persons or institutions (strictly speaking, the money should be given to the governing bodies of the latter institutions, or the corporations established to conduct them, but the word used in the LSA 2000 is 'institutions'[2]). These are (a) persons providing or proposing to provide post-16 education or training, (b) persons providing or proposing to provide goods or services in connection with the provision by others of post-16 education or training, (c) persons receiving or proposing to receive post-16 education or training, (d) persons providing or proposing to provide courses falling within para 1(g) or (h) of Sch 6 to the ERA 1988 (which are courses in preparation for professional examinations at a higher level or providing education at a higher level), (e) institutions within the further education sector or the higher education sector (within the meaning of s 91 of the FHEA 1992) which provide or propose to provide secondary education (which for this purpose does not include post-16 education), (f) persons undertaking or proposing to undertake research relating to education or training, (g) persons providing or proposing to provide facilities described in s 8(1) or (2) of the LSA 2000 (concerning which, see para **16.28**), (h) persons carrying out means tests under arrangements made under s 9 (concerning which, see para **16.25**), and (i) persons providing or proposing to provide information, advice or guidance about education or training or connected matters (including employment).[3]

16.18 The LSC and the CETW can 'secure the provision' of financial resources to the persons and institutions mentioned in the preceding paragraph by either providing the resources themselves, making arrangements for the provision of resources by another person, or making arrangements for the provision of resources by persons jointly (whether or not including itself, that is, the LSC or the CETW as the case may be).[4] When giving (or securing the giving of) money to persons receiving or proposing to receive post-16 education or training, the LSC and the CETW may do so 'by reference to any fees or charges payable by the person receiving or proposing to receive the education or training or to any other matter (such as transport or childcare)'.[5] In other words, the LSC and CETW can make grants to individuals who are receiving or proposing to receive post-16 education or training, either in respect of fees or charges or in respect of other matters such as their transport or childcare costs.

---

1   LSA 2000, ss 25(4) and 47(4).
2   See the discussion in paras **2.163** et seq.
3   LSA 2000, ss 5(1) and 34(1).
4   Ibid, ss 5(2) and 34(2).
5   Ibid, ss 5(3) and 34(3).

Funding of school sixth-forms

16.19 The LSC and the CETW may make grants to LEAs for the funding of sixth-form education. Such a grant is made on condition that it is to be applied as part of the LEA's schools budget for a financial year and with a view to the grant being used for the purposes of, or for purposes connected with, the provision by schools of education suitable to the requirements of persons above compulsory school age.[1]

Conditions which may be imposed in respect of funds

16.20 The LSC and the CETW can impose conditions in relation to the funds which they give others. These include requiring the person receiving the funds to allow the LSC or the CETW, or a person designated by the LSC or (as the case may be) the CETW, to be allowed access to accounts and documents and to be given rights in relation to computers and associated apparatus and material.[2] They also include requiring a person in receipt of funding to give the relevant council any information which it requests for the purpose of carrying out its functions.[3]

16.21 The conditions which the LSC and the CETW may impose also include requiring the person providing or proposing to provide education and training ('the provider') for which funds are to be given to (a) charge fees 'by reference to specified criteria', and (b) 'make awards by reference to specified criteria'.[4] Those conditions also include requiring the provider to recover amounts from (a) persons receiving education or training or (b) employers (or both).[5] The conditions which may be imposed include in addition that the provider makes provision specified in a report conducted under s 140 of the LSA 2000.[6]

16.22 The conditions may include the repayment of some or all of the money (with interest) if any of the conditions subject to which the money was paid are not complied with.[7]

Assessment of performance of education providers

16.23 The LSC and the CETW may, under s 9 or s 32 of the LSA 2000 respectively, 'develop schemes for the assessment of the performance of persons in providing post-16 education and training', and take those assessments into account when deciding how to exercise their funding powers under s 5 (or, as the case may be, s 34).

Power of appointment of up to two governors

16.24 The LSC and the CETW may, under s 11 or s 39 of the LSA 2000, appoint persons to be governors to institutions within the further education sector. However, there may be no more than two governors who were so appointed as members of the

---

[1] LSA 2000, ss 7(1) and 36(1). For the meaning of 'schools budget', see para **7.135**.
[2] Ibid, ss 6(1) and (2)(a) and 35(1) and (2)(a).
[3] Ibid, ss 6(2)(b) and 35(2)(b).
[4] Ibid, s 6(3)(a) and (b); s 35(3)(a) and (b).
[5] Ibid, ss 6(3)(c)–(e) and 35(3)(c)–(e).
[6] Ibid, ss 6(3)(f) and 35(3)(f); as to s 140, see paras **6.186** and **6.187**.
[7] Ibid, ss 6(5) and 35(5).

governing body at any one time. This power was described by Baroness Blackstone, the Government Minister responsible in the House of Lords for the Bill which became the LSA 2000, as a 'last resort measure'.[1]

Means tests

16.25 The LSC and the CETW may carry out means tests, or arrange for other persons to carry out means tests, and take the results of such tests into account in deciding whether to make grants to persons under s 5(1)(c) or (as the case may be) s 34(1)(c).[2]

Promotion of individual learning accounts and arrangements

16.26 The LSC and the CETW may promote 'the holding of accounts which qualify under' s 104 of the LSA 2000, and the making of arrangements which qualify under s 105 of that Act (concerning the making of grants by the Secretary of State or, as the case may be, the National Assembly, under s 108, which form the basis of accounts which qualify under s 104).[3] These are known as 'individual learning accounts'.[4] The LSC and the CETW may each be specified as a body with which arrangements under s 105 may be made.[5] The LSC may be designated by the Secretary of State, and the CETW may be designated by the National Assembly, under s 107(1) or (3), and may 'act in accordance with such a designation'.[6] Sections 107(1) and (3) allow the Secretary of State (or a person designated by him) 'to make arrangements with a body in connection with the making by that body of arrangements which qualify under section 105', and the former arrangements may 'include provision for a person designated by the Secretary of State to carry out on his behalf such of his functions under the arrangements as he specifies'. These sections (ss 105–107) therefore allow the Secretary of State to cause the LSC and the National Assembly to cause the CETW either themselves to administer, or to arrange for others to administer, individual learning accounts.

Encouragement of education and training

16.27 The LSC and the CETW are obliged to encourage (1) individuals to undergo post-16 education and training, (2) employers to participate in the provision of post-16 education and training, and (3) employers to contribute to the costs of post-16 education and training.[7]

Powers in relation to work experience and links with employers

16.28 The LSC (but not the CETW) is empowered to 'secure the provision of facilities for the gaining of work experience by young persons receiving education'.[8]

---

[1] *Hansard*, HL vol 609, col 648.
[2] LSA 2000, ss 9(3) and (4) and 37(3) and (4).
[3] Ibid, ss 10(1) and 38(1).
[4] There is a website dedicated to them: www.dfes.gov.uk/ila.
[5] LSA 2000, ss 10(2)(a) and 38(2)(a).
[6] Ibid, ss 10(2)(b) and 38(2)(b).
[7] Ibid, ss 4 and 33.
[8] Ibid, s 8(1).

Persons are 'young' for this purpose during the period from 1 September onwards in the year (starting then) during which they attain the age of 15 until the end of the year (starting on 1 September) in which they attain the age of 19.[1] The LSC and the CETW are also empowered to 'secure the provision of facilities designed to form links between' (1) employers and (2) persons who (a) provide education or training, or (b) receive education or training and are below the age of 19.[2]

The responsibility of the LSC and the CETW for persons who have special educational needs

16.29 The LSC and the CETW have responsibility for special education in the further education sector, as a result of ss 13 and 41 the LSA 2000 respectively. For example, as a result of s 13(1), in discharging its functions under ss 2, 3, 5(1)(a)–(d) and (g) and 8, the LSC must 'have regard – (a) to the needs of persons with learning difficulties,[3] and (b) in particular, to any report of an assessment conducted under section 140'.[4] In addition, the LSC must in certain circumstances secure the provision of boarding accommodation for persons with learning difficulties.[5] The overlap between (1) the LSC's and the CETW's duties in ss 13 and 41 respectively and (2) the duties of a LEA in relation to pupils with SEN, can be problematic. That overlap is considered in Chapter 6.[6] No further reference is made to the LSC's and the CETW's functions in regard to persons with SEN here, except to mention their power under s 52 of the FHEA 1992 to require the governing body[7] of an institution within the further education sector which provides full-time education suitable to the requirements of persons over compulsory school age who have not attained the age of 19 years, to provide education for a named individual.

Formulation of plans and strategies

16.30 The LSC and the CETW must (as a result of ss 15 and 43 of the LSA 2000) each 'make and publish plans for each of its financial years'.[8] Each of them may in addition make and publish 'such other plans as it thinks fit'.[9] Each of them is also obliged (by s 16 or s 44 of the LSA 2000 respectively) to 'formulate a strategy in relation to its functions and keep it under review'. Sections 43 and 44 require the approval of plans and strategies by the National Assembly, whereas ss 15 and 16 do not require the approval of plans and strategies by the Secretary of State.

---

[1] LSA 2000, s 8(4) and (5).
[2] Ibid, s 8(2) and (3).
[3] Defined by ibid, s 13(5).
[4] See paras **6.186** and **6.187** regarding s 140.
[5] See LSA 2000, s 13(2)–(4).
[6] See paras **6.189–6.192**.
[7] 'Governing body' for this purpose is defined in s 90(1) of the 1992 Act, except that in the case of a designated institution conducted by a company, it means also the company: SI 1993/563, Art 2 and Sch 2.
[8] LSA 2000, ss 15(1)(a) and 43(1).
[9] Ibid, ss 15(1)(b) and 43(7).

Local committees

16.31 In England, the LSC was obliged by s 19 of the LSA 2000 to establish for each area specified by the Secretary of State 'a committee (to be called a local learning and skills council)' (referred to below as 'a local LSC'). In Wales, the CETW was merely empowered by s 48 of, and Sch 5 to, the LSA 2000 to establish regional committees. The functions of such committees differ considerably, as can be seen from a comparison of ss 19–24 of the LSA 2000 with Sch 5 to that Act. For example, a local LSC must prepare annual financial plans, which must be approved by the LSC,[1] whereas there is no such requirement for a regional committee in Wales.

16.32 Under Sch 7 to the LSA 2000, the LSC and the CETW may intervene in relation to what is deemed to be 'inadequate' sixth-form provision made by a school. This power of intervention is referred to further in Chapter 7.[2]

Joint exercise of functions

16.33 Section 82(1) of the FHEA 1992 empowers any two or more councils – which for this purpose means a higher education funding council, the LSC, the CETW, or the Scottish Higher Education Funding Council[3] – to exercise jointly any of their functions where it appears to them that to do so will be more efficient or will enable them more effectively to discharge any of their functions.

Efficiency studies

16.34 Under s 83(1) of the 1992 Act, the LSC and the CETW 'may arrange for the promotion or carrying out by any person of studies designed to improve economy, efficiency and effectiveness in the management or operations of an institution within the further education sector'. The person concerned may require the governing body of the institution in question (and, in the case of a designated further education institution conducted by a company, the company[4]) to furnish such information, and to make available for inspection their accounts or such other documents, as the person may reasonably require for the purpose.[5]

Research

16.35 Sections 12 and 40 of the LSA 2000 empower the carrying out by the LSC and the CETW respectively of research. Those sections also oblige the LSC (and the CETW) among other things to 'establish systems for collecting information which is designed to secure that its decisions with regard to education and training are made on a sound basis'.

---

[1] See LSA 2000, s 22.
[2] See Chapter 7.
[3] See FHEA 1992, s 82(3)(a), read with s 90(2A).
[4] Education (Designated Institutions in Further and Higher Education) (Interpretation) Order 1993, SI 1993/563, Art 2 and Sch 2.
[5] FHEA 1992, s 83(2). The definition of 'governing body' for the purposes of the FHEA 1992 is in s 90(1).

Duty to promote equality of opportunity

16.36 In exercising its functions, the LSC (or the CETW) must 'have due regard to the need to promote equality of opportunity' between persons of different racial groups, men and women, and persons who are disabled and those who are not.[1]

Annual report

16.37 The LSC (and the CETW) is obliged at the end of every financial year (1 April to 31 March[2]) to prepare a report of its activities in that year and to send a copy of it to the Secretary of State or (as the case may be) the National Assembly.[3]

THE INSPECTION OF FURTHER EDUCATION PROVISION

16.38 The inspection of further education was dealt with in the FHEA 1992 very briefly, s 9 of that Act being the only section concerning the assessment of the quality of further education provision. The LSA 2000 introduced a far more extensive statutory framework for such assessment.

The inspection of education for persons aged 16–19

16.39 The Chief Inspector of Schools in England, and the Chief Inspector for Wales,[4] were given an extended remit by Chapters II and IV of Part III of the LSA 2000 (ss 60–68 and 75–88 respectively of the LSA 2000).[5] The wording of the provisions relating to England differs from that which relates to Wales in several material respects, and it is therefore convenient to consider the relevant sets of provisions separately.

England

16.40 The Chief Inspector of Schools is obliged by s 62(1) of the LSA 2000 to inspect all institutions within the further education sector other than those which provide education or training which is 'wholly within the remit of the Adult Learning Inspectorate' (concerning which, see para **16.44**).[6] The Chief Inspector is also obliged, if asked to do so by the Secretary of State, to inspect (a) 'the quality and availability of a specified description of education or training, in a specified area in England, for persons who are aged 16 or over but under 19', (b) the standards achieved by those

---

[1] LSA 2000, ss 14 and 42.

[2] Ibid, ss 29 and 51.

[3] Ibid, ss 28 and 50.

[4] Both of these terms are referred to in the legislation as 'Her Majesty's' Chief Inspector' etc. References to each of them are to be read accordingly. It is of interest that the term 'Chief Inspector of Adult Learning' (concerning which post, see para **16.44**) is not preceded by the words 'Her Majesty's'.

[5] Sections 81 and 82 of the LSA 2000 concern the inspection of careers services. Section 122 of the LSA 2000 extends the remit of the Chief Inspector of Schools in England in relation to careers services.

[6] Sections 63 and 64 of the LSA 2000 contain provision of the sort which applies to other inspections carried out by the Chief Inspector. Section 63 concerns rights of entry and related matters, and s 64 concerns action plans.

receiving that education or training, and (c) 'whether the financial resources made available to those providing that education and training are managed efficiently and used in a way which provides value for money'.[1] This is an 'area inspection'.[2] Such an inspection may include education or training which is within the remit either of the Chief Inspector or of the Adult Learning Inspectorate.[3] That inspectorate may be required to participate in the area inspection.[4] The Chief Inspector of Schools must then ensure that the relevant views of the Chief Inspector of Adult Learning are properly recorded in the report which the former is obliged (by s 66 of the LSA 2000) to publish.[5] The Secretary of State may then direct the LSC or an LEA whose area is wholly or partly in the area covered by the report to prepare an action plan in the light of the report.[6]

16.41 The Chief Inspector of Schools must 'keep the Secretary of State informed' about (a) 'the quality of the education and training brought within the Chief Inspector's remit by this Chapter' (as to which, see para **16.43**), (b) the standards achieved by those receiving that education and training, and (c) whether the financial resources made available to those providing it are 'managed efficiently and used so as to provide value for money'.[7]

16.42 The Chief Inspector may advise the Secretary of State 'on any matter relating to education or training of a kind brought within his remit by this Chapter', and may inspect any education or training of that kind.[8]

The Chief Inspector of Schools' extended remit

16.43 The Chief Inspector of Schools' remit was extended by s 60(1) of the LSA 2000 to (a) secondary education provided in institutions which are in England and within the further education sector, (b) further education which is provided in the further education sector and which is (i) suitable to the requirements of persons aged 16 or over but under 19, and (ii) funded wholly or partly by the LSC, (c) further education provided by LEAs in England for persons aged under 19, and (d) such education and training (including the training of or for teachers or lecturers) as may be prescribed by regulations made by the Secretary of State.[9] For these purposes, the terms 'further education' and 'secondary education' have the same meanings as in the EA 1996.[10]

---

1   LSA 2000, s 65(1). The rest of s 65, apart from those parts which are expressly referred to in the text following this note, concerns the manner in which such an inspection is carried out.
2   Ibid, s 65(9).
3   Ibid, s 65(4).
4   Ibid, s 65(6).
5   See ibid, s 66(2). See also para **16.44** concerning the Chief Inspector of Adult Learning.
6   See ibid, s 67.
7   Ibid, s 61(1).
8   Ibid, s 68.
9   See reg 11 of the Post-16 Education and Training Inspection Regulations 2001, SI 2001/799.
10   LSA 2000, s 60(2). See paras **16.3–16.7** for those definitions.

The adult learning inspectorate

16.44 In England, the Adult Learning Inspectorate (which is a body corporate[1]) (the ALI) is responsible for the inspection of (a) further education for persons aged 19 or over which is wholly or partly funded by the LSC, (b) training for persons aged 16 or over in so far as it takes place wholly or partly at the premises of an employer and is wholly or partly funded by the LSC, (c) further education funded by an LEA in England for persons aged 19 or over, (d) training for persons aged 16 or over which is funded by the Secretary of State under s 2 of the Employment and Training Act 1973, and (e) any other education or training which is prescribed for the purpose in regulations made by the Secretary of State.[2] The Secretary of State is obliged to appoint a chief officer of the ALI,[3] who is known as the Chief Inspector of Adult Learning.[4]

16.45 In exercising their functions, the ALI and the Chief Inspector 'must have regard to such aspects of government policy as the Secretary of State may specify'.[5] The ALI (and not its Chief Inspector) must make an annual report to the Secretary of State, who must lay a copy of it before each House of Parliament.[6]

Common inspection framework

16.46 The ALI and the Chief Inspector of Schools were obliged by s 69 of the LSA 2000 to devise a common set of principles applicable to all inspections conducted under Part III of the LSA 2000 (ss 52 to 72), and to publish that set of principles in a document to be known as the Common Inspection Framework. They were given power by s 69 to revise that document. If a disagreement arises between them in connection with such revision, they may refer that disagreement to the Secretary of State, who may ultimately resolve the disagreement by means of a direction given under s 70(5) of the LSA 2000.

Joint inspections

16.47 Joint inspections of education or training of a kind that is within the remit either of the Chief Inspector of Schools or the ALI may be carried out under regulations made under s 71 of the LSA 2000. Part II of the Post-16 Education and Training Inspection Regulations 2001[7] currently empowers and regulates such inspections. The report of a joint inspection is made by the Chief Inspector of Schools.[8]

---

[1]   LSA 2000, s 52(1).
[2]   See ibid, ss 52–54. Regulation 10 of the Post-16 Education and Training Inspection Regulations 2001, SI 2001/799, prescribes some 'other training' for this purpose. The term 'further education' has the meaning given it by the EA 1996 (as to which, see paras **16.3–16.7**): s 53(3). See s 55 of the LSA 2000 in relation to the report of an inspection carried out under s 54(3). Section 56 confers general powers on the ALI, s 57 concerns rights of entry and offences, and s 58 concerns action plans.
[3]   Ibid, s 52(3).
[4]   Ibid, s 52(4).
[5]   Ibid, s 54(7).
[6]   See ibid, s 59.
[7]   SI 2001/799.
[8]   See LSA 2000, s 71(2)(f).

Wales

16.48 Part IV of the LSA 2000 (ss 73–88) concerns inspections in Wales. The Chief Inspector of Schools in Wales was renamed for all purposes the Chief Inspector of Education and Training in Wales by s 73. No equivalent of the ALI was created by the LSA 2000 in relation to Wales. For the sake of simplicity, references in the following paragraphs to the Chief Inspector are to be read as references to the Chief Inspector of Education and Training in Wales. The Chief Inspector's remit was extended by s 75, and the terms of that section are sufficiently different from those of s 60 of the LSA 2000 (which extend the remit of the Chief Inspector of Schools in England[1]) for full reference to be made to them here.

The Chief Inspector's extended remit

16.49 The Chief Inspector's remit was extended by s 75 to include (a) education or training for persons aged 16 or over where the provider of the education or training is given financial support by the CETW or by an LEA in Wales (either generally or for a specific purpose), (b) education or training for persons aged 16 or over where the CETW or an LEA in Wales is contemplating giving the provider of the education financial support (either generally or for a specific purpose), (c) education or training provided for persons of compulsory school age in an institution in Wales which is within the further education sector, (d) further education provided by a school under s 80 of the SSFA 1998, and (e) 'such other education or training in Wales as may be prescribed by regulations made by the National Assembly'. No such regulations have so far been made.

16.50 The other provisions of Part IV of the LSA 2000 are similar to their equivalents in Chapter II of Part III of that Act, with two exceptions. One is s 85, which empowers the National Assembly to direct the Chief Inspector to carry out a survey of Wales, or a specified area in Wales, 'in respect of specified matters relating to policy concerned with education or training for persons aged 16 or over', or a 'comparative study of the provision made outside Wales in respect of specified matters relating to such education or training'. Section 85 also empowers the Chief Inspector to carry out such a survey or study without being directed to do so. The other exception is that the Chief Inspector is obliged by s 87 to prepare an annual plan of expenditure and income, which must be submitted to the National Assembly for its approval.

DUTY OF CERTAIN BODIES TO GIVE THE LSC AND THE CETW INFORMATION

16.51 Section 54(1) of the FHEA 1992, by imposing a duty on certain bodies to give information to the LSC or the CETW, gives those councils in effect a power to require that such information be given by such a body. The bodies in question are (1)

---

[1] See para **16.43**.

an LEA, and (2) the governing body[1] of (a) any institution maintained by a LEA, (b) a city technology college, (c) a city college for the technology of the arts, (d) an Academy, (e) any institution within the further education sector, (f) any institution within the higher education sector, or (g) any institution which is receiving or has received financial support under s 5 of the FHEA 1992.[2] The information which the body in question is under a duty to give is 'such information as [the relevant council] may require for the purposes of the exercise of any of their functions under any enactment'.

PROVISION OF FURTHER EDUCATION BY LOCAL EDUCATION AUTHORITIES

16.52 The role of LEAs in relation to the provision of further education is now best described as an important residual role.

16.53 As a result of ss 15A(1) and 15B(1) of the EA 1996, an LEA has power to 'secure the provision for their area' of (1) full-time or part-time education suitable to the requirements of persons over compulsory school age who have not attained the age of 19, 'including provision for persons from other areas', and (2) 'full-time or part-time education suitable to the requirements of persons who have attained the age of 19, including for persons from other areas' (but[3] not higher education). These powers include a power to 'secure the provision' of (a) training (including vocational, social, physical and recreational training), and (b) organised leisure-time occupation (including 'such organised cultural training and recreative activities as are suited to their requirements, for any persons over compulsory school age who are able and willing to profit by facilities provided for that purpose') which is provided in connection with the provision of education or such training.[4]

16.54 In exercising these powers, LEAs must 'in particular have regard to the needs of persons with learning difficulties' within the meaning of s 13(5) and (6) of the LSA 2000.[5] They may also do 'anything which appears to them to be necessary or expedient for the purposes of or in connection with the exercise of their' powers under both s 15A and s 15B.[6] The predecessor to ss 15A and 15B was held by Jowett J in *R v Further Education Funding Council, ex parte Parkinson*[7] to be a 'target' power.

16.55 An LEA in England must also secure the provision of education and training in accordance with a plan of a local LSC published under s 22 of the LSA 2000. This duty is enforceable by means of a direction given by the Secretary of State under

---

[1]   As defined in s 90(1) of the FHEA 1992 and the Education (Designated Institutions in Further and Higher Education) (Interpretation) Order 1993, SI 1993/563. Where a designated further or higher education institution is conducted by a company, for the purposes of s 54 the governing body means that company *and* the governing body of the institution: see Sch 2 to those regulations.

[2]   Section 5 has been repealed.

[3]   See EA 1996, s 15B(5).

[4]   Ibid, ss 15A(1A) and 15B(2).

[5]   Ibid, ss 15A(3) and 15B(3).

[6]   Ibid, ss 15A(4) and 15B(4).

[7]   [1997] ELR 204.

s 23(1) of that Act, but the direction is binding only if the LSC 'provides it with any financial resources which the authority reasonably requires to enable it to do so'.

Further education institutions maintained by LEAs

16.56 Where in the exercise of its further education functions an LEA maintains an institution which is not within the further education sector, the LEA may:

'(a) make such provision as they think fit in respect of the government of the institution ... and

(b) delegate to the governing body of the institution such functions relating to the management of the finances of the institution, and such other functions relating to the management of the institution (including the appointment and dismissal of staff), as the authority may determine.'[1]

16.57 Sections 495–498 of the EA 1996 apply to any institution which is maintained by an LEA and provides further education (whether or not it also provides higher education).[2]

16.58 The governing body of any institution providing full-time education which is maintained by an LEA in the exercise of its further education functions, must 'make such reports and returns, and give such information, to the Secretary of State as he may require for the purposes of the exercise of any of his functions in relation to education'.[3] Furthermore, an LEA must publish such information in relation to such an institution as is required by regulations made under s 159 of the ERA 1988.[4]

OFFENCE OF CAUSING NUISANCE OR DISTURBANCE ON THE PREMISES OF ANY FURTHER EDUCATION INSTITUTION

16.59 Section 85A of the FHEA 1992 can usefully be mentioned here. It applies not only to any institution which (a) is maintained by an LEA, (b) is not a school and (c) provides further or higher education (or both), but also to an institution in the further education sector. It is an offence to be present without lawful authority on the premises (including playing fields and other premises for outdoor recreation[5]) of any such institution and to cause or permit 'nuisance or disturbance to the annoyance of persons who lawfully use those premises (whether or not any such persons are present at the time)'. A person may be removed from such premises if either a police constable or a person whom the LEA in the case of such an institution other than an institution in the further education sector, or, in the case of an institution in the further education sector, the governing body, have authorised for the purpose has 'reasonable cause to suspect that [the person in question] is committing or has

---

1   FHEA 1992, s 85(2) and (3). For the definition of 'governing body', see s 90(1).
2   See s 219 of the EA 1988, as substituted by the EA 1996. See Chapter 3 concerning ss 495–497, and para **7.84** regarding s 498.
3   ERA 1988, s 158(1) and (2).
4   No such regulations have so far been made.
5   FHEA 1992, s 85A(2).

committed, the offence in question'.[1] Proceedings for the offence may be brought only by a police constable or an 'authorised person', which means the LEA in the case of an institution maintained by it, and in the case of an institution in the further education sector, a person authorised by the governing body of the institution to bring proceedings.[2]

PROVISION OF FURTHER EDUCATION IN SCHOOLS

16.60   The possibility of the provision by a maintained school of further education needs to be mentioned here. Section 80 of the SSFA 1998 provides that the governing body of a maintained school (meaning a community, foundation, voluntary, or community or foundation special school[3]) is responsible for determining whether or not to provide part-time education suitable to the requirements of persons of any age over compulsory school age or full-time education suitable to the requirements of persons who have attained the age of 19.[4] It appears that there is a power to charge for such further education.[5]

FURTHER EDUCATION CORPORATIONS

16.61   Further education corporations were brought into being by the FHEA 1992. The first ones were created by orders made by the Secretary of State under s 15 of that Act, which applied to the institutions specified in s 15(2) and (3).[6] No more orders may now be made under that section,[7] and new further education corporations may now be created only under s 16 or s 47 of the FHEA 1992.[8] Section 47 allows the Secretary of State (or, in relation to Wales, the National Assembly[9]) by order (made by statutory instrument[10]) to provide for the transfer of a higher education corporation to the further education sector. Section 16(1) empowers the Secretary of State (subject to s 16(2)) by order to make provision for the establishment of a body corporate for the purpose of (a) establishing and conducting an educational institution or (b) conducting an existing educational institution. However, he may not make such an order in respect of an existing institution without the consent of the governing body.[11] Section 16(1) does not apply to any institution which is maintained by an LEA.[12]

---

1   FHEA 1992, s 58A(3) and (4).
2   Ibid, s 58A(5) and (6).
3   SSFA 1998, s 20(7).
4   See further, para **7.175**.
5   The power can be derived by implication from ss 15A(4), 15B(4) and 451 of the EA 1996, as to which, see paras **16.54** and **2.137**.
6   The main order was the Education (Further Education Corporations) Order 1992, SI 1992/2097.
7   See FHEA 1992, s 15(4) and (7).
8   See ibid, ss 17(1) and 47.
9   See the National Assembly for Wales (Transfer of Functions) Order 1999, SI 1999/672. References in this section to the Secretary of State are accordingly to be read as including references to the National Assembly.
10 See FHEA 1992, s 89, as a result of which all orders under ss 16 and 47 must be made by statutory instrument.
11 Ibid, s 16(1).
12 See ibid, s 16(2), as substituted by s 111 of the LSA 2000.

However, the Secretary of State may by order make provision for the establishment of a body corporate for the purpose of conducting an institution which is so maintained and which in his opinion is 'principally concerned with the provision of full-time education suitable to the requirements of persons over compulsory school age who have not attained the age of nineteen years',[1] but only with the consent of the LEA and the governing body.[2]

16.62 No order may be made under s 16(2) or (3) unless a notice of the proposal to make it is published in accordance with s 51 of the FHEA 1992 and the Education (Publication of Draft Proposals and Orders) (Further Education Corporations) (England) Regulations 2001[3] or (as the case may be) the Education (Publication of Draft Proposals and Orders) (Further Education Corporations) (Wales) Regulations 2001.[4]

16.63 The initial name of a new further education corporation is the name given in the order made under s 16 as the name of the institution.[5] The order must provide for the institution to be conducted by the body corporate as from the operative date.[6] The fact that there is a clear distinction made in s 16 between an institution and the body corporate established to conduct it does not mean that such a clear distinction can always safely be made.[7]

Powers of a further education corporation

16.64 The powers of a further education corporation (FEC) are set out in ss 18 and 19 of the FHEA 1992. The corporation's 'principal powers' are set out in s 18(1), and are (1) to 'provide further and higher education', (2) to provide secondary education suitable to the requirements of persons who have attained the age of 14 years, (3) to provide education which is secondary education by virtue of s 2(2B) of the EA 1996,[8] (4) to participate in the provision of secondary education at a school, and (5) to 'supply goods or services in connection with their provision of education'.[9]

16.65 It may be that these powers allow an FEC to trade. However, the better view appears to be that they do not do so and that the fact that an FEC is an exempt

---

[1] FHEA 1992, s 16(3).
[2] See ibid, s 51(3A).
[3] SI 2001/782.
[4] SI 2001/2069.
[5] FHEA 1992, s 16(4). However, the name may subsequently be changed with the approval of the Secretary of State, under Art 20 of all three standard replacement instruments of government made by the Secretary of State in 2001 under s 22(3) of the FHEA 1992. All three of those instruments (and the accompanying articles) of government available on the DfES website. They are referred to further below.
[6] Ibid, s 16(5). The operative date is that which is appointed by order (made by statutory instrument) by the Secretary of State: ss 17(2)(b) and 89.
[7] See further, paras **2.163** et seq.
[8] As to which, see para **7.4**.
[9] See FHEA 1992, s 18(2) and (3) concerning the supply of goods and services for this purpose.

charity for the purposes of the Charities Act 1993[1] imposes a limit on the extent to which it can use the powers in s 18(2) and (3).[2]

16.66 The power of an FEC to provide secondary education (other than by participation in the provision of secondary education at a school) is subject to the duty imposed by s 52A(2) of the FHEA 1992, which applies where the FEC is providing secondary education to persons of compulsory school age. Section 52A(2) applies also where a designated further education institution (concerning which see para **16.81**) provides secondary education to persons of compulsory school age in pursuance of arrangements made either by an LEA or by the governing body of a school on behalf of an LEA. The duty in s 52A(1) is imposed on the governing body of 'the corporation or institution',[3] and it is to secure that 'except in such circumstances as may be prescribed by regulations, no education is provided to a person who has attained the age of nineteen years in a room in which any persons of compulsory school age are for the time being receiving secondary education'. The regulations which prescribe those circumstances are the Education (Secondary Education in Further Education Institutions) Regulations 1999.[4] A teacher must be present except where it would not be practicable and the absence has lasted for less than 5 minutes.

16.67 Section 19 of the FHEA 1992 confers supplementary powers on an FEC. The main such power is set out in s 19(1) and is to do:

> 'anything (including in particular the things referred to in subsections (2) to (4) below) which appears to the corporation to be necessary or expedient for the purpose of or in connection with the exercise of any of their principal powers.'

16.68 Subsections (2)–(4) are for the most part uncontroversial.[5] However, although there is in s 19(4)(c) a power to borrow money, that power 'may not be exercised without the consent of the appropriate council, and such consent may be given for particular borrowing or for borrowing of a particular class.'[6] Furthermore, although s 19(4)(bb) empowers an FEC to subscribe for or otherwise acquire shares in or securities of a company, (1) that power may not be exercised 'for the purpose of conducting an educational institution',[7] and (2) it may not without the consent of the LSC or (as the case may be) the CETW be exercised for the purpose of the provision of education if the provision is secured (wholly or partly) by financial resources provided by the LSC or (as the case may be) the CETW.[8]

---

[1]   See FHEA 1992, s 22A, inserted by s 41(2) of the THEA 1998.
[2]   See also paras **2.155** and **2.156** concerning the possibility of establishing a subsidiary company, and how in some circumstances it would be possible to avoid the problem of the need to make investments in so doing.
[3]   In relation to an FEC, the reference should be to the corporation or the governing body, but not to the governing body of the corporation: see FHEA 1992, s 90(1).
[4]   SI 1999/954.
[5]   But see para **2.156** concerning the power of investment contained in FHEA 1992, s 19(4)(d).
[6]   Ibid, s 19(5).
[7]   Ibid, s 19(4A).
[8]   Ibid, s 19(4B) and (4C).

Constitution and conduct of a further education corporation

Introduction

16.69 A further education corporation's constitution is set out in an instrument of government for the corporation.[1] The instrument must comply with Sch 4 to the FHEA 1992, but may make 'any provision authorised to be made by that Schedule and such other provision as may be necessary or desirable'.[2] The corporation must be conducted in accordance with articles of government, which also must comply with Sch 4 and may also make 'such other provision as may be necessary or desirable'.[3] The instrument and articles of government in the first instance had to be 'such as [was] prescribed by regulations'.[4] The regulations which provided for the initial instruments and articles of government of FECs were the Education (Government of Further Education Corporations) (Former Sixth Form Colleges) Regulations 1992[5] and the Education (Government of Further Education Corporations) (Former Further Education Colleges) Regulations 1992.[6] All of the initial instruments and articles of government of FECs in England were replaced in 2001 by instruments and articles of government made by the Secretary of State under s 22.[7] Before reference is made to the salient features of those instruments and articles of government, two provisions of s 20 can usefully be mentioned.

16.70 Section 20(3) of the FHEA provides that:

'The validity of any proceedings of a further education corporation, or of any committee of the corporation, shall not be affected by a vacancy amongst the members or by any defect in the appointment or nomination of a member.'

16.71 Furthermore, s 20(4) provides that:

'Every document purporting to be an instrument made or issued by or on behalf of a further education corporation and to be duly executed under the seal of the corporation, or to be signed or executed by a person authorised by the corporation to act in that behalf, shall be received in evidence and be treated, without further proof, as being so made or issued unless the contrary is shown.'[8]

Governance of a further education corporation

16.72 An FEC must be governed in accordance with its instruments and articles of government. It must also comply with the applicable principles of public law.

---

[1] See s 20(1)(a) of the FHEA 1992.
[2] Ibid, s 20(2).
[3] Ibid.
[4] Ibid, s 21(1).
[5] SI 1992/1957.
[6] SI 1992/1963.
[7] See para **16.76** concerning s 22.
[8] See paras **2.153** et seq for the principles applicable to education corporations generally.

16.73 The current instruments and articles of government for FECs in England (copies of which – there are three sets – are available on the DfES website[1]) are now largely uncontroversial. They are also in many respects similar to the initial instruments and articles of government (which applied also to Wales), the meaning and effect of which were considered at length in the first edition of this book.[2] A detailed description of the effects of the current instruments and articles of government is therefore not given here. The salient features of the current articles of government include (1) the protection of academic freedom in Art 10, (2) the procedural protections conferred by Art 12 on senior post-holders in relation to their dismissal, and (3) the fact that the FEC must approve the students' union's constitution under Art 15(1).

16.74 One reported case which is of particular interest in relation to the governance of an FEC is *R v City of Bath College Corporation, ex parte Bashforth*.[3] In that case, Dyson J said this in relation to a complaint that the exclusion of a member of an FEC from deliberations concerning his future was unlawful because there was no specific power in the instrument or articles of government to empower such exclusion:

> 'I do not accept that the instrument lays down a complete and exhaustive code for the conduct of meetings. It would be quite absurd if a member of staff had to withdraw from a meeting where his conduct, suspension, dismissal or retirement as a member of staff was being discussed (cl 13(4)(c)), but that the other members did not have the power to require him to leave while his future as a member was discussed. In my view, the corporation could devise such procedures as it saw fit, provided that they were not inconsistent with the instrument of government, and they were fair.'[4]

16.75 The possibility of intervention by the Secretary of State under s 57 of the FHEA 1992 (as substituted by the LSA 2000) in the event of, for example, mismanagement or breach of duty by the governing body of an institution within the further education sector, should be borne in mind. That power is considered in para **16.90**.

Amendment of instrument or articles of government

16.76 The instrument and articles of government for an FEC may be substituted or amended under s 22 of the FHEA 1992. Under section 22(1)(a), the Secretary of State (or the National Assembly) may, where an FEC submits a new instrument of government to him, after consulting the LSC (or, as the case may be, the CETW), by order[5] make a new instrument of government for the FEC in terms of the draft, or in

---

[1] See the Further Education Corporations (Former Further Education Colleges) (Replacement of Instruments and Articles of Government) Order 2001, the Further Education (Former Sixth Form Colleges) (Replacement of Instruments and Articles of Government) Order 2001, and the Further Education Corporations (Former Voluntary Controlled Sixth Form Colleges) (Replacement of Instruments and Articles of Government) Order 2001.

[2] Paragraphs **13.41–13.67**.

[3] [1999] ELR 459.

[4] Ibid, at 469.

[5] An order of any sort made under FHEA 1992, s 22 does not need to be made by statutory instrument: s 89(2).

such terms as he thinks fit.[1] The Secretary of State may also in the same manner modify an instrument of government made under s 22(1)(a).[2] The Secretary of State may not, however, make a new or modified instrument otherwise than in the form so submitted to him unless he has first consulted the corporation.[3] The Secretary of State may also by order modify any instrument of government of any FEC,[4] but only when he has consulted the LSC and each FEC to which the order relates.[5]

16.77 An FEC may, with the consent of the Secretary of State, make new articles of government in place of their existing articles, or modify its existing articles.[6] The Secretary of State may by a direction require FECs, any class of FECs specified in the direction, or any particular FEC so specified, to (a) modify, replace or revoke their articles of government, or (b) secure that any rules or byelaws made in pursuance of their articles of government are modified, replaced, or revoked, in such manner as is specified in the direction.[7] However, such a direction may be made only after the Secretary of State has consulted each FEC to which the direction applies.[8]

Transfer of property and staff to a further education corporation

16.78 The transfer of property and staff to an FEC is governed primarily by ss 23–27 of the FHEA 1992 and related provisions.[9] The provisions regarding the transfer of property were considered in Chapter 17 of the first edition of this book, and the current provisions are referred to in paras **8.48–8.57**. The provisions concerning the transfer of staff are contained in s 26. They largely mirror those in the Transfer of Undertakings (Protection of Employment) Regulations 1981[10] (TUPE), but for practical reasons, those provisions cannot be applied exactly. In any event, the provisions in those regulations were not applied in their entirety.[11] If there is a transfer within the meaning of those regulations, then so far as necessary they apply in addition to the provisions in s 26. Section 26 provides that the contracts of employment of employees who are 'employed by the transferor[12] to work solely at the institution the corporation is established to conduct'[13] have effect from the date when the corporation begins to conduct that institution as if originally made between those

---

1   A reference below in this section to the Secretary of State is to be read as including a reference to the National Assembly, and a reference below in this section to the LSC is to be read as a reference also to the CETW.
2   FHEA 1992, s 22(1)(b).
3   Ibid, s 22(1).
4   Ibid, s 22(2).
5   Ibid, s 22(3)(b). The order may relate to all FECs, any category of FECs specified in the order, or to any FEC so specified: s 22(3)(a).
6   Ibid, s 22(4).
7   Ibid, s 22(5).
8   Ibid, s 22(6).
9   Stamp duty would not be payable on a transfer of property under s 23: ibid, s 88.
10   SI 1981/1794.
11   There was no requirement for consultation with recognised trade unions in respect of the transfer, as is required by reg 10 of TUPE.
12   The transferor is defined for this purpose by FHEA 1992, s 26(6).
13   See ibid, s 26(7) and (8) regarding which employees are to be so regarded.

employees and the corporation.[1] Furthermore, the contracts of employment of employees who are designated by an order made under s 26(1)(b)[2] (which may designate a person either individually or as a member of a class or description of employees[3]) have the same effect.[4]

Dissolution of a further education corporation

16.79 An FEC may be dissolved by an order made by the Secretary of State under s 27 of the FHEA 1992. The order must be made by statutory instrument.[5] The order may transfer property,[6] rights and liabilities of the corporation to 'any person appearing to the Secretary of State to be wholly or mainly engaged in the provision of educational facilities or services of any description', or to 'any body corporate established for purposes which include the provision of such facilities or services'.[7] However, in both cases the person or body concerned must consent to the transfer.[8] Such property, rights and liabilities may also be transferred to the LSC or the CETW or to a higher education funding council (without the relevant council's consent).[9] If the recipient of the transfer is not a charity (within the meaning of the Charities Act 1993) established for charitable purposes (within the meaning of that Act) which are exclusively educational purposes, then any property transferred under s 27 must be transferred on trust to be used for such charitable purposes which are exclusively educational.[10] Section 26 (concerning staff[11]) may be applied (with such modifications as the Secretary of State may consider necessary or desirable) by the order.[12] Before making an order under s 27 in respect of an FEC, the Secretary of State must consult the FEC and the LSC or (as the case may be) the CETW unless, in the case of the LSC or the CETW, the order was made for the purpose of giving effect to a proposal of that council.[13]

16.80 It is of note that the Secretary of State would not be obliged by s 27 to transfer the liabilities of an FEC to a third party. Accordingly, such liabilities might be extinguished on the dissolution of a FEC following an order made under s 27. Presumably, the Secretary of State would need to exercise the discretion not to transfer the relevant liabilities in accordance with the usual public law principles. It is at least arguable that the Secretary of State would have to consult the persons to

---

[1] FHEA 1992, s 26(1)(a) and (2). See s 43 regarding a determination made before a transfer by an LEA concerning the remuneration of transferring employees.
[2] Such an order must be made by statutory instrument: FHEA 1992, s 89.
[3] FHEA 1992, s 26(5).
[4] Ibid, s 26(2).
[5] Ibid, s 89.
[6] Stamp duty and stamp duty land tax would not be payable on a transfer of property under s 27: FHEA 1992, ss 88 and 88A.
[7] Ibid, s 27(2).
[8] Ibid.
[9] Ibid, s 27(3).
[10] FHEA 1992, s 27(4) and (5).
[11] See the preceding paragraph.
[12] FHEA 1992, s 27(6).
[13] Ibid, s 27(7).

whom such liabilities were owed before deciding to follow a course of action which would have the effect of extinguishing the liabilities.[1]

DESIGNATED FURTHER EDUCATION INSTITUTIONS

16.81 Section 28 of the FHEA 1992 empowered the Secretary of State to designate certain educational institutions as eligible to receive support from funds administered by the further education funding councils. As amended, s 28 now empowers the designation, for the purposes of that section, of educational institutions which (1) are principally concerned with the provision of (a) full-time education suitable to the requirements of persons over compulsory school age who have not attained the age of 19 years, and/or (b) courses of further or higher education, and (2) are one of three kinds.[2] The three kinds of institution eligible to be so designated are (a) an institution which is established for the purposes of being principally concerned with either or both of such kinds of education, (b) a voluntary aided school other than one which belongs to a group of schools for which a foundation body acts under s 21 of the SSFA 1998,[3] and (c) an institution which is 'grant-aided or eligible to receive aid by way of grant' (which means that it is maintained by persons other than LEAs, who receive or are eligible to receive grants under regulations made under s 485 of the EA 1996).[4] The Secretary of State may designate a voluntary aided school under s 28 only with the consent of the school's governing body and the LEA.[5] An institution designated under s 28 is known as a 'designated institution' for the purposes of Part I (that is, what remains of ss 1–61) of the FHEA 1992.[6] Such an institution is referred to below, except where the context otherwise requires, as a designated further education institution.

Government and conduct of designated further education institutions

16.82 The government and conduct of a designated further education institution other than one conducted by a company is subject to s 29 of the FHEA 1992, unless the institution is conducted by an unincorporated association and the order designating the institution provides for its exemption from s 29.[7] Section 29 provides that there must be an instrument of government (providing for the constitution of a governing body of the institution) and articles of government (in accordance with which the institution is to be conducted) for the institution which (in each case) has

---

1   Cf *McInnes v Onslow Fane* [1978] 1 WLR 1520.
2   See FHEA 1992, s 28(1).
3   See para **7.17** concerning foundations and foundation bodies.
4   FHEA 1992, s 28(2) and (3).
5   Ibid, s 28(3A).
6   FHEA 1992, s 28(4). For a list of the original designated institutions, see the Education (Designated Institutions in Further Education) Order 1993, SI 1993/1435 and the Education (Designated Institutions in Further Education) (Wales) Order 1993, SI 1993/215.
7   Ibid, s 29(1).

either been approved or made by the Secretary of State.[1] In certain cases the governing body may modify the instrument or articles of government, or both, but, it seems, only with the consent of the Secretary of State.[2] If any other person has a power to modify, replace or revoke the instrument or articles of government, then that power may be exercised only with the consent of the Secretary of State.[3] The Secretary of State may also by order modify, replace or revoke those documents.[4] Before exercising any power under s 29(6) or (8) in relation to any instrument or articles of government, the Secretary of State must (so far as it appears to him to be practicable to do so) consult the governing body of the institution concerned and any persons other than the governing body who have the power to make or modify the relevant document.[5]

16.83 The instruments of government of designated further education institutions which, when designated, were voluntary aided schools,[6] and other institutions which are (1) principally concerned with the provision of full-time education suitable to the requirements of persons over compulsory school age who have not attained the age of 19 years, and (2) specified for the purpose by the Secretary of State, are the subject of special provision in s 30 of the FHEA 1992 (as substituted by s 143 of the LSA 2000). The instrument must provide that the governing body is to include persons appointed for the purpose of securing so far as practicable that the established character of the institution at the time of its designation is preserved and developed, and, in particular, that the institution is conducted in accordance with any trust deed relating to it.[7] The instrument of government must also provide that the majority of the members of the governing body are to be such governors.[8]

16.84 Designated further education institutions conducted by companies are subject to s 31 of the FHEA 1992. The articles of association of the company must incorporate provision with respect to the constitution of a governing body of the institution (which is to be known as the instrument of government of the institution), and provision with respect to the conduct of the institution (which is to be known as the articles of government of the institution).[9] The Secretary of State may give to the persons who appear to him to have effective control over the company such directions as he thinks fit for securing that the memorandum or articles of association of the company, or any rules or byelaws made in pursuance of any power conferred by the articles of association of the company, are amended in the manner specified in

---

[1] See FHEA 1992, s 29(2)–(6). The Secretary of State's power to make either the articles or instrument of government (or both) under s 29(6) is exercisable by order, but the order need not be made by statutory instrument: FHEA 1992, s 89(2).

[2] See ibid, s 29(7) and (8), the latter appearing to restrict the operation of the former.

[3] Ibid, s 29(8), as amended by para 24(4) of Sch 9 to the LSA 2000.

[4] Ibid, s 29(8); the order need not be made by statutory instrument: s 89(2).

[5] Ibid, s 29(9).

[6] See para **7.14** regarding voluntary aided schools.

[7] FHEA 1992, s 30(1)(a). The established character of the institution where it was established shortly before or at the same time as being designated, means the character which the institution is intended to have on its establishment: s 30(4).

[8] Ibid, s 30(1)(b).

[9] Ibid, s 31(2), which must be read with s 31(2A), as inserted by the LSA 2000.

the direction.[1] Apart from in that situation, no amendment of the memorandum or articles of association of the company may take effect until it has been submitted to the Secretary of State for his approval and he has notified his approval to the company.[2]

16.85 As with an FEC, the Secretary of State may intervene in the affairs of a designated further education institution under s 57 of the FHEA in the event of (for example) mismanagement or a breach of duty by the governing body of the institution.[3] Also as with an FEC, the governing body of a designated further education institution may be bound to act in accordance with s 52A(2) of the FHEA 1992. That will be so if the institution provides secondary education to persons of compulsory school age in pursuance of arrangements made by an LEA or by the governing body of a school on behalf of an LEA.[4]

Property of a designated further education institution

16.86 Under s 32(1) and (2) of the FHEA 1992, subject to ss 32(4) and 36,[5] property owned by an LEA and used or held for the purposes of an institution which is to become a designated further education institution, may be transferred. Such property may be transferred only if the order designating the institution under s 28 so provides, or the institution was, before it was designated, either a voluntary aided school or an institution (other than a school) assisted by an LEA.[6] The property is transferred in the case of a designated further education institution conducted by a company, to the company, and, in the case of a designated further education institution which is conducted otherwise than by a company, to 'any persons specified in the order designating the institution as persons appearing to the Secretary of State to be trustees holding property for the purposes of that institution'.[7] Rights and liabilities of the relevant LEA subsisting immediately before the date when the designation takes effect which were acquired or incurred by that authority for the purposes of the institution are dealt with in the same way.[8] However, where the transferees are trustees, they 'incur no personal liability by virtue of any liability so transferred but may apply any property held by them on trust for the purposes of the institution in meeting any such liability'.[9]

---

[1]   FHEA 1992, s 31(3). Before giving any such directions, the Secretary of State must consult the persons who appear to him to have effective control over the company: s 31(5).

[2]   Ibid, s 31(4).

[3]   See further, para **16.90**.

[4]   See para **16.66** concerning s 52A(2).

[5]   Section 32(4) of FHEA 1992 concerns (1) certain loan liabilities, and (2) land which it is agreed under s 32(5), or determined under s 32(6), should not be affected by s 32(2). Section 36 applies to property which is used or held by an LEA or by trustees for the purposes of an institution which is designated under s 28, especially property which is used or held not only for the purposes of that institution.

[6]   FHEA 1992, s 32(1).

[7]   Ibid, s 32(2) and (3). Section 130(5) of the ERA 1988 relating to a designated higher education institution is to the same effect.

[8]   See ibid, s 32(1) to (3). These provisions, and those relating to higher education corporations, are considered in a little more detail in paras **8.48–8.57**.

[9]   Ibid, s 33(2). Section 130(6)(b) of the ERA 1988 relating to designated higher education institutions is to the same effect.

16.87 Any property which is transferred under s 32 to trustees (in other words in the case of a designated further education institution conducted otherwise than by a company) is transferred to be held 'on the trusts applicable under such trust deed relating to or regulating that institution (if any) as may be specified in the order designating the institution, or, if no such trust deed is so specified, on trust for the general purposes of the institution'.[1]

16.88 If any land is transferred to trustees under s 32(3)(b) of the FHEA 1992 after 1 October 2000 in England or 1 April 2001 in Wales, and it is subsequently disposed of, then the trustees must notify the LSC or (as the case may be) the CETW, and then pay such council 'so much of the proceeds of disposal as may be determined to be just' either by agreement, or, in default of agreement, by the Secretary of State or (as the case may be) the National Assembly.[2] The same is true if any land is held by trustees for the purposes of an institution which became a designated further education institution after such date and the land was acquired or enhanced in value wholly or partly by means of money paid under s 65 of the EA 1996 or para 5 of Sch 3 to the SSFA 1998.[3] For these purposes, land is disposed of by the trustees not only in the normal way, but also if they permit it to be used for purposes not connected with the designated further education institution (or any other institution in the further education sector).[4]

Power to provide by order for the constitution as a body corporate of the governing body of a designated further education institution

16.89 Under the FHEA 1992, the governing body of a designated further education institution could be unincorporated. A number of potential problems arising as a result of the lack of corporate status of such a governing body were described in the first edition of this book.[5] A legislative solution to those problems came into existence when Parliament enacted s 143(4)–(6) of the LSA 2000. Those subsections confer on the Secretary of State and (in relation to Wales) the National Assembly a power to make an order (in the form of a statutory instrument which in relation to England does not need to be approved by either House of Parliament[6]) 'providing for the constitution as a body corporate of the governing body' of a designated further education institution.[7] The order may contain various provisions, including 'about the discontinuance of the institution' and 'about the dissolution of the body corporate

---

1   FHEA 1992, s 33(1). Section 130(6)(a) of the ERA 1988 relating to a designated higher education institution is to the same effect. Since a trust for purposes cannot (except with minor exceptions) be valid unless the trust is charitable, the clear implication from s 33(1) is that Parliament regarded the purposes of a designated institution as exclusively charitable. However, even in the absence of the relevant words in s 33(1), it would have been reasonably clear that the purposes of a designated institution were exclusively charitable.

2   See LSA 2000, s 144 (1), (3), (4) and (9). Section 144 applies only to property transferred after its commencement. For the commencement dates, see SI 2000/2559 and SI 2001/1274.

3   See ibid, s 144(2). See para **7.126** concerning para 5 of Sch 3 to the SSFA 1998, and paras 6.91 et seq of the first edition of this book concerning s 65 of the EA 1996.

4   LSA 2000, s 144(7) and (8)(b).

5   Paragraphs 13.79–13.81.

6   See LSA 2000, s 152(1) and (2).

7   Ibid, s 143(4) and (5).

(including provision about the treatment of property, rights and liabilities)'.[1] Before making any such order, the Secretary of State or the National Assembly must consult (a) the governing body of the institution and (b) the trustees of any trust relating to the institution.[2]

SUPERVISION BY THE SECRETARY OF STATE OR THE NATIONAL ASSEMBLY OF AN INSTITUTION IN THE FURTHER EDUCATION SECTOR

16.90 The Secretary of State[3] has power under s 57 of the FHEA 1992, as substituted by the LSA 2000, to give directions to the governing body of an institution in the further education sector. Such a direction may be (a) to remove all or any members of the governing body, (b) to appoint new members if there are vacancies (however arising), and/or (c) such direction 'as he thinks expedient as to the exercise of their powers and performance of their duties'.[4] The power in s 57 arises where (1) the Secretary of State is 'satisfied that the institution's affairs are being or have been mismanaged by the governing body', (2) he is 'satisfied that the governing body have failed to discharge any duty imposed on them by or for the purposes of any Act', (3) he is 'satisfied that the institution's governing body have acted or are proposing to act unreasonably with respect to the exercise of any power conferred or the performance of any duty imposed by or under any Act', or (4) the report of an inspection regarding the institution by for example the ALI 'indicates that the institution has serious weaknesses, or is failing or is likely to fail to give an acceptable standard of education'.[5] In such circumstances, the Secretary of State also has power to declare which of these four conditions is (or are) satisfied.[6]

16.91 A governing body must comply with any directions given to them under s 57.[7] The Secretary of State has power under s 507 of the EA 1996 to direct that a local inquiry is held for the purposes of s 57.[8]

DUTY TO PROMOTE AND SAFEGUARD THE WELFARE OF CHILDREN RECEIVING EDUCATION OR TRAINING AT A FURTHER EDUCATION INSTITUTION

16.92 The governing body of an institution in the further education sector is bound by s 175(3) of the EA 2002 to 'make arrangements for ensuring that their functions relating to the conduct of the institution are exercised with a view to safeguarding and

---

[1] See LSA 2000, s 143(6).
[2] Ibid, s 143(7).
[3] In relation to an institution in Wales, the power to give a direction under s 57 resides in the National Assembly as a result of SI 1999/672: see LSA 2000, s 150.
[4] See FHEA 1992, s 57(5).
[5] See ibid 1992, s 57(1)–(3).
[6] Ibid, s 57(4)(a).
[7] Ibid, s 57(7).
[8] Ibid, s 57(9). See para **3.53** concerning s 507.

promoting the welfare of children who are receiving education or training at the institution'. In considering what such arrangements should be made by them, the governing body must have regard to any guidance given to them by the Secretary of State or (as the case may be) the National Assembly.[1] Since an LEA is bound by an equivalent duty, applicable when it is exercising its functions as an LEA, this duty must be regarded as extending also to further education institutions which are maintained by LEAs.

EDUCATIONAL RECORDS

16.93 Regulations may be made (none have so far been made) under s 202(1) of the EA 2002 'about the compilation, retention and disclosure of educational records of further education institutions'. Such institutions are not only institutions in the further education sector but also institutions which are maintained by LEAs and which provide further education.[2] The regulations may make a duty to provide a copy of a record conditional on the payment of a charge which does not exceed the cost of providing the copy.[3]

HAZARDOUS MATERIALS

16.94 Regulations may also be made under s 203 of the EA 2002 requiring the governing body of an institution in the further education sector to prevent the use in the institution of equipment or materials which is specified by the Secretary of State because he thinks it (or they) might endanger a person's health or safety.[4] The National Assembly may make regulations of a similar (but not the same) sort. The difference is that the regulations must prevent the use of the equipment or materials without the approval of the Assembly.[5] Regulations have currently been made only in England,[6] but a similar provision in the Education (Schools and Further and Higher Education) Regulations 1989[7] remains in force in Wales.

PUBLICATION OF PERFORMANCE INFORMATION

16.95 Institutions within the further education sector in Wales are obliged to comply with the provisions contained in the Education (Further Education Institutions Information) (Wales) Regulations 1993,[8] which were made under s 50 of the FHEA

---

1   EA 2002, s 175(4). See further, para **2.62**.
2   See ss 202(4) and 140 of the EA 2002.
3   Ibid, s 202(3).
4   Ibid, s 203(1) and (2).
5   See ibid, s 203(3) and (4).
6   See the Education (Hazardous Equipment and Materials) (England) Regulations 2004, SI 2004/571.
7   SI 1989/351, reg 7.
8   SI 1993/2169. The equivalent regulations relating to England, SI 1995/2065, were revoked by SI 2003/51.

1992. The regulations require the publication of certain information concerning the performance of the institutions to which they relate.

OBLIGATION TO CO-OPERATE WITH CAREERS ADVISERS

16.96 Section 44(9) of the EA 1997 obliges the governing body of an institution within the further education sector and its principal, 'to secure' that s 44(1), (4) and (6) of that Act (concerning access by careers advisers to relevant students) are complied with. The effect of those provisions is described in paras **11.26–11.28**.

16.97 In this connection, the possibility of the Secretary of State imposing a further duty in relation to careers education, should be borne in mind. That possibility arises from the Secretary of State's power, under s 46 of the EA 1997, by regulations to make provision for requiring the governing bodies of institutions within the further education sector and the principals or other heads of such institutions 'to secure that a programme of careers education is provided for any ... description [specified in the regulations in question] of persons attending such institutions'.[1] Such regulations have been made in relation to Wales only. The Education (Extension of Careers Education) (Wales) Regulations 2001[2] extend the relevant duty to persons aged 16–19 who are attending (whether full-time or part-time) institutions in the further education sector.

VOID PROVISIONS CONCERNING REDUNDANCY PAYMENTS

16.98 Section 49 of the FHEA 1992 provides that any contract made between the governing body of an institution within the further education sector and an employee (other than a contract made in contemplation of the employee's pending dismissal by reason of redundancy) which provides that the employee will not be dismissed by reason of redundancy or, if so dismissed, will be paid an amount in excess of the amount required by Part XI of the Employment Rights Act 1996 to be paid in the event of redundancy, is void and of no effect.

INSPECTION OF ACCOUNTS

16.99 The accounts of a further education corporation or a designated further education institution are open to the inspection of the Comptroller and Auditor General, as a result of s 53(1) of the FHEA 1992.[3]

---

[1]   EA 1997, s 46(3) and (5).
[2]   SI 2001/1987.
[3]   See also s 53(2) regarding the exercise of the power to inspect under s 53(1) and the exercise by the Comptroller and Auditor General of his powers under ss 6 and 8 of the National Audit Act 1983 (concerning examinations into the economy, efficiency and effectiveness of certain bodies, and access to documents and information) which are exercisable by virtue of s 6(3)(c) of that Act. Broadly, those

WITNESSES IN DISCIPLINARY PROCEEDINGS

16.100   One factor which might be relevant to disciplinary proceedings concerning either a student at, or an employee employed to work at, a further education institution, is that a potential witness might be of the same age as a school student. If so, then the Secretary of State's guidance in relation to exclusions from maintained schools[1] is likely to be of assistance by way of analogy. There, in Part 4, it is stated:

> '9.3   To reach a decision, the panel will generally need to hear from those directly or indirectly involved. The Governing Body may wish to call witnesses who saw the incident that gave rise to the exclusion. These may include any alleged victim or any teacher other than the head teacher who investigated the incident and interviewed pupils.
>
> 9.4   In the case of witnesses who are pupils at the school, it will normally be more appropriate for the panel to rely on written statements. Pupils may appear as witnesses if they do so voluntarily and with their parent's consent. Panels should be sensitive to the needs of the child witnesses to ensure that the child's view is properly heard.'

ADDITIONAL PUBLIC FUNDING TO WHICH FURTHER EDUCATION INSTITUTIONS MAY BE ENTITLED

16.101   In addition to funds from the LSC, an institution within the further education sector may be given funds by the Secretary of State, under ss 14–17 of the EA 2002. It is likely that those provisions will be used mainly for the giving of funding which would previously have been given under ss 210 and 211 of the ERA 1988, which were repealed by s 18 of the EA 2002 in relation to England but which continue in force in Wales. Those sections conferred (or, as the case may be, confer) a power to make grants to institutions within the further education sector for the education of travellers and displaced persons and under s 11 of the Local Government Act 1966.[2]

COLLECTIVE WORSHIP AND EDUCATION IN CERTAIN FURTHER EDUCATION INSTITUTIONS WHICH WERE FORMERLY SCHOOLS

16.102   Section 44 of the FHEA 1992, concerning collective worship, applies to any institution within the further education sector which is principally concerned with the provision of full-time education suitable to the requirements of persons over compulsory school age who have not attained the age of 19 years. Unless the institution is of voluntary origin, the governing body of the institution must ensure that at an appropriate time on at least one day in each week during which the

---

powers may only be exercised in, or in relation to documents concerning, a financial year in which the body in question received funding under Part I of the FHEA 1992.

[1]   DfES/0087/2003.
[2]   See para **2.100** in respect of s 11 of the Local Government Act 1966.

institution is open, an act of collective worship which is wholly or mainly of a broadly Christian character is held at the institution which persons receiving education at the institution may attend.[1] An act is wholly or mainly of a broadly Christian character if it reflects the broad traditions of Christian belief; it need not be distinctive of any particular Christian denomination.[2] If the institution is of voluntary origin,[3] the act of collective worship must be 'in such forms as to comply with the provisions of any trust deed affecting the institution' and reflect the traditions and practices of the institution before it joined the further education sector.[4] If the governing body of an institution to which s 44 applies considers it appropriate to do so, it may in addition to the act of collective worship described above, 'provide for acts of worship which reflect the practices of some or all of the other religious traditions represented in Great Britain'.[5]

16.103   Section 45 of the FHEA 1992 concerns religious education in institutions to which s 44 applies. Every such institution must ensure that religious education is provided at the institution for all persons attending it who wish to receive such education.[6] Such a governing body will comply with this duty if religious education is provided at a time or times at which it is convenient for the majority of full-time students to attend.[7]

VARIATION OF TRUST DEEDS

16.104   Under s 46(1) of the FHEA 1992, the Secretary of State may by order[8] make such modifications as he thinks fit in any trust deed or other instrument relating to or regulating an institution within the further education sector, or relating to any land or other property held by any person for the purposes of such an institution. Under s 46(2), the Secretary of State is obliged 'so far as it appears to him to be practicable to do so' to consult certain parties, including the governing body of the institution, before making any modifications of any trust deed or other instrument.[9]

RELATIONSHIP BETWEEN STUDENT AND FURTHER EDUCATION INSTITUTION

16.105   The relationship between a student at a further education institution and the body responsible for conducting that institution is governed by the same principles as those which apply to the relationship between a student at a higher education

---

[1]   See FHEA 1992, s 44(2A)–(4).
[2]   See ibid, s 44(4).
[3]   For the meaning of which, see ibid, s 44(2) as substituted by para 27 of Sch 9 to the LSA 2000.
[4]   Ibid, s 44(3), as amended by para 27 of Sch 9 to the LSA 2000.
[5]   Ibid, s 44(5).
[6]   LSA 2000, s 45(2A).
[7]   Ibid, s 45(3). See s 45(4) and (5) for the content of the religious education and the manner in which it must be provided.
[8]   Made otherwise than by statutory instrument: see s 89 of the FHEA 1992.
[9]   A similar power for the Privy Council in relation to a higher education institution is contained in s 157 of the ERA 1988.

institution and its governing body,[1] with one or two differences. Those differences result in the main from the facts that (1) many further education students will be younger than those at higher education institutions, and (2) no fees will be paid by many students at a further education institution. The former difference may affect the manner in which the law of negligence applies to the situation. The latter may have the effect that a student for whose attendance no fees are payable will have no contract with the institution. This is because it is difficult to see how any contractual consideration can properly be said to have been given by such a student in return for a place at the institution, there being no 'clearing' system in existence.[2] Yet it may be that giving up the chance of a place at another institution would be found by a court to constitute the necessary consideration. If it were found not to have done so, however, then the result would be that public law, rather than the law of contract, would govern the relationship between the student and the governing body of the institution.

16.106   The relationship between students who have mental disabilities and those who are responsible for conducting a further education institution is outside the scope of this chapter, except that of course such disabilities will be relevant in determining the standard of care owed to the student in the law of negligence.

STUDENT LOANS

16.107   The possibility of a further education student receiving a loan from the Secretary of State under regulations made under s 22 of the THEA 1998 needs to be mentioned here. So does the possibility of a further education institution being given functions in relation to such loans by the Secretary of State. Both possibilities are described in Chapter 3.[3]

---

1   As to which, see paras **17.93** et seq.
2   Contrast the situation in *Moran v University College Salford (No 2)* [1994] ELR 187, described so far as relevant in paras **17.93** et seq. Cf *R v Cobham Hall School, ex parte G* [1998] ELR 389, at 398 E–G; [1998] EdCR 79, at 90E–G, per Dyson J.
3   See paras **3.65–3.67**.

Chapter 17

HIGHER EDUCATION

INTRODUCTION

17.1   The law of higher education concerns principally the arrangements for funding higher education, the government (or governance) of higher education institutions, students' unions, and the relationship between a student and the higher education institution at which he is studying or hopes to study. However, there are superficially significant differences between the various types of higher education institutions, and consequential differences concerning the relationships between the student and each type of institution. As with several other areas in the law of education, the law of higher education can probably be understood clearly only by taking into account the history of the law in the area.

HISTORY OF THE LAW OF HIGHER EDUCATION[1]

17.2   Originally, higher education institutions existed in England in the form only of the universities and colleges of Oxford and Cambridge. Over the centuries, further institutions came into existence which (in some cases eventually) were called universities. During the twentieth century, higher education institutions which did not call themselves universities also came into existence, most of which were funded by LEAs. These institutions were known as polytechnics, colleges of higher education or institutes of higher education. Many of those institutions were given independence by the ERA 1988. That Act established independent corporations (higher education corporations[2]) to conduct the institutions which had until then been maintained by LEAs, and transferred their property and operations to those corporations from the LEAs which had maintained them. However, LEAs were allowed by the ERA 1988 to retain certain powers in relation to higher education, and those powers survive today.[3]

17.3   Until the FHEA 1992, there was no uniformity in relation to the constitutional arrangements for the constitution and government of the universities which came into existence from time to time. After that Act, the former diversity remained in relation to the universities created before the Act came into force, but new universities could from then on be created under the procedures originally set out in the ERA 1988. Further, as a result of s 77 of the FHEA 1992, the polytechnics and other relevant higher education institutions were enabled, with the permission of the Privy Council,

---

[1]   For reasons of space, this section contains only a brief overview. A much fuller overview of the fascinating history of higher education institutions is to be found in Chapter 1 of DJ Farrington's *The Law of Higher Education* (Butterworths, 2nd edn, 1998).

[2]   See paras **17.35** et seq.

[3]   See paras **17.29** et seq.

to call themselves universities.[1] As can be inferred, however, the change in name did not in itself result in a change in nature, although it is of interest that s 77(4) provides that an institution whose name includes the word 'university' by virtue of the exercise of the power in s 77(1) 'is to be treated as a university for all purposes unless in that name that word is immediately followed by the word "college" or "collegiate".'

THE PRESENT SITUATION

17.4   Higher education providers therefore cannot be classified by reference to any particular set of criteria, although there is now a statutory definition of higher education.[2] Yet there are some broad categories which can be said to exist, albeit that there is some diversity within at least the category of universities which came into existence before the FHEA 1992. These categories are the latter type of universities (which are referred to below as 'pre-FHEA 1992 universities'), higher education corporations (HECs) established under the ERA 1988, designated higher education institutions (that is higher education institutions designated under s 129 of the ERA 1988) and higher education institutions maintained by LEAs. Higher education corporations and designated higher education institutions may now be called universities, as a result of s 77 of the FHEA 1992. The name 'university' therefore cannot now be taken to indicate any particular kind of organisational or constitutional structure, although only a pre-FHEA 1992 university, an HEC or an institution designated under s 129 of the ERA 1988 may be called a university.[3] As a result, reference is made in this chapter only to pre-FHEA 1992 universities, HECs, designated higher education institutions and higher education institutions maintained by LEAs.

17.5   It may be that in the future the current division between further and higher education will no longer exist, and that there will simply be a division between (1) schools and (2) institutions which cater mainly for persons who are above compulsory school age. At present, colleges of higher and further education are not included within the categories referred to in the preceding paragraph, because they are best described as further education institutions.

17.6   There is, however, one factor which unifies almost all institutions which provide higher education in England and Wales. That is that they almost all receive funds from one of the Higher Education Funding Councils (as to which, see below). (The exception is, apparently, the University of Buckingham, which, although a charity, receives no grant from such a council.[4])

---

[1]   Section 77 of the FHEA 1992 applies to all institutions within the higher education sector (see para **17.14** for the definition of an institution within the higher education sector). The Privy Council has power under s 77(1) to allow such an institution to be called a university only where there is a power to change the name of the institution which is exercisable only with the consent of the Privy Council. The FHEA 1992 has had the effect that higher education corporations and designated higher education institutions all require such consent: see ss 124A and 129A of the 1988 Act.

[2]   See para **17.7**.

[3]   This is the product of ss 77(1)(b) and 91(5) of the FHEA 1992.

[4]   Farrington, op cit, para 1.83.

THE DEFINITION OF 'HIGHER EDUCATION'

17.7   Before turning to consider the arrangements for the funding of higher education, it is necessary to set out the definition of higher education which prevails today. Given the history of the law of higher education, it is perhaps not surprising that the definition is purely technical. The definition is to be found in s 120(1) of the ERA 1988,[1] which provides that higher education is 'education provided by means of a course of any description mentioned in Schedule 6 to this Act'. Schedule 6 provides as follows:

> '1.   The descriptions of courses referred to in sections 120(1) and 235(2)(e) of this Act are the following –
> (a)   a course for the further training of teachers or youth and community workers;
> (b)   a post-graduate course (including a higher degree course);
> (c)   a first degree course;
> (d)   a course for the Diploma of Higher Education;
> (e)   a course for the Higher National Diploma or Higher National Certificate of the Business & Technician Education Council, or the Diploma in Management Studies;
> (f)   a course for the Certificate in Education;
> (g)   a course in preparation for a professional examination at higher level;
> (h)   a course providing education at a higher level (whether or not in preparation for an examination).'[2]

THE HIGHER EDUCATION FUNDING COUNCILS

17.8   The Higher Education Funding Councils came into existence as a result of the FHEA 1992. Before then, there used to be two funding councils, the Universities Funding Council and the Polytechnics and Colleges Funding Council. These were established under ss 131 and 132 of the ERA 1988, to replace the former non-statutory University Grants Committee and the funding by LEAs of institutions which became conducted by HECs established under the ERA 1988.

17.9   Section 62(1) of the FHEA 1992 established a Higher Education Funding Council for England and a Higher Education Funding Council for Wales. The Secretary of State appoints the members of these councils,[3] having regard to the matters referred to in s 62(4). If there is a dispute as to whether any functions are

---

[1]   Section 90(1) of the FHEA 1992 provides that the definition of higher education is as provided for in the ERA 1988.

[2]   A professional examination is at higher level within the meaning of para 1(g) if 'its standard is higher than the standard of examinations at advanced level for the General Certificate of Education or the examination for the National Certificate or the National Diploma of the Business & Technician Education Council': Sch 6, para 2. A course is at a higher level within the meaning of para 1(h) if its standard is higher than the standard of courses providing education in preparation for any of these examinations: Sch 6 para 3.

[3]   FHEA 1992, s 62(2) and (3). In relation to Wales, a reference to the Secretary of State in this chapter must (unless otherwise stated) be read as a reference to the National Assembly: see SI 1999/672.

exercisable by one of the councils, then (including in relation to Wales) it is to be determined by the Secretary of State.[1]

GRANTS FROM THE SECRETARY OF STATE TO THE HIGHER EDUCATION FUNDING COUNCILS

17.10   The funding of the higher education funding councils is given to them by the Secretary of State under s 68 of the FHEA 1992. Section 68(1) empowers the Secretary of State to 'make grants to each of the councils of such amounts and subject to such terms and conditions as he may determine'. Section 68(2)(a) provides that such terms and conditions may impose requirements which apply to 'every institution, or every institution falling within a class or description specified in the terms and conditions'. Section 68(2)(a) also provides that the Secretary of State may require that the terms and conditions are complied with in the case of any institution to which the requirements apply before financial support of any amount or description specified in the terms and conditions is provided by the funding council in respect of activities carried on by the institution. However, the terms and conditions may not otherwise relate to the provision of financial support by the council in respect of activities carried on by any particular institution or institutions.[2] Further, the terms and conditions:

> 'may not be framed by reference to particular courses of study or programmes of research (including the contents of such courses or programmes and the manner in which they are taught, supervised or assessed) or to the criteria for the selection and appointment of academic staff and for the admission of students.'[3]

17.11   Under s 26 of the THEA 1998 (which will be repealed by the Higher Education Act 2004, the effects of which are described in paras **17.126** et seq), the Secretary of State may impose a condition on the payment of grants to the higher education funding councils. That condition is that the grants, loans or other payments made by the higher education funding councils to any specified institution are themselves made subject to a condition. That condition is that the fees payable to the institution in respect of the relevant academic year by 'any prescribed class of persons in connection with their undertaking courses of any prescribed description are equal to the prescribed amount'.[4] This 'prescribed class' and the relevant courses are

---

[1]   FHEA 1992, s 62(8). According to s 62(7), if an institution's activities are carried on principally in, for example, England, then it is to be treated as an institution in England. The Open University is, however, an institution in both England and Wales: ibid.

[2]   Ibid, s 68(2)(b).

[3]   Ibid, s 68(3).

[4]   Ibid, s 26(4), as amended by the LSA 2000. The prescribed amount is 'such amount as may be prescribed for the time being by virtue of section 22(2)(b) as the maximum amount of any grant available for the relevant academic year in respect of fees payable by such persons in connection with their undertaking such courses': s 26(5). The condition does not apply to fees payable by persons who can loosely be described as overseas students: see s 26(7). The Secretary of State may not discriminate between courses in the manner set out in s 26(8) when imposing conditions under s 26(4). The definition of 'fees' for the purposes of s 26 is set out in s 28(1) of the THEA 1998, which allows for exceptions to be prescribed. Such exceptions are provided for by the Education (Student Fees)

provided for by the Education (Fees at Higher Education Institutions) Regulations 1999.[1]

17.12 The terms and conditions imposed by the Secretary of State under s 68(1) of the FHEA 1992 may enable him to require the repayment, in whole or in part, of sums paid by him if any of the terms and conditions subject to which the sums were paid is not complied with, and to require the payment of interest on any sums which are due but not yet paid.[2]

FUNCTIONS OF THE HIGHER EDUCATION FUNDING COUNCILS

The provision of financial support

17.13 The higher education funding councils (HEFCs) do not in the main fund higher education as such. Rather, under s 65 of the FHEA 1992, they mostly fund activities carried on by 'higher education institutions'.[3] Section 65(1) provides that each HEFC is responsible for administering funds made available to the council by the Secretary of State and others for the purposes of providing financial support for activities of the sorts set out in s 65(2), which are as follows:

'(a) the provision of education and the undertaking of research by higher education institutions in the council's area,

(b) the provision of any facilities, and the carrying on of any other activities, by higher education institutions in their area which the governing bodies of those institutions consider it necessary or desirable to provide or carry on for the purpose of or in connection with education or research,

(c) the provision –
    (i) by institutions in their area maintained or assisted by local education authorities,[4] or
    (ii) by such institutions in their area as are within the further education sector, of prescribed courses of higher education,[5] and

(d) the provision by any person of services for the purposes of, or in connection with, the provision of education or the undertaking of research by institutions within the higher education sector.'

17.14 A higher education institution is defined by s 65(5) of the FHEA 1992 for the purposes of ss 65 and 66 of that Act to mean 'a university, an institution conducted by

---

(Exceptions) (England) Regulations 1999, SI 1999/2265 and the Education (Student Fees) (Exceptions) (Wales) Regulations 1999, SI 1999/2862.

[1] SI 1999/603.

[2] FHEA 1992, s 68(4).

[3] As to which, see para **17.14**.

[4] An institution is assisted for this purpose if it is not an institution in the further or higher education sectors, and an LEA 'make[s] to the persons responsible for its maintenance any grant in respect of the institution or any payment in consideration of the provision of educational facilities there': see s 90(5) of the FHEA 1992 and s 579(6) of the 1996 Act.

[5] The regulations prescribing such courses are the Education (Prescribed Courses of Higher Education) Regulations 1993, SI 1993/481, as amended by SI 1998/1970.

a higher education corporation or a designated institution'.[1] An institution 'within the higher education sector' is defined by s 91(5) of the FHEA 1992 as follows:

'References to institutions within the higher education sector are to –
(a) universities receiving financial support under section 65 of this Act,
(b) institutions conducted by higher education corporations, and
(c) designated institutions for the purposes of Part II of this Act (defined in section 72(3) of this Act).'

17.15 The power of the HEFCs to control the activities of the governing bodies of institutions to which they give funding[2] under s 65(3)(a) and of any persons to whom they give funding under s 65(3)(b) derives from their power to make 'grants, loans or other payments ... subject ... to such terms and conditions as the council think fit', which may enable the council to require the repayment in whole or in part of the sums so paid, together with interest in respect of any period during which the money ought to have been repaid.[3] However, such terms and conditions may not relate to the application by such a governing body of any sums derived otherwise than from the council.[4] Those conditions may, as a result of s 26 of the THEA 1998, include a condition with respect to the maximum amount which the governing body can require by way of fees from certain students.[5]

17.16 Before exercising its discretion under s 65(3)(a) with respect to the terms and conditions to be imposed in relation to any grants, loans or other payments, an HEFC must consult:

'such of the following bodies as appear to the council to be appropriate to consult in the circumstances –
(a) such bodies representing the interests of higher education institutions[6] as appear to the council to be concerned, and
(b) the governing body of any particular higher education institution which appears to the council to be concerned.'[7]

17.17 Furthermore, the HEFCs must have regard to the desirability of not discouraging any institution for whose activities financial support is provided under s 65, from maintaining or developing funding from other sources.[8] Finally, in exercising their functions under s 65, as a result of s 66(3), an HEFC must have regard (so far as they think it appropriate to do so in the light of any other relevant considerations) to the desirability of maintaining (a) 'what appears to them to be an

---

[1]   The definition of 'university' is contained in s 90(3) of the FHEA 1992, and is uncontroversial.
[2]   For the definition of 'governing body', see s 90(1) of the FHEA 1992 and the Education (Designated Institutions in Further and Higher Education) (Interpretation) Order 1993, SI 1993/563.
[3]   FHEA 1992, s 65(3) and (4), read with s 65(3A) and (3B). In the case of a designated higher education institution which is conducted by a company, the payments are made to the company and not to the governing body of the institution: Education (Designated Institutions in Further and Higher Education) (Interpretation) Order 1993, SI 1993/563, Art 2, Sch 1.
[4]   Ibid, s 65(4).
[5]   See para **17.11**.
[6]   As defined in s 65(5): see para **17.14**.
[7]   FHEA 1992, s 66(1).
[8]   Ibid, s 66(2).

appropriate balance in the support given by them as between institutions which are of a denominational character and other institutions',[1] and (b) 'any distinctive characteristics of any institution within the higher education sector for whose activities financial support is provided under that section'.

Assessment of quality of education provided by institutions

17.18 The HEFCs are under a duty to 'secure that provision is made for assessing the quality of education provided in institutions for whose activities they provide, or are considering providing, financial support'.[2] They were also under a duty to establish a committee, to be known as the 'Quality Assessment Committee' to give them advice on their function of assessing the quality of education in those institutions.[3] The committee must contain a majority of members who are not members of the HEFC in question, but the committee is otherwise to be treated as a committee of the council.[4]

Payments under section 133 of the Education Reform Act 1988 and section 18 of the Education Act 1994

17.19 Mention has already been made of the power conferred on the HEFCs by s 133 of the ERA 1988 (as substituted by s 67(1) of the FHEA 1992).[5] That is a power to make payments to LEAs, the London Residuary Body, the London Pensions Fund Authority, and the governing body of an institution designated under s 129 of the ERA 1988 as originally enacted,[6] in respect of certain expenditure. The expenditure in question is that incurred in making payments to or in respect of persons employed or formerly employed at an institution which provides or (if the institution has ceased to exist since the employment came to an end) formerly provided higher education or further education (or both), unless the expenditure is incurred by a designated higher education institution. In the latter case, the persons must be or have formerly been employed at the institution. A similar power is conferred by s 18 of the EA 1994 on the HEFCs to make payments to an FEC or the governing body of an institution designated under s 28 of the FHEA 1992, in respect of expenditure which has been or will be incurred by that body in making certain safeguarded salary payments to persons who used before 1 April 1989 to be employed in the training of teachers.[7] The persons must have been employed in a 'college for the training of teachers, or in a department for the training of teachers in any other establishment of further education'.

---

1 FHEA 1992, s 66(4) defines an institution of a denominational character for this purpose.
2 Ibid, s 70(1)(a).
3 Ibid, s 70(1)(b). The majority of the members must satisfy the description in s 70(3): s 70(2)(a).
4 Ibid, s 70(2)(b) and (4). As for the possibility of the joint exercise of functions regarding the assessment of the arrangements for maintaining academic standards in an institution, see s 82(2), concerning which see para **17.25**.
5 Paragraph **2.99**.
6 This means the company where the institution is conducted by a company: Education (Designated Institutions in Further and Higher Education) (Interpretation) Order 1993, SI 1993/563, Art 2, Sch 1. See paras **17.41** et seq concerning institutions designated under s 129.
7 The payments are those made as a result of a direction given by the Secretary of State under reg 3(2) of SI 1975/1092 and regs 15 and 16 of SI 1981/1086, all of which have been revoked.

Supplementary functions

17.20 Section 69 of the FHEA 1992 imposes certain supplementary functions on the HEFCs. As a result of s 69(1), an HEFC must provide the Secretary of State with 'such information or advice relating to the provision for their area of higher education as he may from time to time require', and 'may provide the Secretary of State with such information or advice relating to such provision as they think fit'. Each council must also keep under review activities eligible for funding under s 65 of the Act.[1]

17.21 Under s 69(3), an HEFC may provide 'such advisory services as the Department of Education for Northern Ireland or the Department of Agriculture for Northern Ireland may require in connection with the discharge of the department's functions relating to higher education in Northern Ireland'. Section 69(3) also empowers the making of a charge for such services.

17.22 Where land or other property is or was used or held for the purposes of an institution within the higher education sector[2] and the Secretary of State is entitled to any right or interest in respect of the property, or would be so entitled on the occurrence of any event, the Secretary of State may direct that all or any of his functions in respect of the property are to be exercisable on his behalf by the relevant HEFC.[3] Such functions must be exercised in accordance with such directions as the Secretary of State may give from time to time.[4]

17.23 Finally, the Secretary of State 'may by order confer or impose on a council such supplementary functions relating to the provision of education as he thinks fit'.[5] The order must be made by statutory instrument.[6] A function is supplementary for this purpose if it is exercisable for the purposes of (a) the exercise by the Secretary of State of functions of his under any enactment, or (b) the doing by the Secretary of State of anything which he has power to do apart from any enactment (in other words, presumably, under the Royal Prerogative), and in both cases it relates to, or to the activities of, any institution of the sort referred to in s 69(7).[7] Those institutions are (a) institutions within the higher education sector,[8] and (b) institutions at which prescribed courses of higher education are currently provided and which are either (i) within the further education sector or (ii) maintained or assisted by LEAs.[9]

Efficiency studies

17.24 Under s 83(1) of the FHEA 1992, an HEFC 'may arrange for the promotion or carrying out by any person of studies designed to improve economy, efficiency and effectiveness in the management or operations of an institution within ... the higher

---

1   FHEA 1992, s 69(2).
2   See para **17.14** for the definition of an institution within the higher education sector.
3   FHEA 1992, s 69(4).
4   Ibid.
5   Ibid, s 69(5).
6   Ibid, s 89.
7   Ibid, s 69(6).
8   As to which, see para **17.14**.
9   See footnote 4 in para **17.13** as to what is an institution assisted by an LEA for this purpose.

education sector'.[1] The person concerned may require the governing body of the institution in question (and, in the case of a designated higher education institution conducted by a company, the company[2]) to furnish such information, and to make available for inspection their accounts or such other documents, as the person may reasonably require for the purpose.[3]

Joint exercise of functions

17.25 Under s 82(1) of the FHEA 1992, any two or more funding councils may exercise their functions jointly if it appears to them that it will be more efficient or that it will enable them more effectively to discharge any of their functions. For this purpose, a funding council is an HEFC, the LSC, the CETW, or the Scottish Higher Education Funding Council.[4] In addition, the Secretary of State has power under s 82(2) to direct that two or more such councils make joint provision for the assessment of the arrangements for maintaining academic standards in an institution.[5]

DUTY OF CERTAIN BODIES TO GIVE INFORMATION TO THE HIGHER EDUCATION FUNDING COUNCILS

17.26 Mention may usefully be made here of what is in effect a power given to the HEFCs to require an LEA, the governing body of any institution within the higher education sector,[6] and the governing body of any institution at which prescribed courses of higher education are currently or have at any time been provided, to give information to the relevant council. That power arises under s 79 of the FHEA 1992. The information which the body in question is under a duty to give is 'such information as [the relevant council] may require for the purposes of the exercise of any of their functions under the Education Acts'.

POWER OF THE SECRETARY OF STATE TO GIVE DIRECTIONS TO THE FUNDING COUNCILS

17.27 Each of the HEFCs must, when exercising their functions under Part II of the FHEA 1992, comply with any directions given by the Secretary of State under s 81 of the FHEA 1992. Such directions must be contained in an order, which itself must be contained in a statutory instrument.[7] The Secretary of State may give general directions to an HEFC about the exercise of its functions,[8] and he may also give

---

1   As for an institution within the higher education sector, see para **17.14**.
2   Education (Designated Institutions in Further and Higher Education) (Interpretation) Order 1993, SI 1993/563, Art 2, Sch 2.
3   FHEA 1992, s 83(2). The definition of 'governing body' for the purposes of the FHEA 1992 is contained in s 90(1).
4   Ibid, s 82(3), read with s 90(2A).
5   See para **17.28**.
6   See footnote 2 at para **17.15** and para **17.14** for the definitions of 'governing body' and 'institution within the higher education sector' respectively.
7   See FHEA 1992, ss 81(1) and 89.
8   Ibid, s 81(2).

directions to such a council concerning an individual institution within the higher education sector.[1] However, he may give directions concerning an individual institution only where it appears to him that the financial affairs of the institution 'have been or are being mismanaged'.[2] Before giving such a direction, the Secretary of State must consult the relevant HEFC and the institution.[3] The directions may concern only the provision by the council of financial support in respect of the activities carried on by the institution, and must be such as the Secretary of State considers are necessary or expedient by reason of the mismanagement.[4]

17.28 The Secretary of State may also direct a funding council[5] jointly to:

'make provision for the assessment by a person appointed by them of matters relating to arrangements made by each institution in Great Britain which is within the higher education sector for maintaining academic standards in the institution.'[6]

LOCAL AUTHORITY FUNCTIONS IN RELATION TO HIGHER EDUCATION

17.29 As a result of s 120(3) of the ERA 1988 (as amended by the FHEA 1992), an LEA has power:

'(a) to secure the provision for their area of such facilities for higher education as appear to them to be appropriate for meeting the needs of the population of their area;
(b) to secure the provision of higher education for persons from other areas; and
(c) to do anything which appears to them to be necessary or expedient for the purposes of or in connection with such provision.'

17.30 In exercising their power under s 120(3)(a), the LEA must have regard to 'any facilities for higher education provided by institutions within the higher education sector or the further education sector and other bodies which are provided for, or available for use by persons living in, their area'.[7]

17.31 Where in the exercise of their higher education functions an LEA maintains an institution which is not within the higher education sector, the LEA may:

'(a) make such provision as they think fit in respect of the government of the institution (including replacing any instrument of government or articles of government of the institution made under [Chapter III of Part II or under s 156 of the ERA 1988], and

---

[1] See para **17.14** for the meaning of an institution within the higher education sector.
[2] FHEA 1992, s 81(3).
[3] Ibid. The obligation is to consult the institution (whatever that may mean in this context), and not the governing body of the institution.
[4] Ibid.
[5] Defined for this purpose in s 82(3), as to which see para **17.25**.
[6] FHEA 1992, s 82(2). As for what is an institution within the higher education sector, see para **17.14**.
[7] ERA 1988, s 120(4), as amended by the FHEA 1992. For the definition of an institution within the higher education sector, see para **17.14**, and for the definition of an institution within the further education sector, see s 91(3) of the FHEA 1992, as to which see para **16.2**.

(b)   delegate to the governing body of the institution such functions relating to the management of the finances of the institution, and such other functions relating to the management of the institution (including the appointment and dismissal of staff), as the authority may determine.'[1]

17.32 Sections 495–498 of the EA 1996 apply to any institution which is maintained by an LEA and provides higher education (whether or not it also provides further education).[2] Similarly, s 85A of the FHEA 1992 applies to such an institution.[3]

17.33 The governing body of any institution providing full-time education which is maintained by an LEA in exercise of its higher education functions, must 'make such reports and returns, and give such information, to the Secretary of State as he may require for the purposes of the exercise of any of his functions in relation to education'.[4] Further, an LEA must publish such information in relation to such an institution as is required by regulations made under s 159 of the ERA 1988.[5]

THE CONSTITUTIONS AND GOVERNMENT OF BODIES CONDUCTING HIGHER EDUCATION INSTITUTIONS

17.34 The constitutions and government of bodies conducting higher education institutions is a topic which needs to be considered in relation to (1) HECs established under the ERA 1988, (2) designated higher education institutions within the meaning of that Act, and (3) universities which existed before the passing of the FHEA 1992.

Higher education corporations

17.35 Higher education corporations were first established under s 121 of the ERA 1988. The first such corporations which came into being in that manner are set out in the Education (Higher Education Corporations) Order 1988,[6] which was followed by a series of Orders of the same sort. New HECs may be created under s 122(1) of the ERA 1988, which applies where in the case of any institution maintained by an LEA 'it appears to the Secretary of State ... that its full-time equivalent enrolment number for courses of higher education exceeds 55 per cent of its total full-time equivalent enrolment number'.[7] New HECs may also be created by the transfer of an FEC to the higher education sector under s 122A of the ERA 1988 where the circumstances just mentioned apply in relation to an FEC.[8]

---

[1]   FHEA 1992, s 85(2) and (3). For the definition of 'governing body', see s 90(1).
[2]   See s 219 of the ERA 1988, as substituted by the EA 1996. See Chapter 3 concerning ss 495–497, and para **7.84** concerning s 498.
[3]   See para **16.59** concerning s 85A.
[4]   ERA 1988, s 158(1) and (2).
[5]   There are currently no such regulations.
[6]   SI 1988/1799.
[7]   The full-time equivalent enrolment number is determined in accordance with Sch 9 to the ERA 1988: s 161(3).
[8]   ERA 1988, s 122A. For FECs, see paras **16.61** et seq.

Constitution

17.36 The constitution of an HEC is as provided for in the ERA 1988. The constitutions for corporations established under s 121 or s 122 of the ERA 1988 will be as provided for in Sch 7 to that Act (as amended by the FHEA 1992) unless an instrument of government made under s 124A of the 1998 Act has effect.[1] Where an instrument of government for an HEC has effect under s 124A, the instrument has to comply with Sch 7A to the ERA 1988.[2] The constitution of any new corporation has to comply with s 124A and Sch 7A.[3] The instrument of government of such a corporation is made by the Privy Council.[4] However, the initial appointing authority for the corporation is the Secretary of State.[5] The members of an HEC for which an instrument of government has effect are to be known as the board of governors of the institution conducted by the corporation.[6]

Government

17.37 All HECs must have articles of government in addition to an instrument of government.[7] These are made by the corporation with the approval of the Privy Council, and may be varied in the same manner.[8] The articles of government have to comply with s 125(2)–(7).[9] The validity of any proceedings of an HEC for which an instrument of government has effect, or of any of its committees, is not affected by a vacancy amongst the members or by any defect in the appointment or nomination of a member.[10] Any document purporting to be an instrument made or issued by or on behalf of such a corporation and to be duly executed under the seal of the corporation, or to be signed or executed by a person authorised by the corporation to act in that behalf, 'shall be received in evidence and be treated, without further proof, as being so made or issued unless the contrary is shown'.[11]

Functions of a higher education corporation

17.38 The powers of an HEC are as set out in s 124 of the ERA 1988, the provisions of which are for the most part uncontroversial.[12] One provision which probably affects the powers of an HEC to a considerable extent is s 125A (which was inserted

---

[1] ERA 1998, s 123(3), as substituted by the FHEA 1992.

[2] See ibid, s 124A(4)(a). Section 124C(4) and (5) make consequential provision for the situation: see s 124C(3).

[3] Ibid, s 124A(1).

[4] Ibid, s 124A(2). Such instrument may be modified under s 124A(3). See s 124D of the ERA 1988 regarding (a) the manner in which powers for the purposes of the relevant Part of that Act may be exercised by the Privy Council, and (b) the receipt in evidence of instruments purporting to be signed by the clerk of the Council.

[5] Ibid, s 124C(1).

[6] Ibid, s 124A(8).

[7] Ibid, s 125(1).

[8] Ibid, s 125(1) and (5), as amended by the FHEA 1992.

[9] The question of the effect of a failure to comply with the articles of government of a higher education institution is considered in para **17.82**.

[10] ERA 1988, s 124A(6).

[11] Ibid, s 124A(7).

[12] The most notable provisions are s 124(2)(f), as to which, see para **2.155**, and s 124(2)(h), which empowers an HEC to 'invest any sums not immediately required for' the purpose of any activity which they have power to carry on.

by s 41(1) of the THEA 1998), which provides that an HEC is an exempt charity for the purposes of the Charities Act 1993. The effect of this is probably that any act of an HEC which is not for exclusively charitable purposes or for purposes which are reasonably ancillary to such purposes, is ultra vires (or beyond the powers) of the HEC.[1]

17.39 An HEC is under a duty to keep accounts in accordance with s 124B of the THEA 1998. Such accounts are open to the inspection of the Comptroller and Auditor General.[2] The transfer of property, rights and liabilities, and of staff to an HEC is governed by ss 126 and 127 of the ERA 1988. Trust deeds or other instruments relating to land or other property held by any person for the purposes of an institution conducted by an HEC may be modified by the Privy Council.[3]

Dissolution of a higher education corporation

17.40 Higher education corporations may be dissolved by the Secretary of State under s 128 of the ERA 1988. Where a merger occurs between two or more higher education institutions, s 128 will have to be relied upon in relation to at least one of the corporations involved. Section 128 would also have to be relied upon where the majority of the governing body of an HEC wishes to form a designated higher education institution.[4]

Designated higher education institutions

17.41 Section 129 of the ERA 1988 gives the Secretary of State power to designate institutions as 'eligible to receive support from funds administered by a higher education funding council'. These are either institutions whose full-time equivalent enrolment number[5] for courses of higher education exceeds 55 per cent of its total full-time equivalent enrolment number, or institutions which are, or are to be, conducted by a successor company to an HEC.[6]

17.42 The constitution of a designated higher education institution is regulated by ss 129A and 129B of the ERA 1988. A designated higher education institution which is not conducted by a company and which was not established by Royal Charter must have an instrument of government and articles of government, which must be

---

[1]   See further, paras **2.153** et seq regarding the principles applicable to statutory education corporations generally.

[2]   ERA 1988, s 135(1)(b).

[3]   Ibid, s 157(1) (as amended by the FHEA 1992). Section 157(4)–(6) modify the effect of instruments relating to land or other property held for the purposes of an institution maintained by an LEA which then becomes an institution within the higher education sector, the further education sector, or a grant-aided institution. A grant-aided institution is defined in s 235(2)(c) of the ERA 1988 as a reference to an institution 'maintained by persons who have received grants under regulations made under section 100(1)(b) of the 1944 Act or section 485 of the Education Act 1996 in respect of expenditure incurred or to be incurred for any academic year of that institution current at the time in question'. See para **3.58** concerning s 485. The definition of 'governing body' in s 161(1)(d) of the ERA 1988 may be relevant in relation to the duty to consult contained in s 157(3).

[4]   See ibid, s 129(5)(b) and (e).

[5]   The full-time equivalent enrolment number is determined under Sch 9 to the ERA 1988: s 161(3).

[6]   ERA 1988, s 129(1) and (2). For what constitutes a successor company to an HEC, see s 129(5).

approved for the purpose by the Privy Council.[1] The instrument or articles of government of such a designated higher education institution may be altered, but only by order, or with the consent, of the Privy Council.[2]

17.43 A successor company to an HEC (within the meaning of s 129(5) of the ERA 1988) is an exempt charity while it conducts an institution designated under that section.[3]

17.44 The articles of association of a designated higher education institution which is conducted by a company and which was not established by Royal Charter must incorporate 'provision with respect to the constitution of a governing body of the institution (to be known as the instrument of government of the institution)' and 'provision with respect to the conduct of the institution (to be known as the articles of government of the institution)'.[4] The Privy Council may give to the persons who appear to them to have effective control over the company such directions as the Privy Council think fit for securing that the memorandum or articles of association of the company, or any rules or byelaws made in pursuance of any power conferred by the articles of association of the company, 'are amended in such manner as they may specify in the direction'.[5] The memorandum and articles of association may not otherwise be altered without the approval of the Privy Council.[6]

17.45 Section 130 of the ERA 1988 applies to transfer certain property, rights and liabilities to a designated higher education institution which was, immediately before the date on which the designation took effect, an institution assisted by an LEA,[7] but only where the order designating the institution so provides.[8]

17.46 Section 157 of the ERA 1988 (concerning among other things the variation of trust deeds) applies to a designated higher education institution (other than one established by Royal Charter) in the same way that it does to an HEC.[9] Except for the provisions just described, there are no other statutory provisions which apply to designated higher education institutions as such.

---

[1]   ERA 1988, s 129A(1), (2), (3) and (10).

[2]   Ibid, s 129A(7).

[3]   See Charities Act 1993, Sch 2, para 1(i).

[4]   ERA 1988, s 129B(2) and s 129A(10). For the effect of a failure to follow the articles of government, see para **17.82**.

[5]   Ibid, s 129B(3). The Privy Council must first consult the persons who appear to them to have effective control over the company: s 129B(5).

[6]   Ibid, s 129B(4).

[7]   As for what is an assisted institution for this purpose, see s 579(6) and (7) of the EA 1996: see s 235(2)(c) of the ERA 1988.

[8]   See ERA 1988, s 130(1), which will now only rarely be applicable. See paras **8.48** et seq for a brief overview of the current mechanism for the resolution of disputes over what did, or did not, transfer, and note that this question was dealt with at much greater length in chapter 17 of the first edition of this book.

[9]   ERA 1988, s 157(2)(b). See para **17.39** regarding s 157.

Pre-FHEA 1992 universities[1]

Constitution

17.47 Pre-FHEA 1992 universities were all established under either a Royal Charter or a private Act of Parliament. The universities of Durham and Newcastle are an example of the latter sort.[2] The constitutions of pre-FHEA 1992 universities can therefore be examined only individually, and are outside the scope of this book.

Governance

17.48 The governance of a pre-FHEA 1992 university is a topic which is affected by several matters. The first is the governing instruments of the university, in the form of the confusingly named statutes of the university, and subordinate instruments in the form of ordinances and regulations or rules. As with the constitution of a pre-FHEA 1992 university, these are outside the scope of this book.[3] The second matter relevant to the governance of a pre-FHEA 1992 university is the possible existence of a visitor to the university (although the visitatorial jurisdiction will be abolished by s 20 of the Higher Education Act 2004 in relation to complaints by students or prospective students about the manner in which they have been treated by the university). Finally, there are several statutory provisions imposing duties on those responsible for the governance of universities.

The visitor to an institution

17.49 Where there is a visitor to a university or a college, disputes affecting the governance of the university or college may need to be referred to the visitor.[4] Where that is so, the jurisdiction of the courts is prima facie ousted, except to the extent indicated in *R v Hull University Visitor, ex parte Page*.[5]

17.50 The peculiarity of the universities of Oxford and Cambridge should be mentioned here. Because they are civil corporations, they have long been regarded as not being subject to the jurisdiction of a visitor,[6] although the colleges of both universities are so subject.

---

[1] For the sake of convenience, universities which were in existence before the FHEA 1992 came into force and which were established under a Royal Charter or a private Act of Parliament, are referred to below as 'pre-FHEA 1992 universities'. Institutions which acquired the status of a university under the provisions of the FHEA 1992 are referred to as 'post-FHEA 1992 universities'. It is recognised, however, that new universities may still be established under a Royal Charter or private Act of Parliament, and that in time this distinction may come to be inaccurate.

[2] See the Universities of Durham and Newcastle upon Tyne Act 1963.

[3] But see paras **17.82** et seq regarding the possible effect of a failure to comply with the governing instruments.

[4] For examples of cases where the visitor's jurisdiction has been invoked in relation to students' complaints, see *R v Dunsheath, ex parte Meredith* [1951] 1 KB 127; *Thorne v University of London* [1966] 2 QB 237; *Patel v Bradford University Senate* [1979] 1 WLR 1066; *Oakes v Sidney Sussex College* [1988] 1 WLR 431; *R v University of Nottingham, ex parte K* [1998] ELR 184; *R (Jemchi) v Visitor of Brunel University* [2002] EWHC 2126 (Admin), [2003] ELR 125; and, most recently, *R (Ferguson) v Visitor of the University of Leicester* [2003] EWCA Civ 1082, [2003] ELR 562.

[5] [1993] AC 682; see further, paras **17.59** et seq.

[6] See, in particular, *R v Vice-Chancellor of Cambridge* (1765) 3 Burr 1647, 97 ER 1027.

17.51 A detailed description of the extent of the visitatorial jurisdiction as such is not within the scope of this book, although it is (at present, until s 20 of the Higher Education Act 2004 comes into force) of crucial importance to know when it applies. Accordingly, in what follows there is a brief overview of the visitatorial jurisdiction applied in the context of education. One area which it is nevertheless necessary to examine in detail is the effect of s 206 and related provisions in the ERA 1988 on the jurisdiction of the visitor in relation to disputes between certain employees and the university by which they are employed (although that jurisdiction will also be abolished by the Higher Education Act 2004: see para **17.141**), and that area is accordingly also examined.

THE JURISDICTION OF THE VISITOR

17.52 The leading case on the scope of the visitatorial jurisdiction was determined in relation to the visitor to a university. That case is *Thomas v University of Bradford*.[1] Further, the now fairly extensive literature on the visitatorial jurisdiction was written primarily with reference to the jurisdiction of the visitor to a university.[2] Accordingly, the principles of the visitatorial jurisdiction so far as they apply to educational institutions can be stated with some confidence.

17.53 The visitor to an educational institution[3] will have the right and the duty to determine matters relating to the internal administration of the institution – 'the internal arrangements and dealings with regard to the government and management of the house, of the domus, of the institution'.[4] The following passage from the speech of Lord Griffiths in *Thomas v University of Bradford* makes clear the extent of the jurisdiction of the visitor:

> 'This then leads me to consider what is meant by the reference in the cases to the "domesticity" of the visitatorial jurisdiction. The word is clearly not used with the width of its everyday meaning. Nothing could be more domestic in its everyday sense than the arrangements in the kitchens or for the cleaning of the premises, but no one suggests that the domestic staff of a university fall within the visitatorial jurisdiction. I am satisfied that in referring to the domestic jurisdiction the judges are using a shortened form of reference to those matters which are governed by the internal laws of the foundation. This will include not only the interpretation and enforcement of the laws themselves but those internal powers and discretions that derive from the internal laws such as the

---

1   [1987] AC 795.
2   See, in particular, JW Bridge, 'Keeping Peace in the Universities: the Role of the Visitor' (1970) 86 LQR 531, and PM Smith, 'The Exclusive Jurisdiction of the University Visitor' (1981) 97 LQR 610; 'Visitation of the Universities: A Ghost from the Past' (1986) NLJ 484, 519, 567, and 665; and 'The Jurisdiction of the University Visitor: How Exclusive is Exclusive?' (1994) 2 CLPR 103. See also the further articles referred to by H Picarda, *The Law and Practice Relating to Charities* (Butterworths, 3rd edn, 1999), p 557, n 1, and JW Parlour and LRV Burwood, 'Students' rights' (1995) 7 *Education and the Law* 63.
3   The institution need not be a corporation for the visitatorial jurisdiction to apply: see J Warburton, *Tudor on Charities* (Sweet & Maxwell, 9th edn, 2003), at para 10.63, and *Herring v Templeman* [1973] 2 All ER 581, [1973] 3 All ER 569.
4   *Thomson v University of London* (1864) 33 LJ Ch 625, at 634, per Kindersley V-C.

discretion necessarily bestowed upon those in authority in the exercise of their disciplinary functions over members of the foundation.'[1]

17.54 As for the matter in issue in *Thomas* itself, which was whether or not the question whether the claimant had been validly dismissed by the university was within the exclusive jurisdiction of the visitor, Lord Griffiths said:

'In the present case, the entire dispute is centred upon the statute ordinances and regulations of the university. Were they correctly applied and were they fairly administered? Such a dispute in my view falls within the jurisdiction of the visitor and not the courts of law, notwithstanding that its resolution will affect Miss Thomas's contract of employment.'[2]

THE VISITOR'S JURISDICTION IS EXCLUSIVE

17.55 The jurisdiction of the visitor is exclusive in the sense that where it applies (and it applies only where the existence of the visitor is drawn to the court's attention[3]), the courts have no jurisdiction; the jurisdiction of the visitor is not concurrent with that of the courts, as can be seen from the following further passage from the speech of Lord Griffiths in *Thomas v University of Bradford*:

'What is not permissible is to regard "domesticity" as an elastic term giving the courts freedom to choose which disputes it [*sic*] will entertain and which it will send to the visitor. This approach necessarily involves the concept of a concurrent jurisdiction, and as I have endeavoured to show this is not the way in which our law has developed.'[4]

17.56 The effect of the decision in *Thomas* has been overturned by ss 202–207 of the ERA 1988 in respect of contracts entered into or promotions taking effect after 20 November 1987,[5] but the jurisdiction of the visitor clearly remains effective in relation to matters not affected by those provisions. The argument that this 'approach rooted as it is in mediaeval law has no place in a modern society'[6] was rejected by Lord Griffiths (with whom three other members of the Appellate Committee agreed, although they also agreed with the speech of Lord Ackner). He said that in his view:

'the visitatorial jurisdiction subject to which all our modern universities have been founded is not an ancient anachronism which should now be severely curtailed, if not discarded. If confined to its proper limits, namely, the laws of the foundation and matters deriving therefrom, it provides a practical and expeditious means of resolving disputes which it is in the interests of the universities and their members to preserve.'[7]

---

[1]   *Thomas v University of Bradford*, op cit, at 820F–G.

[2]   Ibid, at 821E.

[3]   See PM Smith, 'The Exclusive Jurisdiction of the University Visitor' (1981) 97 LQR 610, at 629 and the cases there cited: *R v The Chancellor, Masters and Scholars of the University of Cambridge* (1723) 1 Str 557; 2 Ld Raym 1334; Fort 202; 8 Mod 148, at 151 and 152, and *Whiston v Dean & Chapter of Rochester* (1849) 7 Hare 532, at 562, per Sir James Wigram V-C.

[4]   *Thomas v University of Bradford*, op cit, at 820H–821A.

[5]   See paras **17.61** et seq.

[6]   *Thomas v University of Bradford*, op cit, at 821F.

[7]   Ibid, at 825C–D. At 825E–G, Lord Ackner similarly rejected 'the proposition that the visitor's jurisdiction may be an unwelcome survivor from the past, like a ghost, in Lord Atkin's famous phrase

17.57   In recent years, the continuing validity of the visitatorial jurisdiction in the light of the enactment of the Human Rights Act 1998 has been questioned, and it is at least arguable that that jurisdiction is inconsistent with Arts 6 and 14 of the European Convention on Human Rights. However, when s 20 of the Higher Education Act 2004 comes into force, the jurisdiction of the visitor will cease to apply to student complaints within the meaning of that section. There will still be a residual role for the visitor, however, and in any event it is necessary for practical reasons to refer to the current situation, which is that the visitatorial jurisdiction continues to affect universities.

THE POWERS OF THE VISITOR

17.58   It was expressly decided in *Thomas v University of Bradford* that the visitor has the power to order that compensation be paid.[1] In addition, it was determined that the visitor has the power to order reinstatement of an employee.[2] Although, as indicated above, the jurisdiction of the visitor has been ousted in that regard by ss 202–207 of the ERA 1988, these powers would be likely to be of considerable value to a student who was obliged or (depending on one's point of view) able to rely upon the visitatorial jurisdiction.

REMEDY FOR ABUSE OF POWERS BY THE VISITOR

17.59   The only remedy for an abuse of power by the visitor to a foundation is an application for judicial review. However, as a result of *R v Hull University Visitor, ex parte Page*,[3] such an application may not be made on any or all of the usual grounds for review. For example, an error of law within the jurisdiction of the visitor may not be judicially reviewed. The visitor may be judicially reviewed only where he acts outside his jurisdiction (in the narrow sense), where he abuses his powers (for example by acting in bad faith), or where he breaches the rules of natural justice.[4] It is of note that in *R v Her Majesty the Queen in Council, ex parte Vijayatunga*,[5] at a time when the principles in *ex parte Page* had not yet been determined and when accordingly the court's view was that judicial review was possible in a broader range of situations than is now the case, the Court of Appeal nevertheless showed considerable reluctance to intervene in relation to the manner in which the applicant's thesis had been examined. In an extremely pithy judgment, with which Lord Donaldson MR agreed, Mann LJ said this:

> 'The court has a supervisory but not an appellate jurisdiction in regard to the visitor of the University of London. The issue in this case was as to whether the examiners appointed by the university to examine the applicant's thesis were competent so to do. ...

---

in *United Australia Ltd. v Barclays Bank Ltd.* [1941] AC 1, 29 "standing in the path of justice clanking his medieval chains'".

[1]   [1987] AC 795, at 823D–824B.

[2]   Ibid, at 824E–F.

[3]   [1993] AC 682.

[4]   Ibid, at 704F, per Lord Browne-Wilkinson, with whom Lord Keith and Lord Griffiths agreed. The case is subjected to some strong (and cogent) criticism by HWR Wade at (1993) 109 LQR 155.

[5]   [1990] 2 QB 444.

This seems to me wholly a matter of academic judgment in which this court should not interfere.'[1]

17.60 It seems likely that such an approach would be repeated in similar situations arising in the future.

THE OUSTING OF THE JURISDICTION OF THE VISITOR IN RELATION TO CERTAIN EMPLOYMENT DISPUTES AND THE MODIFICATION OF UNIVERSITY STATUTES UNDER SECTIONS 202–207 OF THE EDUCATION REFORM ACT 1988

17.61 Sections 202–207 of the ERA 1988 were intended (among other things) to remove from the jurisdiction of the visitor most disputes between (1) lecturers and others whose employment was subject to that jurisdiction at the time of the passing of that Act, and (2) the universities by which they were employed. Although some of those provisions no longer have effect (see below), some continue to do so, and those which do so can be explained properly only by reference to some of those which are spent.

17.62 Under s 202(1), a new body, the University Commissioners, was established.[2] The Commissioners were given functions in relation to 'qualifying institutions', which are defined in s 202(3) as follows:

'(a) any university or other institution to which, during the period of three years beginning 1st August 1987, grants in aid are or have been made by the Universities Funding Council, or by the Secretary of State acting on the advice of the University Grants Committee;

(b) any constituent college, school or hall or other institution of a university falling within paragraph (a) above; and

(c) any institution not falling within paragraph (a) above which is authorised by charter to grant degrees and to which, during the period of three years beginning 1st August 1987, grants are or have been made by the Secretary of State.'

17.63 In exercising their functions under ss 203–207 of the ERA 1988, the Commissioners were under a duty to have regard to the following needs:

'(a) to ensure that academic staff have freedom within the law to question and test received wisdom, and to put forward new ideas and controversial or unpopular opinions, without placing themselves in jeopardy of losing their jobs or privileges they may have at their institutions;

(b) to enable qualifying institutions to provide education, promote learning and engage in research efficiently and economically; and

(c) to apply the principles of justice and fairness.'[3]

---

[1] [1990] 2 QB 444, at 459F–460B. See further, paras **17.78** et seq concerning a challenge to the exercise of academic judgment.

[2] See Sch 11 to the ERA 1988 (given force by s 202(4)) regarding the appointment and proceedings of the Commissioners.

[3] ERA 1988, s 202(2).

POWERS AND DUTIES OF THE COMMISSIONERS

17.64 The provisions of ss 203 and 204 of the ERA 1998 contained the duties and powers of the Commissioners respectively. The Commissioners were to have these duties and powers initially for a period of only 3 years, but that period was subject to curtailment or extension by an order made by the Secretary of State.[1] The period was extended by a succession of such orders, to end on 31 March 1996.[2]

17.65 Section 203(1) required the Commissioners to exercise their powers with a view to securing that the statutes[3] of each qualifying institution included:

'(a)   provision enabling an appropriate[4] body, or any delegate of such a body, to dismiss[5] any member of the academic staff[6] by reason of redundancy;[7]

(b)   provision enabling an appropriate officer, or any delegate of such an officer, acting in accordance with procedures determined by the Commissioners, to dismiss any member of the academic staff for good cause;[8]

(c)   provision establishing disciplinary procedures determined by the Commissioners for dealing with any complaints made against any member of the academic staff relating to his appointment or employment;

(d)   provision establishing procedures determined by the Commissioners for hearing and determining appeals by any members of the academic staff who are dismissed or under notice of dismissal (whether or not in pursuance of such provision as is mentioned in paragraph (a) or (b) above) or who are otherwise disciplined; and

(e)   provision establishing procedures determined by the Commissioners for affording to any member of the academic staff opportunities for seeking redress for any grievances relating to his appointment or employment.'

17.66 'Good cause' for the purposes of s 203 is defined in s 203(6) to mean in relation to a member of the academic staff of a qualifying institution:

'a reason which is related to his conduct or to his capability or qualifications for performing work of the kind which he was appointed or employed to do.'

Capability and qualifications are defined by the same subsection to mean respectively 'capability assessed by reference to skill, aptitude, health or any other physical or mental quality' of the member of staff in question, and 'any degree, diploma or other

---

[1]   See ERA 1988, Sch 11, para 3.

[2]   See the Education (University Commissioners) Order 1995, SI 1995/604.

[3]   'Statutes' for the purposes of ss 204–206 includes 'any regulations, ordinances or other instruments which, in the opinion of the Commissioners, serve as statutes for the purposes of [the] institution [in question] and are designated as such by the Commissioners': s 203(8).

[4]   The word 'appropriate' in s 203 means in relation to a body or officer of a qualifying institution 'appearing to the Commissioners to be appropriate having regard to the nature and circumstances of the institution': s 203(7).

[5]   Dismissal includes removal from office, and in relation to a contract of employment is to be construed in accordance with Part X of the Employment Rights Act 1996: ERA 1988, s 203(7) (as amended).

[6]   'Academic staff' for this purpose includes 'persons whose terms of appointment or contracts of employment are, in the opinion of the Commissioners, so similar to those of academic staff as to justify their being treated as academic staff for the purposes of [s 203]': s 203(4).

[7]   The definition of redundancy for this purpose is contained in s 203(5), and is to the same effect as that contained in the Employment Rights Act 1996.

[8]   See para **17.66** concerning what is 'good cause' in this context.

academic, technical or professional qualification relevant to the office or position held' by the member of staff in question.

17.67 It is provided by s 203(2) that no member of the academic staff of a qualifying institution may be dismissed by reason of any provision in the statutes made in order to give effect to the duties in s 203(1)(a) or (b):

> 'unless the reason for his dismissal may in the circumstances (including the size and administrative resources of the institution) reasonably be treated as a sufficient reason for dismissing him.'

This wording is to the same effect as that which is in s 98(4)(a) of the Employment Rights Act 1996 regarding unfair dismissal, and is likely to be construed by reference to at least some of the case-law relating to that section.[1] Accordingly, s 203(2) of the ERA 1988 gives a person who is not entitled to the protection of Part X of the Employment Rights Act 1996 – as well as one who is entitled to such protection – a right akin to that not to be unfairly dismissed, and, moreover, a right the remedy for which could be full compensation rather than simply compensation limited to the amount currently specified as the maximum compensation which may be awarded for unfair dismissal.[2]

17.68 It should now be the case that no instrument may now be made which modifies any provision in the statutes of a qualifying institution of the sorts referred to in s 203(1) unless it has been approved by the Privy Council.[3]

17.69 In order to give effect to their duties under s 203, the Commissioners were given power to 'make such modifications of the statutes of any qualifying institution as they consider[ed] necessary or expedient'.[4] However, modifications made for the purpose of securing that the statutes comply with s 203(1)(a) (which concerns dismissal for redundancy[5]) cannot apply to a person unless:

'(a) his appointment is made, or his contract of employment is entered into, on or after 20th November 1987; or
(b) he is promoted on or after that date.'[6]

17.70 Section 204(3)–(6) make extensive provision for determining whether a person was so promoted. Further, modifications made for the purpose of securing that the statutes comply with s 203(1)(b) (which concerns dismissal for good cause[7]) do not

---

[1]   There is no reference in s 203(2) to 'equity and the substantial merits of the case', as there is in s 98(4)(b) of the Employment Rights Act 1996. As a result, it could be argued that the case-law concerning s 98(4) cannot apply. That would, it is suggested here, be a mistaken argument; that case-law must provide at least some sort of guide.

[2]   The amount is specified under s 124(1) of the Employment Rights Act 1996, and is currently £55,000: see SI 2003/3038.

[3]   See ERA 1988, s 203(3).

[4]   Ibid, s 204(1). The Commissioners were empowered also to make incidental, supplementary and transitional provisions: s 204(8).

[5]   See para **17.65**.

[6]   ERA 1988, s 204(2).

[7]   See paras **17.65** and **17.66**.

apply 'in relation to anything done or omitted to be done before the date on which the instrument making the modifications' was approved by Her Majesty in Council.[1]

EXCLUSION OF THE VISITOR'S JURISDICTION – SECTION 206 OF THE ERA 1988

17.71 Section 206 of the ERA 1988 excludes from the jurisdiction of the visitor 'any dispute relating to a member of the academic staff[2] which concerns his appointment or employment or the termination of his appointment or employment', unless the dispute was referred to the visitor before 'the relevant date' or the date when s 206 came into force (which was 29 July 1988).[3] The relevant date for this purpose is defined by s 206(4)(a) to mean 'the date on which the statutes of the institution include such provision as is mentioned in s 203(1)(d) and (e) of this Act' (in other words provision concerning appeals and grievances[4]).

17.72 Section 206(1) does not exclude all matters relating to academic staff from the jurisdiction of the visitor. Section 206(3) provides that the visitor may hear and determine appeals and may hear and redress grievances in accordance with procedures established in pursuance of s 203(1)(d) and (e). This could be interpreted to mean that the visitor may not do so unless such procedures specifically enable him to do so. However, it could also be interpreted to mean that the visitor may hear and determine appeals and hear and redress grievances in accordance with procedures established in pursuance of s 203(1)(d) and (e) even where they make no specific reference to the visitor. It is of note that Lord Irvine LC, acting on behalf of the Queen as visitor to York University in *Burrows v University of York*,[5] said that he thought that s 206(1) did not preclude him from determining a complaint regarding the manner in which a grievance hearing was conducted.

17.73 Section 206(1) appears also not to exclude from the visitor's jurisdiction any dispute which concerns the administration of a qualifying institution but which also coincidentally concerns the rights of the institution as against a member of the academic staff. This is in part because ss 202–207 were addressed at issues arising in relation to academic tenure.[6] Section 206 will be repealed by s 46 of the HEA 2004, which will also end the visitatorial jurisdiction entirely in relation to staff disputes.[7]

---

[1]   ERA 1988, s 204(7) and (9).

[2]   As defined by ibid, s 203(4): s 206(4)(b). According to the Northern Ireland Court of Appeal, a probationary member of the academic staff is not included in this definition: *D v Queen's University of Belfast* [1997] ELR 431, 451F–G and 452F, per Hutton LCJ and MacDermott LJ respectively. Nicholson LJ's primary ground for his decision (which concurred with that of the other two judges) was that the contract of employment of a lecturer who was appointed subject to a period of probation, was conditional. The failure of the condition resulted in the lecturer never being a lecturer within the meaning of the relevant provision in the university's statutes.

[3]   ERA 1988, s 206(1) and (2).

[4]   See para **17.65**.

[5]   [1999] EdCR 586, at 588.

[6]   This can be seen most clearly from the heading to s 202, which is 'Academic tenure'.

[7]   See para **17.141**.

Statutory provisions which affect directly the governance of a pre-FHEA 1992 university

17.74 There are two main sets of provisions which affect directly the governance of a pre-FHEA 1992 university. These are s 43(1) of the Education (No 2) Act 1986 and s 22 of the EA 1994. They are considered separately below.[1]

WHEN CAN A HIGHER EDUCATION INSTITUTION BE JUDICIALLY REVIEWED?

17.75 The extent to which a pre-FHEA 1992 university could be made the subject of an application for judicial review is a matter regarding which there has in the past been some doubt.[2] It has been said that:

'The *ultra vires* doctrine has had a restricted application to corporations created otherwise than by or under statute. Although such corporations are subject to the doctrine in areas regulated by legislation, they seem to be as capable of performing other transactions (e.g. entering into contracts, acquiring land or providing new services) as any natural person.'[3]

17.76 Yet that proposition is based on a line of authorities which can be criticised.[4] Further, there is authority for the proposition that a member of such a corporation can, at least in some circumstances, sue (or at least, where there is a visitor, make an application to the visitor) to restrain the corporation from infringing its charter.[5] In addition, the best approach now seems to be to determine whether any particular corporation has exercised a public function. If it has, then it will in theory be liable to be judicially reviewed in respect of the matter.[6] One thing which is clear, however, is that there is modern authority for the proposition that a pre-FHEA 1992 university may be judicially reviewed in regard to a matter regulated by statute.[7] Further, there is now a considerable body of modern case-law concerning cases where pre-FHEA 1992 universities have been judicially reviewed in regard to matters which were not

---

[1] See paras **17.116** et seq concerning s 43(1) of the EA (No 2) 1986 and paras **17.87** et seq regarding s 22 of the EA 1994.

[2] A comprehensive article on the relationship between a university student and the university was published in 1983 by CB Lewis: 'The Legal Nature of a University and the Student–University Relationship' (1983) 15 *Ottawa Law Review* 249. It is now of mostly historical interest only, although the analysis in it is valuable.

[3] de Smith, Woolf and Jowell, *Judicial Review of Administrative Action* (Sweet & Maxwell, 5th edn, 1995), para 5.14.

[4] The authorities are *Sutton Hospital* case (1612) 10 Co Rep 23a, at 30b; *Wenlock (Baroness) v River Dee Co* (1887) 36 ChD 675, at 685; *Att-Gen v Manchester Corporation* [1906] 1 Ch 643, at 651; *Att-Gen v Leeds Corporation* [1929] 2 Ch 291, at 295; and *Att-Gen v Leicester Corporation* [1943] Ch 86, at 93. For criticism of all except the last of them, see in particular, HA Street, *A Treatise on the Doctrine of Ultra Vires* (1930), at pp 18–22.

[5] *Jenkin v Pharmaceutical Society of Great Britain* [1921] 1 Ch 392; *Dickson v Pharmaceutical Society of Great Britain* [1970] AC 403. See also *Pearce v University of Aston in Birmingham (No 2)* [1991] 2 All ER 469, at 475f.

[6] See *R v Panel on Take-overs and Mergers, ex parte Datafin plc* [1987] QB 815, and de Smith, Woolf and Jowell, *Judicial Review of Administrative Action*, at para 3.25.

[7] See *R v University of Liverpool, ex parte Caesar-Gordon* [1991] 1 QB 124 and *R v University College London, ex parte Riniker* [1995] ELR 213 concerning the application of s 43(1) of the Education (No 2) Act 1986, as to which, see para **17.116**. See also *Kent v University College, London* (1992) 156 LG Rev 1003, CA.

regulated by statute. This includes *University of Ceylon v Fernando*,[1] R *v Aston University Senate, ex parte Roffey*,[2] R *v Oxford University, ex parte Bolchover*,[3] *Glynn v Keele University*,[4] R *v Cambridge University, ex parte Beg*,[5] R *(Persaud) v University of Cambridge*,[6] and R *(Galligan) v Chancellor, Masters and Scholars of the University of Oxford*.[7]

17.77 The question whether an HEC could be judicially reviewed has been considered to be clear because it is a creature of a public and general statute, the FHEA 1992. In any event, there is currently no doubt that an application for judicial review can be made of the decision of an HEC. That has occurred on a number of occasions, including R *v Manchester Metropolitan University ex parte Nolan*,[8] R *v Board of Governors of Sheffield Hallam University ex parte R*,[9] R *v Leeds Metropolitan University, ex parte Manders*,[10] R *v University of Central England, ex parte Sandhu*,[11] R *v Chelsea College of Art and Design, ex parte Nash*,[12] R *v South Bank University, ex parte Coggeran*,[13] *(Burgess) v South Bank University*,[14] and R *(M) v University of West of England*.[15]

---

[1] [1960] 1 WLR 223; noted by SA de Smith at (1960) 23 MLR 428.

[2] [1969] 2 QB 538. The claim was of procedural unfairness.

[3] (1970) *The Times*, October 7. The claim was of procedural unfairness.

[4] [1971] 1 WLR 487. The claim was also of procedural unfairness.

[5] [1999] ELR 404. The claim was advanced on a number of bases.

[6] [2001] EWCA Civ 534, [2001] ELR 480. There it was claimed that the removal of the claimant's name from the register of PhD students was unlawful for a number of reasons, all of which were rejected at first instance. On appeal, those were reduced to two. The appeal (and therefore the challenge) was successful on the basis that there was procedural unfairness.

[7] [2001] EWHC Admin 965, [2002] ELR 494. The court indicated that since that case concerned the relationship between an employee of the university and the university, it would have been slow to intervene even if it had found in favour of the claimant. It is to be contrasted with R *(Evans) v University of Cambridge* [2002] EWHC 1382, [2003] ELR 8, where Scott Baker J ruled that the matter concerned solely the relationship between the applicant and the university acting as her employer, and that therefore the matter was not open to judicial review.

[8] [1994] ELR 380. The case concerned a disciplinary matter.

[9] [1995] ELR 267. That case also concerned a matter of discipline.

[10] [1998] ELR 502. The report is of an application to apply for permission to judicially review the relevant decisions of the university on several bases. The application was unsuccessful.

[11] [1999] ELR 121, [1999] EdCR 594 and (on appeal) [1999] ELR 419, [1999] EdCR 766. That case concerned the lawfulness, including the proportionality, of a sanction of failing to take into account, in awarding a degree, the mark which would have been awarded if a dissertation which was lodged a day late had been lodged in time. The claimant had followed 'a very high risk strategy which had failed' (see [1999] ELR 128C). The claim was unsuccessful: the claimant 'was running the risk that the university would do what they had said in their rules they would do and they did in fact do it': [1999] ELR 134D–E.

[12] [2000] ELR 687. The claim was wide-ranging, and was successful on a number of bases.

[13] [2001 ELR 42. The claim was successful both at first instance and appeal on one public law point, but the case is of most interest for the ruling that a claim of discrimination contrary to the SDA 1975 should not be made in judicial review proceedings but in the appropriate county court: see paras 26 and 30.

[14] [2001] ELR 300. That case concerned the fairness of the university's appeal procedure. Maurice Kay J accepted that there was no reason why a university should not adopt an ad hoc procedure to meet a combination of circumstances: para 42. However, the procedure must be fair: ibid.

[15] [2001] ELR 458. The case concerned the removal from a social work course in the circumstance that the university had found that the claimant would not be able to obtain a social work placement which was necessary to complete the course. The reasons why she would not be able to do so were that (1) her child had twice been placed on the child protection register, and (2) the local social services authorities which the university had approached had, when this was revealed, said that they would not as a result give the claimant a placement. The claim was unsuccessful.

Challenging the exercise of academic judgment

17.78 On a number of occasions, it has been said that the courts will not intervene in relation to matters which concern only the exercise of academic judgment. This was said, for example, in *R v Her Majesty the Queen in Council, ex parte Vijayatunga*[1] (which in fact concerned the visitor's powers), *R v Higher Education Funding Council, ex parte Institute of Dental Surgery*,[2] *R v Liverpool John Moores University, ex parte Hayes*,[3] and *R v University of Portsmouth, ex parte Lakareber*.[4] The *Institute of Dental Surgery* case concerned an academic judgment of the relevant HEFC, but the court made some statements of apparently wider application. Sedley J, giving the judgment of the court, said this:

> 'We would hold that where what is sought to be impugned is on the evidence *no more* than an informed exercise of academic judgment, fairness alone will not require reasons to be given. This is not to say for a moment that academic decisions are beyond challenge. A mark, for example, awarded at an examiners' meeting where irrelevant and damaging personal factors have been allowed to enter into the evaluation of a candidate's written paper is something more than an informed exercise of academic judgment.[5] Where evidence shows that something extraneous has entered into the process of academic judgment, one of two results may follow depending on the nature of the fault: either the decision will fall without more, or the court may require reasons to be given, so that the decision can either be seen to be sound or can be seen or (absent reasons) be inferred to be flawed. But purely academic judgments, in our view, will as a rule not be in the class of case exemplified, though by no means exhausted, by *ex parte Doody* [1993] 3 WLR 154, where the nature and impact of the decision itself call for reasons as a routine aspect of procedural fairness. They will be in the *ex parte Cunningham* [1992] I.C.R 816 class where some trigger factor is required to show, that, in the circumstances of the particular decision, fairness calls for reasons to be given'[6] (original emphasis).

17.79 In the Court of Appeal, as Sedley LJ, the same judge ruled in *Clark v University of Lincolnshire and Humberside*[7] that:

> 'there are issues of academic or pastoral judgment which the university is equipped to consider in breadth and in depth, but on which any judgment of the courts would be jejune and inappropriate.'

17.80 However, there seems to be no good reason why at least in some of the cases the exercise of academic judgment should not be challenged. This is because in at least some cases it is likely to be possible to ascertain with the benefit of expert evidence whether there has been a failure to take reasonable care in assessing a student's work. If, however, there has only been an error of judgment after the exercise of such care

---

1   [1990] 2 QB 444, CA, as to which see para **17.59**. It was applied without analysis by the Court of Appeal in *R v Cranfield University, ex parte Bashir* [1999] ELR 317.
2   [1994] 1 WLR 242.
3   [1998] ELR 261, at 279.
4   [1999] ELR 135, at 139E.
5   In *R v Leeds Metropolitan University, ex parte Manders* [1998] ELR 502, at 504E, Collins J commented: 'Of course, if it is said that there has been bias and a deliberate marking down, that is not a question of academic judgment, but is a specific matter which a student, as I see it, will be clearly entitled to raise on any review'.
6   [1994] 1 WLR 242, at 261B–E.
7   [2000] 1 WLR 1988, at 1992, [2000] ELR 345 at 349F–G.

by a person acting as a reasonably well-informed and competent academic would have done, then it is indeed a matter about which no complaint could properly be made.[1] It is of interest that in R *(Persaud) v University of Cambridge*,[2] Chadwick LJ (with whom May and Schiemann LJJ agreed), said this:

> 'I would accept that there is no principle of fairness which requires, as a general rule, that a person should be entitled to challenge, or make representations with a view to changing, a purely academic judgment on his or her work or potential. But each case must be examined on its own facts. On a true analysis, this case is not, as it seems to me, a challenge to academic judgment; it is a challenge to the process by which it was determined that the appellant should not be reinstated to the Register of Graduate Students because the course of research for which she had been admitted had ceased to be viable. I am satisfied that that process failed to measure up to the standard of fairness required of the university.'

PROCEDURAL EFFECTS OF THE POSSIBILITY OF JUDICIAL REVIEW

17.81 One (perhaps unforeseen) result of the pursuing of claims against universities in what is now the Administrative Court, is that the strict time-limits have been applied to such claims when in reality the claims have in many cases involved matters which could have been regarded as purely contractual and therefore subject to the principles only of private law.[3] Further, in *Clark v University of Lincolnshire and Humberside*[4] the Court of Appeal ruled that private law proceedings may be struck out on the basis that they constitute an abuse of process if they are brought in private law purely to avoid the application of the strict time-limits applicable in public law proceedings. The court did not, however, in so saying distinguish between claims which are for an injunctive remedy and claims which are purely for damages. It would be harsh if a claim purely for damages were to be regarded as precluded merely because it was too late realistically to hope to obtain an injunction or a mandatory order. However, it may be that since a damages claim in those circumstances might require for its resolution at least an estimate of the chances of the claimant's obtaining that which he claims he should have been given by the university (or other higher education institution), and since that question would depend on the exercise of academic judgment, a court might decide that the claim was not justiciable.

---

[1] See, for example, per Lord Diplock in *Saif Ali v Sidney Smith Mitchell & Co* [1980] AC 1989, at 220: 'No matter what profession it may be, the common law does not impose on those who practise it any liability from damage resulting from what in the result turn out to have been errors of judgment, unless the error was such as no reasonably well-informed and competent member of the profession could have made'.

[2] [2001] EWCA Civ 534, [2001] ELR 480, at para 41.

[3] For example this occurred in *R v Leeds Metropolitan University, ex parte Manders* [1998] ELR 502 and *R v University of Portsmouth, ex parte Lakareber* [1999] ELR 135.

[4] [2000] 1 WLR 1988, [2000] ELR 345.

EFFECT OF A FAILURE TO FOLLOW THE GOVERNING INSTRUMENTS OF A HIGHER EDUCATION INSTITUTION

17.82 In any event, as a matter or principle, it seems clear that the result of a failure to follow the governing instruments of a higher education institution should not be affected by the type of institution in question: the outcome should be the same, no matter what the type of institution. However, that may not be the case at present. The position of an HEC is currently as determined by the line of cases referred to above including *R v Board of Governors of Sheffield Hallam University, ex parte R*[1] and *R v Manchester Metropolitan University, ex parte Nolan*.[2] There, the HECs in question were judicially reviewed, and the court quashed the decisions in question on the ground that they were ultra vires. In the public law sphere, the prevailing view appears to be that an ultra vires decision remains valid until a successful challenge results in its being quashed.[3] In *Pearce v University of Aston in Birmingham (No 2)*,[4] Browne-Wilkinson V-C worked on the basis that a threatened breach of the statutes of a (pre-FHEA 1992) university could be prevented before it occurred by an application to the visitor, who would be obliged to 'ensure the lawful conduct of the university in accordance with its regulating document', but that after such a breach had occurred, the visitor could order the university to restore the pre-breach position as far as possible.[5] The implication of this is that the breach would not be ineffective, although it would be capable of being overturned by the visitor or (where appropriate) the court. In the case of a designated higher education institution conducted by a company which has the required articles and instrument of government incorporated in the articles of association of the company,[6] a breach of the articles or instrument of government would not affect the validity of the resulting act, as a result of s 35A of the Companies Act 1985. The situation of a designated higher education institution which is not conducted by a company and which was not established by Royal Charter is anomalous. Such an institution must also have an instrument and articles of association, but the institution need not be conducted by a corporation. Presumably, the institution will then be analogous to maintained voluntary schools before the governing bodies of such schools were incorporated by ss 238 and 239 of the Education Act 1993, in that they will have a governing body but also trustees holding some of the property used for the purposes of the institution. Yet that would not be a true analogy, because the governing body of a designated higher education institution will be given funding for the institution by the relevant HEFC, and the trustees' duties in relation to the institution will be largely superseded by those of the governing body. Further, the governing body will hold the money given to them by the HEFC as trustees. A breach of the instrument or articles of government would then be a matter which would be determinable, as far as individual members of the governing body were concerned, by reference to the principles of trust and charity law alone.

1   [1995] ELR 267.
2   [1994] ELR 380.
3   See de Smith, Woolf and Jowell, *Judicial Review of Administrative Action* (Sweet & Maxwell, 5th edn, 1995), para 5.48.
4   [1991] 2 All ER 469.
5   Ibid, at 475h–j.
6   Under s 129B of the ERA 1988, as to which see paras **17.42** and **17.44**.

However, it is suggested here that those principles would not affect the relationship between a student affected by such a breach.

17.83 It is suggested here that the effect of a decision concerning (for example) a student which would be ultra vires the body conducting a higher education institution if that body were subject to public law principles, should not differ according to the type of institution. Rather, the impact should be the same. This is not least because the type of institution (in terms of legal classification) at which a person studies should not affect the kind of remedies available to him.

STUDENTS' UNIONS

17.84 The relationship between a students' union and the institution as a result of which it was established, can be problematic. The nature of that relationship is considered below first. The statutory provisions affecting that relationship, contained in the EA 1994, are then considered.

The nature of a students' union

17.85 A students' union is properly to be regarded as separate from the institution as a result of which it was established. This is clear from *Baldry v Feintuck*,[1] *Attorney-General v Ross*,[2] and *Commissioners of Customs and Excise v University of Leicester Students' Union*.[3] Those cases, as well as that of *London Hospital Medical College v Inland Revenue Commissioners*,[4] make it clear also that a students' union will almost certainly be regarded as a charity. As Peter Gibson LJ put it in *Commissioners of Customs and Excise v University of Leicester Students' Union*:[5]

> 'The University and the Union have distinct purposes and functions, the Union not existing solely to further the Union's educational purposes, and whilst the law of charity benevolently treats the Union as being an educational charity, the Union is not the same charitable entity as the University.'

17.86 There are several implications arising from this. One is that a students' union will be a separate employer. One result of that is that the transfer of an employee from the employment of the body conducting a higher education institution to the students' union or vice-versa may well break the employee's continuity of employment between the two, unless the transfer is the result of a transfer of a business or an undertaking.[6] Another implication of the students' union being a charity is that the officers of an unincorporated students' union will in law be trustees of the property held for the purposes of the union, and will in any event be trustees for the purposes of the Charities Act 1993.[7]

---

1 [1972] 1 WLR 552.
2 [1986] 1 WLR 252.
3 [2001] EWCA Civ 1972, [2002] ELR 347.
4 [1976] 1 WLR 613.
5 Ibid, at para 33.
6 See *Leicester University Students' Union v Mahomed* [1995] IRLR 292.
7 See ss 96(1) and 97(1) of that Act.

Sections 20–23 of the Education Act 1994

17.87 Parliament has imposed duties on certain institutions in relation to which students' unions were established, in regard to those unions. Those duties are contained in s 22 of the EA 1994. That section applies to students' unions as defined in s 20 of that Act. The definition is fairly complex, and clearly intended to be all-embracing.[1] One salient feature is that although an association or body may be a students' union within the meaning of ss 20–22 in relation to more than one establishment, it cannot be such a students' union in relation to students generally in the United Kingdom or a part of the United Kingdom.[2] The kinds of institution (referred to as an 'establishment' for this purpose) to which a students' union must relate for the duties in s 22 of the 1994 Act to apply in relation to the union, are set out in s 21 of that Act. They include not only most higher education institutions[3] but also most further education institutions.[4] Further, the Secretary of State has an apparently unfettered power by order to designate institutions, or descriptions of institutions, for this purpose.[5] A college, school or hall in an establishment of any of these kinds is also an establishment to which s 22 applies.[6]

The duties in section 22 of the EA 1994

17.88 The duties in s 22 of the 1994 Act are extensive, although they are by no means absolute. The governing body of every establishment to which s 22 applies (which means 'the executive governing body which has responsibility for the conduct of affairs of the establishment and the management and administration of its revenue and property'[7]) must:

> 'take such steps as are reasonably practicable to secure that any students' union for students at the establishment operates in a fair and democratic manner and is accountable for its finances.'[8]

17.89 Such a governing body must also 'take such steps as are reasonably practicable to secure that' a number of requirements are observed by or in relation to a students' union for students at the establishment. Those requirements are set out in s 22(2) and include that the union has a written constitution[9] which is subject to the approval of the governing body and is reviewable by the governing body at intervals of not more than 5 years.[10] The requirements include also that a student has the right not to be a member of the union or (in the case of a representative body which is not an

---

[1] See further, W Hinds, 'The Education Act 1994 – the student union provisions' (1995) 7 *Education and the Law*, 133, at 135–136.
[2] EA 1994, s 20(4).
[3] But not the University of Buckingham, since it does not (as required by s 21(1)(a)) receive support from the HEFC under s 65 of the FHEA 1992, and since it does not come under any other category in s 21.
[4] The reference in EA 1994, s 21(1)(e) to s 6(5) of the FHEA 1992 appears now to be redundant, there being no equivalent of s 6(5) in the LSA 2000.
[5] See EA 1994, s 21(1)(f).
[6] Ibid, s 21(1)(g). See further, Hinds, *op cit*, pp 134–135.
[7] Ibid, s 21(5).
[8] Ibid, s 22(1).
[9] Ibid, s 22(2)(a).
[10] Ibid, s 22(2)(b).

association) a right to signify that he does not want to be represented by it, and that the student has a right not to be unfairly disadvantaged as a result of having exercised that right.[1] The requirements include also that appointment to 'major union offices' should be by election in a secret ballot in which all members are entitled to vote,[2] that the governing body should 'satisfy themselves that the elections are fairly and properly conducted',[3] and that a person should not hold sabbatical union office, or paid elected union office, for more than 2 years in total at the establishment.[4] Presumably the latter requirement means that a person may not hold an office of either or both sorts for more than 2 years in total, that is that it would not be possible to hold an office of one sort for 2 years and then an office of the other sort for 2 years.

17.90   The requirements in s 22(2) include in addition that the union's financial affairs are properly conducted and that appropriate arrangements exist for (1) the approval of the union's budget, and (2) the monitoring of its expenditure, by the governing body.[5] There are also extensive requirements in s 22(2) concerning the affiliation of the union to any external organisation.[6] Finally, there are requirements relating to a complaints procedure for students or groups of students.[7]

17.91   As a result of s 22(3), a relevant governing body was required to prepare and issue, and is required when necessary to revise, a code of practice as to the manner in which the requirements in s 22(1) and (2) are to be carried into effect in relation to any students' union for students at the establishment in question. The code must set out in relation to each of the requirements details of the arrangements made to secure its observance. As a result of s 22(4), the governing body must also bring to the attention of all students[8] at least once a year (a) the code of practice, (b) 'any restrictions imposed on the activities of the union by the law relating to charities', and (c) where the establishment is one to which s 43 of the 1986 Act applies,[9] the provisions of that section, and of any code of practice issued under it, which are relevant to the activities or conduct of the union. As a result of s 22(5), the governing body must also at least once a year bring to the attention of all students, and include in the information generally made available to persons considering whether to become students at the establishment, (a) information as to the right not to be a member of, or to signify that they do not wish to be represented by, the union, and (b) details of any arrangements the governing body has made for services of a kind which a students' union provides for its members to be provided for students who are not members of the union.

---

1   EA 1994, s 22(2)(c). As for what constitutes 'unfair disadvantage', see Hinds, *op cit*, p 141.

2   Ibid, s 22(2)(d). This requirement does not apply in the case of an 'open or distance learning establishment' as defined in s 22(9). As for what constitutes 'major union offices', see Hinds, *op cit*, p 140.

3   Ibid, s 22(2)(e).

4   Ibid, s 22(2)(f).

5   Ibid, s 22(2)(g). See also s 22(2)(h) and (i) regarding the allocation of resources.

6   EA 1994, s 22(2)(j)–(l). The requirement in s 22(2)(l)(ii) does not apply to an 'open or distance learning establishment' as defined in s 22(9). See s 22(8) regarding what may constitute affiliation for the purposes of s 22(2)(j)–(l).

7   See ibid, s 22(2)(m) and (n).

8   As defined by ibid, s 22(6) for the purposes of s 22(2), (4) and (5).

9   As to which, see para **17.118**. Section 43 of EA 1986 does not apply to all the institutions to which s 22 of the EA 1994 applies: see s 43(5) of the 1986 Act and s 21 of the 1994 Act.

Could a body be judicially reviewed in respect of section 22 of the 1994 Act?

17.92   In *R v Thames Valley University Students' Union, ex parte Ogilvy*,[1] Sedley J held that the regime in ss 20–22 of the 1994 Act did not 'invest a students' union ... with a public law or statutory character', with the result that such a union was not susceptible to judicial review in respect of those sections. This is in contrast to the situation of a chartered university, the governing body of which according to *R v University of Liverpool, ex parte Caesar-Gordon*[2] and *R v University College, London, ex parte Riniker*[3] would be susceptible to an application for judicial review in relation to its functions under s 43 of the 1986 Act.[4] Indeed, as a result of those two cases it is clear as a matter of principle that the governing body of any establishment to which s 22 of the 1994 Act applies could be judicially reviewed in respect of its acts or omissions to act in relation to that section.

THE PRINCIPLES OF PRIVATE LAW WHICH APPLY TO THE RELATIONSHIP BETWEEN A HIGHER EDUCATION INSTITUTION AND A STUDENT

In contract

17.93   Despite the now accepted applicability of public law principles to the relationship between a student and a higher education institution,[5] it is clear that a student (including a minor[6]) enters into a contract with a higher education institution.[7] It is now the universal practice to charge fees for courses of higher education. Where a student pays such fees, there will of course be consideration for the provision of the education.[8] In *Moran v University College Salford (No 2)*,[9] it was held that there was consideration for the agreement of a student to enrol, which was to be found in the foregoing by the student of the right to participate in the 'clearing' scheme operated at that time.

---

[1]   (1997) 4 April, QBD; unreported, but see (1997) 4(8) *Education Law Monitor* 6.

[2]   [1991] 1 QB 124.

[3]   [1995] ELR 213.

[4]   See paras **17.116** et seq concerning s 43.

[5]   See paras **17.76–17.77**.

[6]   See *Chitty on Contracts* (Sweet & Maxwell, 29th edn, 2004), at para 8-027.

[7]   The decision of the Court of Appeal in *M v London Guildhall University* [1998] ELR 149 (which, for the reasons set out in para 12.92 of the first edition of this book, can sensibly be said to be a curious decision) can be regarded now as superseded by *Clark v University of Lincolnshire and Humberside* [2000] 1 WLR 1988, [2000] ELR 345. The question of the kind of damages which a higher education institution should pay for a breach of the contract was considered by Judge Charles Harris QC in *Buckinghamshire v Rycotewood College* (case nos OX004341/42 28 February 2003). Somewhat controversially (but by no means clearly wrongly), he held that he could award damages for the distress felt by the claimant former students as a result of the serious deficiencies in their course.

[8]   Consideration for a contract must move from the promisee: *Chitty on Contracts* (Sweet & Maxwell, 29th edn, 2004), at para 3.36.

[9]   [1994] ELR 187, at 197G–198B and 200E–G.

17.94 Where a student has yet to take a public examination, and his admission to the institution is conditional on him achieving a certain grade or grades in that examination, one might have thought that the contract could properly (or should) be regarded as conditional. However, in *Moran v University College Salford (No 2)*,[1] the Court of Appeal held on the facts of that case that there were two contracts – one before matriculation or enrolment, and one after matriculation or enrolment.[2] The case concerned an application for an interlocutory mandatory injunction, ordering the respondent institution to offer the applicant a place to study physiotherapy. The circumstances were that the applicant had been offered a place on the physiotherapy degree course unconditionally, but only as a result of a clerical error on the part of the institution.[3] Although he was (it seems) sufficiently qualified to take the course,[4] the course was fully subscribed, and if there had been a spare place then it would have been offered to another more highly qualified applicant.[5] As Glidewell LJ commented, the outcome of the application for the interlocutory injunction sought was in effect going to be determinative of the case.[6] The Court dismissed the application, but not because the institution was under no contractual obligation. Rather, the application was dismissed because the grant of an interlocutory mandatory order 'might very well create injustice'.[7] Indeed, it was said by Evans LJ that the contract would not be unenforceable on the ground that it involved an element of personal services.[8]

17.95 The rulings of law made by the court were not final, because of the nature of the application. However, the court made rulings which were fairly emphatic. Glidewell LJ held that there was 'a strong case for saying that there was a binding agreement under which UCS committed itself to accept Mr Moran for the physiotherapy course'.[9] Evans LJ referred to there being a need for 'a strong and clear case' to be made out,[10] and then held that the applicant had made out 'a sufficient case for breach of contract to justify the making of the order which he [sought], but that in the circumstances of this case no order should be made'.[11] Waite LJ agreed with both judgments.

17.96 It may be that the fact that the student had satisfied the entry requirements for the course was the cause of the determination by the Court of Appeal that there were two contracts in existence, rather than one. If so, then it is suggested here that the apparent ruling that there are two contracts rather than one (which may be conditional) between a student and a higher education institution should be regarded as confined to the circumstances of the sort which arose in *Moran v University College Salford (No 2)*.

---

1   [1994] ELR 187, CA.
2   Ibid, at 197C–D and 206C.
3   See ibid, at 194F–G.
4   See ibid, at 206A–B.
5   Ibid.
6   See ibid, at 189C.
7   Ibid, at 199B, per Glidewell LJ, with whom Evans and Waite LJJ agreed in this regard (see 206).
8   Ibid, at 206D.
9   [1994] ELR 187, at 197E.
10 Ibid, at 201E.
11 Ibid, at 206E.

The obligations of the institution

17.97 A major obligation owed by a higher education institution under the contract arising on the enrolment of a student will be an implied obligation to use reasonable skill and care in the performance of the contract. That there is such an implied term was confirmed by O'Connor J in *D'Mello v Loughborough College of Technology*,[1] where he referred to the duty 'to exercise professional skill and judgment in conducting the course', although now the matter is governed by s 13 of the Supply of Goods and Services Act 1982. In *Sammy v Birkbeck College*,[2] Marshall J determined the matter slightly more broadly, and decided that the terms of a contract for the course preparing for 'a science degree in the principal subject of physics' were as follows:

> 'Broadly speaking, on accepting the plaintiff as a student – he having paid the recognised fee – the college were contractually bound to provide proper tuition and laboratory facilities. This they agreed to do without personal prejudice ... There was, too, an implied term that the college had the facilities and staff with necessary professional skill to carry out the tuition required for the internal degree examination of the University of London.'

17.98 To the extent that these implied obligations go beyond s 13 of the Supply of Goods and Services Act 1982, they must apply today to the contract between a student and a higher education institution. The courts will not, however, intervene when the claim involves the exercise of academic judgment.[3]

17.99 The express terms of the contract will be found in the prospectus and the documents accompanying the matriculation or enrolment documentation. They may also be found elsewhere, when other documentation is incorporated in the contract by reference.[4] The disciplinary rules of the institution will probably be incorporated in the contract.[5]

The obligations of the student

17.100 The student's main obligations are easier to state. They will be to pay the fees for, and to comply with the express conditions imposed by the institution for continuing on, the course in question.

Excluding liability

17.101 The current trend is for higher education institutions to seek to limit their liability for a failure to deliver what they have agreed to deliver to a student. The major question here, and the one likely to be of most practical importance for a higher education institution in the event of a dispute with a student, is whether they can validly do so. This is a question which used to be determinable by reference mainly to

---

[1]   (1970) *The Times*, June 17.

[2]   (1964) *The Times*, November 3.

[3]   See paras **17.78–17.81**.

[4]   The case of *Price v Dennis* [1999] EdCR 747 (as to which see para **13.35**) is relevant by analogy. The potential application of Sch 2 to the Unfair Terms in Consumer Contracts Regulations 1999, SI 1999/2083 (as to which, see para **17.101**), and in particular para 2(1)(i) of Sch 2, should be borne in mind.

[5]   This also is subject to the Unfair Terms in Consumer Contracts Regulations 1999, SI 1999/2083.

the Unfair Contract Terms Act 1977. However, it is a question which must now be determined in addition by reference to the Unfair Terms in Consumer Contracts Regulations 1999.[1] The application of those regulations is outside the scope of this book, but attention is drawn here to paragraphs 1(c), (i), (j), (k), (m) and (q) of Sch 2 to the regulations, which are terms which may (not must) be regarded as unfair. These are terms which have the object or effect of:

'(c)   making an agreement binding on the consumer whereas provision of services by the seller or supplier is subject to a condition whose realisation depends on his will alone;

(i)   irrevocably binding the consumer to terms with which he had no real opportunity of becoming acquainted before the conclusion of the contract;

(j)   enabling the seller or supplier to alter the terms of the contract unilaterally without a valid reason which is specified in the contract;

(k)   enabling the seller or supplier to alter unilaterally without a valid reason any characteristics of the product or service to be provided; ...

(m)   giving the seller or supplier the right to determine whether the goods or services supplied are in conformity with the contract, or giving him the exclusive right to interpret any term of the contract; ...

(q)   excluding or hindering the consumer's right to take legal action or exercise any other legal remedy, particularly by requiring the consumer to take disputes exclusively to arbitration not covered by legal provisions.'

In tort

17.102   In addition to obligations in the law of contract, an institution will have obligations to a student in the law of tort. It is now clear that such obligations can be co-existent with those in a contract.[2] The most obvious obligation in the law of tort will be that in the law of negligence. Accordingly, even if a contract did not exist in any case, a student could rely upon the law of negligence in seeking redress for a failure to use reasonable skill and care in his education. In doing so, the student would be able to rely upon *Phelps v Hillingdon London Borough Council* [3] by analogy.

17.103   It has been suggested that the role of personal tutor could give rise to liability in the law of negligence.[4] This is on the basis that:

'Universities which encourage students to consult their personal tutor as a first source of advice when they have a problem may be increasing the risk of harm to that student because the tutor does not have the requisite skills and referral options available.'[5]

17.104   One area where a higher education institution clearly could attract liability is in relation to references. Although *Spring v Guardian Assurance plc*[6] concerned references given in respect of employees and those employed under a contract for

---

1   SI 1999/2083, which came into force on 1 October 1999. In relation to a contract entered into between 1 July 1995 and 30 September 1999, the Unfair Terms in Consumer Contracts Regulations 1994, SI 1994/3159, applied.

2   *Henderson v Merrett Syndicates Ltd* [1995] 2 AC 145.

3   [2001] 2 AC 619, as to which, see paras **14.56** et seq.

4   See Mark R Davies, 'Universities, academics and professional negligence' (1996) 12 PN 102.

5   Ibid, at 112.

6   [1995] 2 AC 296.

services, the case would apply by analogy to the relationship between a student and a higher education institution.

17.105 A further situation in which a higher education institution could attract liability in the law of negligence is where a student becomes (for example) extremely drunk. However, liability will probably not arise unless the institution intervenes negligently, as can be seen from the case of *Barrett v Ministry of Defence*,[1] where it was held that it was:

> 'fair, just and reasonable for the law to leave a responsible adult to assume responsibility for his own actions in consuming alcoholic drink ... Until he collapsed, I would hold that the deceased was in law alone responsible for his condition. Thereafter, when the defendant assumed responsibility for him, it accepts that the measures taken fell short of the standard reasonably to be expected.'[2]

17.106 Perhaps the law of negligence is most likely in practice to apply to the relationship between a student and a higher education institution in relation to pre-contractual, or later, statements. The statement might then become a negligent misstatement.

The prospective student

17.107 Indeed, the possible application of the Misrepresentation Act 1967 to what is said to a prospective student in order to induce the student to enter into a contract with the higher education institution should be borne in mind. That Act applies not only to negligent misrepresentations, but also to innocent misrepresentations.[3]

17.108 Otherwise, where there is a visitor whose jurisdiction is invoked, the applicant will have to have recourse to that visitor in respect of any complaint with regard to his rejection, as long as the visitor's jurisdiction applies to the complaint (and, as stated above, s 20 of the Higher Education Act 2004 will end the application of the visitatorial jurisdiction to student complaints; this will include a complaint 'made in respect of an application for admission to the ... institution as a student'). This is clear from certain of the reported cases,[4] and was put beyond doubt by what Lord Griffiths said on the matter in *Thomas v University of Bradford*:[5]

> 'The explanation for the visitor's jurisdiction extending in cases of admission and removal from office (amotion) to those who are not corporators lies in the basis of his jurisdiction, namely, as the judge of the internal or domestic laws of the foundation. It is because those laws invariably provide for the conditions governing admission to and

---

[1]   [1995] 1 WLR 1217, CA.
[2]   Ibid, at 1224F, 1225E–F.
[3]   See s 2 of the Act.
[4]   See, for example, *R Hertford College, Oxford* (1878) 3 QBD 693 and *R v Council of Legal Education, ex parte Eddis* (1995) 7 Admin LR 357.
[5]   [1987] AC 795, at 815H–816A.

removal from membership of the foundation and sometimes of offices on the foundation short of membership that jurisdiction in such matters lies within the visitor.'[1]

17.109   The Unfair Terms in Consumer Contract Regulations 1999[2] will not affect the situation, unless there is a relevant contract in existence.[3]

17.110   The situation where the visitor does not have jurisdiction has been the subject of at least one reported case in England and Wales, and one which is of interest in Scotland. In the English case, *Central Council for Education and Training in Social Work v Edwards*,[4] although the case concerned a polytechnic which was at the time funded by several LEAs and was therefore in the public sector, some wide statements of principle were made. Slade J determined the case initially by reference to the case of *McInnes v Onslow-Fane*.[5] He is reported to have decided that that case showed that 'there was a clear distinction between "forfeiture" cases and "application" cases, and the present case fell into the latter category.' He is reported as having gone on to say:

> 'An educational institution in considering an application for admission as a student was under no obligation to act judicially. Further, such an institution was not bound to give a student a hearing or to assign reasons for refusing to admit him.'[6]

17.111   The passage in the report of the judgment of Slade J following the one just set out is equally apt and interesting:

> 'A further question of law then arose: was the polytechnic under a duty to act fairly if it did in fact interview an applicant? A review of the recent cases showed an increasing willingness on the part of the courts to review administrative decisions of powerful domestic bodies where it was alleged that the decision was reached unfairly, but there was no clear statement of where to draw the line in accepting or rejecting jurisdiction to undertake reviews of the present type.
>
> There was no general proposition of law that a student who was refused admission to any educational establishment had in every case a right to redress from the courts if he could show that his application had been unfairly dealt with. Nevertheless in the present case the court had jurisdiction to review the process by which Mr Vyas's [the student's] application was refused for the following reasons: (1) the polytechnic was a publicly funded educational establishment; (2) the inability to obtain a [Certificate of Qualification in Social Work] would seriously affect Mr Vyas's professional career; (3) the polytechnic had published details of its selection procedures, a copy of which had been supplied to Mr Vyas when he applied for the course.'

---

[1]   As Picarda puts it in *The Law and Practice Relating to Charities* (Butterworths, 3rd edn, 1999), p 568, 'The function occupied by the complainant is irrelevant: it is sufficient that he is mentioned in, and is seeking to enforce his rights under, the domestic law'.

[2]   SI 1999/2083, as to which see para **17.101**.

[3]   See paras **17.95–17.97** for the circumstances in which a pre-matriculation contract may come into existence.

[4]   (1978) *The Times*, May 5.

[5]   [1978] 1 WLR 1520.

[6]   Although no authority was given in the report for this proposition, support can be found for it in the cases referred to in de Smith, Woolf and Jowell, *Judicial Review of Administrative Action* (Sweet & Maxwell, 5th edn, 1995), at paras 6.31–6.32.

17.112   All these three reasons would almost certainly exist in many comparable situations today, but it is not clear whether the approach of Slade J in *Edwards* would now be followed.[1] In particular, the classification of functions as 'judicial' or 'administrative' has become either less common or less important in practice.[2]

17.113   It is of interest that in *Reilly v University of Glasgow*,[3] the Outer House of the Scottish Court of Session allowed an application for judicial review in respect of a refusal of a place to study medicine to proceed, although the application failed on its facts. Yet it appears from the report in *Reilly* that the university did not argue that the matter was not properly the subject of an application for judicial review, and in any event a different test appears to be applied in Scotland from that applied in England and Wales in relation to the appropriateness of an application for judicial review.[4]

17.114   In *R v University College London, ex parte Idriss*,[5] an application for permission to apply for judicial review of a decision to refuse to admit a candidate to study medicine was dismissed, in part because, it was said, the case was not 'one of those cases where fairness [requires] that reasons should be given'.[6]

17.115   It is suggested here that the situation of an applicant for a place to study at a higher education institution should be regarded as subject to the same legal principles no matter what the type of institution to which the application has been made – pre-FHEA 1992 university, post-FHEA 1992 university, or any other kind of higher education institution. Similarly, the applicant should be both able and required to seek the same kind of legal remedy no matter what the kind of institution to which the application has been made. Furthermore, it is suggested here that the law of contract ought to apply where there is a clearly discernible case in the law of contract, but that wherever the law of contract cannot apply (and that must normally be so in respect of an applicant for a course), then the matter should be capable of being judicially reviewed, perhaps on the basis indicated in *Edwards*.

---

[1]   Although the decision in *McInnes v Onslow Fane* is subjected to a critical analysis in de Smith, Woolf and Jowell, *Judicial Review of Administrative Action* (5th edn , 1995), at paras 8.7–8.12, the distinction between applications and revocations in *McInnes* is approved at para 8.27 of that work. Further, at para 10.18 of that work, *Edwards* is cited in support of the proposition that there would not be a need to afford an interview (or hearing) to every applicant for a relatively small number of places on a university course. *Edwards* is also referred to without disapproval in n 76 of para 7.15.

[2]   See, in particular, de Smith, Woolf and Jowell, op cit, paras A.8, A.17–A.21, and A.34.

[3]   [1996] ELR 394.

[4]   See *West v Secretary of State for Scotland* [1992] SLT 636. According to DJ Farrington's *The Law of Higher Education* (Butterworths, 2nd edn, 1998), at para 2.241, however, in *Naik v University of Stirling* [1994] SLT 449, the court 'discerned a tripartite relationship, as required by *West*, between the Queen as the granter of powers to the university and the fulfilment of these powers by the respondent in relation to one of its members, namely a student' (Farrington's words).

[5]   [1999] EdCR 462.

[6]   Ibid, at 465A.

FREE SPEECH – SECTION 43 OF THE EDUCATION (NO 2) ACT 1986

17.116   Section 43(1) of the Education (No 2) Act 1986 requires every 'individual and body of persons concerned in the government of any establishment to which this section applies' to take:

> 'such steps as are reasonably practicable to ensure that freedom of speech within the law is secured for members, students and employees of the establishment and for visiting speakers.'

17.117   That duty includes a duty to ensure, so far as is reasonably practicable, that the use of any premises of the establishment[1] is not denied to any individual or body of persons on any ground connected with (a) the beliefs or views of that individual or of any member of that body, or (b) the policy or objects of that body.[2]

17.118   The establishments to which s 43 applies are:

'(a)   any university;[3]
(aa)   any institution other than a university within the higher education sector;
(b)   any establishment of higher or further education which is maintained by a local education authority; and
(ba)   any institution within the further education sector.'[4]

17.119   The governing body of any such establishment,[5] with a view to facilitating the discharge of the duty imposed by s 43(1) in relation to that establishment, was obliged by s 43(3) to issue, and is obliged to keep up to date, a code of practice setting out certain matters. The code must set out the procedures to be followed by members, students and employees of the establishment in connection with the organisation of meetings and other activities which (in both cases) are of sorts specified in the code and are to take place on the premises of the establishment, and the conduct required of such persons in connection with any such meeting or activity.[6] The code must also deal with 'such other matters as the governing body consider appropriate'.[7] Every individual and body of persons concerned in the government of any relevant establishment must take such steps as are reasonably practicable (including where appropriate the initiation of disciplinary measures) to secure that the requirements of the code of practice for that establishment, issued under s 43(3), are complied with.[8]

---

[1]   The premises of the establishment include for the purposes of s 43 premises occupied by a students' union which are not premises of the establishment in connection with which the union is constituted: s 43(8).
[2]   Education (No 2) Act 1986, s 43(2).
[3]   As defined in ibid, s 43(6).
[4]   Education (No 2) Act 1986, s 43(5), as amended by the ERA 1988 and FHEA 1992.
[5]   The governing body of a university is defined for this purpose in ibid, s 43(6).
[6]   Ibid, s 43(3).
[7]   Ibid.
[8]   Ibid, s 43(4). An LEA is to be taken for the purposes of s 43 to be concerned in the government of an establishment within s 43(5)(b): s 43(7).

17.120   A relevant establishment may not, however, take into account in this context 'threats of "public disorder" outside the confines of the [establishment] by persons not within its control'.[1]

THE AWARDING OF DEGREES

17.121   The power to confer degrees is now subject to regulation. Section 214(1) of the ERA 1988 provides that it is an offence[2] in the course of business to grant, offer to grant, or issue any invitation relating to any award which may reasonably be taken to be an award granted or to be granted by a United Kingdom institution and which is either described as a degree or purports to confer on its holder the right to the title of bachelor, master or doctor and may reasonably be taken to be a degree.[3] As one would expect, this prohibition is subject to exceptions, the main one of which is that s 214(1) does not apply as respects anything done in relation to any 'recognised award'. A recognised award means for this purpose:

'(a)   any award granted or to be granted by a university, college or other body which is authorised by Royal Charter or by or under Act of Parliament to grant degrees;[4]

(b)   any award granted or to be granted by any body for the time being permitted by any body falling within paragraph (a) above to act on its behalf in the granting of degrees; or

(c)   such other award as the Secretary of State may by order designate as a recognised award for the purposes of this section.'[5]

17.122   Further, it is a defence to a charge under s 214(1) to show that authority to grant an award was conferred on or before 5 July 1988 by a foreign institution on the body granting the award, and the defendant took reasonable steps to inform the person to whom the award was granted or any member of the public or particular individual to whom the offer was addressed, that the award was granted by virtue of authority conferred by a foreign institution.[6]

17.123   Proceedings for the offence in s 214(1) may not be instituted except by or on behalf of a local weights and measures authority or the chief officer of police for a police area.[7] It is the duty of such an authority to enforce the provisions of s 214

---

[1]   *R v University of Liverpool, ex parte Caesar-Gordon* [1991] 1 QB 124, at 132D.

[2]   The maximum penalty for which is a fine not exceeding level 5 on the standard scale, which is currently £5,000.

[3]   An educational institution may also contravene the Business Names Act 1985: see *London College of Science and Technology Ltd v Islington London Borough Council* [1997] ELR 162.

[4]   The Privy Council has power under s 76 of the FHEA 1992 by order to specify institutions as competent to grant 'any degree, diploma, certificate or other academic award or distinction'.

[5]   ERA 1988, s 214(2). An award designated by an order made under para (c) may be either a specified award granted or to be granted by a person named in the order, or any award granted or to be granted by that person: s 214(3).

[6]   Ibid, s 214(5); see also s 214(6) and (9) regarding the temporal effect of s 214(1).

[7]   Ibid, s 214(8). The presumption in s 214(4) should be noted, as should s 214(7), which concerns the circumstances in which an officer of a body corporate may commit an offence where the body commits the offence in s 214(1).

within its area, and such an authority must, whenever the Secretary of State so directs, make to him a report on the exercise of their functions under ss 214 and 215.[1]

17.124 If a body is for the time being designated by an order of the Secretary of State as a recognised body for the purposes of ss 214 and 215, then it must be conclusively presumed to be such a body.[2] The Secretary of State must compile, maintain and publish by order a list including the name of every body which appears to him to fall for the time being within s 216(3).[3] A body which falls within s 216(3) is one which is not recognised but which either (a) provides any course which is in preparation for a degree to be granted by a recognised body and is approved by or on behalf of the recognised body, or (b) is a constituent college, school or hall or other institution of a university which is a recognised body.[4]

PROHIBITION OF THE UNAUTHORISED USE OF THE WORD 'UNIVERSITY' IN CERTAIN CIRCUMSTANCES

17.125 Section 39 of the THEA 1998 complements the prohibitions described in the preceding paragraphs relating to the granting of degrees. Section 39(1)–(3) prohibit the making available (or the offering to make available) in any part of the United Kingdom of educational services by, or by any person on behalf of ('through'), an institution within the higher education sector or the further education sector under a name which includes the word 'university' unless the inclusion of the word in that name is (a) authorised by or by virtue of any Act or Royal Charter, or (b) approved by the Privy Council for the purposes of s 39. The fact that a university's Royal Charter provides for the affiliation or association of other institutions to the university, or for the accreditation by the university of educational services provided by other institutions, is not to be taken to mean that the use of the word 'university' by any such other institution is authorised.[5] The Privy Council's power under s 39(1) and (2) does not apply in any case where the inclusion of the word 'university' in the name in question may be authorised by virtue of any other Act or under any Royal Charter,[6] and it is probably because of that that the exceptions to the prohibition in s 39(1) and (2) occur where the inclusion in the relevant name of the word 'university' is either (a) authorised by or by virtue of any Act or Royal Charter, or (b) approved by the Privy Council for the purposes of s 29.[7] When exercising the power under s 39, the Privy Council must 'have regard to the need to avoid names which are or may be misleading'.[8]

---

[1] Ibid, s 215(1). The other provisions of s 215 are consequential in that they confer among other things powers of entry and search, and to detain documents and other items.

[2] ERA 1988, s 216(1). For the purposes of s 216, a 'recognised body' means a body falling within s 214(2)(a) or (b): s 216(4). The current lists are contained in SI 2003/1865 and SI 2003/3124.

[3] Ibid, s 216(2).

[4] The current lists made under s 216(2) are contained in SI 2002/1377 and SI 2002/1667.

[5] THEA 1998, s 39(4).

[6] Ibid, s 39(6).

[7] Ibid, s 39(1).

[8] Ibid, s 39(5).

HIGHER EDUCATION ACT 2004

Introduction

17.126   The HEA 2004 received Royal Assent on 1 July 2004, shortly before the publication of this book. Some of its provisions were, as is usual, commenced by the Act itself, but in operative terms the Act has yet to have effect.

Arts and Humanities Research Council

17.127   Under Part 1 of the HEA 2004 (ss 1–10), a new Arts and Humanities Research Council (AHRC) will be established. It will take the place of the Arts and Humanities Research Board, which is 'a company limited by guarantee which has charitable status and receives its funding through the Higher Education Funding Council for England, the Higher Education Funding Council for Wales, the Scottish Higher Education Funding Council, and the Department for Employment and Learning in Northern Ireland'.[1] The AHRC will be established by Royal Charter 'wholly or mainly for objects consisting of, or comprised in' the purposes set out in s 1 of the HEA 2004. These are:

'(a)   carrying out, facilitating, encouraging and supporting -
   (i)   research in the arts and humanities, and
   (ii) instruction in the arts and humanities,
(b)   advancing and disseminating knowledge in, and promoting understanding of, the arts and humanities,
(c)   promoting awareness of the body's activities, and
(d)   providing advice on matters relating to the body's activities.'

17.128   The AHRC 'will be equivalent to the research councils dealt with in the Science and Technology Act 1965'.[2] It will not be the sole provider of funding for arts and humanities research, since, as a result of s 10 of the HEA 2004, the Secretary of State and the National Assembly will be able among other things to '(a) carry out or support research in the arts and humanities, [and] (b) disseminate the results of research in the arts and humanities'.

Student complaints

17.129   The HEA 2004 will remove from the jurisdiction of the visitor to a higher education institution the power to determine a complaint made 'in respect of an application for admission to the qualifying institution as a student'.[3] It will also remove from the visitor's jurisdiction any complaint which is:

'made by a person -
(a)   as a student or former student at the qualifying institution, or

---

[1]   Explanatory Notes to the HEA 2004, para 23.
[2]   Explanatory Notes, para 13.
[3]   Section 20(1) and (2).

(b)   as a student or former student at another institution (whether or not a qualifying institution) undertaking a course of study, or programme of research, leading to the grant of one of the qualifying institution's awards.'[1]

17.130   Under ss 11–18 of the HEA 2004, a complaint of either sort will, unless it 'relates to matters of academic judgment',[2] be capable of being reviewed in England or Wales under a scheme which (a) satisfies a number of detailed conditions, which are set out in Sch 2 to the HEA 2004, and (b) is provided by a 'designated operator' of the scheme in accordance with the duties set out in Sch 3 to that Act. The 'designated operator' will be designated for England by the Secretary of State and for Wales by the National Assembly. A 'qualifying institution' for all of these purposes is:

'(a)   a university (whether or not receiving financial support under section 65 of the 1992 Act) whose entitlement to grant awards is conferred or confirmed by –
(i)   an Act of Parliament,
(ii)   a Royal Charter, or
(iii)   an order under section 76 of the 1992 Act;
(b)   a constituent college, school or hall or other institution of a university falling within paragraph (a);
(c)   an institution conducted by a higher education corporation;
(d)   a designated institution, as defined by section 72(3) of the 1992 Act.'[3]

17.131   The governing body of every qualifying institution in England and Wales 'must comply with any obligation imposed upon it by a scheme for the review of qualifying complaints that is provided by the designated operator'.[4] Such obligations include 'any obligation to pay fees to the designated operator'.[5]

17.132   The complaints scheme may not require complainants to pay any fees in connection with the operation of the scheme.[6] The scheme must require every qualifying complaint referred under it to be reviewed 'by an individual who – (a) is independent of the parties, and (b) is suitable to review that complaint'.[7] The reviewer

---

[1]   Section 20(1) and (3).
[2]   Section 12(2). The question whether a complaint 'relates to matters of academic judgment' may sometimes be difficult to answer. Parliamentary Under-Secretary of State for Education and Skills, Mr Ivan Lewis, speaking in Standing Committee H of the House of Commons on 12 February 2004 (cols 94–95), commented: 'Any Minister who could define the parameters of academic judgment would be doing exceptionally well. The best that I can do is give examples. Academic judgment is used to decide the marks awarded in examinations or other assessments, and ultimately to decide the class of degree. Only examiners are in a position to make such decisions, and to change that would be a serious infringement of their autonomy on academic matters. However, complaints would qualify if they related to procedural matters such as whether a student had access to an academic appeals committee and whether that committee was properly constituted. The OIA [Office of the Independent Adjudicator] could consider a complaint when a university was attempting to hide behind the excuse that something was a matter of academic judgment and it could be proved that that was not appropriate or reasonable.' However, he said (col 95) that 'the concept of academic judgment' would not 'include a lecturer or tutor who plainly was not giving good lectures or was not qualified to give the lectures in question'.
[3]   Section 11.
[4]   Section 15(1).
[5]   Section 15(3).
[6]   Schedule 2, para 8.
[7]   Ibid, para 4.

may 'dismiss a qualifying complaint without consideration of the merits if the reviewer considers the complaint to be frivolous or vexatious', but must otherwise 'as soon as reasonably practicable' 'make a decision as to the extent to which [the complaint] is justified'.[1] However, if the reviewer decides that the complaint is to any extent justified, he may make only a recommendation to the governing body of the institution to which the complaint relates, and 'may not require any person to do, or refrain from doing, anything'.[2] It is clear that the making of a complaint under the scheme will not preclude the taking of legal proceedings in relation to the matter to which the complaint relates. Indeed, the 6-month time-limit for the making of a complaint of discrimination contrary to the Sex Discrimination Act 1975, the Race Relations Act 1976 or the Disability Discrimination Act 1995, will be extended by 2 months where a complaint is referred under the scheme before the end of that 6-month period.[3]

Student fees and the director of fair access to higher education

17.133   The provisions which eventually formed Part 3 of the HEA 2004 proved to be highly controversial as the Bill which led to the Act was going through Parliament. Under it, a higher education institution may charge higher fees than previously. However, the institution may do so only if it has in place a plan which satisfies the requirements of s 33 of the Act (a s 33 plan) which has been approved under regulations made under s 34 (an approved s 33 plan). Such a plan must 'in relation to each qualifying course in connection with which fees are to be payable to the institution by qualifying persons' specify or provide for the determination of a limit which those fees are not to be permitted to exceed.[4] In relation to England the plan must also include such provisions 'relating to the promotion of equality of opportunity as are required by regulations to be included in the plan', and may include other provisions relating to the promotion of equality of opportunity in connection with access to higher education.[5] In relation to Wales, the plan must include such provisions relating to equality of opportunity or 'the promotion of higher education' as are required to be included by regulations, and may include further such provisions.[6]

17.134   All of these provisions (that is, those which do not impose financial limits) are referred to in s 33 as the 'general provisions' of a plan, and may be of the following sorts:

'(a)   requiring the governing body to take, or secure the taking of, measures to attract applications from prospective students who are members of groups which, at the time when the plan is approved, are under-represented in higher education,

(b)   requiring the governing body to provide, or secure the provision of, financial assistance to students,

---

[1]   Schedule 2, para 5.

[2]   Ibid, para 6. The recommendation may be or include that the governing body of the institution pays money to the complainant: ibid.

[3]   See s 19.

[4]   Section 33(1). This limit is 'the higher amount' within the meaning of s 24(6) and s 28(6) of the HEA 2004: see s 33(1) and (7).

[5]   Section 33(2) and (7).

[6]   Section 33(3).

(c)   requiring the governing body to make available to students and prospective students information about financial assistance available to students from any source,

(d)   setting out objectives relating to the promotion of equality of opportunity and, in relation to Wales, the promotion of higher education,

(e)   relating to the monitoring by the governing body of -
        (i)   its compliance with the provisions of the plan, and
        (ii)   its progress in achieving any objectives set out in the plan by virtue of paragraph (d), and

(f)   requiring the provision of information to the relevant authority.'[1]

17.135   The 'relevant authority' for this purpose in England is the Director of Fair Access to Education within the meaning of s 31 of the HEA 2004 (the Director),[2] and in Wales is 'such person as may be designated for the purposes of [s 30] by regulations made by the Assembly' (which may be the Higher Education Funding Council for Wales).[3] The latter person will, when performing the functions conferred on him by Part 3 of the HEA 2004, have to 'have regard to any guidance given to [him] by the Assembly'.[4] The Director must, in performing his functions under Part 3, have regard to any guidance given to him by the Secretary of State, but must perform those functions 'in such a way as to promote and safeguard fair access to higher education (including part-time higher education in so far as his functions are exercisable in relation to it)'.[5] Further, the Director will have a duty when performing those functions:

'to protect academic freedom including, in particular, the freedom of institutions -
(a)   to determine the contents of particular courses and the manner in which they are taught, supervised or assessed, and
(b)   to determine the criteria for the admission of students and apply those criteria in particular cases.'

17.136   A failure to comply with an approved s 33 plan will be enforced by means of sanctions imposed in relation to the funding of the higher education institution concerned. The mechanism by which such sanctions will be imposed is provided for in relation to England by ss 23, 24 and 37, and in relation to Wales by ss 27, 28 and 38 of the HEA 2004. Section 23 will oblige the Secretary of State when making any grant under s 68 of the FHEA 1992 or s 7 of the EA 1994 to (1) the Higher Education Funding Council for England or (2) the TTA, and s 27 will empower the National Assembly when making such a grant to the Higher Education Funding Council for Wales, to impose a condition under s 24 (or, in Wales, s 28) of the HEA 2004. Such a condition will relate to any grants, loans or other payments made by that body under s 65 of the FHEA 1992 or (as the case may be) s 5 of the EA 1994, and will require the governing body of an institution to which such a grant, loan or other payment is made, to do certain things. One is to comply with 'the general provisions of any [approved s 33 plan] that is in force in relation to the institution during any part of the grant period [ie the period in respect of which the grant, loan or other payment is

---

[1]   Section 33(5).
[2]   Section 30(1)(a).
[3]   Section 30(1)(b) and (2).
[4]   Section 32(4).
[5]   Section 32(1)

made] during which it is in force'.[1] The condition will also require the governing body to secure that if there is no approved s 33 plan in force in relation to the institution, then the fees payable to the institution by a person who falls within any class of persons prescribed by regulations made by statutory instrument for the purposes of s 24 or (as the case may be) s 28 in respect of any academic year (which begins during the grant period) of a course of any description which is so prescribed, 'do not exceed the basic amount'.[2] This amount is also to be so prescribed.[3] If an approved s 33 plan is in force in relation to the institution, then the condition will be that the governing body secures that the fees 'do not exceed such limit, not exceeding the higher amount, as is provided by the plan for that course and that academic year'. That 'higher amount' may not be increased above the rate of inflation before 1 January 2010.[4] An increase in either the 'basic amount' or the 'higher amount' may not occur unless it is the subject of a positive approval by both Houses of Parliament.[5] There is a transitional period to cater for intending students (1) who on or before 1 August 2005 are offered a place to study at a higher education institution but want to wait (for example after finishing at school at the end of the 2004–5 academic year) until the 2006–7 academic year before commencing full-time higher education, or (2) 'who, because of a successful appeal against their A-level results, might miss out on a university place in 2005 and have to start instead in 2006'.[6]

17.137 The clear effect of s 24 (and s 28) is that if there is an approved s 33 plan in place, then its provisions must be complied with in any event, but higher fees than the 'basic amount' may be charged under the plan. If there is no such plan in place, then the fees may not exceed the 'basic amount'.

17.138 The question whether the governing body of a higher education institution has failed to comply with any of the general provisions of an approved s 33 plan or has charged fees for a relevant course which are higher than as permitted under such a plan, is to be determined by the Director in England under s 37 and the relevant authority in Wales under s 38. If the Director is 'satisfied' that it has done so (and it is not to be taken to have done so if it 'shows that it has taken all reasonable steps to comply with that provision'), then he may either (a) direct the Higher Education Funding Council for England or the TTA (or both) to impose specified financial requirements on the governing body under s 24(3) of the HEA 2004, or (b) notify the governing body that on the expiry of the existing plan he will refuse to approve a new plan under s 34 for a specified period. In doing so, he must comply with any regulations made by the Secretary of State under s 37(3) concerning (among other things) the matters to which he is to have regard and the procedure which he must follow. The position in relation to Wales is in broad terms equivalent, but not quite so prescriptive.[7]

---

[1] Sections 23(1), 24(1)(c) and (6) 27(1), and 28(1)(c) and (6).
[2] Sections 24(1)(b) and (6), 28(1)(b) and (6), and 47.
[3] See ss 24(6) and 28(6).
[4] See s 26(2)(b)(ii).
[5] See s 26(2).
[6] See s 25 and the speech of Baroness Ashburton of Upholland, speaking on behalf of the Government in the House of Lords on 1 July 2004, *Hansard*, HL vol 663, col 373.
[7] See s 38.

17.139   Regulations made under s 36 of the HEA 2004 may enable an approved s 33 plan to be varied. Those regulations, and any regulations made under s 34, s 37(3)(b) or s 38(3)(b), will, as a result of s 39, have to include provision requiring any decision of the Director or the relevant authority affecting the governing body of an institution, to have effect in the first instance as a provisional decision.[1] The regulations must also enable the governing body of the institution to 'apply for a review of the provisional decision to a person, or panel of persons, appointed in accordance with the regulations' in relation to England by the Secretary of State and in relation to Wales by the National Assembly.[2] The grounds on which such an application for a review may be made will be prescribed by regulations made under s 39(d). The regulations will have to require 'the relevant authority to reconsider its provisional decision having regard to any recommendation of the person or panel'.[3] This possibility of a review will in practice usually preclude the making of a successful application for judicial review of the Director's or relevant authority's decision under s 37 or (as the case may be) s 38 until the outcome of the review is known.

Amendments to the law relating to student support

17.140   Part 4 of the HEA amends s 22 of the THEA 1998 and related provisions concerning student support. One major change is that regulations made under s 22 will be able to prevent a person's liability in relation to a student loan made under s 22 from being cancelled on the person's bankruptcy.[4] Another major change is that a number of the Secretary of State's functions under or in relation to s 22 will be transferred to the National Assembly.[5]

Abolition of the visitor's jurisdiction in relation to staff disputes

17.141   The final change to be made by the HEA 2004 to which attention is drawn here is the ending by s 46 of the visitor's jurisdiction in relation to (a) any dispute between a higher education institution and any member of its staff concerning the member's appointment or employment, or the termination of that appointment or employment, (b) any other dispute between that institution and the member of staff 'in respect of which proceedings could be brought before any court or tribunal [assuming that the visitor does not have jurisdiction to determine the dispute]', or (c) the application of the statutes or other internal laws of the institution in relation to a matter falling within (a) or (b). Section 206 of the ERA 1988, which went only part of the way towards ending the visitor's jurisdiction in relation to such disputes, will be repealed by s 46(4).

---

[1]   Section 39(a).
[2]   Section 39(b).
[3]   See s 39(e).
[4]   See s 42.
[5]   See s 44.

Chapter 18

DISCRIMINATION LAW; EUROPEAN LAW

INTRODUCTION

18.1   In this chapter, United Kingdom and European Community laws against discrimination in so far as they relate to education are considered. Those which are national in origin are considered first, followed by European Community law. The relevant provisions of the Human Rights Act 1998 and those of the European Convention on Human Rights affecting the provision of education directly, and the case-law concerning the latter, are then considered. The aim of the chapter is to draw attention to the manner in which enactments relating to discrimination affect the provision of education. A comprehensive treatment of the law relating to discrimination is outside the scope of this book. Before turning to the substance of the law, however, it is necessary to state that the provisions of Directive 2000/78/EC (which concern (1) employment and (2) vocational training[1]) established 'a general framework for equal treatment in employment and occupation', aspects of which have now been implemented (in particular in relation to discrimination on the ground of religion or belief and discrimination on the ground of sexual orientation, both of which are referred to further below). However, that Directive has not been implemented fully by the United Kingdom in relation to discrimination on the ground of age or disability. Further, the Directive concerning discrimination on the ground of sex (76/207/EEC) has been amended, and the amendments have yet to be implemented in United Kingdom law (see further below). Changes must therefore be anticipated during the near future in relation to those areas of United Kingdom education law in so far as they constitute vocational training.

SEX DISCRIMINATION ACT 1975

18.2   The provisions of the Sex Discrimination Act 1975 (SDA 1975) have most impact in relation to employment, and most of the case-law concerning that Act has arisen in relation to employment matters. Nevertheless, the SDA 1975 contains provisions which apply specifically to the provision of education.

Definition of sex discrimination

18.3   The definition of discrimination for the purposes of the SDA 1975 is contained in ss 1–5 of that Act. Briefly,[2] there are two types of discrimination on the ground of sex for the purposes of that Act: direct and indirect discrimination. Direct

---

[1]   See Art 3(1). See paras **18.94–18.98** as to what constitutes vocational training for this purpose.
[2]   For a fuller discussion and description of the case-law, see for example, *Harvey on Industrial Relations and Employment Law* (Butterworths, looseleaf) at paras L[244]–L[309].

discrimination is treating a woman less favourably than a man on ground of – that is, because of – her sex.[1] It is also treating a man less favourably than a woman on the ground of his sex.[2] In relation to matters other than employment or vocational training,[3] indirect discrimination consists of the application to a woman of a requirement or condition which applies, or would apply, equally to a man (a) which is such that the proportion of women who can comply with it is considerably smaller than the proportion of men who can comply with it, (b) which the person applying the condition cannot show to be justifiable irrespective of the sex of the person to whom it is applied, and (c) which is to the detriment of the woman to whom it is applied because she cannot in practice comply with it.[4] In relation to employment or vocational training, indirect discrimination consists of the application to a woman of a provision, criterion or practice which applies or would apply equally to a man but which (i) is such that it would be to the detriment of a considerably larger proportion of women than of men, (ii) which the alleged discriminator cannot show to be justifiable irrespective of the sex of the person to whom it is applied, and (iii) which is to the woman's detriment.[5] A man may be indirectly discriminated against in the same way.[6]

18.4   Discrimination on the ground of gender reassignment is unlawful as a result of s 2A of the SDA 1975, in relation to vocational training. This is discrimination 'on the ground that [the alleged victim] intends to undergo, is undergoing, or has undergone gender reassignment'.[7]

18.5   Victimisation of a person where (broadly) a claim has been made or a right has been asserted under the SDA 1975 is defined by s 4 of that Act also as discrimination for the purposes of the SDA 1975. The scope of s 4 is wide. Subject to an exception (mentioned below), discrimination includes for this purpose the treatment by a person (defined for this purpose as the discriminator) of another person (defined for this purpose as the person victimised) in a manner which is less favourable than the manner in which the discriminator treats or would treat other persons 'by reason that' the person victimised has either (a) brought proceedings against the discriminator or any other person under the SDA 1975, the Equal Pay Act 1970, or ss 62–65 of the Pensions Act 1995, (b) given evidence or information in connection with proceedings brought by any person against the discriminator or any other person under any of those provisions, (c) otherwise done anything under or by reference to any of those provisions in relation to the discriminator or any other person, or (d) alleged that the discriminator or any other person has committed an act which (whether or not the allegation so states) would amount to a contravention of any of those provisions.[8] Subject to the same exception, the treatment by a discriminator of a person victimised in a manner which is less favourable than the manner in which the discriminator treats

1   SDA 1975, s 1(1)(a).
2   Ibid, ss 1(1)(a) and 2(1).
3   See paras **18.94–18.98** as to what constitutes vocational training for this purpose.
4   SDA 1975, s 1(1)(b). *Mandla v Dowell Lee* [1983] 2 AC 548.
5   Ibid, s 1(2) and (3). See paras **18.94–18.98** as to what is vocational training for this purpose.
6   Ibid, s 2(1).
7   Ibid, s 2A(1).
8   Ibid, s 4(1).

or would treat other persons 'by reason that the discriminator knows the person victimised intends to do any of those things, or suspects the person victimised has done, or intends to do, any of them', is also discrimination.[1] The exception is that no contravention of s 4(1) will occur in relation to 'treatment of a person by reason of any allegation made by him if the allegation was false and not made in good faith'.[2]

Unlawful acts by bodies in charge of educational establishments

18.6   Discrimination (as defined by s 1 of the SDA 1975) against a woman by one of the bodies responsible for certain educational institutions ('educational establishments') is unlawful in relation to the terms on which that body offers to admit the woman to the establishment as a 'pupil' (meaning a recipient of education there[3]).[4] Such discrimination in the form of a refusal or a deliberate omission to accept an application for the admission of a woman to the establishment as a pupil is also unlawful.[5] Finally, where a woman is a pupil at a relevant establishment, it is unlawful for the relevant body to discriminate against her in the way the body affords her access to any benefits, facilities or services, or to discriminate against her (a) by refusing or deliberately omitting to afford her access to those benefits, facilities or services, (b) by excluding her from the establishment, or (c) by 'subjecting her to any other detriment'.[6] In *Shamoon v Chief Constable of the Royal Ulster Constabulary*,[7] the House of Lords held that a 'detriment' within the meaning of the Northern Ireland equivalent of the SDA 1975 exists if a reasonable employee would or might take the view that the treatment accorded to her had in all the circumstances been to her detriment, and that it is not necessary to demonstrate some adverse physical or economic consequence. This must apply also in relation to discrimination in relation to the provision of education, as must the approach taken by the House of Lords in *Pearce v Governing Body of Mayfield School*,[8] which is that those responsible for the conduct of a school will not be liable for harassment of a relevant sort which is perpetrated by pupils.

18.7   Section 22 applies to the following sorts of establishment: (1) an educational establishment maintained by an LEA, (2) an independent school other than a special school, (3) a special school which is not maintained by an LEA, (4) an institution within the further education sector within the meaning of s 91(3) of the 1992 Act,[9] (5) a university,[10] (6) an institution other than a university which is within the higher education sector (within the meaning of s 91(5) of that Act[11]), and (7) an institution other than those just mentioned which provides full-time or part-time education and

---

[1]   SDA 1975, s 4(1).

[2]   Ibid, s 4(2).

[3]   Ibid, s 22A.

[4]   Ibid, s 22(a). See the following paragraph for the institutions to which s 22 applies, and the bodies which are responsible for those institutions for the purposes of s 22.

[5]   Ibid, s 22(b). See the following paragraph for the institutions to which s 22 applies.

[6]   Ibid, s 22(c).

[7]   [2003] UKHL 11, [2003] ICR 337.

[8]   [2003] UKHL 34, [2003] ICR 937.

[9]   See para **16.2** for the definition of an institution in the further education sector.

[10]   A university college and the college, school or hall of a university are included within the definition of a university for the purposes of the SDA 1975: see SDA 1975, s 82(1).

[11]   See para **17.14** as to what is an institution within the higher education sector.

which is designated under s 24(1) of the SDA 1975.[1] The bodies which are responsible for those establishments for the purposes of that section are as follows. In the case of educational establishments maintained by an LEA, the body responsible is either the LEA or the governors 'according to which of them has the function in question'. In the case of an independent school or a special school which is not maintained by an LEA, it is the proprietor. In the case of all the other establishments, it is the governing body.[2]

Other discrimination by LEAs

18.8   Section 23 of the SDA 1975 provides that it is unlawful for an LEA, 'in carrying out such of its functions under the Education Acts as do not fall under s 22, to do any act which constitutes sex discrimination'.[3] The 'pool' within which comparisons for the purposes of s 1(1)(b) of the SDA 1975 will need to be made is clearly that of the relevant LEA.[4]

18.9   In R *v* *Birmingham City Council, ex parte Equal Opportunities Commission*,[5] the House of Lords held that an LEA contravened s 23 of the SDA 1975 if it knowingly maintained a system of education in its area under which girls had considerably fewer opportunities for selective education than boys. This was so even if the LEA had no power to alter the situation because the relevant schools were voluntary aided, with the results that (1) the LEA could not close the schools without the consent of the Secretary of State, and (2) any initiative for a change in the character of any of the schools would have had to come from the governing body of the school.[6] The House of Lords implicitly recognised these difficulties.[7]

18.10   Subsequently, the same LEA sought to argue in R *v* *Birmingham City Council, ex parte Equal Opportunities Commission (No 2)*[8] that where an imbalance in provision occurred in part as a result of the existence of grant-maintained schools, the LEA was not in breach of s 23. The Court of Appeal rejected that argument,[9] and held that 'in considering the extent of the duty under s 8 of the 1944 Act one looks at all the schools in the area and not merely at the schools which are maintained by the local education authority'.[10] The court further held as follows:

---

[1]   SDA 1975, s 22, table, col 1. An institution may be designated under s 24(1) only if it falls within s 24(2)(b), (c) or (d). Those are establishments (1) in respect of which grants are payable out of money provided by Parliament, (2) which are assisted by an LEA for the purposes of the EA 1996 (which means assisted within the meaning of s 579(5)–(7) of that Act), and (3) which provide full-time education for persons who have attained the upper limit of compulsory school age within the meaning of s 8 of the EA 1996 Act (as to which, see paras **2.40** and **2.41**) but not the age of 19.

[2]   Ibid, s 22, table, col 2.

[3]   The term 'the Education Acts' has the meaning given to it by s 578 of the EA 1996: SDA 1975, s 82(1).

[4]   This is the clear implication of R *v* *Birmingham City Council, ex parte Equal Opportunities Commission (No 2)* [1994] ELR 282.

[5]   [1989] AC 1155.

[6]   See paras **7.26** et seq.

[7]   At 1163D–F and 1191H–1192A.

[8]   [1994] ELR 282.

[9]   Ibid, 297C–D.

[10]   [1994] ELR 282, at 297A–B.

'It is not necessary in the present case to reach a final conclusion with regard to independent schools. It seems to us, however, in considering whether sufficient schools are available, the local education authority has to take account, and only take account, of places which are available free. The relevant "pool", as we would term it, is the pool of free places in single-sex schools providing a grammar school education. This pool may include assisted places at independent schools, but in our judgment it certainly includes grant-maintained schools.'[1]

18.11   The court commented, however, that 'the impact of civil rights legislation in the field of education requires to be looked at comprehensively as a matter of urgency'.[2] However, the problems identified by the court in that case remain. These include that:

'Schools and school places cannot be provided at the drop of a hat. Furthermore, account must be taken of the fact that the risks of discrimination may vary from year to year or even from term to term. Even if precisely equal numbers of places are provided at particular types of school both for boys and for girls, girls may require to achieve a higher mark to obtain admission. Under the present legislation this might constitute a form of unlawful discrimination. But the disparities would be likely to vary from year to year and be due to factors over which local education authorities or governing bodies could not possibly exercise control. It may therefore be right to provide that unlawful discrimination could only be proved if over a period a pattern of discrimination could be established.'[3]

18.12   Some comfort for an LEA can be found in the subsequent decision of the Court of Appeal in R *v Northamptonshire County Council, ex parte K*.[4] There, it was held that where an LEA was under a statutory duty to close a school because it could no longer provide adequate standards of education, the LEA could not 'thereby place itself in breach of the Sex Discrimination Act'.[5]

Discrimination by the LSC, the CETW and the higher education funding councils

18.13   Section 23A of the SDA 1975 provides that it is unlawful for the LSC, the CETW, the Higher Education Funding Council for England or the Higher Education Funding Council for Wales, 'in carrying out their functions under the Education Acts and the Learning and Skills Act 2000, to do any act which constitutes sex discrimination'.

Discrimination by the teacher training agency

18.14   Section 23D of the SDA 1975 provides that it is unlawful for the Teacher Training Agency 'in carrying out their functions under Part I of the Education Act 1994 to do any act which constitutes sex discrimination'.[6]

---

1   [1994] ELR 282, at 297B–C. The assisted places scheme has now been repealed: see para **13.30**.
2   Ibid, 298B.
3   Ibid, 297H–298B.
4   [1994] ELR 397.
5   Ibid, at 402E–F and 403E.
6   See paras **15.3** et seq concerning Part I of the EA 1994.

General duty of certain bodies in relation to sex discrimination under sections 25(1) and 25a(1) of the SDA 1975

Bodies to which section 25(1) applies

18.15   Section 25(1) of the SDA 1975 applies (so far as relevant) to LEAs in England and Wales, and the Teacher Training Agency.[1] Section 25(1) also applies to any other body which is a responsible body within the meaning of s 22 in relation to (a) an educational establishment maintained by an LEA, (b) a special school which is not maintained by an LEA, (c) any institution within the further education sector within the meaning of s 91(3) of the 1992 Act, (d) an institution which is assisted by an LEA for the purposes of the EA 1996, and (e) an establishment in respect of which grants are payable under s 485 of the EA 1996.[2]

The duty in section 25(1)

18.16   Section 25(1) of the SDA 1975 places a body to which it applies, without prejudice to the body's obligation to comply with any other provision of the SDA 1975, 'under a general duty to secure that facilities for education provided by it, and any ancillary benefits or services, are provided without sex discrimination'.

General duty of the LSC and the CETW in relation to sex discrimination in regard to the provision of post-16 education and training

18.17   The LSC and the CETW are under a general duty:

> 'to secure that the facilities [for (a) education, (b) training, and (c) organised leisure-time occupation connected with such education or training, the provision of which is secured by the LSC or, as the case may be, the CETW] and any ancillary benefits or services are provided without sex discrimination.'[3]

Exceptions to the duties in sections 22–25A of the SDA 1975

18.18   There are several exceptions to the various duties contained in ss 22 to 25A of the SDA 1975. They are closely defined, and a little complex.

Section 26 of the SDA 1975 – exception for single-sex establishments

18.19   Section 26(1) of the SDA 1975 excepts from the application of ss 22(a) and (b) (which concern admissions) and ss 25 and 25A any establishment which admits pupils[4] of one sex only, or which would be taken to admit pupils of one sex only if there were disregarded pupils of the opposite sex whose admission is exceptional or whose numbers are comparatively small and whose admission is confined to particular

---

[1]   SDA 1975, s 25(6)(a) and (f).
[2]   Ibid, s 25(6)(c). See para **18.7** as to what is the responsible body in each case for the purposes of s 22. See s 579(5)–(7) of the EA 1996 for what is an institution which is assisted by an LEA for this purpose. See para **3.58** regarding s 485 of the EA 1996.
[3]   Ibid, s 25A(1) and (2).
[4]   A pupil for the purposes of SDA 1975, s 26 'includes any person who receives education' at the establishment in question: s 26(4).

courses of instruction or teaching classes. An establishment of this sort is defined by s 26(1) for the purposes of the SDA 1975 as a 'single-sex establishment'.

18.20 Section 26(2) applies to 'a school which is not a single-sex establishment' which has some pupils as boarders and others as non-boarders and admits as boarders pupils of one sex only (or would be taken to do so if there were disregarded boarders of the opposite sex whose numbers are comparatively small). Section 26(2) provides that ss 22(a) and (b), 25 and 25A do not apply to the admission of boarders, and that ss 22(c)(i), 25 and 25A do not apply to boarding facilities at the school.

18.21 Section 26(3) provides that where an establishment is a single-sex establishment only because the numbers of pupils of the opposite sex are comparatively small and those pupils are confined to particular courses of instruction or teaching classes, the fact that those pupils of the opposite sex are so confined is not to be taken to contravene s 22(c)(i) or the duty in s 25 or s 25A.

Section 27 of the SDA 1975 – exception for single-sex establishments turning co-educational

18.22 Section 27 of the SDA 1975 applies to the situation where the body responsible for a single-sex establishment to which s 22 applies[1] determines to alter its admissions arrangements so that the establishment will cease to be a single-sex establishment. Section 27 also applies where s 26(2) applies to the admission of boarders to a school to which s 22 applies but the body responsible for the school for the purposes of s 22 determines to alter its admissions arrangements so that s 26(2) will cease to apply. In both cases, the responsible body may apply in accordance with Sch 2 to the SDA 1975 for a 'transitional exemption order' authorising discriminatory admissions during the transitional period specified in the order.[2] That order then provides protection against claims under the SDA 1975 as long as its terms are complied with.[3] Where proposals are published under the SSFA 1998 for an establishment to cease to be an establishment which admits pupils of one sex only, and the proposals are sent to the SOC or referred to the adjudicator, such sending or referral constitutes an application for a transitional exemption order within the meaning of s 27 of the SDA 1975.[4] The same is true in relation to a sending of published proposals of the same sort in relation to a school in Wales to the National Assembly under s 28(7) or s 31(6) of the SSFA 1998.[5] Similar provisions apply in relation to proposals made under Sch 7 to the SSFA 1998 regarding the rationalisation of school places.[6]

---

[1]   As to which, see para **18.7**.
[2]   SDA 1975, s 27(1).
[3]   Ibid, s 27(2)–(6).
[4]   See SSFA 1998, Sch 6, para 21. See paras **7.26** et seq concerning the publication of such proposals.
[5]   Ibid, Sch 6, para 22.
[6]   See ibid, Sch 7, paras 16 and 17. See paras **7.48** et seq regarding the directed rationalisation of school places.

Section 28 of the SDA 1975 – exception for physical training

18.23 By virtue of s 28 of the SDA 1975, ss 22, 23, 25 and 25A of the SDA 1975 do not apply to any course in physical education which is (a) a further education course or (b) a higher education course within the meaning of the ERA 1988.

Enforcement of duties in sections 22, 23, 23A, 23C, 23D, 25(1) and 25A

18.24 Sections 496 and 497 of the EA 1996[1] apply to the enforcement of the duties imposed by ss 22, 23, 23A, 23C and 23D and 25(1).[2] Sections 496 and 497 are indeed the *only* means by which the duty in s 25(1) can be enforced, except where the breach is also a contravention of s 22, s 23, s 23A, s 23C or s 23D, which may nevertheless be enforced under s 66 of the SDA 1975 or otherwise.[3] The duty imposed by s 25A on the LSC and the CETW may be enforced only under s 25 or s 47 (as the case may be) of the LSA 2000, unless the breach in question is also a breach of s 23A which may be enforced under s 66 or otherwise.[4]

18.25 Section 66 is indeed the main means by which individuals may enforce the duties in ss 22, 23 and 23A. Section 66(1) provides that a contravention of any duty in Part III of the SDA 1975 (which includes those sections) 'may be made the subject of civil proceedings in like manner as any other claim in tort ... for breach of statutory duty'. The proceedings may be brought only in a county court,[5] but any remedy which would be obtainable in the High Court is nevertheless available.[6] However, no damages are awardable for discrimination which is contrary to s 1(1)(b) of the SDA 1975 (that is indirect discrimination) unless the discrimination was intentional or it concerns vocational training.[7] However, where damages are awardable in respect of an unlawful act of discrimination, compensation may be awarded for injury to feelings, whether or not the damages include compensation under any other head.[8]

18.26 Civil proceedings may not be brought by a person in respect of a claimed contravention of s 22 or s 23 by a body to which s 25(1) applies[9] unless the person (the claimant) has given notice of the claim to the Secretary of State and either the Secretary of State has by notice informed the claimant that the Secretary of State does not require further time to consider the matter, or the period of 2 months has elapsed since the claimant gave notice to the Secretary of State.[10] This restriction does not, however, apply to a counterclaim.[11] It was stated in *R v Bradford Metropolitan Borough*

---

1   As to which, see Chapter 3.
2   SDA 1975, s 25(2).
3   Ibid, s 25(4).
4   Ibid, s 25A(3). See paras **16.15** and **16.16** concerning ss 25 and 47 of the LSA 2000.
5   Proceedings may be brought with respect to an act done on a ship, aircraft or hovercraft outside the court's district, including such an act done outside Great Britain: SDA 1975, s 66(8). The time-limit for a claim is (see SDA 1975, s 76) 6 months, unless the claim is made against a higher education institution and a complaint about the matter is made within that time-limit under Part 2 of the HEA 2004: see s 19 of the latter Act, amending s 76 of the SDA 1975.
6   SDA 1975, s 66(2).
7   Ibid, s 66(3). See paras **18.94–18.98** as to what constitutes vocational training for this purpose.
8   Ibid, s 66(4).
9   See para **18.15** for the bodies to which s 25(1) applies.
10 SDA 1975, s 66(5).
11 Ibid.

Council, ex parte Ali[1] that judicial review proceedings were not covered by the equivalent restriction in the Race Relations Act 1976 (s 57).

Defence of statutory authority

18.27 Section 51A of the SDA 1975 provides as follows:

'(1)   Nothing in –
(a)   the relevant provisions of Part III, or
(b)   Part IV so far as it has effect in relation to those provisions,
shall render unlawful any act done by a person if it was necessary for that person to do it in order to comply with a requirement of an existing statutory provision within the meaning of section 51.

(2)   In subsection (1) "the relevant provisions of Part III" means the provisions of that Part except so far as they apply to vocational training.'

18.28 The reference to vocational training was necessitated by the provisions of the Equal Treatment Directive (as to which, see below[2]). The equivalent provision in the Race Relations Act 1976 is s 41(1), and the decision in R *v Cleveland County Council, ex parte Commission for Racial Equality*[3] concerning that provision is considered above.[4]

Modification of restrictions on certain educational charities

18.29 Under s 78 of the SDA 1975, the Secretary of State may modify or remove certain restrictions in trust deeds or other instruments which concern property applicable for or in connection with the provision of education in any establishment to which s 22 applies.[5] The trust deed or instrument must restrict the benefits available under the instrument to persons of one sex.[6] The Secretary of State cannot act of his own motion; rather, he may act only on the application of the trustees or the responsible body (within the meaning of s 22) relating to the institution.[7] Furthermore, he may act only if he is satisfied that the removal or modification of the restriction 'would conduce to the advancement of education without sex discrimination'.[8]

18.30 Except in certain circumstances, no order may be made by the Secretary of State under s 78 if the trust was created by a gift or bequest, until 25 years after the date on which the gift or bequest took effect.[9] The exceptional circumstances are that the donor or his personal representatives, or the personal representatives of the testator, have consented in writing to the making of the application for the order.[10]

---

[1]   [1994] ELR 299, at 315C–316B.
[2]   Paragraph **18.115**.
[3]   [1994] ELR 44.
[4]   Paragraph **9.39**.
[5]   See para **18.7** for the establishments to which s 22 applies.
[6]   SDA 1975, s 78(1)(b).
[7]   Ibid, s 78(2).
[8]   Ibid.
[9]   SDA 1975, s 78(3).
[10] Ibid.

Law of Education

18.31 Before making an order under s 78, the Secretary of State must require the applicant for the order to publish a notice containing particulars of the proposed order and stating that representations may be made to the Secretary of State within a period specified in the notice.[1] The period must be not less than one month from the date of the notice.[2] The notice must be published in such manner as may be specified by the Secretary of State, but the cost of any publication of the notice may be defrayed out of the property of the trust.[3] Before making the order sought, the Secretary of State must take into account any representations duly made in accordance with the notice.[4]

RACE RELATIONS ACT 1976

18.32 The provisions of the Race Relations Act 1976 (RRA 1976) are in some respects in terms which are almost identical to those of the SDA 1975. However, especially since the enactment of (1) the Race Relations (Amendment) Act 2000 and (2) the Race Relations Act 1976 (Amendment) Regulations 2003[5] (which implemented Directive 2000/43/EC), there are some significant differences between the RRA 1976 and the SDA 1975. In addition to (1) the differing definitions of discrimination in the two Acts (harassment now being included in the definition of discrimination on the ground of race[6] and there now being a new definition of indirect discrimination in s 1(1A), which applies to ss 17–18D of the RRA 1976[7]), and (2) s 19B of the RRA 1976, which provides that it is unlawful for a public authority in carrying out any of its functions to do any act which constitutes discrimination, the main differences between the two Acts relate to the exceptional situations in which the RRA 1976 does not apply. The numbering of the sections of the two Acts differs, however, in part because a number of the provisions in the SDA 1975 are not repeated in the RRA 1976. That is a product of the differences inherent in the situations addressed by the two Acts, which include that there can be no equivalent in the RRA 1976 of the provisions in the SDA 1975 which relate to discrimination on the ground of marital status. There are also some provisions in the RRA 1976 of which there is no equivalent in the SDA 1975. The relevant additional provisions are as follows.

Lawful positive discrimination under section 35 of the RRA 1976

18.33 As a result of s 35 of the RRA 1976, it is lawful to afford persons of a particular racial group preferential access to facilities or services to meet the special needs of persons of that group in regard to their education, training or welfare, or any ancillary benefits.

---

[1] SDA 1975, s 78(4).
[2] Ibid, s 78(5).
[3] Ibid, s 78(6).
[4] Ibid, s 78(7).
[5] SI 2003/1626.
[6] See s 3A, as inserted by the Race Relations Act 1976 (Amendment) Regulations 2003, SI 2003/1626.
[7] See RRA 1976, s 1(1B)(b).

General statutory duty of local authorities under section 71 of the RRA 1976

18.34 Local authorities and the governing bodies of (1) educational establishments which are maintained by LEAs, (2) institutions within the further education sector, and (3) institutions within the higher education sector, are under a general duty under s 71(1) of the RRA 1976[1] (which is without prejudice to any other duty of the authority or body in question under the RRA 1976[2]), in carrying out its functions to 'have due regard to the need (a) to eliminate unlawful racial discrimination; and (b) to promote equality of opportunity and good relations between persons of different racial groups'. The predecessor to this duty (which was in similar terms) was said by the House of Lords in *Wheeler v Leicester City Council*[3] to have no application to the education functions of an LEA.

18.35 Every local authority and each governing body of the educational institutions referred to in the preceding paragraph are also under a duty to comply with the Race Relations Act 1976 (Statutory Duties) Order 2001,[4] which requires them (1) to have a 'Race Equality Scheme', and every three years to review it,[5] (2) to have a written statement of their policy 'for promoting race equality' (their 'race equality policy'),[6] (3) to assess the impact of their policies, including their race equality policy, 'on pupils, staff and parents of different racial groups including, in particular, the impact on attainment levels of such pupils',[7] and (4) to monitor the operation of such policies.[8]

18.36 A code of practice giving practical guidance in relation to the performance of the duties in s 71(1) and (2) has been published by the Commission for Racial Equality (CRE) under s 71C of the RRA 1976.[9] Guidance on race equality policies has also been provided by the CRE, and it is available on their website.[10]

Enforcement

18.37 It is of note that in contrast to the SDA 1975, a breach of the main duties owed by an LEA and an educational establishment under the RRA 1976 is enforceable only in court proceedings, and not also where relevant by means of an application to the Secretary of State under s 496 or s 497 of the EA 1996. This is a product of the repeal by the Race Relations (Amendment) Act 2000 of s 19 of the RRA 1976, without the re-enactment of s 19(2). However, there is still a need to give prior notice to the Secretary of State of a claim to a county court of a breach of s 17 or s 18 of the RRA 1976 (which are the equivalents of ss 22 and 23 of the SDA 1975) by some educational bodies.[11]

---

[1]   As substituted by s 2(1) of the Race Relations (Amendment) Act 2000.
[2]   See RRA 1976, s 71(7).
[3]   [1985] AC 1054, at 1077E–F.
[4]   SI 2001/3458.
[5]   See Art 2, including for the content of such scheme.
[6]   Article 3(1) and (2).
[7]   Article 3(3)(a).
[8]   Article 3(3)(b).
[9]   This was issued in 2002, and is not available on the CRE's website. The ISBN is 1 85442 468 8.
[10] www.cre.gov.uk/publs/download.html, under R.
[11] See s 57(5) and (5A) of the RRA 1976.

DISCRIMINATION ON THE GROUND OF RELIGION OR BELIEF

18.38 As a result of reg 20(1) of the Employment Equality (Religion or Belief) Regulations 2003,[1] it is unlawful for the governing body of an educational establishment to which those regulations apply to discriminate within the meaning of those regulations against a person (a) 'in the terms on which it offers to admit him to the establishment as a student', (b) 'by refusing or deliberately not accepting an application for his admission to the establishment as a student', or (c) 'where he is a student of the establishment (i) in the way it affords him access to any benefits, (ii) by refusing or deliberately not affording him access to them, or (iii) by excluding him from the establishment or subjecting him to any other detriment'. It is also unlawful 'in relation to an educational establishment to which this regulation applies, for the governing body of that establishment to subject to harassment a person who is a student at the establishment, or who has applied for admission to the establishment as a student'.[2]

18.39 Discrimination within the meaning of the Employment Equality (Religion or Belief) Regulations 2003 is defined by regs 3–5 in a manner which is consistent with the new approach taken to the definition of discrimination in the SDA 1975 and the RRA 1976. The educational bodies to which the regulations apply are (a) an institution within the further education sector, (b) a university, and (c) an institution other than a university which is within the higher education sector, unless the institution is within Sch 1B to the regulations.[3] In relation to an institution within Sch 1B, it is possible to refuse to admit a person to the institution if it is 'necessary [for the institution] to give preference in its admissions to persons of a particular religion or belief in order to preserve that institution's religious ethos', except where the course is of vocational training.[4]

DISCRIMINATION ON THE GROUND OF SEXUAL ORIENTATION

18.40 The Employment Equality (Sexual Orientation) Regulations 2003[5] are in very similar terms to those of the Employment Equality (Religion or Belief) Regulations 2003, the effects of which are mentioned in the two preceding paragraphs. Like the latter regulations, the Employment Equality (Sexual Orientation) Regulations 2003 apply to (a) an institution within the further education sector, (b) a university, and (c) an institution other than a university which is within the higher education sector.[6]

---

[1] SI 2003/1660.
[2] Regulation 20(2).
[3] Regulation 20(4) and (4A) (as inserted by SI 2004/437).
[4] See regs 2 and 3 of the Employment Equality (Religion or Belief) (Amendment) Regulations 2004, SI 2004/437.
[5] SI 2003/1661.
[6] Regulation 20(4).

DISABILITY DISCRIMINATION ACT 1995

Introduction

18.41 The provisions of the Disability Discrimination Act 1995 (DDA 1995) were amended by the Special Educational Needs and Disability Act 2001 (SENDA 2001) with the result that Part 4 of the DDA 1995 now applies in a substantial way to education providers. There is, however, a fundamental difference of approach taken by that Act towards (1) the education of children who are at school or who are of school age, and (2) the provision of further education or higher education. Furthermore, claims of discrimination contrary to the DDA 1995 in relation to children who are, or seek to be, provided with education at a school, are not all made to the same judicial body. In addition, the remedies which may be awarded to a person in respect of discrimination contrary to the DDA 1995 differ according to whether the discrimination is related to the provision of education at school, or at a further or higher education institution. Before turning to the provisions of the DDA 1995, it is necessary to state that the provisions of the Employment Directive (2000/78/EC) have not been implemented in regard to disability discrimination concerning vocational training (although they have been prospectively implemented in regard to discrimination concerning employment[1]). Thus, changes to the DDA 1995 should be expected in the relatively near future.

Unlawful discrimination in relation to education at a school or schools

Protection afforded to a disabled person within the meaning of the DDA 1995

18.42 A person who is disabled within the meaning of the DDA 1995 is protected by Chapter 1 of Part 4 of the DDA 1995 in relation to education at school.[2] A detailed analysis of the definition of a disabled person within the meaning of the DDA 1995 is outside the scope of this book. However, it is of interest that the Secretary of State's guidance, issued under s 3 of the DDA 1995, 'on matters to be taken into account in determining questions relating to the definition of disability' states in para C12 that 'severe dyslexia' is obviously within the definition of a disability for the purposes of that Act. By implication, therefore, it is not obvious that mild dyslexia (assuming that there is such a thing) is within that definition. Paragraph C20 of the guidance includes the following words: 'Account should be taken of whether the person has persistent and significant difficulty in reading text in standard English or straightforward numbers'. The examples given in that paragraph of what it would not be reasonable to regard as having a substantial adverse effect on a person's ability to carry out normal

---

[1]   See the Disability Discrimination Act 1995 (Amendment) Regulations 2003, SI 2003/1673, which will come into force on 1 October 2004. See paras **18.94–18.98** as to what constitutes vocational training for this purpose.

[2]   The word 'school' is defined by s 28Q(4) and (5) for the purposes of Chapter 1 of Part 4 of the DDA 1995 to mean (a) a maintained school within the meaning of s 20(7) of the SSFA 1998, (b) a maintained nursery school within the meaning of s 22(9) of the SSFA 1998, (c) an independent school within the meaning of s 463 of the EA 1996, (d) a special school which is not maintained by an LEA but which is approved by the Secretary of State or the National Assembly under s 342 of the EA 1996, and (e) a pupil referral unit within the meaning of s 19(2) of the EA 1996.

day-to-day activities include (a) 'inability to concentrate on a task requiring application over several hours', (b) 'inability to fill in a long, detailed, technical document without assistance', (c) 'inability to read at faster than normal speed', and (d) 'minor problems with writing or spelling'.

The prohibitions

18.43 It is unlawful as a result of s 28A(1) of the DDA 1995 for 'the body responsible for a school'[1] to discriminate (within the meaning of s 28B) against a disabled person '(a) in the arrangements it makes for determining admission to the school as a pupil; (b) in the terms on which it offers to admit him to the school as a pupil; or (c) by refusing or deliberately omitting to accept an application for his admission to the school as a pupil'. As a result of s 28A(2), it is also unlawful for the body responsible for a school to discriminate within the meaning of s 28B 'in the education or associated services provided for, or offered to, pupils at the school by that body'. Regulations may be made by the Secretary of State prescribing what is education or an associated service for this purpose,[2] but none have so far been made.

18.44 It is in addition unlawful for a body responsible for a school 'to discriminate [within the meaning of s 28B] against a disabled pupil by excluding him from the school, whether permanently or temporarily'.[3]

18.45 All of the prohibitions in the preceding two paragraphs apply in the same manner to persons who are not disabled but who are victimised within the meaning of s 55 of the DDA 1995.[4]

Disability discrimination defined

18.46 Discrimination is defined for the purposes of s 28A by ss 28B and 28C of the DDA 1995. Those sections are largely (but not precisely) equivalent to ss 5 and 6 of the DDA 1995 (concerning discrimination in relation to employment, including the adjustments which it is reasonable to require an employer to make for a disabled person), and the case-law relating to those sections will for the most part apply to ss 28B and 28C.[5] The differences between the two sets of provisions (ss 5 and 6 and ss 28B and 28C) include that less favourable treatment is justified if it is the result of a permitted form of selection as defined by s 28Q(9).[6] Selection is permitted by s 28Q(9) if (a) the school in question is designated as a grammar school under s 104 of the SSFA 1998, in which case any of its selective admission arrangements are permitted, (b) the school is not so designated but the selection is authorised by s 99(2)

---

[1]   In relation to a maintained school this is the LEA or the governing body, 'according to which has the function in question'; in relation to a pupil referral unit, it is the LEA; in relation to a maintained nursery school, it is the LEA; in relation to an independent school or a special school which is not maintained by an LEA, it is the proprietor within the meaning of s 579 of the EA 1996: DDA 1995, Sch 4A, para 1, table.

[2]   DDA 1995, s 28A(3).

[3]   Ibid, s 28A(4).

[4]   Ibid, s 28A(6).

[5]   This was confirmed by Silber J in *M Catholic High School v SENDIST* [2003] EWHC 3045 (Admin), [2004] ELR 89, at para 45.

[6]   DDA 1995, s 28B(6).

or (4),[1] or (c) the school is an independent school and it selects any or all of its pupils by reference to general or special ability or aptitude with a view to admitting only pupils of high ability or aptitude.

18.47 Another difference between (1) ss 28B and 28C and (2) ss 5 and 6 of the DDA 1995, is that s 28C does not require a responsible body to '(a) remove or alter a physical feature (for example one arising from the design or construction of the school premises or the location of resources); or (b) provide auxiliary aids or services'.[2] Regulations may be made prescribing (a) circumstances in which it is reasonable for a responsible body to have to take steps of a prescribed description, (b) steps which it is always reasonable for a responsible body to have to take, (c) circumstances in which it is not reasonable for a responsible body to have to take steps of a prescribed sort, and (d) steps which it is never reasonable for a responsible body to have to take.[3] The power to make such regulations was described by Baroness Blackstone, the Government Minister who was responsible for the Bill which became the SENDA 2001 while it was proceeding through the House of Lords, as a 'reserve' power.[4]

Disability rights commission code of practice for schools

18.48 In considering whether it is reasonable to take a particular step in order to comply with its duty to make reasonable arrangements (within the meaning of s 28C(1)) to cater for the needs of disabled persons, a responsible body must have regard to the provisions of any code of practice issued by the Disability Rights Commission (DRC) under s 53A of the DDA 1995.[5] There is an extensive and helpful such code (which is available on the DRC's website[6]). Salient features of the current code include para 6.22, which provides:

> 'Independent schools, where they are educating children at their parents' expense, can make specialist tuition available and can charge parents for this. Less favourable treatment might occur if charges were made at a level designed to deter disabled pupils from coming to the school.'

Confidentiality requests

18.49 Another difference between (1) ss 28B and 28C and (2) ss 5 and 6 of the DDA 1995 is that s 28C(6) (read with s 28C(5) and (7)) provides that in determining whether it is reasonable for a responsible body to have to take a particular step in relation to a person in order to comply with the duty in s 28C(1), regard must be had to the extent to which taking the step in question is consistent with compliance with a request, of which the responsible body is aware, which asks for the nature, or asks for the existence, of a disabled person's disability to be treated as confidential and which either (a) is made by the person's parent or (b) is made by the person himself in the circumstance that the responsible body reasonably believes that he has sufficient

---

1   See paras **9.26** et seq concerning s 99(2) and (4).
2   DDA 1995, s 28C(2).
3   Ibid, s 28C(3).
4   *Hansard,* HL vol 622, col 745.
5   DDA 1995, s 28C(4).
6   See www.drc.org.uk/law/codes.asp.

understanding of the nature of the request and its effect. This is apparently rather different from s 6(6), but in reality it simply (1) reflects the difficulty of determining whether a child is able to give a valid consent for other purposes, and (2) reflects the test for the validity of a consent given by a minor as stated by the House of Lords in *Gillick v West Norfolk and Wisbech Area Health Authority*.[1]

Accessibility strategies and plans

18.50 Section 28D of the DDA 1995 goes some way towards obliging a responsible body to provide the auxiliary aids and services which, as a result of s 28C(2), it is not obliged to provide under s 28C(1). The duties of LEAs differ in some respects from those of other responsible bodies. This is because of the need for what Baroness Blackstone, the relevant Minister of State, speaking on behalf of the Government, called in Grand Committee of the House of Lords: 'strategic planning across a LEA where ... it is considered more cost-effective and sensible to work together and plan provision across a range of schools, than to leave every school to make adjustments'.[2] The differences in the duties of LEAs and the responsible bodies for individual schools are recognised by different nomenclature: LEAs are under a duty to formulate and implement accessibility strategies, and responsible bodies for individual schools are under a duty to formulate and implement accessibility plans.

Accessibility strategies

18.51 An LEA must every 3 years prepare an accessibility strategy in relation to schools[3] for which they are the responsible body (and whether they are the responsible body in relation to any particular function depends on the function in question[4]).[5] An accessibility strategy is a written strategy for (a) increasing the extent to which disabled pupils can participate in the schools' curriculums, (b) improving the physical environment of the schools for the purpose of increasing the extent to which disabled pupils are able to take advantage of education and associated services[6] provided or offered by the schools, and (c) improving the delivery to disabled pupils (i) within a reasonable time, and (ii) in ways which are determined after taking account of their disabilities and any preferences expressed by them or their parents, of information which is provided in writing for pupils who are not disabled.[7] Every LEA must keep their accessibility strategy under review during the period to which it relates, and if necessary revise it.[8]

---

[1]   [1986] AC 112, as to which, see para **14.3**.

[2]   *Hansard*, vol 621, col CWH 173.

[3]   See footnote 4 in para **18.42** for the meaning of the word 'school' in Chapter 1 of Part 4 of the DDA 1995.

[4]   See footnote 1 in para **18.43**.

[5]   See s 28D(1) of the DDA 1995, the Disability Discrimination (Prescribed Periods for Accessibility Strategies and Plans for Schools) (England) Regulations 2002, SI 2002/1981, and the Disability Discrimination (Prescribed Periods for Accessibility Strategies and Plans for Schools) (Wales) Regulations 2003, SI 2003/2531.

[6]   Regulations may be made (in relation to Wales by the National Assembly: s 28D(17)) under s 28D(15) prescribing services which are, or are not, to be regarded for the purposes of s 28D as being education or an associated service.

[7]   DDA 1995, s 28D(2) and (3).

[8]   Ibid, s 28D(4).

18.52 In preparing their accessibility strategy, an LEA must have regard to the need to allocate adequate resources for implementing the strategy and to any guidance issued by the Secretary of State or (as the case may be) the National Assembly as to the content of the strategy, the form in which it is produced, and the persons to be consulted in its preparation.[1] An LEA must also have regard to any such guidance issued as to compliance with the duty imposed by s 28D(4),[2] which is stated at the end of the preceding paragraph.

18.53 An LEA is under a duty to implement its accessibility strategy,[3] and an inspection of the LEA carried out under s 38 of the EA 1997[4] 'may extend to the performance by an LEA of their functions in relation to the preparation, review, revision and implementation of their accessibility strategy'.[5] The duty to implement the accessibility strategy is enforceable under s 28M of the DDA 1995, by means of a direction given by the Secretary of State (or, as the case may be, the National Assembly for Wales), which is itself enforceable by means of a mandatory order made by the High Court.[6] If the Secretary of State or the National Assembly asks for a copy of the accessibility strategy prepared by an LEA, the strategy must be given to him or it.[7] If asked to do so (presumably by any person), an LEA must make a copy of their accessibility strategy available for inspection at 'such reasonable times as they may determine'.[8] These latter duties are also enforceable under s 28M.[9]

Accessibility plans

18.54 The body responsible for a school within the meaning of s 28Q[10] is under a duty to prepare an accessibility plan and further such plans every 3 years.[11] An accessibility plan is a written plan for (a) increasing the extent to which disabled pupils can participate in the school's curriculum, (b) improving the physical environment of the school for the purpose of increasing the extent to which disabled pupils are able to take advantage of education and associated services[12] provided or offered by the school, and (c) improving the delivery to disabled pupils (i) within a reasonable time, and (ii) in ways which are determined after taking account of their disabilities and any preferences expressed by them or their parents, of information which is provided in

---

1   DDA 1995, s 28E(1) and (3).
2   Ibid, s 28E(2).
3   Ibid, s 28D(5).
4   Concerning which, see paras **12.52–12.55**.
5   DDA 1995, s 28D(6).
6   See ibid, s 28M(1), (4) and (7)–(9).
7   Ibid, s 28E(5)(a) and (6)(a).
8   Ibid, s 28E(7).
9   See ibid, s 28M(1), (4) and (7)–(9).
10   See footnote 4 in para **18.42** for what is such a school. In relation to a maintained school, in this context the responsible body is the governing body: s 28D(14).
11   See DDA 1995, s 28D(7) and (8), the Disability Discrimination (Prescribed Periods for Accessibility Strategies and Plans for Schools) (England) Regulations 2002, SI 2002/1981, and the Disability Discrimination (Prescribed Periods for Accessibility Strategies and Plans for Schools) (Wales) Regulations 2003, SI 2003/2531.
12   Regulations may be made (in relation to Wales by the National Assembly: s 28D(17)) under s 28D(15) prescribing services which are, or are not, to be regarded for the purposes of s 28D as being education or an associated service.

writing for pupils who are not disabled.[1] In preparing an accessibility plan, the responsible body must have regard to the need to allocate adequate resources for implementing the plan.[2] During the period to which an accessibility plan relates, the responsible body must keep the plan under review and, if necessary, revise it.[3]

18.55 The responsible body for a school must implement its accessibility plan,[4] and an inspection of the school under the SIA 1996[5] 'may extend to the performance by the responsible body of its functions in relation to the preparation, publication, review, revision and implementation of its accessibility plan'.[6] The duty to implement the accessibility plan is enforceable under s 28M, by means of a direction given by the Secretary of State (or, as the case may be, the National Assembly for Wales), which is itself enforceable by means of a mandatory order made by the High Court.[7] If the Secretary of State or the National Assembly asks for a copy of the accessibility plan prepared by the proprietor of an independent school other than an Academy, the plan must be given to him or it.[8] If asked to do so (presumably by any person), the proprietor of an independent school which is not an academy must make a copy of his accessibility plan available for inspection at 'such reasonable times as he may determine'.[9] These duties are also enforceable under s 28M.[10]

Residual duty of an LEA not to discriminate against disabled pupils or prospective pupils

18.56 An LEA is prohibited by s 28F of the DDA 1995 when exercising any function (other than a prescribed function) under the Education Acts[11] from discriminating against a disabled pupil or a person who may be admitted to a school as a pupil, unless that discrimination is already prohibited by any other provision of Part 4 of the DDA 1995.[12] They are also prohibited in the same manner from discrimination against persons who are not disabled within the meaning of the DDA 1995 by way of victimisation within the meaning of s 55 of that Act.[13] This duty takes effect in the manner provided for by s 28G of that Act, which applies s 28B for the purpose, but with appropriate modifications.

---

[1]   DDA 1995, s 28D(9) and (10).

[2]   Ibid, s 28E(4).

[3]   Ibid, s 28D(11).

[4]   Ibid, s 28D(12).

[5]   Concerning which, see paras **12.13** et seq.

[6]   DDA 1995, s 28D(13).

[7]   See ibid, s 28M(1), (4) and (7)–(9).

[8]   Ibid, s 28E(5)(b) and (6)(b).

[9]   Ibid, s 28E(8).

[10] See ibid, s 28M(1)–(4) and (7)–(9).

[11] The Education Acts means those Acts referred to in s 578 of the EA 1996: DDA 1995, s 28F(7).

[12] DDA 1995, s 28F(1)–(4). There are currently no regulations prescribing functions to which this duty does not apply. See footnote 4 in para **18.42** for the definition of a school for this purpose.

[13] Ibid, s 28F(5).

Enforcement of relevant obligations under the DDA 1995

Appeals to the special educational needs and disability tribunal

18.57 Except where the claim relates to a refusal of admission to a maintained school or an Academy, or to a permanent exclusion from such a school or an Academy, a claim of discrimination contrary to Part 4 of the DDA 1995 in relation to (a) education at a school or (b) provided, or to be provided, for a person of school age, must be made by the child's parent to the Special Educational Needs and Disability Tribunal (or, in Wales, the Special Educational Needs Tribunal for Wales).[1] The procedure in relation to such an appeal is provided for by the Special Educational Needs and Disability Tribunal (General Provisions and Disability Claims Procedure) Regulations 2002.[2] Those regulations are similar to those which apply to appeals to that tribunal which do not concern disability discrimination contrary to the DDA 1995, suitably adapted.[3] Having heard the appeal, the tribunal may, if it considers the claim to be well-founded, declare that the child in question has been unlawfully discriminated against, and if it does so, with a view to obviating or reducing the adverse effect on the person concerned of any matter to which the claim relates, 'make such order as it considers reasonable in all the circumstances of the case', although such an order may not include the payment of any sum by way of compensation.[4]

Claims of unlawful discrimination in relation to a refusal of admission to a maintained school or an academy

18.58 A claim of discrimination contrary to Part 4 of the DDA 1995 in relation to the refusal of a place for a child in a maintained school or an Academy must, as a result of s 28K of that Act, be made to an appeal panel arranged under s 94 of the SSFA 1998 or (in the case of an Academy) under an agreement entered into between the responsible body for the Academy and the Secretary of State under s 482 of the EA 1996. The body hearing the appeal then has the same powers which it would have had if the appeal had not involved a claim of discrimination.[5] Thus the only power which the body hearing the appeal has in relation to the appeal is to dismiss it or order that the child to whom it relates be admitted to the school or Academy in question.

Claims of unlawful discrimination in relation to a decision permanently to exclude a pupil from a maintained school or an academy

18.59 A claim of discrimination contrary to Part 4 of the DDA 1995 in relation to a decision permanently to exclude a pupil from a maintained school or an Academy must, as a result of s 28L of that Act, be made to an appeal panel arranged under s 52(3)(c) of the EA 2002 or (in the case of an Academy) under an agreement entered into between the responsible body for the Academy and the Secretary of State under

---

1   DDA 1995, s 28I(1) and (2), read with s 28Q. This is in contrast to the position in Scotland: see s 28N of the DDA 1995.
2   SI 2002/1985. These apply also to Wales: see reg 1(4).
3   As for the procedure to follow in appeals which do not involve allegations of discrimination contrary to the DDA 1995, see paras **6.120** et seq.
4   Ibid, s 28I(3) and (4).
5   DDA 1995, s 28K(4).

s 482 of the EA 1996. The body hearing the appeal then has the same powers which it would have had if the appeal had not involved a claim of discrimination.[1] In this context, the 'responsible body' in relation to a maintained school includes the discipline committee of the governing body if that committee is required to be established as a result of regulations made under s 19 of the EA 2002.[2] It is of note that a claim of discrimination contrary to the DDA 1995 in relation to a decision to exclude a pupil for a fixed period, may be made only to the relevant SEN tribunal.[3]

Unlawful discrimination in relation to further or higher education

The prohibitions

Further and higher education which is not secured by an LEA or provided by the governing body of a maintained school

18.60 It is unlawful for the body responsible for (a) an institution in the further education sector,[4] (b) an institution in the higher education sector,[5] and (c) an institution which is designated by the Secretary of State in the Disability Discrimination (Designation of Educational Institutions) Order 2002,[6] to discriminate within the meaning of s 28S of the DDA 1995 against a person who is disabled within the meaning of that Act (a) in the arrangements which it makes for determining admissions to the institution, (b) in the terms on which it offers to admit him to the institution, and (c) by refusing or deliberately omitting to accept an application for his admission to the institution.[7] The body responsible for such an institution in the further education sector or the higher education sector is the governing body.[8] In the case of an institution which is designated by the Secretary of State for the purpose, it is the body specified in the order as the responsible body.[9]

18.61 It is also unlawful for the body responsible for any of these types of institution (referred to in Chapter 2 of Part 4 of the DDA 1995 as an 'educational institution', but referred to below as a 'relevant educational institution') to discriminate within the meaning of s 28S against a disabled student 'in the student services it provides, or

---

[1]   DDA 1995, s 28L(4).

[2]   Ibid, s 28L(6).

[3]   According to Margaret Hodge, the Parliamentary Under-Secretary of State for Education and Employment, in Standing Committee B (fifth sitting, 3 April 2001, col 176): 'The simple reason why temporary exclusions have had to go elsewhere is that there is no existing mechanism for them'.

[4]   This means an institution which is conducted by a further education corporation or an institution designated under s 28(4) of the FHEA 1992: DDA 1995, s 28R(6) and FHEA 1992, s 91(3).

[5]   This means a university which is receiving financial support under s 65 of the FHEA 1992, an institution which is conducted by a higher education corporation or an institution designated under s 72(3) of the FHEA 1992: DDA 1995, s 28R(6) and FHEA 1992, s 91(3).

[6]   SI 2002/1459, made under s 28R(6)(c) of the DDA 1995.

[7]   DDA 1995, s 28R(1).

[8]   Ibid, Sch 4B, para 1, table.

[9]   Ibid.

offers to provide'.[1] For this purpose, 'student services' means 'services of any description which are provided wholly or mainly for students'.[2]

18.62 It is in addition unlawful for the body responsible for a relevant educational institution to discriminate within the meaning of s 28S against a disabled student by excluding him from the institution, whether temporarily or permanently.[3]

18.63 The victimisation by the body responsible for a relevant institution of a person, including a person who is not disabled, in relation to a claim of discrimination of the sorts described in the three preceding paragraphs, is also unlawful.[4]

Higher or further education secured by an LEA; further education provided by the governing body of a maintained school

18.64 Discrimination within the meaning of ss 28S and 28T of the DDA 1995 against a disabled person within the meaning of that Act in relation to (a) any course of higher education which is secured by an LEA under s 120 of the ERA 1988,[5] or (b) any course of further education which is either secured by an LEA or provided by the governing body of a maintained school under s 80 of the SSFA 1998,[6] is prohibited in relevant ways by s 28R of the DDA 1995 as modified by s 28U of, and Sch 4C to, the DDA 1995. Those ways are that it is unlawful for the LEA or the governing body so to discriminate against a disabled person (a) in the arrangements which they make for determining who should be enrolled on the course, (b) in the terms on which they offer to enrol him on the course, or (c) by refusing or deliberately omitting to accept an application for his enrolment on the course.[7]

18.65 It is also unlawful for the LEA or the governing body to discriminate within the meaning of ss 28S and 28T against a disabled person who has enrolled on a relevant course 'in the services which they provide, or offer to provide',[8] and for this purpose such services are 'services of any description which are provided wholly or mainly for persons enrolled on the course'.[9]

18.66 Further, it is unlawful for an LEA to discriminate within the meaning of ss 28S and 28T against a disabled person in the terms on which they provide, or offer to provide, recreational or training activities.[10]

---

[1] DDA 1995, s 28R(2).
[2] Ibid, s 28R(11). Regulations may be made under s 28R(12) providing what services are, or are not, to be regarded for the purposes of s 28R(2) as student services. Currently, there are no such regulations.
[3] Ibid, s 28R(3).
[4] Ibid, s 28R(4).
[5] See para **17.29** as to s 120 of the ERA 1988.
[6] See para **7.175** regarding s 80 of the SSFA 1998.
[7] DDA 1995, s 28R(2) as contained in Sch 4C. See s 28R(8) as so contained in relation to enrolment on a course which is split into parts any one of which may be taken by a person without that person also taking another part of the course.
[8] Ibid, s 28R(3) as so contained.
[9] Ibid, s 28R(4) as so contained.
[10] Ibid, s 28R(5) as so contained.

Disability discrimination defined

18.67 Discrimination is defined for the purposes of s 28R by ss 28S and 28T of the DDA 1995. Those sections are largely (but not precisely) equivalent to ss 5 and 6 of the DDA 1995 (concerning discrimination in relation to employment, including the adjustments which it is reasonable to require an employer to make for a disabled person), and the case-law relating to those sections will for the most part apply to ss 28S and 28T. There are two major differences between the two sets of provisions (ss 5 and 6 and ss 28S and 28T). One is that less favourable treatment is justified 'if it is necessary in order to maintain ... academic standards'.[1] The other is that provision is made for a confidentiality request made by a disabled person to be taken into account in determining whether it is reasonable for a responsible body to have to take a particular step in relation to that person.[2]

18.68 In deciding whether it is reasonable to have to take a particular step in order to comply with the duty to make reasonable adjustments imposed by s 28S(1), a responsible body must have regard to any relevant provisions of a code of practice issued by the DRC under s 53A of the DDA 1995.[3] There is a code of practice issued by the DRC relating to 'providers of post-16 education and related services'. This is stated not to apply to 'wholly privately-funded post-16 providers and providers of work-based training', who are instead covered by a code concerning Part 3 of the DDA 1995 relating to the provision of goods, facilities and services.[4]

Leasehold premises occupied by a relevant educational institution

18.69 If (1) the responsible body in relation to (a) a relevant educational institution, or (b) a course of higher education or further education secured by an LEA or further education provided by the governing body of a maintained school,[5] occupies premises under a lease, (2) but for s 28W of the DDA 1995 the body would not be entitled to make a particular alteration to the premises, and (3) the alteration is one which the responsible body proposes to make to the premises, then s 28W provides a route by which the alteration may be lawful. This route is similar to that which existed already under ss 16 and 27 of the DDA 1995.

Enforcement

18.70 The enforcement of the obligations of a further or higher education provider under Chapter 2 of Part 4 of the DDA 1995 is relatively simple in comparison with the enforcement of obligations in relation to schools or children of school age. The obligations under Chapter 2 of Part 4 are enforced by county courts in the usual manner of enforcing obligations not to discriminate on the ground of sex or race.[6] Thus financial compensation is the primary remedy for a claimant, and such

---

[1] DDA 1995, s 28S(6). That subsection contains a power (which has not yet been exercised) to prescribe other standards for this purpose, so that action which is necessary to maintain standards other than academic ones may in the future be justified by s 28S(6).

[2] See ibid, s 28S(3)–(5).

[3] Ibid, s 28S(2).

[4] See p 3 of the code concerning post-16 education.

[5] See DDA 1995, Sch 4C, para 3.

[6] See ibid, s 28V.

compensation may include damages for injury to feelings.[1] However, the amount of any such compensation for injury to feelings may be limited by regulations.[2] Unless a claimant also makes an application for judicial review, a claim of a contravention of Chapter 2 of Part 4 of the DDA 1995 can be made only in a county court.[3] The time-limit for a claim is 6 months (unless the matter is first referred for conciliation under s 31A of the DDA 1995), with the possibility of an extension of time if the court considers such an extension to be just and equitable.[4]

EUROPEAN COMMUNITY LAW AFFECTING THE PROVISION OF AND ACCESS TO EDUCATION[5]

Introduction

18.71 European Community law (Community law) affects in the main access to education rather than its provision. The provision of education as such was not until recently within the scope of the Treaty of Rome, and the Community law provisions which have affected education have in the main been those relating to discrimination on the ground of nationality. A brief overview and history of the Community provisions relating to education is given below, after which reference is made to a number of specific Community legislative provisions which have given rise to decisions in the European Court of Justice (ECJ). Those decisions are examined at the same time.

18.72 In relation to the enforcement of Community Directives, it is necessary to state that the Court of Appeal in *National Union of Teachers v Governing Body of St Mary's Church of England (Aided) Junior School*[6] held that the governing body of an aided school was an emanation of the State for the purpose of the enforcement of Directives. The court did not apply the test laid down by the ECJ in *Foster v British Gas*[7] for what is an emanation of the State, in its entirety. The subsequent decision of the ECJ in *Kampelmann v Landschaftsverband Westfalen-Lippe*[8] confirms the correctness of that approach: emanations of the State are:

'organisations or bodies which are subject to the authority or control of the State or have special powers beyond those which result from the normal rules applicable to relations between individuals, such as local or regional authorities or other bodies which, irrespective of their legal form, have been given responsibility, by the public authorities and under their supervision, for providing a public service.'

---

1   See DDA 1995, s 28V(2).
2   Ibid, Sch 3, para 14. At present there are no such regulations.
3   Ibid, Sch 3, para 12.
4   Ibid, para 13(1)–(3).
5   In what follows, it is assumed that the reader is familiar with the basic principles of European Community law, such as that which relates to the direct applicability, or effect, of Community legislation.
6   [1997] ICR 334.
7   [1991] ICR 84 and [1991] ICR 463.
8   [1998] IRLR 333, para 46.

18.73 On the basis of the decision in the *St Mary's* case, it is clear that the governing body of any maintained school is an emanation of the State for the purpose of the enforcement of Directives. It is also clear that the governing body of an FEC or an HEC may also be an emanation of the State – but it is not clear that they *are* such. That issue has yet to be determined. It may also be the case that the governing body of a chartered university or of a designated further or higher education institution is an emanation of the State, but that is also an untested issue. However, given that it was crucial in the *St Mary's* case that control was exercised by the State (in the form of the Secretary of State and the LEA) over the service of education as provided in maintained schools,[1] and given the lesser degree of control exercised by the State (acting through the LSC, the CETW and the higher education funding councils) over the content of the education provided in institutions within the further and (especially) the higher education sectors,[2] it may be that those institutions are not emanations of the State for the purpose of the enforcement of directives. Yet the ECJ tests for determining what is an emanation of the State are not to be applied as if they were statutory definitions.[3] Accordingly, the question whether the governing body of a further education institution or a higher education institution is an emanation of the State is likely to be regarded by a court or tribunal as, to an extent, one of impression. The statutory underpinning of the constitutions of institutions within the further and higher education sectors could then sway the court or tribunal in favour of determining that those institutions are emanations of the State.

Overview[4]

18.74 Rather than refer to 'education', the Treaty of Rome in its original form referred to 'vocational training'.[5] Article 41 of that treaty provided that in order to achieve the objectives of the common agricultural policy, provision might be made within the framework of that policy for 'an effective co-ordination of efforts in the spheres of [among other things] vocational training'. Article 57(1) provided for the mutual recognition of qualifications. Article 118 obliged the European Commission to promote 'close co-operation between Member States in the social field, particularly in matters relating to ... basic and advanced vocational training'. Article 128 required the Council to lay down 'general principles for implementing a common vocational training policy capable of contributing to the harmonious development both of the national economies and of the common market'. Article 128 has now been repealed and replaced by two new provisions as a result of the Treaty of Maastricht. Those provisions are now Arts 149 and 150 of the consolidated Treaty establishing the European Community ('EC Treaty'). Article 149 is as follows:

[1]   [1997] ICR 334, at 350F–G.
[2]   For the meaning of the phrases 'institution within the further education sector' and 'institution within the higher education sector', see paras **16.2** and **17.14** respectively.
[3]   *National Union of Teachers v Governing Body of St. Mary's Church of England (Aided) Junior School*, ibid, at 350B–D.
[4]   For the development of Community law in relation to education, see J Shaw, 'Education and the European Community' (1991) 3 *Education and the Law* 1; C Barnard, 'The Maastricht agreement and education: one step forward, two steps back?' (1992) 4 *Education and the Law* 123; and H Houghton-James, 'The implication for Member States of the development of an education policy by the Court of Justice' (1993) 5 *Education and the Law* 85.
[5]   See paras **18.94–18.98** as to what constitutes vocational training for the purposes of Community law.

'1. The Community shall contribute to the development of quality education by encouraging co-operation between Member States and, if necessary, by supporting and supplementing their action, while fully respecting the responsibility of the Member States for the content of teaching and the organisation of education systems and their cultural and linguistic diversity.

2. Community action shall be aimed at:
- developing the European dimension in education, particularly through the teaching and dissemination of the languages of the Member States;
- encouraging mobility of students and teachers, *inter alia*, by encouraging the academic recognition of diplomas and periods of study;
- promoting co-operation between educational establishments;
- developing exchanges of information and experience on issues common to the education systems of the Member States;
- encouraging the development of youth exchanges and the exchange of socio-educational instructors;
- encouraging the development of distance education.

3. The Community and the Member States shall foster co-operation with third countries and the competent international organisations in the sphere of education, in particular the Council of Europe.

4. In order to contribute to the achievement of the objectives referred to in this Article, the Council:
- acting in accordance with the procedure referred to in Article 251, after consulting the Economic and Social Committee and the Committee of the Regions, shall adopt incentive measures, excluding any harmonisation of the laws and regulations of the Member States;
- acting by qualified majority on a proposal from the Commission, shall adopt recommendations.'

18.75 Article 150 of the EC Treaty provides as follows:

'1. The Community shall implement a vocational training policy which shall support and supplement the action of Member States, while fully respecting the responsibility of the Member States for the content and organisation of vocational training.

2. Community action shall aim to:

- facilitate adaptation to industrial changes, in particular through vocational training and retraining;
- improve initial and continuing vocational training in order to facilitate vocational integration and reintegration into the labour market;
- facilitate access to vocational training and encourage mobility of instructors and trainees and particularly young people;
- stimulate co-operation on training between educational or training establishments and firms;
- develop exchanges of information and experience on issues common to the training systems of the Member States.

3. The Community and the Member States shall foster co-operation with third countries and the competent international organisations in the sphere of vocational training.

4. The Council, acting in accordance with the procedure referred to in Article 251 and after consulting the Economic and Social Committee, shall adopt measures to contribute

to the achievement of the objectives referred to in this Article, excluding any harmonisation of the laws and regulations of the Member States.'

18.76   As can be seen, neither Art 149 nor Art 150 are likely to give rise to case-law in themselves, and neither appear likely to be held to be directly effective. Furthermore, it is clear that those provisions are not intended to affect the responsibility of Member States for their educational policies.

Regulation 1612/68

18.77   One of the two provisions of Community law which have probably had most effect in practice on the provision of education is a regulation made under what is now Art 39 of the EC Treaty.[1] (The other provision is Art 7 of the Treaty of Rome in its original form. The effect of that provision is considered below.[2]) Article 39 relates to discrimination against workers on the ground of nationality. The regulation in question is that numbered 1612/68. The main relevant provisions of that Regulation are Arts 7 and 12.

Article 7 of regulation 1612/68

18.78   Article 7(2) of Regulation 1612/68 requires Member States to extend to migrant workers all the social advantages which it gives to national workers. It provides as follows:

'[A worker who is a national of a Member State] shall enjoy the same social and tax advantages as national workers.'

18.79   According to Art 7(3):

'He shall also, by virtue of the same right and under the same conditions as national workers, have access to training in vocational schools and retraining centres.'

18.80   A grant of financial assistance for an educational course is a social advantage within the meaning of Art 7(2).[3] The mere fact that a worker has become unemployed does not mean that the worker ceases to be entitled to benefit from the protection afforded by Art 7. However, subject to one exception, there must be 'some continuity between the previous occupational activity and the course of study; there must be a relationship between the purpose of the studies and the previous occupational activity'.[4] The exception is that such continuity may not be required where the worker involuntarily becomes unemployed and is obliged by conditions on the job market to undertake occupational retraining in another field of activity.[5] The mere fact that a contract of employment is from the outset concluded as a fixed-term contract does not necessarily result in the conclusion that once that contract expires, the employee

---

[1]   Unlike many treaty provisions, a Community regulation is directly applicable without more in the courts of Member States.

[2]   Paragraphs **18.92** et seq.

[3]   *Lair v Universität Hannover* [1988] ECR 3161, at 3197.

[4]   Ibid, at 3200.

[5]   Ibid.

concerned is automatically to be regarded as voluntarily unemployed.[1] Thus, when considering whether a person's unemployment is voluntary for this purpose:

> 'the national court may, in particular, take account of circumstances such as practices in the relevant sector of economic activity, the chances of finding employment in that sector which is not fixed-term, whether there is an interest in entering into only a fixed-term employment relationship or whether there is a possibility of renewing the contract of employment.'[2]

18.81   However, this does not mean that a national of a Member State can enter another Member State for the sole purpose of enjoying, after a very short period of occupational activity, the benefit of the student assistance system in that State.[3]

18.82   It was held in *Brown v Secretary of State for Scotland*[4] that the claimant in that case had become a worker for the purposes of Art 7 as a result of undergoing some pre-university industrial training. There, it was said that:

> 'A national of another Member State who enters into an employment relationship in the host State for a period of eight months with a view to subsequently undertaking university studies there in the same field of activity and who would not have been employed by his employer if he had not already been accepted for admission to university is to be regarded as a worker within the meaning of Article 7(2) of Regulation No 1612/68.'[5]

18.83   However, because that employment relationship was ancillary to the education to be pursued, he was:

> 'not entitled, under Article 7(2) of Regulation No 1612/68, to receive for the purpose of his studies an allowance payable to students who are nationals of the host State in respect of their maintenance.'[6]

18.84   The effect of this decision was revisited in *Grzelczyk v Centre Public D'Aide Sociale*[7] but in reality (using domestic legal language) the comments were *obiter*. Nevertheless, it is of interest that the ECJ commented:

> '35. ... since *Brown*, the Treaty on European Union has introduced citizenship of the European Union into the EC Treaty and added to Title VIII of Part Three a new chapter 3 devoted to education and vocational training. There is nothing in the amended text of the Treaty to suggest that students who are citizens of the Union, when they move to another member state to study there, lose the rights which the Treaty confers on citizens

---

[1]   *Ninni-Orasche v Bundesminister fur Wissenschaft Verkehr und Kunst (C-413/01)* [2004] 1 CMLR 19, at para 43.

[2]   Ibid, at para 44.

[3]   Ibid, at para 36. A reference to the ECJ was made by the High Court in *R (Bidar) v London Borough of Ealing*, CO/3091/01, where it was claimed that it was contrary to Art 12 of the EC Treaty to deny a student loan for maintenance expenses to a national of a Member State who had the right of residence in the United Kingdom but who resided there solely for the purpose of receiving education. The determination of that case is currently awaited.

[4]   [1988] ECR 3207.

[5]   Ibid, at 3247.

[6]   Ibid, at 3246, para 28.

[7]   Case C-184/99; [2002] ICR 566, at 598–599, paras 34–39.

of the Union. Furthermore, since *Brown*, the Council has also adopted Directive 93/96,[1] which provides that the member states must grant rights of residence to student nationals of a member state who satisfy certain requirements.

36. The fact that a Union citizen pursues university studies in a member state other than the state of which he is a national cannot, of itself, deprive him of the possibility of relying on the prohibition of all discrimination on grounds of nationality laid down in article 6 of the Treaty.'

Article 12 of regulation 1612/68

18.85   Article 12 of Regulation 1612/68 provides as follows:

'The children of a national of a Member State who is or has been employed in the territory of another Member State shall be admitted to that State's general educational, apprenticeship and vocational training courses under the same conditions as the nationals of that State, if such children are residing in its territory.

Member States shall encourage all efforts to enable such children to attend these courses under the best possible conditions.'

18.86   The ECJ has considered the effect of Art 12 on a number of occasions. The effect of the court's judgments can be summarised in the following manner.

18.87   The words 'under the same conditions' in Art 12 mean 'not only [the] rules relating to admission, but also [the] general measures intended to facilitate educational attendance'.[2] Therefore, financial assistance must be available to children to whom Regulation 1612/68 applies in the same way that it is available to the children of citizens of the Member State in question.[3] A child of a migrant worker is entitled to continue his studies in the relevant Member State after his parents have returned to their home State.[4] Similarly, the child of a migrant worker does not cease to be a 'child' for the purposes of Art 12 until he has completed his education, no matter what his age or whether he remains dependent on his parents.[5] A child's rights under Regulation 1612/68 (such as to financial assistance on the same basis as that on which such assistance is available to the children of citizens of the Member State) cannot be made subject to conditions relating to residence.[6]

18.88   The rights afforded by Regulation 1612/68 supersede and cannot be undermined by an international agreement concluded between an international organisation and the Member State in which a migrant worker is employed.[7] Similarly, a bilateral agreement which reserves scholarships for nationals of the two Member

---

[1]   Concerning which, see paras **18.100** and **18.101**.
[2]   *Casagrande v Landeshauptstadt München* [1974] ECR 773, at 779, para 9.
[3]   This was confirmed in *Echternach and Moritz v Netherlands Minister for Education and Science* [1989] ECR 723, at 761.
[4]   Ibid.
[5]   *Gaal* [1995] ECR I-1031. For a helpful commentary on that case and an overview of the situation, see V Kfjatkovski, 'Equal treatment in education and the children of migrant workers in the EU', (1996) 8 *Education and the Law* 69.
[6]   *Echternach and Moritz* 1989] ECR 723, at 763, para 26.
[7]   Ibid, at 759.

States which are the parties to the agreement cannot prevent the application of the principle of equality of treatment between national and Community workers established in the territory of one of those two Member States.[1]

18.89 The right to equal treatment under Art 12 does not depend on the place where the child concerned pursues his studies.[2] Accordingly, if the child wishes to pursue a course in the home State of his parents, then his application to the host State for financial assistance for that purpose is to be treated in the same way as an application for financial assistance for the same course made by a child of a citizen of the host State would be treated by the host State.[3] Article 7(2) of Reg 1612/68 provides support for this conclusion.[4]

18.90 Where a child has a right of residence for educational purposes as a result of Art 12 of Regulation 1612/68, the parent who is the primary carer of the child has the right, irrespective of his nationality, to reside with the child to facilitate the exercise of the right, even if the parents have divorced or the parent who had the status of a citizen of the European Union has ceased to be a migrant worker in the host State.[5]

Directive 77/486 regarding the education of the children of migrant workers

18.91 The right in Art 12 of Regulation 1612/68 has been supplemented by a Directive, number 77/486/EEC, which applies to 'children for whom school attendance is compulsory under the laws of the host State, who are dependants of any worker who is a national of another Member State, where such children are resident in the territory of the Member State in which that national carries on or has carried on an activity as an employed person'.[6] The host State is obliged by that directive to take appropriate measures to facilitate the initial reception of the children to whom the directive applies, including the teaching (adapted to the specific needs of such children) of the official language, or one of the official languages, of that State.[7] The tuition must be free.[8] The host state must take measures for the training and further training of the teachers who are to provide the tuition.[9] The host State must also promote the teaching of the language and culture of the country of origin of a relevant child.[10]

Prohibition of discrimination in relation to vocational training under the Treaty of Rome

18.92 Article 12 of the EC Treaty prohibits discrimination on the ground of nationality. The predecessor to that Article (Art 7 of the Treaty of Rome) was relied

---

[1] *Matteucci v Communauté française of Belgium* [1988] ECR 5589.
[2] *Di Leo v Land Berlin* [1990] ECR I-4185, at I-4208, para 12.
[3] Ibid, at I-4209.
[4] Ibid, at I-4208–I-4209.
[5] *Baumbast v Secretary of State for the Home Department* [2003] ICR 1347, at 1391, para 75.
[6] Article 1 of the Directive.
[7] Article 2.
[8] Ibid.
[9] Ibid.
[10] Article 3.

upon by the ECJ when ruling, in *Forcheri v Belgian State*,[1] that requiring of 'a national of another Member State lawfully established in the first Member State an enrolment fee which is not required of its own nationals in order to take part in [educational courses relating in particular to vocational training] constitutes discrimination by reason of nationality, which is prohibited by Article 7 of the Treaty'.[2] In arriving at that ruling, the ECJ applied Art 7 to what was then Art 128 of the Treaty.[3]

18.93   In *Gravier v City of Liège*,[4] it was held that 'the conditions of access to vocational training fall within the scope of [Art 7, now Art 12] of the Treaty'. It was later held by the ECJ that indirect discrimination on the ground of nationality in this context is just as unlawful as direct discrimination on that ground.[5] However, in *Brown*, it was held that:

> 'the payment by a Member State to or on behalf of students of tuition fees charged by a university falls within the scope of the EEC Treaty for the purposes of Article 7 thereof, but the payment of grants for students' maintenance does not.'[6]

What is 'vocational training'?

18.94   In *Gravier*, it was held that vocational training for the purposes of Community legislation is 'any form of education which prepares for a qualification for a particular profession, trade or employment or which provides the necessary training and skills for such a profession, trade or employment ... whatever the age and the level of training of the pupils or students, and even if the training programme includes an element of general education'.[7] The claimant in that case was seeking to be enrolled on a 4-year course on the Art of strip cartoons at the Royal Academy of Fine Arts in Liège. The court ruled that that was indeed vocational training of the sort referred to in *Forcheri*.

18.95   It was suggested by the United Kingdom High Court in *McMahon v Department of Education*[8] and held by it in *R v Inner London Education Authority, ex parte Hinde*[9] that only some university courses could properly be considered to be vocational training. However, in *Blaizot v University of Liège*,[10] the ECJ ruled as follows:

> 'With regard to the issue whether university studies prepare for a qualification for a particular profession, trade or employment or provide the necessary training and skills for such a profession, trade or employment, it must be emphasized that that is the case not only where the final academic examination directly provides the qualification for a particular profession, trade or employment but also in so far as the studies in question

---

[1]   [1983] ECR 2323.

[2]   Ibid, at 2336.

[3]   As to which, see para **18.74**.

[4]   [1985] ECR 593, at 613, para 25.

[5]   See *EC Commission v Kingdom of Belgium* [1988] ECR 5445. The indirect discrimination identified in that case was also held to be contrary to Art 12 of Regulation 1612/68.

[6]   [1988] ECR 3205, at 3243, para 19. The continuing validity of this distinction is the subject of the referral to the ECJ in *Bidar* which is mentioned in footnote 6 in para **18.81**.

[7]   Ibid, at 614, para 30.

[8]   [1983] Ch 227.

[9]   (1984) 83 LGR 695, [1985] 1 CMLR 716.

[10]   [1988] ECR 379.

provide specific training and skills, that is to say where a student needs the knowledge so acquired for the pursuit of a profession, trade or employment, even if no legislative or administrative provisions make the acquisition of that knowledge a prerequisite for that purpose.'[1]

18.96 However, 'certain courses of study which, because of their particular nature, are intended for persons wishing to improve their general knowledge rather than prepare themselves for an occupation' are not vocational training.[2]

18.97 In *Blaizot*, the ECJ took the unusual step of limiting the effect of the judgment in that case, so that it had prospective effect only.[3] This was because until 1985 the European Commission did not believe that university education as such would be determined to be vocational training for the purposes of Art 7 of the Treaty (as it then was).

18.98 In *Belgian State v Humbel*,[4] Mr Humbel was undergoing a course of general secondary education provided for persons of compulsory school age. The Advocate-General did not think that this was vocational training,[5] but the ECJ did not rule explicitly on that question. Instead, the court issued the following rather unhelpful ruling:

> 'a year of study which is part of a programme forming an indivisible body of instruction preparing for a qualification for a particular profession, trade or employment or providing the necessary training and skills for such a profession, trade or employment constitutes vocational training for the purposes of the EEC Treaty.'[6]

Relationship between Art 12 of the EC Treaty and reg 1612/68

18.99 It may be helpful to say that Regulation 1612/68 affects rights to benefits (in other words, positive things), whereas Art 12 of the EC Treaty concerns discrimination (in other words, things that must not be done, or negative things). Accordingly, although Mr Brown could not be charged for access to his course in the form of course fees because (1) he was a national of a Community country other than the United Kingdom,[7] (2) the United Kingdom government did not charge course fees to home students, and (3) to charge Mr Brown such fees would have constituted discrimination on the ground of nationality,[8] he was not entitled to the positive benefit of a maintenance grant because he was not entitled to benefit from Regulation 1612/68.[9]

---

[1]   [1988] ECR 379, at 404, para 19.
[2]   Ibid, at 404, para 20.
[3]   See [1988] ECR 379, at 407.
[4]   [1988] ECR 5365.
[5]   Ibid, at 5377.
[6]   Ibid, at 5387, para 13.
[7]   He had dual French and British nationality: see ibid, at 3238, para 3.
[8]   [1988] ECR 3205, at 3243, para 17.
[9]   Ibid, at 3246, para 28.

Right of residence for students

18.100   Students from within the Community now have a potential specific right of residence under Directive 93/96/EEC, which is stated by its preamble to be 'part of a set of related measures designed to promote vocational training'. It is a supplementary directive, as can been seen from Art 1, whose terms are as follows:

> 'In order to lay down conditions to facilitate the exercise of the right of residence and with a view to guaranteeing access to vocational training in a non-discriminatory manner for a national of a Member State, the Member States shall recognise the right of residence for any student who is a national of a Member State and who does not enjoy that right under other provisions of Community Law, and for the student's spouse and their dependent children, where the student assures the relevant national authority, by means of a declaration or by such alternative means as the student may choose that are at least equivalent, that he has sufficient resources to avoid becoming a burden on the social assistance system of the host Member State during their period of residence, provided that the student is enrolled in a recognized educational establishment for the principal purpose of following a vocational training course there and that he is covered by sickness insurance in respect of all risks in the host Member State.'

18.101   As one would expect, this right of residence is limited to the duration of the course of study.[1] Furthermore, the Directive is stated not to 'establish any entitlement to the payment of maintenance grants by the host Member State on the part of students benefiting from the right of residence'.[2]

Is education a service within the meaning of Arts 49 and 59 of the EC Treaty?

18.102   In *Humbel*,[3] the ECJ ruled that publicly funded secondary education is not a service within the meaning of Art 60 and therefore the Treaty of Rome (Art 60 of the Treaty of Rome is now Art 50 of the EC Treaty). Accordingly, there was no need to consider whether there was a restriction on the freedom to provide a service, and therefore (because of the correlative right to receive a service[4]) a contravention of Art 59 (now Art 49 of the EC Treaty). However, it is clear that the provision of education by an independent school or a university could (probably depending on the extent to which the course is paid for by public funds) fall within the definition of a service for the purposes of the Treaty of Rome.

Specific Community programmes affecting education

18.103   A number of Community programmes relating specifically to education have been adopted by means of Community decisions (which have direct effect in the United Kingdom). Those programmes include what are known as the ERASMUS, COMETT, Lingua, and Tempus programmes. The ERASMUS programme (the

---

1   See Art 2 of the Directive.
2   Article 3.
3   [1988] ECR 5365.
4   See *Luisi and Carbone v Ministero del Tresoro* [1984] ECR 377, at 401, para 10.

'European Community Action Scheme for the Mobility of University Students') was initiated by Decision 87/327/EEC,[1] and was intended to:

'achieve a significant increase in the number of students from universities ... spending an integrated period of study in another Member State, in order that the Community may draw upon an adequate pool of manpower with first hand experience of economic and social aspects of other Member States, while ensuring equality of opportunity for male and female students as regards participation in such mobility.'[2]

18.104 In addition to promoting the mobility of students, the ERASMUS programme was intended 'to promote broad and intensive cooperation between universities in all Member States', including by promoting the increased mobility of teaching staff.[3]

18.105 The COMETT programme of co-operation between universities and industry was initiated by Decision 86/365/EEC.[4] It related to training in the field of technology. Its objectives included giving 'a European dimension to cooperation between universities and enterprises in training relating to innovation and the development and application of new technologies'.[5] Objectives also included developing 'the level of training in response to technological change and social changes by identifying the resulting priorities in existing training arrangements which call for supplementary action both within Member States and at Community level, and by promoting equal opportunities for men and women'.[6]

18.106 The Lingua programme was initiated by Decision 89/489/EEC. Its principal objective was to 'promote a quantitative and qualitative improvement in foreign language competence with a view to developing communication skills within the Community'.[7]

18.107 The Tempus programme, implemented by Council Decision 90/233, stemmed from the collapse of communism in Eastern Europe. It was a trans-European mobility scheme for university studies. One of its objectives was 'to enable students from the eligible countries to spend a specific period of study at university or to undertake industry placements within the Member States of the Community, while ensuring equality of opportunity for male and female students as regards participation in such mobility'.[8] It has been extended by Decision 93/246/EEC and Decision 99/311/EC.

---

[1] The history of that Decision is described in JA McMahon, *Education and Culture in European Community Law* (The Athlone Press, 1995), pp 24–29. The decision was amended by Decision 89/663.
[2] Article 2(i) of the Decision.
[3] Article 2(ii) of Decision 87/327/EEC and the preamble.
[4] See also Decision 89/27.
[5] See Art 3(a) of Decision 86/365/EEC.
[6] Ibid, Art 3(d). See further, McMahon, op cit (footnote 1 above), at pp 30–36.
[7] Article 4 of Decision 89/489/EEC. See further, McMahon, op cit, at pp 36–39.
[8] Article 4(d) of Decision 90/233/EEC. See further, McMahon, op cit, at pp 39–42.

18.108   The Leonardo da Vinci[1] and Socrates[2] programmes are also potentially of value in relation to the provision of education. Among other things, the Leonardo da Vinci programme makes specific provision for disadvantaged young people, including those with physical or mental disabilities.[3]

18.109   Most recently, Decision 2317/2003/EC established a programme called Erasmus Mundus, concerning 'the enhancement of quality in higher education and the promotion of intercultural understanding through cooperation with third countries', and Decision 2318/2003/EC adopted a programme 'for the effective integration of information and communication technologies ... in education and training systems in Europe' (the 'eLearning Programme').

The mutual recognition of formal qualifications

18.110   Article 47(1) of the EC Treaty provides as follows:

> 'In order to make it easier for persons to take up and pursue activities as self-employed persons, the Council shall, acting in accordance with the procedure referred to in Article 251, issue directives for the mutual recognition of diplomas, certificates and other evidence of formal qualifications.'

18.111   A number of Directives have been issued under the predecessor to Art 47(1), for example on qualifications in nursing,[4] midwifery,[5] dentistry,[6] pharmacy,[7] veterinary medicine,[8] architecture[9] and medicine.[10]

18.112   It was held by the ECJ in *Broekmeulen*[11] that it is permissible to require more by way of qualifications of a Member State's national workers than of workers from another Member State.[12]

18.113   There is in addition a general Directive on the recognition of higher education qualifications, Directive 89/48/EEC.[13] It is designed to protect the

---

[1]   Decision 94/819/EC, extended by Decision 99/382/EC.
[2]   Decision 819/95/EC, extended by Decision 253/2000/EC.
[3]   See Art 3(h), (i) and (l) of Decision 94/819/EC.
[4]   Directives 77/452/EEC and 77/453/EEC, amended by Directive 2001/19/EC.
[5]   Directives 80/154/EEC and 80/155/EEC, amended by Directive 2001/19/EC.
[6]   Directives 78/686/EEC and 78/687/EEC, amended by Directive 2001/19/EC.
[7]   Directives 85/432/EEC and 85/433/EEC, amended by Directive 2001/19/EC.
[8]   Directives 78/1026/EEC and 78/1027/EEC, amended by Directive 2001/19/EC.
[9]   Directive 85/384/EEC, amended by Directive 2001/19/EC.
[10]   See now Directive 93/16/EEC, implemented by the European Specialist Medical Qualifications Order 1995, SI 1995/3208, as amended by SI 1997/2928, the effect of which was in issue in *R v Specialist Training Authority of the Medical Royal Colleges, ex parte British Medical Association* [1999] EdCR 661. The Directive was amended by Directive 2001/19/EC. The 1995 Order was subsequently further amended by SI 2003/3148, and is prospectively replaced by the General and Specialist Medical Practice (Education, Training and Qualifications) Order 2003, SI 2003/1250, which was amended by SI 2004/1947.
[11]   [1981] ECR 2311.
[12]   See ibid, at 2330–2331.
[13]   It has been supplemented by Directive 92/51/EEC (which was amended by Directive 97/38/EC and Directive 95/43/EC), Directive 99/42/EC, and Decision 2004/108/EC, and amended by Directive 2000/5/EC and Directive 2001/19/EC. Directive 89/48/EEC was implemented in the United

interests of nationals of Community countries who hold 'diplomas' which entitle them to practise in a 'regulated profession' and who cannot rely upon any other directive.[1] Article 1(a) of that Directive contains the definition of a diploma for the purpose of the Directive. It is primarily anything which amounts to evidence of a formal qualification or set of formal qualifications which meets the following requirements. The 'diploma' must have been awarded by a competent authority in a Member State, which is designated in accordance with its own laws, regulations or administrative provisions. The diploma must show that its holder has successfully completed a post-secondary course of education of at least 3 years' duration, or of an equivalent duration part-time, at a university or establishment of higher education or another establishment of similar level. It must also show that, where appropriate, the holder has successfully completed the professional training required in addition to the post-secondary course. Finally, the diploma must show that the holder has the professional qualifications required for taking up or pursuit of a regulated profession in that Member State. If a person has received education and training in the Community which does not amount to a post-secondary course of education of at least 3 years' duration, or of an equivalent duration part-time, at a university or establishment of higher education or another establishment of a similar level, then a diploma awarded as a result of the education and training in fact received will nevertheless entitle the person to be treated as having a diploma entitling him to the benefit of Directive 89/48/EEC if (1) the diploma is awarded on the successful completion of education and training received in the Community and recognised by a competent authority in the Member State concerned as being of an equivalent level, and (2) it confers the same rights in respect of the taking up and pursuit of a regulated profession in that Member State.[2]

18.114   Directive 89/48/EEC applies only to nationals of a Member State who wish to pursue a regulated profession[3] in another Member State either as an employee or as a self-employed person.[4] Article 3 contains the operative provision relating to recognition.[5]

The Equal Treatment Directive and the Employment Directive

18.115   Lastly, reference needs to be made to two Directives. One is mentioned in paras **18.1** and **18.118**, and the other is Directive 76/207/EEC. The latter is commonly known as the Equal Treatment Directive, and concerned discrimination on the ground (only) of sex. It has had most effect in the sphere of employment law, but as a result of Art 4, it applies not only to equal treatment in employment, but also to 'equal access to all types and to all levels, of vocational guidance, vocational training,

---

Kingdom by the European Communities (Recognition of Professional Qualifications) Regulations 1991, SI 1991/824, as amended by SI 2000/1960 and SI 2002/3501. The GTC has an additional function of assisting the Secretary of State to carry out his functions under those regulations: see the General Teaching Council for England (Additional Functions) Order 2004, SI 2004/1886.

[1]   See Art 2, second para.

[2]   Article 1(a), second para.

[3]   Defined in Art 1(c) and (d). A self-regulated profession such as that of solicitors is included.

[4]   See Art 2, first para.

[5]   See also Arts 4–8. There is a detailed description of those provisions and related issues and case-law in McMahon, op cit, pp 84–94.

advanced vocational training and retraining'. Accordingly, Member States are under a duty to take:

'all necessary measures to ensure that ...

> (c)   without prejudice to the freedom granted in certain Member States to certain private training establishments, vocational guidance, vocational training, advanced training and retraining shall be accessible on the basis of the same criteria and at the same levels without any discrimination on grounds of sex.'[1]

18.116   The SDA 1975 appears to have implemented this obligation fully in some contexts. However, bearing in mind the wide interpretation given by the ECJ to the words 'vocational training',[2] it may nevertheless on occasion be of value to an individual to have recourse to this provision in the Equal Treatment Directive in relation to the provision of education by an emanation of the State. Furthermore, Art 4 of that Directive has been applied in a different context from that of the direct provision of education: it availed the successful woman applicant for judicial review in the case of *R v Secretary of State for Education, ex parte Schaffter*,[3] in relation to an allowance made at the time under the Education (Mandatory Awards) Regulations to lone parents who had formerly been married, but not to lone parents who had not formerly been married. A note of caution needs to be sounded, however, in relation to the application of the Equal Treatment Directive to education cases. In *R v South Bank University, ex parte Coggeran*,[4] Mummery LJ (with whom Schiemann and Thorpe LJJ agreed) said that it cannot be assumed that 'the same approach is to be taken to discrimination in education cases' as in employment cases.[5]

18.117   Directive 2002/73/EC amended Directive 76/207/EEC so as to make it consistent with the Employment Directive, 2000/78/EC. The amendments have yet to be implemented in United Kingdom law; the final date for their implementation is 5 October 2005.[6]

18.118   The Employment Directive applies to discrimination on the grounds of (1) religion or belief, (2) disability, (3) age and (4) sexual orientation. Its terms have been implemented in regard to discrimination on the ground of (1) religion or belief and (2) sexual orientation in relation to vocational training,[7] but not yet in relation to age or disability discrimination in connection with vocational training, the final date for the implementation of which is 2 December 2006.[8]

---

1   Directive 76/207/EEC, Art 4.
2   See paras **18.94–18.98**.
3   [1987] IRLR 53.
4   [2001 ELR 42.
5   Ibid, para 30.
6   See 2002/73/EC, Art 2(1).
7   See paras **18.38–18.40**.
8   See 2000/78/EC, Art 18.

THE EUROPEAN CONVENTION ON HUMAN RIGHTS

Introduction

The right to education in the first protocol to the convention

18.119　The Human Rights Act 1998 has now been in force for over 3 years, and it is the subject of a number of specialist texts. Nevertheless, it would be remiss not to refer here to Art 2 of the First Protocol to the Convention and the current case-law concerning it. Article 2 provides:

> 'No person shall be denied the right to education. In the exercise of any functions which it assumes in relation to education and to teaching, the State shall respect the rights of parents to ensure such education and teaching in conformity with their own religious and philosophical convictions.'

18.120　The effect of this Article has been the subject of a number of reported decisions. Their effect can be summarised as follows.

'No person shall be denied the right to education'

18.121　The right in the first sentence of Art 2 is positive, despite its negative wording.[1] However, the first sentence of Art 2 does not require the State to provide any particular kind of education: rather, it confers a right on individuals to obtain access to whatever educational institutions exist at any time.[2] However, the education which is provided in compliance with the right must be effective, although not the most effective possible education.[3] This means that the quality of the education provided must reach a minimum standard.[4] The right conferred by the first sentence of Art 2 is a right to be taught in the, or one of the, national languages of a country (but not merely the language of one's parents' choice),[5] and a right to be given official recognition of the studies completed.[6]

18.122　The first sentence in Art 2 does not require the State to provide special facilities to accommodate particular convictions.[7] Nor does it require the State to pay fees for a child's attendance at an independent special school where the LEA insist that he could be educated at the local comprehensive school.[8] Similarly, the first sentence in Art 2 does not require the State to allow a child to be educated at a State school when the LEA have arranged for him to be educated at a special school.[9]

---

[1]　*Belgian Linguistic Case (No. 2)* (1979–80) 1 EHRR 252, at 280, para 3.
[2]　Ibid; *Holub and Holub v Secretary of State for the Home Department* [2001] ELR 401, para 25; *S v Brent LB* [2002] EWCA Civ 693, [2002] ELR 556, at 564–565, para 9.
[3]　*Holub and Holub v Secretary of State for the Home Department* [2001] ELR 401, para 25.
[4]　Ibid.
[5]　See, in particular, ibid, at 282, para 6.
[6]　Ibid, at 281, para 4.
[7]　*X v UK* (1978) 14 DR 179.
[8]　*Simpson v UK* (1989) 64 DR 188.
[9]　*Ford v UK* [1996] EHRLR 534.

18.123   The positive right to education conferred by the first sentence of Art 2 may be regulated by the State,[1] as long as that regulation does not injure the substance of the right, or conflict with other rights enshrined in the Convention.[2] That power of regulation includes the establishment of compulsory schooling, whether in State schools or independent schools of a satisfactory standard.[3] It also includes the power to take reasonable disciplinary measures,[4] including suspension and expulsion from an educational establishment, provided that the pupil can enrol in another establishment.[5] However, the power of regulation by the State of the right to education conferred by the first sentence of Art 2 does not include a right to inflict corporal punishment against the will of a child's parents.[6] Nor does it include a right to prohibit independent schools.[7]

18.124   Further, as Sedley LJ, with whom Lord Justice Clark and Dame Butler-Sloss P agreed, stated in *A v Head Teacher and Governors of the Lord Grey School*:[8]

'Put broadly, there will be [a denial of the Convention right to education] where [a] breach of domestic law has resulted in the pupil's being unable to avail himself of the means of education which presently exist in England and Wales – not, for example, by being temporarily unable to reach the school premises for want of transport, but by being shut out for a significant or an indefinite period from access to such education as the law provides for him or her.'

18.125   Moreover, as Sedley LJ also said in that case:

'An indefinite exclusion from his school, absent some proper substitute provision ... seems to me to be a pretty unequivocal denial of a pupil's right to education.'[9]

18.126   However, as he also said there:

'an unlawful exclusion during which the pupil is offered no education at all by either the school or the LEA is a different thing in Convention terms from an unlawful exclusion during which adequate or appropriate substitute education is offered.'[10]

Impact of Art 2 on higher education

18.127   Article 2 is 'concerned primarily with elementary education'.[11] However, it is clear from *Douglas v North Tyneside MBC and the Secretary of State*[12] that it applies to

---

1   *Belgian Linguistic Case*, ibid, at 281–282, para 5.
2   Ibid.
3   *Family H v UK* (1984) 37 DR 105, at 108.
4   *A v Head Teacher and Governors of the Lord Grey School* [2003] EWHC 1533, [2003] ELR 517, paras 80–81.
5   *Yanasik v Turkey* (1973) 74 DR 14; *Sulak v Turkey* (1996) 84A DR 98.
6   *Campbell and Cosans* (1982) 4 EHRR 293, at 306–307, paras 40–41.
7   *Jordebo v Sweden* (1987) 51 DR 125, at 128; *Verein Gemeinsam Lernen v Austria* (1995) 82 DR 41, (1995) 20 EHRR CD 78.
8   [2004] EWCA Civ 382, [2004] 2 WLR 1442, [2004] ELR 169, para 45.
9   Ibid, para 50.
10   Ibid, para 53.
11   *X v UK* (1975) 2 DR 50.
12   [2003] EWCA Civ 1847, [2004] 1 All ER 709.

higher education,[1] albeit that on the facts of that case it had no practical effect.[2] Article 2 does not prevent the State from restricting access to limited higher education facilities to those who have attained a level of academic achievement sufficient to benefit most from the courses offered.[3] Nor does it require the State to recognise as valid a professional status acquired in another country.[4]

Parents' right to respect for religious and philosophical convictions

18.128   The two sentences of Art 2 must where relevant be read together.[5] They must also be read in conjunction with Arts 8, 9 and 10 of the Convention.[6]

18.129   The right to respect for religious and philosophical convictions is not merely a right to have the State acknowledge or take into account those convictions:[7]

> 'The verb "respect" means more than "acknowledge" or "take into account". In addition to a primarily negative undertaking, it implies some positive obligation on the part of the State.'[8]

18.130   However, although the obligation to respect parents' religious or philosophical convictions allows them to deny school education to their children and to educate them at home, it does not allow the parents to refuse to allow their children's educational standards to be assessed by an education authority, where the aim of the assessment is to ensure that certain standards of literacy and numeracy are being attained.[9]

18.131   The word 'convictions' in the second sentence of Art 2:

> 'is not synonymous with the words "opinions" and "ideas". It denotes views that attain a certain level of cogency, seriousness, cohesion and importance.'[10]

18.132   Furthermore:

> 'the expression "philosophical convictions" in the present context denotes, in the Court's opinion, such convictions as are worthy of respect in a "democratic society" ... and are not incompatible with human dignity; in addition, they must not conflict with the fundamental right of the child to education, the whole of Article 2 being dominated by its first sentence.'[11]

---

[1]   See at para 44, per Scott Baker LJ.

[2]   See para 65.

[3]   *X v UK* (1980) 23 DR 228.

[4]   *Glazewska v Sweden* (1985) 45 DR 300, at 302.

[5]   *Kjeldsen, Busk Madsen & Pedersen v Denmark* (1979–80) 1 EHRR 711, at 730, para 52; *Campbell and Cosans v UK* (1982) 4 EHRR 293, at 307, para 40; *Valsamis v Greece* (1997) 24 EHRR 294, at 315, para 25. (*Valsamis* is reported also at [1998] ELR 430).

[6]   *Kjeldsen*, ibid, para 52; *Valsamis*, ibid, para 25.

[7]   *Campbell and Cosans*, op cit, para 37; *Valsamis*, op cit, para 27.

[8]   *Valsamis*, op cit.

[9]   *Family H v UK* (1984) 37 DR 105, at 108.

[10]   *Valsamis*, op cit, para 25, referring to the judgment in *Campbell and Cosans*, para 36.

[11]   *Campbell and Cosans*, op cit, para 36.

18.133   The fact that a parent could in theory (if he had the money) send his child to an independent school does not relieve the State of the obligation in the second sentence of Art 2 to respect parents' religious and philosophical convictions.[1] Yet that sentence does not require the State to subsidise the provision of education in any particular manner (such as in a single-sex, selective grammar school) when the teaching which is on offer at a comprehensive school is conveyed in an objective, critical and pluralistic manner.[2] In R *(Begum) v Headteacher and Governors of Denbigh High School*[3] Bennett J decided that a rule precluding pupils from wearing a jilbab did not breach either Art 9 or Art 2, Protocol 1.

18.134   The obligation in the second sentence of Art 2 applies 'not only to the content of the education and the manner of its provision but also to the performance of all the "functions" assumed by the State'.[4] In this connection, the following passage from *Young, James and Webster v United Kingdom*[5] should be borne in mind:

> 'Although individual interests must on occasion be subordinated to those of a group, democracy does not simply mean that the views of a majority must always prevail: a balance must be achieved which ensures the fair and proper treatment of minorities and avoids any abuse of a dominant position.'[6]

18.135   However:

> 'the setting and planning of the curriculum fall in principle within the competence of the Contracting States. This mainly involves questions of expediency on which it is not for the Court to rule and whose solution may legitimately vary according to the country and the era.'[7]

18.136   Nevertheless:

> 'The second sentence of Article 2 implies on the other hand that the State, in fulfilling the functions assumed by it in regard to education and teaching, must take care that information or knowledge included in the curriculum is conveyed in an objective, critical and pluralistic manner. The State is forbidden to pursue an aim of indoctrination that might be considered as not respecting parents' religious and philosophical convictions. That is the limit that must not be exceeded.'[8]

18.137   Yet this does not prevent the communication through teaching or education of information or knowledge of a directly or indirectly religious or philosophical kind.[9] Nor does it prevent the integration in the school curriculum of such information or

---

1   *Kjeldsen*, op cit, at 728–729.
2   *W & DM v UK* (1984) 37 DR 96, at 100.
3   [2004] EWHC 1389, (2004) *The Times* June 18.
4   *Valsamis*, op cit, para 27.
5   (1982) 4 EHRR 38.
6   (1982) 4 EHRR 38 at 57, para 63, to which the court in *Valsamis* referred at para 27 of the judgment.
7   *Kjeldsen*, op cit, para 53.
8   *Kjeldsen*, op cit, applied in part in *Valsamis*, op cit, para 28.
9   See *X, Y and Z v Federal Republic of Germany* (1982) 29 DR 224, where the European Commission on Human Rights (referred to in the rest of this chapter as 'the Commission') rejected as inadmissible a complaint that school curricula imposed an ideology based on a scientific approach to which the complainant parents did not subscribe.

knowledge; otherwise all institutionalised teaching would run the risk of being impracticable.[1] The compulsory integration of sex education into the curriculum for State primary schools may therefore not contravene the second sentence in Art 2 – and did not do so on the facts in *Kjeldsen*.

18.138 The obligation in the second sentence of Art 2 extends also to the administration of education, such as the manner in which discipline is enforced.[2] In *Campbell and Cosans*,[3] it was held that the inability of the applicants and their children to avoid the infliction of corporal punishment breached this obligation. However, in *Valsamis*,[4] it was held by the European Court of Human Rights (ECHR) that that obligation was not breached by the requirement (backed up by a penalty of suspension from school, but not the school's premises, for a day) that all pupils of compulsory school age attend the school parade on National Day (which was otherwise a public holiday). This was despite the facts that (1) the complainants were Jehovah's witnesses, one of whose fundamental tenets is pacifism, (2) their religion 'forbids any conduct or practice associated with war or violence, even indirectly',[5] and (3) the parade was to commemorate the outbreak of war between Greece and Fascist Italy on 28 October 1940. The ECHR commented, however:

> 'While it is not for the Court to rule on the Greek State's decisions as regards the setting and planning of the school curriculum, it is surprised that pupils can be required on pain of suspension from school – even if only for one day – to parade outside the school precincts on a holiday.'[6]

18.139 The reason for the court's rejection of the claim was that it could 'discern nothing, either in the purpose of the parade or in the arrangements for it, which could offend the applicants' pacifist convictions to an extent prohibited by the second sentence of Article 2 of Protocol No. 1'.[7] In the court's view, commemorations of national events such as that in question 'serve, in their way, both pacifist objectives and the public interest'.[8] Furthermore, the court took into account that the penalty imposed for non-attendance at the parade was relatively light, even though it might have some psychological impact on the pupil on whom it was imposed.[9]

18.140 The Commission has on three occasions rejected, on the facts, claims by parents that the failure by the education authorities to comply with their wishes to have their children who had special educational needs educated in a mainstream school, was contrary to the second sentence in Art 2.[10]

---

1   *Kjeldsen*, op cit, para 53.
2   *Campbell and Cosans*, op cit, para 33.
3   Op cit.
4   Op cit.
5   *Valsamis*, op cit, para 6.
6   Ibid, para 31.
7   Ibid.
8   Ibid.
9   Ibid, para 32.
10   *PD and LD v UK* (1989) 62 DR 292; *Graeme v UK* (1990) 64 DR 158; and *Klerks v Netherlands* (1995) 82 DR 129.

18.141   The rights of a natural parent under the second sentence in Art 2 cease if the parent loses custody of the child as a result of a judicial decision.[1] They also cease if the child is adopted.[2]

Independent schools – the obligations of the State under the convention

18.142   It was held by the ECHR in *Costello-Roberts v UK*[3] that the treatment by a headmaster of an independent school of pupils at that school could give rise to responsibility on the part of the State under the Convention, if it breached a right afforded by the Convention.[4]

Convention right not to be discriminated against

18.143   It is appropriate to end this chapter with a reference to the Convention right not to be discriminated against. Article 14 of the Convention provides as follows:

> 'The enjoyment of the rights and freedoms set forth in this Convention shall be secured without discrimination on any ground such as sex, race, colour, language, religion, political or other opinion, national or social origin, association with a national minority, property, birth or other status.'

18.144   The ECHR held in the *Belgian Linguistic Case (No 2)*[5] that Art 14 is not self-standing; rather, it must be read in conjunction with another provision of the convention. Thus if an act of the State does not in itself contravene any other right afforded by the Convention, that may nevertheless contravene Art 14 if it is of a discriminatory nature.[6] So although Art 2 of the First Protocol does not require the State to ensure the provision of any particular kind of educational institution, access to an educational institution established by the State cannot be restricted in a discriminatory way.[7]

18.145   However, the ECHR held in the same case, discrimination is contrary to Art 14 only if it has no objective and reasonable justification. For such justification to exist, the discrimination must pursue a legitimate aim and there must be a reasonable relationship of proportionality between the means employed and the aim sought to be achieved.[8]

18.146   Article 14 almost certainly does not, however, make unlawful the fact that voluntary aided schools may not receive 100 per cent of the cost of the maintenance of their buildings,[9] whereas other maintained schools receive 100 per cent of that

---

1   *X v Sweden* (1977) 12 DR 192.
2   *X v UK* (1977) 11 DR 160.
3   [1994] ELR 1.
4   See paras 26–28 of the judgment, at ibid, pp 9–10.
5   (1979–80) 1 EHRR 252.
6   Ibid, at 283, para 9.
7   Loc cit.
8   (1979–80) 1 EHRR 252, at 284, para 10.
9   See para **7.126**.

cost.[1] Similarly, giving more subsidy to religious private schools than to non-religious private schools was held in the circumstances in *Verein Gemeinsam Lernen v Austria*[2] not to contravene Art 14.

---

[1] See *X v UK* (1978) 14 DR 179, the facts of which would almost certainly be regarded as equivalent to those indicated in the text to this note.

[2] (1995) 82 DR 41.

Chapter 19

POTENTIAL LIABILITIES OF GOVERNORS OF EDUCATION INSTITUTIONS

INTRODUCTION

19.1   Governors of education institutions could in theory be liable as a result of such governorship in a number of ways. However, the likelihood of liability arising in any of those ways is low. In some situations, the possibility of liability as a governor is in any event unclear. In this chapter, brief reference is made first to the main potential liabilities which arise in relation to the membership of any corporate or other body responsible for any kind of business or undertaking. Several issues which are specific to the situations of bodies conducting education institutions are then discussed. Finally, there is a mention of several of the incidents of trusteeship. The latter is because governors of education institutions are likely to be trustees at some time, and because if the analysis set out below is correct, then governors of even statutory education corporations are potentially liable as quasi trustees.

SOME COMMON LIABILITIES

Introduction

19.2   One question which arises here is the extent to which an individual governor may be liable for civil or criminal wrongs committed by the body of which he is a member as well as, or instead of, that body. However, that is a question which can best be examined in context rather than as a question of general application. It is accordingly considered where relevant below. A brief mention is made first of the position in criminal law, after which the position in relation to civil liability is examined.

Liability for criminal acts of the governing body

19.3   A member of any of the relevant kinds of governing body could be liable for a criminal act of the governing body of which he is a member where he is personally responsible to any extent for that act. This could be under a statutory provision which makes natural persons potentially liable in respect of contraventions of the statute in question by other persons (which will normally include for this purpose unincorporated bodies as well as corporations[1]). Examples of statutory provisions of this sort are to be found in ss 36 and 37 of the Health and Safety at Work etc Act 1974.

---

[1]   See Interpretation Act 1978, s 5 and Sch 1.

19.4   A governor could also be potentially liable for a criminal act of the governing body of which he is a member on the basis that he had acted as a secondary party to the crime in question. This would be for example on the basis that he had aided or abetted the crime.

Liability in tort

19.5   The position in relation to a governor's potential liability in tort can best be illustrated by reference to a particular situation. Liability on the part of a relevant governor in the law of tort is most likely to arise (if at all) as a result of the body of which the governor is a member being an occupier of premises. That situation will accordingly now be considered. The manner in which liability on the part of a governor for other torts could arise is, so far as relevant, the same.

19.6   Schools are institutions – whatever that may mean.[1] They and other institutions have to occupy premises. Governing bodies of even maintained schools will have some control of those premises.[2] As a result, the governing bodies of all educational institutions could in theory be liable as occupiers under the Occupiers' Liability Act 1957 and the Occupiers' Liability Act 1984, or in the law of negligence, or both. The scope of the potential liability of a governing body (as such) which could arise as a result of being in occupation of an institution's premises is beyond the scope of this book, and the only observation in that regard made here is that there may be more than one occupier at one time,[3] one result of which is that the governing body of a maintained school may be a joint occupier with the LEA. However, even if that were so in any particular case, it is likely that the LEA would be under an obligation to meet any relevant liability of the governing body. This is because the authority would be under a duty to maintain the school, and because the LEA's duty to maintain the school 'includes' the duty of defraying all the expenses of maintaining it.[4] This is so even where the governing body provides community facilities under s 27 of the EA 2002.[5]

19.7   In any event, the liability of the governing body of any educational institution will usually be corporate (whether because the institution is conducted by a statutory corporation established under one of the Education Acts, by a company established under the Companies Act 1985 or any of its predecessors, or by a corporation established by or conducted under a Royal Charter). Yet despite the incorporation of the governing bodies of maintained schools under (originally) ss 238 and 239 of the Education Act 1993,[6] there will still be occasions when the governing body of an educational institution is an unincorporated association. This is in part because of the existence of designated institutions in the further and higher education sectors – designated under s 28 of the FHEA 1992 and s 129 of the ERA 1988 respectively – which may have unincorporated governing bodies.[7] It is also because some

---

1   See further, para **2.164**.
2   See paras **8.11** et seq.
3   See *Wheat v E Lacon & Co Ltd* [1966] AC 552.
4   See s 22 of the SSFA 1998.
5   See para **7.141**.
6   See para **7.64** for the current provisions.
7   See (1) paras **16.81** and **16.89** and (2) paras **17.41–17.44** respectively.

independent schools may be governed by the trustees of charitable trusts of the premises which are devoted to the use of the school.

Corporate governing body

19.8   Where the governing body of an education institution is a corporate body, the liability of governors under the Occupiers' Liability Acts or in the law of negligence will be very limited. The governors will be capable of being liable in tort under those Acts or in negligence only in two situations which are highly unlikely to arise. The first is if a governor 'procures and induces the [corporation] to commit the tort'.[1] The second is where the governor 'assumes a personal responsibility'.[2]

Unincorporated governing body

19.9   Where the governing body of an educational institution is an unincorporated body, the liability of an individual governor in respect of a breach by the governing body of either of the Occupiers' Liability Acts or in respect of any negligence of the governing body, will depend on the extent to which the governor was responsible for the act or omission in question. However, he will usually be able to call on the funds held by the governing body for the purposes of the institution in order to meet the liability if what gave rise to the liability could properly be said to have occurred in the course of his acting as a governor of the institution in question. The governor would be unable to call on such funds to meet a liability of the relevant sort only if he had acted (or omitted to act) for some extraneous purpose.

Liability in relation to contracts entered into by the governing body

Corporate governing body

19.10   Where a contract is validly entered into by a corporate governing body, the liability under that contract will be the governing body's only. This is because the members of a corporate body will not be personally liable in respect of contracts entered into properly by that body.[3]

19.11   If a governing body purports to enter into a contract which is in fact ultra vires, then (at least in theory) it will be void. A governor might nevertheless in that situation have some liability in relation to the purported contract. That potential liability would be for breach of a warranty of authority. Such a warranty could be one of law or one of fact. If it were one of law, such as that the governing body had power in general terms to enter into the contract, then the best view is that the governor would have no liability.[4] However, if the warranty were one of fact, such as that a

---

1   *Clerk and Lindsell on Torts* (Sweet & Maxwell, London, 18th edn, 2000), para 4.89.
2   Ibid, paras 4.88 and 4.89.
3   *Re Sheffield and South Yorkshire Permanent Building Society* (1889) 22 QBD 470, at 476 per Cave J: 'if a man trusts a corporation, he trusts that legal *persona*, and must look to its assets for payment: he can only call upon individual members to contribute in case the Act or charter [under which the body is incorporated] has so provided'.
4   *Beattie v Lord Ebury* (1872) LR 7 Ch App 777, at 802; *Weeks v Propert* (1873) LR 8 CP 427, at 437. However, statements which could be relied upon to make a governor liable even for a warranty of law

procedure which was required to be followed by the articles of government had been followed when in fact it had not been followed, then the governor undoubtedly could be liable for its breach.[1]

Unincorporated governing body

19.12 An unincorporated governing body would be able to enter into contracts only through one or more members of the governing body entering into the contract. If the contract could properly be said to have been entered into in the exercise of the functions of the governing body, then the member or members who entered into the contract would be able to call on the funds of the institution to meet any liability under the contract. However, if there were insufficient funds, then the relevant member or members would have to meet the liability themselves. This is presumably one of the kinds of liability for which governors may wish to seek insurance.[2]

Liability as fiduciaries

19.13 The members of the governing bodies of all education institutions will almost certainly be regarded as fiduciaries – in other words, as being subject to fiduciary duties to the bodies of which they are members. In two relevant situations, it is already clear that that is so: it is clear that a trustee is a fiduciary (although a fiduciary is not necessarily a trustee), and it is clear that a director of a company is a fiduciary. However, it has not been established whether a member of a corporation established under the Education Acts or established by or conducted under a Royal Charter, is a fiduciary. Yet it can confidently be predicted that such a member is indeed a fiduciary. This is for the following reasons.

19.14 The most apparently coherent statement of principle in academic writings, is that of JC Shepherd in 'Towards a Unified Concept of Fiduciary Relationships'[3] where he says:

---

can be found in other cases, including *Richardson v Williamson* LR 6 QB 276. Yet as pointed out in *Beattie v Lord Ebury*, loc cit, there is no liability for a misrepresentation of law; that being so, it would be odd if there could be liability for a breach by a governor of a warranty of law.

[1] *Firbank's Executors v Humphreys* (1886) 18 QBD 54; *Chapleo v Brunswick Permanent Building Society* (1881) 6 QBD 696.

[2] Whether the governors could use the funds of the institution for the purpose is a different question. The attitude of the Charity Commissioners towards the use of a charitable body's funds for the purpose of paying for insurance to cover governors' liabilities is not entirely clear. Their stance has changed over time, as described by Judith Hill in 'The Trust Versus the Company under the Charities Act 1992 and 1993' (1994) 2 *Charity Law and Practice Review* 133, at 143–144. It seems, however, sensible at least as a matter of policy that insurance could be purchased in respect of even breaches of trust by trustees, as long as those breaches were committed honestly. The position is different for the governors of at least some of the new education corporations. For example, concerning the governing body of a maintained school, see para **7.92**.

[3] (1981) 97 LQR 51, at 75.

'A fiduciary relationship exists whenever any person receives a power of any type on condition that he also receive with it a duty to utilise that power in the best interests of another, and the recipient of the power uses that power.'[1]

19.15 Furthermore, it has been said several times that the categories of cases in which fiduciary duties and obligations arise spring from factual circumstances, with the result that the types of relationship which may be regarded as giving rise to fiduciary obligations are no more closed than the categories of negligence at common law.[2] The fact that in *Att-Gen v De Winston*,[3] a borough treasurer was held to be in a fiduciary position towards the borough council of which he was the treasurer, supports the view that a governor of a statutory education corporation is in the position of a fiduciary as regards the corporation.

19.16 The impact of a person being a fiduciary is not entirely clear. Certainly, the fact that a person is a fiduciary vis-à-vis a body of which he is a member does not necessarily entail personal liability for a misspending of the funds of that body. A fiduciary is under a primary duty to avoid placing himself in a position where his interests conflict with his duties to the body in question, and then to account to that body for any gain which results from that conflict of interest. It may be that a fiduciary is also under a duty to reimburse the body in relation to which he is a fiduciary in respect of loss of any other kind caused to that body by a breach by him of his fiduciary duties.[4] It is of interest that it is argued by Oakley[5] that before the fusion of law and equity by the Judicature Acts of 1873 and 1875, there was an equitable jurisdiction to award compensation for breach of an equitable duty, including breach of a fiduciary duty, and that that jurisdiction 'was lost sight of' after those Acts were enacted.

Liabilities as governors of education corporations

Liability as a quasi trustee

19.17 Education corporations include the governing bodies of maintained schools, FECs and HECs. All those bodies are statutory corporations whose purposes are exclusively charitable. All of them except the governing body of a community or community special school[6] are therefore potentially subject to the jurisdiction of the High Court with respect to charities. However, the governing bodies of maintained schools are in a curious position in that the vast majority of the money which they spend is provided by the LEA, and is in law spent by them on behalf of that authority

---

[1] In the final pages of that article, Shepherd acknowledges that this suggested formulation is open to criticism, but invites the reader to formulate a better one. There is also a very helpful and more recent analysis in AJ Oakley, *Constructive Trusts* (Sweet & Maxwell, 3rd edn, 1997), pp 87–99.

[2] See, for example, DJ Hayton, *Underhill and Hayton, Law Relating to Trusts and Trustees* (Butterworths, 16th edn, 2003), p 21.

[3] [1906] 2 Ch 106.

[4] See chapter 20 of *Underhill and Hayton, Law Relating to Trusts and Trustees* op cit, esp pp 855 et seq.

[5] Op cit, pp 115 et seq.

[6] See in relation to maintained schools, SSFA 1998, s 23(1), in relation to FECs, para **16.65**, and in relation to HECs, para **17.38**. A successor company to an HEC is also an exempt charity: see para **17.43**.

instead of on their own behalf.[1] Accordingly, in that regard the governing body is unlike other education corporations.

19.18 Where any charitable corporation holds money for its general purposes, the best view is that it does so on its own behalf and not as a trustee.[2] However, this does not necessarily mean that a member of the corporation may not be liable for a use of the funds of the body for a purpose which is *ultra vires* the body, including for a purpose which is not charitable. Indeed, if the mere fact that a corporate body is best regarded as holding its property on its own behalf and not as a trustee were regarded as sufficient to absolve its members from any liability, then there would (assuming that no person could be made liable as a constructive trustee) be no person from whom a remedy in respect of a misuse by the body of its funds could be obtained. Further, if the body were a trustee, and misused the property held by it as a trustee, and the members of the body could not be liable as if they were themselves trustees, then an action for breach of trust in respect of the misapplication in question could result only in a diversion of funds from one charitable purpose to another. Accordingly, as a matter of common sense and principle, it would seem that a member of a charitable corporation should be regarded as if he were a trustee in regard to the property of the corporation. Some support for this proposition can be derived from the case of *Harries v Church Commissioners*.[3] There, the members of the Church Commissioners, which is a corporate body, were treated as if they were trustees (or as quasi trustees) as far as their powers of investment were concerned. Further support for the proposition can be drawn from a number of cases, including *Selangor United Rubber Estates Co Ltd v Cradock (No 3)*,[4] where Ungoed-Thomas J, relying on a number of nineteenth-century cases, held that a director of a limited company is answerable as a trustee for any misapplication of the company's property in which he participated and which he knew, or ought to have known, was a misappropriation.[5] As a matter of strict principle, that proposition is inconsistent with trust law, since not all companies are charitable (the majority of course being purely commercial), and (apart from in irrelevant exceptional cases) trusts for purposes which are not charitable are void. However, that factor merely serves to underline the need for a pragmatic approach in this context: if the courts have ignored questions of strict principle in a related context, then they may well do so in this one.

---

[1] See para **7.140**. For recognition of this by the Court of Appeal in relation to the situation before s 49(5) of the SSFA was enacted, see *R v Yorkshire Purchasing Organisation, ex parte British Educational Suppliers* [1998] ELR 195, at 202C–D.

[2] The most recent and most commonly cited authority for this proposition is *Liverpool and District Hospital for Diseases of the Heart v Att-Gen* [1981] Ch 193.

[3] [1992] 1 WLR 1241.

[4] [1968] 1 WLR 1555; see also *Palmer's Company Law* (Sweet & Maxwell, looseleaf, 25th edn, 1992), paras 8.403–8.404.

[5] See most recently *In re Duckwari plc* [1999] Ch 253, where, at 262, Nourse LJ (with whom Pill and Thorpe LJJ agreed) said: 'The assets of a company being vested in the company, the directors are not accurately described as trustees of those assets. Nevertheless, they have always been treated as trustees of assets which are in their hands or under their control. The principle is best stated by Lindley LJ in *In re Lands Allotment Co* [1894] 1 Ch 616, 631'.

Potential defence to an action for breach of trust

19.19 There is a potential defence to an action for breach of trust against a member of an education corporation, contained in s 61 of the Trustee Act 1925. Section 61 applies where a trustee is sued for breach of trust; it allows the court to excuse the trustee if the court determines that the trustee has acted honestly and reasonably and ought fairly to be excused the breach of trust. If a member of an education corporation is properly to be regarded *as if* he were a trustee, then the defence in s 61 of the Trustee Act 1925 should apply to an action for breach of trust brought on that basis as well as to an action brought against a trustee in the strict sense: it would be entirely inconsistent and unfair to hold otherwise. The related defence in s 727 of the Companies Act 1985 appears not to apply. That provision applies only to company directors, and by no reasonable stretch of the imagination could the member of, for example, an FEC be regarded as if he were a company director.

Possible ousting of the jurisdiction of the high court

19.20 There are two possible reasons why the members of a charitable corporation might nevertheless not be subject to the jurisdiction of the High Court with respect to charities. One is that the statutory regime relating to the body might be regarded as having ousted that jurisdiction.[1] The other reason is that there may be a visitor to the institution conducted by the corporation, whose jurisdiction extends to the act in question.[2]

Main relevant potential liabilities as trustees or as quasi trustees

19.21 The potential liabilities of a quasi trustee or a trustee are beyond the scope of this book. However, it may be of value to mention several duties of a trustee which could be relevant. The first is that a charity trustee must use the property of the trust for the express purposes of the charity or for purposes reasonably connected with those purposes. The second is that as a result of s 1 of the Trustee Act 2000, a trustee is obliged to exercise such care and skill as is reasonable in the circumstances having regard in particular to (a) any special knowledge or experience that he has or holds himself out as having, and (b) if he acts as trustee in the course of a business or profession, to any special knowledge or experience that it is reasonable to expect of a person acting in the course of that kind of business or profession.[3]

Liabilities of company directors

19.22 Some educational institutions are conducted by limited companies (whether limited by shares or guarantee). In addition, many charitable institutions have wholly-owned subsidiary companies in order to make lawful trading activities connected with

---

[1] See *Construction Industry Training Board v Att-Gen* [1973] Ch 173. It is highly unlikely that the statutory regime relating to any of the corporations established under the Education Acts would be regarded by the High Court as ousting its jurisdiction. See further, O Hyams, 'The potential liabilities of governors of education institutions' (1994) 6 *Education and the Law* 191, pp 199–200.

[2] As to the jurisdiction of the visitor to an institution, and the extent to which it ousts the jurisdiction of the courts, see paras **17.49** et seq.

[3] See further the discussion in DJ Hayton, *Underhill and Hayton, Law Relating to Trusts and Trustees* op cit, pp 575–577.

the institution and yet retain the profit from those activities. Accordingly, a very brief reference to the liabilities of a company director may be helpful here.

19.23 Apart from the possibility of liability for breach of a director's fiduciary duties as described above, or of liability as a quasi trustee in the manner indicated for example in *Selangor United Rubber Estates Co Ltd v Cradock (No 3)*,[1] a company director's main potential liabilities are towards the company in respect of (fairly serious) negligence[2] or for breach of a warranty of authority made to a third party.[3] Again, the likelihood of liability of either sort arising is low. In any event, s 727 of the Companies Act 1985 affords a company director similar protection in respect of breaches of duty towards the company to that afforded by s 61 of the Trustee Act 1925 to a trustee.[4]

Misfeasance in public office

19.24 The tort of misfeasance in public office deserves a mention here. According to *Clerk & Lindsell on Torts*,[5] 'there is the emergent tort of misfeasance in public office[6] providing a remedy in damages for loss, injury or damage resulting from administrative action which the relevant authority or officer knows to be unlawful. Abuse of public office constitutes a tort'. The requisite mental state is now clear as a result of the decision of the House of Lords in *Three Rivers District Council v Bank of England (No 3)*.[7] It is knowledge that what is proposed will be unlawful, or subjective recklessness (that is, seeing the risk and yet deciding to take it) that it will be unlawful, together with knowledge (of the same sort: either actual knowledge or subjective recklessness) that loss will be caused to the claimant. A governor of an education institution which was established under the Education Acts is probably the holder of a public office for this purpose. It has to be said, however, that it is highly unlikely that a claimant would be able to rely upon this tort in an action against such a governor.

No liability for a governor merely because an education corporation or other body conducting an education institution acts ultra vires

19.25 Finally, it is noted that it has been suggested that if a body conducting an educational institution acts ultra vires, then a governor of that institution is automatically liable for any loss caused as a result of the ultra vires act. It is suggested here that that is mistaken. A governor would in that circumstance be liable to a third party, or the institution in question, only if the governor had breached any of his duties to the institution or some specific duty of the sorts indicated above owed to a third party who had suffered loss as a result of the ultra vires act.

1   [1968] 1 WLR 1555; see further, para **19.18**.
2   See, for example, the discussion in *Gore-Browne on Companies* (Jordans, looseleaf, 44th edn, 1986), para 27.19, and *Palmer's Company Law* (Sweet & Maxwell, 25th edn, 1992), paras 8.406 et seq.
3   See para **19.11** concerning liability for breach of warranty of authority.
4   See para **19.19** concerning s 61 of the Trustee Act 1925.
5   (Sweet & Maxwell, 18th edn, 2000), para 17.134.
6   In *Gizzonio v Chief Constable of Derbyshire Constabulary* (1998) *The Times*, April 29, the tort of misfeasance in public office was specifically referred to by the Court of Appeal as 'emergent'.
7   [2003] 1 AC 1.

INDEX